Continued on back

HANDBOOK OF
PLAY THERAPY

Other Books by Charles Schaefer

How to Help Children with Common Problems 1981

Therapies for School Behavior Problems (With H. Millman and J. Cohen) 1980

Therapies for Psychosomatic Disorders in Children (with H. Millman and G. Levine) 1979

Childhood Encopresis and Enuresis 1979

How to Influence Children—A Handbook of Practical Parenting Skills 1978

Therapies for Children—A Handbook of Effective Treatments for Problem Behaviors (with H. Millman) 1977

Therapeutic Use of Child Play 1976

Developing Creativity in Children 1973

Becoming Somebody—Creative Activities for Preschool Children 1973

Young Voices—The Poetry of Children 1970

HANDBOOK OF PLAY THERAPY

Edited by

CHARLES E. SCHAEFER
The Children's Village
Dobbs Ferry, New York

and

KEVIN J. O'CONNOR
Blythedale Children's Hospital
Valhalla, New York

A WILEY-INTERSCIENCE PUBLICATION

JOHN WILEY & SONS

New York · Chichester · Brisbane · Toronto · Singapore

Library of Congress Cataloging in Publication Data
Main entry under title:

Handbook of play therapy.

(Wiley series on personality processes, ISSN 0195-4008)
Includes indexes.
1. Play therapy. I. Schaefer, Charles E. II O'Connor, Kevin J.
III. Series.
RJ505.P6H36   1982   618.92′891653   82-21818
ISBN 0-471-09462-5

Printed in the United States of America

21 20 19 18 17 16 15 14 13 12

Contributors

DAVID BEHAR, M.D.
Child Psychiatrist
Unit on Childhood Mental Illness
Biological Psychiatry Branch
National Institute of Mental Health
Bethesda, Maryland

RUDOLF EKSTEIN, PH.D.
Clinical Professor of Medical
    Psychology, UCLA
Training and Supervisory Analyst,
    Los Angeles and Southern
    California Psychoanalytic
    Institutes
Annual Guest Professor, University
    of Vienna

AARON H. ESMAN, M.D.
Professor of Clinical Psychiatry,
New York Hospital, Cornell Medical
    Center
New York, New York

RICHARD A. GARDNER, M.D.
Associate Clinical Professor of Child
    Psychiatry,
Columbia University, College of
    Physicians and Surgeons
New York, New York
Visiting Professor of Child
Psychiatry, University of Louvain,
    Belgium

DOUGLAS B. GOLDEN, PH.D.
Assistant Professor of Psychology,
Oregon Health Sciences University
Portland, Oregon

MERLE D. GRIFF, M.S.
Director, Program Development and
    Training
Interactive Arts, Inc.
Canton, Ohio

LOUISE F. GUERNEY, PH.D.
Associate Professor of Human
    Development,
Pennsylvania State University
University Park, Pennsylvania

SUSAN HARTER, PH.D.
Professor, Department of Psychology
University of Denver
Denver, Colorado

ELEANOR C. IRWIN, PH.D.
Assistant Professor of Child
    Psychiatry,
School of Medicine
University of Pittsburgh
Pittsburgh, Pennsylvania

ANN M. JERNBERG, PH.D.
Clinical Director
The Theraplay Institute
Chicago, Illinois

LINDA KUHLI
Clinical Social Worker
San Mateo County Mental Health
    Services
Redwood City, California

GARRY L. LANDRETH, ED.D.
Professor of Counselor Education
North Texas State University
Denton, Texas

HENRY LELAND, PH.D.
Professor of Psychology
Ohio State University
Columbus, Ohio

EBERHARD MANN, M.D.
Associate Professor of Psychiatry and
    Pediatrics
University of Hawaii
Honolulu, Hawaii

JOHN F. MCDERMOTT, JR., M.D.
Professor and Chairman
Department of Psychiatry
University of Hawaii
Honolulu, Hawaii

ALLAN E. MENDELL, M.D.
Child Psychiatrist
Houston, Texas

EILEEN T. NICKERSON, PH.D.
Professor, Counseling Psychology
    Program
School of Education
Boston University
Boston, Massachusetts

KEVIN J. O'CONNOR, PH.D.
Staff Psychologist
Blythedale Children's Hospital
Valhalla, New York

KAY S. O'LAUGHLIN, ED.D.
Psychiatry Department
Lemuel Shattuer Hospital
Jamaica Plain, Maine

CROCKER PEOPLES, PH.D.
Coordinator of Clinical Training
Psychology Department
Eastern Kentucky University
Richmond, Kentucky

JUDITH L. RAPOPORT, M.D.
Chief, Unit on Childhood Mental
    Illness
Biological Psychiatry Branch
National Institute of Mental Illness
Bethesda, Maryland

GEORGE A. REKERS, PH.D.
Professor and Chairman
Marriage and Family Therapy Unit
Department of Family and Child
    Development
Kansas State University
Manhattan, Kansas

MARION K. SALOMON, PH.D.
Bellmore, New York

LENORE C. TERR, M.D.
Associate Professor
School of Medicine
University of California
San Francisco, California

BRENT WILLOCK, PH.D.
Staff Psychologist
University of Michigan
Children's Psychiatric Hospital
Ann Arbor, Michigan

You can do anything with children
if you only play with them.

Prince Otto von Bismarck
1815-1898

Series Preface

This series of books is addressed to behavioral scientists interested in the nature of human personality. Its scope should prove pertinent to personality theorists and researchers as well as to clinicians concerned with applying an understanding of personality processes to the amelioration of emotional difficulties in living. To this end, the series provides a scholarly integration of theoretical formulations, empirical data, and practical recommendations.

Six major aspects of studying and learning about human personality can be designated: personality theory, personality structure and dynamics, personality development, personality assessment, personality change, and personality adjustment. In exploring these aspects of personality, the books in the series discuss a number of distinct but related subject areas: the nature and implications of various theories of personality; personality characteristics that account for consistencies and variations in human behavior; the emergence of personality processes in children and adolescents; the use of interviewing and testing procedures to evaluate individual differences in personality; efforts to modify personality styles through psychotherapy, counseling, behavior therapy, and other methods of influence; and patterns of abnormal personality functioning that impair individual competence.

IRVING B. WEINER

University of Denver
Denver, Colorado

Preface

Although well-known and widely practiced, play therapy is a field whose potential has hardly been tapped. In recent years a variety of new directions and innovative techniques have emerged to invigorate the field. Unfortunately, these advances have not filtered down to practitioners and students. The goal of this handbook is to provide in one volume the available theory and practical knowledge. This *Handbook of Play Therapy* will describe the "state-of-the-art" of play therapy today and, we hope, will serve as a "staging area" for play therapists to launch further developments in the field.

To ensure that the information in this book is both current and valid, we asked leading authorities on particular aspects of play therapy to write original chapters describing recent developments. Interdisciplinary in approach, eclectic in theory, and comprehensive in scope, this handbook should prove to be a landmark volume for years to come.

Handbook of Play Therapy begins with an overview of the major theoretical approaches to play therapy, including psychoanalytic, nondirective, family, and limit-setting schools of thought. The next section describes how one can make therapeutic use of the three developmental stages of play, namely, sensory-motor play, pretend play, and games with rules. The third section presents a variety of innovative play therapy techniques, settings, and practices, and the final section provides guidelines for using play therapy to treat specific childhood disorders.

Psychiatrists, psychologists, social workers, nurses, and counselors at all levels of training and experience will find this *Handbook of Play Therapy* informative, thought provoking, and clinically useful.

CHARLES E. SCHAEFER
KEVIN J. O'CONNOR

Westchester, New York
September 1982

Contents

PART THREE   PLAY THERAPY: SPECIAL TECHNIQUES
AND SETTINGS   189

PART FOUR   PLAY THERAPY FOR SPECIFIC
CHILDHOOD DISORDERS   281

PART ONE

Major Approaches to
Play Therapy:
Advances and Innovations

In the introduction to their 1977 book *Therapies for Children* Charles Schaefer and Howard Millman discussed the concept of the "prescriptive approach" as it applied to therapy with children. This approach emphasizes the therapist's responsibility to determine the most appropriate therapeutic technique for each particular case. "Rather than attempting to force a child into one 'all purpose' therapeutic mold, then, therapists are now trying to individualize, to fit the remedies or techniques to the individual child. Ideally, the prescriptive approach will result in maximum therapeutic effectiveness in the briefest possible time period" (Schaefer & Millman, 1977, pp. 1–2). Although they applied this concept to the field of child therapy in general, thereby including techniques ranging from traditional psychoanalysis to strict behaviorism, it can also be applied within a single category such as play therapy. To use play therapy in a prescriptive way, then, means to choose a specific strategy for each child patient from the wide array of theories, techniques, and variations now encompassed by this particular category of therapy.

With regard to psychotherapy in general, the use of the prescriptive approach has received both intuitive and research support. Historically, the constant development of numerous, new, and diverse techniques has been justified by the fact that previously developed therapeutic strategies were not optimally effective with various subgroups of patients. Within play therapy, for example, traditional psychodynamic therapy has proven most effective for intelligent, moderately disturbed children, whereas more structured techniques have proven more cost-effective with children who have situation-specific difficulties or traumatic reactions. Further, "a number of disorders, such as delinquent and criminal behaviors, have proven refractory to most forms of intervention" (Schaefer & Millman, 1977, p. 3).

Using the prescriptive approach, even within the confines of play therapy, implies the possibility of expanding the therapeutic intervention beyond the individual session if necessary. A frequent research finding indicates that the positive gains made in any one therapeutic setting often are not generalized to the other settings and systems in which the patient is involved. Because of this, therapists have sought to expand their sphere of influence with regard to the lives of their child patients. In doing so, they have broadened the focus of play therapy from the traditional psychodynamic focus on the child's unconscious, to include the child's cognitions, observable behavior, family system, and peer or social system.

Aside from broadening the focus or target of their therapies, play therapists have explored new therapeutic environments, new materials, and new treatment personnel in an attempt to find effective techniques. This search has led to the development of play techniques for use in families, schools, and community settings. Play therapists have used virtually every play material available, including board games, puppets, art materials, music, and food. They have also begun to use paraprofessionals as agents of therapeutic change. But what other modalities are open to therapeutic change? Arnold Lazarus (1973) states that maximum therapeutic effectiveness can be achieved only when the therapist manages the following seven modalities as they affect a particular patient: (1) behavior, (2) affect, (3) sensation, (4) imagery, (5) cognition, (6) socialization, and (7) the somatic or medical aspect.

Beyond assessing and managing these seven modalities as they relate to one's patients, the play therapist who wishes to practice prescriptive play therapy must be familiar with many aspects of the therapy itself. The many aspects of play therapy are the primary focus of this book and include: developing a clear understanding of play and the way it has, historically, been integrated into play therapy; the way play behavior changes over the course of a child's development; the materials and techniques available for dealing with childhood problems; and the ways in which these materials and techniques can be modified to deal with specific patient populations.

It is somewhat difficult for anyone interested in play and play therapy to gain a clear understanding of what is meant by the term "play" because no single, comprehensive definition of the term has been developed. The most often quoted definition was developed by Erikson (1950). He states that "play is a function of the ego, an attempt to synchronize the bodily and social processes with the self" (p. 211). Play is generally thought to be the antithesis of work. It is fun. "It is free from compulsions of a conscience and from impulsions of irrationality" (p. 214).

In reviewing the literature on play it seems that certain elements are generally considered as typifying play behavior. Play is pleasurable (Beach, 1945; Csikszentmihalyi, 1976; Dohlinow & Bishop, 1970; Hutt, 1970; Plant, 1979; Weisler & McCall, 1976). Play is intrinsically complete; it does not depend on external rewards or other people (Csikszentmihalyi, 1976; Plant, 1979). Probably because it is intrinsically motivated, play tends to be person, rather than object, dominated; that is, it is not aimed at acquiring new information about an object but rather at making use of the object (Hutt, 1970; Weisler & McCall, 1976). Furthermore, intrinsic motivation and object independence tend to make play highly variable both across situations and across children

(Weisler & McCall, 1976). Play is noninstrumental: it has no goal, either intra-personal or interpersonal, no purpose, and no task orientation (Berlyne, 1960; Bettelheim, 1972; Goldberg & Lewis, 1969; Huizinga, 1950; Hutt, 1970; Plant, 1979; Weisler & McCall, 1976). Play behavior does not occur in novel or frightening situations (Beach, 1945; Berlyne, 1960; Hutt, 1970; Mason, 1965; Piaget, 1962; Switsky, Haywood & Isett, 1974; Weisler & McCall, 1976). Lastly, Csikszentmihalyi (1975, 1976) talks about the concept of "flow" as it relates to play. Flow, among other things, involves a centering of attention in which action and awareness merge and a loss of self-consciousness in the sense that the child is paying more attention to the task than to his or her own body state. These last two points are evidenced when an adult walks in on a child who is playing. Initially the child will remain oblivious to the adult's presence but when his or her attention is finally broken he or she may seem suddenly embarrassed and then, just as suddenly and quite genuinely, realize that it is time to go to the bathroom.

Variations on the general concept of play behavior include pretending, fantasy, and games with rules. Pretend play is characterized by certain types of communication:

1. *Negation.*   The means, often abrupt, by which the state is broken or terminated.
   (a)   "I stealed your cake."
   (b)   "I don't care. It's not a cake any more."
2. *Enactment.*   The gestures, tone, statements, or attitudes that the actor puts forth to establish or support the pretend situation or character, for example, crying like a baby, speaking sternly like a parent, making noises like a motor.
3. *Signals.*   These support pretense by tipping off the partner and urging him to go along with the play. They include winking, grinning, gig-gling.
4. The preparatory gestures set the stage, supply terms and conditions, and get the ball rolling at the beginning of pretense: "That green tele-phone is the kind that policemen have in their car." "Do you want to play with me?"
5. The final technique is one that involves explicit mention of transforma-tions in or out of the pretend situation or define the terms or roles. "I'm a worklady at work." "Pretend you hated baby fish." "This is the train" (while pointing at the sofa). (Krasner, 1976, p. 20)

Play may become fantasy when it has to be secret. Both play and fantasy are wish-fulfilling situations that allow instinctual discharge which would not be allowed within the framework of existing reality and which modify and correct that reality (Sandler & Nagera, 1963). Games with rules do not generally fit within the standard definition of play, as there is some sense of an implied task or goal. Games are, however, viewed as an intermediate phase between the unregulated play of young children and the often overregulated play behavior of adults.

Not only is the general definition of play behavior varied and sometimes complex, but there also tends to be even greater disagreement as to the function of play behavior. Table 1 summarizes functions which have been proposed in the literature on play. (The general format of the table was adopted from Slobin [1964].)

TABLE 1.   The Functions of Play Behavior

Biological
    Learn basic skills (Boll, 1957; Chateau, 1954; Dohlinow & Bishop, 1970; Druker, 1975; Frank, 1968; Groos, 1898; Slobin, 1964)
    Relax, release excess energy (Schiller, 1875; Slobin, 1964)
    Kinesthetic stimulation, exercise (Plant, 1979; Slobin, 1964)
Intrapersonal
    "Functionlust" (Slobin, 1964; Walder, 1933)
    Mastery of situations (Erikson, 1950; Slobin, 1964)
        Exploration (Druker, 1975; Frank, 1955)
        Develop understanding of the functions of the mind, body, and world (Cramer, 1975; Frank, 1955)
        Cognitive development (Frank, 1968; Piaget, 1962; Pulaski, 1974)
    Mastery of conflicts (Cramer, 1975; Druker, 1975; Erickson, 1950; Frank, 1955; Walder, 1933)
        Symbolism and wish fulfillment (Cramer, 1975; Druker, 1975; Pulaski, 1974; Walder, 1933)
Interpersonal
    Develop social skills (Druker, 1975; Evans, 1974; Frank, 1968; Slobin, 1964)
    Separation—individuation (Mahler, Pine, & Bergman, 1975): Play can serve as a distraction when significant others are absent; it can be used to master the anxiety associated with separation and can utilize objects symbolically to replace significant others who are absent (Corter, Rheingold, & Eckerman, 1972; Cramer, 1975; Druker, 1975; Frank, 1968; Freud, 1962; Pulaski, 1974; Rheingold & Eckerman, 1969; Rheingold & Samuels, 1969; Walder, 1933).
Sociocultural
    Imitate desired roles (adults) (Frank, 1955; Slobin, 1964)

The idea of play having a function seems to run counter to its definition as noninstrumental and intrinsically motivated. What is important to remember is that the function of play is always secondary to its being fun and is seldom, if ever, something of which the child is conscious.

It is precisely these "less than conscious" functions of a child's play behavior which have, historically, induced therapists to incorporate play into their therapy with children. The focus, obviously, has been the intrapersonal or mastery functions of play but, more recently, other functions have been incorporated into the therapeutic encounter. In psychoanalytic, structured, and relationship therapies, play serves a communication function. Through play, children are assisted to expose and subsequently resolve their disturbing emotions, conflicts, or traumas. In contrast, traditional group therapy and many of the new therapy techniques use play to promote developmental growth such as appropriate peer interactions. Finally, limit-setting and behavioral therapies employ play as a medium through which other strategies, such as contingency management, are applied.

Psychotherapy with children was first attempted by Freud (1909) in an attempt to alleviate the phobic reaction of his now historic patient Little Hans. Freud did not treat Hans directly but advised the child's father of ways to resolve Hans' underlying conflicts and fears. Although it was many years before therapists again attempted to work through a child patient's parents, it was this first therapeutic case which laid the necessary foundation for such interventions.

Play was not directly used in the therapy of children until 1919 by Hug-Hellmuth, who felt it was an essential part of child analysis. However, Anna Freud and Melanie Klein wrote extensively on how they adapted traditional psychoanalytic technique for use with children by incorporating play into their sessions. The primary goal of their approach was to help children work through difficulties or trauma by helping them gain insight. Although both women relied on play as part of treatment, they used it in very different ways.

In 1928 Anna Freud began to use play as a way of luring children into therapy. The rationale behind this technique involved the concept of a therapeutic alliance. Traditional psychoanalysis held that the majority of the work of analysis was accomplished once the healthy aspects of the patient's personality joined forces with the analyst to work against the patient's unhealthy self. This joining of forces was termed the therapeutic alliance. Anna Freud was aware that most children do not come to therapy voluntarily; they are brought by their parents, and it is the parents, not the child, who have the complaint. In addition, she realized that the therapeutic techniques of free association and dream analysis were foreign to most children's means of relating. Therefore, to maximize the ability of the child to form an alliance with the therapist, Freud used play—the child's natural medium—with which to build a relationship with her child patients. She used games and toys to interest the child in therapy and the therapist. As the child developed a satisfactory relationship, the emphasis of the sessions was slowly shifted from a focus on play to a focus on more verbal interactions. Since most children were unable to make use of the technique of free association Freud concentrated on the analysis of dreams and daydreams. She found that children were often as able and interested in the work of dream analysis as their adult counterparts. She used the analysis of daydreams to encourage free association with children. She found they were often able to create mental images, and while visualizing their fantasies they were able to verbalize them.

Whereas Anna Freud advocates using play mainly to build a strong, positive relationship between a child patient and the therapist, Melanie Klein (1932) proposed using it as a direct substitute for verbalizations. Klein considered play to be the child's natural medium of expression. She felt that children's verbal skills were insufficiently developed to express satisfactorily the complex thoughts and affects they were capable of experiencing. In Kleinian play therapy there is no introductory phase; the therapist simply starts out making direct interpretations of the child's play behavior. And, whereas Freud thought that analysis was most appropriate for neurotic children whose disorders were primarily anxiety based, Klein thought that any child, from the most normal to the most disturbed, could benefit from her style of "play analysis."

In the late 1930s a technique of play therapy, now known as structured therapy, was developed using psychoanalytic theory as a basis for a more goal-oriented approach. What is common to all of the therapies in this category is: (1) a psychoanalytic framework, (2) at least a partial belief in the cathartic value of play, and (3) the active role of the therapist in determining the course and focus of the therapy. Levy (1938) developed a technique called "release therapy" to deal with children who had experienced a specific traumatic event. Levy would provide the child with materials and toys aimed at helping the child recreate the traumatic event through play. The child was not forced into a set play-pattern, but very few toys were made available to him or her other than those which the therapist thought might be best used to cathect the emotionally loaded event. The concept of this type of therapy was derived from Sigmund Freud's notion of the repetition compulsion. The idea here is that given security, support, and the right materials a· child could replay a traumatic event over and over until he or she was able to assimilate its associated negative thoughts and feelings.

Also in 1938, Solomon developed a technique called active play therapy which was to be used with impulsive/acting-out children. Solomon thought that helping a child to express rage and fear through the medium of play would have an abreactive effect, because a child could act out without experiencing the negative consequences he or she feared. Through interaction with the therapist, the child learns to redirect the energy previously used in acting out toward more socially appropriate play-oriented behaviors. Solomon also places a heavy emphasis on building children's concept of time by helping them to separate out anxiety over past traumas and future consequences from the reality of their present life situations.

Hambridge (1955) set up play sessions in much the same way that Levy did, only he was even more directive in setting up the specifics of the play situation. While Levy made materials available which would facilitate reenactment of a traumatic event, Hambridge directly recreated the event or anxiety-producing life situation in play to aid the child's abreaction. This technique was not used in isolation but rather was introduced as a middle phase in an already established therapeutic relationship with a child: that is, when he was sure that the child had sufficient ego resources to be able to manage such a direct and intrusive procedure. After the situation was played out, Hambridge allowed the child to play freely for a time to recoup before leaving the safety of the playroom.

Also in the 1930s there developed a number of play techniques generally grouped together under the heading of "relationship therapies." The original philosophical basis for relationship therapy comes from the work of Otto Rank (1936), who stressed the importance of the birth trauma in development. He believed that the stress of birth causes persons to fear individuation and thus leads them to cling to their past. He deemphasized the importance of transference and the examination of past events in therapy and instead focused on the realities of the patient–therapist relationship and the patient's life in the here and now.

Taft (1933), Allen (1942), and Moustakas (1959) adapted his line of thinking to work with children in play therapy. All three emphasized the negative role that the birth trauma has on the ability of the child to form deep positive relationships. Because of this trauma, susceptible children may have difficulty separating from their primary caretaker by becoming either clingy and dependent or isolated and unable to relate sufficiently to others. Through therapy the child is given a chance to establish a deep, concerned relationship with a therapist in a setting which, simply because of the basic therapeutic agreement, is safer than any he or she will ever experience again. Taft adopted an existential approach and focused on the interaction between the child and the therapist and the ability of the child to learn to use that relationship effectively. Moustakas focused on helping the child to individuate, to explore interpersonal situations while using the secure relationship with the therapist as a safe base. Despite the tendency to emphasize the child–therapist relationship and to deeemphasize the significance of past events, the Relationship therapists still maintain a strong tie to psychoanalytic theory. Rather than completely abandoning this theoretical framework they seem to have relaxed the "rules" of analysis while retaining the essential element, the therapeutic relationship.

In 1959 Carl Rogers developed the client-centered approach to therapy with adults which was modified by Virginia Axline (1947) into a play-therapy technique. This approach is based on the philosophy that children naturally strive for growth and that this natural striving has been subverted in the emotionally disturbed child. Client-centered play therapy aims to resolve the imbalance between the child and his or her environment so as to facilitate natural, self-improving growth. The basic rules of Axline's play technique (Axline, 1947, pp. 73, 74) are reproduced here because they have become well known as the credo of the approach:

1. The therapist must develop a warm, friendly relationship with the child. Good rapport should be established as soon as possible.
2. The therapist accepts the child exactly as he or she is.
3. The therapist establishes a feeling of permissiveness in the relationship so that the child feels free to express his or her feelings completely.
4. The therapist is alert to recognize the feelings the child is expressing and reflects those feelings back in such a manner that the child gains insight into his or her behavior.
5. The therapist maintains a deep respect for the child's ability to solve his or her own problems if given an opportunity to do so. The responsibility to make choices and to institute change is the child's.
6. The therapist does not attempt to direct the child's actions or conversa-

tion in any manner. The child leads the way, the therapist follows.

7. The therapist does not attempt to hurry the therapy along. It is a gradual process and must be recognized as such by the therapist.

8. The therapist only establishes those limitations necessary to anchor the therapy to the world of reality and to make the child aware of his responsibility in the relationship.

In 1949 Bixler wrote an article entitled "Limits Are Therapy" and, in a sense, ushered in a movement in which the development and enforcement of limits was considered the primary vehicle of change in therapy sessions. Bixler (1949, p. 2) suggests that the therapist set limits with which he or she is comfortable, including:

1. The child should not be allowed to destroy any property or facilities in the room other than play equipment.

2. The child should not be allowed to physically attack the therapist.

3. The child should not be allowed to stay beyond the time limit of the interview.

4. The child should not be allowed to remove toys from the playroom.

5. The child should not be allowed to throw toys or other material out of the window.

Ginott (1959, 1961) felt that the therapist, by properly enforcing limits, can reestablish the child's view of himself or herself as a child who is protected by adults. To say that this technique stresses limits is not to say that other techniques do not use limits. Many other therapists and therapy techniques use limits explicitly but they are not seen as the major effective element of the therapy. The rationale in limit-setting therapy is that children who manifest specific acting-out behavior can no longer trust adults to react in consistent ways and therefore must constantly test their relation to adults. Limits allow the child to express negative feelings without hurting others and subsequently fearing retaliation. Further, limits allow the therapist to maintain a positive attitude toward the child because he or she does not feel compelled to tolerate the child's aggressive acting out.

In this brief history we have attempted to review the early diversification of psychoanalytic play therapy into various clinical approaches. The chapters in Part 1 of this volume discuss the recent advances in some of these approaches and present information on several more recently developed approaches.

REFERENCES

Allen, F. (1942) *Psychotherapy with children.* New York: Norton.

Axline, V. (1947) *Play therapy.* Boston: Houghton-Mifflin.

Beach, F. (1945) Current concepts of play in animals. *American Naturalist,* **79,** 523–541.

Berlyne, D. (1960) *Conflict, arousal, and curiosity.* New York: McGraw-Hill.

Bettelheim, B. (1972) Play and education. *School Review,* **81,** 1–13.

Bixler, R. (1949) Limits are therapy. *Journal of Consulting Psychology,* **13,** 1–11.

Boll, E. (1957) The role of preschool playmates: A situational approach. *Child Development,* **28,** 327–342.

Chateau, J. (1954) *L'enfant et le Jeu.* Paris: Editions du Scarabec.

Corter, C.; Rheingold, H., & Eckerman, C. (1972) Toys delay the infant's following of his mother. *Developmental Psychology,* **6,** 138–145.

Cramer, P. (1975) The development of play and fantasy in boys and girls: Empirical studies. *Psychoanalysis and Contemporary Science,* **4,** 529–567.

Csikszentmihalyi, M. (1975) Play and intrinsic rewards. *Journal of Humanistic Psychology,* **15**(3), 41–63.

Csikszentmihalyi, M. (1976) What play says about behavior. *Ontario Psychologist,* **8**(2), 5–11.

Dohlinow, P., & Bishop, N. (1970) The development of motor skills and social relationships among primates through play. In J. Hill (Ed.), *Minnesota symposia on child psychology,* Vol. 4. Minneapolis: University of Minnesota Press.

Druker, J. (1975) Toddler play: Some comments on its functions in the developmental process. *Psychoanalysis and Contemporary Science,* **4,** 479–527.

Erikson, E. (1950) *Childhood and Society.* New York: Norton.

Evans, M. (1974) Play is life itself. *Theory into Practice,* **13**(4), 267–272.

Frank, L. (1955) Play in personality development. *American Journal of Orthopsychiatry,* **25,** 576–590.

Frank, L. (1968) Play is valid. *Childhood Education,* **32,** 433–440.

Freud, A. (1928) *Introduction to the technique of child analysis.* Translated by L.P. Clark. New York: Nervous and Mental Disease Publishing.

Freud, S. (1909) Analysis of a phobia in a five-year-old boy. In *Standard edition,* Vol. 10. London: Hogarth, 1955.

Freud, S. (1962) Creative writers and daydreaming. In *Standard edition,* Vol. 9. London: Hogarth.

Ginott, H. (1959) The theory and practice of therapeutic intervention in child treatment. *Journal of Consulting Psychology,* **23,** 160–166.

Ginott, H. (1961) *Group psychotherapy with children.* New York: McGraw-Hill.

Goldberg, S., & Lewis, M. (1969) Play behavior in the year-old infant: Early sex differences. *Child Development,* **40,** 21–31.

Groos, K. (1898) *The play of animals.* Translated by E. Baldwin. New York: Appleton.

Hambridge, G. (1955) Structured play therapy, *American Journal of Orthopsychiatry,* **25,** 601–617.

Hug-Hellmuth, H. (1921) On the technique of child-analysis. *International Journal of Psycho-Analysis,* **2,** 287–305.

Huizinga, J. (1950) *Homo ludens: A study of the play element in culture.* New York: Roy.

Hutt, C. (1970) Specific and diverse exploration. In H. Reese & L. Lipsitt (Eds.), *Advances in child development and behavior,* Vol. 5. New York: Academic Press.

Klein, M. (1932) *The psycho-analysis of children.* London: Hogarth.

Krasner, W. (1976) *Children's play and social speech.* Department of Health, Education, and Welfare; National Institute of Mental Health, Maryland.

Lazarus, A. (1973) Multimodal behavior therapy: Treating the basic id. *Journal of Nervous and Mental Disease,* **156,** 404–411.

Levy, D. (1938) Release therapy in young children. *Psychiatry,* **1,** 387–389.

Mahler, M., Pine, F., & Bergman, A. (1975) *The psychological birth of the human infant: Symbiosis and individuation.* New York: Basic Books.

Mason, W. (1965) The social development of monkeys and apes. In I. DeVore (Ed.), *Primate behavior: Field studies of monkeys and apes.* New York: Holt, Rinehart & Winston.

Moustakas, C. (1959) *Psychotherapy with children.* New York: Harper & Row.

Piaget, J. (1962) *Play, dreams, and imitation in childhood.* New York: Norton.

Plant, E. (1979) Play and adaptation. *The Psychoanalytic Study of the Child,* **34,** 217–232.

Pulaski, M. (1974) The importance of ludic symbolism in cognitive development. In J. Magary, M. Poulson, & G. Lubin (Eds), *Proceedings of the third annual UAP conference: Piagetian theory and the helping professions.* Los Angeles: University of Southern California Press.

Rank, O. (1936) *Will therapy.* New York: Knopf.

Rheingold, H., & Eckerman, C. (1969) The infant's free entry in a new environment. *Journal of Experimental Child Psychology,* **8,** 271–283.

Rheingold, H., & Samuels, H. (1969) Maintaining the positive behavior of infants by increased stimulation. *Developmental Psychology,* **1,** 520–527.

Rogers, C. (1959) A theory of therapy, personality, and interpersonal relationships as developed in the client-centered framework. In S. Koch (Ed.), *Psychology: A study of science,* Vol. 3. New York: McGraw-Hill.

Sandler, J., & Nagera, H. (1963) Aspects of the metapsychology of fantasy. *The Psychoanalytic Study of the Child,* **18,** 159–194.

Schaefer, C., & Millman, H. (1977) *Therapies for children.* San Francisco: Jossey-Bass.

Schiller, F. (1875) *Essays, aesthetical and philosophical.* London: Bell.

Slobin, D. (1964) The fruits of the first season: A discussion of the role of play in childhood. *Journal of Humanistic Psychology,* **4,** 59–79.

Solomon, J. (1938) Active play therapy. *American Journal of Orthopsychiatry,* **8,** 479–498.

Switsky, H., Haywood, H., & Isett, R. (1974) Exploration, curiosity, and play in young children: Effects of stimulus complexity. *Developmental Psychology,* **10,** 321–329.

Taft, J. (1933) *The dynamics of therapy in a controlled relationship.* New York: Macmillan.

Walder, R. (1933) The psychoanalytic theory of play. *Psychoanalytic Quarterly,* **2,** 208–224.

Weisler, A., & McCall, R. (1976) Exploration and play: Resume and redirection. *American Psychologist,* **31**(7), 492–508.

CHAPTER 1

Psychoanalytic Play Therapy

AARON H. ESMAN

INTRODUCTION

The role of play in child psychoanalysis is somewhat more ambiguous than is commonly believed. It is striking that in the early literature of the Vienna School (A. Freud, 1926) play is discussed only in passing; Hug-Hellmuth (1921) speaks of the child playing with his own toys in the course of sessions held, as she recommended, in the child's home, while Anna Freud refers to play as a means of promoting the child's verbalization, which is for her the true medium of analysis in latency-age children. Fries (1937), however, gives a fairly detailed account of the use of play in the analysis of a four-year-old conducted under Miss Freud's supervision; the aim of her paper was to delineate the distinctions between the Freudian and Kleinian approaches to the use of play in child analytic work. She presents the role of play as a source of clues to the child's inner life, but emphasizes the desirability of withholding interpretation until the child has, through the systematic working through of his resistances, gained access to his own specific and unique traumatic experiences.

In contrast, the Berlin/London School under the founding guidance of Melanie Klein (1932) conceived of the child's play as equivalent to the "free associations" of adult patients. Accordingly, play activities were and are treated as the primary data on which to base interpretations; further, the child's play was to be translated into the presumed language of the unconscious, generally within the framework of the assumed transference configuration. Thus, as in Klein's classical example, the three-and-a-half-year-old boy who began his hour by banging together two trucks he had selected was told that he was thinking about his parents' sexual intercourse. Hanna Segal (1964) cites the following illustration from the analysis of a five-year-old girl:

> Towards the end of a session which took place a few weeks before a long break, she started spreading glue on the floor of the playroom and on her shoes. She was at that time particularly preoccupied with pregnancies. I interpreted that she wanted to glue herself to the floor so as not to be sent away at the end of the session which represented

the interruption of her treatment. She confirmed this interpretation verbally and then proceeded to smear the glue in a more messy and dirty fashion saying with great satisfaction "But it's also a 'sick' right on your floor." I interpreted that she wanted to glue herself not only to the inside of the room, but also to the inside of my body where new babies grew, and to mess it and dirty it with the "sick." The next day she brought me a big red geranium. She pointed to the stem and the plentiful buds round it and said "Do you see? All those babies come out of the stem. This is a present for you." I interpreted that now she wanted to give me the penis and all the little babies that come out of it to make up for what she felt was the mess that she had made of my babies and the inside of my body the previous day. (p. 15)

The Kleinian method uses play not so much as a means to the end of promoting the treatment relationship and furthering communication, but as an end in itself—as, that is, the definitive communicative mode. This was promoted, no doubt, by Klein's tendency to treat very young children—often, at two-and-a-half or three, barely verbal—whereas the Vienna group were more inclined to treat somewhat older children whose verbal skills were better established.

In any case, the dominant influence in child analytic practice in the United States has been that of Anna Freud, her pupils, and her associates, and it is, by and large, her approach that has dominated the theory and practice of play therapy in clinical work with children in this country. In this essay I shall attempt to spell out the principles of this mode of operation, and to address certain aspects of its clinical application, particularly with regard to issues of maturation and cognitive development. Finally I shall consider the role and requirements of the therapist in such work.

PROCEDURE

Technique: Using Play in Psychoanalytic Child Therapy

It is important in understanding the use of play in psychoanalytic child therapy to know what it is *not* used for. This is not to imply that any of these "non-uses" may not have a place in other therapeutic methods; it serves simply to delimit the psychoanalytic approach from those alternative methods described in other chapters. It should be clear that psychoanalytic therapy with children, as with adults, is predicated on the analysis of resistance and of transference, and that at bottom all interventions are geared to these fundamental ends.

Thus play is not, in child psychoanalytic therapy, used as a means of achieving *abreaction*. Though in Freud's early work this process of affective release seemed to be beneficial, subsequent experience indicated that it is of very limited utility and applicable, if at all, only in rare cases of acute traumatic neuroses (David Levy's "release therapy" [1939] was based on this principle). In the kinds of cases usually brought to psychotherapy or analysis today the structure of the disorder is generally so complex and the determinants of unconscious conflict so varied and manifold that no abreactive process that fails to explore unconscious defenses and ego restrictions is likely to be of more than transitory value.

Further, play is not used to provide the child with *recreation.* Without question, the expansion of the child's recreational repertoire is a valuable goal in the overall treatment process with many children, especially those who are overly constricted, immature, or socially inept. It is not, however, the province of psychoanalytic therapists to provide such experience; on the contrary, were they to do so by entering actively into the child's play, they would severely impair their availability as transference figures and their ability to maintain the position of a neutral observer—a position which is the necessary foundation for their ability to understand the child's behavior. Admittedly it is at times difficult, even impossible, to withhold some level of participation in the child's play; even then, however, the therapist must keep his or her attention focused on the primary goal, which is to serve as *participant observer* rather than playmate.

Finally, play is not used as a means of *educating* the child. Again, play may in other contexts be a legitimate and useful instrument of instruction; indeed, educators commonly exploit its potential in this direction (cf. Piers, 1972). But the function of psychoanalytic child therapy is not to educate the child but to resolve those conflicts that may interfere with his or her ability to utilize the usual educational resources to maximal capacity. Undoubtedly, the child may derive some secondary educational benefits from the treatment process either through identification with the therapist or through the practice of certain kinds of play activities (cf. Beiser, 1979), but the remediation of educational deficits and/or moral education are not the primary aims of the treatment. Where such needs are present, ancillary figures should be called upon for appropriate services.

How then is play used in psychoanalytic child therapy? Briefly, it is used as a means of establishing contact with the child, as a medium of observation and a source of data and, at times, as a device that promotes interpretive communication.

Establishing Contact.   In the early days of child analysis it was thought that a "preparatory period" was required to engage the child's interest and to establish a "positive transference." To this end, as indicated, Hug-Hellmuth and Anna Freud would visit the child in his or her home, even conduct the treatment there, using the child's own toys as a means of promoting what we would now call a "working alliance." Although subsequent work, particularly that of Berta Bornstein (1945) on the technique of resistance analysis, led to the elimination of this "preparatory phase," it remains true that the analyst seeks the best way to facilitate the child's engagement in the treatment process by meeting him or her at the level at which the child can best communicate. For the young child, particularly, this level is that of play. As Sylvester and Cooper (1966) say, "Toys provide a way for the child to relate to the therapist, to modulate distance and closeness or even privacy, [and] to provide as easy a flow of communication as possible" (p. 626).

Accordingly, play materials should be readily available to the child. The therapist should, however, guard against suggesting their use; his or her position should be a permissive but not directive one, bearing in mind the ultimate aim of the treatment—to help the child to verbalize conflicts and make use of the therapist's interpretive efforts.

Promoting Observation.   In the psychoanalytic treatment of adults we rely on the patient's spontaneous associations, in the context of his or her (at least conscious) willing participation in an effort to relieve subjective distress. Since for the child none of these conditions is likely to apply, other means are necessary. For the Kleinians the situation is simple; the child's play is considered fully equivalent to the adult's free associations and equally available for interpretation along the lines of the Kleinian theory of development and symptom formation. For the Freudian therapist, however, the problem is more complex. Play is seen not as the equivalent of "free association" but as an ego-mediated mode of behavior, serving a variety of psychological purposes (cf. Waelder, 1933), yielding a substantial body of data, but requiring supplementation from a variety of additional sources, including the parents. Play is, therefore, only one of the sources from which the therapist derives inferences about the child, but it can be an extremely useful one, both in the process of initial diagnostic assessment and during ongoing treatment. For the former I can cite no better illustration than this one, from an unpublished paper by the late Swiss child analyst Andree Royon (1959):

A girl of five was recently brought to me because of her eating difficulties. Her mother told me that she was quite an easy child except at mealtimes [during] which she would dawdle and play at the table, and keep food in her mouth to a point where, as the mother had put it, she drove her crazy. The little girl was brought in by her mother and made no difficulty about having her leave the office. I asked the child if she knew why she had come, she said, "Yes, because Mommy says I am bad." "Are you?" said I. She replied, "Of course." Then she walked over to the toy shelves and with one sweep of her hand sent a family of dolls to the floor. She then turned to me and smiled the smile of innocence.

What has this little girl in the first act of play communicated to the observer? Verbally she denies the conflict with her mother; by the same token she indicates the stage she has reached in the development of her superego: Mother says I am bad, therefore I am, which is the meaning of her "of course." Her mother's criticisms, however, have not been wholly internalized. They have not yet become self criticism, and she is immediately seeing me as a person who might also criticize. The situation that she is in, which is one of anxiety, calls then for her usual defense system, and what complicates it—as so often is the case—is the combination of defenses: She identifies with the aggressor and performs what she knows to be a reprehensible act; is not she in fact refusing my toys, the equivalent of food offered by her mother? She behaves aggressively, turning her aggression against the very person from whom she expects her aggression. But while reversing the roles of attacker and attacked she is also using the mechanism of denial by her charming smile which seems to mean, "See, I am not naughty at all." The hypothesis which at this point occurred to me was that this child was not eating in order to bring about her mother's anger because she was guilty in the first place. Oedipal conflict? Sibling rivalry? Masturbation? Penis envy? The story in time would be told. What is of interest at this point is to observe the ability of the child at her first communication to tell of the complexity of her problem involving the whole of her emotional life while it had very little to do with eating per se.

Note that the analyst does not interpret to the child on the basis of this sequence; her speculations must await further clarification based on additional data before any intervention is made. This is the cardinal difference between the Freudian and Kleinian modes of using play in child treatment.

Play as a Medium of Interpretation.   By whatever means the analyst arrives at formulations about the child's conflicts, his or her ultimate therapeutic tool is interpretation. It is here that skill, tact, and empathic sensitivity are put to the strictest test; that is, how can he or she best express his or her thoughts so that the patient can accept and make use of them?

With the adult patient the matter is relatively simple; interpretations are phrased in secondary process language, using a vocabulary as close to that of the patient's usual mode of communication as possible. Although this may be the ultimate goal in child analysis as well, its achievement is rendered difficult, and at times impossible, by the immaturities of children's cognitive organization, limitations in their use of language, their dependent attachment on those who figure in their conflicts, and the tenacious character of their resistances. All of these factors frequently combine to dictate a mode of communication referred to by Ekstein and Caruth (1966) as "interpretation within the metaphor." This involves, at various levels, using the play situation and/or the figures represented in it as the subject and object of the interpretive sentence. Such a communication may be a relatively simple one at a low level of displacement, as in the following case:

Peter, a six-year-old boy, was engaged in vigorous play with cowboy and Indian figures. The principal "cowboy" was decimating the ranks of the "Indians," flinging them about the room with noisy abandon. To have suggested that it appeared that he was expressing his rage against his rigid punitive parents would, at this early stage of the treatment, have induced either bland denial or angry resistance. The principal aim of the moment was to connect the action with a named affect—no matter, at that point, whose. Therapeutic tact—and tactics—dictated, then, the comment, "That cowboy sure looks angry at those Indians." "Sure he is," said Peter. "They keep taking his things away from him."

Such an intervention can be considered a preparatory or partial interpretation—to be followed, sooner or later, by "I'll bet you get angry like that sometimes"—or something similar. But the communication within the displaced metaphorical context of the play situation is a necessary starting point for the gradual process of bringing the child's affect and his conflict into the arena of verbal expression.

An infinitely more elaborate, complex, ingenious application of this principle is provided by Ekstein and Friedman (1957), who describe the extended treatment of a borderline psychotic adolescent boy through the use of various levels of "play action, play acting and acting out." Much of the interpretive work is carried on by communicating within the metaphor of delinquent and criminal fantasy played out by the patient, with the therapist functioning always as observer but with varying degrees of participation.

Lewis (1974) has distinguished variant levels of intervention in child analysis. These include: *attention* statements, aimed at bringing to the child's awareness "the basic factual context of his actions and/or verbalizations"; *reductive* statements, which seek to demonstrate unnoticed patterns of behavior by reducing disparate events to a common form; *situational* statements, which seek to make the child aware of those situations that give rise to certain affects or behaviors; *transference* interpretations, which seek to show the child how his conflicts are reflected in his relationship with the therapist; and *etiological* statements, which seek to link for the patient his current behaviors and early developmental events. Again, tact, skill, and a recognition of the child's cognitive capacities will dictate which level of communication the therapist will choose and the degree to which he or she frames his communication within the play metaphor or in direct language.

Materials and Their Use

As with any mode of interaction, psychotherapeutic communication with the child must be attuned to his or her level of affective and cognitive development. This dictum applies, specifically, to the choice and use of play material in child therapy. For each age group, and, despite some current ideologies, for each sex certain materials are appropriate whereas others will gather the dust of disuse. A further principle also applies here—the principle of economy. A plethora of complex play material serves more to confuse the child than to promote his or her engagement; further, it tends to portray the therapist as an inexhaustible gratifier, a subsidiary of FAO Schwarz, an ever-flowing breast if you will, rather than a collaborator in a therapeutic enterprise. As Sylvester and Cooper put it, "What is advocated stems from another basic principle of all theory, which demands that one do the most with the least; a treatment room should be stocked with toys that are simple and durable and provide a minimum of clutter" (p. 626). Finally, the materials should be consistent with the therapist's own sense of comfort and the realities of the available space; one would not suggest the use of finger paints in an office which has no available running water or for a therapist who doesn't like to get his own hands dirty.

A suitable complement of play materials would include (though not necessarily be limited to) a good stock of paper for drawing and cutting; crayons and marking pens; plasticine or Play-Doh for modeling; blocks of various sizes (small and large) for building; small, flexible family dolls and a few pieces of doll furniture; a few hand puppets for dramatic play; a toy nursing bottle and a doll that can be dressed and undressed; a few cars and trucks; two toy guns (yes!); and a soft rubber or plastic ball. For latency-age children (boys especially) a checker and chess set is often useful, and a set of plastic cowboys and Indians is sometimes helpful. For some older latency children, plane and ship models are of value at times, but they can be obtained ad hoc and should not be stocked routinely.

Little else is likely to be required. In particular, complex board games and intricate construction toys should be avoided; like playing cards they tend to serve resistance rather than communication. As much as possible, material should encourage rather than restrict the free play of the child's imagination, and should promote rather than retard the verbalization of fantasy, the expression of affect, and the revelation of characteristic defense mechanisms.

Erikson (1950) has described certain important aspects of the psychogeography and psychodynamics of play that are of clinical importance to the child therapist. In particular he differentiates among various realms in which the child's play and fantasy move—the *autosphere*, referring to the child's own body and bodily functions; the *microsphere*, or the world of play objects and materials themselves; and the *macrosphere*, the larger world of the therapeutic situation *including the therapist himself*. As Erikson points out, the child's play in the microsphere may at times refer to his or her preoccupations in the autosphere (e.g., feeding the baby doll may be related to feelings of oral deprivation), but they may at the same time reflect wishes related to the macrosphere (e.g., the wish to be fed by the therapist). The art of interpretation involves the therapist's judgment as to which of these meanings to emphasize in the interventions. Erikson also demonstrated the currently established principle of "play interruption"; that is, that a break in the sequence and continuity of the child's play is an indicator of anxiety and a clue to the therapist to examine the expressed or latent fantasy content for a significant conflictual configuration at that point. For example:

Toni, age six, was playing with a family of puppets. After a conventional scene in which "mommy" put the children to bed, "mommy and daddy" began to argue, then began hitting each other. Suddenly she dropped the puppets and said, "I have to go to the bathroom." The therapist said, "It's very scary when you hear Mommy and Daddy fighting; it gets you all upset." Toni responded, "They yell a lot"—and forgot all about going to the bathroom.

Such dramatic play is characteristic for preschool and Oedipal-age children. In latency, when verbal communication is more secure, defenses more strongly consolidated, and obsessive–compulsive mechanisms commonplace (cf. Bornstein, 1951; Esman, 1975), such relatively free expression of fantasy and conflict is often replaced by more disguised modes of expression—drawing, complex story telling, or, especially with boys, competitive games. Beiser (1979) has written thoughtfully about the use of games in psychotherapy, about which she is somewhat more enthusiastic than many. Games are useful not only as a means of assessing favored defenses, the capacity to tolerate frustration, and the level of superego development (cheating), but also as a means of generating fantasy and of assessing perceptual–motor skills. Simple pencil and paper games such as tick-tac-toe and "hangman" will often be introduced by the child himself; others, such as dominos and checkers, should be part of the playroom equipment.

By preadolescence the use of play will generally disappear from the treatment experience, which should rely primarily on verbal communication including such devices as dream interpretation as means of exploration. Occasionally, however, the preadolescent and early adolescent child may need to regress defensively to play activities and should be permitted to do so in the context of interpretive efforts to resolve the conflicts that generate such regressive resistance. This may occur, for instance, with boys who find discussion of nascent sexual fantasy and masturbatory impulses too shameful and frightening to discuss, and take recourse to playing "catch" or to compulsive checker playing as means of binding their anxiety.

Characteristics of the Therapist

Certain qualifications are necessary preconditions for the practice of psychoanalytic child therapy. Whatever his or her discipline, the therapist must have a thorough grounding in child development and experience in observation of normal and deviant children in varying situations. He or she must also be thoroughly familiar with the psychoanalytic theory of personality development, structure, and function and must be conversant with the literature in the field. The therapist must, finally, have had extensive supervised experience in the treatment of children in a clinical setting. Such training must be on a graduate level, presupposing adequate basic training and some practical experience in the basic clinical discipline.

Beyond these training requirements, however, the person who purposes to venture into the field of psychoanalytic child therapy must possess certain personality characteristics as well. He or she must be of sufficient maturity and poise to be able to empathize without overidentifying, to permit himself or herself a measure of controlled regression without losing his or her capacity to observe and interpret, and to endure intense affective pressures without loss of control. He or she must be able to deal with provocation without being provoked, with seduction without being seduced. The therapist must be sufficiently comfortable with the resolution of his or her own childhood conflicts to tolerate their reawakening in the treatment situation and their reenactment in the child's play. It is the rare individual who possesses all these resources without having had the experience of personal psychoanalysis.

Above all, the child therapist must possess a genuine interest in children, sensitive curiosity about what makes them tick, and a willingness to subordinate doctrinaire judgments to actual clinical observation. Finally, he or she must be willing and able to be completely honest with both patients and self.

CONCLUSIONS

In the psychoanalytic treatment of children, play has an established and defined function. It promotes the working relationship between patient and therapist, and it allows for the communication of wishes, fantasies, and conflicts in ways the child can tolerate affectively and express at the level of his or her cognitive capacities. The therapist's function is to observe, attempt to understand, integrate, and ultimately communicate the meanings of the child's play in order to promote the child's understanding of his or her conflict toward the end of more adaptive resolution. Play in psychoanalytic therapy is a means to that end. It is conceived of not as a therapeutic agent in its own right, but as one of many instruments through which the child and therapist communicate with one another toward what should become their common therapeutic goal.

REFERENCES

Beiser, H. (1979) Formal games in diagnosis and therapy. *Journal of the American Academy of Child Psychiatry*, **18**, 480–488.

Bornstein, B. (1945) Clinical notes on child analysis. *Psychoanalytic Study of the Child*, **1**, 151–166.

Bornstein, B. (1951) On latency. *Psychoanalytic Study of the Child*, **6**, 279–285.

Ekstein, R. & Caruth, E. (1966) Interpretation within the metaphor: Further considerations. In R. Ekstein (Ed.), *Children of time and space, of action and impulse*. New York: Appleton-Century-Crofts. Pp. 158–166.

Ekstein, R., Caruth, E., & Friedman, S. (1957) The function of acting out, play action, and play acting in the psychotherapeutic process. *Journal of the American Psychoanalytic Association*, **5**, 581–629.

Erikson, E. (1950) *Childhood and society*. New York: Norton.

Esman, A. (1975) The latency period. In G. Wiedeman (Ed.), *Personality development and deviation*. New York: International Universities Press. Pp. 123–234.

Freud, A. (1926) *The psychoanalytical treatment of children*. London: Imago Press, 1946.

Fries, M. (1937) Play technique in the analysis of young children. *Psychoanalytic Review*, **24**, 233–245.

Hug-Hellmuth, H. (1921) On the technique of child analysis. *International Journal of Psychoanalysis*, **2**, 287–305.

Klein, M. (1932) *The psychoanalysis of children*. London: Hogarth Press.

Levy, D. (1939) Release therapy. *American Journal of Orthopsychiatry*. **9**, 713–736.

Lewis, M. (1974) Interpretation in child analysis: Developmental considerations. *Journal of the American Academy of Child Psychiatry*, **13**, 32–53.

Piers, M. (Ed.) (1972) *Play and development*. New York: Norton.

Royon, A. (1959) The Use and Meaning of Play in Child Therapy. Unpublished manuscript. Pp. 13–15.

Segal, H. (1964) *Introduction to the work of Melanie Klein.* New York: Basic Books.

Sylvester, E., & Cooper, S. (1966) Truisms and slogans in the practice and teaching of child psychotherapy. *Journal of the American Academy of Child Psychiatry,* **5,** 617–629.

Waelder, R. (1933). The psychoanalytical theory of play. *Psychoanalytic Quarterly,* **2,** 208–224.

CHAPTER 2

Client-Centered (Nondirective) Play Therapy

LOUISE F. GUERNEY

INTRODUCTION

Axline, the creator of nondirective or client-centered play therapy, makes the major distinction between nondirective and other play therapy methods: "Play therapy may be directive in form—that is, the therapist may assume responsibility for guidance and interpretation, or it may be nondirective; the therapist may leave responsibility and direction to the child" (1947, p. 9). Thus, the other terms applied to play therapy—client-centered, child-centered, or as Axline suggests, self-directed—also are descriptive of the focus on the child as the source of his or her own positive growth and therapeutic direction. In this chapter we use the term client-centered since it has largely replaced the term nondirective in the world of psychotherapy. The role of the therapist is to facilitate the child's growth. For the therapist, the approach is composed of methods which promote this process, which will be described in detail later. For the child, the experience is one of being accepted as he or she is, being given the emphathic understanding, warmth, and security he or she is unlikely to experience in other relationships. It is the special but genuine actions of the therapist which create the therapeutic atmosphere.

More so than any other play therapies, client-centered play therapy grants the individual the freedom to be himself or herself without facing evaluation or pressure to change. Axline (1947) describes the process as "an opportunity that is offered to the child to experience growth under the most favorable conditions," that is, by playing out feelings as he or she brings them to the surface, faces them, learns to control them, or abandons them. The child "begins to realize the power within himself to be an individual in his own right, to think for himself, to make his own decisions, to become psychologically more mature, and, by so doing, to realize selfhood" (Axline, 1947, p. 16). The realization of selfhood via one's own map is the goal of nondirective play therapy. It is assumed, and there is less evidence to dispute it than to support it as will be discussed in outcome studies, that selfhood will not reveal a narcissistic self-indulgent being, but rather a fully socialized one with qualities generally regarded as those of a positively socialized individual.

At this point, the reader may wonder how a mere child can lead him- or herself to such mature stature. Isn't it necessary for a wiser adult, even perhaps one especially trained in psychological dynamics and therapies, to lead the child? One must understand the history and theory behind client-centered play therapy to fully appreciate the rationale behind what is, in fact, a very viable therapeutic approach.

As might be expected, client-centered play therapy parallels the client-centered approach to adult therapy developed by Carl Rogers (1951) and the University of Chicago "School of Psychotherapy." Virginia Axline, who had studied under Rogers, published the primary text describing the method in 1947. It has since been supplanted by no other, although it was reissued in slightly revised form in 1969. Other major contributors to the understanding and development of the method have published excellent, widely used books, namely Clark Moustakas (1973) of the Merrill-Palmer Institute and the late Haim Ginott (1961) of New York University.

Developmental Theory Underlying the Client-Centered Approach

With differences only in method, client-centered play therapies ascribe to the Rogerian theory of personality development and restoration that underlies adult client-centered therapy (Gendlin, 1970; Rogers, 1951). Both approaches derive from the belief that there is a powerful force within each individual that strives continuously for self-actualization. This is a drive toward maturity, independence, and self-direction. In order to achieve self-actualization, the individual needs "permission to be himself," with "the complete acceptance of himself—by himself—as well as others" (Axline, 1947, p. 10).

Says Axline, in explaining the theory of development:

> The behavior of the individual at all times seems to be caused by one drive, the drive for complete self-realization. When an individual reaches a barrier which makes it more difficult for him to achieve the complete realization of the self, there is set up an area of resistance and friction and tension. The drive toward self-realization continues, and the individual's behavior demonstrates that he is satisfying this inner drive by outwardly fighting to establish his self-concept in the world of reality, or that he is satisfying it vicariously by confining it to his inner world where he can build it up with less struggle.
>
> The outward behavior manifestations are dependent upon the integration of all past and present experiences, conditions, and relationships, but are pointed toward the fulfillment of this inner drive that continues as long as there is life. (Axline, 1947, p. 13)

Adjustment versus Maladjustment.   The explanation for maladaptive development presented by Axline is:

> Possibly the difference between well-adjusted behavior and maladjusted behavior could be explained as follows: When the individual develops sufficient self-confidence

. . . consciously and purposefully to direct his behavior by evaluation, selectivity, and application to achieve his ultimate goal in life—self-realization—then he seems to be well-adjusted.

On the other hand, when the individual lacks sufficient self-confidence to chart his course of actions openly, seems content to grow in self-realization vicariously rather than directly, and does little or nothing about channeling this drive in more constructive and productive directions, then he is said to be maladjusted. . . . The individual's behavior is most consistent with the inner concept of self, created in his attempt to achieve complete self-realization. . . . The further apart the behavior and the concept, the greater the degree of maladjustment. (Axline, 1947, pp. 13–14)

Therapeutic Principles in Relation to Rogerian Developmental Theory

The methods of the client-centered therapists are considered to be those which serve as the instrumentation of the Rogerian theoretical postulates. Simply put, they are based on the assumption that the individual of any age has within him or herself, not only the ability to solve his or her own problems satisfactorily, but also a striving for growth which makes mature behavior more satisfying than immature behavior. An illustration is the infant's drive to master walking as opposed to crawling. The client-centered therapist implements these positions in the way in which he or she relates to clients. Axline explains that "regardless of the type of symptomatic behavior, the individual is met by the therapist 'where he is . . . and [the therapist] lets that individual go as far as he is able to go . . . because . . . the client is the source of the living power that directs the growth within himself' " (Axline, 1947, p. 25).

A logical extension to children of adult client-centered therapy, the method incorporates most of the same principles. However, because children are not adults and play includes actions as well as words, the method has included features designed to meet the needs of children and the adult play therapists. Most notable among these is the stress on the participation of the therapist in the play (as directed by the child), and limits on child *behavior* (*not* verbal expression) in order to facilitate the play process for both child and adult.

Translating theory into practice is perhaps most challenging for child therapists. However, as will be seen, the methods do serve as intended: to promote maturity in children without directing them but respecting the directions they set themselves. Most behaviors of the play therapists are designed to facilitate the child's self-direction, self-exploration, and self-growth. In other respects, the nondirective child therapist need not differ notably from many other therapists. As will be detailed later in this chapter, client-centered therapists are empathic with children, participate in their play, are warm and friendly, develop intimate relationships with the children, and place limits on their behavior. The sole difference is that permission is given to the child to be self-directing within certain limits. The therapist reacts to the child instead of initiating action according to his or her own perspective. This does not mean that children have license to be abusive nor are they abandoned into a sterile, distant, cool, interpersonal atmosphere. Quite the opposite: it means that the resources of the therapist, the play setting, and the child are all utilized to meet the child's emotional needs as he or she is currently experiencing them and to *further* their overt expression. It is assumed that these expressions, offered by the child at his or her own time, will be the fastest route to optimal development.

After the initial translation of client-centered adult therapy was made to children by Axline, few methodological changes have been suggested by others. The method has not been modified significantly by secondary developers.

The only significant developments have taken place not in the method but in the therapists employed. The rise of the paraprofessional movement brought into client-centered play therapy the employment of nonprofessional therapists. Guerney (1964) introduced parents as therapists in filial therapy, which will be described later. Stollak et al. (1975) has employed undergraduate students and both he and Guerney have used teachers as therapists with their individual students. Ginsberg (1978) and Goldman (1975) have used parents and teachers to provide nondirective play therapy for groups of children. Guerney and Stover's (1971) study of process with parents indicates that the substitution of parents does not substantively alter the process, although some changes seem to occur more rapidly.

Essentially, then, the process studies which have been conducted, many of them 25 and 30 years ago, can be considered to accurately characterize the process.

Process Analyses

The first to publish a study of process analysis were Landisberg and Snyder (1946), predating even Axline's book. They analyzed both child and therapist session behaviors, verbal and nonverbal, for type and actual frequency. But they also studied the sequence of responses, that is, what behaviors of the therapist preceded child behaviors. They found that three-fifths of all responses were made by the child; two fifths were made by the counselor. Nondirective responses (these will be defined in detail under the methods and procedures section) preceded 84.5% of the child's responses, with 57% of these being reflections of feeling. This is considered a validation of the effectiveness of the therapists' methods for encouraging self-expression in children.

Reflection of feeling (empathic responses) and structuring tended to precede action responses from the children. Less than 10% of therapist responses were simple acceptance (yes and um-hum), contrary to the notion that nondirective therapy is little more than simple acceptance. During the therapy, children were found to release much feeling, increasing the amount through action expression from 50% up to 70% in the later portion of therapy. Negative feelings increased, peaking later in treatment and dropping back down again at the end.

Finke (1947) developed a system for coding play session behaviors which yielded evidence of a three-stage process:

Stage 1.   The child is either reticent or extremely talkative and explores the playroom. If he or she is to show aggression, it will be at this stage.

Stage 2.   Aggression will lessen and the child tests the limits of the playroom.

Stage 3.   The child's efforts are now expanded into attempted relationship with the therapist drawing him or her into games and play.

Stages 1 and 2 are short-lived for most children; Stage 3 occupies the bulk of the sessions.

Lebo (1952) studied the relationship between the age of children and the types of statements they made. Children ranging from 4 through 12 were studied and found to make very different kinds of statements. Older children talked less with the therapist and invited them to join in less. Whereas they voiced more likes and dislikes, they tested limits less. Twelve-year-olds verbalized the least of all ages.

Moustakas (1955) and Moustakas and Scholock (1955) have done the most continuous investigation of process. In a series of studies they described six stages of play therapy which ranged from undifferentiated expression to clear negative and positive feelings, readily discriminated one from the other in their form of expression by the children. At the end, they observed that positive feelings predominated and were generally in line with reality. When comparing normal and disturbed children matched on other variables, Moustakas (1955) found that both normal and disturbed children expressed negative attitudes, but the disturbed had a significantly higher number of negative feelings and expressed them more intensely. These feelings most frequently were hostility and a compulsive need for cleanliness and order. As therapy progressed, the disturbed became more similar to the well-adjusted children in that their negative attitudes were expressed more clearly, directly, frequently, and intensely.

Moustakas and Scholock (1955) compared the responses of children with emotional problems to those of children with no emotional problems. They found that disturbed children spent more time in noninteractive behavior, that is, they excluded the therapist, and were more hostile and dependent. The nondisturbed were more assertive. Interestingly, neither group of children expressed affection in the play sessions.

Lebo and Lebo (1957) investigated children's age and aggression in relation to the amount of speech produced in play therapy. Aggressiveness was classified on the basis of teachers' ratings of classroom behavior, with 26 designated as aggressive, 27 as intermediate in aggression, and 36 as nonaggressive. A total of 89 children aged 4, 6, 9, and 12 were grouped together according to age. Lebo and Lebo found that the aggressiveness of children of similar age, outside of the playroom, did result in different patterns of verbal expression in the playroom. This would suggest that the play therapy experience will vary with age and style of expression and does not have a fixed sequence. Nonetheless, there is general agreement among play therapists and researchers that all children do express both positive and negative feelings; that the latter decrease as therapy progresses, that regressive behaviors often will emerge and later decrease, and that the expressions become more realistically oriented. A generally positive relationship with the therapist emerges slowly.

Sex differences on any variables coded by researchers have not been consistently shown. The most significant findings indicating sex differences involved the expression of negative feelings, defined to include aggression, reported by Fishbein (1974). Normal boys, both older and younger in age, regardless of the types or age level of toys with which they played, consistently expressed more aggression than did girls.

Reif and Stollak (1972) found that when college students, trained in nondirective play therapy techniques, played with normal children randomly assigned to them, permissive behavior on the part of the "therapists" yielded high levels of fantasy expression. It was speculated by the researchers, based on previous research into fantasy in addition to their own findings, that fantasy occurs most easily in "the absence of compelling external stimulation." In the nondirective session, the demands of the adult and the play situation are very few, perhaps permitting the children to be more responsive to their own needs and internal states and thus more able to fantasize them. (A control group in which nondirective methods were not used did not fantasize as much.)

The value of fantasy for helping to control anxiety and master many kinds of internal and external striving has been demonstrated by a number of researchers (Singer, 1974; Yawkey, 1980).

Toy Research

Lebo (1956 a, b) attempted to ascertain the effects of toy qualities on expression of feelings and on activities pursued by children of different ages and different cultures. He was able to demonstrate empirically that toys generally thought of as typical playroom fare were less successful in encouraging expression for older children than younger children. Such standard items as small toy animals, tinker-toys, dolls, and baby bottles seemed to turn off the 12-year-olds, even humiliate them. Lebo states:

> This unpopularity of the usual toys may be one reason nondirective therapy has been believed to be ineffective with children entering their teens. The toys usually do not encourage them to verbalize . . . they seem to feel that such toys are beneath them and the playroom is not theirs. (Lebo, 1956a, p. 236).

As a consequence of such results, ideas on using other items with older children have developed, which will be described in detail in the following section on methods and procedures.

Fishbein (1974) conducted a study to determine whether age-appropriate toys produced greater responsiveness in normal children than toys classified as older or younger than their ages during nondirective play therapy. Forty children were divided into two groups, ages 4–7 and 8–12, and were shown toys both age appropriate and inappropriate; half saw the appropriate first and half the inappropriate. All toys were chosen from recommended toy lists (Ginott, 1961; Lebo, 1955a). Children of both age groups used both age appropriate and inappropriate toys very extensively. There were no significant differences on either condition or age. Moreover, whether the children's age and toy level were matched made no difference in the amount or type of expressions made, either positive or negative. Fishbein's interpretation was that perhaps later when children were more comfortable with the therapist, the toy selection would be more important, but that for the first sessions, any toys served as good props. However, it must be remembered that all play therapy, whether experimental like Fishbein's or clinical, has to get started and that toy props probably serve important purposes until a relationship can be formed.

It is encouraging that the presence of toys may be more critical than their precise nature, since criteria for their selection appear to be unclear.

BASIC METHOD AND PROCEDURAL ISSUES

Qualifications for Therapists

Professional.   Training for professional therapists is generally obtained in clinical courses taken to fulfill the requirements for a degree in a social or behavioral science. Background in psychodynamics, diagnosis, and other helping skills would generally be present. An individual at this level should be able to become a competent therapist after having received quality instruction in the method and having worked with a few cases, either individually or as part of a team offering play therapy to a number of children, provided that supervision is good.

Today, with the widely disseminated concept of the "core conditions" for successful therapy (Carkhuff & Berenson, 1969) incorporated in various helping skills and counseling courses, understanding and practice in the core conditions of empathy, positive regard (acceptance), warmth, and genuineness is rather widespread. Persons trained in creating the core conditions for adults or young people should be primed to learn what is essentially the translation of the core conditions to the playroom by acquiring the techniques necessary for play application.

However, more is necessary than a study of the methods. First, *an openness to the approach* is probably the most important factor. Today, with behavioral approaches so widely recommended for child therapy, there are many who automatically respond with hesitation to approaches that are not strictly behavioral. One must be prepared to entertain alternative methods that have demonstrated their worth and be interested in at least expanding his or her horizons.

Second, *quality of the training and supervision of the play therapist* must be high. Training and supervision must be rigorous, but also supportive, in order to reinforce fledgling efforts into strange waters. Adherence to method must be demanded. Drifting into other methods or typical ways of dealing with children on the grounds that the situation demanded it cannot be tolerated. Situations "demand it" only when the therapist hasn't really mastered the basic methods or has little conviction about their effectiveness. Helping the therapist-in-training to see the point of mastering, and then to provide the means to do so, is the responsibility of the teacher/supervisor.

To be most effective, the initial training should include both didactic and experiential elements. Role playing of the methods prior to the actual undertaking of therapy with a child is probably the best single learning device (Carkhuff & Berenson, 1969).

Third, the possession of certain personal qualities can facilitate the play therapist's ability to learn and maintain the integrity of the therapy. These qualities can make the task easier but are not considered essential. Of course, past training or naturally acquired empathic understanding would be the most useful of these qualities. The author would add a nonauthoritarian attitude toward children as another.

Fourth, ability to self-explore and receptivity toward acquiring self-awareness would help overcome personal struggles with the method. Client-centered therapy can appear to be deceptively easy on first exposure. Commitment to the child, the integrity of the method, and one's own competence in its use requires self-growth potential on the part of the therapist (Carkhuff & Berenson, 1969; Krantz, 1978).

Whether a therapist who has completed training in the use of client-centered play therapy will make it part of his or her therapeutic repertoire probably will be a function of his or her early experience in its application to child cases. If the fledgling therapist adheres to the method, if only out of a conscientious effort to master it, and receives reinforcement from the child's positive response to it, this will serve as a powerful validation of its legitimate place among the therapist's approaches. It is not uncommon to see rabid behaviorists become advocates of client-centered play therapy, at least in cases where the therapeutic task appears to be more complex than the altering of specific behaviors.

Nonprofessional.   Whereas the play therapist typically will have a general background in a clinical area of some sort, there is nothing inherent in the method which mandates that such a background is necessary. Many nonprofessionals, at least non–psychological professionals such as teachers and nurses, have been trained to use these methods with children under professional supervision and have demonstrated themselves able to effect desirable changes in the children, paralleling those created by professionals (Guerney & Stover, 1971). This is actually the same finding that Carkhuff & Berenson (1969) have been able to demonstrate in relation to the mastery of the behaviors related to establishing the core therapeutic conditions. As a matter of fact, Carkhuff has been able to show better performances from some trained non-professionals than many practicing professionals who were presumed to be skilled in these behaviors.

Guerney and others (Kraft, 1973; Hornsby & Appelbaum, 1978) have been training parents, teachers, day-care workers, and others in the use of client-centered play therapy for 16 years with very fine results. Strom & Greathouse (1974) have developed an approach that is very similar. Although not labeled therapy, it is used for modifying mother–child relationships. Stollak (1979) has trained undergraduates in psychology, education, and other fields. The essential element is that each of these groups has some motivation to work with some children—their own or those with whom they associate in the course of their professional duties. Teachers, day-care workers, no less than parents, experience relationship and discipline problems with students. Because of shortages of supportive psychological services or the like, these people find themselves needing some tools to alleviate problems which interfere with their major tasks. Being able to offer play therapy to such children can serve to alleviate these problems. There are also some advantages in having these adults, who relate to the child in primary settings, be the ones to provide the therapy. The generalization process, carrying constructive gains of the play therapy out to the real world, can be facilitated when the same persons are present in both places.

Parents as therapists may not seem as obvious a choice since they would seem to be permanently and inextricably involved with their children's problems. However, this disadvantage also serves as a therapeutic advantage because of the generalization of attitudes and because of the use to which the knowledge of client-centered therapy can be put by the parents in their daily dealings with the children. Their enormous influence on the children can be modified by their offering of the powerful play sessions and by their transferring some of the behaviors of the therapist to their relationship with the child at home. It is typical that parents who couldn't have cared less about empathy find themselves accurately empathizing with their children in real-life situations outside of the play sessions, and reporting on decreases in conflict and defiance as a result. In other words, caregivers can learn a great deal about relating to children in more effective ways from learning how to administer play therapy. In the therapy hour, the children help to demonstrate to the caregivers that their behaviors are tied in with deep needs, that they can be responsible, and that they are eager to relate to the adult, given facilitative conditions. The lessons go a long way toward furthering the relationship not only in the playroom but in other contacts as well.

Whether parents and other nonprofessionals should be employed as primary therapists will be in many instances a function of professional preference. Some therapists see themselves functioning at their "highest and best" in a supervisory role to nonprofessionals who serve as the primary therapists. Others prefer to be the providers themselves at all times; some decide on the basis of the problems or the external circumstances of the case (e.g., distance required to attend a clinic, quality of nonprofessionals available), that persons outside of a psychological center should conduct the play sessions at the home or school, and report in for supervision.

Our own experience in supervising all these categories of therapists, is that the greatest gain in the ecosystem of the school or family, that is, the total constellation of persons in the family or classroom, comes from the use of the primary adults in these systems as therapists. Children seem to experience the play sessions positively regardless of who the therapists are, and show improvements in play session behaviors, progressing through the usual stages, with all these kinds of therapists. The key factor again is supervision. It is a lot easier for adults involved with the children in other settings to revert to non-prescribed therapist behaviors than it is for persons relating to the children only once a week or so, in a playroom. However, various methods of providing close supervision have been developed by Filial Therapists and seem to reduce these drifts to a minimum (Guerney, 1976; Hornsby & Appelbaum, 1978; Kraft, 1973; Stollak, 1979).

Pretreatment Decisions

APPLICABILITY. The concept of the child mapping out the most appropriate route to personal maturity at his or her own pace eliminates the need to set specific behavioral goals for each child's therapy. Since the client-centered school views different kinds of maladjustments simply as different kinds of attempts to assert the frustrated expressions of the independent self, regardless of the form they take, specific ways for handling particular types of maladjustments are generally not required. No goals are set beyond reducing the symptoms of maladjustment and replacing them with evidence of an emerging self-acceptance, independence, and acceptance of others.

The behavior of the therapist is essentially the same regardless of the presenting symptoms. For persons operating in an atmosphere of differential diagnosis and treatment objectives, such an approach may be disconcerting. How can the same therapist behavior be appropriate for nearly all cases presented for play therapy? This is not an unreasonable question in light of the great distance on interpersonal dimensions between aggressive and withdrawn behaviors, social isolation, compulsive need for companionship, and other such dichotomies. The client-centered therapist would answer that the atmosphere created by the therapist seems to permit the child to normalize his or her behavior. That is, it tends to correct for extreme behavior, in the same way that some medications tend to establish normal physiological processes (e.g., Inderal, which regulates blood vessel response, whether the need is for dilation or constriction), regardless of whether the problem is an excess or a deficiency on the relevant dimension.

CONTRAINDICATIONS. Are there any children who lack the capacity to achieve self-actualization? There are many case and experimental studies reported which document the success of client-centered play therapy with children of virtually every possible diagnostic category. Only two groups of children have not been included in these reports of efficacy—the completely autistic and the out-of-contact schizophrenic. What this suggests is that extreme impairments in the individual's physical capacities to generate a concept of self in the context of the social environment would interfere with a therapy that aims to enhance self-development. Straightforward sensory deficits do not necessarily rule out client-centered treatment of emotional problems. Deaf and other sensorially impaired children have been treated successfully. So have the learning disabled and the hyperactive (Guerney, 1976). Children with intellectual impairments and physical handicaps have been included since the earliest days of the method's existence (Axline, 1947).

GROUP VERSUS INDIVIDUAL TREATMENT. Questions of applicability appear to center on differentiating which variation of client-centered therapy would be best. A number of studies have been done using groups with school-aged children (Bills, 1950 a, b) and recently Moulin (1970). Axline (1947), Dorfman (1951), and Ginott (1961) all indicate that there are some children for whom client-centered group therapy is preferable. Ginott is the only one of them who suggests any concrete criteria for the inclusion of certain individuals. His major criterion is evidence of social hunger, which he defined as "a person's desire to gain acceptance by his peers, to act, dress, and talk as they do, and to attain and maintain status in his groups" (Ginott, 1961, p. 17). He states that information concerning a child's social hunger must be available before assigning a child to group therapy. However, he adds that this information cannot be determined by diagnostic procedures but rather from behavior patterns of the children found from the case history.

Unlike individual therapy, there are suggestions for the counterindication of group client-centered therapy. It should be recognized that these counterindications come from one expert, Ginott (1961), and are based on clinical impressions rather than empirical comparisons with individual therapy. The following categories of children he "deems unsuitable" for group therapy: those with intense sibling rivalries, sociopathic children, children with accelerated sexual drives, those who persistently steal, and extremely aggressive children. The reader must be careful to appreciate that Ginott's determination of their unsuitability was not based on possible poor prognosis for the children but rather the possible destructive effects of their behavior on other group members. There is one category of children that he sees as requiring individual therapy as opposed to group for the child's own benefit—these are children with gross stress reactions, generally resulting from the experience of a severe trauma or catastrophe. Distractions from other children would not permit the child to receive the undivided attention of the therapist which is required.

Unless there is a clinical rationale for placing younger children in groups, or an interest in including significant others in the children's lives as part of the therapy, as with Ginsberg (1978) and mothers, and Goldman (1975) with teachers, the present author would suggest that group therapy be reserved for children no younger than 9 or 10 years of age. Younger children typically are centered on the adult relationships in their lives, and are not yet primarily peer oriented. In group therapy, therapeutic effects are generated not only by the therapist but also by the group members. Acceptance by peer group members is one of much greater importance, and hence potential therapeutic impact, for children nine and up than younger ones.

It is for this reason that much has been written about the composition of groups by non–client-centered therapists, Slavson (1947) in particular. Ginott also considered the selection of group members important. Both Slavson and Ginott emphasized that there must be a balance between more and less expressive children so that they "exert a corrective influence upon each other" (Ginott, 1947, p. 50). Ginott further recommends that it is advisable to have one child in a group whose behavior is not disturbed and who will insist on socially acceptable behavior, serving to calm a very active group.

Last, the reader should note that the major difference between individual and group client-centered play therapy is the differential impact of the therapist on the individual child. In group therapy, the therapist effects will be diluted because of the need for him or her to relate to all of the group members as their respective needs dictate. This can make every moment one of decision for the therapist as he or she attempts to evaluate the behavior of each group member, the group as a totality, or of two or more subgroups. Typically, group therapists attempt to attend to both individual and group phenomena. The children's feelings then are dealt with at two levels—in regard to intrapsychic issues of the respective members and their interpersonal issues with the therapist and/or other group members. While a balance must be struck, the therapist will attempt to emphasize in a given session the most pressing issues for the group as a whole.

WHAT ABOUT AGE, SEX, AND MINORITY STATUS?   As mentioned earlier, there have been serious questions raised about the suitability of the individual method, regardless of its basic potential for the child's symptomology, for 12-year-old children (Dorfman, 1951; Lebo, 1956a). (Children over the age of 12, of normal intelligence, have seldom been reported involved in client-centered play therapy.) Ginott (1961), as have many other therapists, saw the method as losing effectiveness as an expressive modality for children between nine and 13. He borrowed a method from Slavson (1947), activity therapy, which permits more realistic games and activities to be made available to children in this age range. To the writer's knowledge, most therapists do provide a different variety of play materials for children 11 and 12. Whether they present the essentially "younger selection" or "adolescent selection" to children 9 and 10 seems to be a matter of personal preference; in all likelihood they are guided by a clinical assessment of what the child would most profit from. It is safe to say that very advanced children intellectually and/or socially would be obvious candidates for the more mature conditions, unless they manifest some evidence that they are able to benefit from some more regressive outlets. Displays of dependence never before revealed or other latent needs would constitute such evidence.

To the author's knowledge there have been no publications citing any differential effects on white versus black or other minority children on any dimension—materials needed, race of therapist, results, or any other. Published reports of group client-centered therapy which included minority members have not revealed differential process issues or results for minority groups (Ginsberg, 1978; Moulin, 1970; Rhinard, 1970). No differential treatment effects have been reported between boys and girls, for any age or any type of problem, to the knowledge of the author.

The Contribution of the Session Materials. Although the therapist does not select or direct the child's play, the play exhibited is believed to be more than a function of the child's own intra and interpersonal dynamics. The ecological principle that expressed behaviors are a function of an interaction between the qualities of the individual and those of the environment is generally accepted by client-centered play therapists. Thus there have been a number of opinion and even empirical papers published on the effects of different toys on verbal and physical experssion.

TYPICAL TOYS. Ginott (1961) was very interested in the relationship of toys to play behavior in the therapy session and contended that even though children do project their emotional needs onto playthings, it cannot be ignored that playroom materials have "behavior propelling" qualities of their own. Thus he recommended that toys be those which tend to elicit acting-out behavior and not those which evoke diffuse hyperactivity. Application of this advice would result in the use of paints and crayons but avoidance of finger paints. He recommends that toys (1) permit reality testing, (2) allow the child to express needs symbolically, and (3) encourage catharsis and insight. A variety of toys thus should be provided, but the collecting of odds and ends, selected on the basis of the therapist's personal predilection, should be avoided (Ginott, 1961, pp. 240–245).

It has been the practice of the writer in setting up playrooms to include the following criteria for selecting playroom toys in addition to those mentioned by Ginott.

1. Choose toys which can be used in many ways. Avoid a rocket ship that only can be fired and select instead a hank of rope, building toys, etc. Even a gun can be employed in several ways. One can shoot for the sake of shooting, or as is often done later in therapy, shooting can become part of a target game format for self-improvement or competition with the therapist.

2. Choose toys that encourage the feelings most difficult to deal with in real life, that is, aggression and dependence. Thus many props that give the message that such feelings may be expressed are provided—bopbags (punch-

ing bags in figure form, usually superheroes or villains). Harmless rubber knives, guns, soldiers, armored cars, etc., are prominent. Equally prominent are baby bottles, dishes, cooking utensils, water, and pouring devices.

3.   Choose toys that can be used by one or two people. This criterion provides the child with the opportunity to include the therapist in the play in the event that she or he wishes to do so. On the other hand, no demand for joint play should be inherent in the quality of the toy, as is the case with certain kinds of board games.

Axline's (1947) original list of toys is probably representative of what most therapists still use, in spite of the many recent innovations in toys. Many of the newer toys on the market do not meet the test of durability which is a major consideration when stocking a playroom. Except for certain "perishables" like crayons, bopbags, and drawing paper, most of the toys will last despite rough use. Axline's list included a doll house, a doll family, and a few pieces of furniture in proper scale. Clay, crayons, drawing paper, toy animals, toy soldiers, toy car, (rag) baby doll, (two) telephones, nursing bottle, hand puppets representing a family, and if possible authority figures, for example, policemen and physicians, and some building materials such as tinkertoys, blocks, and Lego. Axline also recommends a sand table or low sandbox with a seat built part-way around as an ideal setting for placing soldiers, animals, and cars, etc.

The present author would add, at least for children up to age eight, access to water and water paraphernalia: sieves, measuring cups, and pans. If water is running, as opposed to supplied by pitcher, there may need to be a limit set on the height to which water can be run into the basin.

CONTROVERSIAL TOYS.   Axline recommends a toy gun, which many therapists, including the writer, regularly use. It conveys the instant message that "fantasy aggression will be tolerated here." However, since the Kennedy assassinations, there has been an increase in the number of professionals and, in particular, parents who object to the inclusion of guns. This objection stems essentially from a concern about possible generalization from the playroom to the outside world. However, the playroom "gun lobby" contends that the toy gun is a virtually unparalleled means of expressing aggression in fantasy form. For the writer, it seems more honest to actually supply a toy weapon because when it is missing among the playroom toys (both conditions have been used over long periods), the children simulate guns with tinkertoys, their fingers, or other objects. Mild empirical support has been provided via unsolicited reports from parents and teachers, that habituation to the guns takes place; fascination for guns is reportedly decreased when children who were denied them at home are permitted access to them in the playroom.

Whether there should be paints, and in particular finger paints, in the playroom is an unsettled issue among play therapists. The mess that results from their uncontrolled use is difficult for many adults to tolerate. The alternative is to permit paints and set many limits on their free use. The present writer restricts them from the playroom, unless there is a child who particularly wants them for creative expression as opposed to merely making messes. Paints, again particularly finger paints, are a fine medium when the goal is to provide a supervised cathartic or creative experience. When the goal is to provide a permissive atmosphere, alternate means of expression would seem more appropriate. Books, too, are controversial. While the author has often seen books in playrooms, there would appear to be little sound basis for their presence in client-centered therapy sessions. Books are not an expressive outlet but rather provide input. Again, there might be an occasional child who would express a continued desire to read or be read to, in which case the belief in the child's self-direction of his or her special time would dictate that some suitable reading materials be provided.

PLAY MATERIALS FOR OLDER CHILDREN. There is a feeling among many play therapists that older children are not stimulated toward constructive expression, even humiliated (Dorfman, 1951) by the kinds of toys previously described. Except for studies by Fishbein (1974) and Lebo (1955a), there are only case reports or therapist intuition to support or deny this position. The present writer is of the opinion that such toys would stimulate children to express suppressed needs for nurturance, regression, and dependence. However, upon first introduction to the playroom, the selection of toys will contribute to the child's perception of the experience to come. If she or he interprets the recommended toys to mean, "We are going to engage you in some 'baby stuff,' " the child could become very threatened. Later on, however, once the child learns that she or he is free to explore all facets of him or herself, even some lingering immaturities or missing but very much needed nurturance, such toys would not have the same possibly negative effects. Therefore, for the early sessions, it would be safest to select age-appropriate toys for children 10 - 12 and introduce other toys later. Incidentally, it is suggested by most therapists (Axline, 1969; Ginott, 1961) that toys be casually arranged rather than prominently displayed. Obvious emphasis of certain toys will serve to restrict the child to play in a manner consistent with those selected. It is not possible to know in advance which toys will be most appropriate on a given occasion for each child to further his or her own expression of needs.

Since most children of ages 10–12 have entered a period of competition, realistic play, and games playing, appropriate materials should be available. These include target games of all kinds, miniature bowling and basketball games, as well as some board games. If the room were big enough, ping-pong or pool tables would be useful. However, children of this age are not insulted by some of the more usual fare, that is, bop bags, clay, hank of rope, drawing materials, and masks.

If toys that permit fantasy play of a more mature type can be supplied they should also be included. Such toys will encourage a greater range of self-exploration and expression. Tape recorders, "science" equipment (no glass), stethoscopes, and other medical equipment would be examples. Used office equipment is recommended by Durfee (1952) as a very productive medium for children of this age. Dorfman (1951) suggests that older children be given a choice of whether they wish to play in a playroom or an actual office.

There is no reason for play to be confined to a playroom. If the child and therapist would prefer to take advantage of available outside play equipment, weather permitting, they should. This is often extremely facilitative for older children in particular. Outdoor sessions can be held even in the absence of playground facilities. Walks, "street games" the child might initiate, even excursions to places in which the therapist and child can interact freely are possible choices.

Behaviors of the Therapist

The rationale and goals of the therapist, since they are the essence of the therapy, have been explained in the definition of the method. However, the specific behaviors prescribed for the therapist must now be described in detail.

Verbal Behaviors.   The specific tools of the client-centered play therapist are primarily verbal ones.

EMPATHIC RESPONDING.   Sometimes referred to in the client-centered literature as reflections of feeling or reflections of content, empathic responses are those that demonstrate an understanding of where the other person is, and what he or she is experiencing. The highest type of empathic response is considered to be one which addresses the *feelings* that underlie or accompany a thought or action. An example of such a response follows. (The child looks dejected in regard to describing an unpleasant encounter with friends.) Responding to both the facial expression and the words, the therapist says: "It really hurts when your friends won't help you."

In addition to empathic responses to feelings, the therapist should also respond empathically to thoughts and actions in the case of children in play sessions. An example of an empathic response to a purely cognitive issue would be; "You *think* that is for little kids." (Accepting and understanding child's thoughts.)

An action example is "So you are going to put it in the trash can." This statement merely accepts the content of what is going on, not feelings. However, in play sessions, there is generally more content to reflect on than expression of feelings.

These examples of therapist responses may not convey the process of being empathic with another; it actually involves two steps. The first is to be sensitive and receptive to the other in order to understand with accuracy. This is not the way people usually operate, so some typical behaviors must be monitored. The therapist's personal thoughts must be put very much in the background while he or she focuses completely on all aspects of the child. An attitude of complete receptivity expressed with eye contact, facial, muscular, and postural attentiveness must prevail.

The second step involves the wording of the therapist's understanding so that the child knows the therapist understands and does not reject in any way the child's perception. Questions designed to further the therapist's hypotheses or satisfy his or her own curiosity are inappropriate. However, one may ask a question of the child designed to further his or her expression. For example, "I am sorry. I couldn't hear that because of the truck going by. Would you tell me what you said about your dog again?" Or, (role playing) "Do you want me to be the policeman or the principal?" Evaluations and judgments should not be part of the therapist's responses. Empathizing with the other eliminates all responses which derive from the frame of reference of the responder. The emphasis is on the reality of the other as he or she expresses it. Thus, expressing understanding requires the delaying of: opinions, supporting personal example or agreement, or what the therapist would consider positive response in ordinary conversation. The furthering of the "other" is not an ordinary conversational exchange.

STRUCTURING.   Although nondirective therapy is generally considered unstructured, a certain amount of information must be provided so that the child will know what to expect from the therapist and him or herself about the time and the place. Most structuring takes place in the first session and will be described more fully in a later section. However, in considering structuring as a category of therapist response, it can be defined as the providing of information or the arranging of the environment to facilitate situation-appropriate responses from the child. It merely describes interpersonal and physical structure of the play session: how long the session will last, where the child will go afterward, how often the sessions will take place, what the therapist will do, and what the child can do, etc. Physical structuring would entail removing objects from the room (therapist's books, papers, etc.), bolting a door which should not be opened, providing toys of interest to the child, seeing to it that the child is wearing appropriate clothing, and so forth.

After the child develops an understanding of the basic physical and interpersonal structure, most structuring responses will be offered in relation to questions specific to certain activities. For example:

CHILD (talking to the therapist in relation to masks): Which one do you want to be? The clown or the Frankenstein?

THERAPIST (structuring): In the playroom you can decide about all of these things. I will be which ever one you want me to be.

No advice, suggestions, or assistance of any kind is volunteered. Help is given only in minor emergencies (child's chair starts to fall backward) or the child requests it (as when a lid is stuck on something to be opened).

PERSONAL STATEMENTS.   These are limited to statements that further the interactions and are not intended to be even a brief platform for the therapist's opinions. A therapist might provide an answer to an inquiry about something of interest to the child. For example:

CHILD: Do you like football? (Following an expressive sequence by the child about an exciting game, with which the therapist has already empathized.)

THERAPIST: You're hoping that I'm a football fan too. (Therapist perceives that child wishes to have therapist like football too.)

CHILD: Yeah. Do you go to the X team games?

THERAPIST: No, I don't go to the games but I do see them on TV on Monday night football.

This personal information would be important for the child to have so that he or she will be able to make future statements consistent with reality. However, such information should not be volunteered. It should be offered only after it is clear that it is needed by the child.

LIMITS.   Establishment of limits is a very important part of nondirective therapy. They are useful to both child and therapist for the following reasons:

1.   For the child they help to define the areas within which he is free to operate. Enforcement of the limits assures the child that the adult is *not* an uncaring, laissez-faire person to whom freedom means little, but rather that the free range is permitted with the consent of the therapist. This kind of permissiveness is more meaningful. It is a gift when offered by someone who has the power to take it away, but for the sake of the child, does not.

2.   Limits permit the therapist to remain accepting and empathic. If the feelings or physical welfare of the therapist are threatened, the therapist cannot remain accepting.

3.   Limits help the child build self-control since it is the child's responsibility to stay within the defined boundaries.

Playroom limits should be few, but very clear, definable, and enforceable. A limit such as "Be careful not to break the doll" would not be acceptable. A limit must be explicit in terms of the behaviors expected. One must *not* say, "You may not hurt me," if the child were, for example, pinching the therapist with a sharp-toothed puppet. One would say, "I cannot let you bite me with the puppet." Thus the child knows exactly what is prohibited.

Limits should be set for the welfare and safety of the child as well as the therapist. A child would have a right to resent an adult failing to protect him from something that his immaturity or impulsiveness prevented him from seeing as a danger. For example, putting something into a light socket. One should also be certain that aggression against the self, therapist, or property does not reach beyond the psychological tolerance of the child. Guilt and anxiety might result if the limit violated cultural norms. For example, some male therapists do not object to the child bouncing on them, poking at them, in fun. However, since such physical expression could have physical consequences that would make the child feel guilty, one should stop it even if it is not personally aversive.

It is never necessary to recite a list of limits. Merely letting the child know that there are some possible constraints on behavior prepares the child for the time when a limit must be introduced. Some shy and fearful children, even after they become less inhibited, do not break limits. Therefore, it is unnecessary to burden them with them. Furthermore, even few limits sound like a lot when listed, and they are hard to remember when grouped. The "teachable moment" is when a limit issue arises.

Procedures for making and enforcing limits are generally sequenced as follows.

1. First infraction, the rule is stated, "You may not stab the bop-bag with the sharp pencil point."

2. Second infraction, "Remember I explained that you may not stab the bop-bag with the pencil. If it happens again, we will need to (remove the pencil, leave the room)" or whatever else is considered appropriate.

3. Third infraction, "Remember I told you that if the bop-bag were stabbed with the pencil again that you would need to. . . . Now we will (leave the room, put away the pencil) until our next play session."

There is some disagreement in the field as to what limits should be made and what the consequences should be. Ginott and Lebo (1961) conducted a study to determine what limits and enforcements are typically employed by play therapists of all persuasions, not only nondirective ones. Limits regarding destructive behavior were pretty universal, but beyond those, there was little agreement. Regarding the consequences of destructive behavior, some therapists end the session, others remove the offending object, expel the child, or cut the session short. Ginott considers removing the child from the room an unnecessary rejection. Our experience with this limit has been more positive. The therapist always leaves with the child, so that the limit is experienced as the end of the session rather than an expulsion. It must be noted by the student of the method that once the statement of the consequence has been made, the therapist *must* follow it through. If a limit were to be set, for example, that the child must stop playing with an offending rope, the therapist would have to be certain that the child did not have access to the rope again that day. In ending the session, the therapist must see that the child leaves the room with him or her. The limits and consequences should be as predictable and consistent as a brick wall.

This certainty will help children who have trouble in the playroom and in real life dealing with limits. This tendency will be reinforced if there are no real "teeth" in limits. When children know the consequences will certainly occur they will monitor their own behavior to stop short of limits if they value their relationship with the therapist. Since few children do not value this relationship, they will be encouraged to acquire increased impulse control and ego-strength. Assuming responsibility for their expression will also encourage independence. Consequently, the nondirective therapist very often does not intervene to stop a limit from being broken, but rather, leaves it to the child once it is clear that she or he understands. Of course, one would intervene if the child, therapist, or valuable property would really suffer if the child did break the limit. One must also enforce the time limit at the end of the session.

The step-wise sequence from rule establishment to the enforcement of consequences generally permits the therapist to control the situation, although in most instances the ultimate test of limits rests with the child. Thus power struggles should not occur. The most skilled therapists can deal with a limit issue while at the same time attending to a child's feelings about it. It is the *desire* to break a limit that is the important therapeutic phenomenon and it should not be overlooked, even if the behavior itself is not expressed. For example, the following exchange took place after an angry child tried to pull on a forbidden microphone even though he knew that it was against the rules:

THERAPIST: You're so mad, you feel like breaking the rule about the microphone.

CHILD: Yeah. I can if I want to.

THERAPIST: You want to show me who is boss.

CHILD: Yeah (then simply gets down with no further threats).

By dealing with the feelings that relate to the behavior, the need for actually acting out the behavior can often be eliminated.

If the child had actually begun yanking on the microphone, the therapist would have enforced the limit and said:

THERAPIST: You're so mad, you yanked down the microphone even though you know that is against the rule.

CHILD: Yeah.

THERAPIST: Billy, I am sorry but I cannot let you do that. If you continue to do it, we will need to end today's session.

The therapist is certain to capture the child's full attention when dealing with rules by speaking firmly, making eye contact if possible, and speaking the child's name.

Limits help the child acquire the control to verbalize rather than to act out feelings. For example, a child who already knows the rules is angry that he cannot get permission to take something from the playroom that he'd like to bring home when he leaves. He begins grabbing at the object and knocking away the hands of the therapist who is holding onto it, at the same time crying and calling out "You rat." Therapist: "You want that knife so much that you are trying to get it any way you can. Peter, I cannot let you grab at me. You must stop or we will need to end the session." However, the therapist puts no limit on the name-calling. The child stops grappling but continues to call him names. This is acceptable. Therapist: "You will stop grabbing but you're not going to stop calling me names. You want me to know with names how mad you are at me."

Physical structuring is also possible for physical expression; however, it should not be intended to eliminate physical expression, but merely to direct it in an acceptable way. For example, if the child wanted to shoot rubber darts at a forbidden spot, an acceptable target might be suggested instead.

Typically, limits are set on:

1. Physical aggression against the therapist or self.
2. Destruction of expensive or irreplaceable objects.
3. Running in and out of the playroom.
4. Remaining beyond the play period.
5. Undressing (except jackets and shoes).

As settings vary, for example, if the play sessions are held at home or outdoors, additional limits may be necessary.

The present writer also includes what we call "personal limits," which are set sparingly but as firmly as the general limits. These have been introduced in order to allow for individual differences in acceptance of child behaviors, especially when parents and nonprofessionals serve as therapists. For example, when playing with baby bottles, children are fond of squirting water streams around the room as well as directly at the therapist. People vary in their tolerance for this. Some become upset only if they have been directly squirted. Others become upset only if they are worried about their appearance that day. For whatever reason, the therapist may require the child to limit water squirting on a particular day. A personal statement should be used to convey this message. For example: "Janis, today, I must go directly outside in the cold following this session. Therefore, I must ask you, just for today, to keep the water over there away from me." After this statement, the limit should take on the power of any other limit and be fully enforced.

We are not in the least concerned about the children being confused about such "inconsistency." We see this as being a realistic adjustment to changing circumstances. The children are very capable of *understanding* special conditions, and can readily control themselves. Nonetheless, their feelings about being denied a generally expected privilege must be respected. This issue would be dealt with empathically. For example, if the child were to complain about the temporary restriction, the therapist could reply as follows:

THERAPIST: You don't think it's fair to have to stop squirting today. You like to do it and don't really want to have to stop.
CHILD: Yes. You won't catch cold. I go out wet all of the time.
THERAPIST: You think it doesn't really matter.
CHILD: Yeah (goes on to something else).

Unless children are testers of limits, which means that they use defiance, noncompliance, and power plays to express their negative feelings, they are usually satisfied to have respect, attention, and understanding extended to their complaints. They do not feel that it is necessary to act out their objections when warm and genuine empathy has been expressed for their positions.

All four of these tools of the therapist—empathic responding, structuring, personal messages, and limit enforcement—are methods that have been developed and demonstrated to further the superordinate goal of establishing the special relationship of acceptance that must exist between the child in therapy and the client-centered play therapist. As Axline (1969) states:

The structure of this self-directive therapy process embraces complete acceptance of the client as he is. . . . In the warm and friendly relationship which the counselor establishes, the client is able to face himself squarely, feeling secure in this genuinely co-operative relationship . . . in [the] effort to achieve complete self-understanding and self-acceptance. (p. 28)

The ultimate goal, of course, is the child's acceptance of himself. Self-acceptance and high positive self-regard result in higher life performances and better adjustment (Coopersmith, 1967).

Therapist's Activities—Technique.   In addition to verbal behaviors, there are other behaviors of the play therapist that must be considered. At the broadest level, these are issues concerning how involved the therapist should become with the child's activities and how much spontaneity the therapist is permitted. Some critics of the client-centered approach interpret the limited number of acceptable verbalizations permitted the therapist to be crippling for the spontaneity of the therapist. They consider the therapist removed from the relationship and a mere reflector of the child, denied a personal identity, or the right to personal responses. Others believe the client-centered therapists sacrifice personal privacy, a sense of decency, and even safety in a misapplication of permissiveness. Naturally, there will be different responses to the same descriptions of any therapy.

THERAPIST INVOLVEMENT.   Readers undoubtedly will react with a variety of opinions to the views on therapist involvement offered in this chapter. However, it is the opinion of the present writer that some of the criticism of the approach stems from what appears to be two, or even three, unlabeled and undifferentiated subschools of client-centered therapy. When each reports on its form of therapy, it does so under the general title. Readers regard it all as the same, having been given no information to the contrary. If one happens to read about therapy as described by Dorfman (1951) he or she may react with repugnance to the lack of reasonable limits. If one happens to read Ginott, he or she may be disenchanted by the distance to which Ginott (1961) feels the therapist should go to avoid involvement in the child's play.

Noting some of these differences himself, Ginott eloquently lays out *his* position on play participation:

[Some therapists believe] that, in order to get well, children need not only interpretations and insight but also the kind of warmth and tenderness refused to them in infancy. They maintain . . . that this can be supplied best by a therapist who is a loving participant and not just a permissive observer. These therapists do not hesitate to participate actively in children's games and consider such activities a logical part of their "parental role."

Other therapists play with child clients in order to induce regression and eliminate resistance to therapy. They attempt to win the child's confidence by eliminating the traditional distance between adult and child. They intentionally devalue their adult status by participating in playroom activities on the child's level . . . the writer believes that therapy is retarded when the therapist participates whether as "parent" or "play-mate." The unique therapeutic role can be best carried out when the play therapist maintains a non-playing relationship with the child, thus assuring that the session is strictly the child's hour. . . . Effective therapy must be based on mutual respect between the child and the therapist without the therapist's ever abdicating his adult therapeutic role. (Ginott, 1961, pp. 92–93)·

The present writer does not share Ginott's view that only passive observation is facilitative, but does agree that the adult role should not be abandoned. However, she believes that the fourth therapist behavior, that of limit setting and consequence enforcement, communicates very clearly that the therapist has not abandoned *ultimate* responsibility for the session to the child. Thus the therapist can respond freely to requests to join in the play without loss of status.

The child is permitted to express him- or herself without concern for being evaluated, criticized, or judged even when limits are enforced. *This* is what makes the session unique and not the participation or nonparticipation of the therapist. The total focus on the child, with reasonable limits on actions conveys that:

1. She or he is the major object of importance for that hour.
2. All of his or her thoughts and feelings are acceptable for that hour, but not *all behaviors.*
3. Consideration of where the child is, what the child thinks, feels, fantasizes, or acts out, is what the business of therapy is about.

It is this kind of personal, noncontingent attention to the child which characterizes the unique experience. It places a demand on the child to utilize this opportunity for attending to him or herself. She or he meets this demand by reaching into facets of his or her usually unexpressed inner life. Since the therapist never challenges the validity of what the child expresses (unless it violates one of the few limits) the child is free as nowhere else in his experience to look at him or herself as he or she really is, would like to be, or not like to be in relation to others and physical reality. In the opinion of the present writer, such self-examination can best be done with the therapist serving in various roles to help project the child's inner or interpersonal world. The child will request the therapist to assume these roles. The therapist should respond without taking over. Such role playing or activity sharing should not leave the therapist feeling like an impotent shadow of the child. If carried out with genuineness and warmth, it will be an invigorating and satisfying experience for the therapist as well as the child.

A related question regarding therapist involvement: How can one be empathic, responding after the child, and yet play the game or take a role?

Our position is that since the child directs the session, the child should be able to direct the therapist to participate in activities within the legitimate boundaries of the session. Taking this position then makes it possible to role play and play games without conflict. The therapist follows the child's leads while participating. The therapist may ask for information if the child has requested the therapist take a role but has not made clear how it should go. The following sequence should clarify this point:

CHILD: Now we'll play school. You be the pupil and I'll be the teacher. You answer when I call on you. OK, Norman! (looks and waits).

THERAPIST: What kind of answers do you want? Do you want me to be a good kid in school?

CHILD: (Provides information to this question, indirectly.) Yells at therapist: You're always doing the wrong thing. You're a bad boy. I'm going to take you to the principal. Get up!

Sometimes children quickly communicate how the game should go to meet their needs. It is obvious, if they carefully deal all of the aces to themselves, that the purpose of the game is to annihilate the therapist. The same is true if the child stands close to a target and places the therapist much farther away. No questions are required here to emphasize and act upon the child's need to win. If such obvious cues are lacking or the information obtained is confusing, it is advised that the therapist play the game in a casual way. This means that the therapist is not truly competing with the child. However, the therapist is not trying to lose either. In a game of tick-tack-toe, the therapist would go to an obvious spot but not tax him- or herself to find *the* spot that will make the win. However, if the child were to direct the therapist to try really hard, this direction would take priority. *Once clear,* directions from the child should be followed as fully as possible.

The skilled therapist can participate in these roles and games while still attending to the child's feelings and expressed motives and reflecting on them. For example: While adding up target scores, the child always gives herself extra unearned points to get a higher score than the therapist but tries to cover this up.

THERAPIST: You want to do better than I do, one way or the other (and later, as this continues)—

THERAPIST: You're going to get more points than I. You'll see to that.

In this way, the therapist reveals that he or she knows the child is "adjusting the scores" without labeling it as cheating. It is important that the therapist indicate that he or she knows what the child is doing so that the child can understand that the therapist is accepting *that* behavior. Otherwise, the child might feel that the therapist would not be as accepting if he or she knew what the child was really doing. This could be anxiety provoking for the child. If the child denies manipulating the game, the therapist should not challenge the child's position, but rather, indicate that he or she accepts the *complete* position of the child, that is, wanting to win, cheating, and covering up. The therapist would say something to the effect of: "You like to think of yourself as winning without any help." Or "You want me to believe that you can win fair and square."

Such comments on the process can be inserted into the games or roles very easily without disrupting the play.

PHYSICAL POSITION.   There is some controversy in the use of the method regarding how the therapist should be positioned in the playroom since the therapist participates and relates at the direction of the child. In keeping with the warm and friendly attitude of the therapist and the studies of how such attributes are expressed (Carkhuff & Berenson, 1969; Stollak, 1979), it is our practice to have the therapist place him or herself on the same physical plane as the child so that the power of height over the child will be replaced by the more egalitarian face-to-face and eye-to-eye contact. The distance should not violate the 36 inches usually considered the comfortable distance between persons in our culture unless the child comes closer or initiates an activity that includes a closeness component, such as playing a board game or wishing to be held on the therapist's lap to play baby. The rationale here is that closeness can have the effect of crowding some children and violating their personal needs for space. As with other variables, children will communicate when they are ready for greater physical intimacy. The therapist's task is to be ready to respond when the child signals.

Behaviorally, this means remaining three or four feet from the child and moving as he moves, unless closer or greater distance is indicated. (A game involving throwing can require greater distance to be a meaningful experience.)

Another question frequently addressed to the client-centered play therapist is whether the empathic responses are not in fact reinforcements. Implied is the notion that these responses are "teaching the child selectively" whatever provokes a response from the therapist, and shaping the child's behavior toward an increase or decrease of such responses (as would suit the child's dynamics).

It would seem foolish to deny that such expressions of understanding and acceptance are not reinforcing. Countless studies of reinforcement have demonstrated that a mere shake of the head, smile, or touch are reinforcers even to infants. The therapist is aware that by selecting and responding to only some of the material available (it would be impossible to respond to every word and act that takes place for most children), there will be a differential effect upon the child. Therefore he or she attempts to be responsive to all *types* or *categories* of expressions emanating from the child, in order to avoid unintentionally communicating that certain ones have greater value than others. Thus the child's choice of expressions is not limited by the therapist but still rests with the child. For example, a child is throwing rings on a ring-toss.

THERAPIST: Responds to the child's Yea! with: That one landed just where you wanted it (warm tone).

When ring misses spindle, child looks over in a rather expressionless way.

THERAPIST: That one didn't quite make it (in same tone as when ring landed).

The therapist should respond with a comment relating to the child's perception of the situation with about the same amount of emotion in both cases. Without this equal attention, the child might in time begin to feel that the therapist is attracted by success and turned off by failure. The play session must be a place where the child can dare to fail and still be accepted. This basic concept cannot be violated if the therapist wants to maintain the attitude of acceptance believed necessary for full growth in the sessions. Therapists must monitor themselves to be certain that their own spontaneous approvals of certain behaviors do not communicate that these are preferred. A safeguard is to be certain that equal attention and affect are offered the child for success and failure, mature versus immature reactions, pretty versus ugly products. Reviewing tapes of the sessions, receiving supervision, or observer feedback can help the therapist accomplish this important task.

PERMISSIVENESS AND CONFIDENTIALITY.   The final issue to be addressed is raised most commonly by parents and teachers serving as therapists, but is a concern of professionals as well. They voice the fear that the permissiveness of the playroom and the special relationship of the therapist to the child there, will come to be expected by the child outside of the playroom. While this would make sense from learning theory, in actual fact, children quickly recognize the uniqueness of the play session in relation to real life, and rarely attempt to replicate it elsewhere. If the reader finds this hard to believe, as parents sometimes do, it is necessary only to remember how differently each of us behaves, and started doing as young children, in the presence of strangers, at home versus in public, or with Teacher A versus Teacher B. We are all capable of quickly ascertaining the parameters of situations and adjusting ourselves accordingly.

A corollary of this question is how much is discussed outside of the playroom about what went on during the session. A child should be guaranteed that what goes on will not be communicated by the therapist to anyone else. Nor should the child need to feel accountable to parents, teachers, or any other interested parties for providing this information. However, should the child wish to share something, that is his or her privilege. Children will soon learn to monitor their reporting if they do not get the desired response. Many children recognize that most of the thoughts and feelings acted out in the playroom cannot be understood by others and thus never share them, even when probed.

Stages of the Nondirective Play Process

The First Session. The first session has very special significance in the execution of all therapies. Although the perceptions and impressions of this session are not unalterable, in most instances they will have considerable effect on the course of therapeutic events. If, for example, the child feels that the purpose of the therapy is to "shape him up," he will quickly erect defenses to protect against a possible threat to the "self." Maladaptive as a given self may be, even to itself, it is not about to be shanghaied into the service of an alien adult. This is a therapeutic principle recognized by Carl Rogers in formulating the nondirective approach.

It is critical, therefore, that every effort be extended to convey to the child that the atmosphere will be warm, friendly, supportive, and accepting. The therapist initiating sessions with a child should assume he or she is dealing with the most sensitive child imaginable, and should orient his or her own empathic responses accordingly. If the child is known to have been accused of being a sissy, anything that could possibly smack of "sissiness" ought to be excluded until later sessions—a doll for example. If the child has been described as being excessively shy, the therapist should be compulsively cautious not to physically crowd such a child until receiving some cues of emerging relaxation. At the same time, the therapist should express by all means except physical proximity as much warmth as possible, that is, through words, smiles, tone of voice, and relaxed body posture. These children especially, but all children as well, will require simple, short explanations of what the play sessions are all about. The bulk of the structuring takes place in the first session. Telling the child that this is his or her special room and special time "to say anything she or he would like and to *do almost anything*" is the first statement. The "*do almost anything*" is an absolutely imperative phrase. It prepares the child for limits which might need to be set later. A statement should be made to indicate that the child is free to play with any of the toys she or he desires. the toys she or he desires.

The child should be told what the therapist's stance will be during the play time. The therapist should state that she or he will play with the child if the child so desires. The therapist's job will be to try to be sure that he understands the child.

Since all of this structuring adds up to quite a bit of verbiage, it is not necessary to say it all in one long introduction. It can be brought out bit by bit, but at minimum, ground rules must be set about who initiates the interaction. For young children, a simple introductory statement might be, "This is a special room. In here you may play *just about* any way you'd like. If there is anything that you shouldn't do, I will tell you."

Some younger children may need additional structuring to translate such a global statement to specific behaviors, in which case the therapist would quickly add, "There are puppets, chalk, sink, and dishes. You may play with whatever you want. I will be here (on this chair, floor, wherever) and you can talk to me when you want to."

Without being impatient about it, the therapist must provide enough structure to help the hesitant or confused child to make use of his or her time. If necessary, it would be within the nondirective structure for the therapist to sit down and mold some clay or arrange toy animals while offering warm smiles to the child until the child feels free to join in or start his or her own activities. Some children never experience a slow start, and generally even the shyest child will become engaged in un-selfconscious play no later than the fourth session.

Early Sessions.   In the early sessions, the child will explore the realities of the playtime, the therapist as a person, and himself in relation to this different social environment. It is at this time that limits are tested and aggressive behaviors may emerge. Dependent or fearful children will work on their needs for reassurance and direction. The therapist must continue to reaffirm the attitude that it is really the child's direction that counts. The therapist should not infer that hesitations mean the child needs adult direction to play, but rather that the child at that moment is lacking the resources to initiate play alone, without support. Alternatively, the child may not trust the adult not to give subtle or even direct feedback *later* indicating that the child's direction was not what the adult wanted. Children need to learn that the adult really will not judge or criticize. They will then become free to pull on their own latent resources.

Occasionally, if a child has been so deprived of stimulation prior to the sessions or so cowed by adults, as in the case of some abused children, it may be necessary to initiate some open-ended games with them in this early period. The therapist can ease out as soon as it is appropriate.

At this early period it is necessary for the therapist to actively structure his or her own identity for the child. If the child plays silently, perhaps coloring, the therapist should remain attentive, interested, and comment on the *process*, even though the child may have said nothing. A process comment would be, "You're really thinking about what colors you want to use there," or "You decided on black for that one."

Midsessions.   Studies of the behaviors of both child and therapist in nondirective sessions have revealed that aggression tends to level off after the first phase and is followed by a greater expression of regressive behaviors. These are expressed in the form of babytalk, playing baby, or feeding and nurturing dolls and *the self*, the therapist, toy, or pretend animals. These behaviors would appear to be a method of dealing with the inevitable independence-dependence issue. Children's concern for the relationship between nurturing and being nurtured is often dramatically expressed as they move from being the baby to having the therapist play baby.

In this phase, the children seem to be building a relationship of trust and relaxation with an adult that has little to do with the control and power issues of the earlier phase. However, this emphasis on affective as opposed to power concerns does not mean that the latter drop out completely. They are still in evidence but not to the same degree.

It is during the middle sessions that the serious business of personality reorganization and a growing acceptance of the self begin to take place. The accepting, noncritical attitudes of the therapist have had their effect.

Later Sessions. Later sessions tend to be more reality oriented. While some role playing, puppet play, and other fantasy play continue, there are more reality elements in them. For example, one child staged a puppet play week after week in which all of the family members were destroyed by a tornado or other natural catastrophe. As the therapy progressed, the puppets were used to present little entertainments, singing, dancing, acrobatics, and the like, which were neutral in feeling and power.

Aggression will generally not disappear completely, although it drops to a low level. At this stage, aggression is generally circumscribed and related to recent events, for example, frustration regarding schoolwork or parental injustice. Tolerance of frustration for the "here and now" of the play becomes quite good, and the child who previously could not bear to lose card games and cheated to win, later will become able to laugh or be casual about losing. He may even go so far as to help the therapist win. Social behaviors will prevail over antisocial behaviors at this point.

CASE ILLUSTRATION

Description of the Problem

C was an eight-year-old, first born, white female referred for treatment because she appeared to be experiencing an overt rejection of her gender. The parents had been somewhat concerned about this for some time but did not regard it as more than "a stage" until the child was referred to the school psychologist. C was creating anxiety in some of the teachers because she refused to play with anybody in the playground except the toughest, biggest boys, who took advantage of her smaller size (she was small for her age) and lesser strength. No injury would produce tears, however, or even a reduction in her pursuit of such play. In the neighborhood, the pattern was the same. The parents were middle class; the father was a middle-level manager in a large food-service operation. The mother, petite, ultrafeminine, had not worked since the birth of C's little brother, nearly three years ago. She had worked as a secretary from C's early childhood until that time.

The parents were thrilled with their son, who was a "picture poster" looking child, easy to manage, cuddly, with a wonderful disposition, admired wherever he went. He was the "apple of both his parents' eyes," particularly his father's. C had been just the opposite from birth—colicy, "willful," and always on the move. Mrs. P remarked at the intake meeting that it was almost as though nature had fouled up and reversed the sexes of the children. She reported no developmental difficulties or training problems of any consequence with C, however. C had always been bright, alert, quick to learn, verbal, and outgoing with other children, and good at physical activities—swimming, bike riding, and so on. She did have a temper and held grudges, which would lead to prolonged moods and angry accusations of the people she perceived as having thwarted her. She "really loved" her little brother, according to her parents, although she would become moody, vengeful, and "physical" with him if he thwarted her or was made a fuss over by grandparents. Since she was so much "bigger and stronger" they worried about her hurting him. C and her father were not as close since the arrival of the brother, but their relationship had never been an intense one. C was not particularly close to her mother either.

She was referred to a university psychological clinic for treatment, where she was administered the standard test battery, including some projective tests. She was revealed to be a bright child with no academic problems. The projective tests confirmed her rejection of her gender and an ambivalent identification with male power figures. Confusion over a need for succorance and a need to be approved for powerful feats was a repeated theme. Strong feelings of rejection were expressed toward the self. The clinicians were not concerned about C's cross-gender interests per se, but they did see her rejection of her sex as a manifestation of her very negative attitude toward herself. Concerns about possible depression were also expressed. C was recommended for play therapy with a female clinician.

The clinician was of the client-centered persuasion and used only that approach in working with C. The mother was seen only a few times to communicate with her about the situation at home. She and her husband failed to accept the recommendation that counseling would be of value to them. They saw the problem as strictly C's.

The Play Sessions

C did not express self-doubts or self-hatred in the therapy sessions at first. In fact, she was full of bravado about all of the physical feats she could perform. She was extremely competitive with the therapist, always setting up games and activities to defeat her. C preferred gross motor play outside and was moody and uncooperative when weather required staying indoors. She had little trouble expressing her negative feelings and rarely used covert means of communication. Her stories of home life usually included incidents that "put down" the family members, except herself, as incompetent and silly.

By midpoint in her 16 sessions, she was talking about herself in relation to her peers. She did not compare herself favorably to them. She permitted herself to relate to "baby" toys in the playroom, which she earlier would not. At first, she made insulting remarks about children who played with such things, but eventually, getting neither reinforcement nor challenge to these views, her suppressed needs for nurturance surfaced. As the sessions continued she played more regularly with playroom toys, even playing "house" a number of times. When outdoors, she "fell" (totally staged) on four occasions and asked to be carried. Such moments were interspersed with some of her more usual, but less vigorous "bravado" performances.

At this point, the mother reported in a parent interview that C was becoming unbearable around the house because she no longer wanted to play with the boys, and if there were no girls to play with she didn't know what to do with herself. She had few girlfriends to select from since she had not played with them earlier. However, she was accepted by them when they did play.

By the time school was out C was part of a group of girls in the neighborhood that she played with regularly. She refused to play with the boys and even went so far one day to subject herself to their ridicule by pushing a "doll stroller" past the place where they were, daring them to do anything about it. As described by a neighborhood mother who happened to witness it, it was a most dramatic encounter indeed.

After 16 weekly sessions, play sessions were held only on a maintenance basis every three or four weeks since the last four, following the above incident, had become very routine—taking walks and talking about the squirrels and other sights along the way.

By the time school started, the case was closed. Follow-up to see if the return to school had reestablished old patterns revealed that C had a completely new peer group, was relating well to all the children, male and female, and was doing very well in every respect. At home, she was less moody, more cooperative, and starting to be "motherly" occasionally to her little brother. Her grandparents, who had no knowledge of the therapy, were surprised to see how different she was from the way she had been at their Easter visit. Follow-up on projective tests revealed healthy self-attitudes and age-appropriate responses to the stimuli. No evidence of depression was present.

Case Analysis

In the course of less than six months, this little girl developed a new concept of herself as a viable, lovable, and capable person. She accepted herself for what she was—an attractive, bright little girl. She was able to abandon the self of a superstrong, unfeeling pseudo-boy, which she had constructed to compensate for what she must have seen as a crippling deficit—being a girl and thus less able to command attention and respect. Psychoanalytic proponents would probably explain the dynamics in terms of penis envy. Behaviorists would probably be able to identify in family incidents frequent, inappropriate reinforcements for maleness and comparably few reinforcements for age- and sex-appropriate behaviors.

From the client-centered perspective, it would seem that C perceived a differential pattern of reaction from the world to her universally charming little brother. She perceived her femininity as the factor most responsible for herself not sharing in the rewards offered her brother. He had always been reacted to with excessive adult approval, according to Mrs. P's proud accounts. There was clear evidence that C witnessed these scenes too. No effort was made to downplay them around her. Clearly, the parents were building their own egos through the son's attributes. C got lost in the shuffle. Since the problem for C peaked not at her brother's arrival or during his early years when an infant requires so much of a parent's time, but rather when he was three, it would suggest that she was unable to explain his charm any longer on the basis of his being a baby. In her perception of things, it was maleness that accounted for it. The mother suggested also that the father reported looking forward to sports with the son when he got older. Neither parent reported looking forward to any special activities of any sort with C nor sharing any with her at her current age. C solved the problem of loss in the competition by trying to acquire an image of supermale, who could surpass her brother at his own game. As a result of the therapist's ability to accept all facets of C, her bravado, her anger, derision, control, need to regress, and her need to be nurtured by an adult, C was able to accept these aspects of herself. However, the self that emerged at the end of therapy, using Axline's analogy of rearranging pieces in a kaleidoscope, was reorganized into a new pattern. This new self was more realistic, had the potential for greater social reinforcement, and was obviously more satisfying to C.

Discussion

As the reader might have suspected, this case was chosen for presentation here because of its successful outcome via the client-centered approach. However, it is noteworthy not only as an example of success but also as an unusual example of the power of the nondirective and accepting therapeutic strategy. Note that C did not talk about her problem (she didn't even perceive herself as having one; her mother was told to tell her therefore that she was going to have a special playtime with someone at the university); she did not attack any of the issues in the kind of direct way that a therapeutic strategist would have assumed would be necessary. What she did, essentially, was work on accepting herself via a pattern that she programmed according to her own needs. This pattern was certainly not one that anyone else could have programmed in the same way, or any more successfully, regardless of therapeutic wisdom. It is the conviction of the writer that had plans to introduce certain topics, areas of expression, or "needed" activities been used, that it would have encumbered, if not misdirected, the child's efforts to help herself.

Finally, the case is noteworthy in that no other help was given the family, beyond suggesting that they be supportive of C's new efforts to join the "female race." The parents were loving, but saw themselves as very removed from the problem. Efforts to have the mother consider the possibility that the excessive attention to the son might be adversely affecting C and should be monitored were totally rejected. Her need for her perception of the situation to be the "correct" one was too strong to process any different perceptions. C essentially undertook and completed the whole process on her own within the special interpersonal atmosphere of the child-centered play session. The contribution of the family was merely that they avoided sabotaging her. This is no minor contribution, but it is not the active one that parent counselors would advocate and perhaps believe essential. Axline (1947) refers to children improving without the aid of parents or caregivers in the first writings of the process. As a matter of fact, as we shall see in the section on evaluation research, a number of definitive studies of the client-centered approach have been concerned with the question of the success of therapy without parental participation.

EVALUATIVE RESEARCH

Compared to many therapeutic approaches, there has been a considerable amount of outcome research in client-centered play therapy. It has consistently demonstrated positive treatment effects. Following the empirical heritage of the so-called Chicago School, many of the studies have been more than simple pre–post changes and single case studies. Control groups, sometimes of two kinds, have frequently been employed. For brevity, only the research that has employed some sort of control condition will be included here.

Significant Studies with Professional Therapists

The client-centered researchers were considerably more active when the approach was first introduced than they have been in recent years. The earliest report on outcome appeared at almost the same moment as Axline's book in 1947. Conducted by Fleming and Snyder (1947) it analyzed group play therapy, comparing maladjusted children to a group of normal control children. The controls did not improve on the criterion measures, which included two sociometric devices, while the treatment children did.

Cox (1953) chose two matched groups of children living together in an orphanage (a controlled environment). One group received 10 weeks of client-centered play therapy. Pre–post comparison of the Thematic Apperception Test (TAT) and sociometric measures revealed significant changes for the treatment group, while the control group showed no gains at all. Since their environment was as similar as is reasonably possible in clinical studies, the therapy was the only factor to which the gains could be attributed.

Bills (1950a) tested the treatment children at four points in time. First, six weeks prior to treatment (a "wait period"), immediately before the start of play therapy, at the end of the six weeks of therapy, and a follow-up six weeks later. The wait period data provided a baseline for the change expected without treatment. The children were selected for "retarded reading" achievement

(1-2 grades below grade level) and maladjustment. The measures used to assess the effectiveness of play therapy were reading achievement tests. Previous studies had looked only at personality variables. Bills found significant gains in reading achievement following play therapy and none during the wait period. Gains remained at follow-up.

Bills (1950b) repeated the same study with well-adjusted retarded readers and found no improvement in their reading ability. He concluded that the gains in reading in the first study were related to improvement in personality adjustment and that when personality problems are at the root of reading problems, client-centered play therapy is effective; otherwise it may not be.

This comparison study is very important because it makes clear that the gains in Bills' first study (1950) were due specifically to the child-centered therapy rather than nonspecific factors, for example, attention, suggestion, teacher effectiveness, and experimenter demand.

With these early successes, the client-centered play therapists knew that they had a "viable" treatment, the first step in evaluation.

The study conducted by Dorfman in 1958 became a model for evaluation research by virtue of its built-in control baseline—the wait period—in addition to a no-treatment control group matched to the treatment children. The study included a follow-up 1½ years later. After an average of 19 therapy sessions on an approximately weekly basis, the maladjusted treatment children showed significant improvement on personality and adjustment measures in the treatment period over their scores in the wait period and relative to the no-treatment group. Scores at follow-up did not decrease significantly from their level at the end of treatment. Scores on two measures were actually higher than they were immediately following treatment.

Dorfman stressed the significance of the fact that the therapy was conducted in school with children rated maladjusted by teachers, and that the changes took place without contact with parents. The early client-centered researchers regarded with much interest their ability to attain therapeutic gains in children without concomitant parent involvement. They saw this as having practical implications, in that lack of parental involvement need not mitigate against undertaking child treatment. They also interpreted it as a validation of their belief in the individual potential of the child to attain optimal development in a therapeutic climate.

The next published study of significance was conducted by Seeman, Barry, and Ellinwood (1964). The study demonstrated very positive results using children designated as lowest in adjustment on teacher rating scales and personality tests. A new methodological refinement was added by assigning these children randomly to treatment or control conditions. A follow-up at one year was made. The most interesting finding concerned aggression. All of the children in both treatment and control groups started out higher on aggression than their better adjusted classmates. At follow-up, all children in the treatment (male and female alike) had lower aggression scores than the average, whereas all control children still had higher than average aggression scores. The researchers commented that despite the commonly held belief that aggressive children need a controlled therapeutic environment, these children showed a striking reduction in aggressiveness as the result of a permissive therapeutic climate. They further pointed out that no work had been done with parents. "This finding suggests that even children as young as seven or eight years may change in the absence of systematic environmental alteration" (p. 66).

A study conducted in West Germany (Schmidtchen & Hobrucker, 1978) added an interesting touch of precision. Employing a treatment group along with a placebo treatment and a no-treatment control group, the researchers were able to show significant improvements for the treatment children on social and intellectual flexibility, and an increase in self-concept, as well as a decrease in anxiety and behavior disorders. The inclusion of a placebo control group indicates that improvements were not due simply to contact and attention.

Evaluation of Nonprofessionals Conducting Therapy

Stollak and associates (Reif & Stollak, 1972; Stollak, Scholom, Green, Schreiber, & Messe, 1975) have conducted two large studies which used undergraduate students, not professionals, as therapists. The earlier study (Reif & Stollak, 1972) was conducted with the goal of demonstrating that undergraduate students, trained and supervised in conducting child-centered therapy, could produce therapeutic conditions and demonstrate positive changes in essentially normal children. The control group was offered a placebo therapy—playing with untrained students who "just did what came naturally" to provide the child with a positive experience. Extensive coding of therapist responses indicated that the trained students did adhere to nondirective methods. As already described in the section of this chapter on process studies, it was found that the children receiving child-centered play sessions were more expressive and fantasized at higher levels; that the higher fantasy levels "more often contained references to intrapersonal and interpersonal situations" and demonstrated resolution of those situations, that is, the appropriate expression of aggression. Their fantasies also showed greater pre–post increments in identification with adult role behavior than did those of children receiving non–child-centered play sessions.

In a second evaluation study, Stollak et al. (1975) utilized trained undergraduates to treat actual clinical cases under the supervision of advanced graduate students. A small group of control children were assigned to untrained undergraduates for simple play times which were considered placebo treatments. Post–test data indicated that significant decreases in the problem behaviors of treatment children were reported by fathers, mothers, and teachers. No significant changes occurred for any of the control children.

Evaluation of Treatment Using Parents as Therapists

Guerney and associates (1964), in developing Filial Therapy (wherein parents conduct the play sessions), compared the therapeutic abilities of mothers trained to conduct play sessions with the abilities of untrained mothers (Stover & Guerney, 1967). They were able to demonstrate that mothers could be trained to carry out play sessions according to therapeutic definition. They were more empathic, permitted greater self-direction to the child, and were more involved (showed more attention and responsiveness) in the play sessions.

Guerney and others then researched the effects of mothers' therapy on children. They found that children's pre–post problem behaviors decreased significantly and the behaviors coded in the playroom showing greater leadership (independence) and less aggression (Guerney, B., 1976; Guerney, L., 1975; Guerney & Stover, 1971). In contrast, after the same period of time as the therapy, a group of normal children who were not involved in therapy but were matched on demographic variables exhibited no such changes. This indicates that maturation and time alone do not produce the kinds of changes evidenced in the treatment children (Oxman, 1971).

A follow-up study conducted one to three years after the end of treatment (Guerney, L., 1975) indicated that only one of the 41 children whose parents responded to the follow-up questionnaire (51 had finished the treatment) had required any further psychotherapy. Four other children failed to maintain treatment gains, four remained the same, and 32 improved in adjustment after finishing treatment.

Using a different sample of children, most of whom received play therapy from both mother and father, Sywulak (1977) showed that parents' ratings of the children's behavior did not change during a four-month wait period. After the children were in treatment for four months, they showed a significant improvement. Further, the parents' acceptance of the children increased in the therapy period.

A follow-up study of this group (Sensue, 1981) revealed even higher scores at the finish of treatment (approximately six months) and no significant losses two to three years later. *At the time of follow-up*, the treated children, who before treatment tested as maladjusted, were as well adjusted as a control group of normal children. Moreover, the parents who had participated in their children's therapy had higher scores on acceptance of their children than the normative sample.

Evaluation of Client-Centered Play Therapy in Contrast to Other Treatment

With a series of controlled studies, many of which lack an aspect that would remove all question about efficacy in relation to untreated children, the client-centered therapists have been able to demonstrate that positive changes consistently take place in therapy for children between the ages of three and ten, even when inexperienced, nonprofessional therapists are providing the treatment. That positive changes have been achieved in client-centered play therapy seems clearly established. Whether gains are less or more likely to take place in client-centered than in other effective therapies is the question that must now be addressed.

Difficult as it is to conduct therapy evaluation with control groups (and the client-centered therapists have really done well on this level), it is even more difficult to find comparable samples of children who have had comparably competent therapists in different, appropriate treatments with which to make comparative analyses. Aside from the logistical problems in conducting such studies, there is the bigger problem of therapists being willing to submit their favorite approach to comparison against other approaches. Ideally, comparable children should be assigned randomly to the treatments being evaluated. This brings up the question of treatment match, a subject dear to the hearts of clinicians. It should be said that evaluation studies should compare only those treatments which have been demonstrated to be viable treatments for the clinical populations in question. Therefore, the ethics and logic of assignment of treatment will not be violated. Regardless of how cooperative therapists might be for evaluation purposes, there is no question that such comparative studies will be extremely difficult to execute. Attrition and maintenance of genuinely comparable conditions of time, external factors, and other relevant but hard to control factors will prevent the gathering of uncontroversial results. Nonetheless, if imperfect but at least minimally adequate studies were repeated with many samples, many therapists, in many places, and if similar results were consistently obtained, one could begin to feel assured that those results were reliable and meaningful.

A study by Wall (1979) has come closest to a genuine comparison. Three variations of play therapy were conducted: (1) by graduate therapist trainees; (2) by parents who were not trained; and (3) by parents under the supervision of therapist trainees who observed and gave guidance to parents on how to conduct the play sessions via radio transmitter. Sessions by therapists and trained parents alike were in the "Axline/Moustakas tradition." Changes in parents and children's behavior were evaluated in play sessions and by written measures. Parents who participated in guided play therapy improved their ability to communicate empathically with children. For the children, there was only one significant difference in 14 cross-treatment comparisons. This finding favored the parent-guided condition, leading Wall to conclude that acceptance of negative feelings by a parent has a more powerful impact on children than does acceptance by a therapist.

SUMMARY AND CONCLUSIONS

The reader who has never witnessed a client-centered play session may not be able to appreciate how completely rewarding such a session can be for both child and therapist. As children express themselves confident of acceptance and understanding, they will engage in creative play and make original, uninhibited statements. The sessions can be touching and poignant as children explore less pleasant sides of themselves or come to grips with some of the limitations of their world. They can also be very dramatic, explosive, or exhausting as children act out their needs for power or control by reversing roles and putting the therapist through an exaggerated version of what they perceive as excessive adult demands. But even this can be rewarding as the basic comedy of an adult playing, for example, the role of a superobedient child is processed. At times the children will convulse with laughter at such antics and follow-up with affectionate responses, verbal and/or physical. It is wonderful for them to have someone to whom they can express any part of themselves that needs expressing, and still be accepted.

The introduction to this section was written in the hope that the reader will be able to sense the basic warmth, involvement, and congruity that are part of the properly employed client-centered approach. However, as one witnesses such an expressive session, he or she would eventually realize that the lively participation of the therapist is actually controlled, always centered on the child, and attuned to his or her communications, even the subtle ones. And, in turn, these therapist behaviors stimulate the child to greater expressiveness. For this is not "just playing" as it might appear to be, but a very special, cognitive, and receptive kind of playing that only the skilled therapist can make look spontaneous.

If the reader were to watch a particular therapist carry out a number of such sessions with different children, she or he would note that the style of the therapist is always the same but that the play of the children is extremely variable. It would also be evident that the differences in the content of the sessions is a function of the children.

An examination of the process would soon reveal to the observer that there are two features which differentiate child-centered therapy from most other kinds of child therapy. First, it is an approach that does not require different methods for different problems presented by the children and is effective across a wide range of problems, including serious ones. However, it can also be used for preventive purposes—to maximize what appears to be adequate development (Baruch, 1949), since the therapeutic process is conceptualized as optimizing growth to maturity from *wherever* it currently is. To put it simply, it can be said that the client-centered approach is viewed as promoting the process of growth and normalization. If the child is too aggressive, treatment would encourage the child to give up these non–self-enhancing, unadaptive behaviors. So it would go with the child who is withdrawn. The therapeutic conditions create an atmosphere which permits the child to abandon the inappropriate and move toward the norm (i.e., that which is adaptive to his or her self-development within his or her own environmental realities).

The second feature is that the therapist must rely on the child to direct this process at his or her own rate. The therapist skillfully establishes the therapeutic conditions of empathic understanding, acceptance, warmth, congruity, and behavioral limits. He or she must also stimulate the child to express himself yet at the same time learn adaptive self-controlling processes. The latter comes in part from the limit enforcement aspects of the sessions.

If the therapist does not follow the tenets of the approach and, for example, tries to direct the child's discussions or behaviors in ways the therapist deems helpful, the full potential of the method will not be utilized and less than complete effects may be achieved. Such a practice will indicate to the child that the "therapist's direction is best" and he or she will be reluctant to rely on him or herself, just as the therapist was reluctant to rely upon the child. Thus, manipulating the child's expression in an attempt to speed up the process will only serve to interfere with therapy. The child will perceive that the therapist makes judgments about his or her session behavior. Thereafter, the child will consciously or unconsciously monitor his or her expression to please (or frustrate) the therapist. Self-discovery and expression will thereby be hampered.

This is not because some vague "self-force for growth" would be disrupted, but rather because the client-centered approach is an integrated system, an entire complex of rationales and procedures designed to stand together. If used as a system, it can have enormous impact on all significant aspects of personality development. If only selected methods of the approach are used the techniques will become mechanical and isolated. A system is not fully functional unless fully utilized.

However, one need not be only a client-centered therapist to the exclusion of all other approaches. One need not ascribe to the theory of self-growth and self-development from which the approach evolved in order to employ the system successfully. One need only adhere to the approach in a total and systematic way and not indulge in what many practitioners erroneously call eclecticism. Eclecticism really involves, by dictionary definition, the bringing together of what is considered the best of two or more approaches into a new *integrated whole.* An example of genuine eclecticism would be the *Multi-Modal Therapy of Lazarus* (1981) in which many approaches are utilized in a planned way according to the tenets of the system. A little of this and then a bit of that is not eclecticism but rather a flying-by-the-seat-of-one's-pants approach.

There are many therapists, well educated in several therapeutic approaches, who regard themselves as multidisciplinary. They employ different therapies with different kinds of cases depending on the problems, the treatment goals, and their own therapeutic strengths and weaknesses with different personality or symptom styles. If such a therapist were to employ the client-centered system in its totality for a given case, one which he or she believed would be suitable, there is no reason to assume that lack of singular commitment to the client-centered approach would be a handicap. If the therapist had the goal of activating the full strengths of the system in behalf of an appropriate client, this would be sufficient dedication for it to be effective.

Furthermore, it is the writer's view that there is no reason why this same therapist could not offer a second, different treatment to the same client at a different time, or even concurrently with the client-centered one, provided that the client were sufficiently intelligent and old enough to understand that "on this day we play and on this other day we will give you training in social skills." As a matter of fact, although the writer and her colleagues are passionately committed to the client-centered system, we also employ another integrated system in our work, that of behavior therapy. This might be employed before or after a series of play sessions. Actually, we utilize, at our Consultation Center at Pennsylvania State University for adolescents and their parents, another therapy system which integrates behavioral and client-centered approaches into a systematic training program. This is known as Relationship Enhancement (Guerney, 1978). We view such behavioral methods as behavioral rehearsal and assertive training, when used following a series of client-centered sessions, as the most efficient means of providing the skills to implement the insights and newly defined goals of clients whose defenses have been removed and self-concepts enhanced via client-centered therapy. We believe that the client-centered approach is the most efficient and effective means for the removal of defenses and the building of a positive image of one's potential. Once "the blinders" of defensiveness are removed, however, new skills must be acquired to permit behaviors consistent with new perceptions and goals.

The need for additional approaches is more likely for adolescents and adults in verbal therapy than for children in play therapy. If the client-centered play therapy is allowed to run its full course, the child can perfect more adaptive behaviors through his or her play.

In our view, many therapeutic approaches tend to develop techniques or procedures that do not follow from their tenets. Conversely, some of the tenets are poorly reflected in the methods employed. Therapeutic change can be explained by different theories. For example, it is possible to explain the success of client-centered methods in terms of reinforcement theory, in much the same manner that Dollard and Miller (1950) explained Freudian phenomena in terms of learning theory.

If therapeutic phenomena can be translated into the terms of opposing theories, and trained therapists can execute them well, as long as they maintain the integrity of the respective approaches, then are there any real differences among the approaches except in techniques?

In our view, the most fundamental differences between approaches lie in the method of dealing with psychological defenses (transference phenomena being less fundamental). Psychodynamicists will confront them head on (Klein, 1948); Behaviorists will try to ignore their existence (Wolpe & Lazarus, 1966); Cognitive Behaviorists will teach the client to make nondefensive or counterdefensive self-statements (Mahoney, 1974). The client-centered therapists will try to create an atmosphere that is so nonthreatening, supportive, and accepting that the client is free to uncover basic longings and fears and then to seek personal rewards from the environment in more direct and successful ways, including specific training in new skills.

The procedures, techniques, and methods developed by Rogers have become widely used as standard tools for helping professionals (Carkhuff & Berenson, 1969). One should not confuse the use of one or more of these helping behaviors with the use of the whole system. It is common to hear people say that they use a few "nondirective techniques" or that they are "basically Rogerian" when in fact they mean that they encourage the client to do most of the talking or that they occasionally use empathic responses among questions and confrontations and otherwise engage in defense-raising behaviors. It is apparent that they have not been adequately trained to understand that the client-centered method is an integral system for dealing with defenses, and that its methods and techniques cannot be dabbled in if any meaningful results are expected.

Continuous supervision is required during the training and early practice of therapists learning this approach. (Nonprofessionals should always be supervised when using them.) "Drift" can otherwise set in. Supervision is always important, but for client-centered approaches it is more critical because of the amount of self-control and commitment required. For all of us, it is much easier to come in with our own idea than it is to permit the client to progress in a circuitous way. Genuine and true empathy with the client will serve as partial protection against such intrusions. Positive development of this skill should facilitate the development of appropriate self-restraint.

In closing, the writer would like to suggest that when feasible, parents or significant other figures in the children's lives be regarded as the first choice to serve as primary therapists. This strategy has many advantages. Parents, with professional supervision, provide therapy that appears to be equally, if not more powerful than that provided by professionals. Professionals producing improved child behavior do not necessarily improve the *parent–child relationship*. Sometimes, uninvolved parents are not able to adjust to a child relieved of symptoms and may disrupt the treatment or create new problems. Parents who serve as therapists are ego-involved in the therapy process and motivated to help promote adjustment rather than intimidated by it. In the Filial Therapy approach, parents are taught to change their behaviors in play sessions. However, parents usually wish to carry lessons of the playroom back to real life. When they are ready to do so, the Filial approach has methods for facilitating this transfer.

As demonstrated by the previously cited studies, client-centered play therapy does not require parental involvement of any kind to effect meaningful changes. However, utilizing parental potential to its fullest does seem to be more efficient and to increase the probability of success. When the client-centered therapist works with the child directly, rather than training a parent to be the child therapist, it is nonetheless a most challenging and rewarding experience. As the professional observes a child using intricate imagery to unlock boxes within boxes to arrive at a therapeutic destination, it is clear that the map for traversing that route could not be known better by anyone but the child.

REFERENCES

Axline, V. (1947) *Play therapy.* Cambridge, MA: Houghton Mifflin.

Axline, V. (1969) *Play therapy*, rev. ed. New York: Ballantine Books.

Baruch, D. (1949) *New ways in discipline.* New York: McGraw-Hill.

Bills, R. E. (1950a) Non-directed play therapy with retarded readers. *Journal of Consulting Psychology,* **14,** 140–149.

Bills, R. E. (1950b) Play therapy with well-adjusted readers. *Journal of Consulting Psychology,* **14,** 246–249.

Carkhuff, R., & Berenson, B. (1969) *The sources of gain in counseling and psychotherapy.* New York: Holt, Rinehart & Winston.

Cox, F. (1953) Sociometric status before and after play therapy. *Journal of Abnormal and Social Psychology,* **48,** 354–356.

Coopersmith, S. (1967) *The antecedents of self-esteem.* San Francisco: Freeman.

Dollard J., & Miller, N. (1950) *Personality and psychotherapy.* New York: McGraw-Hill.

Dorfman, E. (1951) Play therapy. In C. Rogers (Ed.), *Client-centered therapy.* Boston: Houghton Mifflin.

Dorfman, E. (1958) Personality outcomes of client-centered child therapy. *Psychological Monographs,* **72,** No. 3, Whole No. 456.

Durfee, M. B. (1952) Use of ordinary office equipment in play therapy. *American Journal of Orthopsychiatry,* **12,** 495–503.

Finke, H. (1947) Changes in the expression of emotionalized attitudes in six cases of play therapy. Unpublished masters thesis, University of Chicago.

Fishbein, C. (1974) The relationship between age-related toys and therapeutic expression in non-directive play therapy. Unpublished master's thesis, The Pennsylvania State University.

Fleming, L., & Snyder, W. (1947) Social and personal changes following non-directive group play therapy. *American Journal of Orthopsychiatry,* **17,** 101–116.

Gendlin, E. (1970) In Hart, J., & R. Tomlinson (Eds.), *New directions in client-centered therapy.* Boston: Houghton Mifflin.

Ginott, H. (1961) *Group psychotherapy with children: The theory and practice of play therapy.* New York: McGraw-Hill.

Ginott, H., & Lebo, D. (1961) Play therapy limits and theoretical orientation. *Journal of Consulting Psychology,* **25**(4), 337–340.

Ginsberg, B., Stutman, J., & Hummel, J. (1978) Notes for practice: Group filial therapy. *Social Work,* **23**(2), 154–156.

Goldman, I. (1975) Manual for non-directive play sessions in a school setting. Mimeographed manuscript.

Guerney, B. (1964) Filial therapy: Description and rationale. *Journal of Consulting Psychology*, **28**, 303-310.

Guerney, B. (1976) Filial therapy used as a treatment method for disturbed children. *Evaluation*, **3**, 34-35.

Guerney, B. (1978) *Relationship enhancement.* San Francisco, CA: Jossey-Bass Publishers.

Guerney, B., & Flumen, A. (1970) Teachers as psychotherapeutic agents for withdrawn children. *Journal of School Psychology*, **8**(2), 107-113.

Guerney, B., & Stover, L. (1971) Filial therapy. Final report to NIMH on MH18264.

Guerney, L. (1975) A follow-up study on filial therapy. Symposium paper presented at the Annual Convention of the Eastern Psychological Association, New York.

Guerney, L. (1976) Filial therapy program. In D. Olson (Ed.), *Treating relationships.* Lake Mills, Iowa: Graphic Publishing Co. Pp. 67-91.

Hornsby, L., & Appelbaum, A. (1978) Parents as primary therapists: Filial therapy. In L. Arnold (Ed.), *Helping parents help their children.* New York: Brunner/Mazel.

Klein, M. (1948) *The psychoanalysis of children.* London: Hogarth Press.

Kraft, A. (1973) *Are you listening to your child?* New York: Walker and Co.

Krantz, P. (1978) The play therapist: The student, the struggle, the process. *Journal of Psychiatric Nursing and Mental Health Services*, **16**(11), 29-31.

Landisberg, S., & Snyder, W. (1946) Nondirective play therapy. *Journal of Clinical Psychology*, **2**, 203-213.

Lazarus, A. (1981) *The practice of multimodal therapy.* New York: McGraw-Hill.

Lebo, D. (1952) The relationships of response categories in play therapy to chronological age. *Child Psychiatry*, **20**, 330-336.

Lebo, D. (1955a) The expressive value of toys recommended for non-directive play therapy. *Journal of Clinical Psychology*, **11**, 144-148.

Lebo, D. (1955b) Quantification of the non-directive play therapy process. *Journal of Genetic Psychology*, **86**, 375-378.

Lebo, D. (1956a) Age and suitability for non-directive therapy. *Journal of Genetic Psychology*, **89**, 231-238.

Lebo, D. (1956b). The question of toys in play therapy: An international problem. *Journal of Education and Psychology*, **86**, 375-378.

Lebo, D., & Lebo, E. (1957) Aggression and age in relation to verbal expression in nondirective play therapy. *Psychological Monographs*, **71**, No. 20 (Whole No. 449).

Linden, J. L., & Stollak, G. E. (1969) The training of undergraduates in play techniques. *Journal of Clinical Psychology*, **25**, 213-218.

Mahoney, M. (1974) *Cognition and behavior modification.* Cambridge, Mass: Ballinger.

Moulin, E. (1970; The effects of client-centered group counseling play media on the intelligence, achievement, and psycholinguistics of underachieving primary school children. *Elementary School Guidance Counselor*, **98.**

Moustakas, C. (1955) The frequency and intensity of negative attitudes expressed in play therapy. *Journal of Genetic Psychology*, **86**, 301-325.

Moustakas, C. (1973) *Children in play therapy*, rev. ed. New York: Jason Aronson.

Moustakas, C., & Scholock, H. (1955) An analysis of therapist–child intervention in play therapy. *Child Development,* **26**(2).

Oxman, L. (1971) The effectiveness of filial therapy: A controlled study. Unpublished doctoral dissertation, Rutgers University.

Reif, T., & Stollak, G. (1972) *Sensitivity to children: Training and its effects.* East Lansing: Michigan State University Press.

Rhinard, L. (1970) A comparison of the effectiveness of non-directive play therapy and behavior modification approaches. *Dissertation Abstracts* 5696, **30** (12-B), June.

Rogers, C. (1951) *Client-centered therapy.* Boston: Houghton-Mifflin.

Schmidtchen, S., & Hobrucker, B. (1978) The efficiency of client-centered play therapy. *Praxis Der Kinderpsychologie and Kinderpsychiatric,* **27**(4), 117–125.

Seeman, J., Barry, E., & Ellinwood, C. (1964) Interpersonal assessment of play therapy outcome. *Psychotherapy: Theory, Research, and Practice,* **1**(2), 64–66.

Sensue, M. (1981) Filial therapy follow-up study: Effects on parental acceptance and child adjustment. Unpublished doctoral dissertation, The Pennsylvania State University.

Singer, J. (Ed.) (1974) *The child's world of make believe.* New York: Academic Press.

Slavson, S. (1947) *The practice of group therapy.* New York: International Universities Press.

Speers, R. (1976) Play; An essential component of development. *Children in Contemporary Society,* **9**(3), 40, 61–62.

Stollak, G. (1979) Elaboration and extension of filial therapy. Paper presented at the American Psychological Association, New York.

Stollak, G., Scholom, A., Green, L., Schreiber, J., & Messe, L. (1975) Process and outcome of play encounters between undergraduates and clinic-referred children: Preliminary findings. *Psychotherapy: Theory, Research, and Practice,* **13**, 327–331.

Stover, L., & Guerney, B. (1967) The efficacy of training procedures for mothers in filial therapy. *Psychotherapy: Theory, Research, and Practice,* **4**, 110–115.

Strom, R., & Greathouse, B. (1974) Play and maternal self-concept. *Theory into practice,* **13**(4).

Sywulak, A. (1977) The effect of filial therapy on parental acceptance and child adjustment. Unpublished doctoral dissertation, The Pennsylvania State University.

Wall, L. (1979) Parents as play therapists: a comparison of three interventions into children's play. Unpublished doctoral dissertation. The University of Northern Colorado.

Wolpe, J., & Lazarus, A. (1966) *Behavior therapy techniques.* Oxford: Pergamon Press.

Yawkey, T. (1980) An investigation of imaginative play and aural language development in young children, five, six, and seven. In D. Williamson (Ed.), *Play in human settlements.* London: Croonhelm Publishers.

CHAPTER 3

Family Play Therapy

MERLE D. GRIFF

HISTORY AND INTRODUCTION

Family Play Therapy is an eclectic technique, combining elements from play and family therapies in addition to the methods of adult education. This technique includes parent(s), child(ren), and a therapist together in a preplanned play situation.

Historically, play therapists have dealt primarily with children, although at times they have permitted parents to be passively present in the playroom, such as in the work of Axline (1947) and Moustakas (1953). In spite of the fact that during the evolution of the technique, play therapists have revised their choice of play objects and materials and alternate between nondirective and directive roles, the basic tenet of "children only" remains an underlying foundation in the majority of play therapy encounters. Parents, when seen, are usually involved in such ancillary forms of treatment as marital or individual counseling.

Emphasizing the fact that children exist within a family system, practitioners of Family Therapy created techniques which have incorporated entire families in their sessions. Bell (1961) justifies the exclusion of children under nine years of age by emphasizing that they do not possess the verbal abilities necessary to participate in family interviews. More recently, techniques have been developed that attempt to include even the youngest of children. In treatment approaches such as those of Villeneuve (1979) and Ziegler (1980), play is incorporated into family sessions so as to include young children. Such techniques as the Family Puppet Interview developed by Irwin and Malloy (1975) and Family Sculpture as discussed by Simon (1972) involve the families in a play situation during some part of the session and have proved to be successful. However, up to this point, the play technique has been considered subordinate to traditional individual therapy and has served as a secondary aid in therapeutic assessment of the family's problems—providing insights that serve as a basis for discussion following the play period.

D. Safer (1965), in introducing the Conjoint Play Therapy technique, refocused attention from discourse and discussion as the main object of the session to the play itself. Safer requires both the parent(s) and himself to participate in play activities chosen by the child in a spontaneous and random fashion. Safer perceived his role as active and directive and considered his most important treatment techniques to be demonstration, education, and interpretation. Like play therapy, this treatment approach implies a fluid and ongoing process.

Family Play Therapy

Family Play Therapy expands many of these basic tenets in goal-oriented play or activity sessions which are planned in advance by the therapist in conjunction with family members. Sessions can be held in a variety of settings and include parent(s), child(ren), and the therapist. This is a short-term technique which has been designed to fill what the author perceived as a "missing link" in her work with children and their families. It is intended to be used at the therapist's discretion as an adjunct to other kinds of intervention techniques rather than as a therapeutic entity in and of itself.

The idea for combining parents and children together in planned play sessions was developed during the time the author spent working with emotionally disturbed children ranging in ages from two to seven years of age. Staff members were often frustrated with parents who failed to follow through on suggestions concerning new child management techniques and/or styles of communication and interaction. When parents failed in their attempts to adopt these changes, staff members in their own frustration considered these parents to be unmotivated or uncaring or both. Based on an intuition that some of these parents simply did not know how to incorporate these suggestions into their daily lives, the author planned activities which incorporated previous staff suggestions and to which all family members were invited. The primary emphasis of these sessions became parental education and the assimilation of new skills. Parents who had previously exhibited an "unwillingness" to cooperate began, over a period of time, to demonstrate significant changes on various levels. Since that time the author has continued to utilize this technique with families in a variety of settings. Aspects of this approach have thereby been discarded and refined.

Andragogy

In his book, *The Adult Learner: A Neglected Species,* Malcolm Knowles (1973) proposes a new theory of adult learning and education which he referred to as Andragogy. The principles of his work have had considerable effect on educators in universities and colleges and trainers in all settings. Formal therapeutic techniques, however, continue in many instances to relate to adults in traditional ways. For example, the therapeutic task is not completed if the therapist only helps families solve those problems which initially motivated them to seek help and does not also teach basic problem-solving skills with which these families can resolve future conflicts and promote a healthy, independent, emotional existence. Because of these considerations, any therapeutic system must to some extent incorporate techniques of reeducating parents which are suited to their adult methods of receiving and assimilating new information. Some of the principles of adult education, such as creating a climate of openness and respect, are already present in our therapeutic environments. Other principles of andragogy as stated by Knowles (1973) that are incorporated in the Family Play Therapy technique are as follows:

1. Adults enjoy planning and carrying out their own learning experiences.
2. Adults need to be involved in evaluating their own progress toward self-chosen goals.
3. Less use is made of transmittal techniques; more of experiential techniques.
4. Adults need the opportunity to apply and try out learning quickly.

Thus, the Family Play Therapy technique incorporates these principles into the therapeutic sphere in work with adults. The particular adults that this approach involves are also parents, existing within a family system and requiring a technique that will include their children. The inclusion of children always returns us to the recognition of the importance of play as a primary mode of communication between parents and children. Play, as stated by Amster (1943), "can be used to establish a working relationship and can be used to develop a child's (and adult's) play interest which can be carried over into daily life." Family Play Therapy provides an approach wherein parents can learn more effective parenting skills and styles of interaction in an environment that not only facilitates their receptiveness to this information, but also provides a medium that is comfortable for their children. This technique allows the therapist to be a role model for parents who previously had been exposed to deficient role models. It also provides a controlled and non-threatening environment in which parents can comfortably experiment with change.

THE PROCEDURE

In implementing this technique, one is advised to take full advantage of its flexibility. It can be utilized at any point during treatment and, as previously stated, as part of a total treatment plan. This approach does seem, however, to be more easily implemented and successful when a relationship of mutual trust exists between the therapist and the family. In the few instances in which the author has attempted to implement this technique without any previous contact with the family, it has not proven to be as effective. It may be that the act of playing is so foreign or anxiety provoking for many adults that they can only become "children" once again in an atmosphere of trust.

Goals and Contracts

Choosing the goals of the session, planning the activities, and approving the contract is a process which primarily involves the parents. Children's input should not be disregarded but the parent's cooperation "to play" is difficult to elicit and is the most important requirement for a successful therapeutic encounter. If they take advantage of Knowles (1973) insights and principles of adult education, parents can become major participants in planning and carrying out their learning experiences. Including the parents in the learning process relieves them of the role of passive recipient and makes them active, contributing members of the "team." By being asked to accept responsibility for planning, parents often learn and assimilate methods for problem organization which will help them in future family affairs.

Only one or two specific goals should be chosen. As the contract for Family Play Therapy sessions should only extend for 8 to 10 sessions, the therapist should choose goals with a mind to their successful accomplishment within this time period. At the end of this cycle a new or modified contract may be written for another cycle of sessions. Whittaker (1979) states that in most instances parents have previously tried to alter their child's troublesome behavior and have failed. "Their feelings of helplessness and frustration is rekindled when they are asked to be directly involved in a helping relationship." However, a short-term approach with limited goals appears to distract parents from these experiences of failure. By breaking down a long-term goal into smaller, more attainable, and successive steps, parents are able to see progress and experience some measure of success. This experience teaches the family an approach in which change occurs in small, successive steps over a period of time and makes less important the illusion of sudden, overnight, major transformations.

As with other therapies, this technique can be modified within certain guidelines throughout the process. Usually the necessity for modification occurs when patterns of interaction and new dynamics appear which were not observable in other counseling situations, even if conducted by the same therapist. This usually occurs within the first two sessions and may lead to modifications in the contract. If these modifications adhere to the guidelines of avoiding generalizations and being short term, they usually do not disrupt the treatment process.

Based upon consideration of the goals, the therapist will decide which family members to include. As an example, the author was seeing a family in which the parents had a fairly strong relationship with each other as did the father with their only child, a two-year-old boy. The mother was extremely uncomfortable and awkward in relating to her son and was afraid that she would abuse him. She had a history of multiple family problems for which she was being seen on an individual basis. It was mutually decided to begin the Family Play Therapy sessions to help her learn ways of relating comfortably with her son. All family members attended the first session but the father in his love of playing so overpowered her that he was asked not to attend the remaining sessions in order to afford the mother an opportunity to increase her skills. Sessions were held with both parents to discuss the father's role with his wife and his son, and he returned to the second cycle of sessions when she had become more confident.

Activity Planning

Planning of activities is a seemingly complex, but worthwhile process. Parents and sometimes children are asked to list their favorite games or play activities. For parents, this is often a matter of asking them to remember what they enjoyed playing when they were children This produces a picture of their style of play Questions such as whether they enjoy structured or unstructured games, competitive or noncompetitive play may then be answered. This enables the therapist to begin choosing the types of activities family members may find enjoyable. Activities are reviewed according to the guidelines of activity analysis, a method taken from occupational therapy and applied by VanderVen (1972) to activity programming. This method analyzes an activity for such elements as the magnitude of body coordination and motion required, amount of competition and interaction involved, and the degree of structure inherent in the activity. As the activity itself is not the focus of therapy, but the interactions surrounding it, activities should be chosen which match as closely as possible the play style of the family. This method will help avoid failure, for example, merely because a parent does not possess the coordination required to play a particular game.

There are infinite possibilities in choosing a location. The author has used various facilities including a play therapy room, a gymnasium, and a family home. The most important element is one of environmental control, as optimally there should be minimal, if any, interruptions. Although this appears to imply only an office setting, therapists working in milieu facilities can reserve, in advance, gymnasiums, art rooms, and even swimming pools. Control can even be accomplished within a home by taking telephones off the hook and placing a "Do not disturb" sign on the front door. It is important to remember that the range of possible activities increases as the facilities expand in size and variety.

The Therapist's Role

The therapist's role in the Family Play Therapy technique is a multifaceted one; it includes educator, play facilitator, role model, and player. Family Play Therapists should obviously have some training and experience in the therapeutic use of play, family systems, and psychodynamics. This person should feel secure in playing and possess a working knowledge of how to utilize the milieu as part of the treatment approach. As the therapist is so exposed during these sessions, he or she should be secure and familiar with his or her therapeutic role. The therapist must assume an active and direct involvement in the therapy and must be prepared to serve as a role model.

The treatment process usually proceeds in three major stages and the therapist's role will change as these stages unfold. In the first two sessions the therapist introduces and leads the activities. Since this is usually the therapist's first exposure to the family in a more natural setting, it also provides an opportunity for the therapist to observe and assess once again individual and familial patterns while at the same time serving as a support for an often awkward beginning. In the following three sessions the therapist usually assumes a more active and directive role, modeling new patterns and skills and aiding parents in their first attempts to "try on" these new patterns. In his study of role modeling, Berchter (1973) found that a considerable amount of contact between model and observer is necessary for imitation to occur. Therefore, these sessions offer the therapists an excellent opportunity to educate the adult learner in a practical, experiential manner. The final three sessions are devoted to encouraging the parents and/or child to initiate and implement independently their new skills. The presence of the therapist provides an opportunity for direct feedback, support, and immediate reinforcement in what are often a family's courageous attempts at change in the face of previous debilitating failure.

CLINICAL DATA

The original qualitative study involved Terry R., a four-year-old boy who had been enrolled in a therapeutic nursery school for five full morning sessions for almost a year. Terry appeared quite different from the boy who had been referred for lack of speech, inability to accept directions or limitations, and extremely aggressive and impulsive behavior. Terry's energies were now primarily and firmly invested in people and objects outside himself. Although he still experienced some outbursts, especially in times of great stress, these outbursts were far less frequent and their intensity greatly diminished. Terry's vocabulary had increased to the point where he could utilize words to aid himself in controlling his behavior.

Mrs. R. had been seen for individual counseling for two years by a social worker at a community mental health center. One of the major themes of these sessions was Mrs. R.'s great fear in separating from her mother. She also explored the nature of her relationship to a father and husband who were both alcoholic and physically abusive to her. Mrs. R. was seen on a weekly basis, arriving punctually and regularly, and continued to work diligently on her treatment contract.

Mr. R., an alcoholic, was separated from his wife. Mr. R. lived with his parents, who supported him financially and emotionally. Although he attended a few counseling sessions it was believed that his parents' protection was a major roadblock in Mr. R.'s recognition of his problem.

At the time Family Play Therapy sessions began, the author had been seeing Mrs. R. for individual counseling sessions on a weekly basis. Mrs. R.'s case had been transferred approximately six months previously when her counselor left the agency.

The author had developed a rapport with Terry through daily interaction in the classroom in addition to conducting individual play sessions with him on a weekly basis. Although Terry and Mrs. R. had made significant personal gains, Mrs. R. especially had not been as satisfied with the change and development in their relationship with each other. Mrs. R. was very concerned about what she described as Terry's "sudden showing of temper and anger," and expressed her frustration at his play with toy tanks, soldiers, and guns.

Mrs. R.'s obvious difficulty in reacting positively to her child's "aggression" seemed to be founded in her early experiences with male aggression, specifically that of her father and husband, as previously stated. Although a team meeting concerning Terry had revealed a feeling among all staff that this type of play was within expected developmental limits for Terry and was not regarded as a regression to earlier patterns, Mrs. R. was still unable to view any form of aggression as being within "normal" limits. She could not express these feelings directly to her young son, but did so in a manner marked by great ambivalence.

Planning

It was therefore decided to begin a series of Family Play Therapy sessions to help Mrs. R. accept some amount of aggression in Terry's play, to alleviate her feelings of discomfort in playing with Terry in other types of activities, and generally to provide an opportunity to facilitate their interaction with each other. Planning took place during Mrs. R.'s weekly individual sessions. The Family Play Therapy sessions were to be held once a week for a period of six weeks in one of the playrooms of the school, an area with which both parent and child were familiar. (It was later found that a minimum of eight sessions allowed a slower, more desirable pace for the therapist during the sessions.)

Essential equipment in the room included toy guns and holster, construction vehicles, a large army jeep, playhouse with family life dolls, building blocks, two simple puzzles, cookies, juice, and a large plastic ball that has one opening large enough to allow a child to crawl into the hollow shell. The same play materials were placed in the room for every session.

Aggression in Play

At the beginning of the first session, Terry entered the room, quickly scanned all of the toys and immediately picked up the toy guns and holster. He grinned broadly, asking the author to help him put on the holster. Mrs. R. sighed, then quickly stated that she would help. Mrs. R. took the holster in hand, bent down to her son and proceeded to put the holster on backwards three consecutive times. This pattern was repeated until the fifth session when she finally succeeded in putting the holster on correctly the first time and also participated in Terry's gun play for the first time.

When Terry was actually playing with the guns, Mrs. R. attempted to divert his attention to other toys although she almost always failed in this task. In the first session, Mrs. R. attempted to seduce Terry into building a fort with the blocks and at one point even pleaded her own inability to do so, although this failed. When it was impossible for her to avoid Terry's gun play she attempted to structure her own anxiety and thus his play. In the second session, when Terry was aimlessly shooting one of the guns at the wall clock, Mrs. R. tried to structure this episode of "aggressive play" by insisting that Terry shoot at the number one and then at the number two on the clock. When Terry was unable to follow through on her request, she turned to the author saying "I guess he still doesn't know his numbers."

In the third session the author participated with Terry in playing "cops and robbers." Mrs. R. was shocked and interpreted her acceptance of Terry's aggression as a personal betrayal. When she arrived for her counseling session during that week, she was very angry. The main points of their discussion were as follows:

1. Generally, why did this display of so-called aggressiveness cause her so much anxiety?
2. What relationship did Terry's display of aggressiveness, in his play, have to do with her own history of being physically abused by both her father and husband?
3. Did she view Terry's aggressive play as a display of the same kind of aggressiveness expressed in his earlier aggressive outbursts?
4. A discussion of "normal" aggression within the "normal play of children."

Although it is difficult to separate the results of the counseling sessions in helping to produce a notable change in Mrs. R.'s subsequent behavior from the results of the Family Play Therapy sessions, the author believes that the mere verbalization of her feelings would not have sufficed. By the fifth session Mrs. R. had decided to attempt to actively participate in the gun play and responded to Terry's repeated requests to "join in." Although her participation in this play was marked with tension she expressed in the tautness of her body, Mrs. R. played with the guns a second time following a period of passive play. Before leaving she turned in the doorway and said, "I've spoken to my sister-in-law and some of the other mothers in the neighborhood and they don't think that playing with guns makes you into a murderer or anything like that at all."

Mrs. R. again participated with Terry in the gun play during the final session. Although her body movements and facial expressions were still significantly awkward, her general muscle tone expressed far less tension than it had the previous weeks. Only after having observed the author's participation in aggressive play with her child and the author's capacity to delimit the aggression in the Family Play Therapy sessions was the mother able to collaborate with her child in a play theme involving aggression. Without the assistance of such modeling the mother's anxiety seemed to paralyze her as a play partner and thus seemed to forbid active progressive work in the channeling of aggression.

Family Play Therapist as Model

In the Family Play Therapy sessions Mrs. R. was not only directly encouraged to participate in types of play that evoked ambivalent feelings in her, but she could also observe the author's style of play and interaction and use her as a role model.

Mrs. R. also experienced difficulty in responding to Terry's needs, as expressed in his dominant choice of play activities. During the fifth session, as previously stated, Terry pleaded with his mother to join in his play with the guns. The first sequence of gun play in which the mother participated was notable as her movements, including what she used as her pretend gun, were almost an exact copy of the author's style of play with her son. In both the fifth and sixth sessions the author brought to Mrs. R.'s attention how much Terry seemed to enjoy playing with her during these times. She smiled shyly and agreed that he did seem especially happy when they both participated in the gun play.

The mother's agreement to respond to Terry's developmental needs in participating in "aggressive" play generalized to other activities. For example, previous to the fifth session Mrs. R. had attempted to interest Terry in a relatively passive game which she had created and referred to as the "mailman game." Terry had either reluctantly complied or had refused to acknowledge these requests. During the fifth session the author initiated Mrs. R.'s mailman game with Terry after they had both participated in a sequence of gun play. However, this time Terry willingly agreed to play the "mailman game" with the therapist and his mother. In this session, as in the sixth session, Mrs. R. was more willing to allow Terry to initiate play activities and sequences and Terry, in turn, agreed to cooperate in play that he had originally resisted because it was his mother's imposed choice. Thus, the author could not only show Mrs. R. how she could choose to interact with her son on a newer level, but also was able to directly support her movements in this direction.

Comments and Discussion

Originally the Family Play Therapy model was designed for use with families having children between the ages of 18 months and 9 years. Since its inception the author has implemented this technique with children within these ages who have been diagnosed as emotionally disturbed. Child Care Workers and Educateurs in Canada report great success with this technique with adolescents in residential treatment centers. One limitation that has been found is the failure of this approach to be effective with children who are mentally retarded or functioning at a very low level as a result of an organic disorder. It has always seemed necessary to resort to some type of behavior modification training in order to accomplish the goals of Family Play Therapy. Also, highly disturbed, psychotic children do not appear to be as responsive to this technique.

Parameters such as sociocultural factors do not adversely effect the treatment process. Economic status becomes a factor only when choosing play materials and activities. For example, it would not be prudent to "teach" a family from a lower socioeconomic background activities that require more expense than the family is able to afford. As this technique continues to be implemented in families experiencing varied problems and having family members at varying developmental levels, more complete information will become available.

RESEARCH IDEAS

The presentation of this technique has been qualitative rather than quantitative. As Family Play Therapy was designed to be used in conjunction with other types of therapeutic intervention, it will become necessary to devise an evaluation system that is capable of ascertaining how much behaviorial change was a direct result of the Family Play Therapy sessions and how much change was due to other interventions. Using the methods of occupational therapy, one could devise studies along similar lines for Family Play Therapy sessions to determine the differential effects of the components of such activities on the group as a whole and the individuals.

SUMMARY

A more circumspect examination of parental "unwillingness" or "refusal" to accept changes often discloses a lack of information, an absence or deficiency in appropriate role models, and often a genuine feeling of "I don't know how," or "I'm too frightened to try." Attempts at change learned in therapy but attempted only outside the therapeutic arena are performed, if at all, in the absence of immediate reinforcement, support, and feedback. Even when there is a positive return from the child, the parent for whom negatives have become a habit will often fail to perceive these positive advances. In the Family Play Therapy sessions, the therapist is in an optimal position to be an appropriate role model: demonstrating new ways of interaction and communication and facilitating the experiential learning of these new skills. The therapist is readily available to provide immediate reinforcement and can impart objective, but caring support for family members in new behaviorial ventures. Parents begin learning in a manner that communicates respect for their adulthood, taking them from the role of the "bad" parent passively receiving advice from the "good" parent–therapist to a contributing, active role in the therapeutic process.

As a result of specific short-range goals and contracts terminating within a specified period of time, parents and their children can usually begin to experience for themselves some feelings of success. Parents and children suddenly begin to be refueled, no longer lacking the energy or motivation to try "just one more time."

Family Play Therapy does not commit one to a specific technique that may or may not match a particular family and their problems. It is designed to be a conjunctive method; it is to be utilized at the therapist's discretion. Inherent in this model is a flexibility in use, location, and mode. It, therefore, becomes a highly practical technique: short-term, flexible, and designed to remove families from their recurring cycles of failure and fear concerning change itself.

REFERENCES

Amster, F. (1943) Differential uses of play in treatment of young children. *American Journal of Orthopsychiatry*, **13**, 62–68.

Axline, V. M. (1947) *Play therapy*. New York: Ballantine.

Bell, J. (1961) Family group therapy. *Public Health Monograph*, **64.**

Berchter, H. J. (1973) The child care worker as a role model. *Child Care Quarterly*, **2**, 178–191.

Irwin, E. C., & Malloy, E. S. (1975) Family puppet interview. *Family Process*, **14**, 179–191.

Knowles, M. (1973) *The adult learner: A neglected species*. Houston: Gulf Publishing Co.

Moustakas, C. E. (1953) *Children in play therapy*. New York: McGraw-Hill.

Safer, D. (1965) Conjoint play therapy for the young child and his parent. *Archives of General Psychiatry*, **13**, 320–326.

Simon, R. (1972) Sculpting the family. *Family Process*, **11**, 49–59.

VanderVen, K. D. (1972) Activity programming. In G.W. Foster, et al. (Eds.), *Child care work with emotionally disturbed children*. Pittsburgh: University of Pittsburgh Press. Pp. 203–257.

Villeneuve, C. (1979) The specific participation of the child in family therapy. *American Academy of Child Psychiatry*, 44–53.

Whittaker, J. (1979) *Caring for troubled children*. San Francisco: Jossey-Bass.

Ziegler, R. G. (1980) Task-focused therapy with children and families. *American Journal of Psychotherapy*, **34**, 107–118.

CHAPTER 4

Fair Play Therapy

CROCKER PEOPLES

Fair Play Therapy is based on the proposition that children need to be dealt with equitably and that troubled children have probably not had this kind of experience. The aim of this approach is to construct conditions in which such a child can begin to learn relatively adaptive ways of solving problems and building interpersonal relationships. The focus on appropriate give and take requires that the therapist be actively involved in the play, at times leading and at times following, and even, at times, taking the relatively passive role of observer/interpreter. This approach differs from traditional play therapies in that the therapist is more active and makes more explicit demands for acceptable behavior on the part of the child.

INTRODUCTION AND THEORETICAL BACKGROUND

To trace the theoretical background of this position will require some arbitrary decisions. The present form of the position represents a point on an evolutionary process which is continuing, as such processes are wont to do. Also, in common with other evolutionary processes, this particular one has a multitude of roots, many of which are buried in an unclear past. At least the major ones can be discerned and will be identified and described in the following discussion.

The whole idea of interacting helpfully with children in what might appear to be a frivolous activity seems strange to some people, even some who specifically intend to engage in play therapy. Recently I had a student who was planning to begin therapy with a five-year-old boy, and she became increasingly concerned as the first session approached. On the day before the planned first session, she and I were talking, and in an effort to reassure her, I pointed out to her, "Katherine, all you have to do is go in and play with the kid." She replied, "I just have to *play* with him?" We then went on to discuss her involvement with the child from what was a new perspective for her, free of all the heavy burden of "expert performance" with which she had laden herself.

The point is that play therapy should indeed involve play, and this seems to have been lost sight of by more than just my student. Children really do communicate important things about themselves through play and usually do so more freely and easily than they can through direct verbalizations about themselves.

Play therapy differs in various important ways from naturally and spontaneously occurring play. The most important difference, from the perspective of this position, is the presence and participation of a therapist in the play situation. Naturally occurring play may indeed have growth-inducing or restorative properties, but in therapy this process is guided and generally facilitated by the intervention of a skilled therapist.

Approximately 25 years ago, at the time I began studying play therapy, there were a few well-defined theoretical positions, and I found the Rogerian ideas as interpreted by Virginia Axline to be useful and compatible with some of my convictions. The optimism inherent in Roger's formulation appealed to me and helped me define some problem children in a beneficial way. To relate to these children in the permissive and indulgent manner which Rogers and Axline advocated was sometimes more difficult than to formulate their problems from a Rogerian perspective. I found it difficult to consistently maintain the degree of saintliness which Axline seemed to advocate.

Increased experience and a generally broadened theoretical perspective enabled me to begin to modify my own practice and teaching of play therapy. Whereas Axline had insisted that the child must always take the lead in the play situation, it began to seem more efficient to me for the therapist to take the lead at times. It seems possible to do this and still preserve the child's basic personal worth. To do this requires that the therapist understand the child and have a clear idea of how the child needs to change. I became increasingly willing to make those kinds of decisions, or at least to be more straightforward about doing so. I mention this last consideration with the old charge in mind that the "nondirective therapist" is not really so nondirective after all.

To plan a preferred direction of change requires that one have some kind of framework, either explicit or implicit. My own framework consists of a complex mixture of ideas from Abraham Maslow, R.W. White, Sigmund Freud, B.F. Skinner, and Albert Bandura, to name some of the more prominent. William Glasser (1965) and Robert Genthner (1976) have provided formulations compatible with my own directions and in some instances have provided more succinct formulations than I had made for myself.

Whatever the most important problem for a child presented for therapy, it seems reasonable to assume that some of his or her important needs are being frustrated and that it is advisable to attempt to identify those needs. Another basic consideration is to attempt to determine what faulty learning patterns the child has developed, since it is assumed that some kind of inappropriate learning has occurred. In this same vein, it seems wise to ascertain what, in the child's experience, is serving to maintain the maladaptive habits. A decision must always be made as to whether the child's parents or, indeed, the entire family must also be worked with. There seems to be little point in attempting to assist the child in learning to behave more adaptively if he or she is to continue to be mismanaged when away from the therapy setting.

The therapist's obligation to "formulate the case" is not fully met by simply deciding what kinds of maladaptive habits the child may have learned, the roadblocks the child may have encountered which have precluded natural and effective growth, or other deficit-related understandings. It is also necessary to construct a plan for intervention, and the theoretical positions previously mentioned are somewhat deficient in this respect. That is, they provide relatively little in the way of explicit criteria for effective functioning. For that guidance, the writings of Genthner and Glasser are instructive.

Robert W. Genthner has written fairly extensively about personal responsibility and its place in adaptive living. His major contention is that the more personally responsible a person is, the more productively and effectively he or she is likely to function. While most of his work has dealt with adults, his findings appear to hold for children as well. As with many other human phenomena, it appears to be necessary to make allowances for developmental differences in personal responsibility. That is, one would not expect a six-year-old to accept responsibility for as many of his or her experiences as one would expect a 16-year-old to accept. The notion of personal responsibility has direct applicability in the playroom, as will be made explicit in a later section.

William Glasser, in his formulations regarding Reality Therapy, has also provided ideas which are directly applicable to Fair Play Therapy. Although he also talks about responsibility, he approaches this concept somewhat differently than Genthner does, and provides useful additional perspective. Glasser has one concept in particular which is entirely consistent with the Fair Play position. This is his contention that an individual can meet his or her legitimate needs entirely without encroaching on the equally legitimate prerogatives of any other person. Assiduous adherence to that principal is an integral part of Fair Play Therapy.

In addition to the important theoretical considerations previously described, there are certain others which are basic to this position. Whereas these considerations may well be inherent in other therapeutic positions, they have at least a slightly different emphasis in this position. For example, the therapist's rights and prerogatives are given an important place here. It is deemed necessary that the therapist not engage in any behavior, nor tolerate any behavior from the child, which would in any manner diminish the therapist as a person. Thus the notion of "therapeutic genuineness" is enlarged to include the further implication that the therapist has rights which are also worthy of protection.

Consistent with an earlier observation is the expanded role ascribed to the therapist in this position. Since the therapist has an understanding of where the child is and some possible desirable directions and goals, it is incumbent on the therapist to pursue these changes actively. This means that he or she should not be content to merely sit back, observe, and interpret the child's play, rather, the therapist should take the lead when necessary to ensure that the child engages in productive play. This is intended to be a very general guideline and can take many different forms in specific situations.

BASIC METHODS AND PROCEDURES

Logistics

The setting and materials for Fair Play Therapy are not unusual for this kind of activity. A room specifically designed and equipped for play is most desirable although the therapy can be applied in other, less specialized settings. The materials needed are common play objects, the less specialized or "single purpose" the better. A sandbox and washbasin are also desirable but not essential. Some kind of storage facility is highly recommended for the orderly maintenance of toys and supplies. The floor and walls should be finished in durable, easy-to-clean materials, and cleaning equipment and supplies should be readily available, preferably in the playroom. These are intended for relatively superficial straightening and cleaning, not a thorough endeavor.

Indications and Contraindications for Fair Play Therapy

Little mention has been made thus far about the kind of children who are best suited for Fair Play Therapy. A minimum consideration is that the child must be amenable to social stimuli and controls. A child who would respond only to electric shock or the direct application of such a positive reinforcer as chocolate candy would probably not do well in Fair Play Therapy. A child who is so withdrawn as to be uninterested in playing also would probably not do well in Fair Play Therapy.

The vast majority of children with troubled behavior could be assumed to be suitable candidates for Fair Play Therapy since they should probably be amenable to social stimuli. It is probably the case that the more deviant the child, the more skillful and creative the therapist should be.

Fair Play Therapy is appropriate for children with a wide variety of problems. A child who is inappropriately hostile, withdrawn, manipulative, anxious, phobic, or responding maladaptively to situational stress might be helped. A decision must always be made whether to see only the child, or perhaps the child in conjunction with his or her family, one or both parents, and perhaps involving another therapist. In only very rare instances would it be appropriate to work only with the child. Working with one or both parents in addition to the child is usually the preferred approach. Involving both parents in the intervention is preferable and should be done as long as both parents were willing. The parents should ordinarily be seen separately from the child and the focus of the sessions should be on developing more effective ways of relating to the child. This would not preclude dealing with other issues as they became important and relevant to the central focus.

Preliminary Work

The privacy and confidentiality of the sessions with the child are maintained with certain provisos. In my teaching setting the child is informed that he or she may be observed as well as videotaped during the play sessions. (This last *caveat* is hardly necessary in our facilities, since the video cameras are located in the playroom and the child is quite aware when they are whirring and turning as they follow the action during the therapy hour. This activity quickly becomes commonplace and the child is apparently undisturbed by it.) Although the child has little say in these arrangements, he or she ordinarily accepts them without apparent concern. Of course, the therapist is obligated to handle any and all records of individual sessions and the overall intervention in accord with ethical constraints.

Prior to beginning therapy with the child or whomever else is involved in the intervention, an understanding of the problem must be developed. The "diagnostic workup" may be as simple as an interview with one or both parents, but would ordinarily involve at least the child in addition to one or both parents. The administration of one or more formal diagnostic procedures might be appropriate. The conservative therapist will require that the child have been examined by a physician within the relatively recent past to rule out any likely medical explanation for the problem behavior.

Therapist Characteristics and Variables

The preliminaries are eventually dispensed with, and the therapist is presented with a real child with a specified problem. The therapist has taken care to dress in casual clothing since he or she must be prepared to interact freely with the child without fear of damaging or soiling expensive or fragile attire. In addition to good judgment in selecting clothing for the play session, the therapist needs other qualities. Perhaps most important of these is a kindly feeling toward children. Without a basic affinity for children, a would-be child therapist is almost certain to fail in his or her attempts at being genuinely helpful. This attribute does not appear to be "teachable" in the sense that either didactic or experiential procedures in a formal academic setting can assist the would-be therapist in its acquisition. Rather, it appears to be an outgrowth of life-long experiences preceding entry into a training program in psychotherapy.

Another highly desirable, if not mandatory attribute is a characteristic the psychoanalysts have called "regression in the service of the ego." This ability to slough off the appurtenances of mature, adult behavior and to reassume the cognitive and behavioral flexibility that characterizes childhood can greatly facilitate the establishment of an effective therapeutic atmosphere. This regression must be carefully controlled, of course, since the therapist continues to maintain responsibility for monitoring and controlling the course of the therapeutic interaction. The point is that stiff, formal, and overcontrolled behavior on the part of the therapist is likely to be inimical to a variety of potentially useful experiences for the child and the therapist.

Fair Play Therapy requires that the therapist be unusually willing to trust his or her judgment in the playroom on a moment-by-moment basis. Along with the freedom to engage the child in a more proactive manner than other positions endorse goes the responsibility for selecting and devising appropriate strategies and tactics in a timely manner. Therefore it is important that the Fair Play Therapist have a good level of self-confidence and reasonable decisiveness. A therapist must often make decisions on the basis of relatively subtle cues, and a person who needs overwhelming evidence before taking action would probably feel out of place as a Fair Play Therapist. The more creative the therapist can be, the better. To "go with the flow" of action in the playroom often requires that the therapist be able to shift quickly from one role to another. The therapist is free to draw from an array of theoretical concepts and is limited only by his or her own level of sophistication in the interest of understanding the child. The therapist can take comfort in the understanding that a therapeutic opportunity seldom occurs only once, and if missed, is not gone forever. Any important conflicts or problems of whatever kind are virtually certain to be reflected in the child's behavior many times, allowing the therapist repeated opportunities to deal with them in a facilitative way.

In preparing to function as a Fair Play Therapist, the student would be well advised to become comfortable with children in a play setting. The theoretical understandings which a neophyte therapist should develop include the postulates of Rogers, Skinner, White, Freud, Maslow, Genthner, Glasser—in short, all the theorists mentioned earlier in this discussion. Further, the student should have an awareness of developmental stages and processes from birth through childhood, a working knowledge of social learning theory, and an awareness of the emotional problems of children. The preparation of the Fair Play Therapist should include a suitable period of supervised practice. The neophyte therapist may be initially intimidated by the freedoms and responsibilities inherent in the Fair Play position. It takes time to develop the confidence necessary to take useful advantage of offered opportunities. This development can be considerably enhanced through timely and accurate feedback from a knowledgeable and sympathetic supervisor. This supervision time should also help the student develop an optimistic expectation regarding the likely efficacy of play therapy which is a desirable part of the play therapist's armamentarium.

It was previously claimed that the therapist is expected to respond with honest emotion in the playroom. Implicit in this claim is the expectation that the therapist will not only respond honestly but appropriately as well; this requires that he or she be a well-integrated person. It appears to be the case that the more comfortable an individual is with his or her feelings, the more effective he or she is likely to be as a Fair Play Therapist.

Therapy Procedures and Goals

The first goal of the play therapist with a new client is to establish the conditions necessary for psychotherapy, as spelled out by Carkhuff (1973). This objective is accomplished in the playroom, in general terms, by responding to and dealing with the child's play rather than focusing on verbal language, as one would with an adult.

The Fair Play Therapist works to create a situation in which the child with a problem can learn to feel cared for and approved of. One important characteristic of the Fair Play situation, however, is that the child must meet certain conditions in order to earn approval; unconditional positive regard is not a component of this position.

If a child is behaving in such a way as to require the corrective experience of play therapy, it seems apparent that certain aspects of the child's functioning are unacceptable. It seems most appropriate to focus on these unacceptable phenomena and to design therapeutic play to eliminate or significantly diminish their frequency. Thus, in general terms, the approval that the child earns in play therapy depends on his or her development and maintenance of behaviors other than those deemed unacceptable by the therapist and others interested in the child's welfare.

Limit setting is of major concern in Fair Play Therapy. The therapist must not only predict the kinds of limits which will be necessary and plan accordingly, but also devise methods of implementing these limits without obstructing the goals of psychotherapy. Indeed, shrewd and skillful implementation will have a facilitative rather than an obstructive effect on play therapy.

While it is impossible to lay down hard and fast rules for every situation a play therapist is likely to encounter, it is possible to describe certain principles and procedures which have proven useful in this context. Ordinarily, it is appropriate for the therapist to describe general rules to the child prior to the first play session. This should of course be done in a kindly and supportive manner, and should include such cautions as most children would expect in regard to play activities indoors. For example, the usual strictures against deliberate damage to the physical facilities, physical attacks on the therapist, and deliberate damage or destruction of equipment are appropriate. One general rule of limit setting should be mentioned, and will be assumed throughout this discussion: *Never announce a limit which cannot be imposed.*

In addition to the obvious and basic limits just mentioned, there are other limits which are equally basic to the Fair Play position. These have to do with the conviction that each child should do his or her share in the interest of any enterprise he or she is engaged in, including play therapy, and that this expectation should be made explicit and be a continuing aspect of the play therapy experience. One obvious application of this principle is in the maintenance of the playroom and equipment. The child should be required to help set the room and equipment in order after use in a manner appropriate to his or her age, strength, housekeeping skills, and so on. Skillful management on the part of the therapist can result in this potentially troublesome experience proceeding without trauma.

The overall aim of limit setting should be kept in mind during this discussion. Limits are necessary to ensure that each individual's rights and prerogatives are protected and that no one is taken advantage of. The therapist can do much to facilitate limit setting by providing a model of accepting, friendly cooperation not only with regard to limit setting, but also in every aspect of the experience. It is good to remember that the therapist is the child's cohort, among other roles, and is not just an overseer.

As to specific procedures for enforcing limits, almost any penalty or control short of corporal punishment is appropriate. As was observed many years ago, "a soft answer turneth away wrath," in the playroom as well as in other situations. The therapist is well-advised to be as low-key and matter-of-fact as possible in imposing limits and by all means to avoid being antagonistic or provocative. The therapist's relative sophistication and ability to maintain the proper perspective can be as helpful in effective limit setting as in other areas of therapeutic functioning.

Foresight can pay great dividends in play therapy, and this is nowhere more apparent than in limit setting. Proper planning will enable the well-prepared therapist to suggest an alternative activity to a child if he or she is testing the limits the therapist has established and can thus avoid a "battle of wills."

Although most children will find the playroom sufficiently attractive that therapists will therein find "leverage" for use in limit setting, occasionally, children will prove to be either so passive or so defiantly sullen that therapists must be more proactive in establishing reward values for themselves and/or the total situation. The well-prepared therapist will be ready with some kind of activity which he or she finds enjoyable and which can be engaged in alone. The activity should also, of course, be likely to pique the child's curiosity. With shrewd planning and proper application, the therapist will be able once again to engage the child and resume productive play.

Consistent application of established limits is essential. Although the therapist is not on guard, he or she should anticipate possible challenge at any point and be ready to deal with it. The child cannot be forced to do anything except remain in the room for the stated time. He or she should be taken to the rest room and allowed a drink of water by the therapist or another caretaker prior to the therapy hour. It can be assumed that any child with normal self-control can then avoid the need for additional drinks or further trips to the rest room until the end of the session. If a child should "have an accident," it would be appropriate for the therapist to commiserate with the child in his or her subsequent discomfort, but to insist that the child stay in the playroom until the end of the stated time. This is consistent with the general expectation that the child should be helped to learn to experience the natural consequences of his or her behavior.

How Therapy Proceeds. A general description of a series of sessions of Fair Play Therapy will help define its character further. In the first sessions the primary purpose of the therapist is to become thoroughly acquainted with the child and to develop an understanding of the problems requiring attention. Another important goal in the early sessions is for the therapist to establish credibility, reinforcement value, and the other conditions necessary for therapeutic interaction. The therapist engages in a number of activities in the interest of these various goals, including giving careful and continuing attention to the child and commenting aloud on the child's behaviors and his or her understanding of these behaviors. While engaged in this activity, the therapist must be careful to maintain a level of transparency appropriate to the child's sophistication and to the general nature of the therapeutic relationship. While no attempt should be made to mislead the child, care must be taken not to overwhelm him or her with "brutal frankness."

As further understanding of the child develops and the therapist begins to be important to the child in the sense that the child begins to value the therapist's approval, the therapist can begin to take a more active role in the therapy. It is at this stage of therapy that modeling is likely to become appropriate. The therapist will begin to understand which feelings the child needs to learn to handle more effectively, which situations pose particular problems for the child, and the like. The therapist can effectively and directly instruct the child regarding more adaptive behaviors via modeling. A host of specific props and devices will facilitate this kind of activity, including finger puppets, doll families, modeling clay, Play-Doh, to name only a few. It is also possible, of course, to use conventional athletic equipment in the interest of very therapeutic growth, and an example of this will be given later.

The end stage of Fair Play Therapy is characterized by helping the child consolidate gains made earlier. Activities at this time would probably encourage explicit rehearsal of desired behavior, and be accompaned by verbal descriptions, justifications, and explanations of these behaviors, as appropriate. Care should be taken at every step of the way to ensure that all conversation be carried on at a level appropriate to the child's understanding. Everyday language should be employed and jargon deliberately avoided.

The Therapist and the Child. Along with directing the activities of each session, defining and enforcing limits, establishing and maintaining an effective therapeutic atmosphere, and maintaining a continuing understanding of the child, the therapist is also responsible for acting like a real human being. This means that he or she should respond in a manner appropriate to the feelings he or she experiences. Fair Play Therapy is designed to be fair for the therapist as well as for the child. Neither should suffer at the hands of the other, and this includes the freedom to express honest feelings in an honest manner. Fairness to the child requires that this be done; fairness to the therapist requires the same.

This kind of therapist transparency represents a fairly distinct departure from traditional therapeutic practices. The justification for this procedure is at least twofold. First of all, the child clearly needs to understand the nature and magnitude of feelings he or she stimulates in other people. This understanding can best occur if the therapist shows these feelings in an unmistakable way. Furthermore, the therapist is human and would suffer various predictable, negative consequences if required either to deny or disguise his or her feelings in the therapeutic situation. To be able to function freely and genuinely is one of the most highly desired therapeutic goals for therapists as well as for clients. This goal can be achieved and maintained only in an atmosphere which encourages relatively unencumbered expression of feeling.

The point was previously made that Fair Play Therapy does not imply unconditional positive regard. The straightforward expression of legitimate feelings seems far preferable to the endorsement of every action of a client, however inappropriate or offensive such action might be. While unconditional positive regard might have certain theoretical or hypothetical merits, the children worked with in Fair Play Therapy live in a real world and it is the purpose of Fair Play Therapy to equip them to deal with the real consequences of their behavior. It is assumed that the child's experience of the therapist as a real, honest, human being is excellent preparation for dealing with other flesh-and-blood people.

CLINICAL EXAMPLES OF FAIR PLAY THERAPY

A few brief examples will make some of the important characteristics of Fair Play Therapy more explicit. These examples have been chosen because of their variety and relevance to various important tenets of this position. Selections from work with more than one child were chosen in the interest of illustrating a wider range of therapeutic problems and their possible resolutions.

Luke was referred for play therapy by his first-grade teacher, Mrs. Jones. She had observed Luke to be quite withdrawn and fearful and reported that he would frequently cry when she left the classroom, even for brief periods. Luke avoided contact with the other children, and at recess would stay close to the teacher. However, when she would approach him and try to comfort and reassure him, he would pull away from her.

The therapist observed Luke on several occasions prior to beginning therapy and his observations were consistent with Mrs. Jones' reports. On one fairly typical occasion, Luke spent the recess quite near the porch area where the teacher stayed, walking around with his hands in his pockets, kicking at the ground, pulling grass, and frequently looking in the direction of the other children playing together. When approached by another child, he would apparently respond verbally to the child who had spoken to him, but would not accompany or interact physically with the other child, even in the area near the teacher.

In the playroom, the first several sessions were characterized by quiet play and relatively little interaction between Luke and the therapist, Stan. Luke spent most of his time in solitary play, knocking over plastic dinosaurs by rolling glass marbles at them. After a few play sessions, he began to talk more freely to Stan, telling of events at home and the like.

Stan initiated play with some building blocks and Luke soon joined him. He developed a practice of making cars out of the blocks and rolling them off the table onto cushions on the floor. Stan also did this, and Luke noticed and commented that Stan's cars always lasted better than his since his came apart so easily. Stan offered to show Luke how to make them more sturdily, and Luke was obviously very pleased with the result. His cars then survived just as many crashes as Stan's did.

Another important development involved the cushions. Luke discovered that he enjoyed stacking a number of them up and running and jumping on them. He then asked Stan to hide behind the stack of cushions, which Stan did, whereupon Luke ran and jumped onto them once more, landing on Stan as well. They repeated this play on numerous occasions, rolling around the floor, struggling with each other and the cushions in a very well-controlled, muted, aggressive display.

The foregoing example is meant to illustrate several important features of Fair Play Therapy. The therapist took the lead in interrupting a relatively sterile pattern (the "Marbles and Dinosaurs" game), provided direct instruction in more competent functioning (building sturdier cars), and accepted appropriate aggressive display. Through all this, he was able to experience and communicate his genuine enjoyment of the child.

Tommy was a five-year-old boy whose mother requested help with him because of his increasingly numerous fantasies. She had recently divorced her husband and was trying to cope with both Tommy and a young baby, and felt that Tommy was becoming increasingly difficult for her to control. She was uncomfortable with the vivid nature of some of his fantasies and the vigor with which he would act them out.

In the playroom, Tommy proved to be a very active and fanciful little boy. His therapist, Sandra, was a very warm and caring young woman who found herself quite comfortable with Tommy's fantasies. These involved his being a "bionic man" with many fabulous powers. These special capabilities went far beyond mere physical strength and included special recipes known only by him for producing a variety of concoctions, the principal ingredients of which were sand, water, and dried pigment. In the process of mixing these concoctions and using them in the production of various paintings and the like, Tommy and Sandra created a significant mess in the playroom. After one such occasion, when time came to clean up, Tommy simply refused, hit Sandra in the face with the punching bag, taking her completely by surprise, and walked out. She was nonplussed, felt out of control of the situation, and cleaned up the playroom by herself.

At the next session, Tommy and Sandra involved themselves in much the same activities as before, but this time Sandra took care to point out to Tommy that after they cleaned up the playroom, they would go and look at the videotape which was being made of the session. This idea greatly appealed to Tommy, and he made it a point to hold several of his paintings and other productions directly in front of one of the cameras. He then did his part in the cleanup without complaint.

After he and Sandra watched several minutes of the videotape of their session, Tommy suddenly became very rigid in his posture and announced that he was blind and frozen. He then began walking around, bumping into the walls and calling out to Sandra that he could not find her. She kept calling to him, telling him which way to turn, and so on, but he still did not come to her. He approached relatively closely to her at one point, she grabbed him and hugged him, saying, "Here I am!" and he replied, "You unfroze me!" Tommy then went quietly to meet his mother.

From the previous example, it is evident that efforts at limit setting are not always successful, but that failure can be avoided through careful planning. Also, failure on a single occasion does not mean that all is lost. Indeed, Sandra was able to persist and to continue to provide acceptance and understanding for Tommy. She perceived his fascination with omnipotent and omniscient fantasies as reflecting his keen sense of helplessness in the face of family disintegration and was able to let him know of her understanding by cooperating effectively and "realistically" in his play. She specifically recognized his strength and uniqueness while, at the same time, she understood and satisfied his need for nurturance. She responded to his oblique and disguised need for physical contact in a very direct, straightforward, and accepting manner.

Melvin was a seven-year-old boy who had caused considerable distress for his father by attiring himself in his mother's discarded dresses and high-heeled shoes and walking around in the yard. At the same time, Melvin was reluctant to play with other boys in the neighborhood, including his nine-year-old brother, John. He stated that the other boys played too roughly, and besides, he was no good at such games as baseball.

Jim, the therapist who was assigned to work with Melvin, decided on a very straightforward intervention after conferring with the therapist who was chosen to work with Melvin's parents. After establishing a reasonable helping relationship with Melvin, Jim proceeded to teach him "how to be a boy." This involved engaging Melvin in increasingly vigorous play in the playroom, culminating in gentle wrestling. Jim had taken the lead in developing a modified version of "King of the Mountain" in keeping with the constraints implicit in the physical properties of the playroom. Subsequent to that activity, Jim worked with Melvin both inside the playroom and on the playground in developing skills specific to baseball and football. Melvin proved to be an apt pupil, and quickly became adequately proficient in the basics of both games.

During the sessions when Jim worked with Melvin, the parents were seen for counseling. They were given instructions in permitting and encouraging Melvin to be more "boyish" around the house. This included instructing the mother specifically to stop referred to Melvin as "my little girl." She had developed that unfortunate habit early in Melvin's life as a consequence of wanting a daughter prior to his birth. She agreed readily to stop this practice when its obvious consequences were pointed out to her. Other suggestions made to the parents referred to involving Melvin more frequently in his father's activities, situations the father had avoided only because of fear of his wife's disapproval. After our conversations, she was quite willing for Melvin and her husband to do these things together.

In the previous example, the teaching and modeling function of the Fair Play Therapist can be clearly seen. It should also be apparent that these problems required the parents to develop new understandings of their roles and to agree to change some of the ways they responded to the child. Indeed, it was imperative not only to agree to these changes, but actually to make the changes in their family life. This was done, and to very good effect.

END NOTE

Fair Play Therapy can offer some unique contributions to work with troubled children. Most, if not all, of the differences from traditional play therapy are relatively modest, but their total impact can be considerable. The work with the child can be well-formulated on the basis of the empathic understanding recommended in this position, and the total intervention can be relatively brief and efficient. The emphasis on fairness and equity for everyone concerned seems to have a widespread appeal, no doubt related to the broader culture we all share. The therapist who is bold enough to employ this approach will learn to be comfortable with the greater freedom inherent in the role, while also accepting its concomitant responsibilities. Although these expectations are demanding, learning to meet them is proportionately rewarding.

REFERENCES

Carkhuff, R. (1973) *The art of helping.* Amherst, MA: Human Resource Development Press.

Genthner, R.W. (1976) An empirical investigation of the Personal Responsibility rating system. *Journal of Psychology*, 53–56.

Glasser, W. (1965) *Reality therapy.* New York: Harper & Row.

PART TWO

Developmental Approaches to Play Therapy

A number of the major theoretical approaches to play therapy were presented in Part One of this handbook. These chapters represent a small part of the diversification which child psychotherapy has undergone since it was first proposed by Freud in 1909. Contributing to this diversification of therapeutic approaches is the ever-increasing body of theoretical and research material on child development. Since Freud (1905/1953) first postulated a stage model for the psychosexual development of children, virtually every aspect of childhood has been subjected to scrutiny from a developmental perspective. Aspects which have received particular emphasis are the cognitive, social, and motor development of children. Exploration of these areas led, in turn, to the formulation of numerous stage models for the development of play behavior. The major theoretical models in each of these areas are summarized in Table 2. The reader may note, in perusing the table, that all of the models appear interrelated; this observation has received considerable research support. That is, the child's acquisition of behavior in any one area (cognitive, social, motor, or play) is dependent on his or her acquisition of behavior in the other areas. Since it is inconceivable that all of a play therapist's patients would fall within the same developmental level in each of these areas, it becomes apparent that developmental concepts are of considerable importance. With this in mind we will now examine the ways in which a therapist's knowledge of developmental concepts may enhance his or her ability to practice prescriptive play therapy.

As previously mentioned, one aspect of the prescriptive approach involves the ability of the therapist to modify his or her particular approach to the patient's individual needs. In determining the needs of a child patient it behooves any therapist to assess the child's cognitive–developmental level, as this may affect so many aspects of the therapy. On the simplest level an awareness of the child's cognitive stage may help the therapist communicate with the child appropriately. Second, the expectatations the therapist has for the child's behavior may need to be adjusted to fit the child's cognitive level. For example, the basic decision as to whether to use a play or verbal thera-

TABLE 2. General Developmental Stages Versus Play Development

Child's Age (years)	Cognitive Piaget (1952, 1962, 1967)	Psycho-social Erikson (1950)	Psycho-sexual Freud (1905/1953)	Play Piaget (1962)	Play Erikson (1950)	Play Parker (1977)	Play Pulaski (1974)	Play Howes (1980)	Play Peller (1954)	Play Linford and Jean-renaud (1968)	Play Sutton-Smith (1967)
0	Sensori-motor	Trust vs. Mistrust	Oral	Sensori-motor	Auto-cosmic (body centered)	Solitary play	Sensori-motor		Body	Preplay exploration	Imitative play
1		Autonomy vs. shame and doubt	Anal	Practice/solitary	Micro-sphere (toy centered)	Parallel play	Practice	Parallel play[a]	Pre-oedipal	Conditioned responding	Exploratory
2						Shifting group play					
3	Preoperational	Initiative vs. guilt	Phallic	Symbolic (pretend)	Mac-rosphere (other focused)		Symbolic (1) Project into environment	Parallel with mutual regard; Simple social	Oedipal	Creative play	

90

#	Piaget	Erikson	Freud	Play	Games with rules	Social	Cooperation games
4							Games with powerful "it" (tag)
5		Industry vs. inferiority	Latency	Organized cooperative play; (2) Use body symbolically		Reciprocal/complimentary	
6	Concrete operations			(3) Dramatization			
7					Games with rules	Reciprocal social; Sibling	
8							Games with "it" requiring cooperation (frozen tag); Cooperative games (Red Rover)
9							
10	Formal operations						
11		Identity vs. conformity	Genital				Elaborate cooperation (Kick the Can)

[a] Howes states that the stages he lists do not correspond to a particular age, only to a developmental stage of the child.

peutic approach is generally based on the child's ability to express him or herself verbally, which is, in turn, related to his or her cognitive level. Lastly, the goals the therapist may reasonably set for a patient also depend on the child's cognitive–developmental level. Some of the typical therapeutic goals which might be affected include: the child's ability to understand and express affect, his or her ability to understand the motives of behavior, and his or her ability to understand aspects of the self. The implications of each of these points are discussed at length in Susan Harter's chapter, "Cognitive-Developmental Considerations in the Conduct of Play Therapy."

Another tactic of the prescriptive play therapist is to employ completely different techniques, not just modify a standard approach, to meet each patient's needs. To this end a number of play therapy techniques have been devised which are based on elements of Piaget's (1952, 1962, 1967) model of the development of play behavior. Piaget proposed three stages: sensorimotor play, pretend play, and games with rules.

Sensorimotor play begins at birth and continues until the child is 18 to 24 months old. According to Piaget (1962) the primary function of this type of play behavior is the assimilation of sensory information into the child's cognitive processes. As a result of the gradual assimilation of sensory data, the child's play changes over the course of this stage. Initially the child engages in purely reflexive behavior: he or she grasps objects which are touched, orients toward sounds, and blinks at sudden visual stimuli. These behaviors become play when, at 1–4 months of age, the child begins to repeat movements for their own sake, that is, reflexive movements come under conscious control. Eventually the child becomes less interested in his or her own movement and more interested in the various objects toward which those movements are directed. For example, the 1–4-month-old hits a mobile and is fascinated with the process of hitting. Visually, he or she attends to his or her arm more than to the mobile and may repeat the arm motion, with pleasure, even when the mobile is not present. For the 4–8-month old the mobile is the fascination and the arm motion is generally not observed unless the mobile is present. By 8–12 months, behaviors in which the child engages usually have some purpose, and the purpose is often "to have fun." By this time the child has assimilated the sensory stimuli associated with numerous objects and people, he or she will now seek out novel situations, and will explore them with great interest. During this period the child has come to know the world on a very primitive level. He or she is aware of events as collections of stimuli; perceptions are unencumbered by complex adult type cognitions. If this reception of stimuli has been a positive experience, then the child's sensations, his or her perceptions, and the objects associated with those perceptions are assimilated in a positive way; the child trusts. If this has not been a positive period, then the child is not likely to develop an adequate sense of trust and, in turn, this may inhibit his or her ability to assimilate additional stimuli and experiences. Ann Jernberg's belief in the fundamental value of this stage of play as it relates to a child's overall development led her to formulate the Theraplay technique which focuses on sensorimotor play and the child's relationship to a "safe" adult. In Chapter 6, "Therapeutic Use of Sensorimotor Play," she discusses current advances in this particular technique.

The second stage proposed by Piaget (1962) is based on the child's development of symbolic or pretend play, which is the primary type of play behavior observed in children between the ages of two and six years. Pulaski (1974) broke this stage down into three subparts based on the complexity of the play behavior. Initially the child pretends simply by projecting his or her own wishes, impulses, etc. onto the environment. At this level it is the toy bear who wants a second piece of candy, not the child. Later the child is able to use his or her own body symbolically, pretending to be a lion or a tree, for example. Still later the child is able to reproduce both real and fantasized events through dramatic play. The crucial development in this stage, according to Piaget (1962), is the child's ability to assume the "as if" position. The child has assimilated enough stimuli and organized them into perceptions of objects which are consistent enough to allow him or her to act as if objects are present even when they are not. Later on, actions may be internalized in association with objects; at this point the child is able to anticipate the consequences of his actions. He or she is no longer dependent on trial and error. The child is also able to anticipate the effects his or her actions will have on other persons, that is, to take another's point of view. It is generally assumed, regarding the therapeutic value of pretend play, that unless a child has gone through this stage, he or she may not develop the concomitant problem-solving skills. Consequently, the child will have difficulty managing his or her impulses and emotions, developing social skills, and developing more abstract cognitive skills. Further, pretend play is often assumed to have a strong communication function and therefore is an integral part of the more analytically oriented therapies. Elaborating on these ideas in "The Diagnostic and Therapeutic Use of Pretend Play," Eleanor Irwin discusses the value of pretend play and its uses in child psychotherapy.

The last stage of play development proposed by Piaget (1962) is characterized by the child's participation in games with rules and begins around age six. Although games with rules eventually take on a competitive and outcome-oriented tone as the child enters adolescence, during this earlier stage it is the process of playing which the child enjoys. The goal is not so much the winning or losing but having fun while playing. Sutton-Smith (1967) notes that games the child plays during this stage often reflect ongoing psychic development. He particularly notes that the role of the "it" in children's games changes over the course of this stage. Early in this stage the child enjoys games with the all-powerful "it," such as tag, which reflect his or her ongoing view of adults as all powerful. By age seven or eight the child begins to play games in which the group must cooperate to overcome the power of the individual who is "it," such as in frozen tag. This is postulated to reflect the latency-age child's move away from his or her adult protectors and into the peer group. Finally, the child develops an interest in cooperative games, which become more elaborate with age and include team sports. Not only does this substage reflect the child's total involvement with peers, but also the fact that outcome becomes more important to the child, possibly as an indicator of his or her ability to function within the social structure of the peer group. Whereas the other two stages of play behavior were closely linked to the child's intrapersonal development, games with rules have a strong interpersonal or social component. Not only must the child learn to cope with success or failure on a personal level but he or she must also learn to cope with the constant interpersonal contact such games require. Since a frequent therapeutic goal in working with children is the increase of appropriate social behaviors, the use of games in therapy seems entirely appropriate. Further, the structure of the game situation may help to allay a child's interpersonal anxiety and provide an arena for teaching the child basic social skills. This approach is discussed in the last chapter of Part Two, "The Therapeutic Use of Games" by Eileen Nickerson and Kay O'Laughlin.

REFERENCES

Erikson, E. (1950) *Childhood and society.* New York: Norton.

Freud, S. (1905) Three essays on the theory of sexuality. In *Standard edition,* Vol. 7. London: Hogarth, 1953.

Howes, C. (1980) Peer play scale as an index of complexity of peer interaction. *Developmental Psychology,* **16**(4), 371–372.

Linford, A., & Jeanrenaud, C. (1968) Report: A behavioral model for a four-stage play theory. In G. Kenyon (Ed.), *Contemporary psychology of sport.* Chicago: Athletic Institute.

Parker, A. (1977) *Family development.* Brunswick, N.J.: Rutgers University, Leaflet No. 545.

Peller, L. (1954) Libidinal phases, ego development and play. *The Psychoanalytic Study of the Child,* **9,** 178–198.

Piaget, J. (1952) *The origin of intelligence in children.* New York: International Universities Press.

Piaget, J. (1962) *Play, dreams and imitation in childhood.* New York: Norton.

Piaget, J. (1967) *Six psychological studies.* New York: Vintage.

Pulaski, M. (1974) The importance of ludic symbolism in cognitive development. In J. Magary, M. Poulson, & G. Lubin (Eds.), *Proceedings of the third annual UAP conference: Piagetian theory and the helping professions.* University of Southern California Press.

Sutton-Smith, B. (1967) Children at play. *Natural History,* December, 175–181.

CHAPTER 5

Cognitive–Developmental Considerations in the Conduct of Play Therapy

SUSAN HARTER

INTRODUCTION

We are currently witnessing an era in which cognition has become a conceptual cornerstone in our attempts to understand a wide variety of human behaviors. Cognitive theories now dominate the fields of social psychology, learning and perception, developmental psychology, social learning theory, personality, and clinical psychology. This trend is particularly salient among those who are studying the developing child. Piaget's theory has not only had a major impact but has also spawned numerous neo-Piagetian formulations which emphasize the need to employ a cognitive-developmental perspective in understanding the social and affective realms of the child's life. With regard to our clinical approaches to child behavior, cognitions have also been considered critical by those psychodynamically oriented therapies which emphasize insight as a major goal. More recently, the new cognitive outlook has found its way into the bastion of behaviorists, who are now espousing a variety of treatment programs under the general rubric of cognitive–behavior modification.

Although cognitive processes have come to play a prominent role in our therapeutic efforts with children, we have yet to devote sufficient attention to the implications of cognitive–developmental change. This chapter will explore several avenues for applying our knowledge of cognitive development to the treatment process. The purpose of this chapter is *not* to propose a particular cognitive therapy for children. Rather, the goal is to sensitize child clinicians to certain cognitive–developmental principles which may be applicable across a wide variety of therapeutic techniques. For the purposes of this handbook, emphasis will be placed on the applicability of such principles to the play therapy setting.

In the first section, we will examine why play in children is often viewed as the therapeutic analogue of free association with adults. Specifically, what are the cognitive–developmental limitations which preclude the use of free association with children? The second section will deal with three goals which are common to many forms of play therapy: (1) understanding and expressing emotions, (2) understanding the motives or causes underlying one's behavior, and (3) the child's understanding of self. We will examine the pattern of normative cognitive–developmental change within each of these three realms, and then will explore the implications for therapeutic intervention. The third section will address the transition from play to talk within the play therapy context. I will describe an interpretive process which has evolved in my own work with children, a gradual process which proceeds according to several phases designed to facilitate the child's verbal understanding of his or her behavior. The fourth and final section will attempt to illustrate how our interpretive efforts are part of a larger conceptual endeavor combining both the inductive and hypothetico-deductive methods of scientific inquiry. From this perspective, one can examine how our *own* cognitive–developmental level as therapists influences the nature of our formulations. This, in turn, raises the issue of precisely what we can and cannot meaningfully convey to those child clients who are functioning at less mature cognitive levels.

ISSUES AND EVIDENCE

Why Can't Children Free Associate?

A common assertion in play therapy texts is that children are unable to free associate, and therefore play is employed as an alternative medium of expression. When one considers that the natural mode of thought for the young child is associative in nature, upon first glance such an assertion may seem somewhat paradoxical. The young child happily produces a chain of associations as he or she flits from one thought to another in seemingly illogical fashion. So what does it mean to say that free association is developmentally inappropriate? I will first examine the reasons suggested by those psychodynamically oriented therapists, and then attempt to indicate how the application of cognitive–developmental principles provides a complementary set of explanations.

Anna Freud (1965) offered the most comprehensive account of the reasons why children do not make use of free-associative techniques and why they resist the verbal interpretations offered by the analyst. The psychodynamic considerations she raises can be cast into a general two-stage developmental framework, examining the reasons why free association is unworkable with both the (1) oedipal and the (2) latency-age child. It should be noted that the general psychoanalytic task is to bring unconscious material into consciousness.

Several reasons can be offered for why the young, *oedipal* child is unable to make use of free association toward this goal:

1. The natural mode of expression for the young child is *action*. Thus the oedipal child prefers to "act out" thoughts, fantasies, and conflicts rather than to talk about them, since the verbal facility for such expression is relatively weak.
2. The expression of id impulses may be too threatening. The analysis of primary process material depends upon strongly developed secondary thought processes, which have not yet been developed by the young child.
3. Unlike adult patients, the young child is less likely to accept a contract with the therapist to obey the "rules" of treatment, one of which involves free association.
4. The young child cannot adopt a long-term perspective in which temporary anxiety, experienced in the short run, is tolerated because it is viewed as necessary for long-term gain. Thus the young child chooses simply to avoid activities which cause immediate anxiety and discomfort.

Somewhat different reasons are invoked to explain why the *latency-age* child cannot make use of free association:

1. Latency, by definition, is a period during which id impulses are stifled, made latent. Numerous defenses and resistances are called upon to prevent the surfacing of threatening unconscious material.
   a. Since the ego is precariously balanced and extremely fragile during the emergence of this new stage, the defenses which are mobilized may be particularly rigid.
   b. Since emerging new defenses join the existing more primitive defenses, the repressive barrier is exceedingly difficult to penetrate.
2. Related to these changes in latency is an amnesia for the past and the urge to outgrow or reject the events in one's early childhood. The unveiling of id material runs counter to the ego's desire for mastery.
3. During latency there is also little motivation to engage in a contract with the therapist. The child does not understand the need to go "backward" in order to progress "forward."
4. Furthermore, there is a tendency for the child to *externalize* conflict; environmental solutions are thus preferred to internal or intrapsychic analysis and change.

What does a *cognitive–developmental* understanding add to this psychodynamic explanation? In order to answer this question, it is first necessary to distinguish between three related aspects of free association as a therapeutic technique with adults: the actual process itself, the intended effect, and the therapeutic goal:

1. The actual *process* requires that the patient suspend logical thinking and report everything that passes through his or her mind; one is urged not to censor thoughts.
2. The *effect* of so doing is to sidetrack or overcome repression and thereby to bring forth unconscious material into consciousness.
3. The *therapeutic goal* is to make interpretive connections by the analyst possible, and, as a result, bring unconscious material into the range of the patient's conscious insight.

A cognitive–developmental analysis of why this technique cannot be employed fruitfully with children can be directed toward two Piagetian stages of development, the preoperational and the concrete operational period, which correspond to the oedipal and latency periods, respectively. The natural mode of thought for the preoperational child is by definition associative or "transductive" as Piaget described it; the child does not reason inductively or deductively, but cognitively moves from one thought to another, stringing them together nonlogically. Thus, the actual *process* of free association would not seem to be the problem for the young child.

The limitations of the preoperational period which make use of free association problematic would appear to be as follows:

1. The *effect* of the free-associative process, to bring unconscious material into consciousness, may not be tolerated by the young child. Fantasy material, directly produced by the child, may be extremely frightening to the extent that the tendency toward "realism" is operative during this period. That is, the child's confusion between fantasy and reality may cause him or her to interpret a scary thought as a "real" event and not just the product of his or her thoughts or imagination. This, in turn, would stifle further productions.

2. Whereas the young child may *generate* associations, the prelogical child is unable to appreciate the connections and to view them as casually or meaningfully related. The lack of logical thought makes it impossible for the young child to understand, much less accept, the therapist's analysis of the free-associative productions. Thus, the therapeutic *goal* cannot be achieved.

3. The *egocentrism* of the preoperational period further mitigates against the acceptance of an interpretation by the therapist, since the young child cannot yet adopt the psychological perspective of another person. Thus, the young child cannot utilize different perspectives as a potential means of correcting his or her own perspective.

4. Finally, Inhelder and Piaget (1958) have pointed out that the form and

complexity of adult language, not yet mastered by the young child, is unsuited to his or her affective needs. For this reason young children create their own system of symbols and signifiers, those found in make-believe play. Therefore, direct interpretations made by the therapist are not likely to be understood.

Assuming that certain limitations of preoperational thought are overcome during the period of *concrete operations,* why should the use of free association also be problematic at this more advanced stage?

1. The advent of concrete operations brings with it a general penchant for the logical organization and classification of the objects, events, and occurrences in the child's world, a thrust which runs counter to the demands of free association. Thus, the concrete–operational child would have considerable difficulty engaging in the actual process of free association.

2. The newfound logical abilities which emerge during this period are directed toward an analysis of concrete events in the external world, as the title of this stage implies. The child shows little interest in analyzing internal events such as thoughts, wishes, or fantasies. To the extent that one can coerce a child of this stage to produce associations, they will tend to be a logical ordering of publicly observable phenomena in the real world, that is, lion, tiger, elephant, zebra, kangaroo, or Staubach, Plunkett, Bradshaw, Tarkenton! Thus, the intended *effect* of the free-associative process will not be achieved.

3. The very *ability* to think about one's thinking, to reflect on one's thoughts, may simply not be present at this cognitive–developmental level. The analysis of free-associative material may well depend upon a form of introspection which requires higher level skills of abstraction that do not emerge until the period of formal operational thought, at adolescence. Thus, although the child of this stage is able to think logically about certain concrete events, the therapeutic goal will not be realized given that he or she cannot treat his or her own internal thoughts as an object of reflection.

From this type of analysis, then, we can appreciate why free association is an inappropriate technique for children. Clinicians have long been aware of this fact, an awareness which has promoted the search for alternative therapeutic techniques. However, this conclusion has typically been based on psychodynamic considerations. There has been much less emphasis on how cognitive–developmental factors influence or limit the effectiveness of free-association as a technique. The primary purpose of this examination and review has been to illustrate how a consideration of the developing child's cognitive level can illuminate our understanding of how effective a particular form of therapeutic intervention might be. As such, it sets the stage for the next section, which will explore how cognitive–developmental factors influence the child's understanding of emotions, motives, and the self.

Developmental Changes in the Understanding of Emotions, Motives, and the Self

Multidimensional Emotions in a Unidimensional Mind.   Both the expression and the understanding of emotions, whether verbalized directly or projected in play, are common goals of many therapeutic approaches. Until recently, however, we have not devoted sufficient attention to deveopmental changes in children's understanding of emotions. My own interest in this topic began in the play-therapy room, with clients of normal or above intelligence between the ages of six and nine. Independent of the particular symptoms or presenting problem, these clients all shared a common limitation in describing their emotions: they could only acknowledge the existence of one feeling at a time. They were unable to appreciate the fact that one could have two (or more) emotions simultaneously, particularly emotion pairs where one feeling was positive, for example, happy, and the other feeling was negative, that is, sad or mad (see Harter, 1977).

Thus, they would assert that they were "all happy" in situations where sadness or anger was also warranted; or, they would claim to be "all mad" in situations where positive feelings were also appropirate. For example, one young client was "all happy" about her dad, despite the fact that her step-father was often inappropriately punitive. This six-year-old had already experienced considerable loss in terms of several significant adult figures in her life, and the potential fear of losing yet another may have contributed to the all-positive focus on her stepfather. Another client could express nothing but anger for her younger brother. This eight-year-old girl, the third daughter in a very orthodox Jewish family, felt displaced by the long-awaited son who was finally bestowed upon these parents, leading her to feel jealousy, resentment, and rejection.

My brief synopsis of these two cases may imply that a psychodynamic interpretation of these emotional reactions is sufficient. However, it seemed that there might be other factors influencing the difficulty young children have in acknowledging that two different feelings can occur at the same time, in the same mind. Thus, I hypothesized that cognitive–developmental limitations were also contributing to this phenomenon, limitations which can be extrapolated from Piagetian theory.

From the performance of preoperational children on such Piagetian tasks as conservation and multiplication of classes, we know that one cognitive limitation of this period is children's inability to focus on more than one perceptual dimension at a time. For example, in the conservation task, when the young child insists that there is more water in the taller and narrower beaker, his or her judgment is dominated by the perception of the single most salient physical dimension, in this case height. (See Harter, 1977, for a more complete analysis.) Thus, it seemed reasonable to infer that when a young child attempts to understand his or her *emotions,* such cognitive limitations might also make it difficult to acknowledge that two feelings can occur simultaneously.

We sought to examine this general formulation, and embarked upon a program of normative-developmental research, relying heavily on interview techniques with children between the ages of four and 12 (see Harter, 1980, 1981d). Our initial studies revealed a three-stage sequence. In the *first* stage, children simply deny that two feelings can co-occur. Our youngest subjects were quite vehement on this issue. Some of them merely asserted that this was not possible: "There's *no way* you can have two feelings together!" Others attempted to document their statement: "You can't have two feelings at the same time because you only have one mind!," or "I've never had two feelings at the same time, I've only lived six years you know!"

The *second* stage marks the first ability to think about the co-occurrence of two feelings, however, they can only be experienced *sequentially*, not simultaneously. Examples are: "I was happy we were going to see *Star Wars* again, but sad when we got there late"; "I was scared in the haunted house and then happy going on the merry-go-round."

The ability to conceptualize two emotions *simultaneously* defines the *third* stage. Examples of such responses: "I get angry and upset when my brother messes up my stuff"; "I was happy that I was watching T.V., but scared my mom was going to punish me for not cleaning my room."

The ability to conceptualize two emotions *simultaneously* has been our particular interest, since it seems to have the most interesting clinical implications. Our subsequent research has revealed that there are two additional dimensions which contribute to the ease or difficulty of conceptualizing the simultaneous co-occurrence of two emotions. One such dimension we have labeled "valence" of the emotion, whether it is possitive or negative. Emotion pairs may be of *similar* valence, both negative (mad or sad) or both positive (happy and proud), or they may be of *opposite* valence, that is, happy and sad. Another dimension which has emerged from our data involves the *target* toward which the emotion was directed. Two emotions may simultaneously be directed toward the *same* target, or, one emotion may be directed toward one target, while the second emotion is focused on a different target.

Our findings now suggest four substages in the conceptualization of the simultaneity of two emotions which are based on the combinations of these two dimensions, valence and target. These substages define an hypothesized developmental sequence which we are currently testing.

1. Feelings of *similar* valence directed toward the *same* target. This combination appears to be the easiest and represents the first acknowledgment that two feelings can occur at the same time. Responses here take the form of virtually "synonymous" emotion labels, "I'd be happy and glad if Grandma came to visit"; of highly "compatible" feelings, "I get angry and upset when my brother messes up my stuff"; and "blends" of two feelings, "I can be happy and proud when I hit a home run."

2. Feelings of *similar* valence directed toward *different* targets. Given that the two feelings are either both negative or both positive, it seems less natural,

and therefore perhaps more difficult, to direct similar emotions toward different targets. However, examples do occur: "I'd be bored 'cause there was nothing to do and mad 'cause my mom punished me"; "I'd be proud that we won the game and happy that we were going to the movies."

3. Feelings of *different* valence directed toward *different* targets. The data suggest that emotion pairs of different valence are more difficult than those of same valence just described. Moreover, when different valence feelings can first be conceptualized, one is directed toward one target, and the second is directed toward a different target. For example, "I was scared my mom was going to punish me for not cleaning my room and happy that I was watching T.V." The key to the greater difficulty of different valence pairs, in comparison to same valence pairs, would appear to inhere in having the opposition of both a positive and negative feeling in the same mind at the same time. When requested to give such an example, children often revert to sequentiality as a strategy for handling this question, for example, "First I felt happy about watching T.V. and then I got scared." That is, they seem not be able to comprehend simultaneity.

4. Feelings of *different* valence directed toward the *same* target. The most difficult task seems to involve the acknowledgment that one can have both a positive and a negative feeling directed toward the same target at the same time. For example, as one 10-year-old told us, "I was happy I got a bike for Christmas, but sad that it was only a three-speed 'cause I wanted a ten-speed." We are hypothesizing that *within* this category, the greatest difficulty involves a positive and negative feeling directed toward the same *person* as the target. There were no *spontaneous* comments of this type of "ambivalence" or "conflictual" feelings in our normative sample, nor did we explicitly probe for it. Yet it would appear that this combination is the most interesting clinically, in that we are frequently faced with child clients (or even adults) who manifest very all-or-none thinking about a significant person in their life and who seem unable to appreciate both sides of the emotional coin. For example, one child client of mine became rather depressed when her favorite grandmother moved to a far-away city, and she could only acknowledge sadness. It was only after considerable therapeutic work that she could acknowledge that she was happy to have her grandmother, sad that she moved away, and mad, also, because the grandmother didn't write often enough.

Although we have yet to document this detailed developmental sequence systematically, the general trends are quite clear. The youngest children deny that two feelings can co-occur; the first appearance of the co-occurrence involves the sequential experience of two feelings, which reduces, in effect, to having only one feeling at a time. The first examples of two feelings experienced simultaneously typically involve emotions of the same valence. The most advanced conceptualization requires that one acknowledge the simultaneous co-occurrence of a positive and a negative feeling directed toward the same target, particularly when this target is a person.

With this as a normative cognitive–developmental backdrop, we can begin to explore the implications for child therapy. It is highly likely, for example, that in a specific area of conflict a child will be at lower stages in the sequence than for areas which are less fraught with anxiety. Thus, whereas the child previously mentioned had great difficulty acknowledging her ambivalence toward her grandmother, she had much less trouble talking about seemingly contradictory feelings toward her schoolfriends, an area where she was relatively successful. To the extent that we can document this type of pattern, the level of emotional understanding may be taken as a diagnostic barometer of problem areas for the child. That is, interview procedures or observations during the initial phases of therapy may highlight differences in the level at which children can describe their emotional reactions to different life situations.

The interpretation of this type of unevenness may appear paradoxical on the surface. One would expect that descriptions communicating the *least* verbalized amount of conflict, namely the all-or-none emotional descriptions, would be indicative of the greatest amount of psychological conflict for the child. That is, in problem areas the child has more difficulty appreciating both sides of the emotional coin. This type of interpretation would only be warranted for children who also had the capacity to describe the coexistence of two opposing feelings for a different and presumably less emotionally charged life situation, such that one could make a meaningful comparison. If the child is cognitively limited by age or some conceptual impairment, then one would anticipate that the simultaneous occurrence of feelings would not be observed at all.

Can we facilitate the acknowledgment of seemingly contradictory feelings where there is reason to believe that the child has the cognitive capacity to put these feelings together? Elsewhere (Harter, 1977, 1980) I have described a drawing technique which holds promise as a means of facilitating children's understanding that they can have more than one feeling at a time in a given situation or toward a particular person. The technique began by drawing a circle with a line down the middle. The circle represented the child, and the two halves designated two feelings, for example, happy and sad, which could coexist within the child. The therapeutic use of this technique has been described in detail with one child client in the article previously cited. After one demonstration of such a drawing, this client continued to produce the circle, session after session, often with her own variations. It seemed to serve as a graphic metaphor to aid her in realizing that she could have both positive and negative feelings toward the same person. It also facilitated a more direct expression of her feelings. For example, after depicting with the circle drawing how she had happy, angry, and sad feelings toward the grandmother, this client then wrote and mailed a letter to her grandmother communicating her feelings. She wrote: "Dear Grandma, I love you very much, I am sad that you moved away, but why don't you ever write me!"

We should be cautious, however, not to equate circle drawings with a technique, per se. A variety of tasks, activities, and media for expression may potentially be employed, depending upon their appropriateness for the client in question. For example, with other clients who enjoy drawing people, I have introduced "bifurcated balloons" over the heads of the illustrations, in which we write the seemingly contradictory messages that may come from the person depicted. A new doll recently introduced into our play therapy rooms has also proved its potential. These small wooden figures have a head, around which is painted three emotional expressions, happy, sad, and mad. The head can revolve inside a "helmet of hair" such that only one of these facial expressions is visible at any given point in time. However, the other two feelings, while not manifest facially, are nevertheless still there, in the head or the mind of the doll. The attractive feature of this type of doll figure lies in its symbolization of how a child can be experiencing or manifesting one feeling, while at the same time have other feelings which exist, albeit more latently. As such, it appears to illustrate the phenomenological emotional experience in question.

It is unlikely that we actually *experience* two opposing feelings simultaneously. When we are mad at someone we love, we may well *feel* "all mad" at the time, although we know, *cognitively* that we also love that person. The disentanglement, as it were, of immediate emotional reactions from a more enduring emotional attitude toward another person appears to be the major developmental advance in achieving the most difficult conceptualization of feelings identified in our sequence, acknowledging both positive and negative feelings simultaneously toward the same person. The doll figure described provides a nice vehicle for communicating that one can be manifestly angry, while at the same time retaining a positive emotional attitude toward that person.

Developmental Changes in the Appreciation of Manifest versus Latent Feelings. The previous discussion suggested that the key to acknowledging two contradictory feelings lies in the ability to realize that one feeling may be more manifest while the second feeling is more latent. The work of Selman (1980) reveals that the very ability to think about latent or hidden feelings undergoes a fascinating developmental progression. At Level 1 in Selman's formulation, the young child does not realize that people can hide their inner or "true" feelings. Although the young child appreciates the fact that one can have feelings "inside," these feelings are reflected in one's overt, manifest behavior, that is, when you cry you must feel unhappy.

At Level 2, the child becomes aware that feelings can be hidden, that emotions are not necessarily obvious from overt behavior. At this level one can purposely cover up inner feelings and prevent others from determining how one might really feel. At Level 3, there is a further advance. The mind is granted the ability to control consciousness in that it can put thoughts and feelings out of one's awareness. Through particular conscious actions, for example, repeating to yourself that you don't have a particular feeling, painful thoughts or feelings can be forcibly removed from the mind.

It is not until Selman's fourth level, during adolescence, that the *unconscious* emerges as a natural explanatory construct. The adolescent comes to realize that no matter how much effort or will one might try to exert over the mind, there remain certain thoughts and feelings which are not readily available to conscious awareness. As a result, such emotions resist self-analysis.

An appreciation for this developmental progression has obvious implications for the type of interpretation we make about a child's emotional experience. For example, as therapists, we may infer that a given child has deep-seated unconscious feelings of anger or anxiety; however, interpretations to this effect may have little impact until early adolescence, according to Selman's analysis. On the other hand, if the child is aware of these feelings, but is either trying to hide them from the therapist (Level 2) or from him or herself (Level 3), the interpretive focus may be an illumination of these defensive attempts on the part of the child to deal with his or her emotions. For the young Level 1 child, who is judged to be in transition to Level 2 but who does not yet seem to appreciate that true feelings can be hidden, the initial approach may be more didactic. That is, one may want to focus on examples which illustrate that while people show some emotions on the outside, they can also have other feelings on the inside.

An awareness of potential differences in the way children conceptualize their emotions dictates that we first attempt to determine at what particular level the child is functioning. Interview questions such as Selman's may facilitate this initial goal, for example, "Is it possible to hide your feelings from other people? Can you hide them from yourself?" Follow-up questions ("Why not?" or "How can you do this?") can then be asked to encourage the child to elaborate on his or her theory of emotional understanding. This information, in turn, should suggest what level of interpretation is most appropriate for that child.

Children's Understanding of Parental Feelings. The discussion thus far has centered on children's understanding of their own emotions. However, it may be equally important to assess the child's understanding of the *parents'* emotions, especially in cases when the child's problem is intimately related to the family situation. Our own work (Harter & Barnes, 1980) reveals interesting developmental differences in children's conceptualizations of parental emotions.

One set of findings reveals that young children, ages four to six, have difficulty disentangling their emotional states from those of their parents. We asked children how *they* would feel in reaction to four parental emotions, happy, scared, mad, and sad. The overwhelming majority of the youngest children indicated that they would experience the same feeling as the parent. For two emotions, mad and sad, there was a developmental decrease in the report of identical feeling over the 7- to 11-year age range. Emotional responses to a parental display of anger shift to fear or anxiety, and responses to parental sadness evoke feelings of being sorry for the parent. (Responses to parental happiness and fear did not show this developmental trend. Children of all ages indicated that they would experience similar feelings, suggesting that these particular emotions are more "contagious." When the parent is happy, this tends to provoke happy feelings in the self; and when a parent is scared, it may well be appropriate to share this feeling.) The developmental differences for the emotions of anger and sadness, however, suggest that the younger the child, the more likely one is to unreflectively adopt the parental emotion as one's own. Thus, the younger the child, the more help he or she may need in correctly identifying the sources of his or her feelings.

In this same study (Harter & Barnes, 1980), another interesting developmental sequence was revealed with regard to children's understanding of the *causes* of parental emotions. Children were first asked what would cause *them* to feel each of the four basic emotions investigated: happy, sad, mad, and scared. They were then asked what caused both their mother and father to experience each of these same four emotions. Photographic stimuli, in which a mother model and a father model displayed facial expressions easily identifiable by all children as these four emotions, were utilized. A content analysis of children's responses revealed a three-stage sequence:

1.   The *same event* which evokes a given *child* emotion was seen to evoke that emotion in the parent. Thus, if the child told us that losing a toy would make him or her sad, losing a toy was also offered as the cause of parental sadness. In all of these responses, the children appear to egocentrically project the causes of their own emotions onto the parents. Other examples were: "Daddy would be mad if he couldn't stay up and watch 'Hulk' on television." "Mommy would be scared because there might be monsters under her bed." The young child cannot yet differentiate the causes of his or her feelings from those of the parent, and thus seems to project his or her own emotions onto the mother and father.

2.   The child is the *cause* of the parental emotion. Examples here were: "Mommy would be happy if I cleaned my room." "Daddy would be sad if I hurt myself." "Mommy gets mad because I fight with my brother." "Mommy would get scared if I got lost." At this level, a somewhat different form of egocentrism is apparent in that the child places him or herself at the casual center of the parents' emotional life.

3.   Events in the parents' life which do not involve the child provoke parental emotions. Responses coded in this category were: "Dad would be mad if someone wrecked his new chiropractor's table." "Mom is happy if Dad remembers their anniversary and takes her out to dinner." "Dad would be scared if he lost his job." In these responses we see some appreciation for the fact that parents have an emotional life outside of the child, and that events in the adults' world also provoke feelings.

This sequence would also appear to have implications for therapeutic intervention. For the youngest children, who simply project the causes of their own emotions onto the parent, it may be difficult to promote a realistic understanding of parental feelings unless the child appears to be in transition. Although the child at the second stage in our sequence has made certain developmental advances, there are potential misunderstandings during this period of middle childhood. While it is certainly true that children do directly cause any number of parental emotional reactions, the child may overgeneralize and erroneously see himself or herself as responsible for feelings which actually result from other causes in the parents' life. Children's reaction to divorce represents one such example in that many children feel responsible, or at fault, for the parents' marital problems. Therapeutically, therefore, we need to be sensitive to this type of overgeneralization and to assist children in discriminating between those situations in which they actually are the cause of a parental feeling and those situations in which there are other causes, independent of the child.

Our findings indicate that feelings of responsibility for parental *anger* are extremely prevalent at every age, from four through 11. Eighty percent of our entire sample saw themselves as the cause of this parental emotion. Thus, while our most mature subjects *generally* gave the highest level responses indicating their awareness of emotion-provoking events *other* than the child, this was not the case for parental anger. Thus, we cannot assume that children move unilaterally through these stages with regard to their understanding of all parental emotions. Unevenness appears to be the rule in our normative–developmental sample, and individual differences in the particular level at which different parental emotions are interpreted may be of diagnostic significance.

Children's Understanding of the Motives and Causes for their Behavior.

INTENTIONALITY. Piaget (1965) first alerted us to developmental differences in the child's understanding of intentionality in his studies on the moral judgment of the child. These studies revealed that the young child's judgments of the moral rightness or wrongness of an act were based on the objective consequences of the act, whereas for the older child intentionality and the underlying motives of the person performing the act were more salient. Thus, for the young child, breaking ten cups is a more serious moral act than breaking one cup, independent of the intention of the actor. In contrast, the older child views the intentional destruction of one cup as more morally wrong than breaking ten cups accidentally. Piaget's descriptions of developmental differences preceded his articulation of the four-stage theory identifying the sensorimotor, preoperational, concrete operational, and formal operational periods. The shift from judgments based on objective consequences to judgments based on intentionality roughly corresponds to the shift from preoperational to concrete operational thought, although the ages are quite variable.

Selman (1980) has integrated the construct of intentionality into his stage model of the development of interpersonal understanding. At his earliest Level 0, young children manifest confusion between the physical and psychological realms leading to erroneous causal inferences. For example, the child at this level may acknowledge that they are good *because* they are big. In the moral sphere, this orientation is consistent with Piaget's observations and with Kohlberg's extension of Piaget, in that objective consequences, in the form of the magnitude of physical damage and the severity of the punishment, define the morality of the deed.

It is not until Selman's Level 1, beginning somewhere between the ages of five and nine, that children view people as intentional beings and impute motives to their behavior. During this stage children more clearly differentiate psychological and physical causality, although their understanding of the nature of motives undergoes further refinement during subsequent stages. For example, at Level 2 (ages 7–12), the child becomes aware that one's motives can be concealed from others. At Level 3 (ages 10–15), the child comes to realize that one can have mixed or conflicting motives, as well. However, one can also try to "fool oneself" if one "wills" it, and actively banish a given intention from the mind. Moreover, the Level 3 child also realizes that one can observe or reflect upon one's own motivations, and that this type of analysis can lead to a greater understanding of the causes of one's behavior. It is not until Level 4, during adolescence and beyond, that conflicting motives are integrated into higher-order psychological constructs. For example, wanting to approach as well as to avoid a particular social situation is not simply viewed as two competing motives, but as a distinct psychological experience which may be construed as "ambivalence." Another major advance of Level 4 is the understanding that one's motives may be *unconscious,* and thus even the most intensive attempts at introspection may not reveal the causes of one's behavior.

For many clinicians, an important therapeutic task is to aid the child in understanding the motivations underlying his or her behavior. Selman's formulation implies that it is not until Level 3 (somewhere between the ages of 10 and 13) that the child has the cognitive capacity to engage in the type of self-awareness typically associated with insight therapy. During this level, the child develops a penchant for observing the self as an object of reflection. Prior to this level, attempts to produce "ahha" experiences in our child clients will undoubtedly be futile.

This does not imply that there is nothing that can be done of a therapeutic nature. For the Level 2 child, the therapist may serve the function of the observing ego, and begin to make inferences about the motives underlying the child's behavior. *Modeling* the observing ego, as it were, may encourage the child to adopt this function, thereby facilitating the transition to Level 3.

For the Level 1 child, however, the most fruitful therapeutic strategy would appear to be the identification of contingencies between behaviors and outcomes, bypassing an interpretation of motives altogether. Thus, for the aggressive child whose popularity is suffering as a result, one can emphasize the cause and effect link between the child's aggressive acts and the avoidance or counteraggressive reactions of his or her peers. Many of the recent cognitive–therapeutic models designed for children (e.g., Spivack & Shure, 1974; Camp,

Blom, Hebert, & Van Doorninck, 1977) include problem-solving exercises designed to facilitate this type of causal thinking. At this level, then, emphasis should be placed on "What happens when you do X-behavior?" in contrast to *"Why* do you think you *do* X?" The latter inquiry is unlikely to be a successful therapeutic strategy until later levels, particularly Level 3 and beyond.

A MULTIDIMENSIONAL APPROACH TO CHILDREN'S UNDERSTANDING OF THE CONTINGENCIES GOVERNING THEIR BEHAVIOR.   During the recent years, there has been a burgeoning interest in an attributional construct initially labeled locus of control (Rotter, 1966; 1975), a construct which also relates to people's understanding of the causes of their behavior. At a general level, this construct refers to peoples' perceptions of who or what controls the positive and negative outcomes in their lives. Rotter, and most others who have pursued this issue, have focused on the distinction between *internal* perceptions of control, where one takes personal responsibility for behavioral outcomes, and *external* perceptions of control, where responsibility is attributed to people or other forces external to the self. Levenson (1972) has further distinguished between two sources of external control: powerful others and chance. From self-report measures designed to tap this construct, a single score can be obtained which is interpreted as a generalized control orientation operative across a wide variety of life situations.

My colleague, Jim Connell, has for several years been investigating this construct in children from a developmental perspective. Initially, he questioned the sensitivity of the single-score approach, hypothesizing that children may have differing perceptions of control in different domains of their lives. The domains he elected to study were those found to be meaningful in my own research on children's competence (Harter, 1978, 1981b, c) where it has been demonstrated that children make meaningful distinctions between three competence domains; cognitive or scholastic competence, social competence with peers, and physical competence at athletics. Following the Crandalls' (Crandall, Katkovsky, & Crandall, 1965) lead, Connell reasoned that children might also have differing perceptions for their *successful* outcomes in contrast to their *failures.* For example, the same child might take internal responsibility for scholastic successes, but attribute scholastic failures to an external source, such as a lousy teacher. For this same child, a different pattern might emerge with regard to another domain. In sports, the child may feel that he or she is not responsible for successes (the coach likes and puts me in), whereas he or she does feel in control of failures due to lack of sufficient practice.

In constructing a multidimensional perception of control scale to tap these perceived contingencies in children, Connell initially adopted the three potential sources of control which had been reported in the adult literature: internal, powerful others, and chance. His empirical efforts eventually led him to conclude that children do not make systematic attributions based on chance or luck. What he did discover, however, is that children will acknowledge that they simply *don't know* who or what is responsible for a success or failure outcome in a particular competence domain. Thus, a separate subscale, labeled *Unknown* source of control, was created and can be compared to the two sources of *known* control, namely, internal and powerful others.

The pattern of developmental findings emerging from the interaction of several dimensions built into this scale is extremely complex (see Connell, 1980). However, one very striking trend for the Unknown Score should be noted. Across grades three through six, this score gradually decreases, indicating that with increasing age during the elementary school years, children are less likely to acknowledge that they don't know who or what is responsible for outcomes. The implication is that with increasing age up through the sixth grade, they feel they do know. However, the Unknown Score takes an abrupt rise in seventh grade, indicating that the first-year junior high pupils no longer seem to understand the contingencies governing their successes and failures. The Unknown Score then gradually drops during the eighth and ninth grades, suggesting that the adolescents come to learn what are undoubtedly the new rules and contingencies appropriate within the junior high school context. This general developmental pattern suggests that in our intervention efforts we should be particularly sensitive to the potential lack of knowledge about the contingencies governing the outcomes in one's life during the early elementary grades as well as the first year of junior high.

Beyond these normative-developmental trends, a multidimensional approach offers a compelling framework within which to view the individual child. Our examination of individual profiles clearly reveals that the majority of children make very different attributions for successes and failures in the different domains of their lives. For the clinician interested in the causes of a child's academic problems or difficulties in peer relationships, information concerning the child's *perceptions* of these causes is critical. The child who blames himself or herself for school failure is cognitively and psychodynamically in a very different place than the child who blames these failure on others. These two children, each claiming to possess *some* form of knowledge about their plight, may also differ dramatically from the child who helplessly acknowledges that he or she simply doesn't know who or what is responsible.

Based upon some understanding of a child's particular attributions concerning control in the various domains of his or her life, one can then proceed to determine how *realistic* these perceptions might be. Moreover, in so doing, it is necessary to move beyond value judgments about the nature of a child's perceptions of control. Both the literature and lore would have us believe that an external locus of control is somehow less desirable than an internal locus of control. In certain contexts, however, an external orientation may be extremely realistic, perhaps even more so for children who are naturally subordinate to a number of powerful others in the form of parents, teachers, scout leaders, coaches, counselors, ministers, doctors, dentists, etc. For some children, their difficulties may indeed reside in the attitudes or behavior of such powerful others, whereas other children may be projecting onto others their own failures due to lack of personal effort. One's therapeutic strategy would be very different in these two cases. In order to select the strategy of choice, therefore, one needs first to ascertain the child's perceptions of control and then to determine how realistic these perceptions actually are.

INTRINSIC VERSUS EXTRINSIC MOTIVATIONAL ORIENTATION. The perceptions of control construct just discussed refers to attributions concerning the causes of successful or unsuccessful outcomes in one's life. A different, but related, construct involves the child's motivational orientation, namely what is motivating the child to *engage* in a particular behavior. In our own work (Harter, 1978, 1981a, b), we have distinguished between an intrinsic and an extrinsic motivational orientation. To date, we have focused primarily on classroom learning as the behavior in question. Thus, the intrinsically motivated child prefers challenge, is inherently curious, and enjoys figuring out problems independently whereas the extrinsically motivated child prefers easy assignments, seems to work primarily to please the teacher and obtain good grades, and attempts to enlist the teacher's assistance when he or she encounters difficulty on an assignment or problem.

Our findings reveal striking developmental trends over the age range investigated so far, third through ninth grades. Third graders manifest the highest level of classroom intrinsic motivation, with a steady linear shift toward an extrinsic motivational orientation which reaches its maximum during the junior high school years. Interpretations for this shift from intrinsic to extrinsic motivation have been advanced elsewhere (Harter, 1981c, 1982a). The relevance of these findings for the present chapter lies in our need to appreciate the developmental norms which may serve as a backdrop for our understanding of a particular child. Given the large number of clinic referrals which involve school learning problems, it behooves us to attend to the age appropriateness of a child's motivational orientation. Our normative data suggest that an extrinsic classroom orientation in a third or fourth grader may be grounds for more concern than a similar pattern in a junior high pupil, for whom such an orientation is more typical.

We have yet to extend this research on children's percepions of their motivations to other domains. It may well be, for example, that while intrinsic motivation for classroom learning decreases developmentally, there are increases in intrinsic motivation for other domains, such as social relationships, athletic activities, or cognitive endeavors outside of the school context. Thus, this type of analysis needs to be extended beyond the classroom in order to provide a more comprehensive picture of developmental differences in children's motivational orientation.

Developmental Differences in the Concept of the Self.

CHANGES IN SELF-DEFINITION. Many of our therapies with children focus not only on facilitating children's understanding of their emotions and motivations but also on their understanding of the characteristics which define them as a person. Within this context, a common goal is to help children develop a realistic sense of self. As a developmental backdrop, therefore, it behooves us to appreciate the age-related changes in the very nature of the self-descriptors which children employ. This knowledge may, in turn, guide the form and content of our interpretations and interventions with regard to the child's understanding of the self.

Rosenberg's (1979) findings suggest a general three-stage sequence, based on interview data in which children ranging in age from 10 to 18 were asked to describe a number of facets of the self. His youngest subjects typically defined themselves in terms of *observables*. These included physical attributes (I'm short with blond hair), preferred activities (I like to play baseball), possessions (I have a baseball mitt, and a dog), membership (I'm part of the Ferguson family), and "territory" (I live on Blake Street and I go to Richmond Elementary School). For Rosenberg the child at this level functions very much like a radical behaviorist in that his or her self-descriptors are limited to attributes which could potentially be observed by others as well.

With increasing age, children shift their focus to *traits* as the most salient features which define the self. The earliest traits involve competencies (I am smart, good at sports) as well as "character" traits (I am nice, a good person, helpful, brave). During this period there is increasing emphasis on *interpersonal* traits, such as popular, shy, attractive, friendly, including the emergence of descriptors which emphasize emotional control, that is, I don't lose my temper, or get into fights. The child at this level, therefore, functions very much like a trait theorist, according to Rosenberg's analysis.

During adolescence, there is a shift toward the self-definition of one's "psychological interior." Thus, there is emphasis on one's inner thoughts, feelings, wishes, and attitudes: I'm a dreamer, I don't always understand myself, I'm moody. More abstract traits or membership categories also begin to appear: I'm assertive, a procrastinator, introspective, a liberal, an atheist. For Rosenberg, the adolescent functions very much as a Freudian clinician, manifesting an intense interest in analyzing the psychological self.

Elsewhere (Harter, 1982b) I have suggested that this sequence may be even more differentiated, drawing upon our own research in conjunction with the theorizing of Fischer (1980) and Selman (1980). My own clinical observations of children in play therapy (Harter, 1977) led me to conclude that children not only have difficulty integrating two seemingly conflicting emotions, but they also have difficulty acknowledging that they can possess what appear to be conflicting attributes or trait labels, such as, smart and dumb. My clients referred for school learning problems would typically view themselves as all dumb, without a smart bone in their bodies. Clients with problems in the control of impulses and aggression would see themselves as all bad, without any redeeming features. Other clients would tend to vacillate, describing themselves in terms of one trait (e.g., smart) on one occasion or in one situation and then describing themselves in terms of its opposite (dumb) in other situations.

Integrating these observations with the findings of Rosenberg, as well as with the developmental models of Fischer and Selman, we can postulate a four-stage sequence, with two levels at each stage. The first two stages roughly correspond to Piaget's descriptions of preoperational and concrete-operational thought. The third and fourth stages parallel changes during formal-operational thought. Movement from the first to the second level *within* a stage involves *differentiation*. Movement to the *next stage* involves *integration*. A more complete description of these stages and levels can be found in Harter (1982b).

1. During the first stage, behaviors and observable attributes define the self. At level one, these tend to be global descriptions couched in positive terms, for example, "I can run fast. I have a lot of friends"; the child's egocentricity and limited experience do not permit him or her to put these claims to a realistic test. At the second level, the child may alter his or her self-descriptions across situations or domains. Thus, one may be fast at running, but not have very many friends. The child's self-descriptions become more differentiated.

2. During the second stage, the first level involves an integration of these behavioral descriptions in the form of the first trait labels, that is, smart and dumb, popular or unpopular. However, within any given domain where the traits can be construed as opposites, the child is only able to control cognitively one trait label in the pair, thereby concluding that he or she is either all smart or all dumb. Opposites cannot coexist at this point, and through this all-or-none thinking, trait is overgeneralized across situations. The second level of this stage involves the differentiation of trait labels, such that one can be smart in some situations, say, in language and reading, but dumb in others, such as math, science, and history. Thus, the advance of this level is greater differentiation in terms of the situation specificity of trait labels; however, these self-concepts exist side by side, as it were, each restricted to a separate domain.

3. A more advanced type of integration is achieved at the third stage, in the emergence of abstractions. The budding adolescent combines the existing trait labels to form what Fischer (1980) labels a single abstraction. Thus, the child who is smart (in language and reading) as well as dumb (in math, science, and history) may conclude he or she is only of average conventional intelligence. However, there are the potential dangers of overgeneralization at this level, as well. The young adolescent may initially believe that his or her intellectual capabilities are modest in all domains. Then, at the next level, single abstractions are formed in other sphere's of one's life, and thus several single abstractions become differentiated. For example, this same adolescent may combine his perception of himself as a skilled writer of poetry and short stories with his perceived talents at drawing and painting to form another single abstraction of him- or herself as an artistic, creative person. This second abstraction is differentiated from the abstraction about his or her conventional intelligence. However, the adolescent at this level is not yet able to integrate these *abstractions*. As a result, he or she may appear confused or perplexed about what seems to be a contradiction: How can one be of only average

intelligence in conventional areas of knowledge but seemingly very gifted in other spheres?

4.   In the fourth stage, therefore, these single abstractions become further integrated into higher order abstractions such that they no longer appear contradictory, and the self no longer seems fragmented. For example, the young adult may come to define him- or herself as a Bohemian, one who rejects the conventional intellectual values of the society in favor of artistic endeavors. Moreover, higher order abstractions in other areas may be differentiated and then combined. For example, one's Bohemianism in the intellectual sphere may be integrated with a radical political ideology as well as an atheistic stance toward organized religion to lead to the conclusion that, in general, he or she is an iconoclast.

As therapists, an awareness of these stages and levels may help us identify where a given child might be in terms of self-description. This knowledge, in turn, may sensitize us to developmental phases during which the child may need some assistance in constructing a realistic self-image. For example, during the first levels of the second and third stages, there is a tendency to overgeneralize, either at the level of trait labels (Stage 2) or abstractions (Stage 3). Helping the child to differentiate further his or her understanding of self beyond this type of all-or-none thinking may be a focal point of therapy. For other children and adolescents who have already undergone this type of differentiation, we may wish to assist them in conceptually achieving the next step, integrating these different self-descriptions at a more advanced cognitive level.

For children with emotional problems in a given domain, one may find that their level of reasoning about the self in this area lags behind their self-descriptions in other areas of their lives where they are more successful. This may be particularly evident in the tendency toward all-or-none thinking, either in terms of trait labels (Stage 2) or abstractions (Stage 3) about the self. In the therapy case which has been described in detail elsewhere (Harter, 1977) the client, at age seven, was manifesting Stage 2, Level 1, all-or-none thinking regarding her intellectual ability. On the basis of her difficulty with math and reading, she concluded that she was "all dumb" despite the fact there were other indications that she was also smart. The drawing technique briefly described in a previous section of this chapter was also utilized here, to help her develop a more differentiated picture of her capabilities. One half of the circle drawing which depicted the self was labeled with an "S," to represent her smart aspects, and the other half, designating areas in which she was having difficulty, were labeled "D" for dumb. Not only did this client frequently reproduce this drawing, but she integrated it into her play, in which school-work was a constant theme. For example, when she enacted problem-solving in math, she would record the correct solutions on the S side, and keep track of incorrect responses on the D side. In so doing, she was attempting to differentiate between smart and dumb traits on the basis of the particular behaviors which defined each one.

This example illustrates the importance of providing the behavioral evidence upon which trait labels are constructed. That is, we need to go beyond therapeutic interpretations couched solely in terms of the trait labels themselves: merely telling the child that she is smart. From a cognitive perspective, trait labels represent a logical construction based upon the combination of concrete behavioral characteristics. As such, we can facilitate the child's cognitive construction of traits. An interpretation such as "*I* think you're smart even though *you* don't seem to think so" may not have much impact on the child at this level. A more facilitative interpretation, according to this analysis, would be: "I know that *part* of you is smart because you got some of your math problems right, you know these five spelling words, and now you can read the stories in the first grade reader." We know that good clinicians intuitively make this kind of an interpretation, describing the particular behaviors which lead to the inference. I am merely trying to illustrate how it follows from a cognitive–developmental analysis of children's changing self-perceptions.

Changes in Self-awareness.   Insight-oriented therapies place considerable emphasis on the client's ability to observe the self as an object of reflection. However, evidence suggests that it is not until middle or late childhood that this ability emerges (see Harter, 1982b; Selman, 1980). Selman describes this phenomenon within the context of his stage theory of perspective taking. For the very young child (Level 0) there is little differentiation between the perspectives of the self and other. At Level 1, the child can observe certain characteristics in another, and can engage in the first form of perspective taking. But the child does not realize that others can also observe the self's perspective, nor can the child mentally step outside the self to observe his or her perspective.

It is not until Selman's Level 3 (between the ages of seven and twelve) that the child demonstrates this type of self-reflective behavior. The key to this ability is postulated to lie in the child's initial appreciation that others are observing and describing the self. As scholars of the self (e.g., Cooley, 1902; Mead, 1934) have postulated, the child must first be able to adopt the perspective of others toward the self, a perspective which one gradually comes to adopt, including the particular descriptors and traits which others ascribe to the self. In this manner, the looking-glass self, in Cooley's terminology, is formed and consists of the reflected appraisals of others. After the self as actor or observer adopts this perspective, it can take this self as an object of its own reflection.

There is a further advance at Selman's Level 4 (ages 10 to 15) as the child consolidates the various reflected appraisals into what Mead termed the "generalized other." Furthermore, the older child can not only observe the self as an object of reflection, but can also view the self as the actor who is engaging in the observation process itself. At Selman's Level 5 (adolescence and beyond), there is the further appreciation of the unconscious self. Although Selman does not make the following distinction, one could further postulate that the first awareness of the unconscious would apply to the self as *object*, in that one recognizes that he or she has hidden thoughts, emotions, and motivations which cannot easily be analyzed through introspection. Subsequently, one may become aware of the self as an unconscious *actor* or protagonist in the process of relegating such contents to the unconscious. That is, one comes to appreciate that the unconscious also involves the active engagement of defense mechanisms which make such repression possible.

An important goal in certain forms of therapy is to make clients reflectively or analytically aware of their emotions, motives, and thoughts, to encourage them to invoke the observing ego. The analysis just offered suggests that the ability to do so will not be evident until later childhood or early adolescence, depending on the individual child. When a child does begin to manifest such an awareness of the self, he or she will undoubtedly be extremely sensitive to the evaluations or appraisals of others. Rosenberg's findings indicate that the specific others which emerge as most significant during this period are the child's peers. To the extent that the child develops a meaningful and trusting relationship with the therapist, the opinions and evaluations of the therapist may also have a powerful impact. Undoubtedly, however, the various significant others in the child's life, parents, siblings, peers, teachers, therapist, will not speak in the same evaluative voice. Thus, a major therapeutic task may involve helping the child realistically sort out which evaluations should be taken seriously in forming his or her self-definition. The child who is receiving very conflicting appraisals from different significant others may find it particularly difficult to develop a clear sense of the "generalized other" which can be incorporated into a unified sense of self.

The extrapolation from Selman's fourth level, during which an appreciation for the unconscious develops, also has interesting implications. The adolescent may well acknowledge that there are thoughts and motives which define aspects of the self, but which are beyond introspection. Until he or she is able or willing to take responsibility for actively banishing such thoughts to the unconscious, attempts to interpret defenses may meet with continued resistance. A major contribution of such ego analysts as Anna Freud (1946, 1965) has involved a shift in focus from the direct interpretation of id contents, to the initial interpretation of the defense mechanisms which are responsible for the repression of those contents. Until the individual has the cognitive capacity to appreciate this psychodynamic possibility, therapeutic efforts may well meet with frustration or failure. In attempting to account for the latency-age child's resistance to interpretations, Anna Freud highlights the rigidity of the defenses which the child of this age necessarily constructs, as described in the first section of this chapter. We may now postulate an additional cognitive-developmental factor which may influence the child's seeming resistance to interpretation. At this stage of development, the child has not yet acquired the *cognitive* ability to conceptualize defenses as purposeful strategies which the self, as an unconscious actor, employs to relegate thoughts to the unconscious.

In this section, I have attempted to highlight the importance of recognizing how the individual's very *theory* of mind, motives, emotions, and self changes with developmental level, which in turn has implications for therapeutic intervention. The most general implication is that we identify the particular developmental level at which the child is operating, in the sphere that is most critical to our choice of treatment strategies. Interpretations or interventions may then begin at that level, or may encourage the child to psychologically reach for the next level if that seems appropriate. Intervention at levels considerably below or above the child's existing level are probably not likely to be harmful in most cases. However, they are likely to be ineffective.

THERAPEUTIC APPLICATIONS AND CLINICAL MATERIAL

From Play to Talk: Phases in the Therapy Process

In the first section of this chapter, it was noted that many clinicians view play with children as the therapeutic analogue of free association with adults. Play serves additional functions as well. From the psychoanalytic perspective, the opportunity to project one's thoughts, feelings, and conflicts onto play characters provides immediate tension release. In addition, it provides a symbolic haven in which children can affectively master emotional conflicts and the perplexing experiences of reality. Inhelder and Piaget (1954) echo this psychoanalytic theme in their description of the functions of make-believe play. For these theorists, the symbolic activity of play serves to meet the affective needs in the young child's life, needs which cannot yet be met through his or her active interchange with the social and physical environment. Thus, in play, one observes the symbolic neutralization of fears, liquidation of conflicts, and corrections of reality.

The observation of children at play certainly bears witness to these forms of symbolic affective mastery. However, for many child therapists, myself included, the model of therapy involves a transition from the indirect expression of needs and conflicts in play to the more direct verbal expression of these issues. The general rationale behind such a model is that one must first bring thoughts, feelings, and conflicts into conscious awareness in order to promote an understanding of behavior, which in turn might permit actual changes in reality.

The previous section provided cognitive–developmental guidelines for the level at which we might expect a given child to understand his or her behavior, emotions, motivations, and the self. As such, these developmental norms provide suggestions for the *content* of our interpretations and interventions, namely *what* we might say. The present section will focus on the form of the interpretive process itself, that is, *how* these interpretive messages are delivered. The suggestions to be presented have evolved out of my own therapeutic endeavors with children. As such, they are offered here as one of many possible models of the interpretive process.

The phases to be described are first divided into a *diagnostic* phase and a phase of *interpretation*. Within the phase of interpretation, four subphases will be identified. Across this overall sequence, three general shifts will be documented:

1. With regard to the therapist's role, there is a gradual shift from relatively passive participation in the play to more active participation.
2. There is a gradual shift from indirect to increasingly direct interpretations.
3. The content of the sessions will gradually shift from a predominance of play activity to a predominance of verbalization on the part of both therapist and child.

Illustrative material from one case, a client I will call K, will document these changes. K was six and in first grade when she came into treatment. Her presenting problem involved school learning difficulties; she seemed unable to master the basic skills of reading and arithmetic. She was living with her mother, her stepfather, an aunt, and a brother two years older than she.

Diagnostic Phase. The therapist is often described as a participant–observer during the initial phases of treatment; participation involves following the child's lead. Whereas the therapist has been made aware of the child's presenting problems and symptoms, there are typically few clues as to the etiology of these problems. Thus, in the earliest phase of treatment, the child is allowed to structure the play, to choose the materials, activities, or the doll characters he or she desires. K eagerly sought out the dollhouse, selected her cast of characters, and welcomed me to join her. When I asked her to decide whom she wanted to be and what characters she wanted me to portray, she took on the roles of the mother and an aunt, and assigned me the roles of the young sister and brother. (The father doll was side-armed out of a rear window.) K's assignment of characters is quite consistent with the general principle of role reversal which we see in child play. The child adopts the role of the adult figures in his or her life and assigns the child roles to others, in this case to the therapist.

The next task to be faced in undertaking this type of play involves *directing the dialogue.* The child is encouraged to begin, and her character utters the first pronouncement. Thus the mother doll admonishes: "You better get down here Sissy and eat your breakfast or you'll be late for school!" As the speaker for the doll, Sissy, I could easily come up with a response. However, I am much more interested in what my *client* K might have Sissy say, since her perspective will have the greatest diagnostic utility in helping me understand K's perceptions of the younger sister doll who is most like her in reality. Thus, I attempt to direct the dialogue in this fashion, having my client K speak for Sissy as well. The strategy I employ involves my stepping back from the play, and as Dr. Harter, I whisper to my child client, K, "What should I have Sissy say?" K willingly whispers back "She says she doesn't want to go to school today." We then both move back into the play, at which point I whine: "Ah, Mom, I don't want to go to school today. Do I have to?" K harshly speaks the mother's line: "You better get down here quick, and if you don't, I'm going to tell your father!" Once again, I step outside the scenario to request help from my client in knowing how my doll character, Sissy, should respond to the mother. K whispers to me: "She's kind of scared of her father, so she says she'll come down, even though she really doesn't want to go to school." So I have Sissy reluctantly reply: "OK, in a minute, but, Mom, I really don't want to go to school."

By engineering the dialogue in this fashion, my client thus speaks for all of the characters present, even though I am also participating in the play. Thus, during this diagnostic phase, I come to learn my *client's* perceptions of *each* of the characters, including the doll most like herself in reality. Thus, I can begin to piece together a picture of the family dynamics which might illuminate her problems. I have found this technique of stepping outside of the play and enlisting the help of the child client in creating the dialogue to be extremely successful with virtually all of my clients who engage in doll play. It can also be used effectively with puppet play, or any similar activity where there is a dialogue between characters. Its effectiveness lies in having the child create the entire scenario, rather than having the therapist create part of the dialogue which may or may not be relevant, given the lack of information during the earliest phases of treatment.

Interpretive Phases.   Presumably, through the type of play interaction just described, the therapist begins to develop hypotheses about the nature of the child's problems or conflicts. In at least some areas, the therapist may feel that he or she wishes to make certain interpretations, perhaps initially to clarify the client's feelings about the situation which have been portrayed in play. However, the client, in all likelihood, will resist a *direct* interpretation such that denial or play disruption will result. Therefore, the first phase of interpretation is confined to the play scenario.

INTERPRETATIONS BY CHARACTERS WITHIN THE PLAY SCENARIO.   In this initial phase, the therapist actively chooses to have one of his or her play characters make an interpretation about the doll character most like the client. With my client, K, at this point in treatment, I had pieced together a picture of her fear of going to school, given what she perceived to be censure from the teacher and ridicule from her peers. Thus, during one session of our doll play, I took the initiative and spoke for the brother doll who said to the sister doll: "Sissy, I think the reason you don't want to go to school is because the teacher gets mad at you for not doing your work, and the kids make fun of you." I then ask my client, K, stepping outside of the play, what Sissy says in return. From K's response, I can determine whether she is willing to accept such an interpretation *within* the play, or whether even this is too threatening to think about. In K's case, the interpretation was sufficiently distanced in the form of the play characters that she could have Sissy acknowledge that the teachers and the other kids really did upset her. Eventually, through this type of interpretation within the play scenario, I came to learn that my client, under the guise of Sissy, was extremely anxious at school, and this anxiety was preventing her from concentrating on even the simplest arithmetic and reading exercises which she should have been capable of mastering. However, if I attempted to suggest to K *directly* that she might be experiencing these feelings, she would not accept my interpretation.

INTERPRETIVE LINK BETWEEN A PLAY CHARACTER AND THE ACTUAL CHILD CLIENT.   In moving from interpretations within the play to direct interpretations there is in intermediate subphase which is often successful. Without confronting the child directly, the therapist merely comments on how the child client is like one of the doll characters. Thus, during one session I commented to K: "I just noticed something really interesting. You know how Sissy doesn't want to go to school because she gets nervous about what the teacher and the kids think, and then she can't do her work? Well, I think you're kind of a little bit like Sissy! You don't want to go to school either, maybe because you get nervous there too!" The child may or may not accept this interpretive link between the play character's dilemma and her own. If she doesn't, then one remains at the previous level of interpretation within the play. If she does accept it, then the child is indicating some readiness to deal with her difficulties more directly.

INDIRECT INTERPRETATION ABOUT THE CHILD HIMSELF OR HERSELF.   This particular subphase has emerged only recently in my own therapeutic endeavors and seems particularly effective with child clients of average or above average intelligence who also seem to respond to playful humor. The format of the interpretation is as follows. The therapist says: "I have this friend, named (client's name) that I'd like to tell you about." In certain cases, where the use of the client's name might bring things too close to reality, I have described the physical appearance of the child; for example, "She's got blond hair, she's wearing a blue skirt and red blouse, and she likes to play school." One then proceeds to describe "this friend" in terms of the interpretive material one wishes to communicate. Children who accept this form of an interpretation often do so with a rather whimsical smile, communicating their conspiracy in this playfully thin disguise. These children seem willing to accept an interpretation in this form, whereas a more direct intervention might be rejected. The "friend" metaphor seems to distance the interpretation just enough for the child to be able to entertain the content of the message communicated.

DIRECT INTERPRETATIONS TO THE CHILD.   The final subphase involves interpretive comments made directly to the child. With K, for example, we finally reached a point where we no longer needed even the thin disguise. We could discuss her feelings of anxiety about school, and begin to explore some of the reasons causing her to feel so anxious. Together, we could also plan for her to receive help in a resource room where she would be removed from her regular teacher and the peers she felt were taunting her. Because she was willing to talk directly about her feelings and difficulties, she could be actively involved in at least a partial solution. Thus, the personal control afforded by her ability to discuss these issues would appear to be a particularly critical outcome of this type of interpretive process.

It is important to point out that whereas these phases may define a general progression in treatment, there is considerable unevenness across the different areas of a child's life with regard to the particular level of interpretation the child can handle. At any one point in time, therefore, children may talk directly about certain topics, whereas for other issues, they may only be able to accept links between their behavior and a play character, or very indirect interpretations made within the play scenario. The particular level at which a child can accept an interpretation should provide some indication of how conflictual a given issue might be. The more conflicted or troubled a child is about a given topic, the greater the likelihood that the interpretations will need to be couched indirectly, as defined by the earliest phases in the sequence. For example, in the case of K, although she could talk directly about her feelings in school, interpretations concerning her fearful–dependent relationship with her stepfather could only be approached through the doll character's utterances within the play itself. Thus, in a given therapy session in which different themes arise, certain topics may be expressed entirely through play, other issues may be dealt with at one of the intermediate levels described, and some may be discussed through direct interpretive conversation.

The timetable governing the child's movement through these phases will vary considerably, given the severity of the conflict and the particular child. Thus, the process may take weeks, months, or years. Furthermore, regressions are to be expected. A child who may seem to be moving toward an acceptance of more direct forms of interpretations may encounter a setback, such that he or she regresses to earlier levels in the sequence. Moreover, as new issues are revealed, the therapist may find him- or herself at the diagnostic phase of play for topics just surfacing, whereas the interpretation of conflicts which have been explored at some length can be dealt with more directly. An understanding of the unevenness across domains in the child's life allows one to appreciate why a given play therapy session may appear so disjointed, as child and therapist seem to move from one level to another. It is the skilled therapist who can make these necessary transitions and match his or her interpretive mode to the particular level at which the child can accept an interpretation.

Hypothesis Testing within the Play Therapy Setting

For many laypersons and practitioners alike, the therapeutic endeavor is likened to an art form, an intuitive interpersonal process bearing little resemblance to the scientific enterprise. From this perspective, there is a conceptual chasm between psychoanalysis and factor analysis! I would like to argue that in the hands of skilled analysts, of both persuasions, the processes are actually quite similar.

Science is typically associated with the hypothetico-deductive method. One postulates formal hypotheses, engages in a series of experiments, and on the basis of the results deduces whether there is support for the hypotheses put forth. In contrast, *inductive* methods may be construed as science with a small "s." Here the theorist begins with observations, often single cases, and gradually comes to appreciate commonalities leading to a more general formulation which ties these observations together. The earliest formulations of Freud, for example his studies on hysteria with Breuer, fit this model. Case observations with a number of individual patients eventually led them to formulate a general picture of the symptomatology and causes of hysteria.

I would concur with many that some of the best science involves the *combination* of the inductive and deductive methods. I would like to argue further that this very combination also results in the best therapy. In so doing, I will develop this position in relation to the phases of therapy proposed in the preceding section.

During the diagnostic phase, the therapist proceeds very much like the inductive theorist, attuned to behaviors on the part of the child without the benefit or hindrance of hypotheses. Gradually observations begin to coalesce into more general patterns. I notice, for example, that my client is very upset over the death of an uncle. In addition, she seems concerned that several aunts have moved into her house; with each she has attempted to develop a relationship, but each has subsequently left, sometimes abruptly. My client also became very depressed when her favorite grandmother moved to a far-away city.

On the bases of these observations, I begin to piece together a *hypothesis*— not a conclusion, but a hypothesis. In the case of this client, I speculate that she has a particular conflict regarding people leaving her, a conflict which may cause her to avoid establishing close relationships in the future. How, then, is such a hypothesis to be tested, following the model of science? The scientific method would have us systematically test this hypothesis through a series of experiments. What is the therapeutic analogue of the experiment? I would submit that it is the *interpretation.* Just as "good" science involves repeated experiments under slightly different conditions, "good" therapy involves repeated interpretations which converge on the same conclusion. These interpretations or interventions are analogous to experimental manipulations.

The scientific enterprise requires that in testing hypotheses, we specify not only what would count as evidence in support of the hypothesis, but also what constitutes disconfirming evidence. What, then, constitutes evidence *for* the appropriateness or correctness of a given interpretation in the therapeutic milieu? Certainly a very straightforward acceptance of our interpretation by the client will serve to confirm our hypothesis. However, it would appear that we also treat two additional types of reactions as confirming evidence. If the patient vehemently *denies* the interpretation, we view this response as an indication that we are at least on the correct interpretive path. Secondly, if the intervention provokes a *play disruption,* accompanied by anxiety, this also serves as a confirming alert.

Within this framework, what would constitute evidence *against* our hypothesis? From my own experience, *no* reaction seems to represent the major source of disconfirming evidence. The child neither accepts nor rejects the interpretation, nor does it result in a play disruption or other forms of anxiety and distress. Lack of any of these reactions suggests that the hypothesis may have been somewhat misguided. Our strategy, then, is to design another experiment, to attempt a different type of interpretive intervention and try again. Although others may have somewhat different criteria for what constitutes evidence for and against the correctness of an interpretation, the point is that in essence, at our best, we are functioning as scientists. We generate hypotheses based on our observations and then proceed to test these hypotheses as systematically as possible within the play therapy context.

Our next task is to *communicate* the knowledge gained through this form of inquiry. I will concentrate here on how we communicate our formulation to the *child client,* although we also have a responsibility to communicate our knowledge to parents, teachers, etc. Talent in the form of data gathering to support one's hypothesis does *not necessarily* translate into skill at communicating this information to the child in the service of therapeutic gain. (Freud himself, while modestly acknowledging his brilliance as a diagnostician and theorist felt much less adequate in his clinical attempts to utilize this knowledge in treatment to improve the mental health of the patient.)

Child clients may pose a particular challenge in this regard. If we are truly utilizing the hypothetico-deductive model, then we, as therapists, are functioning at Piaget's highest stage of reasoning, formal operations. Our child clients, prior to the emergence of this stage during adolescence or beyond, do not have the benefit of this type of reasoning. What are the implications, then, of this lack of concordance between the cognitive level of the therapist and the cognitive level of the child?

The child will be unable to appreciate the process of logic underlying the conclusions the therapist has deduced. Not only does the child not have the ability to understand the process of hypothetico-deductive thinking, but it is also unlikely that he or she would accept denial, distress, or play disruption as confirming evidence. The child may, on the other hand, treat his or her direct *acceptance* of an interpretation as some indication for the correctness of the therapist's conclusion.

It would seem, however, that the child functioning in the concrete operational period would be able to appreciate the *inductive* component of the enterprise if he or she were provided with the evidence on which the initial inference was based. An interpretation to my client, to the effect that I think she has a problem with important people leaving her, may have little impact. However, this same interpretation in conjunction with the specific examples she had given me would provide the data base, as it were, from which she could appreciate the generalization. A similar point was made in the section describing developmental changes in the child's self-concept. There it was suggested that in order to convince the child that she is smart, one needs to present a number of concrete behavioral descriptions which can be combined to construct a trait label. In conclusion I suggest that to *arrive* at an acceptable formulation of the child client's conflicts, the therapist must make use of both inductive and deductive approaches. In *communicating* these findings, however, the therapist must sensitively employ procedures which focus on the inductive features of this process in order to maximize the child's understanding of his or her behavior and personality.

SUMMARY AND CONCLUSIONS

The general purpose of this chapter has been to highlight normative cognitive–developmental changes which may have implications for our therapeutic interventions with children, with particular emphasis on the play therapy process. The very fact that we employ play as a medium of expression, rather than free association, is itself a function of the cognitive limitations of the developing child. These specific limitations were described.

In the next section, developmental changes in children's understanding of emotions, motives, and the self were discussed. With regard to emotions, our own research reveals developmental differences in children's ability to appreciate that two seemingly contradictory affects, for example, happy and sad, can coexist. Children first deny that such feelings can co-occur, then acknowledge that they can occur *sequentially,* and eventually appreciate the fact that they can simultaneously occur. It is suggested that the most difficult conceptual task is to realize that one can have two opposing feelings, say, love and anger, toward the same *person* at the same time. Possible techniques for helping children appreciate that they in fact can have such multiple feelings were described. Developmental differences in children's understanding of parental emotions and the implications for treatment were also discussed.

A developmental sequence involving children's understanding of manifest versus latent feelings was also presented. The very young child does not realize that feelings can be hidden, whereas at a later age this is appreciated. The next advance is marked by the child's belief that one can consciously control these affects, and actively banish negative feelings from one's mind. It is not until adolescence that an appreciation for the unconscious emerges, including the understanding that unconscious emotions may not be readily available to conscious awareness and analysis. A similar sequence was described with regard to children's understanding of their motives. Initially children do not appreciate the fact that behavior is motivated; gradually they move through a series of stages, culminating in adolescence with an appreciation for unconscious motivation. These developmental patterns suggest that interpretations of intentionality will not be understood or accepted by children until middle childhood, and that an appreciation of how behaviors and affects might be unconsciously motivated or repressed will not be possible until adolescence.

Developmental differences in children's understanding of the factors which control their successes and failures were also highlighted. Whereas some children feel that they are responsible for the outcomes in their lives, others see authority figures as primarily responsible. Our findings reveal that there are also children who simply report that they don't know who or what is responsible. It was urged that we not only attempt to determine a given child's perceptions of control, but also evaluate how realistic these perceptions might be. While there is a tendency for many therapists to consider an "internal" sense of control as somehow "better," there are situations in which an external authority orientation or even ignorance of the factors in control may be much more realistic. Developmental norms were presented for certain of these control dimensions as well as for another construct our group has studied, intrinsic versus extrinsic motivational orientation. It was suggested that we need to appreciate these developmental norms as a backdrop for assessing the individual child.

Given the focus of many to enhance the child's understanding of the self, developmental differences in self-descriptions were discussed. A four-stage model was presented, moving from self-descriptions based on discrete behaviors, to traits, to single abstractions, and finally to higher order abstractions. Two levels within each stage were described. At the first level of a given stage, behaviors, traits, or abstractions are typically global and overgeneralized. These become more differentiated and situation specific at the second level. Thus, for example, the child with school learning problems who is at level one of the *trait* stage may overgeneralize and feel that he or she is all dumb. Therapeutically, for such a child, our efforts should be directed toward helping him or her develop a more differentiated picture, realizing that there can be both dumb and smart components to the self. For other children or adolescents who feel that the coexistence of opposites is somehow contradictory, our task will be to help them integrate these concepts at a higher level of understanding.

It is not possible to present a single stage model incorporating all of the dimensions of developmental change, given the tremendous unevenness across the domains described. For example, children may be at one level of understanding with regard to the behavioral attributes which define the self but at another level in regard to their ability to understand their emotions and motivations. Furthermore, there are tremendous individual differences in the rate of movement through the stages described. Thus, some appreciation for the *sequence* is required, rather than a rigid adherence to age norms. The cognitive–developmental perspective also highlights the need for the therapist to be actively didactic in certain situations, rather than merely interpretive. Once we have identified the child's particular level of understanding in a given domain, we may be able to facilitate the child's movement to the next level if that is deemed appropriate.

The actual therapeutic *process* described in this chapter focused on the transition from play to talk. A phase model was described which highlighted how interpretations, initially couched in terms of the play scenario, become increasingly more direct. Particular interpretive techniques were illustrated for each of the phases.

Finally, the need to view our therapeutic efforts as a scientific enterprise, rather than an intuitive art form, was underscored. It was suggested that the best therapists function much like scientists employing a combination of inductive and hypothetico-deductive methods. However, since it is unlikely that the majority of our child clients can cognitively appreciate hypothetico-deductive reasoning, suggestions for how to communicate our findings and formulations to our clients were offered. Underlying all of the suggestions in this chapter is the assumption that our therapeutic efforts should help the child to understand his or her behavior and personality. However, this can only be achieved if we as therapists have an understanding of the developing child.

REFERENCES

Camp, B., Blom, G., Hebert, F., & Van Doorninck, W. (1977) "Think aloud": A program for developing self-control in young aggressive boys. *Journal of Abnormal Child Psychology,* **8,** 157–169.

Connell, J. P. (1980) A multidimensional measure of children's perceptions of control: A comprehensive assessment of the development of children's perceptions of control. Unpublished masters thesis, University of Denver.

Cooley, C. H. (1902) *Human nature and the social order.* New York: Charles Scribner's Sons.

Crandall, V. C., Katkovsky, W., & Crandall, V. J. (1965) Children's beliefs in their own control of reinforcement in intellectual academic achievement situations. *Child Development,* **36,** 91–109.

Fischer, K. F. (1980) A theory of cognitive development: The control and construction of hierarchies of skills. *Psychological Review,* **87,** 477–531.

Freud, A. (1946) *The ego and mechanisms of defense.* New York: International Universities Press.

Freud, A. (1965) *Normality and pathology in childhood.* New York: International Universities Press.

Harter, S. (1977) A cognitive–developmental approach to children's expression of conflicting feelings and a technique to facilitate such expression in play therapy. *Journal of Consulting and Clinical Psychology,* **45,** 417–432.

Harter, S. (1978) Effectance motivation reconsidered: A developmental model. *Human Development,* **21,** 34–64.

Harter, S. (1980) Children's understanding of multiple emotions: A cognitive–developmental approach. In *The proceedings of the Jean Piaget Society.* Hillsdale, N. J.: Lawrence Erlbaum.

Harter, S. (1981a) A new self-report scale of intrinsic versus extrinsic orientation in the classroom: Motivational and informational components. *Developmental Psychology,* **17,** 300–312.

Harter, S. (1981b) A model of intrinsic mastery motivation in children: Individual differences and developmental change. In Collins (Ed.), *Minnesota symposium on child psychology*, Vol. 14. Hillsdale, N.J.: Lawrence Erlbaum.

Harter, S. (1982a) A developmentalist's perspective on some parameters on the self-regulation process in children. In Kanfer & Karoly (Eds.), *The psychology of self-management: From theory to practice.* Elmsford, N.Y.: Pergamon Press.

Harter, S. (1982b) Developmental perspectives on the self-system. In Hetherington (Ed.), *Carmichael's manual of child psychology*, Volume on *Social Development.* New York: Wiley.

Harter, S. (1982c) The perceived competence scale for children. *Child Development,* 53, 87–97.

Harter, S. (1982d) A cognitive–developmental approach to children's use of affect and trait labels. In F. C. Serafica (Ed.), *Social cognition in context.* New York: Guilford Press.

Harter, S., & Barnes, R. (1980) Children's understanding of parental emotions. Unpublished manuscript, University of Denver.

Inhelder, B., & Piaget, J. (1954) *The growth of logical thinking from childhood to adolescence.* New York: Basic Books.

Kohlberg, L. Stage and sequence: The cognitive-developmental approach to socialization. In D.A. Goslin (Ed.), *Handbook of socialization theory and research.* Chicago: Rand McNally 1969.

Kohlberg, L. Moral stages and moralization. In T. Lickona (Ed.), *Moral development and behavior.* New York: Holt, 1976.

Levenson, H. (1972) *Distinction within the concept of internal–external control.* Paper presented at the American Psychological Association Convention, Washington, D.C.

Mead, G. H. (1934) *Mind, self, and society.* Chicago: University of Chicago Press.

Piaget, J. (1965) *The moral judgment of the child.* New York: Free Press.

Rosenberg, M. (1979) *Conceiving the self.* New York: Basic Books.

Rotter, J. B. (1966) Generalized expectancies for internal versus external control of reinforcement. *Psychological Monographs,* **80** (1, Whole No. 609).

Rotter, J. B. (1975) Some problems and misconceptions related to the construct of internal vs. external control of reinforcement. *Journal of Consulting and Clinical Psychology,* **43**, 56–67.

Selman, R. (1980) *Interpersonal understanding.* New York: Academic Press.

Spivack, G., & Shure, M. (1974) *Social adjustment of young children: A cognitive approach to solving real-life problems.* San Francisco: Jossey-Bass.

CHAPTER 6

Therapeutic Use of Sensory-Motor Play

ANN M. JERNBERG

INTRODUCTION: ASPECTS OF SENSORY-MOTOR PLAY

Definition

Sensory-motor play is the play of the concrete, self-centered, predominantly biological infant. Sensory-motor play permeates both the baby's own movements through space and his or her handling of objects in the outside world. Both large- and small-muscle movements over this first period of life progress from crude and undifferentiated to directed and refined. As the infant develops coordination and experience his or her body wriggling changes to deliberate goal-oriented efforts. There is a progression also in the baby's dealing with objects in the outside world. First he or she just "studies" objects, then manipulates them, and finally perfects highly skillful maneuvers with them. During the first third of the sensory-motor period the infant is not really aware of the properties of the world. Then gradually he or she develops three concepts: object constancy, cause and effect, and time and space. The infant begins to understand that whether or not they are concretely visible at the moment, objects (and people) can be counted on to maintain an existence of their own. He or she begins to anticipate that a tower will fall if kicked. The child recognizes that there is a special time for breakfast and a special place for his or her blanket. In the final stage of the sensory-motor period the child is able to conceive of action even in the absence of objects. The way is thus paved for later symbolizing, make-believe, fantasy, and pretense.

During this important first period, the period of sensory-motor intelligence (0–2 years), the infant moves from a neonatal reflex level of complete self–world undifferentiation to a relatively coherent organization of sensory-motor action, vis-à-vis his immediate environment. The organization is an entirely "practical" one, however, in the sense that it involves simple perceptual and motor adjustments to things rather than symbolic manipulation of them. (Flavell, 1963, p. 86)

Piaget separates the sensory-motor period into six distinct developmental stages (Piaget, 1952). In Stage I (0–1 month) the reflexes with which the infant was born are the primary determinants of his or her actions. In Stage II (1–4 months) these reflexes become modulated through experience and begin to coordinate with one another. Of this period, Susanna Millar (1968) writes, "The infant's behavior now goes beyond the reflex stage. New elements become embodied in the circular reaction between stimuli and responses, but still only as repetition. Such repetition 'for its own sake' is the forerunner of play." In Stage III (4–8 months) behavior becomes directed to external happenings and to things outside the infant's body. To quote Millar, "looking and touching have become coordinated and the child learns that to push the toy hanging from its cot will make it swing or rattle. Once learned the action will be repeated again and again. This is play." In Stage IV (8–12 months) the infant does what he does with a definite purpose. "Having learned to remove covers to find toys and other objects, removing covers and screens itself becomes an enjoyable game" (Millar, 1968, p. 54). In Stage V (12–18 months) the infant experiments and actively pursues new avenues simply because he or she enjoys their novelty. In the final stage (18 months–2 years), internal representations, symbolization, pretense, and make-believe replace concrete trial and error. The child draws upon fantasy for the invention of new solutions. Throughout his conceptualization of the child's sensory-motor development, "Piaget has no need to assume a special impulse to play," writes Millar (1968, p. 54), "since he regards it as an aspect of assimilation, i.e., the repetition of an achievement to fit it in and consolidate it."

Description

If we close our eyes for a moment and picture a three- to six-month-old boy at play in his crib we see him lying on his back, perhaps, cooing happily or gurgling through a little bubble on his lips. Perhaps he is fascinated by his fingers and alternates plunging them into and pulling them out of his mouth with intertwining them and fanning the air with them widespread so as to allow the sunlight rhythmically to filter through the spaces between them.

Now let us close our eyes once again and this time introduce his mother. Her face, let us say, is close to his. When they are not gazing into each other's eyes, she is tickling his cheeks with her hair and blowing on his eyelids. All the while she is imitating his sounds as he babbles, coos, and chuckles. Then, she backs out of sight, reappearing instantly to the accompaniment of his delighted squealing. Or she may plant the soles of his feet up against her stomach and pretend surprise and feign toppling over backward as he gives a little push. She may sit in a chair and alternate between bouncing him upon her knees and unexpectedly dropping him down between them. She may suspend him in the air or let him climb up and then slide down her legs. Or perhaps it is a time of quiet cuddling, stroking, nuzzling, caressing, and lullabies. At the very beginning of the sensory-motor phase of development the infant is already responsive. LeBoyer (1975) describes the sensitivities of the newborn in this dramatic way:

The baby's senses are at work. Totally. They are sharp and open—new. . . . These sensations are not yet organized into integrated, coherent perceptions. . . . Sight: The infant does perceive light vividly. Hearing: The . . . baby is marked by its mother's voice, its nuances, its inflections. . . . Touch: . . . its skin, thin, fine, almost without a protective surface layer—is as exposed and raw as tissue that has suffered a burn. The slightest touch makes it quiver.

This degree of sensitivity to stimuli, of course, diminishes in time. Indeed, provided it is neither more than the infant can comfortably integrate nor less than he or she is equipped to handle, the infant actually comes to seek out stimulation and complexity (Fantz, 1967). And, most important of all, verbal and nonverbal communication with the mother becomes more and more enjoyable, his or her attachment to her grows stronger every day.

Delimitation

For Piaget (Flavell, 1963) the sensory-motor stage of play begins at birth and continues to approximately two years of age. This period is divided up into six stages: 0–1 month; 1–4 months; 4–8 months; 8–12 months; 12–18 months; and 18 months–2 years.

Growth-Producing Functions

In that it sets the stage for many later perceptions, abilities, strategies, behaviors, and relationships, the sensory-motor phase of development has far-reaching, growth-determining implications. It is in the sensory-motor phase that attachment and bonding are set into motion, that the child's view of him or herself and of the world are first formulated. The quality of his or her earliest attachment colors the child's self-image as lovable, interesting, effective, special, and beautiful or as unworthy, bad, and ugly; and affects whether he or she comes to see the world as empathic, responsive, enjoyable, loving, engaged, and exciting or as hostile, distant, rejecting, punitive, and cold. Through the consequences of his or her acts, furthermore, the child learns that purposeful, goal-directed, and determined behavior can make a significant impact, for, already in his or her earliest weeks, the infant learns that he or she can produce a reaction in others with crying and smiling—cries signaling needs for relief from discomfort, smiles entreating others to approach and interact. This same sense of impact occurs when the child learns that through the intensity of sucking he or she can control the rate of flow of milk; that he or she can grasp and cling; that objects can be followed with his or her eyes; that jiggling the cradle will make the mobile dance; that moving his or her tongue quickly while humming produces lovely songs and babbling. Gradually, as the child learns that sucking a rattle brings sensations only to the mouth whereas chewing his or her big toe results in two sensations simultaneously, the infant becomes familiar with the boundaries of his or her body. From this familiarity the child forms a mental body image, and from that mental picture he or she develops self-esteem. A natural curiosity, all the while, is leading the child to sort objects into groups—the rudiments of scientific method. Stephenson (1980) gives the following example of primitive sorting. "At little more than a year old, my daughter, in visits to the London Zoo, called all animals of the feline family 'puss-puss'—tigers, lions, pumas, panthers, ocelots, lynxes, and every smaller member of the family Felidae. Nor was any dog, large or small, anything other than a 'bow-wow.' " This same curiosity is leading the child to discriminate between objects—the kind of discrimination necessary for learning to read. Out of a systematic, organized interpretation of the world, in time will come a rudimentary memory. Out of associating sights and sounds and movement together will come cognition. A playful imitation of surrounding sounds serves two purposes: It not only engages the child in pleasurable interactions with others and helps to master that which is bewildering, it also prepares him or her for the development of language. Thus, in summary, each piece of behavior and each step accomplished during the sensory-motor phase can be seen to have very special growth–enhancing properties which will show up in very special ways at later phases. "The kinds of circumstances that facilitate the acquisition of the specific skills of the early months," writes White (1975), "simultaneously seem to result in a more interested, cheerful and alert child."

RESEARCH FINDINGS

Research into sensory-motor play and the essentials of the sensory-motor phase of development (e.g., attachment) has attempted to determine its universality (e.g., across species and cultures) and its origins (instinctual versus learned). The overall goal of these studies, of course, is to determine those conditions in which human beings will be optimally creative and will function at their very healthiest. In explaining the study of attachment in animals, F.V. Smith (1969) writes:

There is evidence that the type of attachment achieved in early life, and indeed the failure to achieve an attachment, may have important consequences for the subsequent normality of the individual. The studies with bees, fish and birds are of intense biological interest, and despite the differences in evolutionary development represented by these different species, it is natural that many people concerned with delinquency and the impaired emotional intellectual development of children should look to studies with other species, particularly mammalian species, for possible cues for insight and research.

With respect to sensory-motor play specifically, much research effort, primarily with animals, has been directed to understanding its purpose and its importance. Animals have been used for behavioral research because, as Schaffer (1977) explains, "investigators have found it more profitable to examine the problem [of whether specific events have a formative influence] in animals where it is much easier to program experience and ensure that only single events are studied without the influence of others."

There have been studies of animals deprived of the opportunities for sensory-motor play, studies of animals offered sensory enrichment, and studies of the effects of overstimulation (Wachs et al., 1967). Melzack and Scott (1957) demonstrated the poor coping skills of dogs reared in restricting cages; Beach and Jaynes (1954) have shown that animals reared in sensorially restrictive environments display diffuse, random activity. And Lessac (1966) shows that isolation of puppies during the early developmental period not only hampers normal behavior but in fact destroys previously developed abilities. A University of Illinois study referred to in the "NOVA" television series (Dec. 9, 1980) describes clear damage to the structures of the cerebellum of monkeys permitted to see but prevented by a glass pane from touching one another. Studies at the University of Colorado Medical Center ("NOVA," Dec. 9, 1980) show that, even after the psychological effects clear up, the physiological ones (including damage to the immune system) persist in monkeys temporarily separated from their mothers. Also, as a consequence of early tactile deprivation, monkeys later fail to socialize (Harlow et al., 1962). Goldfarb (1955) characterized children isolated and institutionalized during their first years of life as less intelligent, more concrete, emotionally impoverished, and incapable of attachment. Studies by Ribble (1944), Provence and Lipton (1962), Foss (1961), and Spitz (1945) corroborate these findings. Studies of enrichment, on the other hand, paint quite a different picture. Rats reared in a visually enriched environment show, at autopsy, to have increased brain size and brain chemistry in the optical area, whereas rats provided auditory enrichment show increased brain size and brain chemistry in the auditory area (Krech, 1962). Premature human infants at the Maternity Hospital in Cambridge, England placed on lamb's wool for 24 out of every 48 hours gain half an ounce over and above their usual weight gain during those days spent on the lamb's wool (NOVA, Dec. 9, 1980). In addition, studies by Rheingold, Gewirtz, and Ross (1959) found that infant intelligence is affected by short-term multisensory stimulation. Other studies indicate a positive relationship between engagement of mothers (looking at, touching, holding, or talking to their infants) and their infant's intrigue with unfamiliar objects six weeks later (Rubenstein, 1967). In a study of 20 12-week-old infants, response decrement (decrease in fixation time to familiar stimulus) is greater in infants whose mothers did the most touching, looking, holding, and smiling (Lewis & Goldberg 1969). There are filmed sequences, furthermore, to show what happens to babies when their mothers suddenly behave as though they (the mothers) have "turned to stone" (Tronick et al., 1978). By the same token, studies by Yarrow (1961) indicate that attachment is absent or delayed in infants whose care is the responsibility of many different caretakers. Attachment has been found to be heightened when mothers respond to their infant's signals (Ainsworth, 1972; Schaffer & Emerson, 1964). In addition to the previously mentioned follow-up studies of understimulated infants, there are case studies of blind babies (Fraiberg, 1977) and autistic children—autism being seen by DesLauriers as a manifestation of sensory deprivation (DesLauriers & Carlson, 1969).

White (1967), studying institutionalized babies in their first month of life, demonstrated that extra handling correlated with visual attentiveness and found that 2-month-old babies with accelerated visual-motor skills came from visually stimulating environments. Caldwell et al, report (Caldwell, Herder, and Kaplan, 1966) that "the kinds of circumstances that facilitate the acquisition of the specific skills of the early months simultaneously seem to result in a more interested, cheerful, and alert child." White (1975) advises parents, "Therefore, good early child-rearing includes seeing that your baby (especially after the first 6–8 weeks) is regularly involved in activities that interest him."

One "NOVA" program titled "The Pinks and the Blues" quotes studies by Zella Luria and Jeffrey Rubin showing that fathers tend to touch and vocalize more to newborn sons than to newborn daughters, whereas mothers vocalize more to daughters. Parke and Sawin (1980), observing families in the hospital and at home, found mothers to be more involved with daughters whereas fathers look at, talk to, and play more with their sons than they do with their daughters. Jacklin and Maccoby (1974) found that fathers, to a greater extent than mothers, had body contact with their sons. They conclude that the father, far more than the mother, is responsible for sex-typed play in children. Block (1973) finds these differences to be a function of the parental expectation that sons be independent, control their feelings, and assume responsibility, whereas daughters should be trustworthy, truthful, physically close, obedient, intimate, and warm.

Tasch (1952) has conducted studies which show that fathers view their daughters as more delicate and sensitive than their sons. He also found that if their daughters resemble an ultrafeminine mother, fathers are especially likely to treat them as female. They may reject those daughters they view as large and unattractive. If they have no sons and the daughters are energetic and strong, fathers may treat them as boys (Biller, 1974).

Studying seven- and eight-month-olds, Lamb (1976) found mothers initiating and spending more time playing with daughters than with sons. Fathers, on the other hand, did not initiate more play with children of either sex. Both fathers and mothers held boys for longer periods than they did girls, "a large proportion of this physical contact being for soothing." As for differences in infant responsiveness by sex, Lamb found girls to be more positively responsive than boys to play with visitors and with their fathers.

The ultimate outcome, as suggested by Block (1976), is a clear difference between boys and girls in the following seven areas: (1) aggression, (2) activity, (3) curiosity and exploratory behaviors, (4) impulsivity, (5) anxiety, (6) social behavior, and (7) self-concept. Although little research has been done regarding the absence of fathers during the sensory-motor period specifically, Hetherington (1966) has concluded that father absence before the age of four has a retarding effect on masculine development. And Burton (1972), studying cross-sex identity in Barbados, writes, "cross cultural evidence indicates early father absence is often associated with sex-role conflict among males in other societies."

With regard to differences in parental play as a function of social class, Lamb reports, "There were fewer social-class differences [than sex-role differences] suggesting that, at least with very young infants, parents of different socio-economic status play with their children in essentially the same manner and to essentially the same extent" (Lamb, 1976. p. 320).

It appears from several studies that the nature of sensory-motor play differs in different social classes. Optimum development seems to occur when a small number of familiar adults interact with the child often and for reasonably long periods of time—more typically the situation in middle-class families than in the typical high-risk lower class family where adult figures tend to come and go more often and with less predictability. In addition, of course, the *quality* of stimulation is of paramount importance. In the high-risk family, for example, too much stimulation, and inappropriate *kinds* of stimulation, include indiscriminate television exposure, street noises, and haphazard lifestyle. The child reacts by shutting out these disturbing stimuli and thereby shutting out growth opportunities and skills for learning. Stimulation, as such, therefore, cannot always be evaluated as simply "too much" or "too little." For, whereas some research has shown that increase in infant IQ's is a function of amount of stimulation in the home (Caldwell et al., 1966), other studies report that "overstimulating" homes (regarding noise level and activity particularly) produce infants with the slowest cognitive development (Wachs et al., 1967). As early as the first year, differences can be observed and ascribed to social class. Kagan (1971) acknowledges as one possible predisposing factor the absence in lower class parents of "faith that they can influence the child's mental development" (p. 188). In one such study, infants were shown three kinds of portraits: (1) large photos, (2) drawings, and (3) "scrambled" versions of photos or drawings (e.g., a mouth substituted for an eye). Normal infants, as young as eight weeks of age, seemed to demonstrate a "discrepancy principle" (Kagan, 1971), that is, they took more time studying a picture which was "moderately discrepant" than they did a "totally familiar" picture (as for example, of their mother's face) or a "totally novel" one. "Middle class infants," says Kagan, "have a longer fixation time than lower class infants," because "the inner representation of the face is less well developed in the lower class infant compared with middle class . . . an out-growth of less face-to-face contact with the mother and less reciprocal smiling and vocalizing. There has simply been less exposure to a face than would be expected in middle class homes" (Kagan, 1971, pp. 77–80). This lack of face-to-face contact in early life is thought to lead to impaired attachment and ultimately to poorer learning capacity in later life. Faced with a too-familiar stimulus, on the other hand, 18-month-old middle-class children appear to become "bored" more quickly than do lower class children, and two years later it is these boredom-prone children who have higher IQ's. Three-month-old infants showing this same tendency to boredom-with-the-too-familiar had mothers who did the most touching, looking, holding, and smiling (Lewis & Goldberg, 1969).

Escalona (1968) reports that frequent mother–infant contacts together with a high degree of stimulation at home occurred in conjunction with accelerated development. If they are to develop early language skills, infants need to be spoken to long before they appear to understand. Studies indicate that of perhaps greater importance than the *frequency* with which a mother speaks with her baby is *what* she says, how she says it, and when she says it—including tempo and complexity (Streissguth & Bee, 1972). Deprived of appropriate verbal stimulation, the child can be expected to suffer delays in speech and language development.

As to whether children develop differently as a function of the culture into which they are born, there have been many studies investigating cross-cultural differences in mother–child interaction and variations in child personality and behavior. Among them, Arai, Ishikawa, and Toshima (1958), looking at over 750 infants, attribute their initially slow motor development to limited attention and their constricting clothing. By the same token, some black infants from unrestrictive groups were found to have advanced motor development relative to black children from groups which discouraged contact with adults and freedom of movement (Williams & Scott, 1953). One study compares recent Polish and Italian immigrant fathers interacting with their preschool sons (Marschak, 1979), and another (Marschak, 1975) compares the parent–child relationships in kibbutzim with those of city-reared children in Israel. These and many similar studies point to the impact a child's culture has, first upon his or her parents, and then, through the way the parent is expected to interact with the child, upon the developing child.

THERAPEUTIC USES

How can our understanding of the normal development of sensory-motor play help in our therapeutic efforts with children who are *not* developing normally? Stephen Bennett, in describing interactions between infants and their caretakers, states "Maternal ebullience and skill in handling can lead to extraordinarily complex combinations of arousal and calming. These in turn can create a striking involvement between mother and infant . . . by rocking, tickling, singing to, and stroking the infant's face, they can produce a state of aroused vigilance evidenced by an intensely animated expression" (Bennett, 1976, pp. 79–80).

Broussard (1976), studying 100 first-born children, found a positive correlation between mothers' views of their infants within the first month of life and psychological adjustment 10 and 11 years later. Fifty percent of the babies described by their mothers as being "better" than average were later assessed as emotionally healthy; 7.7% of those viewed by their mothers as not being "better" than average were later judged to be emotionally healthy.

Given that we would like to see both positive maternal judgment and "aroused vigilance evidenced by an intensely animated expression" in all children, and understanding that whenever it does not occur its absence may be a function of infant temperament, child–parent misfit, "maternal apathy and depression" (Bennett, 1976, p. 79), or environmental impediments, still, the fact remains that no matter what the cause, children suffering from a painful, rejecting, or inadequate environment in early life may well show later pathological development. It can be assumed that if provided joyful, adoring nursery experiences, a child will grow up viewing him or herself as worthy, lovable, competent, unique, and appealing and will grow up viewing the world as pleasurable, giving, exciting, reliable, and loving. In the absence of such a joyful life in the nursery, it is possible that he or she will grow up with a self-image of "bad," unlovable, ugly, and impotent and an image of the world as harsh, cold, painful, and grim. How this self-image and world-view might lead the child to behave is our next question. Given this negative image of self and this untrustworthy view of the world, will he or she behave with confidence, optimism, trust, *joie de vivre?* Or will the child behave with aggression, hostility, mistrust, defeat, self-injury, withdrawal, and failure? If the latter is how we see the child behave at home or in the classroom, then what might we do to make him or her "feel better"? Would we discuss the gloomy outlook, review his or her "miserable" infancy, and listen to descriptions of nightmares? Or would we scoop the child up in our arms and cheerfully rock him or her, plant kisses on his or her cheeks, and blow upon his or her eyelids? Would we encourage the child to come to "understand" his or her fears and fantasies? Or would we tell the child that he or she is "beautiful" and "strong" and "special"? Would we "interpret" the reasons for accidents or would we show the child that we know how to take good care of his or her cuts and bruises? Would we reward "appropriate" behavior or, rather, regardless of how "good" he or she is, cuddle and feed, play peek-a-boo, and count his or her freckles? In the hope that we could "produce a state of aroused vigilance evidenced by an intensely animated expression" might we not perhaps do well to "rock, tickle, sing to and stroke" the child just as Bennett describes? Might we not do well to let the child know, as Broussard's work suggests, that he or she is the apple of our eye? In an effort to help children with emotional and behavior problems, Theraplay, a new form of child therapy, has been developed to replicate the joyful and adoring features of the parent–infant interaction. Theraplay requires the therapist, like the mother in the nursery, to take the initiative and remain in charge (i.e., to communicate, "We're going to do what I have planned for you because, as the adult, I know what will ultimately make you feel better"). The Theraplay therapist, like the nursery mother, is adoring and physical and joyful, yet is empathic with a child's underlying needs. Although Theraplay therapists are nurturing, they are so on their (the therapists') terms alone and do not indulge the child beyond his or her appropriate needs.

In their *Structuring* they are neither arbitrary nor rigid. In their *Intruding* they neither impose their own needs nor cause pain. And in their *Challenging* they first make certain that the child is ready to "move ahead." The dimensions of Structuring, Challenging, Intruding, and Nurturing (SCIN) generally encompass both the actitivities of Theraplay and those in the nursery.

Needless to say, different Theraplay dimensions are appropriate for different kinds of children. What may be pleasurable or integrating for one kind of child may be painful and confusing for another. Thus, whereas a compulsive or autistic child, for example, may respond well to intrusive, surprising activities such as "drop the rider in the ditch" or peek-a-boo or tickling, an overactive or schizophrenic child may become further disorganized. By the same token, nurturing activities like gentle rocking or soft stroking may be fine for wildly aggressive children but may permit a dreamy, withdrawn child to fall into a deeper trance. Sessions will vary with age (developmental rather than chronological) of the child, of course, but not nearly to the extent that might be expected. Even children of school age respond remarkably well to having their backs powdered or hand lotion applied, to encouragement to spit watermelon seeds or hide behind a blanket. The adolescent, for face-saving reasons, often requires some modification of this endeavor. Although this is not always the case, haircombing or pedicures may have to replace rocking and lullabies for a teenager.

Theraplay is helpful for children with a large variety of presenting problems (e.g., school problems, pseudomaturity, fearfulness, hysteria, schizophrenia, somatization, and immature, withdrawn, or aggressive behavior). It is definitely not helpful for one group of children and could even be harmful for a second. Sociopathic children, although they enjoy their Theraplay sessions, seem to derive no benefit from the experience. It appears that these children are not available for therapeutic work until their parents are faced with the severity of the problem and are confronted with the possible family "needs" being served by the maintenance of the behavior. At this point, family therapy, not Theraplay, becomes the treatment of choice. The second group for which Theraplay is contraindicated consists of children who have experienced a recent trauma. A child who has just lost a parent, for example, or been sexually molested, could not benefit from, and may actually be damaged by tickles, swings in the air, or "horsey" rides. Traditional crisis intervention methods and nurturing, in the form of soothing, stroking, or an arm around the shoulder, may be appropriate, but structuring, intruding and challenging are not.

ASPECTS OF THE TREATMENT AND CASE MATERIAL

The Course of Treatment

As the treatment course unfolds, the child and the sessions can be expected to take a generally predictable direction marked by six more or less distinct phases. (This is not to say that every child's response is identical to every other child's. But it does suggest that therapists are well-advised to alert parents and teachers to the likelihood of temporary atypical behavior.)

1. *The Introductory Phase.*   The therapist greets the child with a cheerful, vigorously engaging first encounter. The introductory phase is the time to set out these rules, not in words but by implication:

> The sessions will be fun.
> The sessions will be clearly directed by the therapist.
> The sessions will be action-, not talk- or insight-oriented.
> The sessions will be clearly delineated as to scheduling, the use of space in the room, and so forth.

2. *The Exploration Phase.*   The therapist and child come to know each other and how they are alike and different with respect to hair color and curliness, size of toes, strength of muscle, etc.

3. *The Tentative Acceptance Phase.*   During this phase the child appears to be accepting the Theraplay experience but the appearance may, in fact, be deceptive. His or her only purpose in being so "willing" seems to be to "get the therapist off his or her back."

4. *The Negative Reaction Phase.*   This is the period when the child's true feelings of resistance and mistrust at last emerge. It is as though the child were saying, "I've let you come too close and that's too tempting. From here on in, I'm backing off." Yet this negative phase does not last forever, for with the therapist's continued insistence on engagement the child soon enters the next phase.

5. *The Phase of Growing and Trusting.*   In this phase the child and therapist interact with one another with all the warmth, pleasure, and spontaneity of any normal relationship. Having begun to grow and trust, the child is finally ready for Phase 6.

6. *The Termination Phase.*   This phase covers the preparation for terminating, the announcement to the child that after a few more sessions Theraplay will be over, and the final session itself.

Children react in different ways to various points in the treatment course. Underactive (withdrawn) children, for example, may go through a period of aggressive, angry acting out before settling into behavior which is neither withdrawn nor aggressive. Overactive (aggressive) children may become withdrawn (depressed) before ending at a normal midpoint. Immature children may become pseudomature initially, and pseudomature children may initially

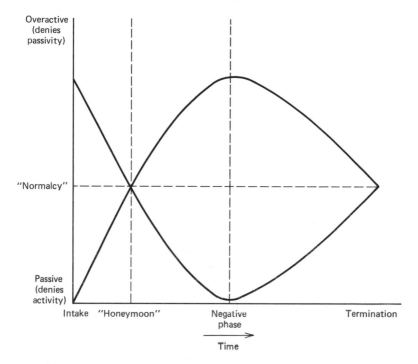

Figure 6.1.   The effect of theraplay on overactive versus passive children.

become immature. Figure 6.1 reflects the difference in the paths toward health (normalcy) typically taken by overactive/aggressive children in contrast to that taken by those who are underactive/withdrawn. Figure 6.2 reflects the path of the "immature," "developmentally delayed" child, compared with that of the pseudomature child.

Even within each Theraplay session predictable steps are followed. Each session has an opening (including a greeting and a series of "checkup" activities), followed by the session proper, and ending with a two-part closing. In part one the child and therapist separate. In part two the therapist helps the child make the transition into the "real world."

Therapist Variables

Theraplay therapists, in addition to being well-versed in Theraplay theory and method, must possess certain important personality features. They must be cheerful, energetic, imaginative, and optimistic. They must be neither hesitant to "engage" nor uneasy about "taking charge." Above all else, they must have available sources of narcissistic supply other than their clients. Thus, the overriding question, "Is this activity being done for the child's needs or for my own?" must always be answered, "For the child's," and *never*, "For my own." Because Theraplay is so physical, so regressive, so fast-moving and so intensely personal, it is essential to avoid possible acting out by the therapist.

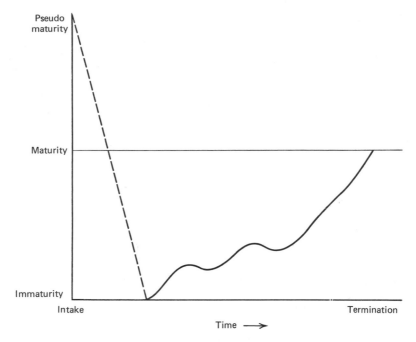

Figure 6.2.   The effect of theraplay on immature or pseudomature children.

Theraplay therapists, therefore, should have expert supervision available.

In our experience, neither age nor race need to be tailored to the child. The sex of the therapist, however, is an exception. In the selection of male or female therapist the child's past sexual history and present developmental level must be seriously considered. A little girl who has experienced sexual molestation or lives in a sexually overstimulating household, for example, should not be assigned a male therapist. The decision as to the sex of the therapist is crucial for adolescents regardless of their history.

Variations of Therapy

Family Theraplay is one variation involving the family. Although not realistically feasible in Day Care, residential, and some Head Start, or other populations, Family, rather than individual, Theraplay provides the ideal Theraplay therapy format. It should not, however, be used with children referred with severely disturbed or profoundly damaged diagnoses. Family Theraplay is short term and time limited. The treatment is divided into the following segments: (1) Intake; (2) The Marschak Interaction Method (MIM); (3) MIM#2 (for two-parent families); (4) Feedback session; (5) Theraplay, parent and child apart; (6) Theraplay, parent and child together; (7) Quarterly check-ups; (8) Annual check-ups.

1.   *The Intake*   (Jernberg, 1979, pp. 138–154). The first visit, scheduled for

parent(s) only, is for a traditional intake of information including history, presenting problem, family dynamics. Throughout this interview the intake worker formulates hypotheses and attempts to answer the question, "Before treatment strategies can be determined, what aspects of the parent–child relationship still need in-depth assessment?"

2. *The Marschak Interaction Method*   (MIM) (Marschak, 1979; Jernberg, 1980). This diagnostic method taps the following aspects of the adult–child relationship: (1) purposive behavior; (2) attachment; (3) alertness to the environment; and (4) stress reduction. The MIM Kits span these levels: infant; toddler; preschool age; schoolage; and adolescent/adult. Parent and child perform the tasks together sitting side by side at a table (infants lying, propped up, or sitting in parent's lap). In an effort to confirm, elaborate, or refute particular issues raised in the intake interview (Step 1), certain areas (e.g., attachment, direction-giving, stress reduction) more than others become the focus of the MIM. Specific tasks (e.g., squeaky animals, tower imitation, doll caretaking) are selected to tap those areas.

3. *MIM #2.*   In two-parent families the MIM is administered to the other parent.

4. *Feedback.*   Parents are scheduled for one session of discussion of MIM findings. If the MIM has been videotaped then it is during this appointment that tapes are shown and discussed.

5. *Theraplay, Parent and Child Apart.*   Parents sit with an interpreting therapist and observe their child in interaction with his or her Theraplay therapist. (The child, of course, knows he or she is being observed.) As they watch, parents are "taught" the principles of Theraplay, are provided guidance in relating to their child, are helped to see the relevance of their and his or her history and the dynamics of the family as they relate to their child's present-day behavior.

6. *Theraplay, Parent and Child Together.*   Sessions continue as before except that for the last 15 minutes of each of the remaining half-hour sessions, parents go into the Theraplay room to join their child in his or her Theraplay session, again with guidance from the therapist(s).

7. *Quarterly Check-Up Visits.*   Following termination: Once every three months during the next one-year period, parents and child return for a session similar to Step 6 sessions.

8. *Annual Check-Up Visits.*   Once annually, following the first year, the family returns for a repeat of Step 7.

Family Theraplay is particularly useful for children whose bonding/attachments were never accomplished as they should have been. Most notable, of course, are autistic children who "warded off" early parental bonding efforts, and foster or adopted children whose placements, beginning in infancy, made it impossible for them to form a first attachment. Both groups are ideal candidates for bonding/attachment Theraplay which, of necessity, includes their natural (in the case of autism), adoptive, or foster parents. In these sessions the parents are helped to do belatedly what parents of newborns do at birth, that is, view the child as a newcomer, check him out physically, become familiar with him in other ways, cuddle him, mirror him, bottle feed him, etc.

Group Theraplay is another variation of Theraplay. In Group Theraplay a team of two or more therapists works in close interaction with four to six children in a group. The children, under the "direction" of the therapists, serve as "therapists" to one another. They may play leapfrog, scoot under human "tunnels," walk over human "bridges," swing one child in a blanket, guess whose hidden feet are wiggling, or take turns allowing others in the group to mold them into "statues," imitating the kind of activity which is that particular child's favorite activity (e.g., swimming, sleeping, eating). Although the goal and the activities are essentially the same, Brody's (1978) Developmental Play takes place within a slightly different format. For one hour, once a week, within a school setting, a group of six to eight teacher-referred, emotionally disturbed children meets for six months with six to eight trainee-status adults and one supervisor for a specifically assigned, one-on-one, playful, mother–infant-like interaction. The session is divided equally into individual time and "Circle Time." The play is delighting, concrete, and physical. "The goal of the program," writes Brody, "is to assist the child to become a separate and differentiated person by first becoming attached and then becoming separate."

Research into the effectiveness of Theraplay is only just beginning. "Before and after" test comparisons and later follow-ups have been done on individual cases by Jernberg (1979), Koller (1976), and for the film *Here I Am* (Jernberg et al., 1969). Although no testing is involved, another film, *There He Goes* (Jernberg et al., 1975), does show before, after, and follow-up behavior. Further comparisons of children seen individually (in Speech Theraplay) have been carried out by Bligh (1977a; 1977b; 1979), Kupperman et al. (1980), Rubin (1978), and Searcy (1979). Brody et al. (1976) have studied teachers' reports and changes in IQ of children who have participated in weekly sessions of "Developmental Play." Without exception, the results of these studies show improved intellectual and emotional functioning.

Case Illustration

Brian, age six, has been referred for treatment because of his hyperactive, destructive behavior at school and his tantrums in the neighborhood. The following dialog occurred at the first session.

THERAPIST: (Meeting Brian in the waiting room): Hi Brian. I see you brought two rosy cheeks and two great feet along.

BRIAN (attempting to crawl out of view behind his mother's chair)

THERAPIST: And you know what? Those feet are just right for skipping down the hall with me. Ready now, we're going to hold hands this way and skip with our feet like this.

BRIAN (reluctantly drags along)

THERAPIST: Oh, I see you know just how to skip! (arriving at Theraplay room) In we go. (lilting voice) Close the door.

BRIAN (tries to hesitate)

THERAPIST: (gives him little chance to hesitate): Sit down. I got to check out those dimples (studies them). Ah! Just as I thought; there are two of them. I'll bet when you smile. . . .

BRIAN (smiles in spite of himself)

THERAPIST: Ah! Ah! Sure enough! When you smile those dimples make you look even more handsome. And how many toes did you bring along today? 3? 17? Let's check (takes shoes and socks off)

BRIAN (tries to get up to leave)

THERAPIST: We need to count your toes. Sit down. Oh, you're so wiggly!

BRIAN (wriggles to free himself)

THERAPIST: I never have seen a better wiggler! You got to show me how you do that. Here, let's see . . . like this?

BRIAN (grinning, he begins to demonstrate, then stops short): No.

THERAPIST: Oh when you say "no" like that I can see your tongue. It looks like a beautiful, rosy, pink tongue. Here let's look at it in the mirror (guides him to the mirror). Now let's see all the tricks you can make that tongue do.

The session continues with these kinds of activities alternating with nurturing and with further structuring for this kind of overactive child. After 20 minutes Brian is nestled in his therapist's lap, their eyes gazing at one another as the therapist sings a soothing lullaby such as this one, "Twinkle, twinkle little star, what a handsome boy you are. Two nice ears and rosy cheeks, bright blue eyes from which you peek. Twinkle, twinkle little star, what a handsome boy you are." * Twenty-five minutes into the session his therapist playfully puts Brian's socks and then his shoes back on, stands him up, tucks his shirt into his pants, smoothes his hair, gives him a big hug, and then walks with him out the door.

After a few sessions of struggle and resistance Brian settles into a markedly sad period with calm despair followed by uncontrolled weeping as his therapist cradles him in her arms and rocks him. Eventually Brian becomes relaxed and friendlier and eventually appears as a much happier, less defensive boy. Eighteen half-hour sessions later his school reports that he has calmed down markedly, and there are no further complaints from the neighbors. Termination seems appropriate. Brian and his therapist plan that in the next session they will assemble paper plates and spoons and party hats for the following session, the goodbye party. The goodbye party may include a parent, a teacher, or a classroom or neighborhood friend. Or it may consist of Brian and his therapist alone. The party is a time for reviewing tricks and skills, measur-

* Courtesy of Charles West.

ing height and comparing it to the marker put up five-months ago, comparing weight, foot size, muscle strength, and changes in number of teeth. The party ends with the singing of a familiar song and the making of an appointment three months later for the first of the quarterly check-up visits. Annual check-ups are scheduled after the first year.

SUMMARY AND CONCLUSIONS

As Theraplay as a child therapy technique becomes more familiar, we see that it is used more widely, more imaginatively, and with more reports of success. In addition to its benefits, Theraplay clearly demonstrates that inexpensive treatment carried out by students and paraprofessionals is a viable alternative to the more costly, long-term therapy conducted by traditional professionals. Because it is so "natural" and so reminiscent of wholesome parent–child interaction, Theraplay appears almost simple to the untrained eye. Yet we find these playful, physical, and intensely personal experiences all-too-often absent, despite their profound importance for the development of every child. It is our hope someday to find maternity staffs teaching these engagement techniques to new mothers and to find pediatricians and high school teachers reinforcing them in parent conferences and in education-for-parenthood classes. If every baby were to begin life with all the joy, touching, and positive personal attention necessary and appropriate for his particular biological make-up, if all parents were to relate to their children with sure knowledge about what kind and how much excitement and tranquility, freedom and control, tenderness and firmness, gentleness and roughness meets their individual child's unique needs, then we would undoubtedly find ourselves much closer to a society of healthy children, happy families, and accomplishing citizens.

REFERENCES

Ainsworth, M., Bell, S., & Stayton, D. (1972) Individual differences in strange-situation behavior of one-year-olds. In H. R. Schaffer (Ed.), *The origins of human social relations.* London: Academic Press.

Arai, S., Ishikawa, J., & Toshima, K. (1958) Psychomotor development in Japanese children. *Review Neuropsychiatry Infant,* **6,** 107.

Beach, F. A., & Jaynes, J. (1954) Effects of early experience upon the behavior of animals. *Psychological Bulletin,* **51,** 239–263.

Bennett, S. (1976) Infant-caretaker interaction. In Rexford et al. (Eds.), *Infant psychiatry.* Cambridge, Mass: Harvard University Press.

Biller, H. B. (1971) *Father–child and sex role.* Lexington, Mass.: Heath.

Biller, H. B. (1974) *Paternal deprivation.* Lexington, Mass.: Heath.

Bligh, S. B. (1977a) Theraplay: Opening the door for withdrawn and autistic children. Paper presented to Illinois Speech and Hearing Association, Chicago. April.

Bligh, S. B. (1977b) Theraplay: Facilitating communication in language-delayed children. In J. Andrews & M. Burns (Eds.), *Selected papers in language and phonology,* vol. 2: *Language remediation.* Evanston, Ill.: Institute for Continuing Education.

Bligh, S. B., et al. (1979) Activating communication skills in autistic children: Five case studies. Unpublished paper, available from author, Speech Clinic, Elmhurst College.

Block, J. (1973) Conceptions of sex role: Some cross-cultural and longitudinal perspectives. *American Psychologist,* June.

Block. J. (1976) Issues, problems and pitfalls in assessing sex differences: A critical review of the psychology of sex differences. *Merrill-Palmer Quarterly,* **22,** No. 4.

Brody, V., Fenderson, D., & Stephenson, S. (1976) *Sourcebook for finding your way to helping young children through developmental play.* State of Florida, Department of State. Distributed by Pupil Personnel Services Demonstration Project, All Children's Hospital, 801 6th St., St. Petersburg, Fla. 33701.

Brody, V. (1978) Developmental play: A relationship-focused program for children. *Child Welfare,* **57,** No. 9, 591–599.

Broussard, E. R. (1976) Neonatal prediction and outcome at 10/11 years. *Child Psychiatry and Human Development,* **3,** 85–93.

Burton, R. V. (1972) Cross-sex identity in Barbados. *Developmental Psychology,* **6,** 365–374.

Caldwell, B., Herder, J. & Kaplan, B. (1966) The inventory of home stimulation. Unpublished manuscript, Syracuse University.

DesLauriers, A., & Carlson, D. (1969) *Your child is asleep: Early infantile autism.* Homewood, Ill.: Dorsey.

Escalona, S. (1968) *The roots of individuality: Normal patterns of development in infancy.* Chicago: Aldine.

Fantz, R. L. (1967) Visual perception and experience in early infancy: A look at the hidden side of behavior development. In H. Stevenson, E. Hess, & H. Rheingold (Eds.), *Early behavior: Comparative and developmental approaches.* New York: Wiley. Pp 181–224.

Flavell, J. (1963) *The developmental psychology of Jean Piaget.* New York: Nostrand.

Foss, B., (Ed.) (1961) *Determinants of infant behavior.* New York: Wiley.

Fraiberg, S. (1977) *Insights from the blind.* New York: Basic Books.

Gewirtz, J., & Ross, H. (1959) Social conditioning of vocalizations in the infant. *Journal of Comparative Physiological Psychology,* **52,** 68–73.

Goldfarb, W. (1955) Emotional and intellectual consequences of psychologic deprivation in infancy: A re-evaluation. In P.H. Hock & J. Zubin (Eds.), *Psychopathology of childhood.* New York: Grune and Stratton. Pp. 105–119.

Harlow, H. F., & Harlow, M. K. (1962) The effect of rearing conditions on behavior. *Bulletin of Menninger Clinic,* **26,** 213–224.

Hetherington, E. M. (1966) Effects of paternal absence on sex-type behaviors in negro and white preadolescent males. *Journal of Personality and Social Psychology,* **4,** 87–91.

Jacklin, C., & Maccoby, E. (1974) *The psychology of sex differences.* Stanford: Stanford University Press.

Jernberg, A., Hurst, T., & Lyman, C. (1969) *Here I Am.* 16mm film, available from The Theraplay Institute, 333 N. Michigan Ave., Chicago, Ill. 60601.

Jernberg, A., Hurst, T., & Lyman, C. (1975) *There He Goes.* 16mm film, available from The Theraplay Institute.

Jernberg, A. (1979) *Theraplay.* San Francisco: Jossey-Bass.

Jernberg, A., Booth, P., Koller, T., & Allert, A. (1980) *Manual for the administration and the clinical interpretation of the Marshak Interaction Method (MIM).* Available from The Theraplay Institute.

Kagan, J. (1971) *Change and continuity in infancy.* New York: Wiley.

Koller, T. (1976) Changes in children's intelligence test scores following Theraplay. Paper presented at workshop for Comprehensive Mental Health Center, Laporte County, Indiana. April.

Krech, D., Rosenzweig, R., & Bennett, E. L. (1962) Relationship between brain chemistry and problem solving among rats raised in enriched and impoverished environments. *Journal of Comparative and Physiological Psychiatry,* **55,** 801–807.

Kupperman, P. (1977) Speech Theraplay: High impact articulation therapy. Paper presented at the American Speech and Hearing Association, Chicago, November.

Kupperman, P., Bligh, S., & Goodban, M. (1980) Activating articulation skills through Theraplay. *Journal of Speech and Hearing Disorders,* **45,** No. 4, 540–548.

Lamb, M. (1976) *Role of the father.* New York: Wiley.

LeBoyer, F. (1975) *Birth without violence.* New York: Knopf.

Lessac, M. S. (1966) The effects of early isolation and restriction on the later behavior of beagle puppies. Unpublished doctoral dissertation. University of Pennsylvania. Order No. 66–279.

Lewis, M., & Goldberg, S. (1969) Perceptual–cognitive development in infancy: A generalized expectancy model as a function of mother–infant interaction. *Merrill-Palmer Quarterly,* **15,** 81–100.

Marschak, M. (1975) *Two Climates of Israel.* Film, available from New York University Film Library.

Marschak, M. (1979) *Parent–child interaction and youth rebellion.* New York: Gardner Press.

Melzack, R., & Scott, T. H. (1957) The effects of early experience on the response to pain. *Journal of Comparative Physiological Psychology,* **50,** 155–161.

Millar, S. (1968) *The psychology of play.* Middlesex, England: Penguin Books.

NOVA. (1980). PBS Television series. "A Touch of Sensitivity." Original broadcast, December 9, 1980. Copyright by WGBH, Boston, Massachusetts.

Parke, R., & Sawin, D. (1980) The family in early infancy: Social interactional and attitudinal analyses in F. Pedersen (Ed.), *The father–infant relationship: Observational studies in a family context.* New York: Praeger. P. 54.

Piaget, J. (1952). *The origins of intelligence in children.* New York: International University Press.

Provence, S., & Lipton, R. (1962) *Infants in institutions.* New York: International University Press.

Rheingold, H. L., Gewirtz, J. L, & Ross, H. W. (1959) Social conditioning of vocalization in the infant. *Journal of Comparative and Physiological Psychology, 52,* 68–73.

Ribble, M. A. (1944) Infantile experience in relation to personality development. In J. McV. Hunt (Ed.), *Personality and the behavior disorders.* New York: Ronald Press. Pp. 621–651.

Rubenstein, J. (1967) Maternal attentiveness and subsequent exploratory behavior in the infant. *Child Development, 38,* 1089–1100.

Rubin, P. (1978) Theraplay in the public schools: Opening the door to communication. Paper presented at the Illinois Speech and Hearing Association Convention, Chicago. April.

Schaffer, H. R., & Emerson, P. E. (1964) The development of social attachments in infancy. *Monograph of the Society for Research in Child Development, 29,* No. 3.

Schaffer, R. (1977) *Mothering.* Cambridge, Mass.: Harvard University Press.

Searcy, K. (1979) The mercy approach to Theraplay. In M. Burns & J. Andrews (Eds.), *Selected papers: Current trends in the treatment of language disorders.* Evanston, Ill.: Institute for Continuing Education.

Smith, F. V. (1969) *Attachment of the young: Imprinting and other developments.* Edinburgh: Oliver and Boyd.

Spitz, R. A. (1945). Hospitalism: An inquiry into the genesis of psychiatric conditions in early childhood. *Psychoanalytic Study of the Child, 1,* 53–74.

Stephenson, W. (1980) Newton's fifth rule and Q methodology. *American Psychologist,* **34,** No. 10, 883–884.

Streissguth, A., & Bee, H. (1972) Mother–child interactions and cognitive development in children. In W. Hartup (Ed.), *The young child,* vol. 2. Washington, D.C.: National Association for the Education of Young Children.

Tasch, R. J. (1952) The role of the father in the family. *Journal of Experimental Education,* **20,** 319–361.

Tasch, R. J. (1955) Interpersonal perceptions of fathers and mothers. *Journal of Genetic Psychology,* **87,** 59–65.

Tronick, E., et al. (1978) The infant's response to entrapment between contradictory messages in face-to-face interaction. *Journal of American Academy of Child Psychiatry,* **17,** 1–13.

Wachs, T. D., Uzgiris, I. C., & Hunt, J. McV. (1967) Cognitive development in infants of different age levels and from different environmental backgrounds. Paper presented to the Society for Research in Child Development. New York, March.

White, B. L. (1967) An experimental approach to the effects of experience on early human behavior. In J. P. Hill (Ed.), *Minnesota symposia on child psychology,* vol. 1. Minneapolis: University of Minnesota Press. Pp. 201–225.

White, B. L. (1975) *The first three years of life.* Englewood Cliffs, N.J.: Prentice-Hall.

Williams, J. R., & Scott, R. B. (1953) Growth and development of negro infants. *Child Development,* **24,** 103–121.

Yarrow, L. (1961) Maternal deprivation: Toward an empirical and conceptual re-evaluation. *Psychological Bulletin,* **8,** 459–490.

CHAPTER 7

The Diagnostic and Therapeutic Use of Pretend Play

ELEANOR C. IRWIN

INTRODUCTION

Play is indeed a serious activity, as Huizinga (1955) has said, but it is also a perplexing one since there is rarely agreement on its nature, function, or purpose. Bax (1977, p. 4), discussing this phenomenon, offered some sage advice: "One should be very precisely concerned to say what activity one is describing and leave it to others to decide whether it fits into their category of . . . play." With that thought in mind, this chapter will focus on a special form of play—pretend play—outlining its roots in the course of the child's development and its diagnostic and therapeutic use in the treatment of children.

Although observations and deductions about the meaning of child play have been made by many, it was probably Freud (1920) who stimulated interest in play as a vehicle for understanding the emotional life of children. Describing the play of a "good little boy" of 18 months, he noted the child's "distinct habit" of throwing his toys in the corner and crying "Gone!" One day the child added another dimension to his play repertoire. He repetitively threw a reel out of his cot ("Gone!"), but then pulled it back, joyfully greeting its return ("There!"). Disappearance and return, Freud speculated, was a "game" invented to master the experience of mother's departure. In devising the game, the child became active instead of passive and demonstrated "the instinct for mastery." "It is clear," Freud wrote, "that in their play children repeat everything that has made a great impression on them in real life, and that in doing so they abreact the strength of the impression and . . . make themselves master of the situation" (p. 17).

Freud's observations on play and his treatment, through the father, of a phobic child named Hans (Freud, 1909) provided an impetus for work in child therapy by Hug-Hellmuth (1921), Klein (1932), A. Freud (1946), and others who saw the possibility of the symbolism in child play serving as a substitute for the free association of adults. Despite distinct theoretical differences among various schools of thought, there is general agreement that the child's spontaneous "acting out" of concerns in therapy is a kind of language to be examined and understood.

When a child spontaneously enacts a story in a therapeutic setting, she or he is simultaneously playwright, actor, director, and critic. Projecting something from his or her inner world into the play sphere, the child sets the scene, becomes the various characters in the story, and, through action, speech, gesture, and pantomime, acts it out. Current and past events become organized (more or less) into a script. The drama reflects an admixture of things experienced and imagined, an amalgam of past and present, impulse and defense, will and counterwill. And if, as sometimes happens, the play doesn't suit "the critics" (i.e., the conscience), then play disruption occurs and the show does *not* go on. Because of the richness of this kind of symbolic communication, pretend play is welcomed in treatment and is utilized according to the therapist's theoretical orientation.

Acting things out in treatment (as opposed to "acting out," a special form of remembering, in which action is a substitute for recollection) is viewed as an attempt at mastery. Proposed by Erikson (1950), this was echoed by Woltmann (1964):

> The spontaneous and self-generating activities of the child enable him to conceptualize, to structure, and to bring to tangible levels of activity his experiences and the feelings with which he invests them. Play . . . furnishes the child with opportunities to "act out" situations which are disrupting, conflicting, and confusing to him. (p. 21)

Ekstein (1966, p. 171), underscores the importance of play within the treatment context, commenting: "Whatever the patient produces, acts out, plays out, or talks out, is to be understood within the framework of the psychotherapy as the communication of the unconscious conflict that has driven the patient to seek the help of the psychotherapist."

Most children referred for treatment are able to pretend and communicate their view of the world through stories of imaginary events and fantasies. Play diagnostic interviews (to be described later) can elicit this kind of material, enabling one to learn many things about the child. Symbolic material and the behavior during the diagnostic interview can provide clues about:

1. *The child's view of him or herself,* through self-presentations, including the roles she or he assumes.

Six-year-old Hetty covered her eyes and refused to look at the puppets, saying they were dirty and bad. Finally curiosity overcame fear and she "peeked," picking a puppet which she said was a good one—a nice dragon with no teeth, who doesn't bite and is clean." She then played a story wherein the dragon sprinkled "magic dust" on all the animals making them "friendly, not bad."

In Hetty's choice of the dragon character she revealed something of herself as *she wished to be*—clean, good, not orally aggressive or bad. Her reaction formation, the beginning of character traits, were clear as were her conflicts over orality and aggressiveness.

2.   *The child's view of others,* as one gets a glimpse of his or her emotional world.

Nine-year-old Diana had a double loss. Her father had left the family and her mother was ill, dying of cancer. Outwardly this placid child was the picture of a devoted, loving daughter; only her hypochondria gave a hint of underlying difficulties. In her sand play, she enacted a story of a mother who had killed her husband ("drove him to his death") and was trying to "bury her daughter alive." The mother was portrayed as being controlling, critical, and powerful; the daughter could do nothing but "swallow it" and mutter under her breath, "You make me sick."

3.   *The child's worries, wishes, and conflicts, including his or her defenses.* Sometimes children's stories are peopled with characters, other times they are sparse. Sometimes they are fantasy oriented, sometimes embedded in the concrete of reality. All are different; all are considered to be derivative of the inner world of fantasy.

Five-year-old Theresa's mother had just been killed. She made a line of animals in the sandbox, led by the baby giraffe. The mommy giraffe had gotten killed by the "bad monsters" and the baby giraffe was leading "all her friends" into the forest to find the mommy and unearth her, to bring her back to life. Teresa's play poignantly spoke of her pain, her denial in fantasy, and the strong wish that she, like the baby giraffe, might find and resurrect her mother.

Ten-year-old Tammy's mother had also died, but her play was very different. Her sandbox construction gave clues about her own attempts to defend herself against a flood of feelings, especially sadness. She made a village with strong walls reinforced to contain the "spring flood waters" which threatened to sweep the village clean.

4.   *The child's usual way of viewing the world, habitual reasoning and thinking patterns, including intellectual capacities and problem-solving abilities.*   The core of the pretend play is the conflict which ensues. In the drama, the child shows us how she or he struggles with (or avoids) conflict. Play is sometimes repetition compulsion, as Freud (1920) has said, but it is also an active attempt at problem solving, a visible externalization of impulses causing both pleasure and pain in a search for resolution.

Nine-year-old Billy hardly talked. He filled the sandbox with as many aggressive animals as he could find and enacted a fierce dinosaur war which ended in total destruction. Asked for a moral, he said, "Never start a war with a dinosaur, or there'll be a fight to the end."

Given attention, materials, and empathic support, most children can engage in pretend play and thereby reveal inner conflicts. In working with children, however, it is always necessary to be familiar with what constitutes normal development so as to recognize those who do not have serious problems as well as those whose development is deviant. Some youngsters do not engage in symbolic play; a knowledge of the developmental stages of play can help determine where the child is functioning and perhaps why. Many children, too, in the course of treatment, experience regression and/or fixation in both the form and content of their play. Being aware of the hierarchical development of play can help the therapist be sensitive to shifts in functioning and deal with them not only theoretically, but practically as well, via appropriate media and materials. Before outlining procedures of diagnostic play interviews, therefore, a brief discussion of developmental levels of play will be undertaken; some attention will be given to the "poor player" who may be overlooked as a candidate for pretend play.

DEVELOPMENTAL ROOTS OF PRETEND PLAY

Acting things out, whether in the home, school, or playroom, is natural for most children; but for the young child, play does not begin immediately and automatically, as we know from Piaget's (1962) careful studies. Instead, play follows a sequence of development which is dependent not only on cognitive and language development, but also on environmental, cultural, and familial factors. The infant doesn't know how to play; it is only with experience (and crucial help from a mother or caretaker) that she or he builds a repertoire of behaviors that emerge into organized patterns of investigation. Sucking, biting, throwing, grasping, dropping—the infant learns about him or herself and the surrounding world in the first stage of play, the *sensorimotor period*, which extends from infancy through 18 to 24 months. Over time, the child "assimilates" new activities into already existing patterns of behavior and "accommodates" his or her perceptual and motor behavior to the outside world of reality (Piaget, 1962). There is a gradual progression from undifferentiated random actions to meaningful activity, until, between 18 and 24 months, the child begins to indicate a representational use of toys.

The second stage in the developmental sequence of play is made possible by cognitive as well as linguistic growth. During this period, commonly called the *symbolic play* stage and occurring between two and six years, the child shows a different kind of activity—imitating and pretending. The ability to symbolize, evident in pretending, is uniquely human. In children the ability to pretend coalesces into thematic play and signifies a major advance in development, the visible result of the synthesis of many prior events. The child is able to assume an "as if" stance, using one thing to "stand for" or represent (symbolize) another, to which it may be vaguely, accidentally, perhaps unconsciously, related.

In pretending, the child imitates people and objects, creates new situations, and puts real and imagined experiences together in new combinations. The result is "pretending" wherein the child takes roles, creates a loosely structured plot and a make-believe setting, and uses props to enact experiences that she or he has experienced or fantasized. The play activities of this period are spontaneous and self-generating, voluntary, ends in themselves, and therefore goalless or unrelated to "work" (Lowenfeld, 1967; Huizinga, 1955; Piaget, 1962; Ward, 1957).

Pretending seems easy, being simply an elaboration and enactment of the story—the who, what, where, when, and why. In actuality, however, it is not that simple; a certain level of cognitive, lingual, and emotional maturity is necessary before a child can symbolize experiences through pretend play. Smilansky (1968), in a study of disadvantaged children in Israel, outlined six elements she felt were important for pretend play (which she called socio-dramatic play or social dramatic play):

1. Imitative role play—taking roles and enacting characterizations via appropriate speech, gesture, and pantomime.
2. Make-believe with objects—using real or imaginary objects to "stand for" other things.
3. Make-believe in regard to actions and situations—pretending according to time and place and agreeing upon certain conventions in the play.
4. Persistence—sticking with the play for a designated time period.
5. Interaction—working with another in shared pretend play.
6. Verbal communication—using words to elaborate on the story with others. (Pp. 7–10).

Like Anna Freud (1965), Smilansky considered that play was related to work in that the skills rehearsed in play are necessary for the "school game" of the next stage. When children reach school age, however, pretending becomes less overt, more covert. Rather than act things out, older children do more fantasizing and carry on *monologues intérieurs* ("interiorized play"), as emphasized by Piaget (1962), Singer (1966), and Sarnoff (1976). In this stage of *games with rules,* from ages six to 12, children turn toward reality and their use of reasoning and symbols becomes more logical and objective. Play and fantasy become more realistic, and the child realizes that overt pretend play is not socially acceptable. Fantasy play, therefore, gradually becomes internalized. Singer (1966) suggests that fantasy-play material becomes stored as a series of images or impressions, to be recalled later on demand. Even though fantasy goes partly underground, as it were, one can still see in it the child's interests and preoccupations as they change over time. For example, we have Sam's play; *

When Sam was four and five, he and his friends enjoyed rough games of cops and robbers, with its "bang bang, you're dead" quality. At eight and nine, their favorite game was "Detective."

Making badges and writing reports of past (imaginary) successful exploits, Sam and Company made elaborate plans to watch for "suspicious moves" in the neighborhood. Careful maps and drawings were made of houses and streets, walkie-talkies and telescopes were constructed, secret passwords rehearsed. Much time was spent devising

* All of the vignettes reported here are of patients seen by the author, with the exception of Sam, who was related to the author. The names of the children have been changed for purposes of confidentiality.

"correct" procedures and regulations by which the detectives operated. Occasionally the area was secretly surveyed (usually at twilight) to see if there were any untoward changes. Anchored partly in reality and partly in fantasy, the game was rooted in a shared wish to know and learn the secrets of the grown-ups.

INDICATIONS FOR INTERVENTION: WHEN CHILDREN CAN'T PRETEND

Poor Players

To the observing adult, pretend play seems effortless, artless. And to most children, it is. But there are some youngsters, many of whom come for treatment, who cannot play so easily. Their play doesn't "hang together"; it may seem a disconnected, fragmented puzzle, hardly a way for them to learn about themselves and the world around them.

Laura, a pretty five-year-old, could not sustain or enjoy play. She alternated between listlessness and uncontrolled aggression which usually resulted in play disruption. Observed in the kindergarten room, she was standing at the doll house, listlessly flipping the doll's arm up and down, displaying no visible affect. After a minute or two, she suddenly picked up the doll and with great force, threw it to the floor. She laughed, throwing her head back, arching her back, emitting a high pitched sound. Picking up the baby again, she said, to no one in particular, "Gotta give her a shot. . . ." She looked around the room, perhaps for the doctor's kit, but then she seemed to lose interest.

Almost absentmindedly, she dropped the doll and wandered away. A wooden truck caught her eye and she pushed it with her foot, watching it roll away. She circled the room, wandered to the play corner, and began to examine the costume jewelry, two fingers from one hand in her mouth, the other hand rooting in the box. During this time, she made no contact with other children and seemed not to see Tammy's smile and attempt at eye contact, perhaps a signal to play together in the doll corner.

When "poor players" like Laura are referred for play therapy, they present a puzzle. What can one do with a child who cannot sustain play or become invested in materials? Therapists trained to recognize the psychodynamic meanings of play, cautioned about the danger of contamination or intrusion in play, are often bewildered by such children. Bypassing attempts at pretend play, some therapists use physical games to engage the child; some try checkers or other table games. They may hope that physical games with motoric outlets or structured games with definite rules might serve as a "holding environment" (Winnicott, 1971) while the boundaries of the relationship are explored.

Unfortunately, poor players like Laura are not a rarity. They come from diverse backgrounds, their inability to play often reflecting complex problems. Experience and research, however, suggest that assessing the child's symbolic play skills during a play diagnostic session can aid in making decisions about the course of treatment, help the therapist formulate a plan of action, and provide the most congenial modality and materials for the child's needs.

If, for example, it appears that the child either cannot play or sustain play at the symbolic level, it would be helpful to generate some educated guesses about why this might be so. Sometimes emotional factors interfere; sometimes there are developmental delays or cognitive, linguistic, or sensory impairments; sometimes the child lacks play opportunities or strong adult identifications which help promote pretend play. Each of these possibilities carries with it a line of investigation and a suggestion for remediation.

Pretend Play and Emotional Turmoil

Laura, whose play was briefly described earlier, is an example of a child in emotional distress; her constant anxiety interfered with the externalization of thoughts and ideas via play. Laura had a history of physical and sexual abuse. While in treatment, she played with baby dolls, which she abused—dropping, hitting, stabbing, and drowning them. Her play was fragmented, confused, and confusing. Once a relationship was established, she allowed the therapist to "mirror" her play and thus enter into it with her. This made it possible for the play eventually to be shared, elaborated, sustained, and finally talked about. Over time, she went beyond abreaction and externalized her own needs in play, caring for the babies as she wished to be cared for. Slowly her perception of herself changed, and this change was mirrored in her self-representations. She no longer portrayed herself as the victim deserving to be hurt, or as the aggressor inflicting pain. Instead, she became the nurturer, giving the babies "good things, not bad things" (Gould, 1972).

Pretend Play and Developmental Lags or Other Impairments

Some youngsters have handicaps or impairments and show marked delays in their ability to pretend. Although the delays may be due to cognitive handicaps, they may also be due to a lack of play opportunities and stimulation for pretend play. For youngsters who present a mixed diagnostic picture, it may be helpful to give them a structured play assessment to determine whether they are functioning at the sensorimotor level, representational or symbolic level, or beyond. The research and play interviews of Chappell and Johnson (1976), Lowe and Costello (1976), Rosenblatt (1977), Kalverboer (1977), and Largo and Howard (1979) are all attempts of this kind. In these interviews, children are given toys in a prescribed way and encouraged to play while the examiner observes the play patterns and responses to the materials. This enables the examiner to arrive at an evaluation of the child's present level of maturity as expressed in play. This information is then compared with estimates of other functions (e.g., nonverbal and linguistic) which can help determine what other line of investigation or remediation might be undertaken to promote overall development.

This chapter will focus on ways in which the therapist can assess the child's personality and functioning through pretend play. In an attempt to cover a range of approaches (and bypass some of the other issues which inevitably complicate the treatment picture), assessment procedures have been emphasized. However, it should be understood that these methods are equally applicable to treatment as well.

PRETEND PLAY IN ASSESSMENT WITH CLINICAL EXAMPLES

In treatment, adults use words as the currency of exchange; children use play. A variety of approaches found to be helpful for both diagnosis and treatment will be summarized in the following pages. In each, dramatic play materials are used to stimulate fantasy and play. Each offers an opportunity to observe the child's verbal and nonverbal responses; the thinking and decision-making process; the response to and use of materials; the process, form, and content of the play; and the child's interaction with the therapist (Irwin & Rubin, 1976). Used with other clinical material, these data can give a multidimensional picture of the child and his or her functioning and can help with the formulation of treatment recommendations.

Experience has indicated that a variety of diagnostic approaches are helpful, as each gives data about different aspects of personality functioning. In addition, variety allows for the child's idiosyncratic responses to materials and media and gives the adult a chance to learn about natural interests and preferences. Experience also suggests that many of these procedures are useful not only with children but also with adolescents and adults. Slight modifications for different ages are, of course, required (Irwin & Malloy, 1975; Lowenfeld, 1970).

Two important factors in the success of any diagnostic or therapeutic procedure are the therapist's comfort with the materials and his or her willingness to intervene in the play if necessary. Intervention may be needed to facilitate play for the inhibited child, limit regression for the overstimulated child, or help the youngster who has experienced play disruption to manage the resulting anxiety. If such intervention is necessary, the therapist who is comfortable with his or her activity and who is aware of the possible implications of the intervention is likely to be of maximum help to the child.

Murphy's Miniature Toy Interview

For young preschool or early latency children, Murphy's (1956) miniature toy interview provides rich opportunities for observing free play in a relatively unstructured way. A series of miniature toys are put on the floor in a semicircle. Figures of people and animals, both domestic and wild, transportation toys, sensorimotor materials, etc., are available for use. The child is asked to play with the toys in any way she or he likes. The therapist observes, perhaps taking notes to record the process, and intervenes according to therapeutic orientation in order to gather further information.

Murphy comments that the interview enables one to observe both the content or *what* the play is about and the form or *how* the child plays. While the content gives clues as to *what* the child is disturbed about, the form reveals *how* disturbed she or he is and "the character of his cognitive, motor, and emotional processes, their variation and appropriateness" (p. 15). The purpose of the miniature toy interview is "to see the child's needs, drives, problems, and ego structure in relation to his temperament and his perception of his life space" (p. 23).

Five-year-old Marcella entered the room slowly, eyes downcast, body hugging the wall. She eyed the materials carefully before "sliding" to the pile of toys nearest her. Avoiding eye contact and verbal.communication, body stiff and head bent down, she looked at the toys a long while before she began to play. Slowly she reached for the animals and farm toys, including fences, all items within her reach. Never moving from her chosen spot, she began to "fence in" the animals. When the therapist commented on her play, her body stiffened, but she did not verbally respond, her nonverbal behavior communicating her own "defense" against spontaneous play. At the end of the session, when told that she had five minutes left, she fingered her last enclosure. A dinosaur was posed at a water fountain, a bird perched nearby. Slowly and deliberately, with her finger, she knocked the bird from its perch and whispered something. Asked to repeat, she said in a low voice, "He (the dinosaur) say, 'git away; there ain't nuff for us 'boff.' " The therapist replied, "Poor bird . . . you want some too." Marcella looked up and made eye contact, nodding her head slowly.

Lowenfeld's Sand World Technique

One productive but rarely used activity which can stimulate fantasy play is that devised by the British analyst Margaret Lowenfeld. While helpful with most latency children, this technique seems to be most fruitful with children at the extremes of the behavior continuum—those who are inhibited and resist play (or lack the skills for play) and those who are hyperactive and find it difficult to focus and attend. The permission to turn away, as it were, from the therapist and to obtain tactile, sensory pleasure through the shaping and forming of the sand seems to exert a focusing influence through which inchoate fantasies can be externalized.

In this procedure, children are asked to create "a picture in the sand" and are given a collection of miniature toys, including people, animals, transportation toys, and unstructured materials such as plasticine, paper, wood, and stones (Lowenfeld, 1964). Through this "vocabulary of play materials" children are helped to talk, to cross the bridge that often separates adult and child. Lowenfeld found that children created "worlds" which were defined as "the planet on which we live, with its mountains and lakes, its forests and deserts, its animals . . . people . . . their way of seeing and feeling, of wishing and working, of loving and hating, different for every individual" (1970, p. xi).

Lowenfeld writes that this approach grew out of her attempts to find a way of helping children to talk "without the use of language," a method whereby they could "describe to themselves and to the adult the nature of their experience" (1964, p. 5). She describes this process as "non-verbal thinking," a kind of primitive thought activity "carried out more through concrete images than in words" (1964, p. 37). The process of such play seems to help children to express the inexpressible, to make visible that which is indefinable, elusive, a way of projecting the inner world of feeling.

Whereas Bühler (1951) and others (Lowenfeld, 1970) have devised a variety of scoring procedures, this author has used the technique in a different way. After the world has been created and the child sits back to contemplate what has emerged, she or he is invited to tell a story about what has happened. The youngster is encouraged to think of the world as a stage on which something has happened or will happen. It is as though the constructed image represents action frozen in time, a kind of personal, three-dimensional Thematic Apperception Test (TAT). The child is asked to project his or her fantasies on the self-created world, to bring it to life, and to act it out if she or he wishes. Preadolescents, wary of "kid stuff," are asked to think of their creations as a "movie set" and are encouraged to think of what might happen next, when "the cameras begin to roll." Some children like Joseph, described as follows, seem unable to confine their play to the play sphere. They demonstrate their developmental and psychodynamic difficulties in session behavior and in their interactions with the therapist. Most children, however, either proceed to enact a story spontaneously as they handle and choose materials, or accept the therapist's invitation to tell a story about what has been constructed. To illustrate the range of reactions, two case examples will be cited.

JOSEPH: IMPULSIVE ACTING OUT DURING THE SESSION

Eight-year-old Joseph was enuretic and encopretic. When the therapist met him and his mother in the lobby for the first time, Mrs. T. circled her son with her arms, pressed his face to her bosom, and spoke to the therapist. She wondered if her session and her son's would end simultaneously. She then gave Joseph a hardy kiss as he departed.

Once Joseph was shown the sandbox and given the materials, he began to coax the therapist to play with him. "Why won't you? My mom always does; it's more funner when someone plays with you. . . ." The therapist sympathized with his wish for a partner but said that when kids come to the Center, they play alone; that way the therapist can be of most help to them. Still unhappy, Joseph searched for a solution: "I know! We'll have a *war!* You be the bad guys and I'll be the good guys, okay?" Carefully he chose all the intact or "good" soldiers, planes and ships for himself and all the damaged or "bad" materials for the therapist. Set for battle, he once more tried to get the therapist to play with him, finally deciding that he would take turns, shooting the dart gun for both of them.

Alas, with the first shot, Joseph "accidentally" shot one of his own men. A few seconds later, a fecal smell filled the room; Joseph looked distraught, then hurriedly exited to the bathroom. When he returned, he said that he guessed he wouldn't play war, he hated wars, they were never any fun. He then asked the therapist to give him the white plane he had used, as it was the "bestest" he'd ever had. If only his mom would give him a plane like that, it would make him happy.

For Joseph, the process of the play stimulated fantasies which likely frightened him and precipitated his regression. His sudden bowel accident disrupted the play and seemed to mirror his anxiety about aggression.

Whereas Joseph's sand play and its symbolic theme of destruction brought his play to a halt, other children, like Timmy, find release in sand play. They seem to respond to the soothing pleasure of this medium, the gratification of the infantile wish "to mess." Temporary forms, created in the sand, can be wiped out or destroyed in a moment and quickly remade. For many children, this brings gratification on many levels—tactile as well as psychic—and involves fulfillment as well as denial of aggressive and/or loving impulses.

Timmy: Enjoying the Tactile and Psychic Pleasures of the Medium

Five-year-old Timmy was enuretic and encopretic. His kindergarten teacher reported sudden angry outbursts and destructive behavior in the classroom. Mrs. K. said that Timmy had achieved bowel and bladder control at age two-and-a-half but began soiling a year later. When Timmy was three, his parents were separated, and he had not seen his father since.

Timmy reluctantly accompanied the therapist to the playroom, but hung back. Once in the room, given directions and shown the materials for the sand world interview, he still stood near the door, eyes darting about, visually active, physically inactive. While the therapist sat down and took out her notepad, Timmy neither spoke nor moved. After a few moments, the therapist said, "Sometimes it's hard to get started." When Timmy was still unable to begin, she got up and pointed out the available play materials once more, naming each one. Timmy moved from his spot and accompanied her around the room, then moved to the sand table, running his fingers through the moist sand. His body and face gradually softened and he sighed, expressing pleasure in the feel of the sand. He glanced at the rubber people figures and spoke for the first time asking, "You got any men?" The therapist invited him to look on the shelf. He chose a female figure, threw her into the sand box, then threw sand over her. He took a boy figure and said, "He's throwing sand on her. She's in a sandstorm." He patted the sand neatly around the buried female figure. Then somewhat hurriedly, he buried the boy figure also. He then took a second boy figure and began to dig in the sand, unearthing the two buried ones.

Putting the figures aside, he began to build a "volcano" in the sand box. He explained that volcanoes sometimes erupt and spill "stuff" on the city. He put the figures to one side, as though they were watching the eruption. Then, as sand spilled out of the volcano, he said, "What do you expect? I'm supposed to erupt!" When the therapist wondered who said that, he replied, "The voice of the volcano—it's erupting." He rebuilt and exploded his volcano again, this time spilling sand everywhere, out of the sandbox and onto the floor. As he rebuilt the volcano for the third time, the therapist suggested that he follow "the rule" about keeping the sand in the sandbox. While he was working, she asked him if he knew of anyone or anything that exploded like the volcano. He grinned and responded, "Me!" Asked how he might be like a volcano, he talked about how he "bad mouths" his mother, shoots off his mouth, gets into trouble, and how he got into a "big fight" at school. . . .

Messing with sand reminded Timmy of his own "messes." He associated volcanoes with his own blowups. Although some, like Bühler (1951) omit the use
of sand in this procedure, it has been this author's experience that the sand not
only provides tactile pleasure but also provides clues to the thinking that
accompanies the feeling as the child makes "dreamlike" forms in the sand.
Like other play techniques, this procedure offers symbolic protection and disguise and reduces the need for words, but at the same time, as Lowenfeld
suggests, provides its own possibilities for communication.

Puppetry in Child Treatment

Puppetry, a form of drama in which human or fantasy characters imitate life,
is an art form which has its origins in the religious rituals of the early theater.
Because they provide safe. vicarious outlets for impulses and fantasies, puppets have been used in a variety of clinical settings. Woltmann (1940, 1951,
1971) was one of the first to write of his therapeutic experiences using mario-
nettes and puppets both as formal theater for inpatient audiences and as therapeutic techniques for youngsters in individual and group work.

The puppets' ease of manipulation, combined with the rich symbolism of
the spontaneously enacted story, has led many therapists to use hand puppets
in work with children, groups, and families (Howells & Townsend, 1973; Irwin
& Malloy, 1975; Irwin & Shapiro, 1975; Rambert, 1949). For many, communicating through puppets is physically safe and fun. Used as a tool in assessment, puppet play provides symbolic, nonverbal, and interactional data. As in
any diagnostic procedure, however, it is important to have a *range* of puppets
available, as well as an adequate *choice* of materials within each category.
Categories could include realistic as well as royalty family figures, wild and
domestic animals, and symbolic types, like the devil, ghost, witch. Choice, in
terms of specificity, degree of disguise and range, are crucial if the emergent
material is to have validity.

Some structure is necessary to help youngsters produce a spontaneous story.
A range of puppet types can be spilled out on the floor in a pile, and the child
invited to select whatever appeals to him or her. After the carefully noted
selection process is finished, the child is asked to go behind a small stage or
table and begin the puppet story by "introducing" the selected characters.
With an overcontrolled or undercontrolled child, it often helps to lengthen the
initial "warm-up" by engaging in friendly dialogue with the puppets (not the
child) to help the child focus, pretend, and feel more comfortable. It's important, of course, not to "lead the witness" and thereby contaminate the data but
to ask open-ended questions which can lead to ease of associations for the
story to follow (Irwin & Shapiro, 1975).

Once the characters are introduced, the therapist can announce the beginning of the show and become the audience–observer. According to style and
preference, some clinicians tape-record the session; others take notes on di-

alogue, character, and conflict; still others are able to capture and recall the essence of the spontaneously enacted story without recording aids.

When the child is finished, the format of the show can be extended by interviewing puppet(s), puppeteer, or both to elicit further associations and thus help unravel the story's many meanings. In a sense, the enacted story is similar to the manifest content of a dream; it is full of distortions and disguises meant to protect and obscure. To decipher the story without the child's associations is to engage in wild analysis; both therapist and child need to work to understand the latent meanings of the story through the child's associations and elaborations. Like all other clinical work, sensitivity, skill, and practice are required. To highlight some of the diagnostic data elicited in such an interview, case examples will be presented.

Selection Process.   It often seems that children respond quickly, perhaps on a less-than-conscious level, to the materials and the invitation to play. Materials evoke strong responses in the child. An array of cognitive, affective, and sensory impulses emerge as the child is presented with an aesthetically pleasing selection of toys. Obsessive-compulsive rituals, ambivalences, and other peculiarities of behavior are evoked, along with the child's usual sensory approach. Often materials stimulate fantasies which, for some youngsters, are not confined to the play space, but are acted out with the therapist. Nine-year-old Robert offers an example of a child who had a strong reaction to the materials; this stimulated a fantasy which at first was enacted in play, then "acted out" with the therapist.

Immaculately dressed, Robert was on time for his appointment, waiting in the lobby with his mother. He came with the therapist readily and expressed surprise and curiosity about the puppets. After being given directions for the puppet interview, he began to look through them, handling them tentatively, as though not quite sure what to do.

Robert at first chose the devil, looked at it closely, then remarked with some dismay, "Hey! The eye is missing—I don't want that!" With sudden energy, he threw the devil away and rooted through the pile until he found another devil, this one "intact." He chose a policeman next, looked at it carefully and commented, "looks like he lost his stick." He found a second policeman puppet, compared the two and pointed out that the first one had a slightly longer moustache and beard; he would use that one. Picking up the witch puppet, he exclaimed, "Boy, she has a pretty crooked nose!" Looking at the devil puppet, he noticed that part of the stitching was undone; he pushed his forefinger in the hole, making the separation greater, and commented, "You need to do a job here; looks like he needs some sewing." From this, his attention turned to himself, as he noticed that *he* had an imperfection—a small spot of mud on his sleeve. He rubbed it vigorously until it was almost gone; then he turned his attention back to the puppet.

Noticing the dragon and the alligator, he put one hand in each and began an interplay between them. The dragon bit the alligator and vice versa; as they acted aggressively against each other, a gleam came to his eye, he smiled broadly, then moved aggressively against the therapist, using the dragon's mouth to pull at the therapist's nose. He laughed uproariously, if anxiously, at this surprise attack.

Content. The content of the story gives clues about the child's preoccupations and his or her ways of dealing with them. The latter is important, for as Murphy (1956, p. 6) writes, "The content of a child's problems tells us little about his adjustment; the way he handles them is the crucial factor." The dialogue following this play gives the therapist a chance to learn more about the child's associations to the story. Listening to the material, one must be alert to spoken as well as unspoken concerns and be sensitive to:

1. The child's seemingly random comments, as she or he selects the materials and begins the task.
2. The conscious verbalization of what the story is about (i.e., the manifest content).
3. Associations to the content, reflected in the title, in comments about the characters, and in the postpuppet dialogue and discussion.
4. The implied (latent) content, evident in the form and process.

One listens for the main theme of the story, the degree of disguise, the representation of self and others. The child's representations or self symbols are often disguised, and one needs the child's help in deciphering them. These self representations may be the way things really are or may be projections of the child's fantasies; they may be what the child wishes or fears himself to be. Often different aspects of the self are represented through various characters within the puppet material. Eight-year-old Danny, for example, seemed to be *the pirate* who had impulses to steal what did not belong to him; *the alligator* with the big, biting mouth; and *the policeman* who vainly but ineffectively tried to restore law and order. These data are utilized the same way other projective data are used—as impressions to be verified, refuted, or altered in the course of ongoing work.

In addition to the characters in the story (whether people, animals, or inanimate objects), one can look at the *setting*. Maria set her scene on a "far-off planet" with people circling in a spacecraft, worried about oxygen supply; Kent always set his dramas in a kingdom, fighting fierce battles with the king; and Billy's scenes were usually in a primeval forest, where dinosaurs fought battles to the death. Similarly, the *time element* gives further clues about the child's thinking; Tommy said that his story took place when "a little boy went swimming without his mother . . ." and Louise set her story "in the dark time. . . ."

It is important to help the child think about the story and consider some of its many meanings; one reason is the need to assess the child's capacity for introspection and his or her degree of self-awareness. Toward this end, children might be asked who, of all the people (or things) in the story, they would *most* like to be, and, similarly, who they wouldn't want to be! It is of course *not* helpful to ask a child "Who are you in the story?," as one clinician did, wondering why this question did not bring much information. Similarly, one might ask, as Gardner (1971) suggests, what the lesson or moral of the story might be, or whether the story reminds him or her of anything previously seen or heard. Such questioning must be done sensitively, with respect for the child's defenses and vulnerabilities, because children often reveal their "life histories," so to speak, in this symbolic mode and may need the protection and disguise offered therein. The following story, with its painful theme of abandonment, illustrates Randy's own concerns about abandonment in his telling of the "dog" who was left behind, to die of thirst in the desert.

Following the initial introduction in the lobby, Randy began to talk nonstop about a baseball game he had seen; there were no pauses in his long monologue. Spying the dictaphone, he asked to make a tape of the baseball game "to hear my voice." Once he began, the story "dried up" and he became almost immobilized with indecision. He didn't know which game, which inning, which commercial to talk about; he asked the therapist to decide these things for him.

With relief he saw the puppets and began to talk nonstop again, saying that he used to be a puppeteer. He selected the policeman, devil, dog, and walrus for a show. Compared to his earlier agonizing attempts in decision making, the puppets were easily selected. He announced that his story was entitled, "How do I get Home and Find some Water?" It would take place in the desert and the story began with the dog gasping for breath.

DOG: Wa . . . wa . . . wa . . . water. I need water. Help me, help me. Oh, I need water. Water . . . wa . . . I need water.

(Just as the dog was about to pass out, the walrus appeared)

WALRUS: What's the matter wi' chu?

DOG: I need water . . . water.

WALRUS: Wonder what's the matter with him? Oh brother . . . I need water too. I'm thirsty, too.

(Just then the devil appeared)

DEVIL: Brother, brother . . . what's the matter with them? Can't they stand this beautiful heat? It feels *so good!* I feel like I'm at home . . . hey, dummies! Wake up!

DOG: I need water. Ah, water. Give me water.

DEVIL: Brother! Did they goof it!

NARRATOR: That's all folks. That's the end. Stay tuned for part two.

Randy then said that "part two" would take place somewhere else in the room, since they weren't in the desert any more. Asked what happened, he said, "I don't know, but this dog, well, they had a camp out there once and the dog got lost. This walrus got there cause he was just laying there. The circus was out there and they saw the walrus coming back, just laying there so the circus went away and they just forgot about him." After a moment's reflection, Randy said, "Well, I think . . . they said he was just lost in the desert. The dog was lost so they went away and left him there, lost, all by himself."

The therapist asked how the dog felt, being left in the desert, and Randy said, "Well, he felt lonely. He thought he was lost *for good,* so he tried to find his way back home. He got halfway home but he was very thirsty on the way back . . . very, very thirsty . . . and that's all there is to the story, so stay tuned for part two."

When the therapist said that sounded like a sad story, he said "Well, I'll tell you the rest. You want to hear? I'll whisper it to you . . . What really happened was, I think, that the dog died of thirst . . . that's what really happened." Randy then said he didn't think he wanted to play part two; it was really a little sad . . . maybe next time.

Form.   The form of the stories, however, is often overlooked. It is harder to "see" yet may be an even more important source of data, as Murphy has suggested. She writes, "Forms and structures then are important for what they tell us about how a child conceptualizes his observations, his needs, his feelings as well as for what they tell us about his way of controlling impulses, or freedom in space" (Murphy, 1956, p. 7). Stories can be described according to their formal or configurational characteristics. They may be static or fluid, disorganized or finished, original or stereotyped, balanced or unbalanced. All of these elements provide the observer with clues about the child's internal state and degree of organization.

Formal characteristics help one to see how the child copes with emerging impulses, multiple stimuli, and the feelings and fantasies aroused by such experiences. Chuck's disjointed, illogical, and fragmented story seemed to mirror his own shattered self:

Eight-year-old Chuck has a long history of physical abuse and had been removed from his family two years earlier. A blonde, freckled youngster with marked astigmatism and cluttered, ungrammatical speech, Chuck had a wide smile which seemed to accent the prominent scar on his forehead. His appearance was slovenly; his socks and T-shirt were on inside out, his pants were baggy and torn. He related warmly to the therapist until directed to the task, then, in a passive-aggressive way, he seemed not to hear or understand.

On the tape recorder, he insisted on reciting a series of stories, real and imagined. He pointed to his many scars and told of a boy who was tied to a bed and beaten; he told a second story of "Fire, cancer, broken windows, and blood, blood all over da kitchen floor." He took the puppets, as though to enact a story, but recited the following:

"One day, an old grouch man . . . meet old girl . . . old and dead. Da man's bite me . . . owww. Smack dat man . . . smack dat dog, he's biting me. Owww!!! (The story continued in this vein, with his burying "the old girl" and the old grouch man who was dying of cancer. In a chorus of "dat dead," he pointed, one by one, to each puppet as though unable to stop). Dat cat dead; dat old mudder dead; girl's dead; old witch dead; all dead. Three-hundred funeral . . . dead . . . dead . . . dead. What's dat? See dat man doing dat woman, dat man, killing da woman, dat woman's killed . . . dat old mudder, dat dead."

After reciting this litany of death, he listened to it on the tape recorder, repeating it half aloud, walking back and forth, immersed in his reality/fantasy world.

Chuck had many play disruptions and confusions. He often imagined that he, instead of the puppets, was being bitten or killed. His reality testing was poor, he flooded with affect, and had difficulty separating himself from his pretend story. He had marked difficulty with boundaries between self and others, his body and the world around him, fantasy and reality. Such formal characteristics point to severe difficulties. In Chuck's case these were of psychotic proportions.

Whereas Chuck seemed to flood, Shirley was tight and constricted. This listless eight-year-old youngster told a story, which, like Chuck's, was narrated, not acted out. Her associations were concrete, sparse, devoid of affect, reflecting pervasive ego constriction, a barren inner life.

This is a little girl. This is a little boy. They're dark. Let's go play ball. Have to go and eat dinner. Sit down. Next morning—let's have breakfast. They play a little, then come in for lunch. Dance. Have to eat dinner. Then go to sleep. That's the end.

Improvisational Dramas

In diagnosis as well as treatment, therapists attempt to elicit spontaneous role playing and pretending in an effort to assess:

1. The child's ability to take on and elaborate a role or roles, thus revealing not only his or her ability to differentiate between self and others, but also his or her role repertoire and role flexibility.
2. The content of the improvised play (i.e., the thoughts and fantasies consciously and unconsciously selected for portrayal, including the characters, setting, themes, ending, overall affective tone and so forth).
3. The form or structure of the improvised play (i.e., the degree of organization, balance, complexity, spontaneity, or creativity).
4. The process of the play, which gives clues about the child's ability to present and solve a problem, tolerance for frustration, and capacity to use language.
5. The interaction with the therapist.
6. The ability to talk about and reflect on the experience, including a discussion of feelings about the "product" which has just been created.

Because it is indicative of personality and "style," it is not surprising that role play and pretending have been the heart of many forms of treatment, such as psychodrama, gestalt therapy, and certain forms of behavior therapy, including most recently, assertiveness training. Role play procedures have been utilized both with adults (McReynolds & DeVoge, 1971) and with children (Elmer, 1977; London & Bowers, 1973).

In order to create a situation in which individuals can express their fantasies in free play, the author uses an improvisation interview. After being shown the contents of a costume and prop box, youngsters are asked to look through them, select some, and make up a story. The costume box contains masks, hats, makeup in the form of soap crayons (which can be washed off easily), and costume pieces. There is also a prop box which contains jewelry, guns, badges, hats, cigars, fake money, medical kit, etc. While selecting from such projective stimuli, children gradually begin to elaborate a story.

Generally, children play all the roles themselves. Occasionally, however, this is not feasible or possible, and the therapist may choose to play but makes it clear that it is the child's story and is to be played under his or her direction. The therapist must then play a "believable" role, being careful not to contaminate the material unduly, remaining aware of the possible results of the intervention. If the play becomes unclear, the child might be asked to "reverse roles," a common psychodramatic procedure, which gives information from the child's point of view.

Gary was a 10-year-old street "tough" who had been deserted by his parents, both of whom were alcoholics. He had not been in school for six months when picked up by police. He was hospitalized while undergoing an assessment and awaiting a decision about placement.

Gary was brought to the diagnostic interview by his two workers who expected to be able to observe a puppet session. Instead, Gary greeted the therapist with a stream of swear words, insisted he was not going to do anything. The therapist said the time was his and he could use it as he wanted. Opening the prop and costume box, she invited him to look around the room. Still cursing, he pulled things from the cupboard in a random fashion, but soon became interested in a sparkling crown. Placing it on his head, he began to stride around the room, giving orders as though he were a powerful king. The therapist showed him how to complete his costume with a robe and other accoutrements of the office, and he proudly surveyed himself in the mirror. He began to bark orders, as though surrounded by slaves. The therapist said it looked as though he had an idea for a story; how could it be played out? If they were to set the scene, where would it take place? He announced that he needed a throne and a makeshift one was created.

As the child worked, he became more involved and felt more grandiose and powerful. Eventually he developed the story of a king who banished a man and a woman from his kingdom. Evil people, they had left their children unattended to forage for themselves in the forest and to be attacked by wild dogs. Delighted with his story, he asked to return the following week and videotape the story, and this was done. A few weeks later, he proudly showed his tape to his peers on the unit. In doing so, he spontaneously began to relate horror stories of his own childhood, and how he, like the children of the "evil couple" in the story, had also been left by his parents.

Sometimes a prop or a costume piece stimulates a fantasy, as with Ruth and Lois, reported below.

In her first session, Ruth was titillated by an oversized cigar she found in the costume cupboard. She shoved it in her mouth and strutted around the room. Then she found some men's clothing and dressed herself as a man. To the therapist she said, "You be the mother and give me what I want, okay?" What she wanted, she said, was to be "special" and to be given special things—food, favors, and evidence of mother's preference for her over the other siblings. After the story was dramatized, asked about her choice of a main character, Ruth, somewhat embarrassed, said she guessed that she'd always thought it would be better to be a boy than a girl. Her mother, she thought, preferred her brother. If she had three wishes, the first would be to be a boy.

Lois found a crinoline skirt which reminded her of a princess's. Taking pieces of cloth, she decorated a throne and set up furniture as though in a palace. As she set the scene, she gradually elaborated on a plot. There was a beautiful princess who was about to be killed by a bad witch who wanted to poison her. Why might the witch want to do that, the therapist wondered. "Well, because she hates me . . . I don't know why," Lois responded. Going to the sink, she began to mix up some paints to make the "poison potion." She laughed aloud to think about how the witch would drink the potion and die. Following the enactment of this drama wherein she played both the princess and the dying witch, she began to make a witch puppet. As she worked, she began to speak of her experience with foster mothers, who, she asserted, were really, really mean.

Materials like props and costumes are semistructured and carry with them their own possibilities for projective play. Like puppets, they are intermediary objects, reflecting both reality and fantasy, aiding in the "willing suspension of disbelief." Intrigued by them, most children begin by selecting something that strikes a responsive inner chord, and continue by constructing a fantasy around it, much as these youngsters did.

As the "warm-up" process continues, the child completes the costume, puts on makeup and sets the scene. She or he elaborates on the theme and, with the therapist's interest and empathic support, begins to play it out. If necessary, the therapist helps with the structure, asking, for example, where the story might take place, who might be in it, and what is needed to set the scene. Such play is akin to free association, serving, as Erikson (1950) has said, as the royal road to the unconscious. Like puppet play, there is a dreamlike quality to improvisation and one can examine, with the child's help, both its manifest and latent meanings. Erikson (1950, p. 17) reminds us that "any item of human behavior shows a continuum of dynamic meaning, reaching from the surface through many layers of crust to the 'core.'" The improvisation can be examined, in the same way as the configuration of the dream, for its interpersonal aspects (i.e., the dreamer or "player," the "population" of the dream, including people, objects, aspects of nature); affective tone (whether happy, impatient, anxious, etc.); the spatial dimensions (details of the setting, including references to body parts); and the temporal aspects (whether in the present, past or future). The child's associations and idiosyncratic as well as more common symbols can lead the way to understanding the underlying meaning and the connections between the manifest and latent content.

THERAPY CONSIDERATIONS

The Goal of Pretend Play in Treatment

Through play, the therapist can help the child learn about him or herself and acquire the skills necessary to express feelings and ideas, thus gaining control over behavior. There are two parts to the pretending process in treatment: playing things out, and talking things out. Whereas *some* children need help in learning to pretend, *most* need help in learning to talk things out, making sense of the play, tying it to experience. As children gradually gain control of their inner world of feelings through the use of language, they can learn to manage anxiety by connecting events, extracting meanings from experiences, and making changes in their behavior and thus in their lives. Through the playing out of thoughts and feelings, children can learn to tolerate delay and endure frustration and, in time, make the transition from more primitive modes of thought to more verbal ones (i.e., from primary to secondary process functioning or from what Ekstein [1966] calls *play action* and *play acting* to talking out).

Alternatives to Therapy: The Play Tutor

In determining the type of intervention to be made, the therapist should consider whether there have been opportunities for the child to learn to pretend, and whether he or she has had the kind of relationship with an adult which facilitates such play, rather than view a youngster's poor play skills as solely a manifestation of cognitive or emotional problems. Given the basic developmental attributes, the ability to play grows out of a relationship with a caring adult who stimulates, facilitates, and models play for the child. The adult is the child's first play companion and tutor and serves to validate play, providing appropriate and stimulating materials, investing play with socially conventional meanings. In this "play space" the child gradually develops the confidence to be alone and to play alone (Winnicott, 1971).

If the child has not had this kind of identification with an adult, play skills will likely be poor and the psychological and cognitive functioning which are reflected in play will probably be impaired as well. In treatment, therefore, through the relationship (and its inherent possibilities for growth through identification), the therapist attempts to promote play, thus stimulating development.

Using Pretend in Play Therapy

Helping a child to adopt an "as if" attitude in treatment involves a variety of factors: a safe environment, appealing materials, and the therapist's own personality, including sensitivity, ability to play, and training.

Environment and Materials.   Most people learn best and function most effectively in an environment that is psychically as well as physically safe, where they feel accepted, understood, and have a feeling of belonging. In an atmosphere of respect where exploration is encouraged, children can learn to examine their behavior and feelings. A facilitative climate encourages openness; a closed or unsafe climate reinforces defensiveness and shame and is antithetical to growth, whether in the playroom, classroom, or home.

The environment should be "child proof," with durable materials and easy-to-care-for furniture. This minimizes worry for the child as well as the therapist. If there is a sandbox or large plastic container with sand, a puppet stage (even one made of cardboard) or a table which can serve as a stage, and a sink nearby, children can move at will from one activity to another during the hour.

Materials help, as they carry their own invitations to pretend. Puppets, miniature life toys, and props should be readily available. Range, variety, and durability are important considerations. A devil invites a different response from a king puppet, and a friendly animal invites a different response from a fierce one. A plain piece of material, on the other hand, serves a variety of purposes—a witch's cape, a king's robe, or a cover for a cave. Materials which are too real or specific can prematurely structure play. Thus a female doll figure is preferable to a "bride" doll, a male figure is preferable to a G.I. Joe doll.

Therapist Variables.   One of the keys to the pretending process is the personality of the therapist who, through attitude, action, and interest, demonstrates a willingness to invest in the child and the play. Self-awareness, a remembrance of the pleasures and pains of his or her own childhood, and an acceptance of the unconscious can enable the therapist to accept and be of help to others. At times, merging and blending with the child is necessary and inevitable, but awareness of this process and of one's own boundaries is crucial. Especially when engaging in pretending with a child, it is important to be able to step back, think about what has happened, and make decisions about how to proceed according to the therapeutic needs of the moment. Being alert for the child's signs of readiness to play, one can read nonverbal clues and transform a play gesture into a play dialogue, as in the following exchange:

Depressed and listless, Tess had no interest in the toys or puppets. She showed no energy, affect, or investment. She found some plastic disks and began repetitively to cover and uncover a smaller disk with a larger one. This action, in a way, seemed to reflect her own attempt to "keep in" her thoughts and impulses. Teasingly, the therapist said, "Better keep it in there!" Tess looked up, surprised, a wisp of a smile flashing across her sad face. The therapist congratulated her for keeping "that thing" inside. When asked what would happen if it got out, she said, "Eat you up," thus giving a clue about her struggle. Feigning shock, the therapist said it *needed* to be kept inside! She invited the child to help find something "stronger" to contain the thing, which later Tess called "the eating up monster." A plastic shoe box was found; Tess added a pillow and a blanket made of kleenex for it; it was put in a safe place. In subsequent sessions, this developed into a fantasy of the monster force-feeding all the dolls and puppets, giving them "delicious" sand to eat, punishing them if they did not.

Acceptance of the irrational, along with a willingness to explore its myriad forms, enables the therapist to enter the world of the disturbed child, becoming a partner in the exploratory process.

Four-year-old Jimmy was referred because he did not relate to peers or adults; he talked in a high-pitched voice, saying things that didn't seem to make sense. He began to play in treatment by engaging in sensorimotor play; after nine months, tentatively relating to the therapist, he began dramatic play. In a frenzy, Jimmy pretended to set fire to the room (including all the furniture *and* the therapist); ate up everything including the therapist; and then spat it all out again. The theme was destruction and restoration. Along with his wild play came external changes: a willingness to reinvest in a relationship with his parents, especially his mother, who had left him at an early age in the care of a rigid and rejecting babysitter.

With some youngsters who find it difficult to talk about the play, several techniques have been found to be helpful. At times, the therapist can enter the story as a "newspaper reporter" interviewing the child (in role) about what has just transpired. Sometimes a written record of the session, or a taped narration, can extend the reflection process. In this way, the therapist helps the child to learn to reflect and observe, think and talk, moving from an action orientation to a more verbal one.

Helpful as techniques are, however, there are no magic tricks in treatment for either therapist or child. Sensitive observation, empathy, and introspection are the therapist's best tools and form the basis for psychological understanding and an emotional engagement with the child. Katie, described as follows, neither talked nor played. She initially rejected the dramatic play materials but communicated something of her concerns through art. Only when she felt physically and psychically safe did she begin to engage in pretend play. Then she used neither props, costumes, sandbox nor puppets. Sometimes she played all the roles herself; sometimes she asked the therapist to play a role. At times she first explored themes in a more disguised way through art, then more directly in drama. Although there was no set pattern, she led the way and the adult followed. Both worked to understand the multiple determinants which lay behind her elective mutism.

Four-year-old Katie's parents were concerned because she spoke only to a few family members. She did not talk to teachers, peers, friends, or most relatives. Born with a cleft palate, Katie had been hospitalized at 14 months for repair of the cleft but seemed to recover well from the hospitalization and surgery.

In the initial session, Katie was hesitant to leave her mother. Once in the room she would not talk, play, or move. Finally the therapist picked her up and showed her the materials, pointing out the options for play. Reluctantly Katie nonverbally indicated her preference for paper and magic markers. The process of "playing around" seemed to reflect her preoccupations. Making seemingly random marks on the paper, Katie momentarily hesitated before intersecting or crossing any lines. When two lines joined or crossed, she would stop, then abruptly "push" one line into another, using much force. It was as though she were playing a nonverbal game on paper, one with the theme of "separate" and "together." Therapist and child communicated nonverbally at first, with eye contact, then smiles as the lines joined. When the pattern seemed clear, the therapist described the process. Katie giggled and increased the rhythm, tempo, and energy.

In the next two sessions, Katie continued the game, but chose larger paper and markers, moving from table to the floor. She went over the "boundaries" of the paper, at times making marks on the floor. There was increased freedom in body movement, greater emotional involvement, more body language and even a few softly whispered words. In sessions four through six, Katie developed a yes–no game. She would ask for an item, but when given it, she pretended that she had asked for something else. She made a face, stomped her foot, and acted as though something was being withheld from her. This became a ritualistic yes–no game. This otherwise quiet, self-contained child would then have a (pretend) temper tantrum, scream NO! or YES! in a loud voice, having a glorious time being "bad."

From the fourth to the ninth months of treatment the theme of defiance and opposition grew. It was explored in ritualistic activities at first, games which permitted little variation. As she gained in freedom and spontaneity, however, Katie began to use free flowing dramatic play with variations on a theme and a changing plot. She developed a story of a monster (Katie) who tied a little girl (the therapist) to a chair, locked her behind "500 steel doors for 100 years." Katie would then whisper instructions on how the therapist should attempt to escape, but alas, the monster would always thwart her efforts. This game was elaborated over time with countless variations. One of these variations seemed to replicate Katie's early hospital experience. In this play, Katie tied the therapist's hands to the "bed" and ordered her to try to suck her thumb. She then forcibly restrained her, tying her even tighter. She ordered the therapist to "spit out the red stuff" given her to drink. This led to memories of her hospitalization. Katie said she didn't think she had ever been in the hospital, but she remembered "reading" about it. In actuality, Katie had broken her restraints twice following surgery (trying to suck her thumb) and this had provoked an angry reaction from the hospital personnel. Later Katie asked her mother about the experience, learned she had been given red gelatin to drink and was fascinated by pictures taken before and after the event. It was as though the playing out of the theme of power and control exacerbated these traumatic memories, made them available for working through, and aided in their integration.

Freeing her body and feelings brought Katie the freedom to use words. In treatment Katie became loud, talkative, and spontaneous, revealing a delightful sense of humor. Outside of treatment there were changes as well. She was less fearful of separation, of anger, and began to talk to relatives, teachers, and peers. Although still a quiet and somewhat shy child, she gave up the symptom of not talking, often sang to herself and others, and surprised her family by even talking on the telephone. In her final treatment sessions, she began by drawing pictures of a jack-in-the-box, then a jack-out-of-the-box. She explained that he was lonely being closed up all the time and decided to come out and play. She played this story out and in the discussion that followed, showed she understood that she was talking about herself and her self-imposed isolation. She, like the toy, had changed because it was "more funner" to be out of the box.

Many youngsters are like Katie. When they learn they can use pretend play to express inner concerns, they have less need for props and costumes, for concrete help and psychic disguises. They learn how to enact and talk about things more directly, and in the process, they learn about themselves and how they can make changes in their lives.

SUMMARY

This chapter discussed the historical and developmental roots of dramatic, or pretend, play and elaborated on a number of techniques which can be useful in diagnosis and treatment. Dramatic play materials, such as miniature life toys, puppets, props, and costumes can be helpful in eliciting idiosyncratic as well as universal symbols and fantasies. The miniature toy and sand world interviews, along with the puppetry and improvisational techniques were discussed, and the resultant diagnostic and treatment data illustrated through case examples. Like dreams, such material, in the context of the patient–therapist relationship, can point the way to the unconscious, linking current reality with the recent as well as the distant past.

With appropriate materials and empathic support, many children can be helped to use pretend play. The therapist who is comfortable with such play can help the child to elaborate on his or her fantasies and thus symbolically chart the path of treatment and change. Skill and sensitivity, empathy and introspection are needed to elicit and understand the play, which the therapist encourages within his or her usual frame of reference and mode of treatment. In this way, children are helped to express, explore, work through their difficulties, putting together the pieces of the puzzle of who they are and who they would like to be.

REFERENCES

Bax, M. (1977) Man the player. In B. Tizard & D. Harvey (Eds.), *Biology of play.* London: Heineman.

Bühler, C. (1951) The world test: A projective technique. *Journal of Child Psychology,* **2,** 4.

Chappell, G. E., & Johnson, G. A. (1976) Evaluation of cognitive behavior in the young nonverbal child. *Language Speech and Hearing Services in the Schools,* **7,** 17–27.

Ekstein, R. (1966) *Children of time and space, of action and impulse.* New York: Appleton-Century-Crofts.

Elmer, E. (1977) *Fragile families, troubled children.* Pittsburgh, Pa.: University of Pittsburgh Press.

Erikson, E. H. (1950) *Childhood and society.* New York: Norton.

Erikson, E. H. (1954) The dream specimen in psychoanalysis. *Journal of the American Psychoanalytic Association,* **2,** 5–56.

Freud, A. (1946) *The psychoanalytic treatment of children.* London: Imago.

Freud, A. (1965) *Normality and pathology in childhood.* New York: International Universities Press.

Freud, S. (1909) Analysis of a phobia in a five-year-old boy. In J. Strachey (Ed. and Trans.), *The Standard Edition of the Complete Works of Sigmund Freud,* Vol. 10, London: Hogarth, 1932.

Freud, S. (1920) Beyond the pleasure principle. In J. Strachey (Ed. and Trans.), *The Standard Edition of the Complete Words of Sigmund Freud,* Vol. 18. London: Hogarth, 1955.

Gardner, R. (1971) *Therapeutic communication with children: The mutual story-telling technique.* New York: Science House.

Gould, R. (1972) *Child studies through fantasy.* New York: Quadrangle Books.

Howells, J. G., & Townsend, D. (1973) Puppetry as a medium for play diagnosis. *Child Psychiatry Quarterly*, **6**(1), 9–14.

Huizinga, N. (1955) *Homo ludens*. Boston: Beacon Press.

Hug-Hellmuth, H. (1921) On the technique of child analysis. *International Journal of Psychoanalysis*, **2**, 287–305.

Irwin, E., & Malloy, E. (1975) Family puppet interview. *Family Process*, **14**, 179–191.

Irwin, E., & Rubin, J. (1976) Art and drama interviews; Decoding symbolic messages. *Art Psychotherapy*, **3**, 169–175.

Irwin, E., & Shapiro, M. I. (1975) Puppetry as a diagnostic and therapeutic technique. In I. Jakab (Ed.), *Psychiatry and art*, Vol. 4. Basel: Karger.

Kalverboer, A. F. (1977) Measurement of play: Clinical applications. In B. Tizard & D. Harvey (Eds.), *Biology of play*. London: Heineman.

Klein, M. (1932) *The psychoanalysis of children*. London: Hogarth.

Largo, R. H., & Howard, J. A. (1979) Developmental progression in play behavior of children between nine and thirty months: I: Spontaneous play and imitation. *Developmental and Medical Child Neurology*, **21**, 299–310.

London, P., & Bowers, P. (1973) The dramatic acting test; A role playing test for children. University of Illinois Ph.D. Service Research Grant, NIMH.

Lowe, M., & Costello, A. J. (1976) *The symbolic play test*. National Foundation for Educational Research.

Lowenfeld, M. (1964) *The non-verbal thinking of children and its place in psychotherapy*. London: Waterlow and Sons. (pamphlet)

Lowenfeld, M. (1967) *Play in childhood*. New York: Wiley.

Lowenfeld, M. (1970) *The Lowenfeld technique*. R. Bowyer (Ed.). Oxford: Pergamon Press.

McReynolds, P., & DeVoge, S. (1971) The use of improvisational techniques in assessment. In P. McReynolds (Ed.), *Advances in psychological assessment*. Palo Alto: Science and Behavior Books. Pp. 222–277.

Murphy, L. (1956) *Methods for the study of personality in young children*, Vol. I. New York: Basic Books.

Piaget, J. (1962) *Play, dreams and imitation in childhood*. New York: Norton.

Rambert, M. (1949) *Children in conflict*. New York: International Universities Press.

Rosenblatt, D. (1977) Developmental trends in infant play. In B. Tizard & D. Harvey (Eds.), *Biology of play*. London: Heineman.

Sarnoff, C. (1976) *Latency*. New York: Jason Aronson.

Singer, J. (1966) *Daydreaming*. New York: Random House.

Smilansky, S. (1968) *The effects of sociodramatic play on disadvantaged pre-school children*. New York: Wiley.

Ward, W. (1957) *Playmaking with children*. New York: Appleton-Century-Crofts.

Winnicott, D. W. (1971) *Playing and reality*. London: Tavistock.

Woltmann, A. G. (1940) The use of puppets in understanding children. *Mental Hygiene*, **24**, 445–458.

Woltmann, A. G. (1964) Concepts of play therapy techniques. In M. R. Haworth (Ed.), *Child psychotherapy*. New York: Basic Books.

Woltmann, A. G. (1951) The use of puppetry as a projective method in therapy. In W. W. Anderson & G. L. Anderson (Eds.), *An introduction to projective techniques.* New York: Prentice-Hall.

Woltmann, A. G. (1971) Spontaneous puppetry by children as a projective method. In A. I. Rabin & M. R. Haworth (Eds.), *Projective techniques with children.* New York: Grune and Stratton.

CHAPTER 8

The Therapeutic
Use of Games

EILEEN T. NICKERSON and KAY S. O'LAUGHLIN

INTRODUCTION

One of the contemporary developments in the area of child and adolescent therapy has been the utilization of games and game theory (Boocock, 1967; Crocker & Wroblewski, 1975; Varenhorst, 1973). This development has largely taken place in school settings because of the demonstrated usefulness of such games in classroom instruction (Gorden, 1969; Hackett, 1972; Henderson & Gaines, 1971; Humphrey, 1969; O'Toole, 1967). The therapeutic antecedents of this development can be traced to the original use of play by Anna Freud (1964) as a means of assessing and working with children and the work of Slavson and his collaborators (Schiffer, 1969; Slavson, 1946; 1947; Slavson & Schiffer, 1975) who developed what Slavson termed Activity Group Therapy, a noninterpretative form of group therapy for latency-aged youth.

A systematic survey of the more recent developments in the use of games for therapeutic purposes is important at this point, as is an attempt to determine their usefulness and the techniques which require further work. Hence, a broad survey of this contemporary development will be made in the present chapter, including an assessment of the therapeutic usefulness of this approach in working with children.

Before pursuing the question of usefulness, let us first examine the rationale behind the employment of games in therapeutic endeavors. A number of authors have attested to the role and significance of play and playing games in a child's life (Bettelheim, 1972; Crocker & Wroblewski, 1975; Erikson, 1963; Nickerson, 1974; 1975; 1980).

The Role of Games and Play Activities in Development

Play and playing games serve a number of purposes in a young person's life. Play is, first of all, one of the chief and most significant ways in which a child

174

learns. It is the means by which a child tries out activities and social roles and comes to terms with objects and people in his or her environment. Opie and Opie (1976) discuss the nature of games: "A true game is one that frees the spirit. It allows for no cares but those fictitious ones engendered by the game itself." They make a distinction between games and play: "Play is unrestricted, games have rules. Play may merely be the enactment of a dream, but in each game there is a contest" (p. 394).

We should also remember that play and playing games is not only cathartic, self-revealing, and instructive in nature, but also fun. Hence, it is self-motivating. The very essence of play is *not* taking it "for real" (i.e., too seriously). And so, though play is part of the serious business of childhood by which a child learns to handle the environment, it need not be taken excessively seriously by the child. In playing games, children can feel relatively spontaneous and free to be themselves, to have fun "trying things out." Usually we do *not* have to work at getting a child to play. Play and games are, hence, an educational and therapeutic medium which is naturally attractive and important in the overall development of children.

RESEARCH

Most of the evidence related to the usefulness of games as a therapeutic modality comes in the form of testimonials (quotations from case histories and clinical experiences) with an occasional therapeutic warning. Crocker & Wroblewski (1975) put it this way: "Games: an aid, not a panacea!" (p. 459).

Jernberg (1973) and Schachter (1975), however, present promising theoretical models which merit extensive experimental examination of their effectiveness. Jernberg (1973) points to two bits of evidence to document the effectiveness of Theraplay, namely, the "extra long list of child referrals and parent volunteers for the Theraplay training" (p. 5); and the three-year retesting and refilming of the two children in the film *Here I Am* (Wurthington Hurst Associates, Chicago). Of course, this evidence in itself is not sufficient or satisfactory for the purposes of better understanding the nature of the Theraplay intervention or the effects of the interaction of the recipient, therapist, and environmental milieu. Nor is there any attempt made to compare this intervention with others and/or with "no-treatment" conditions.

Schachter's (1975) work represents a more serious attempt to measure the effectiveness of Kinetic Psychotherapy (KPT), a group game therapy format, with 48 public elementary school students referred for classroom behavior problems. The subjects were randomly assigned to KPT and no-treatment groups. The treatment group showed some promising but non–statistically significant improvements which included the lowering of measured achievement anxiety, the raising of measured self-esteem, and observable reduction of disruptive classroom behavior. However, Schachter's design does not include a comparison with other treatment modalities nor a follow-up.

There remains a need, therefore, to compare game therapy with other interventions in a systematic, well-planned set of comparative studies over time. Such research must also explore the complex interactions of nature, causation, life situation, and condition of the recipient, characteristics of the therapist, and so forth. "Clinical witnessing" is an important first step in the development of game therapy. We have made that significant beginning; we now need to press on in our exploration of the process and promise of game therapy.

THERAPEUTIC USES

The rationale for incorporating play and game media in work with children is based on the following concepts:

1. Play and games are a child's natural medium for self-expression, experimentation, and learning in general.
2. The child feels "at home" in a play setting and can readily relate to toys and "play out" concerns with them.
3. A game medium facilitates communication and expression.
4. A game medium also allows for a cathartic release of feelings, frustrations, anxieties (i.e., an opportunity to ventilate and put concerns into perspective).
5. Game playing experiences can be renewing, wholesome, and constructive.
6. An adult can more fully and naturally understand the world of children by observing them playing games. The adult can more readily relate to the child via play activities than by trying to induce entirely verbal discussions of their lives.

The Role of Games In Counseling and Therapy

Referring specifically to games, Capell (1968) points to four aspects which make them particularly useful as (psychoanalytically oriented) assessment and therapeutic tools:

1. The gross perceptual and judgmental distortions which regularly occur.
2. The overemphasis placed on outcome.
3. The profound affective involvement that commonly accompanies the play.
4. The obvious intensity of fantasy and motor activity by both participants and onlookers (p. 309).

Crocker and Wroblewski (1975) list six possible helping functions resulting from the use of games in counseling or therapy:

1.   The use of games serves as a projective assessment tool. The process observation and related discussion period, such as that employed by Crocker and Wroblewski (1975) in the commerical game of "Risk" or by Schachter (1974, 1975) in his Kinetic Psychotherapy approach tend to sensitize players and therapist to significant behavioral patterns not previously acknowledged or understood for their interpersonal significance.

2.   The use of a game may set up a situation in which anxiety about certain conditions can be confronted and worked through. For example, Capell (1968) hypothesizes that "Monopoly" enables players to deal with the anxiety caused by feelings of poverty and helplessness and thereby gain mastery over such feelings.

3.   The use of games may also offer a player an opportunity to learn to deal with the "rules of the game" as an analogy to living responsibly by acceptable norms of society and seeing one's rights and privileges in relation to those of others.

4.   The use of games may also allow a player's playfulness and fantasy activity to emerge (regardless of age) and in the process may free creative potential for living and problem solving.

5.   The use of games, like any playful fantasy situation, tends to create a safe and permissive climate in which a person can experiment with new behaviors. As previously noted, behavioral patterns may become more apparent through the processing of the way the players play the game. This increased self-awareness may subsequently enable the person to acknowledge and try out new behaviors in the game situation and perhaps generalize them to other life situations.

6.   Hence, therapeutic game playing tends to lead to newer and more adequate coping behaviors. Exploring the personal meaning of winning and losing in the safer therapeutic context of playing a game can help the person learn varied skills of coping with aggressiveness, defeating others, accepting defeat, receiving criticism, hostility, or rejection from others, etc.

The Use of Specific Games for Specific Aims

Nearly every known game, commerical or otherwise, and every known game-like experience has been used as a therapeutic medium, from blocks, checkers, chess, bombardment, hide-n-seek, and jacks, to trips, films, and picnics. We have already made reference, for example, to Capell's (1968) use of "Monopoly" as a vehicle for mastering feelings of helplessness and powerlessness. Bettelheim (1972) also discusses the psychological significance of such games as blindman's bluff, poker, and chess, and outlines the ways he uses these games. Crocker and Wroblewski (1975) employ gambling, bluffing, and bidding games to focus on the "dynamics of taking and avoiding risk" (p. 456); "Monopoly" to focus on power and helplessness; and "Risk" to focus more directly on aggressiveness and helplessness. They also employ "Mother, May I?" and "Simon Says" to "explore group members' experience with control and dependence" (p. 457).

Gardner (1969), as another example, details the use of checkers as a diagnostic and therapeutic tool in child psychotherapy. Although Gardner grants that many of the therapeutic benefits he ascribes to checkers could be equally derived from other games, he asserts that there are certain elements of checkers which make it unique, especially for the perceptually impaired child. Gardner feels that checkers is appropriate for providing a sense of mastery and competence for both the normal and disturbed child.

Some helping professionals have designed their own games or have modified existing ones. Teeter, Teeter, and Papai (1976) developed the game of "FRUSTRATION," replete with instructions for construction and use, to "show incoming high school students some of the ordinary hazards of the high school experience which partly determine whether the four years will be completed on schedule" (p. 265). They also propose that it be used to demonstrate the vagaries of occupational choice and as a tool to identify prospective runaways and dropouts. They advocate the development and use of this and similar games as an alternative, action-oriented style of group educational and career counseling.

Another example is the "Family Contracting Game" developed by Blechman (Crocker & Wroblewski, 1975). It is a board game in which players must negotiate with each other in order to move around the board. In this way players supposedly "develop a contract that is mutually pleasing and germane to their problem." What is to be emphasized is the interdependence of the family or group, and participants learn the process of behavior contracting through a low-threat method (p. 457).

The Use of Games to Reduce Therapeutic Resistance

Games have also been used specifically to deal with the inherent resistance to traditional talking, insight-oriented therapies. Thus, the limited ability and unwillingness of children (including latency-aged children) to discuss their problems and feelings directly has stimulated the use of play and games for the assessment and therapeutic handling of repressed and suppressed material. Child psychotherapists, therefore, have sought additional projective gamelike modalities for the communication of thematic material by latency-aged youth who tend to resist direct questioning.

Claman (1980), for example, developed the "Squiggle Drawing Game" as an adaptation of Winnicott's (1971) Squiggle Technique and Gardner (1971) and Kritzberg's (1975) storytelling approaches. Winnicott (1971) introduced the squiggle technique in an effort to communicate by metaphor with children. The goal of his "squiggle-drawing" was to establish communication with the child's inner thoughts and feelings through an interchange that "unhitches something at the place where the patient's development is hitched up."

Gardner (1971) and Kritzberg (1975) developed more systematic techniques of therapeutic communication by metaphor for children, namely, the Mutual Storytelling Technique which later evolved into the Talking, Feeling and Doing Game (a board game which utilizes written verbal cues to elicit thematic material). Kritzberg (1975) built on Gardner's earlier work and developed two games: TASKIT (an adaptation of the popular Scrabble) and TISKIT (a game almost identical to Gardner's Board of Objects Game).

As Gardner (1971) notes, these gamelike, therapeutic approaches serve the therapeutic purpose of bypassing the superego (and its resistances to revelation) by speaking directly to the ego. In these games then, the child and the therapist carry out a thematic exchange of unconscious and sub-conscious material in a structured, highly interactive fashion. The feelings and concerns of the child are reputed to be usefully revealed and therapeutically handled in this creative type of game interaction.

Games as Central to a Therapeutic System

To some therapists, games serve merely as one instrument or tool in the therapeutic approach (e.g., Gardner, 1969), yet to others, games are a central, basic feature of the therapeutic approach. One such system is that developed by Schachter (1974, 1975), called Kinetic Psychotherapy. It is defined as a form of group therapy consisting of a number of familiar games (e.g., tag, bombardment) modified to mobilize feelings and stimulate interaction among participants. It is characterized by three aspects:

1. Once a participant shows evidence of a feeling during one of the activities, the game is stopped and the participant is taught by the leader and the group to identify and verbalize the feeling.
2. During the activity period, participants exhibit characteristic coping behaviors. As these become evident, participants are taught by the leader and the group to try alternative modes of coping. They may then experientially try different ways of responding to feelings and situations.
3. After the activity period, participants engage in an interpersonal verbal exchange and are encouraged to associate their experiences with the preceding game to other situations.

In contrast to Schachter's system, Wurthington Hurst Associates (Jernberg, 1973, 1979) advocate a system called Theraplay for urban disadvantaged and emotionally disturbed preschoolers. Theraplay is characterized by the emphasis that therapeutic games played with children be fun, physical in nature, and insistent. Thus, the usual early infancy games like "Peek-a-Boo," "What's This?" and "I've Got Your _____!" are interspersed with cooing, rocking, tickling, piggyback rides, and continued playful, physical interaction. The verbal processing of Schachter's approach is absent. The pleasurable and continuous physical relatedness with the therapist is considered to be the necessary and sufficient condition for filling the hypothesized void in early infant inter-personal relatedness and sensory experiences which led to the emotional difficulties.

Physical Challenge and Initiative Games in Therapy

In the past decade physical challenge activities and initiative games have also gained in acceptance and popularity as forms of group therapy for all ages.* Winn (1981) describes the rationale of physical challenge approaches to ther-apy and gives examples of a "ropes course" and various initiative games as therapeutic activities. Winn states that the physical challenge format offers an effective alternative to therapeutic techniques that rely mainly on verbal and cognitive processes, and he notes that physically disabled clients may be espe-cially receptive to an intervention which fosters a sense of physical integrity. Winn cites the potential benefits for clients whose primary mode of communi-cation is action and, conversely, for those whose psychological problems in-volve limited kinetic functioning (such as depression).

Initiative games involve a clearly defined problem or task which group members can solve only by working together to find a solution. These games, which involve little or no equipment, foster the use of cognitive skills such as planning, evaluating, and decision making. They also encourage interpersonal growth as participants seek group solutions to problems. For example, Winn describes an initiative game called "Electric Fence":

> The group's task is to get all members over an imaginary electric fence. Anyone who touches the fence dies. A piece of rope, which is tied between two chairs or two trees and set at various heights depending on the group's physical abilities, serves as the electric fence. The only other equipment at the group's disposal is an eight foot beam. Since it is very difficult to remain unnoticed by the group because everyone must try to get over the fence, the experience becomes a useful opportunity to examine one's role in an interpersonal process. A variety of personal and group issues emerge as participants try to solve the problem. Conflicts about death, failure, power or physical appearance can be discussed as individuals review their experiences in a processing session.

Physical challenge activities are often incorporated into programs which em-phasize personal development, self-actualization, and learning teamwork. Rice (1979), for example, describes a physical challenge Outward Bound program for executives in which nine days of wilderness experiences were related to managerial situations. Although a great many different physical challenge ac-tivities and games have been used in therapy, they share a common theoretical premise: games provide a nonthreatening atmosphere in which behavior can be observed and discussed in relation to real-life situations.

---

* Physical challenge approaches emphasize the development of physical motor skills and the experimentation with new behaviors that eventually translate to increased competence elsewhere. The active use of one's body to confront a physical problem generalizes to the use of one's psyche to master psychosocial challenges within and beyond the therapeutic environment (Winn, 1981).

PROCEDURAL GUIDES AND CASE ILLUSTRATIONS

Procedural Guides

Nearly all of the advocates of games as a therapeutic medium discuss the "how" and "why," as well as the interpretive implications of using games (Bettelheim, 1972; Capell, 1968; Crocker & Wroblewski, 1975; Gardner, 1969; Jernberg, 1973; Schachter, 1974; Teeter et al., 1976). Interesting elucidation and clinical examples of the applicability of games in counseling and therapy are replete in the literature cited. The case discussion material from a variety of theoretical orientations furnishes helpful guidance to the novice interested in exploring this medium. Bettelheim (1972), Capell (1968, Gardner (1969), and Jernberg (1973) specifically address themselves, however, to issues of *individual* therapy, whereas Crocker and Wroblewski (1975), Schachter (1974, 1975), and Teeter et al. (1976) are particularly concerned with games as a *group* therapeutic technique.

Considerable attention has been paid in the literature to the nature and selection of the game(s) employed, with reference to the preference of certain games for "pulling forth" specific issues (e.g., "Monopoly" for issues of help lessness and powerlessness). Additional criteria for selection of the appropriate game include:

1. The game should be either familiar or easy to learn.
2. The game should be appropriate for the individual or group in terms of age level and development.
3. The game should have clear, inherent properties which are related to the therapeutic outcomes desired.

Perhaps the overriding differences in the use of games as a therapeutic medium lie in the theoretical orientation of the therapist and in the centrality of games to the therapeutic process itself. For example, Gardner's (1969) psychoanalytic orientation leads to consideration of phenomena such as "countertransferential hostility" (p. 145), whereas Jernberg (1973) conjectures about "emotionally positive infantile sensory experiences" (p. 2). In these cases the procedures seem to be clearly related to their theoretical stance; in others, they seem less so. Schachter (1974, 1975) and Crocker and Wroblewski (1975) both consider group processing of the game experience as crucial, despite the different theoretical frameworks from which they operate.

These latter differences—conceiving of games as central to the therapeutic process or seeing games as an aid or adjunct to therapy—constitute the poles of a continuum for ordering "game proponents." It is perhaps obvious that the former position has resulted in a more carefully conceptualized theoretical "game" framework, relating process (the game content) in a central fashion to objective and outcome (e.g., Jernberg, 1973; Schachter, 1974, 1975). This position merits serious attention by proponents of game and other action-oriented therapeutic media.

Jernberg (1973) starts from a more narrow theoretical framework (i.e., Austin DesLaurier's theory relating deficient infantile sensory experiences to later emotional disturbances) than does Schachter (1974, 1975), who borrows from Adlerian theory and attempts to integrate it with a social learning framework. There are commonalities in their positions, however, and these underlie the general position of the game therapy approaches, namely that:

1. Problem behaviors are an attempt to communicate.
2. Feelings and behaviors are explored through the medium of games.
3. Feelings and behaviors are explored in an atmosphere in which there are outlets for the expression of feelings, as well as means for their sublimation, and where new behaviors can be learned by observing, modeling and trying them out.

Case Illustrations

In the following description of a child's use of a game to do grief work, Thorne (1982) takes note of the child's choice of a game activity that seems designed to best aid him therapeutically while working through the stages of grief through his game play. The stages of grief have been described by Erich Lindemann (1965) as: delineating the relationship with the deceased; experiencing positive and negative feelings related to the loss; freeing oneself from bondage to the deceased; forming new social contacts and interacting in an environment in which the deceased is now missing.

Background Information.   Bill, age nine, was the only child of an unwed mother on welfare. His home environment was disrupted by his mother's transitory relationships with men. Physical violence, not to the child, but to the mother, figured in these relationships. The mother had never followed up on outreach efforts, and had not been able to benefit from mental health services. Threats of Protective Services involvement had helped in motivating her to better their living situation substantially. Through its outreach program, our clinic staff was able to place Bill in a boys' therapy group, and involve the mother peripherally. Bill attended the group for a year and a half, and made some progress in controlling impulsivity and in decreasing behavior that made him the group scapegoat.

In the middle of the second year of group work, group leaders noted regression in Bill's behavior. In response to minor frustrations or with no apparent provocation, he screamed, threw materials, and attacked other group members. Physical restraint and removal from the group were the only interventions that stopped him.

Finally, the mother told us that Bill's grandfather, an important person in his life, had died six months earlier, and that Bill had been the first person to discover the body. Furthermore, Bill was demonstrating similar behavior at home and was refusing to watch certain television shows or engage in sports activities that he had enjoyed with the grandfather.

At a joint session with his mother, when the subject was brought up, Bill began to grieve actively for the relationship. Because of the mother's previous denial, this was something he had not been able to do.

A contract was made with him for eight individual sessions in which to do the grief work. Because Bill did not keep appointments each week, the work extended over three months instead of two.

Treatment.   Bill chose to play the game "Clue" in all of his sessions. This is a board game in which the object is to choose among several suspects, weapons and rooms, to solve a murder. He used the game in the first three sessions to help him describe his grandfather's death. As he became threatened by the material, he refocused on the game, placing it between him and his feelings and thoughts. The game, with its descriptive vocabulary for violence and death, allowed him to talk symbolically about the act of dying. Bill chose one of the characters to represent him and his fear that actions resulted from feelings—that he was responsible for his grandfather's death.

Bill reminisced about the relationship with his grandfather. At first he substituted the characters and a room on the board. This led him to gradually talk about real, past, shared experiences and to feelings about the relationship and its loss.

Feelings of warmth and sadness were present throughout the second and third sessions and anger emerged as the dominant affect in sessions four and five. Bill repeatedly shifted back and forth from concentrating on actually moving pieces in the game, to having characters express feelings, to direct expression of and acknowledgment of feelings. He spoke of the functions that the grandfather had fulfilled in his life and his resentment at being left to manage on his own. While he talked about this, he allowed the therapist's piece to move far away from him on the board. The therapist could then point this out, and help him verbalize the painful experience of being alone.

By the sixth and seventh sessions Bill had begun to talk about other aspects of his life. There was a refocusing on the game. This time the focus was on the competency involved in playing it. Bill talked about games he had played with his grandfather and ways his grandfather had played. In the last session Bill decided to attempt to win the game by playing fairly. We discussed his competence at using the game to work through his grief, and at the game itself. These were ways in which he could identify with the grandfather, and yet be his own person. Follow-up showed that Bill's disruptive behavior in school and group had stopped. His mother reported that he was easier to manage at home, and that he was doing the things that he had previously avoided.

In summary, Bill's therapeutic use of this game demonstrated his movement from a delayed grief reaction, through the stages of grief, to homeostasis. He chose an activity that gave him permission to talk about death, and provided a structure in which to do so. His play, in this example, shows the shifting of defensives previously described. Through the use of displacement, he could, in various ways, give expression to material too threatening to deal with directly. Within the safety of the structure he could tie the material to his substituted character, and finally to himself. Bill mastered the game and his grief in the process.

SUMMARY AND CONCLUSIONS

The utilization of games is a contemporary development in therapeutic work with children and adolescents. Nearly every known game, commercial or otherwise, and every known game experience, has been used as a therapeutic medium. The educational antecedents of this development lie in the demonstrated usefulness of games in classroom instruction (Gorden, 1969) Hackett, 1972; Henderson & Gaines, 1971; Humphrey, 1969). The therapeutic background lay in the earlier use by Anna Freud (1964) of play as a means of assessing and working with children; as well as the work of Slavson and his collaborators (Schiffer, 1969, Slavson, 1946, 1947; Slavson & Schiffer, 1975), who developed "Activity Group Therapy," a noninterpretive form of group therapy for latency-aged youth.

Games may be used either as an adjunct to the overall therapeutic process or as central to the therapeutic process itself. In the former instances, games are often used to "free up" blocked therapeutic transactions and/or reduce resistance to the more direct verbal processing of problems and feelings (e.g., Gardner, 1969, 1971; Winnicott, 1971). In the latter case, games are used as the central, major therapeutic medium (e.g., Jernberg, 1971; Schachter, 1974, 1975) in which feelings and problems are "played out" rather than "talked out."

Games furnish a particularly significant therapeutic medium since they allow for the communication of feelings, concerns, and issues at the same time they provide an outlet for these feelings; they provide an opportunity to experiment with and try out new behaviors, new solutions to old or continuing needs and preoccupations. Games, while being an excellent, highly interactive and participatory projective vehicle, are not for real. One's fantasy life and creativity can be less hesitantly involved. Yet, there are, as in life, the constraints of the reality of the games' rules—rules which in turn may be tested out for their consequences, limits, and degree of flexibility. The game may represent life, and hence, an opportunity to tangle with and master its complexities and vagaries in a telescoped and therapeutically focused manner.

It is obvious that games are fun. They are cathartic, emotion and energy engaging and releasing. Yet, the question raised in an earlier paper (Nickerson, 1980), namely "Games are fun, but will they work?" remains a significant one. For although the groundwork has been laid for development of game therapy, mainly in the form of clinical detailing and witnessing of the effectiveness of this approach, systematic, comparative research is now needed to explore the promise of this action-oriented approach to therapy. We believe, but we need to believe with sound empirical reason.

REFERENCES

Avedon, E. M., Sutton-Smith, B. (1971) *Study of games.* New York: Wiley.

Bettelheim, B. (1972) Play and education. *School Review,* **81,** 1–13.

Blackham, G. J., & Silberman, A. (1975) *Modification of child and adolescent behavior,* 2nd ed. Belmont, Calif. Wadsworth.

Boocock, S. (1967) The life career game. *Personnel and Guidance Journal,* **46,** 328–334.

Boocock, S., & Schild, E. O. (Eds.) (1968) *Simulation games in learning.* Beverly Hills, Calif.: Sage.

Brandes, N. S., & Gardner, M. L. (1971) *Group therapy for the adolescent.* New York: Jason Aronson.

Capell, M. (1968) Passive mastery of helplessness in games. *American Imago,* **25,** 309–330.

Casella, D. A., & Scharder, D. R., (1975) "Tripping" with borderline dropouts. *The School Counselor,* **23**(1), 48–50.

Claman, L. (1980) The Squiggle-Drawing Game in child psychotherapy. *American Journal of Psychotherapy,* **34**(3), 414–425

Crocker, J. W., & Wroblewski, M. (1975) Using recreational games in counseling. *Personnel and Guidance Journal,* **53**(6), 453–458.

Dinkmeyer, D. *Developing Understanding of Self and Others: Play Kit and Manual.* Circle Pines, Minn.: Publishers Building.

Erikson, E. H. (1963) Toys and reasons. In *Childhood and society.* New York: Norton.

Erikson, E. H. (1964) The meaning of play. In M. R. Haworth (Ed.), *Child psychotherapy: Practice and theory.* New York: Basic Books.

Freud, A. (1964) *The psychoanalytic treatment of children.* New York: Schoken.

Gardner, R. A. (1969) The game of checkers as a diagnostic and therapeutic tool in child psychotherapy. *Acta Paedopsychiatry,* **38,** 140–153.

Gardner, R. A. (1971) *Therapeutic communication with children: The mutual storytelling technique.* New York: Jason Aronson.

Gorden, A. K. (1970) *Games for growth and educational games in the classroom.* Chicago: Science Research Associate.

Gorden, W. I. (1969) Academic games in the speech curriculum. *Central Statistics Speech Journal,* **20,** 269–279.

Gorden, W. I. (1970) Rhetoric communication concepts illustrated by several academic games. Metaphor and mystique at play. *Today's Speech,* **19,** 27–32.

Gumaer, J., Bleck, R., & Loesch, L. C. (1975) Affective education through role playing: The feelings class. *Personnel and Guidance Journal,* **53**(8), 604–608.

Hackett, V. (1972) Games in the English class. *English Journal,* **61,** 100–103.

Henderson, B. G., & Gaines, W. G. (1971) Assessment of selected simulations and games for the social studies. *Social Education,* **35,** 508–513.

Hendricks, G., & Wills, R. (1975) *The centering book: Awareness activities for children, parents and teachers.* Englewood Cliffs, N.J.: Prentice-Hall.

Humphrey, J. H. (1969) Active games as a learning medium. *Academic Therapy,* **5,** 15–24.

Jernberg, A. M. (1973) Coming alive through theraplay. Paper read at the American Personnel and Guidance Association, San Diego, February 9-15.

Jernberg, A. M. (1979) *Theraplay*. San Francisco: Jossey-Bass.

Klaiman, A., & Hochman, S. R. (1960) Chess: Play to learn. *Instructor*, **78**(5), 49.

Kritzberg, N. I. (1975) *The structured therapeutic method of game analytic psychotherapy*. Hicksville, N.Y.: Exposition Press.

Lindemann, E. (1965) Symptomatology and management of acute grief. In H. Parad (Ed.), *Crisis intervention: Selected readings*. New York: Family Service Association of America.

Lovelace, J. C. (1975) *The use of a social simulation game in an attempt to modify white suburban adolescents attitudes towards blacks*. Unpublished doctoral dissertation, Boston University.

Nickerson, E. T. (1973a) Recent trends and innovations in play therapy. *International Journal of Child Psychotherapy*, **2**(1), 53-70.

Nickerson, E. T. (1973b) The application of play therapy to a school setting. *Psychology in the Schools*.

Nickerson, E. T. (1974a) *Helping children: Readings in recent approaches to the practice of therapy with children*. Lexington, Mass.: College Xerox Publishing.

Nickerson, E. T. (1974b) The use of art as a play therapeutic medium in the classroom. *Journal of Art Psychotherapy*, **1**, 293-297.

Nickerson, E. T. (1975) Bibliotherapy: A therapeutic medium for helping children. *Psychotherapy: Theory, Research and Practice*, **12**(3), 258-261.

Nickerson, E. T. (1980) It's fun, but will it work? The use of games as a therapeutic medium for children and adolescents. *Journal of Clincial Child Psychology*, pp. 78-81.

Nickerson, E. T. & O'Laughlin, K. S. (1978). *Action therapies: Readings in the practice of working therapeutically with children and adolescents*. Lexington, Mass.: College Xerox Publishing.

O'Brien, C. R., & Johnson, J. L. (1976) Cinema therapy. *The School Counselor*, **24**(1), 39-47.

Olman, R. (1977) *Investigation of trust and suspicion free game playing behavior of symbiotic and socio-pathio paranoid childhood schizophrenia*. Unpublished doctoral dissertation, Boston University.

Opie, I., & Opie, P. (1976) Street games: Counting out and chasing. In J.S. Bruner et al. (Eds.), *Play—Its role in development and evolution*. New York: Basic Books.

O'Toole, C. A. (1967) Monopoly in the classroom. *Clearing House*, **42**, 145.

Rice, B. (1979) Going to the mountain. *Psychology Today*, pp. 65-80. (December)

Schachter, R. S. (1974) Kinetic psychotherapy in the treatment of children. *American Journal of Psychotherapy*, **28**(3), 430-437.

Schachter, R. S. (1975). *A study of the relative effectiveness of Kinetic Psychotherapy with a group of school-aged boys*. Unpublished doctoral dissertation, Boston University.

Schiffer, M. (1969) *The therapeutic play group*. New York: Grune & Stratton.

Slavson, S. R. (1946) Group therapy with children. In W. Lewis & B. Pacella (Eds.), *Modern trends in child psychiatry*. New York: International Universities Press.

Slavson, S. R. (1947) *The Practice of Group Therapy.* New York: International Universities Press.

Slavson, S. R., & Schiffer, M. (1975) *Group psychotherapies for children: A textbook.* New York: International Universities Press.

Smith, J. P. (1968) Academic games in the classroom. *School and Society,* **96,** 184–185.

Stoll, C. (1970); Games students play. *Media and Methods,* **7,** 37–41.

Teeter, R., Teeter, T., & Papai, J. (1976) Frustration—A game. *The School Counselor,* pp. 264–270. (March)

Thorne, E. M. (1982) A child's use of a game to do grief work. In E. T. Nickerson & K. S. O'Laughlin, *Helping through action.* Amherst, Mass.: Human Development Press.

Varenhorst, B. (1973) Game theory, simulation and group counseling. *Educational Technology,* **13**(2), 40–43.

Winn, W. A. (1981) Physical challenge approaches to psychotherapy. In F. T. Nickerson & K. S. O'Laughlin, *Helping through action.* Amherst, Mass.: Human Resources Development Press.

PART THREE

Play Therapy: Special Techniques and Settings

In the first two parts of this volume we have looked at recent advances in several major theoretical approaches to therapy with children and also at the way in which developmental concepts have been integrated into play therapy. This material forms the foundation upon which the therapist who wishes to practice prescriptive play therapy can build. Having chosen a general theoretical framework or even a particular therapeutic methodology, the prescriptive therapist will still want to add specific strategies to his or her therapeutic armamentarium in order to manage atypical problems as they arise. The problems to which we refer are those that interfere in any way with the therapy process. Specific therapeutic interventions may be aimed at increasing the therapist's diagnostic accuracy, the availability and consistency of therapeutic interventions, the sphere of the therapist's influence, and the level of affective or creative communication on the part of the child.

The use of play in diagnostic work with children has risen in recent years primarily because of the increased awareness of the relation between play and development, as discussed in Part Two of this volume. As therapists learned that observation of child play could reveal levels of cognitive, social, and emotional development, they became eager to adopt this method as an aid in evaluating and diagnosing children not amenable to traditional verbal interview techniques. For example, Csikszentmihalyi (1975) and Fein and Apfel (1979) found that elements of play behavior were related to the child's level of intelligence, development, and degree of psychopathology. They suggested that observation of a child's play could be used to assess these levels and measure their change over time.

The increased ability of various practitioners to identify children at risk for psychological disturbance has, in part, contributed to an increase in the demand for psychological services. The use of play therapy in settings other than the traditional private office has allowed therapists to make therapy more available and has also increased the consistency of their contacts with patients. In making therapy available to more children, therapists have moved into schools, hospitals, medical clincis, and community-based social service agencies.

Providing therapy in these settings increases consistency because it decreases both the child's and the therapist's dependency on the parents as agents of contact. If the child is seen in school or in a hospital, then the parents are no longer in the position of having to make appointments, transport the child, and, in general, accommodate their lifestyle to the therapy schedule. In addition, contacts may be more consistent because the child is more motivated to attend therapy if it interferes with something like class time than if it interferes with after-school playtime.

Another dimension to having therapists treat children in a wide variety of settings is that it allows the therapist to influence additional aspects of the child's life, often expediting the therapeutic process. If a child who is having difficulty in school can be treated in that setting, then the therapist has the child's teacher, the child's classmates, and the resources of the school available to him or her in helping to effect change. The therapist is available to see the reality of the situation and to deal with it firsthand. The same applies to a child who is hospitalized. If the therapist treating the child is a part of the hospital system, then he or she has access to the child's physician, nurses, and to the other hospitalized children, and may thereby work out solutions to some "hospital" problems directly. An example of such a problem which has received a great deal of attention recently is anxiety regarding medical procedures. Therapists working in hospital settings are able to familiarize themselves with medical procedures, relay this information to their child patients through brief, directed play sessions, and, subsequently, achieve a significant decrease in the child's hospital-related anxiety. The important point here is that whenever a therapist works with a child in an institutional setting, a significant amount of the therapist's impact may be mediated through his or her role as a liaison between any combination of the following: the child, the parents, the institution's staff, the institution's administration, and other institutions which may become involved. This role is generally available to the therapist no matter what type of therapy he or she is conducting.

Regardless of the child's diagnosis or the treatment setting, therapists frequently find themselves in need of special techniques or materials in order to resolve difficulties within the therapy. Usually, the difficulties involve the communication between child and therapist. Children may find traditional techniques or materials too threatening, they may not have sufficient skills to communicate their thoughts and feelings on any level, or they may resist becoming involved in the therapy right from the beginning. Whatever the underlying problem, the end result is that the therapist and the child cannot work together because they lack an avenue for interaction. To overcome this difficulty therapists have devised a number of new materials and very specific techniques.

Traditionally, therapists have used a wide variety of both structured and unstructured play materials. Psychoanalytic play therapists tend to favor the less-structured materials such as clay, paint, water, sand, and the like on the assumption that these allow the child maximum freedom of self-expression. Slightly more structured toys which are used in virtually all types of play therapy might be called "props for pretending"; these include a doll house with furniture and a doll family: baby dolls; toy soldiers, animals, guns, knives, and telephones; play sized tables, chairs, stove, refrigerator, and sink; costumes; and puppets. The therapy may be more or less structured simply by limiting the child's choice of toys or requiring that the toys be played with in a certain way, as is done in Release Therapy.

Recent additions to the therapist's arsenal of materials and techniques seem aimed at (1) making playing or talking more attractive to the child, (2) structuring play in such a way as to make it less threatening, and (3) creating materials which are appropriate to a very specific setting or child. Many recent technological advances fall into the first category, particularly audio and videotape recorders. Gardner (1975) has made extensive use of these tools and has found that there are very few children who will not respond to the opportunity to hear themselves on tape or to see themselves on television. The second category consists primarily of some specially constructed "therapeutic" games (Gardner, 1971) and some structured programs aimed at teaching children more appropriate ways of responding or behaving. The teaching programs include the Developing Understanding of Self and Others (DUSO) program (Dinkmeyer, 1970), Teaching Children Self-Control (Fagen, Long, & Stevens, 1975) and the Social Skills training program (Spivak & Shure, 1974). Although these programs are very structured and goal oriented they still involve a great deal of play and children generally perceive them as fun: they tend to focus on the process rather than the goals. The materials which fall in the last category are often items made by creative therapists which may not be widely available. A therapist in a school setting might use a toy school to encourage a child to play out school-related problems. In the late 1970s Barbara Aiello developed a set of puppets which represent various physical disabilities. For example, one puppet has a wheelchair and another puppet has a hearing aid. These puppets have been incorporated into "The Kid's Project" (Picker, 1979), a puppet show and play program in New York State which is designed to help nonhandicapped children adjust when a handicapped child is placed in their regular school classroom.

Each of the following chapters presents a particular technique, material, or setting for play therapy. The strategic technical variations outlined in each chapter are not proposed as independent therapeutic interventions. Instead, each special technique, material, or setting is meant to assist the therapist in overcoming certain treatment problems within the context of his or her overall theoretical or methodological approach to therapy.

MATERIALS AND PROGRAMS

Aiello, B. *Handicapped puppets.* Washington, D.C.: Kids on the Block, Inc.

Dinkmeyer, D. (1970) *Developing understanding of self and others: Play kit and manual.* Circle Pines, Minn.: Publishers Building.

Csikszentmihalyi, M. (1975) Play and intrinsic rewards. *Journal of Humanistic Psychology,* **15**(3), 41–63.

Fagen, S., Long, N., & Stevens, D. (1975) *Teaching children self-control.* Columbus, Ohio: Merrill.

Fein, G., & Apfel, N. (1979) The development of play: Style, structure and situations. *Genetic Psychology Monographs,* **99,** 231–250.

Gardner, R. (1971) *Therapeutic communication with children: The mutual storytelling technique.* New York: Jason Aronson.

Gardner, R. (1975) *Psychotherapeutic approaches to the resistant child.* New York: Jason Aronson.

Picker, D. (Director) (1979) *The kid's project.* Albany: New York State Office of Mental Retardation and Developmental Disabilities.

Spivak, G., & Shure, M. (1974) *Social adjustment of young children.* San Francisco: Jossey-Bass.

CHAPTER 9

Play Observation and
Psychiatric Diagnosis

DAVID BEHAR
JUDITH L. RAPOPORT

INTRODUCTION

Whatever play is, it is easily recognized in a vast array of mammalian young as well as in human children. Play seems nearly irrepressible. Like speech and social living, it develops, giftlike, from the meeting of unspecified brain structure and the slightest environmental provocation. One might think then that psychiatric disorders would affect play quality and quantity in consistent ways. But do observations of play facilitate the diagnosis of these diseases? In this chapter, we will review the research addressing this question.

The behavior of young children is highly variable and more directly affected by the immediate situation than behavior of older pediatric groups. Nevertheless, clinicians do make assumptions about reliability and validity of play behavior and use these assumptions in their diagnostic formulations. We feel it is helpful to review the few experimental studies which examine the diagnostic usefulness of psychiatric play interviews.

TECHNIQUE

The diagnostic play interview seems particularly important for children before they have found more adult, or structured outlets. Older children's sports and games have restrictive goals and rules and require less self-expression and more skill. The verbal interview becomes increasingly germane and fruitful after mental age seven when verbal skills, memory, and social sophistication begin to unfold. By age 10, a child may consider unstructured diagnostic play observation to be patronizing. For example, puppet use considered to have high communicative and rapport value was judged to be no more effective than interviewing in separating a group of disturbed from control children between the ages of seven and nine (Graham, 1979). Naturalistic observation of structured tasks with somewhat playful qualities, however, is useful for children up to the age of puberty.

Play observation must be therapeutically useful in a fashion consistent with the rising standards of modern psychiatric diagnosis. In addition, sufficient interrater reliability needs to be established. Almost no studies have included measures to factor out chance agreement. We will review those studies which indicated at least some concern for reliability and validity.

Most systematic studies of play diagnosis have examined specific play activities which were tailored to particular diagnoses. There are no valid diagnostic protocols that apply to random clinic children. The following is a review of the literature on the use of play diagnosis with normal children, for general clinical screening, and for the diagnosis of autism, retardation, hyperactivity, aggressiveness, and gender identity disorder.

Normal Children

In a study duplicating a typical 30-minute play interview between a normal child and a therapist, it was found that systematic observation correlated well with more formal ratings by parent, teacher, and psychologist. Time required for separation from parent correlated inversely with emotional independence on the Benet Behavior Scale. A high verbal articulation score was associated with greater relatedness to the interviewer, participation in play, and perceived benefit from the experience. There was agreement on the degree of immaturity as reported by parents. The frequency of toy switching correlated inversely with parental reports of attention. In brief, this play interview met reliability standards and reflected the child's everyday behavior, although actual correlations were low (Stephens et al., 1980).

General Clinical Screening

In a study screening the entire three-year-old population ($N = 110$) of Martha's Vineyard, Massachusetts, the judges felt the most useful diagnostic information was a description of the child's relatedness to the examiner. Clinical ratings of severity of "caseness" based on written summaries of the play interview and on the Behavioral Screening Questionnaire, a parental scale, showed a correlation of 0.74 ($p < .001$) This study represents a unique study of play which did not limit itself to a particular disorder.

In a case finding of a totally different nature, dolls with anatomical accuracy have been used to elicit information on suspected sex and physical abuse from toddlers and children who had not developed the required vocabulary (see Chapter 18 of this book).

Autism and Retardation

Retarded children and normal children of the same mental age (3.3 years) were compared in free-play observation which was later rated on a scale of organization of play behavior (Hulme & Linzer, 1966). There were no differ-ences in elaboration of free play or ability to order objects (beads), although language responses, retention of models, and ability to correct errors in model building were inferior in the retarded. Clinically, play interviews are often unreliable in the evaluation of retarded children and this study supports the use of other techniques for identifying these patients.

In a comparison of retarded, autistic, and normal children, the greatest and most discriminating difference was found to be the "combinatorial" use of toys (Tilton & Ottinger, 1964; Weiner et al., 1969). This was defined as putting toys together, as in building with blocks, filling a truck, or putting a cup on a saucer. The autistics were the most deficient in this area. Their play also in-cluded repetitive manipulations and inappropriate chewing of toys. Freeman et al. (in press) made a systematic comparison of play observations of carefully diagnosed autistic, retarded, and normal children matched for chronological age. They made up the Behavioral Observation Scale to record the frequency of a wide variety of activities. They found that the items which differentiated the normals from both autistic and retarded were mouthing, sniffing, de-creased eye contact, less social smiling, leading adults by the hand, ignoring the examiner, babbling, communicative speech, deviant ball play. Autistic be-haviors infrequently seen in the other two groups included sound repetition, ear covering, looking at hands, scrutiny of visual detail, rubbing of surfaces, inappropriate top spinning, hand flapping, finger flicking, whirling, and toe walking. The authors point out the clinical significance of single behaviors or symptom changes with the mental age of the subject. However, they did find that babbling, uncommunicative speech, and ritual use of objects alone accu-rately classified more than 85% of the children in the normal or autistic and retarded categories. Hand flapping and absence of social smiling accurately separated 72% of the retarded from the autistic (Freeman et al., 1978). Whereas the parental interview is the most important diagnostic tool for au-tism, clinical interview discrimination is not difficult. Thus, experimental re-search is not as important in this case as it is in other conditions.

Hyperactivity and Aggressiveness

Many overactive children considered unmanageable by parents and teachers appear nonchalant and composed in the initial visit to a physician's office. A few studies have addressed this issue specifically.

Routh et al. (1974) divided a small playroom into four quadrants with tape on the floor. They showed that the amount of activity as measured by tape crossings decreased with age in normal children. The findings in this study may be used as normative age standards. Kantosky (1976) adopted this ap-proach and confirmed the frequent classroom observation that hyperactive children stand out more from their peers during restricted play and classroom activity than during free play.

Roberts (1979) then sought to discriminate between three groups of dis-turbed children: pure hyperactives, pure aggressives, and combined hyperactives and aggressives. Although this project was designed to facilitate research on these often confused conditions, it does have potential clinical applications in that hyperactivity and attention deficit alone (but not aggressiveness) may be alleviated with stimulant medication. Aggressiveness also speaks for relatively poor prognosis but is rarely exhibited in the intimidating confines of a strange office. Laboratory and home observations have not yielded satisfactory discriminating ratings (reviewed in Roberts, 1979).

Careful clinical diagnoses were made. Roberts observed free and restricted play in a playroom containing a number of toys. After playing with any toy they wished, the children were restricted to playing with an Etch-a-Sketch at one of four tables in the room. These were replaced by five worksheets during a restricted academic observation. Each period took 15 minutes. The greatest differences between hyperactives and normals in free play were in the number of grid crossings, activity measured by ankle actometer (an altered self-winding watch), proportion of time spent out of seat, and proportion of time on task. In a restricted play setting, 85% were correctly classified. The same variables were useful again in a classroom setting to correctly classify 90% of the children.

The groups of hyperactive and hyperactive/aggressives were then tested. The restricted academic period was the most telling. And the single variable of "proportion on task" was most effective (86% correct). Fidgetiness and vocalizing were not helpful measures. In the other settings, discrimination was less adequate. Age seemed to improve worksheet performance and decrease motor activities. Socioeconomic status and IQ were irrelevant.

In both experiments, the clearest discrimination took place in a classroom-like setting, rather than in a play interview. Aggressive children acted like controls, while hyperactive children were distractible and overactive; boys with both conditions manifested even greater abnormalities on the same measures.

A replication of this approach indicated correct classification was 76% in free play and 67% in the academic setting. Using these play observations helped to demonstrate the independence of hyperactivity and aggression. The two factors tend to get blurred and to intercorrelate when only teacher and parent rating scales are used (Milich et al., 1982).

Gender Identity

In a series of clinical studies, Green defined effeminacy as a preference in boys for feminine activities and an explicitly stated desire to "become a girl." When given a choice in a playroom, effeminate boys aged 4 to 10 chose "feminine" toys more often than not and "masculine" toys much less often than typically masculine boys (Green et al., 1972a). The truck and the doll were the most discriminating toys. When asked to "draw a person" 57% of feminine boys drew a girl first compared to 82% of normal girls and 20% of normal boys. The masculine boys drew boys first (76%) (Green et al., 1972b). One advantage of this test, according to Green, is that it does not relate directly to effeminacy. A child who wants to hide his beliefs is less likely to sabotage this test than a scale questionnaire or direct interviewing. When given a selection of dolls representing all members of the family in the Family Doll Preference Test, girls and feminine boys spent significantly more time than masculine boys holding female and infant figures (Green & Fuller, 1973). During storytelling associated with these dolls, effeminate boys preferred situations involving "infant care."

DISCUSSION

Formal diagnosis of childhood disorders should rely on standardized, reliable, clinical criteria. Play observation may be a particularly useful accessory function under the following circumstances:

1. Contradictions or doubtful assertions are found in the reports of parents and teachers.
2. A discrepancy is sensed between reports and clinical observation.
3. The child is too young mentally to be interviewed verbally, or for a variety of reasons, the verbal communications are suspect.
4. The child is too shy or withdrawn to be otherwise engaged.

For school-age children, there are valid diagnostic interviews which will permit useful research on diagnosis in child psychiatry. One of these is based on DSM III criteria (Herjanic & Campbell, 1977). Another is that developed for the World Health Organization (Rutter et al., 1975). Neither of these addresses the particular problems of the diagnostic play interview.

We have deliberately not discussed the clinical, intuitive, hypothesis generating process which play interview provides. Furthermore, just the contrast between play data and the history obtained from parent or teacher may provide useful information about plasticity and reactivity of the child. There is room for a great deal of research confirming the usefulness of particular play techniques for identifying problems in young children. From the limited number of studies to date, particular points emerge.

There are no standardized play interviews designed to elicit a specific symptom or which point to a particular diagnosis. It is therefore advisable to obtain a rough idea of the diagnosis from verbal reports and to then apply the techniques previously described for each area of pathology. The formulation of specific questions or hypotheses for testing seems most fruitful. In play interviews, children should be given the opportunity to demonstrate:

1. Style of interaction with a parent.
2. Style of separation from parent.

3. Quality of relatedness to the examiner.
4. Use of toys in free play that are appropriate to mental age.
5. Spontaneous behavior in a restrictive setting similar to the classroom without benefit of one-to-one limit setting.
6. Play behaviors often involving doll play relevant to the working diagnosis.

In conclusion, play observation may be necessary and important for diagnosing the young or nonverbal child. Despite the absence of standardization, play interviewing represents an important area for research in child psychiatry. Specific hypotheses concerning discrepancies between play behavior and parent/teacher reports are particularly needed. Furthermore, while initial studies suggest that both mood and activity are poorly rated on an initial diagnostic play interview, these areas are of such importance that the findings must be replicated. Finally, whereas play behavior to some extent replicates the actual behaviors of everyday life, systematic study of just those deviations from everyday functioning which appear in diagnostic interviews would be interesting.

With older children, information about mood swings, fears, and guilt is reliably obtained only from interviews with the child (Orvachel et al., 1981). It remains to be determined by similar studies comparing information from parent and child, what unique information is available from play interviews with young children.

REFERENCES

Freeman, B. J., Ritvo, E. R., Tonick, I., Guthrie, D., & Schroth, P. (In press) The Behavior Observation Scale for autism (BOS): Analysis of behaviors among autistic, mentally retarded, and normal children.

Freeman, B. J., Ritvo, E., Guthrie, D., Schroth, P., & Ball, J. (1978) The Behavior Observation Scale for autism: Initial methodology, data analysis, and preliminary findings on 89 children. *Journal of the American Academy of Child Psychiatry,* **17,** 576–588.

Graham, B. D. (1979) *The effectiveness of hand-puppet use by children in obtaining diagnostic information in interviewing.* Unpublished thesis, University of Missouri, Kansas City.

Green, R., Fuller, M., Rutley, B. R., & Hendler, J. (1972a) Playroom toy preferences of fifteen masculine and fifteen feminine boys. *Behavior Therapy* **3,** 425–429.

Green, R., Fuller, M., Rutley, B. (1972b) It-scale for children and Draw-A-Person Test: 30 feminine versus 25 masculine boys. *Journal of Personality Assessment,* **36,** 349–352.

Green, R., & Fuller, M. (1973) Family doll play and female identity in pre-adolescent males. *American Journal of Orthopsychiatry,* **43,** 123–127.

Herjanic, B., & Campbell, J. W. (1977) Differentiating psychiatrically disturbed children on the basis of a structured interview. *Journal of Abnormal Child Psychology,* **5,** 127–135.

Hulme, I., & Linzer, E. A. (1966) Play language and reasoning in subnormal children. *Journal of Child Psychology and Psychiatry,* **7,** 107–123.

Kantosky, M. A. (1976) A behavioral method for assessing overactivity in hyperactive children. Unpublished Master's thesis, University of Wisconsin.

Milich, R., Loney, J., & Landau, S. (1982) Independent dimensions of hyperactivity and aggression: A validation with playroom observation data, *J. of Abnormal Psychology* **91,** 183–198.

Orvachel, H., Weissman, M., Padian, N., & Lowe, T. (1981) Assessing psychopathology of children of psychiatrically disturbed parents: A pilot study. *Journal of Child Psychiatry,* **20,** 112–123.

Roberts, M. A. (1979) A behavioral method for differentiating hyperactive, aggressive, and hyperactive plus aggressive children. Unpublished doctoral thesis. University of Wisconsin.

Routh, D. K., Schroeder, C. S., & O'Tuama, L. A. (1974) Development of activity level in children. *Developmental Psychology,* **2,** 163–168.

Rutter, M., Shaffer, D., & Sturge, C. (1976). *A Guide to a Multi-Axial Classification Scheme for Psychiatric Disorders in Childhood and Adolescence.* London: Frowde & Co.

Stephens, R. G., Bartley, L. S., Rapoport, J. L., & Berg, C. (1980) A brief preschool playroom interview. *Journal of the American Academy of Child Psychiatry,* **19,** 213–224.

Tilton, J. R., & Ottinger, D. R. (1964) Comparison of the toy play behavior of autistic, retarded, and normal children. *Psychological Reports,* **15,** 967–975.

Weiner, B. J., Ottinger, D. R., & Tilton, J. R. (1969) Comparison of the toy play behaviors of autistic, retarded, and normal children: A reanalysis. *Psychological Reports,* **25,** 223–227.

CHAPTER 10

Play Therapy in Elementary School Settings

GARRY L. LANDRETH

INTRODUCTION

During the past decade, school personnel have begun to recognize and accept play therapy as an effective therapeutic intervention approach with children in school settings. The absence of play therapy programs in elementary schools is for the most part the result of four factors. First, play therapy is quite young. The use of play in therapy originated with Sigmund Freud's (1909) classic case of Little Hans. Although it was then used by several psychoanalysts in Europe, Klein (1955) reported that as late as 1929, play, as part of the therapeutic procedure with children, was little used in the United States. Second, counselors, school psychologists, and social workers were not added to elementary school staffs until the 1960s. Third, school personnel have not understood what play therapy is. Fourth, few counselor education programs, departments of social work, or departments of psychology offer specific training in play therapy. The assumption seems to be that counselors, school psychologists, and social workers will be able to use verbal exchange effectively with children. Such an approach shows little understanding of the world of the child.

Rationale for Play Therapy

Children must be approached and understood from a developmental perspective. Words are abstractions and thus are often foreign to the child whose natural means of communication is the concrete world of play. Efforts to communicate with children on an exclusively verbal level assume the presence of a well-developed facility for expression through speech and thus confine children to a medium which is often awkward and unnecessarily restrictive.

Play is to the child what verbalization is to the adult. It is a medium for expressing feelings, exploring relationships, describing experiences, disclosing wishes, and achieving self-fulfillment. Play is the natural and comfortable medium of expression for children. Seldom do children discuss their feelings; they demonstrate or show their feelings by acting them out. As Ginott has stated, "the child's play is his talk and the toys are his words" (1961, p. 51). Since play is something children have always known, they are more likely to express themselves honestly through that medium. Axline describes the play therapy experience as a place where "there is an honesty, a frankness, and a vividness in the way children state themselves" (1950, p. 68). Dimick and Huff (1970) suggest that until children reach a level of facility and sophistication with verbal communication that allows them to express themselves fully and effectively to others, the use of play media is mandatory if significant communication is to take place between child and counselor. It would seem then that it is not a question of whether the elementary school counselor, psychologist, or social worker should use play therapy, but rather how play therapy should be utilized in elementary schools.

The ultimate objective of elementary schools is to assist the intellectual, emotional, physical, and social development of children by providing adequate learning opportunities. Therefore, a major objective of utilizing play therapy with children in an elementary school setting is to help children get ready to profit from the learning experiences offered. Children cannot be made to learn. Even the most effective teachers cannot teach children who are not yet ready to learn. Play therapy, then, is an adjunct to the learning environment, an experience which assists children in maximizing their opportunities to learn.

Advantages of Play Therapy in Elementary Schools

Too often, elementary school counselors, school psychologists, and social workers with years of accumulated experience drift into a pattern of "get things done in a hurry" as a natural reaction to the stress of their jobs. Jobs must be done in a hurry. Tasks must be completed in a minimum amount of time to avoid accumulation and accompanying pressure. Unfortunately, under such circumstances, the focus is often on things rather than children, on problems rather than the child as a person, and thus on "making" children change to get quick results. The objective becomes one of talking *to* children rather than talking *with* children and "straightening children out" rather than trying to understand them.

The significant adults in the lives of children would do well to remember that attempting to carry on a conversation while sitting in a large chair, from which the child's feet dangle in midair, in an office containing a huge desk and tall file cabinets may be an awkward and anxiety-producing experience for children. Everything about such settings including the "official" telephone, large stuffed chair for the counselor, papers on the desk, bookcase, and fragile decorative items communicates to children "this is a place for big people."

In many elementary schools a visit to the office of the counselor or school psychologist is perceived by children to be synonymous with "being sent to the office to receive punishment for getting in trouble." On the way to the school psychologist's office for a counseling session, children are often asked by classmates, "What did you do?" implying some rule has been violated or some unacceptable act has been committed. In the minds of children "the office" quickly becomes a place to avoid. This is certainly not the image counselors want to project.

The use of toys and play materials in elementary schools by counselors, school psychologists, and social workers offers unique advantages seldom found in counseling sessions which are restricted to verbal means of communication. The presence of toys and creative materials indicates to children an understanding of their world. When a child enters a room or area in which toys and materials are displayed, the immediate message communicated to the child is, "In here is different. This is a place for children and it's OK to be a child here." Such materials provide an environment that is freeing to children. Thus, they experience less initial awkwardness and anxiety in the counseling experience.

Play media materials invite the child's participation and establish a natural means of communication which does not require verbal interaction. The play of the child becomes the medium of exchange and is utilized by the counselor not only to understand the child but also to build a therapeutic relationship.

The presence of play media materials in the elementary counselor's office can quickly change the atmosphere of the relationship from "hurry" to "this is your time, set your own pace." A logical consequence is that the child typically maintains a high level of interest during the session. The child no longer experiences pressure to change and is thus free to explore those positive and creative aspects of self which could not emerge in environments which attempted to "make" him or her change. Attempts to "make" a child change typically result in a defending of the old self. In the play therapy setting, the therapist must focus on the child and try to understand his or her communication of experiences and self-perception.

Since play is the language of the child, play provides a medium for building the essential relationship between counselor and child. The counselor is able to enter into the child's emotional world as it is freely revealed and acted upon by the child. Play media materials thus facilitate the development of a dynamic living relationship because the child is able to act upon and experience the totality of the immediacy of his or her behavior. The child is not restricted to discussing what happened; rather he or she lives out, in play, a moment of his or her life. The child's play is current, concrete, and specific.

After analyzing the differential uses of play in the treatment of children, Amster (1943) concluded that irrespective of the specific purpose in using play, diagnostic and therapeutic values are present. "As all play helps a child to share himself and, in varying degree, to re-enact, re-live and release, all play has some therapeutic value. . . . Play activity . . . must be recognized always as a complex, distorted assortment of the child's conscious and unconscious expressions (Amster, 1943, p. 68).

Amster (1943, pp. 62–67) has listed six uses of play in the therapy setting:

1. Play can be used for diagnostic understanding of the child.
2. Play can be used to establish a working relationship.
3. Play can be used to break through a child's way of playing in his daily life and his defenses against anxiety.
4. Play can be used to help a child verbalize certain conscious material and associated feelings.
5. Play can be used to help a child act out unconscious material and to relieve the accompanying tension.
6. Play can be used to develop a child's play interests which he can carry over into his daily life and which will strengthen him for his future life.

The specific therapeutic values of play therapy as suggested by Solomon (1940, p. 763) are "(1) release of hostility toward parents, siblings, etc.; (2) alleviation of guilt feelings; (3) opportunity to express freely all love fantasies; (4) incorporation of therapeutic suggestions in direction of growth; and (5) desensitization by means of repetition."

Difficulties in Using Play Therapy in Elementary Schools

Although adequate physical space for learning experiences and other school activities is already a problem in many elementary schools, we should not consider it a major limitation or deterrent to the use of play therapy. Granted, space is necessary, but it is my contention that every elementary school has some space that will adequately accommodate a play therapy program. Therefore, the question of where to conduct a play therapy program will be dealt with later in this chapter.

The most frequently expressed concern about a play therapy program is that play is often noisy. This is a valid concern since it is perhaps unrealistic to expect to have a soundproof room located at some distance from other occupied areas. Play as the child's natural expression may take the form of destructive as well as constructive actions. However, the amount of time spent by children in noisy and/or destructive activities in the play therapy experience is minimal when compared to the amount of time spent in quieter play (Hendricks, 1971; Withee, 1975). The greatest potential difficulty is not in the amount of noise but rather in the administrators' and teachers' reactions to the noise. Therefore, it is essential that they be informed about what to expect and helped to understand the significance of what may be expressed through play. It might be helpful to explain that some children need active release of tension, anger, frustration, or aggression and that a part of the release experienced is the noise itself. Through the process of expressing such feelings and experiencing the counselor's appropriate responses of therapeutic limit setting which provides a choice of more acceptable expression, the child learns to gain control. The administrators and teachers may need to be reminded that self-control and self-direction are also goals in every classroom, and that the freedom and permission to express feelings noisily in the play area results in the child having less need to act out those feelings in a disruptive manner in the classroom.

The cost of equipping and maintaining a playroom or area is a potential hindrance since most elementary schools provide little or no funds for a counseling budget other than what is required for a testing or diagnostic program. However, as is discussed in a later section of this chapter, a special, fully equipped room is not essential. A play therapy program can be established with a very small budget and in some schools with no money supplied by the school. Most of the toys and materials described later in this chapter can be obtained inexpensively from garage sales, donations from parents whose children have outgrown the toys, or community sources. For example, the telephone company will supply, without cost, telephones which are no longer serviceable, and the local newspaper will give away end runs of newsprint roll. In addition, Parent-Teacher Associations are often eager to provide a small yearly budget when they understand the nature and purpose of the play therapy program. Some local service organizations will collect the required materials. The prerequisite is to get invited to speak to the organization about the needs of children and how a play therapy program can help. A final reminder regarding cost is to anticipate that some toys will be broken and materials such as paste and paints will need to be resupplied.

For those counselors, school psychologists, and social workers who have a need for things to be neat and clean, the messiness that is inherent in play therapy can be a source of frustration and thus a deterrent. Contrary to what Ginott (1961) recommends, play therapy programs in most schools will not have the services of a maid to clean up after each session. This will be reserved in most situations for the play therapist who used the room. There are three possible solutions to this problem. Play therapists who have strong needs for orderliness would do well to examine their own value systems and strive to avoid imposing their needs on children. Second, limits can be utilized to restrict the amount of messiness, thus helping the play therapist to be more accepting, and third, messy play therapy sessions can be shortened a few minutes to allow the counselor time to clean up. Requiring the child to clean up may result in a power struggle, or the child may feel punished for being messy. My own experience has shown that children in play therapy tend to move toward the mean or to reach a balance of expression. That is to say, children who are messy begin, on their own without any prompting by the play therapist, to clean up their messes and children who are compulsively neat begin to tolerate some lack of orderliness in their play.

TECHNICAL ASPECTS

What to Call the Play Therapy Program

Most school personnel and many parents react with anxiety and apprehension to the term "therapy" because they do not understand what the term means.

For them, "therapy" is synonymous with "severity" and "deep psychological problems." Therefore, it is recommended that play therapy programs be referred to by some other term or title that will cause less reaction. Play therapy programs in schools could be referred to as play media programs, counseling with toys, emotional growth through play, developmental growth through play, or a similar title. The play therapist will be the best judge of the degree of acceptability of the term play therapy in the individual school setting.

Potential Settings for Play Therapy in Elementary Schools

Although the traditional setting for play therapy has been a private office or playroom in an agency or clinic setting, a fully equipped playroom is not essential for children to express themselves. What is important is that children be provided with an opportunity to choose the mode of communication which is most natural for them. For some children, this may be a combination of the two modes available play and verbalization. An immediate therapeutic dividend resulting from being allowed to choose is that children can set their own directions and assume responsibility for doing so.

Play therapy sessions can be held in the corner of the cafeteria, a storage closet, a workroom, the nurse's office, the library, the corner of a regular classroom, or the counselor's office to which the counselor brings a small bag or box of materials for each session. I am acquainted with an innovative elementary school counselor who utilizes space in the bookroom after textbooks have been removed from it and distributed at the start of the school term. She displays the toys and materials on several of the empty bookshelves and the children play in the floor space and on the shelves. Although far from the ideal 150–200-square-foot playroom recommended by Ginott (1961), she reports significant results in this setting. Another counselor obtained permission from a church adjoining the school grounds to use one of their Sunday School classrooms. Other counselors have reported satisfactory results using the stage of the auditorium or cafeteria. These areas are often unused and a portion of the stage or off-stage area can be made more private by closing the stage curtains. A broad guideline to follow in selecting a place for play therapy: Where there is sufficient space and privacy, the play therapy process can be pursued.

Wherever play therapy sessions are held, every effort must be made to protect the confidentiality of the sessions. When complete privacy and confidentiality are not possible, the child should be informed that what he or she does may be heard and/or seen by others.

Toys and Materials

A few carefully selected play media items can provide children with an opportunity to act out feelings and difficulties they experience. Thus, the counselor is allowed to experience and participate in the emotional life of the child. Since the child's total being is thrust into the play, expressions and feelings are experienced by the child as being specific, concrete, and current. The counselor can, therefore, respond to the child's present activities, statements, feelings, and emotions rather than past circumstances. Toys are utilized in the act of play by the child to communicate a personal world to the counselor, school psychologist, or social worker.

Children can communicate a wide range of messages and feelings with a limited number of toys and materials. The following items are considered to be the minimal requirements for conducting a play therapy session: crayons, newsprint, blunt scissors, nursing bottle (plastic), rubber knife, doll, Play-Doh (place in a small plastic container to keep pliable—the top of the cardboard Play-Doh can will fray and allow air to enter the can), dart gun, handcuffs, toy soldiers, empty vegetable can (doubles as container for toy soldiers), plastic or tin play dishes (a complete set is not necessary), spoons (avoid forks because of sharp points), small airplane, small car, telephone, hand puppets or bendable doll family, a small cardboard box with rooms indicated by strips of tape (could double as a container for some materials), dollhouse furniture, small plain mask (Lone Ranger type), Nerf ball (a rubber ball bounces too much), bendable Gumby (nondescript figure), Popsicle sticks, pipe cleaners, pounding bench, old cap or hat, and egg cartons to stack, color, or smash. If storage space is available, an inflatable plastic punching toy would be a special asset. Additional toys and materials can be added by counselors who have a permanent "home."

For the counselor who must travel between several schools, or whose "office" is whatever space happens to be free in the school, these materials can be easily transported in a tote bag. Open display of these play media materials prior to each session helps children feel more comfortable; they invite participation and convey permissiveness. To avoid having to set unnecessary limits and in keeping with budgetary considerations, small quantities of such materials as paste, tempera paint, and finger paints should be displayed.

Toys and materials to avoid include (1) sharp, pointed, or glass items which could hurt the child, (2) elaborate, expensive, complicated or mechanical toys and materials since they may interfere with, rather than facilitate, children's expressions, and (3) highly structured materials such as games, because they do not promote creativity and exploration. Puzzles are a particular problem since at least one piece of the puzzle is invariably lost and the child will be prevented from experiencing a sense of completion and success. Broken toys should always be removed because they promote unnecessary frustration. In addition, materials containing hundreds of pieces such as the larger sets of Lincoln Logs and Tinker Toys should not be included in order to avoid situations requiring the counselor to hunt 20 minutes for all 379 pieces after a particularly messy session.

**Special Considerations When Using Play Therapy
in a School Setting**

Effective implementation and utilization of a play therapy program in an
elementary school setting requires attention to the unique aspects of the school
environment and setting. Unlike play therapy programs in agencies and other
institutions, in elementary schools, careful attention must be given to informing school personnel about what play therapy is, how it helps children, how it
fits into the overall scheme of educational objectives of the school, and what
play therapy can realistically be expected to accomplish.

The playroom or play area should be located as far as possible from classrooms and administrative offices. Schiffer (1969) suggests that greater distance
between play area and classroom fosters psychological separation between
permissive and nonpermissive environments. The greater distance also helps
to insure fewer noise disruptions of classrooms. If the playroom or area is
adjacent to classrooms, toys or equipment with a potentially high noise level
may have to be kept to a minimum or in some cases excluded, depending on
the attitude of the school personnel.

Because the counselor-to-student ratio is high in most elementary schools,
and the amount of time available to work with students is often limited, the
play therapy sessions may have to be kept to 30-minute sessions rather than
the typical 50-minute sessions. My experience has shown that a 30-minute
session can be quite beneficial to most elementary school children.

Another special consideration is the scheduling of children for play therapy
sessions as it will in most cases necessitate their removal from classes. Teachers
should be consulted to avoid disruption of classes which the teacher considers
to be most significant to the child's development. If a teacher is reluctant to
release a child from *any* class activities, it might be helpful to spend time
building the case for play therapy and responding in a supportive, understanding way to the teacher's underlying feelings about the importance of the classroom learning activities and concern for the child's welfare. There is a positive
aspect to a disruptive child missing class instruction. At least for that period of
time the teacher and other students will be less distracted, and the learning
environment enhanced.

A related concern is the movement of the children to and from the play
area. Is the helping professional to accompany the child? Are children to be
allowed to assume full responsibility for themselves? One solution is to use
monitors from upper grade classes to escort children to and from the play area
(Schiffer, 1969).

The counselor, school psychologist, and social worker who use play therapy
in a school setting will find it necessary to set more limits on the child's behavior than would normally be required in a clinic setting. This is particularly true
if there is not a play therapy room. Less noise can be tolerated, the room and
other accommodations will need more protection, and more attention will be
directed toward what is off limits for the child.

Parents may not be as readily accessible as in agency or clinic settings because they do not have to transport the child to and from the play therapy sessions. Obviously it is much easier to interview and consult with parents when they accompany the child to your office each week. Due to the size of the counselor's case load, it may be unrealistic, and in many cases unnecessary to attempt to involve all parents. Dorfman (1951) points out that children can and do benefit from play therapy without concurrent parent counseling. One alternative to "missing parents" is to schedule short-term parent group counseling sessions in the evening for parents of children in play therapy.

Many children who could benefit from the developmental aspects of play therapy do not need a full 50-minute experience each week. Indeed, it might be best to schedule some children for 10- or 15-minute sessions twice a week if they do not need an intensive relationship with the play therapist. Children with specific problems such as a school phobia would benefit more from a 5- or 10-minute session in the playroom every morning before going to class than they would from a 50-minute session once a week.

Special consideration must also be given to the restrictions placed on the play therapy process by the lengthy Christmas holiday, spring vacation, and end of the school term. The relationships with the children may have to be interrupted for a week or two at a crucial time or terminated at the end of the school term before it is advisable to do so. Children should be helped to anticipate the break in their routine, and in the case of premature termination of severe cases for the summer, the possibility of referral should be explored with parents. It is also not advisable to schedule a new case the week before a major holiday break in the school schedule because the resulting second session two or three weeks later will be almost like a first session for the child. For the same reason, avoid scheduling a new case during the last three weeks of the school year unless you will be able to see the child two or three times a week.

Play Therapy Clientele in an Elementary School Setting

Unlike most play therapy experiences in clinics and agencies which primarily involve crisis situations, play therapy in an elementary school setting can be preventive and developmental by facilitating the normal child's growth and understanding of self. The adjusted child who is experiencing conflict because of stressful situations such as death, divorce, remarriage, moving, or a new baby in the family can be helped in play therapy to work out temporarily disturbing feelings (Moustakas, 1951). Brief experiences in the playroom can be helpful for the fearful child or the child who has excess physical energy. Brief experiences in the playroom can also help the school phobia child by providing initial contact, upon first arrival at school, with toys and materials the child enjoys and can identify with. Stress is then reduced on the child, parent, and teacher.

Since play therapy in the school setting is an integral part of the total educational program, a large segment of the student population requiring the play therapist's attention will be broadly defined as learning disabled because learning disabilities rarely exist in isolation. Landreth et al. (1969) suggest children's problems are global in nature and that disturbances reverberate throughout the child's organism. The child with a speech difficulty may also have distorted emotional reactions. The child who is not able to read may exhibit highly disruptive classroom behavior. The individual child is not a fragmented personality and the child's problems do not exist apart from self or another person.

Play therapy has been demonstrated to be an effective treatment approach for a variety of children's problems which have an emotional basis or emotional effect, including the correction of poor reading performance (Axline, 1947, 1949; Bills, 1950; Bixler, 1945; Mehus, 1953; Pumfrey & Elliott, 1970; Winn, 1959), increased academic performance in learning disabled children (Axline, 1949; Holmer, 1937; Jones, 1952; Machler, 1965; Moustakas, 1951; Sokoloff, 1959), correction of speech problems (Axline & Rogers, 1945; Dupent et al., 1953; Reynert, 1946; Winn, 1959), decreased emotional and intellectual problems of the mentally retarded (Leland & Smith, 1962; Miller, 1948; Moyer & Von Haller, 1956; Pothier, 1967), and better social and emotional adjustment (Andriola, 1944; Axline, 1948, 1964; Baruch, 1952; Conn, 1952; King & Ekstein, 1967; Miller, 1947; Moustakas, 1951; Pothier, 1967; Schiffer, 1957).

Innovations and Extensions of the Role of the Play Therapist

Successful intervention in learning disability failure patterns can be aided by the development of a systematic, interdisciplinary team approach (Landreth et al., 1969) which matches the global nature of children's problems by bringing together such units as the teacher, speech therapist, counselor, school psychologist, social worker, remedial reading teacher, and school nurse. Since the counselor, school psychologist, or social worker is typically in a better position to conceptualize the dynamic, interrelated structure of the child, they are in a unique position to unite in staffing sessions the disparate units concerned with the child's total learning development. Because of his or her unique personal relationship with the child, the play therapist will be able to share insights and understandings with the teacher and other members of the interdisciplinary team in a very concrete way without violating the child's confidentiality. Alexander (1964) views the play therapist as attempting to create a therapeutic attitude throughout the school system through his or her intimate sharing which helps teachers to develop more therapeutic attitudes toward all students.

Kranz (1972) reported an innovative approach to meeting the psychological needs of school children in the early grades by initiating a program in which

12 volunteer elementary school teachers were given 10 weeks of training in play therapy in preparation for conducting play therapy sessions with children in their own schools but not from their own classrooms. Sessions were scheduled before school, during teacher free periods, and after school. All the teachers reported the experience to be positive. Kranz reported positive changes in the children as evidenced by their being more relaxed and open to educational experiences and more adequate peer relationships. Children who had experienced difficulties with adult authority figures were less threatened and more comfortable in the presence of those adults.

SUMMARY

Play therapy in elementary school settings offers a unique opportunity for children to experience growth under the most favorable conditions. In addition to recognizing that play is the child's natural medium of expression, the basic rationale for utilizing a play therapy program in schools is to maximize children's learning opportunities by helping them work out those problems which interfere with learning. The process of play is viewed as the child's effort to gain control over the environment in which he or she finds self. The problems children experience do not exist apart from the people they are. Therefore, play therapy matches the dynamic inner structure of the child with an equally dynamic approach.

The issue of play therapy theory or therapeutic approach has not been addressed in this chapter because counselors, school psychologists, social workers, and other helping professionals are encouraged to be creative in their selection of the play therapy procedures which will be most appropriate for their own personality and work environment. What technique to use, the question of structured or nonstructured approaches to play therapy, as well as related issues will be dictated by the play therapist's value system, the prevailing attitude in the school and the needs of the child.

Dibs' reaction to his play therapy experience perhaps best summarizes the underlying message of this chapter. "You're not a mother. You're not a teacher. You're not a member of mother's bridge club. What are you? It does not really matter. You are the lady of the wonderful playroom" (Axline 1964, p. 204).

REFERENCES

Alexander, E. D. (1964) School centered play therapy program. *Personnel and Guidance Journal,* **43,** 256–261.

Amster, F. (1943) Differential uses of play in treatment of young children. *American Journal of Orthopsychiatry,* **13,** 62–68.

Andriola, J. (1944) Release of aggressions through play therapy for a ten-year-old patient at a child guidance clinic. *Psychoanalytic Review*, **31**, 71–80.

Axline, V. (1947) Nondirective play therapy for poor readers. *Journal of Consulting Psychology*, **11**, 61–69.

Axline, V. (1948) Play therapy: Race and conflict in young children. *Journal of Abnormal and Social Psychology*, **43**, 300–310.

Axline, V. (1949) Play therapy: A way of understanding and helping reading problems. *Childhood Education*, **26**, 156–161.

Axline, V. (1950) Entering the child's world via play experience. *Progressive Education*, **27**, 68–75.

Axline, V. (1964) *Dibs: In search of self.* Boston: Houghton Mifflin.

Axline, V., & Rogers, C. R. (1945) A teacher-therapist deals with a handicapped child. *Journal of Abnormal and Social Psychology*, **40**, 119–142.

Baruch, D. W. (1952) *One little boy.* New York: Dell Publishing.

Bills, R. E. (1950) Nondirective play therapy with retarded readers. *Journal of Consulting Psychology*, **14**, 140–149.

Bixler, R. H. (1945) Treatment of a reading problem through nondirective play therapy. *Journal of Consulting Psychology*, **9**, 105–118.

Conn, J. H. (1952) Treatment of anxiety states in children by play interviews. *Sinai Hospital Journal*, **1**, 57–63.

Dimick, K. M., & Huff, V. E. (1970) *Child counseling.* Chicago: William C. Brown.

Dorfman, E. (1951) Play therapy. In C. R. Rogers (Ed.), *Client-centered therapy.* Boston: Houghton Mifflin. Pp. 235–277.

Dupent, H. J., Landsman, T., & Valentine, M. (1953) The treatment of delayed speech by client-centered therapy. *Journal of Consulting Psychology*, **18**, 122–125.

Ginott, H. G. (1961) *Group psychotherapy with children.* New York: McGraw-Hill.

Hendricks, S. (1971) A descriptive analysis of the process of client-centered play therapy. Unpublished doctoral dissertation, North Texas State University.

Holmer, P. (1937) The use of the play situation as an aid to diagnosis, a case report. *American Journal of Orthopsychiatry*, **7**, 523–531.

Jones, J. W. (1952) Play therapy and the blind child. *New Outlook for the Blind*, **46**, 189–197.

King, P., & Ekstein, R. (1967) The search for ego controls: Progression of play activity in psychotherapy with a schizophrenic child. *Psychoanalytic Review*, **54**, 25–37.

Klein, M. (1955) The psychoanalytic play technique. *American Journal of Orthopsychiatry*, **25**, 223–237.

Kranz, P. L. (1972) Teachers as play therapists: An experiment in learning. *Childhood Education*, **49**, 73–74.

Landreth, G. L., Jacquot, W. S., & Allen, L. (1969) A team approach to learning disabilities. *Journal of Learning Disabilities*, **2**, 82–87.

Leland, H., & Smith, D. (1962) Unstructured material in play therapy for emotionally disturbed brain damaged, mentally retarded children. *American Journal of Mental Deficiency*, **66**, 621–628.

Machler, T. (1965) Pinocchio in the treatment of school phobia. *Bulletin of the Menninger Clinic*, **29**, 212–219.

Mehus, H. (1953) Learning and therapy. *American Journal of Orthopsychiatry,* **23,** 416–421.

Miller, H. E. (1947) Play therapy for the problem child. *Public Health Nurse Bulletin,* **39,** 294–296.

Miller, H. E. (1948) Play therapy for the institutional child. *Nervous Child,* **7,** 311–317.

Moustakas, C. E. (1951) Situational play therapy with normal children. *Journal of Consulting Psychology,* **15,** 225–230.

Moyer, K., & Von Haller, G. (1956) Experimental study of children's preferences and use of blocks in play. *Journal of Genetic Psychology,* **89,** 3–10.

Pothier, P. C. (1967) Resolving conflict through play fantasy. *Journal of Psychiatric Nursing and Mental Health Services,* **5,** 141–147.

Pumfrey, P. D., & Elliott, C. D. (1970) Play therapy, social adjustment and reading attainment. *Educational Research,* **12,** 183–193.

Reynert, M. I. (1946) Play therapy at Mooseheart. *Journal of the Exceptional Child,* **13,** 2–9.

Schiffer, M. (1957) A therapeutic play group in a public school. *Mental Hygiene,* **41,** 185–193.

Schiffer, M. (1969) *The therapeutic play group.* New York: Grune and Stratton.

Sokoloff, M. A. (1959) A comparison of gains in communicative skills, resulting from group play therapy and individual speech therapy, among a group of non-severely dysarthric, speech handicapped cerebral palsied children. Unpublished doctoral dissertation, New York University.

Solomon, J. C. (1940) Active play therapy: Further experiences. *American Journal of Orthopsychiatry,* **10,** 763–781.

Winn, E. V. (1959) The influence of play therapy on personality change and the consequent effect on heading performance. Unpublished doctoral dissertation, Michigan State University.

Withee, K. L. (1975) A descriptive analysis of the process of play therapy. Unpublished doctoral dissertation, North Texas State University.

CHAPTER 11

Play Therapy for Hospitalized Children

DOUGLAS B. GOLDEN

INTRODUCTION

Play intervention for children in hospital settings is an unqualified necessity.
The play therapist's puppets are every bit as important as the surgeon's knife
in helping a child leave the hospital healthier than when he or she arrived.
This premise is explored in the present chapter. The effects of hospitalization
on children are discussed, followed by a presentation of the rationale for play
programs. Some elements in setting up play programs, such as staffing, the
play room, and its use are considered. Various aspects of play intervention
then pursued, including group play versus individual play, the age of the child,
structured versus nonstructured play, separation, autonomy and mastery,
medical information and medical procedures, surgery, injections, chronic disability, and parental involvement. This chapter is meant to serve as an overview; references are offered for a more specific inquiry.

The topic of play with hospitalized children has provoked the interest of
individuals in many different disciplines, particularly nursing, pediatrics, and
psychology. The literature in this area consists primarily of descriptive accounts of established play programs and brief case presentations of the children who participate in them. Research studies have been the exception
(Burstein & Meichenbaum, 1979; Cassell, 1965; Clatworthy, 1981; Katz et al.,
1980; Schulz et al., 1981). Most of the research studies have focused on the
effects of play programs in reducing stress and anxiety in children.

The application of play intervention for hospitalized children has had international recognition. Articles cited herein have been taken from British, Swiss,
and Australian journals. In the United States, a great deal of work in this area
is done by the Association for the Care of Children's Health, referred to as the
Child Life Program. This program strives "to promote optimum development
of children, adolescents and families, to maintain normal living patterns and
to minimize psychological trauma" (ACCH, 1979). Their goals include "mini-

mizing stress and anxiety for the child and adolescent, providing essential life experiences and providing opportunities to retain self-esteem and appropriate independence" (ACCH, 1979). Child Life programs exist in virtually every major hospital in the United States.

Effects of Hospitalization and Illness on Children

The effects of hospitalization and illness on children is a topic that has received considerable attention. Whereas it is generally agreed that the impact of hospitalization and illness can be mild to severe, hospitalization predictably raises a measure of uncertainty and apprehension in the child. The literature abounds with descriptions of various changes in behavior that occur when children are hospitalized (Adams, 1976; Cassell, 1965; Chan, 1980; Clatworthy, 1981; Freud, 1952; Harvey, 1980; Katz et al., 1980; Linn, 1978; Prugh et al., 1953; Tisza et al., 1970). These behavioral changes seem to differ according to the age of the child, and without intervention, may persist for the duration of hospitalization and continue well beyond discharge. Children have been described as withdrawing by staying in their beds, becoming immobile and nonverbal, refusing to eat, and staring blankly. Developmental regressions which include the loss of hygiene skills, toileting habits, neuromuscular abilities, social skills, and appropriate emotional maturity have been noted. Children in hospitals are known to have excessive periods of crying and vomiting. They may cling to adults and protest loudly when released. Descriptions of children awakening from bad dreams and not wanting to be left alone are common. Conversely, children have also been described as acting resentful and angry. Full-blown temper tantrums may be observed. Some children may act aggressively toward other children on the ward or use hostile language. At times these children may become destructive. An uncooperative attitude may prevail in which the child will refuse to take medications, submit to injections, get up and walk after surgery, or lie still for an x-ray. Other children may cooperate, yet be tentative and fearful, asking a great many questions that disclose confusion and a lack of knowledge. These behavioral changes are such a common occurrence in hospitalized children that hospital staff members may become more concerned if they do *not* occur.

Several primary causes of these behaviors have been proposed. They include (1) separation and relocation in a new environment, (2) loss of autonomy and control, and (3) fear of injury and/or death.

Separation from parents is one of the most difficult problems for hospitalized young children (Adams, 1976; Bowlby, 1960; Chan, 1980; Freud, 1952; Robertson, 1958; Tisza et al., 1970). Children under four years of age are consequently vulnerable to excessive anxiety that can cause healthy coping mechanisms to deteriorate. In this strange and nonhomelike environment of the hospital (Billington, 1972), with strangers dressed in white and acting in an unfamiliar manner, the child attempts to deal with his physical discomfort and is uncertain of his parents' return. In addition to simply needing the physical comforting that a knowing parent can provide, the child, in attempting to accommodate all this new information, may conclude that he is abandoned. This can be a frightening and panic-ridden experience. Robertson (1958) outlines three stages of separation for children in hospitals: protest, despair, and denial. In the first stage the child is very aware of his need for his parents, and utilizing those behaviors that have been successful in the past he cries loudly, hoping to secure their return. When they do not return, the child acts calmer outwardly, although continues to be psychologically troubled. In the second stage the child goes through a period of grieving, conscious of his desire for his parents, yet feeling hopeless about their return. While generally calm, there may be bursts of anger. When they do return, the child may vent these feelings, bringing repressed anger and resentments to the surface. In the third stage the child begins to repress his or her feelings due to their continued intensity and his or her need to quiet internal stress. The child may begin to take what appears to be a lively interest in his or her surroundings. This third stage usually does not occur unless there is an extended period of separation; remediation of the parent–child relationship may take considerable time and effort. A number of variables may contribute to the difficulty of separation for the child, including the amount of time parents are actually present in the hospital, the total length of time the child requires hospital treatment, the intrusiveness of medical procedures, the actual physical pain experienced, the degree to which the child returns to normal physical health, confinement to the bed, preparation for hospitalization, activities while sick, the ego strength of the child, and the relationship with health professionals while in the hospital. Whereas transitional objects such as a blanket or teddy bear from home often assume a great importance for these children, they are usually insufficient. A relationship with an adult who is present on the wards, who can be trusted, and who helps the child reestablish common patterns of the adult–child relationship may be required in order for separation anxieties to subside.

Any adult who has been hospitalized knows the *feeling of having to give up some control* when being cast into the routinized experience of the institution (Freud, 1952). Not in control of his daily activities, the adult may feel that he or she is being treated like a baby. One might think that because of the similarity to the infantile experience, and the closer in time the child is to this experience, he or she would suffer less from hospital nursing. The opposite may be true. Although the loss of autonomy for the adult may be considerable, the development of the ego, independent of the parent, is complete. With the realization that they can admit or discharge themselves at any time and thus exercise choice in the treatment of their own illness, the adult can maintain a sense of mastery. Not only is this choice unavailable to the child, but the development of an independent ego is not complete. Being unable to continue the development of mastery over bodily functions, the child may slip into a regressive role, lose previously acquired skills, and require total care. This regression may extend beyond hospitalization and require relearning in such areas as toileting, hygiene, or eating. Other children who have a strong resistance to this enforced regression may become belligerent, refuse attempts by nurses to provide care and become uncooperative when undergoing medical procedures. The seemingly arbitrary nature of hospital events further underscores the loss of control by reducing predictability. In attempting to master even some small part of the experience, the resistive child may create a ruckus that has a predictable outcome, thus reestablishing previous patterns of behavior.

Children's concepts of their own illness and pain may also be quite distorted and lead to confusion, panic, and guilt. The abilities required to understand the interaction between internal and external factors bringing about the child's illness may be beyond his or her cognitive level (Bibace et al., 1980). The child may view his or her illness as a mystical event or may associate it with something he or she has done wrong (Freud, 1952). The child may view hospitalization as punishment for "bad behavior" and even "bad thinking." Surgical procedures may produce feelings of dread that a body part will be cut off or that the body will be mutilated. The actual physical experience of pain may be altered by the psychological experience of pain. The child's fear of the invading needle and the thought of being poisoned may lead an unknowing observer to the conclusion that the child may be very sensitive to pain when in fact the actual pain may be minimal.

Thus, in reviewing the effects of hospitalization on children, we find a set of experiences that, in the absence of intervention, can put a child at risk for an acute reactive emotional disturbance which may have long-term consequences.

Rationale for Play Programs

Because of the stresses of hospitalization on children, health professionals have considered ways for children to cope with these hospital stresses and have developed a rationale for the implementation of various programs of intervention. Unfortunately, hospitals create an environment that is often not conducive to the free expression of children's feelings (Linn, 1978). If a child assumes that his or her illness and confinement in the hospital is the result of his or her own presumed negative behavior, he or she may be reluctant to act out negative and angry feelings for fear of further inflictions or retributions. The child needs an opportunity to ventilate feelings and gain clearer understanding. Yet he or she is inhibited by the hospital's focus on routine in addition to the power of the health professionals who can inflict more pain. In such a strange environment it may be difficult to trust a strange adult enough to express a secret thought or bottled-up feeling. This problem is further exacerbated by the child's brief contact with hospital staff; it thus becomes difficult for the child to unfold at a slow pace, to develop an awareness of feelings, a willingness to express them, and a trusting relationship through which to express them.

Hospitalization creates a situation in which many new experiences and a large body of information must be rapidly assimilated by the child. Most children require more time to comprehend what is happening to them than the few hours it takes to go through the admitting process. To gain a good understanding, a child may need to approach questions one at a time in a piecemeal fashion (Tisza et al., 1970). Children benefit most if they are able to utilize all of their senses when trying to understand equipment that will be used, rooms they will be in, how meals are served, how to use the bathrooms, and details of the medical procedures. Physical contact with medical instruments such as stethoscopes, tongue blades, and syringes can speed the child's processes of assimilation and help to answer their emotion-laden questions (Chan, 1980).

Attempting to cope with the stress of hospitalization through the use of denial has been shown to be less effective than confronting the feared stimulus and arousing a small amount of anxiety (Burstein & Meichenbaum, 1979, Clatworthy, 1981; Jolly, 1968). Burstein & Meichenbaum call this the "work of worrying." In their investigation they hypothesize that if a child chooses to play with toys symbolically loaded for medical content, thoughts and fantasies about forthcoming hospital procedures will be stimulated. By experiencing these thoughts and images, the child is able to develop a more differentiated view of the feared stimuli and create self-assurance mechanisms for coping with the stresses the stimuli invoke. Defensive retreat from the feared stimuli delays recovery from the anxieties these stimuli invoke. Social isolation further exacerbates the defensive posture, preventing adaptation (Adams, 1976). The safety of the playroom allows for active confrontation of the feared fantasies through exploration and manipulation of medical instruments and materials, by role playing medical procedures, and by sharing concerns with other children. Thus, coping strategies can be developed in an incremental fashion.

One of the primary features of the play therapy approach is its emphasis on the development of trust. This is accomplished through the formation of the therapeutic relationship. In other contexts, the development of a trusting relationship may be a primary therapeutic goal, whereas for hospitalized children it is also the means by which other therapeutic goals are met, such as increased expression or the willingness to participate in preparatory enactments. In individual play therapy the adult–child relationship is emphasized. In group play therapy both the adult–child and the child–child relationships are emphasized. Both types of relationship are important for the child's healthy adjustment to hospitalization. The development of these relationships can help when comfort and reassurance is needed. They can also help remove roadblocks to expression, generate further understanding, enhance the feelings of normalcy, and build self-esteem as ego boundaries become more established.

To encourage consonance with previous experience, it is desirable for hospitals to help create an environment that in some way approximates the home environment. Homey furniture, familiar toys, available living spaces, and permission to play as the child might at home helps to create a normalized environment. A messy playroom filled with familiar toys and the lifting of restrictions that may apply in other parts of the hospital can help the child attain a sense of well-being (Harvey, 1980). The playroom also provides a somewhat more natural setting in which to observe children, thus helping physicians to more accurately estimate illness and recovery (Azarnoff & Flegal, 1975). The playroom itself emphasizes health through activity, freedom of choice, mobility, and space. It allows patients to change from a passive sufferer to an active agent in their own medical care (Tisza et al., 1970). It is well recognized that play is of a fundamental importance to normal growth and development from infancy on (Axline, 1947; Bruner et al., 1976; Erikson, 1950; Freud, 1965; Harvey, 1980; Noble, 1967). Virtually all areas of development seem to be influenced by play: social, fine motor, cognitive/symbolic, gross motor, and emotional. Through play the child learns to master his or her environment, to learn how to cope with daily stresses and strains, and to form relationships with other children. A large body of experimental research points to the detrimental effects of disruption and restriction of play activities during the early developmental years (Harlow & Harlow, 1962; Suomi & Harlow, 1971). The activities of the playroom can help bring about the sense of normalcy for the child (Chan, 1980), fortifying and keeping intact the basic schemata of his or her identity.

Thus, the development of play programs in hospitals has a great many benefits. Foremost, these programs assist in providing better health care to the children (Azarnoff et al., 1975). Anxieties associated with illness and hospitalization may be reduced or at least kept from increasing (Clatworthy, 1980; Cassell, 1965). As psychological health improves, physical recovery becomes more rapid. Children are more cooperative, and thus examinations are quicker, and medical procedures can be carried out more smoothly. There is a greater willingness to return among those children who may need future hospital treatments (Cassell, 1965). Play programs also have the potential for assisting families. Parents are comforted with the knowledge that the emotional needs of their children are being met. Staff members can assist parents with their own anxieties and can help them develop adult–child interactional skills. These skills become particularly useful after the child's return home when the parent may have to help him or her resolve emotional conflicts through play.

TECHNICAL CONSIDERATIONS AND METHODS

Setting up Play Programs

Staffing.   Commitment to a play program in the hospital requires hiring trained staff to run it. The practice of having nurses provide this service to the children in their spare time is not adequate, as when workloads increase, it is the play activities that suffer (Azarnoff et al., 1975). Also, the use of women's auxiliaries or other volunteer organizations does not sufficiently provide for the full-time staffing needs of the playroom (Goldman et al., 1978; Leffman & Murton, 1977). Consistency and constancy of staff is important in the development of trusting relationships—the backbone of a successful play program. Playroom staff should be relieved from other duties and not called away from the playroom. The job of playroom director must be viewed as a full-time job. Uncertainty as to the presence of playroom staff may actually exacerbate problems of separation as it indicates to the child that even the most trustworthy person in the hospital may not be there when needed. This may be worse than not having a chance to develop that expectation in the first place. Jolly (1968) has cautioned, however, that hospial administrators be careful not to assign only medical procedure duties to the rest of the ward staff. This, he states, creates a system in which some staff may be viewed by the child as "nice" while others will be viewed as "mean." This is not only unrealistic for the child, but also quite difficult on the morale of the staff. He suggests that all staff spend time in the playroom and involve themselves in play activities. The need for a play intervention can occur at any time of the day or night; since the play therapist is not available at all hours other staff need to serve as back-ups.

Play is the type of specialty that can be claimed by no single discipline and the broad, multidisciplinary interest and involvement in this topic make it unique. A hospital play therapist may receive training from a number of different disciplines, for example, psychology, social work, child development, education, occupational therapy, recreational therapy, nursing, pediatrics, sociology, and counseling. No matter what the field, the individual needs a good background in child development. Standards for the training of the Child Life Specialist includes:

academic preparation at the bachelor's degree level with supervised experience in the health care setting and competence in the following areas: growth and development, family dynamics, play and activities, interpersonal communication, developmental observations and assessment, the learning process, group process, behavior management, the reactions of children to hospitalization and to illness, interventions to prevent emotional trauma, collaboration with other health care professionals, basic understanding of children's illness and medical terminology, and supervisory skills. (ACCH, 1979)

The Playroom.   On hospital wards, the playroom needs to be accessible. If children have independent mobility, they ought to be able to get out of their beds in the morning and proceed to the playroom on their own (Harvey, 1980). The playroom need not be a sanctuary that isolates the child from the hospital. It is not the purpose of the playroom to shield the child from the hospital, rather it is to help him or her cope with the hospital (Jolly, 1978). However, if the safety of the playroom is lost by using it for threatening, painful, or embarrassing procedures, its therapeutic usefulness may be compromised. For the playroom activities to be most beneficial, anxieties should be aroused to a high enough level to activate an adjustment and healing process but at a low enough level to be manageable. Some hospitals may be unable to provide a separate room for play and in this case a section of another room may be used. Another concept that has been developed is that of the play cart (Azarnoff et al., 1975). This is used in two ways: One in which the cart is used for the storage of toys only and the other in which the cart becomes a piece of play equipment itself. In the former, it would be used to convert to a playroom an existing room that is regularly used for some other purpose. In this case, the cart needs to be designed for maximum use of space, storage, and easy accessibility. In the second case, mobility is a primary function as the cart will be taken from room to room in the hospital and used at the bedside. The cart may be built so that it converts into a table and easel. Sometimes by necessity the playroom will have to be locked. Hours should, therefore, be carefully explained to the children, the parents, and the ward staff. The room may also be used at times for free play and at other times for directed play with specific children. Again, this would need to be carefully posted so that a child wouldn't feel excluded.

Careful consideration need always be given to the toys that are used in the playroom. Even in the most unstructured form of play therapy, the toys themselves dictate the nature and scope of the play. Both structured and unstructured toys need to be available as they would be in most playrooms (Leland & Smith, 1965). Emphasis should be given in this special playroom to the inclusion of various pieces of hospital equipment. This might include such things as: syringes, stethoscopes, a play examination table, white coats, and masks. Puppets will also be important in this playroom as there may be times when specific medical procedures need to be demonstrated to the child. This may best be accomplished with the use of puppets. Puppet play is also useful for social dramatic play. It promotes the use of language by creating a distance between the play activities and events of the real world. By remaining in the "microcosm" (the world of fantasy and small toys), disruptions of play produced by intrusion of material from the "macrocosm" (the world of big people), is held at a minimum (Erikson, 1950). The puppets also offer an outlet, otherwise not available, for boys who may think that play with dolls is for girls only.

Whereas the primary emphasis of this chapter is on play therapy within the inpatient hospital, some consideration should be given to the outpatient program. In this setting, the primary time available for play intervention is while the child is waiting to see the health professional. Anxieties may also be highest in the waiting room as the child experiences exaggerated and horrifying expectations. Zilliacus and Enberg (1980) have suggested that waiting rooms be sectioned off in such a manner as to provide an area suitable for play with toys readily accessible in storage cabinets. Establishment of this type of playroom not only humanizes what is generally a rather austere environment, but also helps reduce some of the tensions that are created by long periods of waiting. Leffman et al. (1977) discuss the use of a separate playroom in the outpatient unit. The playroom has a full-time therapist and children come and play before their own appointments, when their parents have appointments, or when a brother or sister has an appointment. Intercoms are set up between the regular waiting room and the playroom so that the playroom staff know where the parents are at all times.

Use of the Playroom.   Children have questions and anxieties from the moment they enter the hospital until the moment they leave, and play therapy is appropriate and useful for them at any time. Admission anxieties can be reduced immediately if the child sees the hospital environment is not so foreign and contains elements of the world that was left behind. The recognizable toys of the playroom and the familiar patterns of interacting with other children can have an immediate effect in slowing, stopping, or rapidly reducing increasing tensions. Following an intrusive medical procedure, such as surgery, children may have anxieties, including concern about the disfigurement of their bodies and their ability to return to the prehospital type of normal play. Play then becomes important in reaffirming normalcy to the child. Although this may be accomplished over time without specific intervention efforts, a more rapid resolution will allow the child to suffer less and have a better overall hospital experience.

There are two distinct approaches on the matter of when children should use the playroom. One approach allows for the playroom to be available to the children during all hours of the day (Jolly, 1978). The other approach is for there to be specifically designated times for the children to be involved in play therapy sessions. Clatworthy (1981), in choosing the latter approach, conducted 30-minute sessions with individual children on a daily basis. Several rationales have been proposed for the open playroom approach. First, there is the argument that free play is a normal part of development and, therefore, play opportunities need to be readily available throughout the day, otherwise a disruption of the developmental process may result. Restricting the use of a playroom in this case would be seen as restricting normal developmental activity. Second, play activities are assumed to be less anxiety provoking than lying in bed and, therefore, provide a better use of time for the child throughout the day in the hospital. Third, based on the assumption that a child needs immediate attention at the arousal of acute anxiety, the playroom will need to be available at any time. Fourth, more children get greater use of the playroom if it is always available.

By contrast, there are also rationales for the use of a playroom in a structured and time-restricted manner. Sometimes a play therapist will have a specifically organized set of activities that he or she wishes to conduct with a child, such as preparing the child for surgery. In this case the therapist may want to set limits and have a child pay close attention to what the therapist does or says. Other children in the playroom with different concerns and the freedom of the children to come and go as they please may be too disruptive. With only one play therapist in the playroom, the number of children allowed in may have to be limited. The size of the room and the number and kinds of toys will certainly present limitations. The use of the playroom for children of different ages may also present some scheduling problems, such that young children might use the playroom in the morning and adolescents might use the playroom in the afternoon (Goldman et al., 1978). Some hospitals try to compromise by having certain times each day designated for closed sessions and certain times designated for open sessions. Others try to equip a large playroom with enough toys and additional staff so that both types of activities can occur simultaneously. Still other hospitals use two separate rooms.

Play Intervention Strategies

Group Play versus Individual Play. The decision to conduct group play or individual play rests on several variables. Clatworthy (1981) points out that the development of an adult relationship is of primary importance for the young child experiencing separation anxieties. Her study has shown that these young children do not play unless the adult relationship is established. Although this may not preclude contact with other children, it might necessitate closer adult–child contact. Individual play therapy may have increased value for a child who has had emotional difficulties before coming to the hospital and/or for a child who faces a long hospitalization. Children who are chronically ill or have terminal and progressive illnesses may also profit from an individual approach. Apart from considerations regarding the establishment of the adult–child relationship are issues of the uniqueness of the child's problems, the need of the child to have individual attention for the development of a trust relationship that helps him or her venture into symbolic exploration of anxieties, and the necessity for structuring various specific procedures. The intensity of the hospital experience is greater for children facing extended hospitalization than for children undergoing the average five-to-seven-day visit. Thus, the intervention tends to be more intense. Both individual and group play therapy that incorporates interaction with other children will be important. For the school-age child, these interactions may be even more important than interaction with adults. Interaction with children who have already gone through a medical procedure can be of great assistance to a child who is facing the same experience.

Play Intervention Based on the Age of a Child. Children aged two to four are most susceptible to anxiety as a result of hospitalization (Adams, 1976). Because of their level of development, they lack the cognitive sophistication to understand their illness and resultant hospitalization as well as the social maturity required for separation. The lack of experiences and the need for security make it difficult to accommodate the new situation of the hospital. Even when presented with play material, they may refuse to play (Tisza et al., 1970). They may regress to the degree that they are unable to play until the love object relationship can be replaced and the threat to their egos removed. These children may cling to their mothers and cry in panic when they leave. It may become very difficult to assess the child's level of play under these cir- cumstances, as it may not only regress with regard to developmental level, but also the breadth of play may suffer. A child may be found in the playroom occupying one distinct location, and, if engaged in object play, it may be rudimentary or even self-stimulating (repetitious manipulation without any apparent exploration). The child may be quite tentative about approaching an adult or other children.

Having the parents in the playroom during admission helps in the transi- tion. However, eventually, the parent has to leave and gentle firmness may be required to help the child until the beginning of the parent's next visit. Usually it takes several trials of going and coming for a child to realize that the parents will in fact return. Meanwhile, the transitional attachment to another adult assists the child in using play to work out fear, anger, sadness, and confusion. Usually by the third day of hospitalization, and often by the second, the child will engage in more open displays of affect, and regressions will diminish. This will occur given the efforts of a therapist to establish a relationship with a child.

Children aged four to seven, while not suffering the separation anxieties of the younger children, worry about mutilation to their bodies (Adams, 1976). Socially, they are more active with other children, yet they maintain a preoc- cupation with adults. Authority issues become pronounced as these children try to take a measure of control over their lives. They may continually test limits. Cognitive development may still not be sufficient for them to under- stand the need for medical procedures. No longer being burdened with the overwhelming anxiety of separation, they may experience a great deal of anger at perceived injustices and the assaults against their bodies. This anger may be withheld by children who think that expression of these feelings will increase the length of their hospitalization or cause them to get more injections. Other children who do not feel this limitation may become very active, giving the dolls innumerable shots or acting out malicious surgical acts. This type of expression is useful, yet the play therapist should explain that, in reality, these things would not happen and that there are good reasons for the various medical procedures. Of course, if toys begin to be broken or other children or the play director are attacked through a total lack of impulse control, limits must be imposed.

The child eight-years-old to puberty is concerned about mastery in peer relationships. For medical problems that are chronic or terminal, these chil- dren may have to try to understand death. Unlike younger children, these children can begin to grasp the reasons for their hospitalizations. They may become involved in the use of hospital jargon when trying to explain what has been done to them or what is going to happen. Other children describing their own experiences will greatly help to put these children at ease. With much better impulse control, they will be more involved with table activities, general conversation, and role plays. They may be interested in what is happening with their friends at school, and a visit from a school friend can be very significant. Because of their need to know detailed explanations of the disease process and medical procedures, a partial explanation may prove to be very frustrating. The seemingly more adult way of acting can disguise a continuing need for nurturance, which will be welcomed if it is given along socially acceptable lines.

Structured versus Nonstructured Play.   Perhaps one of the most controversial aspects of the play therapy approach is the degree to which therapy sessions should be structured. In nonstructured approaches, the therapist uses skills such as tracking, describing, and/or reflecting. It is thought to be effective therapeutically based on the following hypothesis: Play is the natural medium the child uses to work through conflicts; extreme anxiety inhibits play; helping a child play assists him in reducing inner stress (Axline, 1947). The use of themes, metaphors, and interpretations gives more direction to this approach and is thought to help the child make cognitive connections that assist conflict resolution.

Directed or structured play therapy often tends to be based on a learning/ behavioral model of development. The therapist may attempt to help a child understand new material by teaching new meanings or he or she may attempt to change the behavior of the child as it is exhibited during the play therapy sessions. It is assumed that new learning and behavioral changes are generalized to non-playroom situations. Symbolic use of play may not be stressed as much as the process of play (Golden, 1978).

Deciding on an approach depends on the therapeutic goals. A distinction might be made for intervention with children who are preoperative and postoperative (Welch, 1977). Goals for preoperative children often include preparation for the impending surgery. Because very specific information is to be conveyed, a structured teaching approach might be favored. On the other hand, postoperative goals may involve allowing the child an opportunity to ventilate and regain a sense of mastery. In this case, the nonstructured approach may be most helpful. Hospitalized children who lose impulse control may need a structured approach to help them regain control; children who use defenses of denial and rigidity to deal with hospital anxieties may need to be encouraged within a nonstructured play environment.

Clatworthy (1981) states that children who are in a relatively sound state of physical and mental health are more likely to engage eagerly in play, whereas children who are in a period of conflict with their emotional and coping responses require more direction from the therapist. If a child does not immediately begin playing upon entering the play room, the play therapist should not conclude that the child needs direction out of a supposedly "withdrawn" state. One needs to distinguish carefully between stresses the child may experience as emanating from the playroom (and the play therapist) and those stresses the child brings into the playroom from external sources. A period of quiet in which questions are not asked and directives are not given may be equally appropriate for the child who doesn't play. For young children, anxiety levels may be so high that this period of quiet may have no effect, thus necessitating a more structured intervention. Because of the varying needs of hospitalized children, hospital play therapists need to be well-versed in both forms of intervention.

No play program can be free from the imposition of limits. Even if the approach primarily uses catharsis, limits become necessary in defining the boundaries of expression. When a child understands these limits, he or she no longer has to unnecessarily restrict expression out of a fear of retaliation. When the consequences are clear and certain to be enforced, the child can stop testing. The three major groups of behavior that need to be limited are (1) physically hurting others, (2) physically hurting oneself, and (3) destroying property. Energy directed into any of these behaviors in the hospital needs to be redirected toward some other object such as a punching bag, drawing images of the hated person, toy trucks that can be crashed, or toy block structures that can be pushed over. Other methods include pounding pillows or acting out anger with the use of puppets or dolls. Other behaviors in the playroom that may require limitation include excessive noise making or excessive messiness with such items as paint, sand, and water. It may be difficult to establish a clear threshold on noise and, thus, many therapists do not attempt to. Messiness lends itself more easily to the establishment of boundaries; however, this may depend on individual therapeutic needs For example, an obsessive-compulsive child may need less external structure, whereas the oppositional or hyperactive child may need more external structure. When using an open playroom or conducting group play therapy, different sets of limits based on individual differences will have to give way to compromise and consistency (and sometimes conservatism).

Dealing with the special problems of children in hospitals

SEPARATION. As has been previously discussed, separation is one of the most difficult problems for the young, hospitalized child. Play intervention in this area can be highly beneficial in reducing the negative impact of hospitalization. Several factors contribute to a healthy adjustment for the child. One of the most important factors is the relationship that the child develops with the play therapist. The therapist needs to be flexible in developing different kinds of relationships with different children. Some of these relationships may be calm whereas others may be active, but they all need to be nurturant (Jernberg, 1979). In nurturant relationships there may be considerable touching, cuddling, rubbing, and reinforcing. The therapist's behavior should not be directed at getting the child to "do" anything. The therapist communicates caring through physical contact, eye contact, proximity, laughter, and soft tones. This is done in a nonintrusive manner through the use of following, describing, and imitating. Other relationships may be more active and include wrestling (thumb, arm, leg, full body), lifting the child, rolling and playing together in finger paints or water. Giving and receiving massages can also be used.

The development of this nurturant relationship is seen as transitional in the same sense that an object from home might be transitional. The relationship helps the child in the transition between the parents' departure and their return. It also helps keep the child from repressing and denying feelings of attachment. When denial does occur, especially after a long period of hospitalization, it can be difficult for the child to reestablish intimacy with a parent or any other adult (Robertson, 1958). The child might appear to be more content at this stage, but the stage of protest is preferable as its resolution is more quickly achieved.

If parents can be involved during the formation of this relationship, it helps the child who might have loyalty issues. In this case it is important for the therapist to encourage the parents to support the therapist–child relationship in front of the child. In general, it is important for parents to be able to spend time on the wards with their children. If some of this time can be spent in play with the play therapist, it can be mutually beneficial to the parent and the child. Because of the young child's poor concept of time, the return of the parent may be difficult to anticipate. It is often useful to relate the parent's return to a specific event such as a television show or a meal (Kunzman, 1972).

AUTONOMY AND MASTERY.   The practice of modern medicine, particularly in hospitals, casts the patient into the role of the passive recipient of an active treatment which is formulated and carried out by the often nameless (and faceless) health professionals. While there has been quiet criticism of this approach over the years, the protests have recently become louder. Norman Cousins poignantly brought this issue to the attention of the medical world with "Anatomy of an Illness," which was published in the *New England Journal of Medicine.* He was one of the first non–health professionals to write an article for this journal. This piece and many subsequent books and articles attest to the debilitating effects on an individual when he or she feels a loss of control while in the hospital. Children suffer the same indignities and the play therapist can help the child restore a sense of mastery through play therapy.

The goal of the play therapist is to help the child become involved in his or her own treatment (even if only in some small way) and to help the child retain a sense of competence. The first goal can be carried out by giving the child a choice with regard to hospital treatment. He should have a selection of the type of food he eats and when he can get out of bed. When receiving an injection, he might be given a choice by the nurse as to a preferred location.

Just taking the effort to inform the child about his treatment, within the limits imposed by his or her ability to understand, involves the child. Helping a child to feel competent can be done within play. The child can be encouraged to demonstrate skills in many ways. Creative skill can be shown through drawings, paintings, modeling with clay, paper folding or cutting, or writing. Stacking blocks, building houses or forts, pounding wood, stringing beads, assembling puzzles, and pasting can all help the child demonstrate construction skills. In fact, almost any type of play other than ventilation of feelings can be used to help a child experience his strengths. Whenever it is at all possible, the child should be encouraged to do things on his or her own. If he or she is confined to bed, activities can be brought in which can be done while lying down. Even sports activities can be carried out in bed with a little inventiveness. Azarnoff et al. (1975) gives the example of a boy playing basketball in bed by using a sponge ball with an attached cord and a hoop made out of a coat hanger. The first step in making a child an active agent in his or her own health care lies in getting him or her to be active. Activity itself and subsequent involvement in the medical process can help the child achieve autonomy and mastery while in the hospital.

MEDICAL INFORMATION AND MEDICAL PROCEDURES. Regardless of age, most children profit from some type of pre-exposure to medical equipment before it is used on them. Much of this equipment can be brought into the playroom and demonstrated, whereas other equipment, such as the x-ray machine or the casting tools might best be demonstrated in another room. The depth of understanding with regard to the purpose of the procedures will vary with the age of the child. For older children, greater knowledge of medical information can give them a sense of mastery, and efforts should be made to answer all of their questions. This understanding, however, may be secondary to dispelling false fantasies. Children may think that the electrodes of an EKG machine puncture the skin or that it will slow down, speed up, or stop the heart. The EEG machine may be thought to have mind-reading abilities. The cast cutter is typically thought to be able to cut into the skin, like a saw, and thus raises fears that a limb will be cut off. Venipuncture may raise fears that the blood will be drained out of the body. X-rays may be thought to burn. Whether the child raises these fears or not, it is useful to anticipate and dispel them by clearly showing and explaining the limits of commonly feared procedures. Performing the procedures on a large doll is useful as this enactment can then be repeated by the child on his own. The sensitive physician often becomes involved in these role plays and demonstrations, thus becoming less mysterious and ominous. Demonstrations can be carried out in the playroom even if the equipment is not going to be used on all the children who are there. Children sometimes become very frightened because of a procedure that is to be done on someone else. Attempting to trick a child through deceit or surprise is rarely successful. Medical personnel may do this as much to allay their own fears as to help the child. As has been previously discussed, a small measure of anxiety is helpful for the child in developing coping skills. The surprise method has the disadvantage of undermining trust, and warns the child to guard against future surprises. In a trusting atmosphere, reassurance and nurturance go a long way in helping a child.

SURGERY.   Although the data base in this field is small, the bulk of research pertains to specific surgical interventions, such as cardiac catheterizations, tonsillectomies, and appendectomies (Burstein & Meichenbaum, 1979; Cassel, 1965; Chan, 1980, Linn, 1978; Schulz et al., 1981). Most of this research has been directed at the measurement of the effectiveness of a play intervention in reducing or preventing an increase in presurgical and postsurgical anxiety. The research findings support the effectiveness of these methods. Chan (1980) discusses how impending surgery can raise a great many questions and conflicts for the child. As has been previously discussed, these may involve feelings that a body part is going to be cut off or that the body will be mutilated. Chan stresses the importance of working through issues one at a time and states that the child may never be "fully" prepared. There are common misconceptions about anesthesia. Some children think that they are going to be put to sleep and never wake up. Kunzman (1972) discusses a young boy who was not afraid of being put to sleep but was afraid of waking up when the surgeon cut him with a knife. He reasoned that if he were cut with a knife while he was sleeping at home he would most certainly wake up. Children with these types of misconceptions need to be helped in understanding the difference between natural sleep and "sleep" induced by anesthesia.

Cassel (1965) uses a method of puppet play that begins with the therapist playing the role of the doctor and later reverses roles so that the child can play the health professional. It is done in this way so that the adult can first give a full disclosure to the child of the upcoming events. In reversing the roles, the therapist gives the child a chance to assimilate this information and then accommodate it, both cognitively and emotionally, by acting it out. Linn (1978) makes a point of not allowing children to act out a surgical event spontaneously with the puppet unless they can give a reason(s) for why the surgery is being done. Through enforcement of this rule, she helps clarify the children's misconceptions about surgery, giving them the message that a surgical insult to the body is done for a good reason.

INJECTIONS.   Chan (1980) and Linn (1978) state that injections are one of the most common themes in the play of the children with whom they work. Dramas are often repeated with shots being given to puppets, dolls, the therapist, and other children. Linn discusses that, in most cases, the children with whom she works want the receiver of the shot to cry and, if this does not occur, the children remind her to "make the puppet cry." Needles are often frightening to children and, again, the purpose of receiving a shot may not be understood by the child. Chan (1980) cites examples of children telling a doll that he needs hundreds of shots because he hit his sister and is bad, or that the syringes contain poison, or that doctors drink the blood after it is taken. Tolerating the pain of an injection is made more difficult by these distortions or by thinking that it has no reason. It becomes important for the play director to (1) help children understand (at their level) the reasons they are receiving an injection, and (2) open an avenue of expression for the children so that they might ventilate about this seemingly brutal act.

CHRONIC DISABILITY.   Children who are chronically disabled and repeatedly return to the hospital present additional concerns for the play therapist. They may suffer feelings of inferiority, insecurity, feeling excluded, and lack of motivation. In working with these children, effort must be made to keep them active and involved. Although they have to recognize and accept their differences, these differences should be kept in perspective. Emphasis should be placed on the whole child so that they don't become preoccupied with their medical problems. To the degree possible, these children should participate in the normal playroom activities. They will be encouraged to demonstrate their competencies, such that they can be recognized by other children and staff. Group play therapy is often the treatment of choice after these children are four to five years old, so as to prevent them from becoming socially isolated and to force them to learn social skills at an early age. These children may exhibit considerable anger and frustration with their physical limitations and may need to be helped to develop ways of expressing these feelings in socially acceptable ways.

Whereas hospitalization is known to cause difficulties for children, some children react so severely that a more vigorous intervention is required. More typically it is children who are hospitalized for over a week who are at risk. Hospital staff usually become aware of these children through their severe withdrawn behavior, infantile regressions, loss of cognitive skills, excessive somatization, and emotional lability. Although the specific behavioral changes may be the same as in other children, the degree is heightened and they do not respond to regular interventions. In these cases, it may be useful to consult with outside professionals.

PARENTAL INVOLVEMENT.   The need for parental involvement in the hospitalization of young children has been acknowledged for many years. Many hospitals do try to permit parent visitation during most hours of the day. Perhaps it was both the active and passive protests of these children that helped the professionals realize the potential danger in unprepared and extended separations. In spite of this, it is still with some reluctance that hospitals permit the involvement (in contrast to visitation) of families in the health care of patients at all age levels. Parent involvement not only helps to ease anxiety in the children, but also in the parents themselves.

The play program in the hospital also offers an excellent opportunity for parents to expand their knowledge and develop skills in new areas. Most noticeably absent in our public educational process are classes on parenting and child development. Hospitalization provides an opportunity for parents to learn about normal growth and development, children's response to hospitalization (Goldman et al., 1978), and some positive parenting or child-directed play skills. It occurs at a time when their motivation is high and the need for child-oriented play skills will be even greater than usual. With an open door policy in the playroom, parents can be taught basic attending skills, use of eye and body contact, verbal description and reflection, imitation and praise. In carrying out these interactional skills, the relationship can become "anchored," providing for children's exploration into new areas and increasing he parents' ability to set limits. Through modeling and verbal description, the play director can teach the parents the procedures that are being used in the playroom with the children. In this relaxed and nonthreatening atmosphere, parents can practice new skills which they can carry on with their children after discharge. Through this type of involvement with parents, play treatment is not only effective at addressing the problems at hand, but also encourages the learning of preventive skills by the parents.

SUMMARY AND CONCLUSION

The vast literature on the effects of illness and hospitalization on children make it increasingly clear that there is a considerable potential for emotional damage to children. Separation anxieties, loss of control, and misconceptions about pain and illness all combine to produce difficulties in their adjustment. Play, as the natural medium of expression and conflict resolution in children, can become the pathway to a healthy adjustment. Play activities can help children pace themselves by confronting anxieties one by one so they don't become overwhelming. The play therapist helps children develop trust so they can more successfully deal with the inhibiting factors of the hospital in the more familiar climate of play. Consideration must be given to a number of issues when setting up play programs, including staffing, the playroom, and its use. The play therapy approach must vary according to such factors as the age of the child, the specific illness, the length of the hospital stay, previous hospital experience, the chronicity of the illness, the temperament of the child, the child's current and past relationship to the parents, and the specific medical procedures.

Although the research is limited, it consistently shows lower levels of anxiety in the experimental group (those receiving play intervention). Therapy outcome research is difficult and the area of hospital play is no exception. Nevertheless, a broader experimental base addressing specific forms of play intervention is needed. In spite of these research limitations, the experiences of professionals working in the field make it overwhelmingly clear that play intervention must be a regular part of the pediatric hospital program.

REFERENCES

Adams, M. (1976) A hospital play program: Helping children with serious illness. *American Journal of Orthopsychiatry,* **46**(3), 416–424.

Ainsworth, M. (1966) The development of infant-mother attachment. In B. Caldwell and H. Riccuiti (Eds.), *Review of child development Research.* Chicago: University of Chicago Press.

Association for the Care of Children's Health. (1979) Child Life Activity Study Section Position Paper.

Axline, V. (1947) *Play therapy.* New York: Ballantine.

Azarnoff, P. (1974) Mediating the trauma of serious illness and hospitalization in childhood. *Children Today,* **3**(4), 12–17.

Azarnoff, P., & Flegal, S. (1975) *A pediatric play program: Developing a therapeutic play program for children in medical settings.* Springfield: Charles C. Thomas.

Barton, P. H. (1962) Play as a tool of nursing. *Nursing Outlook,* **10**(3), 162–164.

Bibace, R., & Walsh, M. E. (1980) Development of children's concept of illness. *Pediatrics,* **66**(6), 912–917.

Billington, G. F. (1972) Play program reduces children's anxiety, speeds recoveries. *Modern Hospital,* **118**(4), 90–92.

Bowlby, J. (1960) Separation anxiety. *Journal of Child Psychology and Psychiatry,* **1**, 251–269.

Brooks, M. (1970) Why play in the hospital? *Nursing Clinics of North America,* **5**(3), 431–441.

Bruner, J. S., Jolly, A., & Sylva, K. (Eds.). (1976) *Play—Its role in development and evolution.* New York: Basic Books.

Burr, S. (1977) Play for children in hospital. *Nursing Times,* **73**(10), 5–6 (ABPN Supp.).

Burstein, S., & Meichenbaum, D. (1979) The work of worrying in children undergoing surgery. *Journal of Abnormal Child Psychology,* **7**, 127–132.

Cassell, S. (1965) Effect of brief puppet therapy upon the emotional responses of children undergoing cardiac catheterization. *Journal of Consulting Psychology,* **29**(1), 1–8.

Chan, J. M. (1980) Preparation for procedures and surgery through play. *Paediatrician,* **9**, 210–219.

Clatworthy, S. (1981) Therapeutic play: Effects on hospitalized children. *Journal of the Association for the Care of Children's Health,* **9**(4), 10–113.

Cousins, N. (1976) Anatomy of an illness (as perceived by the patient). *New England Journal of Medicine,* **295**(26), 1458–1463.

Digby, M. (1975) The hospital play therapist. *Child: Care, Health and Development,* **1** (4), 233–237.

Erikson, E. (1950) *Childhood and society.* New York: Norton.

Freud, A. (1952) The role of bodily illness in the mental life of children. In R. S. Eissler, A. Freud, H. Hartmann, & E. Kris (Eds.), *The Psychoanalytic Study of the Child,* Vol. VII. New York: International Universities Press. Pp. 69–81.

Freud, A. (1965) *Normality and pathology in childhood.* New York: International University Press.

Ginott, H. (1961) *Group psychotherapy with children.* New York: McGraw-Hill

Golden, D. B. (1978) A comparison of the Leland-Smith play therapy approach with other therapeutic modalities. Presented at the Annual Meeting of the American Association on Mental Deficiency.

Goldman, M., Sponseller, D., & Ream, B. (1978) A play program in a community hospital. *American Journal of Maternal Child Nursing,* **3**(1), 42–45.

Harlow, H. F., & Harlow, M. K. (1962) Social deprivation in monkeys. *Scientific American,* **207**, 137–146.

Harvey, S. (1980) The value of play therapy in hospital. *Paediatrician,* **9**, 191–197.

Jernberg, A. M. (1979) *Theraplay.* San Francisco: Jossey-Bass.

Jolly, H. (1968) Play and the sick child. *Lancet,* **2**, 1286–1287.

Jolly, H. (1969) Play is work: The role of play for sick and healthy children. *Lancet,* **2**, 487–488.

Jolly, H. (1978) The work of the play specialists in Charing Cross Hospital, London. *Journal of the Association for the Care of Children's Health,* **6**(2), 4–10.

Katz, E. R., Kellerman, J., & Siegel, S.E. (1980) Behavioral distress in children with cancer undergoing medical procedures: Developmental considerations. *Journal of Consulting and Clinical Psychology,* **48**(3), 356–365.

Kunzman, L. (1972) Some factors influencing a young child's mastery of hospitalization. *Nursing Clinics of North America,* **7**(1), 13–26.

Landsman, E. (1972) The function of a play program in pediatrics. *Pediatric Annals,* **1**(3), 64–69.

Leffman, J., and Murton, J. (1977) The children's waiting room at Charing Cross Hospital. *Child: Care, Health and Development,* **3**, 241–245.

Leland, H., & Smith, D. E. (1965) *Play therapy with mentally subnormal children.* New York: Grune and Stratton.

Linn, S. (1978) Puppet therapy in hospitals: Helping children cope. *Journal of the American Medical Women's Association,* **33**(2), 61–65.

McDonnell, L. (1979) Paraverbal therapy in pediatric cases with emotional complications. *American Journal of Orthopsychiatry,* **49**(1), 44–52.

Narwold, S. (1975) Coping with hospitalization through play. *Journal of Physical Education and Recreation,* **46**(5), 35.

Noble, E. (1967) *Play and the sick child.* London: Faber & Faber.

Prugh, D. G., Staub, E. M., Sands, H. H., Kirschbaum, R. M., & Lenihan, E. A. (1953) A study of the emotional reactions of children and families to hospitalization and illness. *American Journal of Orthopsychiatry,* **23**, 70–106.

Robertson, J. (1958) *Young children in hospitals.* New York: Basic Books.

Schulz, J. B., Raschke, D., Dedrick, & Thompson M. (1981) The effects of a preoperational puppet show on anxiety levels of hospitalized children. *Journal of the Association for the Care of Children's Health,* **9**(4), 118–121.

Smith, A. M. (1941) *Play for convalescent children in hospitals and at home.* New York: Barnes.

Suomi, S. & Harlow, H. F. (1971) Monkeys without play. In J. S. Bruner, A. Jolly, & K. Sylva (Eds.), *Play—Its role in development and evolution.* New York: Basic Books.

Tisza, V., Hurwitz, I., & Angoff, K. (1970) The use of a play program by hospitalized children. *Journal of the American Academy of Child Psychiatry*, **9**, 515-531.

Welch, C. (1977) The nurse's role in play. Nursing Care, **10**(1), 14-15.

Whitted, B. A., & Scott, R.B. (1962) The significance of a play program in the care of children in a general hospital. *Journal of the National Medical Association*, **54**(4), 488-491.

Zilliacus, K., & Enberg, S. (1980) Play therapy in the pediatric outpatient department. *Paediatrician*, **9**, 224-230.

CHAPTER 12

Art as a Play Therapeutic Medium

EILEEN T. NICKERSON

INTRODUCTION

Art as a therapeutic medium has been particularly important through the ages as an area of expressive and creative activity. From the earliest days art has been used to enrich life. Useful objects were decorated—either for the joy of it or to instill magic in them. Their symbolic representations may have offered a feeling of control over external forces as well as forces of an internal nature, thus serving as a meeting ground for the world outside and the world inside.

These symbolic representations also served, from the earliest times, as a form of communication. One's own personal story, emotions, or the group's history and values were conveyed through graphic efforts. Thus, art represents an emotional and physical outlet which forms a communicative bond between the product and the recipient of that production, whether the recipient be the artist or others.

Art as Therapy

Although art has been used for self-expression and as a means of exploring one's relationship to others since prehistoric times, the use of art expression as a therapeutic modality in and of itself came into its own in the 1940s with the pioneering efforts of Margaret Naumburg. Naumburg (1966), relying heavily upon psychoanalytic theory, encouraged clients to draw spontaneously and to free associate to their pictures. She was followed in the 1950s by Edith Kramer (1971), who worked extensively with children. Kramer emphasized the integrative and healing properties of the creative process which do not require verbalized reflection and insight. More recent developments include the expansion of the use of art therapy into work with children in school settings (Nickerson, 1973a, b, c); as well as in family settings and family therapy (Burns & Kaufman, 1970; Kwiatkowska, 1967).

Thus, art therapy has been broadened from its initial use as an adjunct to psychodynamically oriented insight therapy with neurotic-type conflicts to use

234

with a range of symptomatology from minor to major psychiatric designations, and to those who strive to enhance growth in everyday problems of living (Wadeson, 1980). Similarly, in work with children, art has been increasingly employed as a therapeutic medium (Kramer, 1971; Rubin, 1977); or in combination with other expressive modalities incuding play (Heimlich, 1972; Nickerson, 1973a, b; Nickerson & O'Laughlin, 1978, 1982; Rubin & Shapiro, 1975). Art has also been used in conjunction with play with an increasing range of children, including normal and retarded children (Nickerson, 1973a, b, c; 1980; Roth & Barnett, 1979; Wilson 1977); and in a variety of settings including schools, as previously noted (Nickerson, 1973a, b, c; 1980).

Play as Therapy

Play therapy has evolved along lines paralleling those of art therapy. The field originated in the work of Anna Freud (1946), who employed play as a diagnostic and rapport-building adjunct to the more formal psychoanalysis of children. It has been extended, much as art therapy has, from an adjunct to insight-oriented, talking therapy to use as a principal therapeutic medium in and of itself (Axline, 1969). In this later orientation, children are reputedly provided a safe, permissive, and accepting environment, in which they "play it" rather than "talk it out." Hence, the play itself is felt to hold the key to the curative process.

Play has also been considered as serving a number of educational and therapeutic purposes in a child's life. It is first of all one of the chief and most significant ways in which a child learns. It is the way in which a child tries out activities and social roles and comes to terms with objects and people in his or her environment. Play is also the child's chief medium of communication. It is in a child's play that ideational and fantasy preoccupations are revealed. Play is not only instructive and cathartic in nature, but it is also self-revealing and can obviously be used to better understand a child's concerns and feelings. As Hartley et al. (1952) have indicated, "to read the language of play is to read the hearts and minds of children." In this connection, it is also one of the major avenues for experimentation with and mastery of verbal interpersonal communication. Children in play rehearse and act out what they see and hear, and hence, reveal as well as master themselves and their world.

We should not forget that play is not only cathartic, self-revealing, and instructive in nature, but it is also fun and therefore self-motivating. The very nature of play means *not* taking it "for real" (i.e., too seriously). And, so, though "play" is part of the "serious business" of childhood by which children learn to handle themselves and their environments better, it need not be taken that seriously by them. Hence, children can feel relatively free and spontaneous in play to be themselves, to have fun "trying things out." Thus, usually we do *not* have to "work" at getting a child to "play"—play in and of itself tends to be an inviting means by which we can aid children to realize themselves.

Role of Art as a Play Therapeutic Medium

As noted previously, both art and play have been employed as significant self-expressive therapeutic media for people of varying ages, conditions, and diagnostic status and for varying therapeutic goals and purposes. Rather than exploring the totality of either approach, in this chapter we attempt to delineate the use of art as type of play medium which is particularly suitable for use with children as a beneficial and significant opportunity for their personal self-growth and fulfillment.

Play therapy, as we have seen, provides a child with a natural, easy, and nonthreatening opportunity to reveal fears, hopes, and fantasies through play. Thoughts and feelings which are perplexing and troubling are revealed through play whether representational or symbolic. Art is one form of this kind of symbolic communication which offers an opportunity for therapeutic enactment and resolution.

In this context, art is instant graphic communication directed toward someone or the self as an expression of emotion. Thus, art as one form of play media can help children express themselves more openly and help us understand problems they are unable to talk about. Through art activities the child can reveal concerns more readily and with greater ease than with the usual unraveling process of verbal therapy.

There are a number of similarities between art and play therapy as well as some significant differences. The use of toys in play, for example, involves objects whose functions are largely predetermined, whereas the use of art allows the child to create form and function. These creations may be as varied, imaginative, and personal as the child wishes. No two art productions are the same and each one represents a personal statement.

In summary, the rationale for incorporating art with play as a therapeutic medium includes:

1. Art media facilitates communication with children despite possible barriers of language, culture, repressed experiences, and resistance.
2. Art activities encourage creativity, spontaneity, self-expression, and disclosure.
3. Art productions furnish a catharticlike projective media in which feelings, ideas, and concerns can be projected, explored, and ultimately understood and worked through.
4. Since in art work there is a definitive end product, working in an art medium is an active, creative, intuitive process which allows feelings of mastery and competence to emerge.

APPLICATIONS: METHODS, SETTINGS, MATERIALS

Art as a "play therapeutic medium" offers children an opportunity to communicate through the use of a variety of materials. Children represent through scribbling, drawing, painting or interacting with materials such as clay and finger paints, feelings and concerns that bother them but which they may not fully understand or be able to "talk out" directly with a therapist. And for the emotionally repressed, the nonverbal, multilingual, or retarded child, the art-making process offers a special form of self-expression that may be cathartic, revealing, meaningful, and therapeutically beneficial.

Space, Furnishings, and Materials

The use of the art-making therapeutic process requires sufficient space, furnishings, and materials. Kramer (1972), for example, feels that art therapy should be conducted in a room exclusively reserved for this activity. Wadeson (1980) insists there should be ample space, adequate lighting, suitable art materials, cleanup equipment, and a room with furnishings which don't need to be protected from stains, etc.

Furnishings of the art therapy room include movable tables, chairs, easels, blackboards, as well as closets, racks, and shelves for storing art supplies and finished and unfinished projects, a sink, cleanup area and art supplies. Since not all clients or patients are mobile and can come to a fixed location, a portable art therapy kit should be made up to include easily manipulated materials that require little preparation and cleanup.

Materials

A variety of materials may be used in art therapy (see Table 12.1 for a listing of these materials). As is the case with other elements of the therapeutic transaction, the materials should be selected purposefully and with a sensitivity to the client's needs. In order to make a wise selection, it is necessary to be familiar with what may be evoked by the different materials and what their relative advantages and limitations are. Two of the important considerations in material selection, according to Wadeson (1980), are the dimensions of control and facilitation. Some materials, for example, are easier to control than others—a pencil lends itself to tight control whereas watercolors and clay are more difficult to control.

In reference to the facilitation of therapeutic progress, a variety of colors, adequate sizes of paper or canvas, and similar elements tend to facilitate spontaneity, although an overabundance of materials can be confusing and overwhelming. Frustrating materials such as fragile paper or newsprint should be avoided. Sometimes changing the medium can help an individual who is in a rut. At times, the opportunity to smear with finger paints can help an inhibited

TABLE   12.1
Art Therapy Materials[a]

Paint	Clay	Printing
Tempera	Ball clay	Linoleum
Oil	Plasticine	Silkscreen
Acrylic	Terra-cotta	Batik
Watercolor	Porcelain	Potato
Finger paint	Play dough	Vegetable
Food coloring	Carran D'Ache	Sponge
Enamel	Bread dough	
India ink		

Sculpture	Handwork	Crafts
Plaster	Knitting	Leather
Wax	Crochet	Popsicle sticks
Soap	Macramé	Ceramic tiles
Wood	Appliqué	Models
Wire	Quilting	Plexiglass
Metal	Doll making	Beading
Junk	Needlepoint	

Papers	Utensils	Adhesives and Other
Drawing	Crayon	Elmer's glue
Manila	Pencil	Rubber cement
Construction	Magic markers	Contact cement
Canvas board	Charcoal	Epoxy
Tissue	Ink Pen	
Corrugated	Cray Pas	
Foil	Pastels	
Oak tag	Conte crayon	
Cardboard	Brushes	
Sandpaper	Sponge	Sandbox
Newspaper	Rich art markers	Polaroid camera
Velour	Flair pens	Videotape
Wax	Palette knife	Tape recorder
Paper towels	X-Acto knife	Typewriter

[a]From A. Robbins & L.B. Sibley, *Creative Art Therapy*. New York: Brunner/Mazel, 1976, p. 209.

individual, although initially it might be frightening. Thus, the timing of the use of materials is as important as their nature and use.

Procedural Issues

A variety of therapeutic process choices and issues are involved in the use of art by a play therapist. There is a diversity of possible goals, settings, and structures which depend on the population treated, the needs to be attended to, the setting, and so forth.

In general, after the goals are set, the process and structure are then designed to facilitate them. If, for example, insight-oriented therapy is prescribed, then the art activities are used in an adjunctive fashion to alleviate blocks and impasses in the therapeutic process, to reduce sporadic resistance, to bring forth deeply repressed material. On the other hand, if the objective is to reduce a child's inhibited demeanor and increase the child's creativity and spontaneity, unstructured, projectivelike art material such as finger paints may be the principal format employed in a permissive and accepting but non–insight-oriented framework. If socialization is an objective though, then a group art project (or projects) may be set up and collaboratively decided upon, conducted, and/or discussed. If the goal is to help a child deal with a family crisis, then all family members may be invited to attend the session(s) and to draw pictures related to the crisis.

Theoretical orientation also affects the goals that are set and the role and use of the art activities employed. As noted previously, psychoanalytically oriented therapists such as Anna Freud (1946) and Margaret Naumburg (1966) tend to use play and art in an adjunctive fashion to shed light on the child's unconscious feelings, thoughts, and motivations; they then employ verbal, insight-oriented techniques such as interpretation to insure the overall goal of ego strengthening and integration. On the other hand, client-centered humanistically oriented therapists, such as Axline (1969) and Rubin (1977), believe in the basic curative value of the art and play activities themselves, and, hence, employ fewer verbal interpretations as a means of producing change.

Irrespective of therapeutic goals and theoretical orientation, nearly all play therapists using art agree upon the necessity of certain structural features such as clearly defined space and time dimensions, without which "inner growth does not happen" (Allan, 1978, p. 3). That is, it is usually considered essential to meet with the child at the same time and place each week. And, as noted earlier, ideally, the place should be free from outside distractions and interruptions and should be specially designated as a safe and protected therapeutic environment.

The duration or length of treatment depends on the child's improvement. That is, the child is seen, simply put, until therapy is no longer needed. This is obviously not always possible, due to such factors as geographical moves and premature terminations. Also, in some settings such as a school, the length of the school year usually determines the duration of treatment. The treatment needs to be structured with this knowledge and reality in mind. In all instances, it is considered desirable that the child be informed of the nature and probable duration of the "therapeutic contract," and that the necessary groundwork for termination be laid in the earliest stages and therapeutically carried out when the time comes.

Also, as previously noted, care in the selection and use of art materials is also considered essential; materials should be employed on the basis of therapeutically established goals for the child (or children). Generally, the therapist's skills, understanding, and ability to relate to the child in a caring, supportive, empathic and nonjudgmental fashion are also basic requirements of successful therapeutic transactions. The therapists' own activity level, degree of interaction, and verbal input usually depend on the therapist's theoretical orientation, combined with the therapist's assessment of the child's needs and resources.

Specific Approaches/Techniques

A proliferation of specific types of therapeutically oriented art approaches or techniques has accompanied the development of art and play therapy. One of these is "Serial Drawing," a therapeutic approach advocated for use with young children (Allan, 1978). The objectives of this approach are twofold according to Allan—namely to provide an opportunity (1) to rework some aspects of the parent–child attachment relationship in which the child begins to feel truly cared for, liked, and respected; and (2) for the child's unconscious to be expressed in symbolic form (through the art activity) and to "tap into the healing potential of the psyche."

Essentially, the Serial Drawing approach consists of seeing a child alone for a regularly scheduled 15–20 minute period and asking the child during this period to "draw-a-picture" as Allan suggests: "This will be our time together and I wonder if you can draw me a picture. Any picture that you want to do. . . ." And in the early phases of therapy, Allan sees the helpers' role to be that of a listener who waits for the child to talk, except for the end of a session when the therapist is instructed to ask three TAT-like queries, namely:

"What's going on in the picture?"
"What happens next?" ("What's the outcome?")
"Does it have a title?"

Allan then goes on to delineate three stages in the Serial Drawing Approach:

1. An initial stage, lasting 2–3 sessions, with three main aspects to the drawings which give a view of the child's internal world, reflect the child's "stuck" position, and represent the vehicle for establishing the initial interaction with the therapist.
2. A middle stage, lasting 4–7 sessions, marked by a separation out of the ambivalence with a clearer expression of the painful feelings, and a deepening of the relationship with the therapist with the child sharing deeper feelings more freely.
3. And the termination stage, lasting 8–10 sessions in which there is a rapid movement toward resolution of the deeper feelings and pain, with positive images of mastery and control emerging.

With more serious disturbed children Allan notes that the therapist tends to become more active in the middle stage, relating the drawings to the reality of the child's outer world and the nature of the present therapeutic relationship.

Psycho-Iconography.   Psycho-Iconography (Brown, 1960) is an illustration of an art technique developed principally for work with more disturbed (i.e., psychotic) clients. In this technique the therapist begins by slowly drawing a dot on a piece of paper with a felt-tip pen. The child is then given the piece of paper and asked to draw anything that comes to mind, whether a doodle or a picture. The therapist then uses this material to assess the child's emotional/psychological status and uses the highly repressed material revealed in the art in future therapeutic transactions. As in all approaches with highly disturbed persons, the therapist takes a highly directive stance, tightly structuring and "managing" the therapeutic process. Usually, with these individuals, the art activity as in Psycho-Iconography is used in conjunction with other therapeutic interactions and over a long period of time.

Squiggle-Drawing Game.   The Squiggle-Drawing Game is an art activity aimed at latency-aged children in contrast to the Serial Drawing approach advocated for young children or the Psycho-Iconography mode recommended in an adjunctive manner for highly disturbed youth. The Squiggle-Drawing Game has been adapted by Claman (1980) from Winnicott's Squiggle Techniques (1971) and from the storytelling approach of Gardner (1971). It is recommended as a useful technique (Claman, 1980) for obtaining thematic material and communicating through artistic and storytelling metaphors with latency-aged children who tend to resist direct questioning of their problems and feelings.

The Squiggle Technique itself was introduced by Winnicott (1971) to communicate by metaphor with his child patients. The goal of the technique is to establish communication with the child's inner thoughts and feelings through an interchange which bypasses the inherent resistances and leads to revelation of repressed and personally unacceptable thoughts and feelings. Essentially, it consists of asking the child to make a drawing out of the squiggle which the therapist first draws—a squiggle being any variation of a straight, curved, or wavy line.

In the Squiggle-Drawing Game, as noted, Claman elaborated on this basic procedure by asking the child to make up a story about the drawing and asking a few of the usual questions about the drawing (e.g., What's going on in it?). Then Claman reverses the procedure with the child starting with a squiggle, the therapist making the squiggle into a drawing, telling a story about it and the child asking questions. Simon (1978) uses the Squiggle Technique in conjunction with another drawing procedure called "Fold-Over." In the Fold-Over approach both players draw a head at the top of separate strips of paper and then fold the paper forward to leave only the base of the neck showing. They then exchange papers and draw bodies from the neck to the waist.

Again, the papers are folded and exchanged with clue marks left visible. Next the body is drawn from waist to ankles and then the feet. Simon claims that these drawing games "tend to bypass blocks and to tap and order hidden resources" (p. 75) as well as "supplement and induce speech . . . encourage copperation, etc." (p. 84).

The Therapeutic Use of Art in the Classroom

One of the present educational trends is toward the incorporation of "thera-peutically oriented" materials and techniques into the classroom curriculum, particularly in curriculum areas such as the language arts, the social sciences, physical education (dance, etc.) and the arts (painting, music, drama) them-selves. As Kramer says in *Art as Therapy with Children* (1971), in this world of increasing mechanization where children are accustomd to sit and accept pas-sively, just to do something actively creative is therapeutic in itself since it allows children to express their own thoughts, feelings, and dreams. There is a universal human need for mastery and self-expression to counteract feelings of anxiety and the helpless inability to cope with one's environment. Art can help expand one's knowledge of his or her environment and help develop a sense of identity. In the classroom situation, as in the therapy or counseling situation, the child who experiences the self through art can increase self-confidence, a general sense of mastery, and can build self-esteem.

It is not necessary to have a formal art education to use art as a growth-producing, therapeutic medium in the classroom. One can encourage art ex-pression without forcing it into a straitjacket of conventionality. The process, not the product, is important. The child is encouraged to see who she or he is and might become, rather than what she or he has produced. Conventional art standards and perfectionistic expectations may be eliminated with the follow-ing techniques:

1. The scribble, or automatic drawing technique in which a spontaneous random line is developed into a meaningful picture.
2. The free wash technique, with blobs of paint dripped onto wet paper and developed into a free painting.
3. Interactive drawing or drawing completion, where the picture is built conjointly by more than one person.

Many more techniques with paint, pen, paper and paste, clay, and other mate-rials can be found in the literature of art therapy and art education. The important consideration is to use materials which are easy to control and take no great expertise to achieve expressive results. In doing so, encourage the child to think about what the colors selected mean—that is, what feelings she or he gets from the atmosphere created on paper. Through reaching her or his deepest feelings the child may find her or his own creative self. This increases feelings of self-validation and helps the process of maturation.

Some additional expressive art activities which could be adapted to classroom settings:

1. Have the students practice drawing rhythmic lines which express feelings. Ask them if their lines are smooth, spiky, wavy, heavy, light, etc. (If possible, use oil art crayons, which are easy to control and won't smear.) Suggest they find their own tempo—is it tense, relaxed, excited, calm, etc. Do at least ten pages.

2. Now encourage them to use this same technique to do an abstract self-portrait, showing the feelings they have at the moment. Suggest they use color, form, lines to express their state of tension or mood, etc.

3. Then, ask them to share their self-portraits.

4. On the basis of what they have seen and heard from each group member (and the leader), ask them to do a symbolic portrait of the other class members. Now, have them go around the circle, presenting each person with his portrait. (This is how I see you. You are _____.)

5. Using a large piece of paper ask them to work together with one or two others on a joint drawing. This entire experience needs to be completely non-verbal. Suggest they notice these things: How did you get together? Did you choose, or wait to be chosen? How were decisions made? What did you experience as you worked together? Later, each person may describe the experience and how he or she worked things out within the larger group.

6. Ask each child to draw two group abstracts: the group as he or she sees it and the group as he or she would like it to be. Discussion of the group abstracts of the various class members could then focus on such features as their desired classroom climate.

7. Ask each student to take a piece of clay which is comfortable to their hands. Ask them to close their eyes and silently manipulate it. Instruct them to gradually work it into a form which is them. In doing so, recommend they notice what they feel, and what changes it goes through on its way to the final product. Suggest they let this evolve and that they not think too much about it. Then ask them to share their experience with the group.

8. Scrapbooks, art posters, collages, and collections could be employed to encourage students to explore various aspects of their experiences and themselves. For example, they could be developed around themes like:

> My favorite things
> Bad moments
> When I'm mad
> When I'am afraid
> My favorite stories
> What helps me to get over my anger
> Love is. . . .
> Families are for. . . .

In these art experiences, it is important the teacher not just be an adult directing, setting a task, sitting back, and being objective. The students create together with the teacher's encouragement and acceptance. There is no right or
wrong. Art is presented as a tool for enjoyment and self-exploration. After a
few practice exercises, common graphic language is shared which expresses
individual feelings. Since the interaction is not all verbal or intellectual, superficial misunderstandings one hopes will be avoided. Deeper meanings evolve
slowly as students interact with each other via art media and eventually talk
about their work. An opportunity then to share one's experiences both nonverbally (initially) and verbally (eventually) is afforded.

Therefore, basic to the therapeutic employment of art activities in the classroom is:

1. An opportunity for self-expression through guided artistic activities.
2. A further opportunity to view one's own and others' efforts, perceptually, motorically, and verbally.
3. Additional opportunities to share one's experiences with others.

CASE ILLUSTRATIONS

Whereas art may be employed as the sole medium of interaction with a child,
it is also frequently used in conjunction with other play modalities such as
blocks, dolls, toy animals, and so forth. In the case of Carla to be discussed as
follows, art materials were made available and introduced at the beginning of
the session—for example: "I have some finger paints and paper available for
you today if you would like to use them and make a picture." There were,
however, other toys and objects available in the room to play with. Carla
usually chose to become engrossed with the art materials and then increasingly
employed this as a means of interacting with other materials. For example,
once she made clay meatballs which she force-fed to the dolls that were
nearby.

Carla

Carla was a five-and-a-half-year-old girl with a younger sister, Laura. She was
referred in the middle of the school year for treatment of socially inappropriate and periodically disruptive behavior while attending kindergarten. Carla
would, for example, cry for a period of time after being left at school. She
would also alternate between a withdrawn stance or striking out by hitting at
other children. At times, she would angrily tear up something she was working
on or she would push or jostle another child at work. She was friendless, and
the other children, for the most part, ignored her.

Three parent conferences were arranged by the school personnel during
this period, only one of which the father attended. The mother appeared

apprehensive and harried during these conferences (as she did when leaving Carla off for kindergarten), fidgeting all the while and reiterating that she was doing her best, yet expressing concern about Carla and her sister, Laura.

The family history included a "forced marriage" as a result of Carla's unplanned arrival, the mother being a senior in high school and the father finishing his second year at a nearby technical college. The early marriage and onset of parenthood produced economic stresses in the already tenuous relationship and reportedly necessitated the father's working two part-time jobs while finishing college. The father continued to bury himself in work after leaving college even though the family finances had improved. The second child was planned in an aim to "cement the marriage."

Carla's mother reportedly put anxious effort into parenting and keeping the house neat. She described Carla as being delicate and young for her age and felt that she wasn't really ready for kindergarten. Diagnostically, it was felt that mother and daughter were suffering from separation anxiety due to the mother's repressed anger with Carla and Carla's repressed feelings of rejection, of "being in the way at home."

The treatment plans included marriage counseling for the mother and father and a combined art and play therapy program to help Carla deal with her angry and hurt feelings. Twice weekly, meetings of 50 minutes each were scheduled. Carla originally began working with finger paints. In the initial half-dozen sessions Carla used dark colors primarily and smeared them together intensely, often spilling paint over the sides of the paper. She resisted efforts to confine her work to the paper and showed little interest in the other play materials. She also insisted on taking these initial paintings with her to show her mother, and would periodically ask where her mother was or if the mother could join in Carla's activities.

As the sessions progressed (the next 15 sessions) she showed greater control, definition, and organization in her art productions, as well as a greater flexibility in the choice of art materials. Periodically she would choose to incorporate some of the other available play items in her art work, such as when she made clay meatballs and force-fed them to the dolls. Occasionally, she would display angry outbursts and would regress into a period of messing the art materials or tearing up something she had done and angrily throwing it away. She also began to verbalize her feelings of anger, frustration, and sadness as she played with the toys and worked with the materials.

Her parents, meanwhile, were making progress in their couple therapy, with her mother requesting additional sessions for herself with a separate therapist. In these she expressed an interest in finding something for herself and improving her relationship with both of her daughters. Undoubtedly, this helped Carla indirectly in her own therapy. About midway through the middle period of Carla's therapy, she began relating more directly to the therapist, informing her that she could keep her pictures and at one point handing her one which she had marked proudly with a "C" saying, "This is for *you!*" She became increasingly task oriented for sustained periods, saying that she wanted, for example, to finish something before she left. Her nursery school teachers reported that her withdrawn behavior was disappearing and that she was now a firmly entrenched member of a four-child group that often played together in the kindergarten room and on the playground.

Because of an impending family vacation as the summer began and because Carla's schoolwork improved, the remaining eight sessions were structured around termination. Carla increasingly used more structured materials, such as clay in conjunction with a set of dolls, and played and talked out the family's situation, their plans for the summer, and the new school she would go to in the fall. Periodically, she would ask the therapist to come home with her to continue playing and this was interpreted as her understandable reluctance at leaving the therapy experience. Her last production was a huge picture of herself, smiling, and waving goodbye, which she gave to the therapist.

The case of Mark represents a different type of orientation for the use of art, that is, to work through feelings of guilt and pain associated with loss and in this case, loss which was felt to be negligently caused by the child.

Mark *

Mark's brother, Scotty, died one week after a fire that both inadvertently started. Feeling guilty, Mark disobeyed his parents, provoked fights with his friends, and apparently sought punishment. He ate compulsively, started fires, and hit and bit himself. Two years later he was brought to a child guidance clinic and diagnosed as having neurotic anxiety and depressive reactions. Mark looked lonely and as if waiting to be punished. Presumably for two years he had had unresolved conflicts of self-accusation, self-forgiveness, anger, and confusion over his ambivalent feelings toward his brother. His parents did not express grief openly. Mark was ignored and not given any consolation or opportunity to express his feelings.

Initially, in art therapy, Mark was silent, responded in monosyllables and did not use the art materials. In a programmed fashion, he mechanically told the story of Scotty's death, adding that he himself should have also been burned. After four months of painting age-appropriate pictures, he began to accompany his drawings with talk about his dreams—red hot fires that consumed him. While painting, he asked his therapist why he had not been allowed to go to the hospital or funeral, why his parents would not talk to him about Scotty, and why he also did not die. After two months of this type of materials, his therapist suggested that he paint scenes about accidents. Evidently, no one had used the word "accident" with reference to the tragedy. Mark drew a series of stick figures on one large sheet. There were seven separate drawings. Each scene showed part of the accidental fire; the final one

* C. E. Schaefer and H. L. Millman, *Therapies for Children.* San Francisco: Jossey-Bass, 1977, pp. 68–69.

showed scarred Scotty being held by his mother. Mark complained that they took Scotty away and his parents never said anything about it again.

During each drawing, Mark cried as he relived the past tragedy. His therapist encouraged him to continue talking about each scene. After saying that he could now see that he had not killed his brother, he accepted the accidental nature of the event. Presumably, he had felt guilty and defensively employed repression and denial. Mark remained in art therapy for an additional three months, by which time all referral problems had been eliminated.

Mark's parents were concomitantly seen for counseling by a social worker. At home, Mark and his parents began to express their feelings with each other. Mark was told that they had never held him responsible for Scotty's death. At one point, they openly expressed and shared their grief together.

SUMMARY AND CONCLUSIONS

Art has been used as a means of self-expression and exploration of the larger universe since prehistoric times. In the 1940s both art and play began to be used as a serious therapeutic medium. Initially, both were employed in an assessment-oriented, adjunctive fashion to aid in building rapport and uncovering repressed and troublesome feelings, thoughts, and concerns.

The use of both art and play as a therapeutic medium has expanded, resulting in an increasing recognition of the inherent therapeutic properties of both activities. These properties include: the emotionally cathartic and freeing nature of the media, their communicative and expressive properties, and their greater appeal over direct verbal inquiry and discussion for all children and especially those who were emotionally disturbed, not verbally oriented, or from differing linguistic, ethnic, and racial backgrounds. These approaches, hence, serve to reduce resistance to acknowledgment of underlying issues and fears; in psychoanalytic language, they help to bypass the superego and speak directly to the ego. They tend to be sought out by children for the pleasure they offer as well as the opportunity to create, learn, become more competent and integrated, and to master the world about them.

This chapter focused on the ways in which art is being used by play therapists and other helping professionals who work with children. Art is viewed as a play therapeutic medium which offers children the opportunity to communicate and work through conflicts and issues using a variety of art materials. The choice of the art activities or materials themselves are posited as representing significant opportunities to focus selectively on a child's concerns or problems with certain therapeutic goals or objectives in mind.

Specific examples of the employment of art as a play therapeutic medium include the use of the Squiggle and Fold-over techniques as well as the Squiggle-Drawing approach, in which the therapist and the child collaborate in a pictorial fashion to gradually unfold and work through conflict-laden concerns. Attention is also given to the preventive use of art activities as a growth-enhancing experience to be used in school settings. Throughout the chapter, examples of the uses of art are coupled with therapeutic considerations as to structure, procedure, and process.

Populations successfully treated with this medium include normal, neurotic, psychotic, handicapped, and disadvantaged children. Art therapy employed as a play therapeutic treatment modality is particularly appropriate for those children who tend to be nonverbal, are retarded, or represent a linguistic, ethnic, or racial minority. It is also particularly useful as an adjunctive assessment or therapeutic medium and when used to deal with various crises and specific symptoms such as phobia(s).

While the use of art for therapeutic and growth-enhancing development is promising, the promise is marred by the lack of carefully designed and controlled studies of its efficacy. Unfortunately, there is presently a dearth of such studies. We are presently still inclined to insist that what we do "works." While enthusiasm and faith are important in motivating all of us to make greater efforts, these virtues alone are insufficient as a solid basis for therapeutic decisions. Systematic investigation into the efficacy of all art therapy approaches must be firmly wedded to our commitment to improve our therapeutic potentiality.

REFERENCES

Allan, J. A. B. (1978) "Serial Drawing": A therapeutic approach with young children. *Canadian Counselor,* **12**(4), 223–228.

Axline, U. M. (1969) *Play therapy.* New York: Ballantine Books.

Brown, W. L. (1960) Psycho-iconography. *Spectrum* (January), 2–6.

Burns, R. C., & Kaufman, S. H. (1970) *Kinetic family drawings (KFD).* New York: Brunner/Mazel.

Claman, L. (1980) The Squiggle-Drawing Game in child psychotherapy. *American Journal of Psychotherapy,* **34**(3), 414–425

Dinkmeyer, D. (1970) *Developing understanding of self and others: Play kit and manual.* Circle Pines, Minn.: Publishers' Building.

Erikson, E. H. (1964) The meaning of play. In M. R. Haworth (Ed.), *Child psychotherapy: Practice and theory.* New York: Basic Books. Pp. 3–11.

Erikson, E. H. (1963), Toys and reasons. In *Childhood and society.* New York: Norton. Chapter 6.

Freud, A. (1946) *The psychoanalytic treatment of children.* New York: Schocken.

Gardner, R. A. (1971) *Therapeutic communication with children: The mutual storytelling technique.* New York: Jason Aronson.

Ginott, H. G. (1961) *Group psychotherapy with children.* New York: McGraw-Hill.

Gordon, A. K. (1970) *Games for growth and education games in the classroom.* Chicago: Science Research Associates.

Hartley, R. E., Frank, L., & Goldenson, R. M. (1952) *Understanding children's play.* New York: Columbia University Press.

Hartley, R. E., & Goldenson, R. M. (1963) *The complete book of children's play,* rev. ed. New York: Thomas Y. Crowell.

Heimlich, E. P. (1972) Paraverbal techniques in the therapy of childhood communication disorders. *International Journal of Psychotherapy,* **1**(1), 65–83.

Herron, R. E., & Sutton-Smith, B. (1971) *Child's play.* New York: Wiley.

Kellogg, R. (1967) Understanding children's art. *Psychology Today,* **1**, 16–25.

Klinger, G. (1969) Development of imaginative behavior: Implications of play for a theory of fantasy. *Psychological Bulletin,* **72**(4), 277–298.

Kramer, E. (1971) *Art as therapy with children.* New York: Schocken.

Kramer, E. (1972) The practice of art therapy with children. *American Journal of Art Therapy,* **11**, 89–110.

Kramer, E. (1977) Art therapy and play. *American Journal of Art Therapy,* **17**, 3–11.

Kwiatkowska, H. (1967) Family art therapy. *Family Process,* **6**, 37–55.

Linderman, E. W., & Herberholz, D. W. (1964) *Developing artistic and perceptual awareness,* 2nd ed. Dubuque, Iowa: William C. Brown Co.

Millar, S. (1968) *The psychology of play.* Baltimore: Penguin.

Moreno, J. L. (1970) *Psychodrama,* Vol. 1, 3rd ed. Beacon, N.Y.: Beacon House.

Moustakas, C. E. (1973) *Children in play therapy.* New York: Jason Aronson.

Mulac, M. E. (1971) *Educational games for fun.* New York: Harper & Row.

Muro, J. J. (1968) Play media in counseling: A brief report on experience and some opinions. *Elementary School Guidance and Counseling,* **3**, 104–110.

Myrick, R. D., & Moni, L. S. (1972) The counselor's workshop. *Elementary School Guidance and Counseling,* **6**(3), 202–205.

Naumburg, M. (1966) *Dynamically oriented art therapy: It's principles and practices.* New York: Grune & Stratton.

Nelson, R. C. (1966) Elementary school counseling with play media. *Personnel and Guidance Journal,* **45**(1), 24–27.

Nelson, R. C. (1967) Pros and cons of using play media in counseling. *Elementary School Guidance and Counseling,* **2**, 143–147.

Nelson, R. C. (1972) Play media in counseling. *Guidance and counseling in the elementary school.* New York: Holt, Rinehart & Winston. Pp. 200–217.

Nickerson, E. T. (1973a) Psychology of play and play therapy activities in classroom activities. *Educating Children: Early and Middle Years,* Spring, 1–6.

Nickerson, E. T. (1973b) Recent approaches to and innovations in play therapy. *International Journal of Child Psychotherapy,* **2**(5), 53–70.

Nickerson, E. T. (1973c) The use of art as a play therapeutic medium in the classroom. *Art Psychotherapy,* **1**, 293–297.

Nickerson, E. T. (1980) More recent approaches ot working therapeutically with children and teenagers. Paper read at Division 29 (Psychotherapy) American Psychological Association Mid-Winter Conference, San Diego, (1973a) February.

Nickerson, E. T., & O'Laughlin, K. S. (1978) *Action therapies.* Lexington, Mass.: College Xerox Publishing.

Nickerson, E. T., & O'Laughlin, K.S. (1982) *Helping through action.* Amherst, Mass.: Human Resources Development Press.

Robbins, A., & Sibley, L. B. (1976) *Creative art therapy.* New York: Brunner/Mazel.

Roth, E. A. & Barnett, R. P. (1980) Parallels in art and play therapy with a disturbed retarded child. *Arts in Psychotherapy,* **7,** 19-26.

Rubin, J. (1977) *Child art therapy: Understanding and helping children grow through art.* New York: Van Nostrand.

Schaefer, C. E., & Millman, H. L. (1977) *Therapies for children.* San Francisco: Jossey-Bass.

Simon, E. (1978) Drawing games in art therapy with children. *American Journal of Art Therapy,* **17,** 75-84.

Sutton-Smith, B. (1971) Child's play—Very serious business. *Psychology Today,* **5**(7), 67-69, 87.

Torrance, E. P. (1970) *Encouraging creativity in the classroom.* Dubuque, Iowa: William C. Brown Co.

Ulman, E., & Dachinger, E. (Eds.) (1975) *Art therapy in theory and practice.* New York: Schocken.

Ulman, E., & Levy, B. F. (1973) Art therapists as diagnosticians. *American Journal of Art Therapy,* **13,** 35-38.

Wadeson, H. (1980) *Art psychotherapy.* New York: Wiley-Interscience.

Wilson, L. (1977) Theory and practice of art therapy with the mentally retarded. *American Journal of Art Therapy,* **16,** 87-97.

Winnicott, D. W. (1971) *Therapeutic consultations in child psychiatry.* New York: Basic Books.

CHAPTER 13

The Color-Your-Life Technique

KEVIN J. O'CONNOR

INTRODUCTION

Within the context of play therapy techniques, therapists often experience difficulty when trying to help their child patients make the transition from an action-oriented way of behaving to a more verbal style. Children in therapy often are perfectly willing to play in order to avoid discussion. Some children keep their sessions so programmed and busy that they can virtually "tune out" the therapist. This tends to be the pattern with many impulsive and aggressive children as well as younger children. Whereas encouraging verbalization on the part of the child may not be particularly important with younger children it becomes increasingly important as the child matures cognitively (Harter, Chapter 5, this volume). In fact, it is the introduction of verbal mediators into a child's behavior which is considered to be the primary goal of many cognitively oriented therapy techniques (Bornstein & Quevillon, 1976; Douglas, Parry, Marton, & Garson, 1976; Fry, 1978; Meichenbaum & Goodman, 1971; Moore & Cole, 1978; Pelham, Bryan, & Paluchowski, 1978). In each of these programs self-verbalization or the presence of verbally mediated behavior is seen as the major factor in helping children to develop self-control and, subsequently, more socialized behaviors. The assumption is that in young children thoughts move very quickly into action without an intermediate stage in which the child contemplates the implications of the desired behavior. Although this is typical behavior for young children it is also hypothesized to be the underlying difficulty in children who are impulsive, who act out aggressively, or whose socialization skills are underdeveloped.

One aspect of the verbal mediation and self-control process stressed by a number of large-scale, educational–therapeutic programs is the ability of the child to manage affects and affective material appropriately (Dinkmeyer, 1974; Ellis, 1972; Fagen, Long, & Stevens, 1975; Wood, 1975). Managing one's affects involves a number of subskills such as: (1) an awareness of the variety of affective states, (2) the ability to relate those affects to situations in one's own life, and (3) verbalizing affects in appropriate ways. A difficulty encountered, not only by these programs but by play therapists in general, is how to give young children, who tend to be so concrete, a way of conceptualizing and discussing something as abstract as affects.

The Color-Your-Life Technique was designed by the author as an educational-play method of providing children with a fairly concrete referent for understanding and discussing affects. Specifically the goals of the technique are:

1. To enhance children's awareness of different affective states.
2. To encourage children to discuss events on an affective level.
3. To help children make the transition from a purely action-oriented way of behaving to one that is more verbal.
4. To assist therapists in obtaining information about the child's past and present affective status jn a way which is less threatening than traditional verbal interviews.

To accomplish these goals children are taught to pair affects and colors, such as red/anger, blue/sad, and yellow/happy. Although most of the color–feeling pairs are derived from Western cultural and aesthetic norms, the point of this technique is not specifically to teach these norms. Instead the colors are meant to serve as a mnemonic, a code if you will, for a variety of affects. What differentiates this technique from something purely educational and makes it play is the choice of materials, the format of presentation, and the focus on process rather than product.

Very familiar, simple materials are used in the Color-Your-Life Technique: crayons, paint or chalk, and white paper. These materials were selected for their simplicity and because children tend to see them as a natural, non-threatening, and enjoyable medium of self-expression (Nickerson, Chapter 12, this volume). The format in which the color-feeling pairs are presented and developed is one of open discussion. When the author has particularly wished to stress the playful element in the format he has had children think of the colors as a code for feelings which seems to quickly engage even the more resistant child. Lastly, in keeping the technique enjoyable and thereby optimally productive, it is necessary that the therapist stress the process elements of the technique rather than the product the child ends up creating. Each of these aspects of the technique will be discussed at some length in the following two sections.

METHOD

Therapist Variables

The Color-Your-Life Technique can be adapted for use by anyone working with children. On the simplest level it is merely a tool for teaching youngsters about affects and their expression. In this context it could be used by a parent, teacher, or psychology paraprofessional. On a second level it may be used to gather information about the affective life of the child and in this sense is probably better managed by individuals with at least a moderate level of psychological training. Finally. the technique can be used to elicit intense feelings on the part of the child as well as detailed discussions of specific affects and the life events the child associates with them. In this type of work it is best if the technique is used by a trained therapist.

Child Variables

The technique has been used by the author with a wide variety of children. It seems to be the most productive with children between the ages of 6 and 12 who are of average intelligence, although older children often seem to enjoy the technique a great deal. A basic prerequisite is that the child have sufficient cognitive abilities to recognize and name colors as well as different affective states.

The technique is also adaptable for use with either individual children or groups. The author has found that using the technique with a group of children often leads to excellent in-depth discussions which can be followed over several sessions. Further, the technique can be repeated at intervals to gauge the affective level of a group as a whole. With individual children the technique usually becomes more of a teaching exercise, although several children who have been in therapy with the author have subsequently used the color-feeling pairs as a way of communicating their feelings during a session.

Obviously the technique requires a certain level of concrete and associative thinking and is, therefore, probably not appropriate for use with psychotic children. The author has not used it with a severely disturbed population but has found it to be useful with children who were diagnosed as having psychosomatic illnesses, impulse control difficulties, aggressive behaviors, and neurotic or intrapsychic conflicts.

Materials

The materials used in the Color-Your-Life Technique are any type of coloring instrument (paint, crayons, chalk, etc.) and plain white paper. A wide variety of colors may be made available, but yellow, green, blue, black, red, purple, brown, and gray are basic.

Technique

Since the purpose of the Color-Your-Life Technique is to encourage children to verbalize regarding their feelings, active discussion is encouraged throughout. The therapist generally begins by asking if he or she can pair an affect with a particular color. For example:

THERAPIST: Can you tell me what feeling might go with the color red?

CHILD: Uhm, I don't know.

THERAPIST: Can you think of a time when people get very red in the face? Think about cartoons you have seen. When do the characters scrunch up their faces and get red?

CHILD: When they are mad!

THERAPIST: That's right. Most people think that the color red goes along with being angry.

This type of exchange continues as each color is associated with a particular affect, as follows: red, anger; purple, rage; blue, sad; black, very sad; green, jealousy; brown, bored; gray, lonesome; yellow, happy. Although most of these pairings are somewhat arbitrary, some are consistent with art therapy interpretations, such as yellow for happy, brown or black for sad, and red as fire for anger. Further, this author has found them to be fairly consistent across children, especially the first five listed. It also seems helpful to have the child describe each affect in terms which are as concrete as possible. Anger can be differentiated from rage by saying that rage is a kind of anger which is so strong it makes a person want to hurt somebody or break something. Feeling blue, or sad, is differentiated from the feeling that goes with black by saying that black is for the kind of feeling that a person has when someone or something they care a lot about dies. (Black is the color at most funerals.) This type of discussion proceeds until the therapist feels reasonably sure that the child can differentiate between each of the color–feeling pairs.

Other pairs may be added as they seem appropriate for a particular child or group. The author has found orange, pink, and blue-green to be other useful colors. Orange may be used to represent excitement, like right before one's birthday or Christmas Eve. Pink and blue-green are discussed together and are associated with traditional sex-role stereotypes. Pink is used to represent feminine feelings and activities such as cooking, taking care of babies, and feeling soft, tender, or sensitive. Blue-green represents masculine feelings and activities, such as playing sports, and feeling strong, tough, and proud of being male. These last two color–feeling pairs are difficult concepts to convey and are usually poorly understood by children of less than average intelligence. With normally intelligent children, however, they may give the therapist useful information as to how much a child sees his or her behavior as corresponding to traditional sex-role stereotypes.

The number and variety of color–feeling pairs is limited only by the materials available and by the ingenuity of the therapist. It is generally wise, however, to limit the number of pairs presented at any one time to eight or nine as this seems to be a number most children can manage successfully. It also behooves the therapist to remember the color–feeling pairs used with each particular child or group as the children may fall back on the color terms later when trying to describe a certain feeling or state.

Once the color-feeling pairs are established each child is given a piece of blank paper and told that this paper is going to be filled up with colors to show the feelings they have had in their lives. Some explanation is generally necessary at this point to help the child or children get started. The therapist might say "If you have been happy about half the time in your life then half the paper should be yellow. If you have been happy your whole life with no other feelings then you should color the whole paper yellow." The therapist adds that the child may complete the coloring in whatever way he or she chooses, using squares, circles, designs, and so forth. The therapist continues to clarify the instructions as necessary for the particular person or group.

At this point the therapist continues to encourage verbalization on the part of the child or group but does much less talking of his or her own. The discussion may focus on life events, the relative quantity of the different colors in the child's project, and certainly on anything the child mentions spontaneously. When the technique is used with a group the children may spontaneously compare their productions; this may lead to some particularly lively discussions if the therapist feels sufficiently comfortable to guide the discussion and prevent it from becoming hostile or derogatory for any one group member.

CASE EXAMPLES

Rather than give the reader a general outline of a case and the results of the Color-Your-Life Technique for that case, brief examples will be pulled from a number of cases. All of the children discussed in the following were part of an ongoing therapy group for children with chronic asthma; all were inpatients in a medical hospital for the duration of their psychotherapy.

D. was a 12-year-old male who tended to be a negative leader within the hospital setting. He often encouraged other children to act out against the medical staff and demanded that the younger children on the ward do favors for him. His Color-Your-Life picture consisted of a page of scribbled red and blue. His accompanying statement was that he did not usually feel happy, most of the time he felt mad and sad and the two were always getting all mixed together. This was D's first attempt at verbalizing his feelings and seemed to open him up to becoming much more positively involved with the other children in the group.

S., another 12-year-old male, colored in words on his picture. He chose to write "Happy Father's Day." Of the five letters in "happy," three were done in colors representing sad feelings, one was done in red for angry, and one was done in yellow for happy. The word "father" was done by alternating red and purple, anger and rage. Then, because he had used the unhappy colors for so many letters he chose to write the word "day" twice so he could use the other colors. Much later in therapy S. was able to confront some of his angry feelings toward his father who tended to doubt the validity of S's asthma attacks.

B., a seven-year-old female, appeared to be precocious in her social skills and tended to be particularly seductive in all her interpersonal contacts. Her parents were divorced, and although her father remarried, the biological parents continued to battle for B's affections. The battle to win B's loyalty also meant that the parents tended to create numerous situations in which B, felt compelled to choose between them. Initially B's Color-Your-Life picture was divided into three equal parts: one red, one purple, and one yellow, representing anger, rage, and happiness. B, soon decided, however, that this was not an accurate drawing and colored over most of the yellow with purple and black (very sad). Later on in therapy she constantly referred to this picture, which hung on the wall in the group room, to show how much she had improved since her first few weeks in therapy.

The last case to be discussed is that of M, a seven-year-old male who was of above-average intelligence who tended to be very immature in his interactions with both adults and peers. With adults he tended to be clingy and demanding. With older peers he withdrew, while with younger peers he was constantly giving directions and being a "know it all." Soon after he was admitted to the group, which consisted primarily of older children, the Color-Your-Life Technique was used. There was nothing remarkable about M's production regarding the colors used, but the extreme lightness of his picture seemed directly proportional to his timidity within the group. Several months later when M, seemed much more comfortable with the group the technique was used again. This time there was a relative increase in the use of cheerful colors and they were much more boldly applied to the paper. Obviously in this case the quality of the production was at least as significant as any other aspect.

Besides these specific examples, certain generalities have been observed by the author in using the Color-Your-Life Technique. First, the order of the colors used tends to be less significant than their relative quantity. As was seen in the description of J's picture, the quantity of each color is somewhat flexible no matter what the order. Second, most children seem to color in blocks or stripes and when they do not it is usually significant. This can be seen in D's choice of scribbles, reflecting his impulsivity and affective confusion, and it can be noted in S's decision to use words instead of an abstract design. Third, most children fill up the page with colors, sometimes they even overflow onto the back. When the colors fill only a small part of the paper it seems to indicate either emotional constriction or poor self-esteem or both. Scribbles, on the other hand, seem to be characteristic of impulsive, overactive children. Fourth, the technique tends to pull for negative emotions. At this point it is unclear whether this is related to some aspect of the technique or to the populations with which it has been used. Last, the reader should also keep in mind that this technique has only been used within ongoing therapy and therefore these observations are general to a patient population, not to a "normal" population.

SUMMARY

The Color-Your-Life Technique was developed by the author specifically to help children bridge the gap between action and verbalization. The technique uses a commonly enjoyed play medium of children, namely coloring or painting, and attaches to it numerous affective terms and concepts. Children, who as a general rule are fascinated by secret codes and symbols, seem to fall easily into the task and to see it as fun, rather than threatening. The assignment of certain affects to certain colors is largely arbitrary although some pairings are based on cultural norms. When creating the color–feeling pairs with the child it is important to allow him or her to help, so that the colors take on enough meaning that he or she wants to use them. It does not seem to matter whether the technique is used within individual or group therapy but a group format tends to make it more of a game/play situation and to elicit more spontaneous verbalizations. Further, the technique is not a freestanding diagnostic or therapeutic tool. It is intended for use by a therapist in ascertaining the child's affective self-image and in helping the child learn about and express a variety of affects within the framework of ongoing interactions and contacts.

REFERENCES

Arlow, J., & Kadis, A. (1946) Finger painting in the psychotherapy of children. *American Journal of Orthopsychiatry,* **16,** 134–146.

Bornstein, P., & Quevillon, R. (1976) The effects of a self-instructional package on overactive preschool boys. *Journal of Applied Behavior Analysis,* **9,** 179–188.

Dinkmeyer, D. (1974) Developing understanding of self and others is central to the educational process. In G. Williams and S. Gordon (Eds.), *Clinical child psychology: Current practices and future perspectives.* New York: Behavioral Publications.

Douglas, V., Parry, P., Marton, P., & Garson, C. (1976) Assessment of a cognitive training program for hyperactive children. *Journal of Abnormal Child Psychology,* **41,** 389–310.

Ellis, A. (1972) Emotional education in the classroom: The living school. *Journal of Clinical Child Psychology,* **1**(3), 19–22.

Fagen, S., Long, N., & Stevens, D. (1975) *Teaching children self-control.* Columbus, Ohio: Merrill.

Fry, P. (1978) Resistance to temptation as a function of the duration of self-verbalization. *British Journal of Social and Clinical Psychology,* **17,** 111–116.

Meichenbaum, D., & Goodman, J. (1971) Training impulsive children to talk to themselves: A means of developing self-control. *Journal of Abnormal Psychology,* **77,** 115–126.

Moore, S., & Cole, S. (1978) Cognitive self-mediation training with hyperkinetic children. *Bulletin of the Psychonomic Society,* **12**(1), 18–20.

Pelham, W., Bryan, B., & Paluchowski, C. (1978) Social skills training with hyperactive children: A preliminary evaluation of a coaching procedure and a reward system. Paper presented at the *Annual Meeting of the Association for the Advancement of Behavior Therapy.*

Wood, M. (Ed.) (1975) *Developmental therapy.* Baltimore: University Park Press.

CHAPTER 14

The Talking, Feeling, and Doing Game

RICHARD A. GARDNER

The Talking, Feeling and Doing Game was originally devised to engage resistant and uncooperative children in meaningful psychotherapeutic endeavors. The instrument has also proved useful for less resistant children as an additional therapeutic modality. The basic rationale of the game will be presented and its method of utilization described. Then, some examples of the ways in which the therapist might respond to selected cards will be discussed, with particular focus on the therapeutic implications of these responses.

INTRODUCTION AND THEORETICAL CONSIDERATIONS

To the best of this author's knowledge, von Hug-Hellmuth (1913) was the first to describe the value of children's self-created fantasies as a rich source of information about their underlying psychodynamics. This observation first appeared in the English literature in an article published in 1921. Von Hug-Hellmuth used such fantasies psychoanalytically, believing that the best way to alleviate children's neurotic disturbances was to help them gain insight into the underlying meaning of their fantasies. Both Anna Freud and Melanie Klein, although differing significantly with regard to their interpretations of children's fantasies, agreed that helping children gain insight into the underlying meaning of their fantasies was the most effective way to bring about therapeutic change.

Many psychotherapeutic techniques have been devised to help children. Many rely heavily on the elicitation of self-created fantasies, but therapists have long experienced frustration in getting children to take a psychoanalytic stance and attempting to gain insight into the psychoanalytic meaning of their fantasies. Conn (1939, 1941a, 1941a,b, 1948, 1954) and Solomon (1938, 1940, 1951, 1955) dealt with the problem of children's unreceptivity to psychoanalytic inquiry by responding at the allegorical level. They held that one could impart important therapeutic messages by discussing the child's fantasy at the symbolic level. They were certainly receptive to the notion of helping children gain insight into their fantasies, but believed that important therapeutic changes could be brought about by discussing the fantasy at the symbolic level, for example, "Why did the fox bite the wolf's tail?" "Was there a better way the fox could have dealt with his anger toward the wolf than biting his tail?"

This author has also directed his attention to the question of how to utilize therapeutically the self-created fantasies of children who will tell stories, but who are unreceptive or unwilling to analyze them. The mutual storytelling technique (Gardner, 1971, this volume, Chapter 19) deals with this problem by having the therapist create responding stories, using the child's own characters and setting, but introducing healthier modes of adaptation and resolution than those exhibited in the child's story. For children who are somewhat unreceptive to telling stories, the author has found that a series of games utilizing standard board game play and token reinforcement (1975a,b) proved useful in facilitating the creation of stories and other fantasy material of therapeutic value. However, there were still some children who, in spite of these games, were unwilling and/or too resistant to tell self-created stories freely or to provide other therapeutically useful fantasy material. It was for such children that the author developed The Talking, Feeling, and Doing Game (1973).

THE GAME AND ITS USE

The Talking, Feeling, and Doing Game (Figure 14.1) is similar in format and appearance to many of the typical board games with which most children are familiar. The game begins with the child and the therapist each placing their playing pieces at the START position. They alternate turns, throwing the dice and moving their playing pieces along a curved path of squares which ultimately ends at the FINISH position. If the playing piece lands on a white square, the player takes a Talking Card; on a yellow square, a Feeling Card; and on a red square, a Doing Card. If the playing piece lands on a square marked SPIN, the player spins the spinner, which directs the player to move forward or backward or to gain or lose chips. In addition, there are GO FORWARD and GO BACKWARD squares. The spinner and the latter squares are of little psychological significance. They merely add to the child's fun and thereby enhance the likelihood of involvement. It is the questions and directions on the Talking, Feeling or Doing cards, of course, that are of primary importance and the child is given a reward chip for each response provided. The first person to reach the FINISH position gets five extra reward chips. The winner is the person who has the most chips after both players have reached FINISH, or after the game has been interrupted because the session is over. Active competition for the acquisition of chips is discouraged, rather, the therapist plays at a slow pace and tries to use each response as a point of

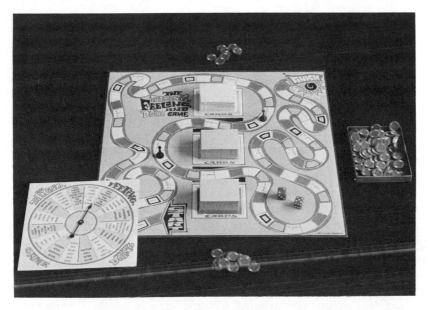

Figure 14.1.   The Talking, Feeling, and Doing Game

departure for a therapeutic interchange. Obviously, the greater the breadth and depth of such discussion, the greater the likelihood it will be of therapeutic value.

The core of the game, of course, are the questions and directions on each of the cards. As is implied by their titles, the Talking Cards direct the child to make comments that are primarily in the cognitive and intellectual realm. The Feeling Cards focus on emotional issues. And the Doing Cards involve some kind of physical activity and/or play acting. There are 104 cards in each stack. The questions in each category range from the very nonthreatening (so that practically any child will be able to respond) to the moderately anxiety provoking. If the child responds (and the most liberal criteria are used—especially for the very inhibited child), a token reward chip is given from the "bank."

None of the cards directs the child into areas that would be as anxiety provoking as relating self-created stories or free fantasy expression. The main purpose of the low-anxiety cards is to ensure the child's providing a response and gaining a chip. These enhance the likelihood that the child will remain involved. Some typical low-anxiety questions: "What's your favorite flavor ice cream?" "What is your address?" "What present would you like to get for your next birthday?" "What is your lucky number? Why?" and "How do you feel when you stand close to someone whose breath smells because he hasn't brushed his teeth?" It is the questions which provoke moderate anxiety that are the most important and these make up over 90% of all the cards. Some typical questions: "Suppose two people were talking about you and they didn't know you were listening. What do you think you would hear them saying?" "A boy has something on his mind that he's afraid to tell his father. What is it that he's scared to talk about?" "Everybody in the class was laughing at a girl. What had happened?" "All the girls in the class were invited to a birthday party except one. How did she feel? Why wasn't she invited?" "What things come into your mind when you can't fall asleep?" "If a fly followed you around for a day, and could then talk about you, what would it say?" "If the walls of your house could talk, what would they say about your family?"

The child's responses are usually revealing of those psychological issues that are most important at the time. The questions cover the broad range of human experiences, and issues related to the responses are likely to be of relevance to the etiology of the child's psychological disturbance. One does well to view symptoms as the most superficial manifestations of underlying unresolved problems. The problems that are being handled inappropriately via symptom formation are generally the same problems with which all of us deal. Accordingly, the topics raised by the cards are likely to relate to issues that are at the very foundation of the psychopathological process. Each response should serve as a point of departure for therapeutic interchanges. The therapist does well to get "as much mileage" as possible from each response. Merely providing the child with a reward chip and then going on with the game defeats the whole purpose of this therapeutic instrument. However, the therapist should use his or her discretion when deciding how much discussion is indicated for each patient. The more resistant and defended child will generally not be able to tolerate an in-depth discussion as well as the child with greater ego-strength.

The therapist plays similarly to the child and also responds to the questions, which should be left randomized. The therapist's knowledge of the child's problems, as well as the responses that have been given to previous cards, can provide guidelines for his or her own responses. The game requires considerable judiciousness on the therapist's part regarding responses to his or her cards. The therapist must always be aware that a response should be selected that is in the child's best interests. Many of the cards ask personal questions about the therapist's life. This brings up an important therapeutic question regarding self-revelation. It is the author's belief that therapists who strictly withhold information about themselves certainly enjoy the advantage of getting more free associations from the patient—associations uncontaminated by the reality of the therapist's life. However, a price is paid for this benefit. I believe that it reduces the humanity of the therapeutic relationship and fosters unrealistic ideas about what other human beings are like. Elsewhere (1975a) this author elaborated in detail on the question of the therapist's revelation versus nonrevelation. In accordance with this position, I answer each question honestly, even when a response involves the revelation of personal material. However, such divulgences are not made indiscriminately. Some personal experience is selected that will not only be revelant to the child, but will not compromise my own privacy and/or that of my family. I often find it useful to relate an experience that occurred at the time in my life when I was at the age at which the child is at the present time. This generally enhances the child's interest in my response, because children usually enjoy hearing about the childhood experiences of their parents and other significant figures.

It is rare that I do not answer a question. However, I give children the opportunity not to answer if they do not wish to. In such cases I will often inform such children that failure to answer will result in their not getting a reward chip and thereby lessening the likelihood of winning the game. This can serve to motivate some children at least to try to respond to the card. It is not immediately appreciated by many therapists that the main determinant as to who wins the game is much more luck than anything else. If each player were to answer each card, then the determinant as to who wins would be the dice. If a player gets a large number of high throws, then he or she will reach FINISH earlier and thereby acquire fewer chips. On the other hand, if a player gets a large number of low throws, then more chips will be acquired in the course of going from START to FINISH. Because high and low throws tend to average out for each player, the number of wins and losses also averages out over time.

CLINICAL MATERIAL: EXAMPLES OF TYPICAL RESPONSES

In this section I discuss some of the common responses I give to some of the cards. It is important for the reader to appreciate that these are not my invariable replies. Each response is tailored to the particular needs of the child. However, there are some responses that I commonly give because they are so uniformly useful. And it is these that I will focus on here.

Talking Cards

If a fly followed you around for a day and could then talk about you, what would it say?

For the impulsive child I might give an answer like: "Dr. Gardner certainly thinks in advance before he does anything. He tries to figure out what the consequences of his actions will be, before he does anything. In this way he avoids a lot of trouble for himself."

What do you think about a girl who sometimes wished that her sister were dead?

This card can be particularly useful for the child who feels excessively guilty over the usual angry thoughts and feelings that enter most children's minds. But even with the less inhibited, I often answer along these lines: "It's perfectly normal for a girl to wish that her sister were dead—especially if they had a big fight or when her sister has done something that she thinks is very cruel. But there's a big difference between having such thoughts come into her head and *really wanting* her sister to die. In my opinion, she'd be pretty sick or weird if she really wanted her sister to die. But she'd be normal if she just had such wishes from time to time—especially when she's very angry at her."

If a child, however, is extremely inhibited in the expression of anger, I might talk about a girl who is extremely inhibited over such thoughts and thinks that having them is a terrible sin or crime. I would then elaborate upon the fact that she felt so guilty about these thoughts that she feared telling anyone, even her best friends. While depressed over such preoccupations one day, she encounters a teenager (the supreme authority, in the view of most younger chldren) who inquires into the sources of her despondency. In the ensuing discussion he attempts to assuage her guilt by impressing upon her the normality of such thoughts and feelings. In the course of providing such reassurance, he might make a comment like: "You're like everybody else with regard to having such thoughts and feelings. The only difference between you and others is that you feel so bad, so guilty, over these normal thoughts."

What do you think about a girl who doesn't take care of her dog?

"I think that the parents of such a girl should warn her that if she doesn't start taking good care of her dog, taking it out, feeding it, and doing all the other things that a dog owner should do, that they will no longer let her keep the dog. Then, if she doesn't 'shape up' and start taking care of the dog, they might give it away for a few days or weeks to a kennel or a friend. Often this will help her remember to do the thing she's supposed to do. If, however, after the dog is brought back and she still doesn't start taking care of it, then I would suggest that they find a new home for the dog because the girl is not living up to her responsibilities." This card can be especially useful for children who have little sense of commitment to their responsibilities and are somewhat oblivious to the consequences of their failure to assume them.

What do you think about a girl who curses at her mother?

"I think it's completely normal to *think* curse words at your mother. When people get angry these words normally come into their minds. However, it's generally not a good idea to *say* such words to a parent. Generally, it's usually wiser to use words that are *more polite* than those that come into your mind. The important thing is to let the anger out and tell the parent what is causing you to be angry. You want to use the anger to help change the situation that is causing you to be angry in the first place. If you do this with polite words you're more likely to be successful. If you use curse words, you're more likely to get the parent even angrier and then you'll not only accomplish nothing, but make things worse. Sometimes letting out your anger helps and sometimes it doesn't. Even if it doesn't you'll at least feel better about yourself for having tried to change the thing that has made you angry. The important thing is to let out your anger, but in words that are more polite than the ones that come into your mind.

Everybody has one or a few bad habits. Name some of yours.

"One of my bad habits is that I work too hard. There are some people who don't work hard enough. They try to get through doing things as quickly as possible and don't take things very seriously. One of my problems is that I sometimes take things too seriously. It's best to be somewhere in the middle." This is the kind of response that I would tend to give to a child who is slipshod in his or her attitude toward school work and the assumption of obligations. It is very important that therapists provide children with examples of their own deficiencies—when the situation warrants such revelation—in an uncontrived way. All too often (and this is especially true in the classical psychoanalytic approach), the patient comes to view the therapist as perfect. This negative comparison between the patient and the therapist is antitherapeutic, the benefits to be derived from such therapy notwithstanding. The Talking, Feeling, and Doing Game provides the therapist with an opportunity to expose deficiencies in an uncontrived and natural way. Such exposures help to prevent the aforementioned ego-debasing, unfavorable comparison between the patient and the therapist.

What sport are you worst at?

"It's really hard to pick one sport that I am worst at, because I'm so poor at so many. I don't get enough exercise and this is one of the reasons why I'm so poor at so many sports. I'm particularly bad at basketball, which requires a lot of practice if one is to be good. I know that if I practiced more, I could be better." This response helps the child view the therapist as a human being with liabilities of his or her own. It tends to narrow the antitherapeutic gap that often exists between the patient's view of him or herself and that of the therapist—the patient being the "sick" one and the therapist being the "healthy" one. I also introduce the element here that this deficit could potentially be reduced if I were to dedicate myself to practicing more. The advice I am providing for myself, of course, is also being given to the patient.

A girl was standing at the window, staring out for a long time. What was she looking at?

There are a wide variety of responses that I will give to this question. It is closer to the blank card of the Thematic Apperception Test (Murray, 1936) than many of the other verbal projective questions posed in this game. For the child who is scapegoating other children, I might respond: "She was looking at a big boy picking on a little boy. She knew that the big boy thought he was quite a 'big shot' for being able to beat up the little kid. She thought that really, in his heart, he knew that it wasn't such a great feat to be beating up a little kid. He also thought that the kids who were watching were very impressed with him. Actually, if he knew what they were thinking, he wouldn't be so proud of himself. If he knew that they thought that he was really a *coward* for picking on little kids, he'd be ashamed of himself, not proud of himself."

For the child who is frequently scapegoated, I might respond: "She's watching a bigger boy pick on a smaller boy. The smaller boy, even though he is a little smaller, is fighting back quite hard. The bully is quite surprised when the smaller kid gives him a big punch in the belly and then another one in the face. But the smaller boy realizes that the bully is still bigger than him and could probably still win the fight. So he runs away as fast as he can and gets some of his friends. They come back and then chase the bully away. The smaller boy feels good about himself for having stood up to the bully."

Through the same window, the girl here observes many other things. For example, she will watch school-phobic children slowly desensitize themselves to their separation anxiety and gradually accomplish successful school attendance. She will watch children who are fearful of sleeping over at other children's homes bravely squelch their fears and make the visits. She will watch children who have "goofed off" throughout the school year shamefacedly return home with their report cards, sorry that they had not paid closer attention to their school work during the year. She will watch children who cheat at games being asked to leave the group by their irate peers.

What is one of the smartest things a person can do? Why?

For the impulsive child I might answer, "One of the smartest things a person can do is to think in advance about the consequences of his or her acts. People who think in advance are less likely to do things that cause trouble to themselves as well as others."

For the child who utilizes denial mechanisms as a primary defense, I might respond, "One of the smartest things a person can do is to look honestly at and think carefully about a problem. People who try to hide their problems hardly ever solve them. Those who look at their problems are more likely to solve them. For the older child, I might elaborate upon the fact that withdrawal, avoidance, and hiding may make one initially comfortable in that one may protect oneself from certain anxieties. However, I point out that ultimately these maneuvers are counterproductive and even detrimental in that the individual does not then deal with the basic problem.

A girl was the only one in the class not invited to a birthday party. Why do you think she wasn't invited?

For children who are self-indulgent and egocentric, who have little capacity to put themselves in the position of others, I might respond: "The girl was mean and selfish. She only thought of herself and not others. She always wanted to be first and never thought how badly others felt when she insisted that she be first."

For the disruptive, agitated child I might respond: "She was always making a lot of fuss and noise. She didn't sit still very long and was always bothering other people. Also she often made a lot of noise. So they didn't invite her because they thought that she would ruin the party with all her noise and fussing and make it harder for others to have fun."

Make up a message that you would put in a bottle that you would throw into the ocean.

To the "know-it-all" I might respond: "Please help us. We're stranded on a small island about 5 miles east of Cape May, New Jersey. We were wise guys and didn't listen to the storm warnings. The radio warned that all small craft should leave the water because the weather was going to be bad and windy. We didn't listen and now we're sorry. Please help us."

What things come into your mind when you can't fall asleep.

"When I can't fall asleep I usually think about 'unfinished business' of the day. If I haven't finished something that I should have, it may linger on my mind and interfere with my going to sleep. I may feel worried about what might happen because I didn't do what I was supposed to do. However, when I do all the things I'm supposed to do, then I don't have this trouble and I fall asleep right away." The answer is obviously designed for the child with poor follow-through and emphasizes the inner (rather than the outer) consequences of such negligence.

Feeling Cards

The Feeling Cards deal with affective and emotional issues. They encourage the child to express feelings and they are particularly useful for children who are inhibited in this regard. I believe that a common error which therapists frequently make is to view the expression of feelings as an end in itself in therapy. I view the expression of feelings as a first step toward the alleviation of difficulties. The feelings serve to enhance one's efficacy in reaching goals. We fight harder when we are angry, we run faster when we are frightened, we mourn more effectively when we cry, we love more ardently when we are sexually excited, we eat more fully when we are hungry, and we sleep more deeply and effectively when we are tired. This goal, of feeling expression, is an extremely important part of the therapeutic process. The Feeling Cards provide the therapist with an opportunity to help the patient deal effectively with feelings.

Tell about something you did that made you very proud.

Unfortunately, most of the cards in *The Talking, Feeling, and Doing Game* will elicit material of a negative nature. Therapy, by necessity, requires focusing on undesirable and often embarrassing traits if it is to be effective. However, the therapist should make every reasonable attempt to focus on assets and other ego-enhancing qualities as part of the therapeutic procedure. Some of the cards in the game provide such an opportunity for the child. The response I commonly give to this card is: "I'm very proud to have made up this *Talking, Feeling, and Doing Game.* Lots of psychiatrists, psychologists, and social workers use it and that makes me feel very good because it helps many children talk about their problems."

For a child who shows poor motivation in school I might respond: "I was very proud on the day that I graduated from medical school. It took many years and it was a lot of hard work, but it certainly was worth it. Sometimes when I really didn't feel like studying, and I would have preferred to go out and have a good time, I stayed in and studied because I knew that it was important to do so if I were to become a doctor someday. I've never been sorry that once in a while I missed out on good times in order to become a doctor. I think I made the right choice. This doesn't mean that I never had good times; I certainly did while I was a medical student. It was just that I had to give up some of the good times in order to study to become a doctor."

How do you feel when you stand close to someone whose breath smells because he hasn't brushed his teeth?

This question is particularly useful for Minimal Brain Dysfunction (MBD) children who often have trouble putting themselves in other people's position. For such children I will often respond: "I think that's a pretty disgusting habit. The person's breath smells and it's often nauseating to stand near such a person if you have to smell his breath. It can make you sick to your stomach. I think that person doesn't think about how he affects others. If he did, he would brush his teeth."

What do you think about a boy who sometimes plays with his penis when he's alone?

This card is obviously designed for the sexually inhibited child. I generally respond: "I think that's perfectly normal for a boy to play with his penis *once in a while* when he's *alone*. However, if he does it so much that he neglects doing his homework or playing with other children, then I would consider it a problem. Also, if he does it in front of other people, it shows that he hasn't learned proper manners. Although it's perfectly normal and healthy to do such a thing, most agree that it's a private, personal matter that should be done alone." There is a similar question for a girl regarding playing with her vagina and I respond similarly.

A girl was very angry at her father and wished that he would be hit by a car. Later that day he was hit by a car. How did she feel? What did she think?

To the child with an anger inhibition problem, I might respond: "The girl thought that her wishing that her father be hit by a car actually caused him to be hit by a car. However, when she discussed it with her mother, her mother convinced her that her thinking was wrong. Her mother convinced her that wishing for something to happen, no matter how hard she wished, could not make that thing happen. She also helped her feel less guilty about her thoughts. She helped her realize that when you're angry at someone you often think of harmful things happening to them, even though you really don't want them to. And this is what happened with this girl. She was angry at her father and had the wish that he would get hit by a car, but she *really* didn't wish that it would happen. The thought just came into her head. One of the main lessons she learned from this was that angry thoughts can't harm. Another lesson she learned was that when you're angry at somebody all kinds of terrible things may enter your mind that you really don't want to happen. Such thoughts are normal."

Say three curse words. What do you think of people who use these words?

This card is designed for the child who is inhibited in the proper use of profanity in socially acceptable ways and situations. The child may be initially astounded to hear me use such words—believing that it is inappropriate for a doctor to utilize profanity. Generally, I will respond with: "Shit. Crap. Fuck. I think these words are fine to use if you're having a fight with a friend of yours outside your home. They serve a useful purpose. They get out anger without *actually* hurting the other person. However, it's a bad idea to use these words in front of parents, teachers, and other adults. They usually get very upset and angry and will tell you that it's not proper to use these words in front of others. So, it's often best to use words that are *more polite* than these if you want to get something accomplished. There are times when these words are the best words to use. If another kid speaks to you with such words, it can often be useful to use similar words back. There's an old saying, 'Sticks and stones may break my bones, but names will never hurt me.' This tells very well what I said before about dirty words helping you get and use anger without actually hurting anyone."

What do you think is the purpose of crying?

This card can also be useful for children who are emotionally inhibited. To such a child I might say: "Crying helps you get out feelings. After you've had a good cry your chest feels clearer and you feel better. But it's also important to talk about the problem that's making you cry so that you can try to solve it."

Everybody in the class was laughing at a boy. What had happened?

For the child who is inattentive in school I will sometimes answer: "He wasn't listening while the teacher was talking. Then she asked him a question. He guessed an answer and it was not only wrong, but it was funny. That's why everybody laughed at him. He was then sorry that he hadn't paid attention."

What do you think is the ugliest thing in the whole world? Why?

"I think the ugliest thing in the whole world is a human being who has wasted his or her life. An example would be some of the bums you see on the street who are drunkards and have no place to live. It's very sad. If they had worked harder when they were younger and tried to do things to help themselves, they might not be where they are today." One can argue that this is very heavy medicine for a child. I have not, however, found it to be specifically psychologically detrimental.

What was the worst punishment you ever got in your whole life? What had you done wrong?

"When I was about eight or nine, my brother and I didn't come home at 6 o'clock when we were supposed to. Instead, we played out in some fields near my house and didn't come home until way after dark—until after 10 o'clock. My parents were very upset and angry and were worried about us. My father gave me a big spanking, a spanking that I never forgot. I was sorry then that I didn't think about their feelings and about how worried they'd be about us when we didn't tell them where we were." The question not only helps the child appreciate the consequences of being insensitive to other people's feelings, but also helps the child see me as a real human being with real parents and as someone who has also made mistakes in his life. As mentioned, this lessens antitherapeutic, unfavorable comparisons.

You accidentally break a window and are quite sure that no one saw you do it. Tell about what you would then do.

For children with weak superegos, who need some strengthening in that area, I might respond: "I would probably want to walk or even run away as fast as possible so that nothing would happen to me. However, I personally wouldn't do that. I'd think about the person whose window I broke, how bad he or she would feel, and how angry that person would be about having to pay money to buy a new window. Because of my feelings for that other person, I would go into the house, tell what I did, and offer to pay for the window. Then I would feel much better about myself. If I ran away, I'd feel bad about myself. I'd feel guilty and feel that I was a coward. I really wouldn't have much respect for myself then. To avoid having these feelings I'd pay for the window."

Doing Cards

The Doing Cards, as their name implies, focus primarily on physical activity. Generally, the topics covered are not as emotionally charged as those in the Talking Cards and Feeling Cards stack. They do, however, still provide a good deal of meaningful therapeutic material. They also help children become freer in expressing themselves physically.

Make believe that someone grabbed something of yours. Show what you would do.

This card is designed to help children with self-assertion problems. My common answer is: "I would first try to use talk before using action. I'd tell the child to give it back and threaten to grab it back if he or she doesn't return it. If the child was my size or a little taller, I'd try to grab it back, providing it wasn't something that could break. If it was something that could break and/ or the person was bigger, I would threaten to call the teacher or my parent(s) if it wasn't given back immediately. I might ask a friend or two to help me get it back. But I wouldn't just stand there, say nothing, and let the person get away with it."

Make believe you're reading a magazine showing pictures of nude ladies. What do you think about such magazines?

This card is designed for children who are sexually inhibited. While making believe that I am thumbing through a magazine I, with a gleeful expression on my face, will say, "Gee, these pictures are great. It's really fun to look at these pictures of these nude women. I'm not saying that I do it all the time. It's just fun to look at them once in a while."

You're standing in line to buy something and an adult pushes himself in front of you. Show what you would do.

"I would tell the person that this is my place in line and that I would appreciate his going to the back of the line and waiting his turn like everyone else. If the person looks like he's crazy, someone who might do dangerous things, I wouldn't make a big deal out of it. There are times when it's smart not to speak up and fight for your rights, but most often it's wise to do so. The important thing is to size up the situation, and get a lot more information before acting. Otherwise, you may find yourself in a lot of trouble."

Make believe you're dreaming. What is the dream about?

"I'm dreaming that I'm a kid again and that I'm going into the classroom to take a big test. Unfortunately, instead of studying a lot the night before, I watched television all evening. So I'm not prepared for the test and I'm very scared that I'm going to fail it. And when the teacher gives out the test, I see that the questions are very hard. I'm very sorry that I didn't study and I'm scared of getting a failing grade. I feel terrible and I'm getting increasingly frightened as I can't answer question after question. I'm thinking about what the teacher will think about me as well as my parents. I'm very scared and sad at the same time. Just then I wake up and *boy, am I relieved,* because it was only a dream." My response, of course, emphasizes the consequences of not fulfilling one's obligations—a common problem for children in treatment.

Make believe you're speaking to someone on the phone. Whom are you speaking to? What are you saying?

"I'm speaking to the principal of a girl who is seeing me in treatment. He's asked my advice about whether or not she should be required to repeat the third grade. He tells me that she really isn't ready to go into the fourth grade, because her work has been so poor, and she hasn't really tried all year. However, he thinks that she'll be very upset if she were not promoted, especially because all her friends will be. I tell him that the reason for promotion is learning what you're supposed to have learned. If she hasn't learned what she was supposed to learn, then I would suggest that she repeat the third grade. I tell him that if she goes on to the fourth grade, without understanding what she should have learned in the third grade, she's going to get into a lot of trouble and may lose interest in school altogether. He takes my advice and decides to keep her in the third grade. He thanks me and that's the end of our conversation." In general, I'm very much against psychological and social promotions. The response, of course, informs the child of this philosophy and serves to tell him or her that I will not be supportive of such a promotion at the end of the school year.

Make believe you're opening up a letter that you've just received from someone. What does the letter say?

"It's a letter from the mother of a child I once treated. It says, 'Dear Dr. Gardner: It's been a year now since you last saw Jimmy and I want to tell you how well he's doing. He's studying much harder in school and he has many more friends. He told me that he learned some important and useful things from you and he still talks about you from time to time. He also said that he learned a lot of useful things from your book, *Stories About the Real World.* At first, he didn't take you very seriously. But later, when he did, he realized that coming to see you could be very useful. I hope all is going well with you. Sincerely, Mrs. Jones.'" My purposes here are self-explanatory: I encourage serious receptivity to treatment and promise a reduction and alleviation of problems for those who take the therapy seriously.

SUMMARY

The clinical material just reviewed represents only a few of the possible responses to some of the cards in each category.This particular material was selected because it was representative. I have described some of my common responses and I well recognize that each therapist has his or her own collection. It is imporant for the reader to appreciate, however, that these *common* responses are not my *standard* or *stock* responses. There are many children who receive entirely different responses to their cards because their problems do not warrant the aforementioned responses. Just as the responding story in The Mutual Storytelling Technique is specifically designed to relate to the particular problems that the child is revealing through the stories, the therapist's responses to the cards in The Talking , Feeling, and Doing Game should also be tailored specifically to the particular psychological needs of the child. Accordingly, there is little place for standard answers and the responses I have described above are not exceptions to this principle. This is a crucial point for the therapist to keep in mind.

REFERENCES

Conn, J. H. (1939) The child reveals himself through play. *Mental Hygiene,* **23**(1), 1–21.

Conn, J. H. (1941a) The timid, dependent child. *Journal of Pediatrics,* **19**(1),1–2.

Conn, J. H. (1941b) The treatment of fearful children. *American Journal of Orthopsychiatry,* **11**(4), 744–751.

Conn, J. H. (1948) The play-interview as an investigative and therapeutic procedure. *The Nervous Child*, **7**(3), 257–286.

Conn, J. H. (1954). Play interview therapy of castration fears. *American Journal of Orthopsychiatry*, **25**(4), 747–754.

Hug-Hellmuth, H. von (1913) *Aus dem Seelenleben des Kindes*. Leipzig, Germany: Deuticke.

Hug-Hellmuth, H. von (1921) On the technique of child analysis. *International Journal of Psychoanalysis*, **2**(3/4), 285–305.

Gardner, R. A. (1971) *Therapeutic communication with children: The mutual storytelling technique*. New York: Jason Aronson.

Gardner, R. A. (1973) *The Talking, Feeling, and Doing Game*. Cresskill, N.J.: Creative Therapeutics.

Gardner, R. A. (1975a) *Psychotherapeutic approaches to the resistant child*. New York: Jason Aronson.

Gardner, R. A. (1975b) Psychotherapeutic approaches to the resistant child (2 one-hour cassette tapes). Cresskill, N.J.: Creative Therapeutics.

Murray, H. (1936). *Thematic Apperception Test*. New York: The Psychological Corporation.

Solomon, J. C. (1938) Active play therapy. *American Journal of Orthopsychiatry*, **8**(3), 479–498.

Solomon, J. C. (1940) Active play therapy: Further experiences. *American Journal of Orthopsychiatry*, **10**(4), 763–781.

Solomon, J. C. (1951) Therapeutic use of play. In H. H. Anderson & G. L. Anderson (Eds.), *An introduction to projective techniques*. Englewood Cliffs, N.J.: Prentice-Hall. Pp. 639–661.

Solomon, J. C. (1955) Play technique and the integrative process. *American Journal of Orthopsychiatry*, **25**(3), 591–600.

CHAPTER 15

The Use of Two Houses
in Play Therapy

LINDA KUHLI

INTRODUCTION

References in therapeutic literature to the use of houses in play therapy are relatively few. Erikson (1937) noted that the house is the only regularly occurring representation of the whole human form found in children's play: "The house a child creates often reveals how he perceives his body and what he feels about it" (p. 143). House structures are also described as symbolic expressions of a child's mental state (such as being caged) that can frequently be traced to early traumatic experiences (p. 141). They can indicate the level of a child's object relations, self-esteem, and identification within the family (p. 153). Moustakas (1953) described a little girl's play sessions in which she verbally depicted two homes, one wild and one peaceful, indicating ambivalent feelings towards her home situation (p. 84). Klein (1961) interpreted a boy's drawing of an old deserted house as his mother whom he saw as unprotected and in danger of being injured (p. 214).

In modern society, children face an increasing number of relocations, dissolutions, and family crises. Littner (1956) notes that it is painful for children to be placed away from the family for day care or long-term placement. Their anxieties must be recognized and dealt with if they are to benefit from these experiences (p. 5). Repression is used as a defense against feelings of abandonment, helplessness, and anger. This can result in self-destructive behavior which damages a child's ability to be receptive to a new placement and sets him up for rejection by the new parenting figures (p. 17). Fraiberg (1962) goes

I would like to thank Genevieve B. Oxley, Lecturer, School of Social Welfare, University of California, Berkeley, and Joel S. Saldinger, Medical Director, Lincoln Child Center, Oakland, California, for their consultation in writing this paper. Parts of this chapter have appeared previously in slightly altered form in the *American Journal of Orthopsychiatry*, **49**(3), 431–435. Copyright © 1979 the American Orthopsychiatric Association, Inc. Reproduced by permission.

further to state that the ability to form new object relationships may become permanently impaired.

Clinicians in placement agencies are often faced with children who have moved through numerous placements and have never worked through the initial separation process. Expanding the use of houses in therapy may enhance treatment for children working through separation trauma.

TREATMENT PROCEDURE AND CASE MATERIAL

Setting

This case history describes an experience with a child in Lincoln Child Center's residential treatment facility for emotionally disturbed children. The therapist's office contains a typical assortment of toys and includes a large, two-story house inhabited by several dolls. A box of blocks provides material for building another house.

Subject

Emily was the third of four siblings. Her home life was characterized by extreme neglect and reports of physical abuse. Her mother first noticed withdrawn unresponsive behavior when Emily was four months old. Developmental landmarks were described as late but normal. With the birth of her younger sister Laura, when she was three, Emily regressed further and became enuretic. Laura received the bulk of the mother's affection and protection, leaving Emily feeling worthless, unloved, and good only to the extent she could model herself after her younger sister. Emily's growth from that time was characterized by the increasing conflict with her mother and peers, and with immature psychosocial development. She was excluded from the first grade due to extreme hyperactivity, distractibility, and refusal to follow directions in kindergarten. Sensory integration and speech evaluation indicated poor form recognition, a lack of focused and cohesive thought patterns, and a need to simplify incoming stimuli. Her IQ tested at 81. At the time of placement at age seven, Laura was the only other child not removed from the home.

Emily's ability to function in the new setting at Lincoln Child Center was considerably below age level. Her needs for attention and affection from staff took the form of excessive whining and clinging behavior. Rather than verbalize her feelings, she threw tantrums or became withdrawn. She sought help with even the simplest tasks, such as bed-making, but staff felt that she was often more capable than she presented herself to be.

During Emily's first year and a half of weekly psychotherapy, she primarily focused on the dollhouse and the theme of trying to put order in a disorderly environment. She found everyone a place to sleep, regardless of how cramped the space. Her style of communication was one of endless questioning and perseverance, with a very flat and depressed affect and self-protection from challenge or overstimulation.

Emily appeared to be struggling with her repression of a tremendous amount of rage, fear, and guilt over the inadequate mothering she and her siblings experienced. While physically she was in the latency stage, her doll play indicated a more primitive fixation and preoccupation with nurturing. She had a limited sense of control over her environment and limited ability to assert her own identity. Direction in therapy was focused on helping Emily conceptualize areas of conflict within the dollhouse in order to work through repressed fears and fantasies. It was felt that her severe organic impairments and difficulty hearing and responding to her therapist considerably limited her ability to use play therapy.

After a year and a half of placement, another sensory integration evaluation concluded that all efforts should be made to simplify the types and degree of stimuli presented to Emily due to gross vestibular system deficits. Within the context of individual psychotherapy, it was suggested that her most commonly chosen media of play, the house, be made less complex. Emily was encouraged to focus her attention on a more simply constructed dollhouse consisting of blocks to form an adult's and a child's room, with furniture suited to match large and small proportions. In time, it became evident that Emily began to attribute special meaning to this new structure and see it as a release from an anxiety-ridden situation which had had no solution within its own boundaries. Although this was originally designed to help construct order in her physical environment, it proved to fill a need on an emotional level. As the therapist realized this, she began using the two houses as the metaphoric symbols they represented to the child.

Results

The process of problem solving went through several definable stages and resulted in rejection of past parenting and identification with new standards of care offered in residence. First, movement of the family figures between the two houses enabled Emily to identify the dangers she saw within her home environment. The big playhouse represented her own home where robbers entered through unlocked or broken windows to rape, steal, and kidnap children. Family pets proved to be monsters who tried to hurt people. Conflict and tension were at a continuously high level.

Once her fears were clearly portrayed, a guest entered the big home and served as a "good" mother who took care of the children, while the real mother stood by passively as a neutral figure. In other sessions, the family was put to bed safely in the second house, and when they became frightened the surrogate figure came to reassure and protect them. The warmly portrayed surrogate figure symbolized the counselors in Emily's unit.

At this point, Emily depicted a family meeting in her home where a social worker said, "You have problems little girl. You have to leave!" The doll was sent to another home where the children prepared for her coming by making up a special bed for her (an act of no small significance to Emily). For the first time in treatment, Emily had consciously identified her perception of herself as a "problem" to her family. Then in a turn of fate the introduction of the small playhouse seemed to open up to her the possibility of an alternative home where there could be order and caring. Her ability to play out her rejection was facilitated by her recognition that she had found something better. She tested the new homes' dependability by asking if it was a place where kids could stay a long time. Her conception of an alternative home took months to incorporate as she continually moved herself and the family back and forth between the two houses.

Her use of two houses demonstrated a tentative trial in play toward a solution to the dilemma of splitting allegiance between two homes. As described by Greenacre (1959), "by repeatedly going over an experience, it becomes more real and familiar to the child, allowing fears to give way to recognition" (p. 65). With this method, Emily had an opportunity to reverse her real-life role as the receptor, and took on a position of power within the play.

With determination and no small feeling of guilt, Emily often tried to reestablish the family within the old house, only to feel overwhelmed by its size and lack of structure. She again began perseverative questioning about where everyone would sleep and how everyone would be warmly covered. Due to her frustration, she was gently encouraged to return to the second playhouse where things were less crowded and everyone had his own place. Gradually, Emily worked through many of her feelings of rejection, and integrated the concept of a family being separated from itself and its home.

Meanwhile Emily began defining and asserting her own concept of a nurturing home environment, separate from her mother's. Having established a place of safety, she went back to the old dollhouse to master fears her mother instilled in her. She began to restore a sense of order to the old house as if to give it a new beginning. Broken windows had paper securely taped over them to keep the family safe and warm. Loose nails in walls were hammered in solidly. Dependence on mother for her frame of reference decreased.

Ten months after the introduction of the second playhouse, Emily's identification with the parenting she received at the child center became discernible. The little girl doll went to her doll mother and told her that the new home turned out to be a nice place after all where "the kids get help with their problems and get presents too!" A new self-esteem was evident in her attempts to make pretty things for the children to wear, and to size furniture to their proportions. Constant references to her sister diminished. Contact with her family was maintained in play through pilgrimages to her first home to be reunited with the family for holidays.

Emily became increasingly capable of verbalizing her feelings about the poor parenting she received from her mother on visits home. She preferred being with staff and children at the child center. She declined her mother's request to go home for her birthday and clearly laid out ground rules for her own protection when her sister asked to make a visit. How Emily wanted things done in her environment began taking priority over how others wanted them done.

The culmination of this growing confidence and assertiveness was her decision not to go on overnight visits with her mother when the circumstances of the visits frightened her (broken windows and being left at home alone with her younger sister at night). She began observing her mother's poor judgment and difficulty handling problems at home. She also talked of her younger sister's previously "perfect" behavior, which she now saw as inappropriate. Meanwhile, in therapy, the release of energy hitherto bound in frustration enabled a gradual development of interest in cognitive tasks requiring frustration tolerance, concentration, and perceptual decoding abilities. A lifting of her depression was also apparent.

In the living unit, Emily evolved from using passive resistance as her only mode of control, and she became noticeably more assertive in situations. Staff observed improvement in her ability to see she could make choices in her life and get her needs met. She began to act much happier and began paying attention to her appearance. An increased use of humor and initiative contributed to her becoming the focus of more attention. There was also an increase in demanding, unreasonable behavior, characteristic of the "terrible twos" which was seen as a precursor to further growth.

Performance in school was the slowest area to change due to the feelings of failure it induced. At times she would be quite dull, lethargic, and unable to focus on tasks, whereas on other days she seemed brighter and more animated. Her teachers noticed that perseverative questioning was slowly decreasing and becoming more logical and directed. Sensory integration testing indicated very slow but steady growth.

On the occasional home visits, mother was pleased with Emily's increased responsiveness, cooperativeness, and inquisitive nature.

IMPLICATIONS

There are many traumatic situations that children face which could be applicable to a two-house approach. Change in a family structure to accommodate stepparents and siblings is a common cause for stress among children. For a child in outpatient therapy, this approach could serve as a setting for "testing out" new family members, and expressing anger toward them in a safe environment. A child could also use two houses to deal with the birth of a new sibling by playing out the process of entry into the family and what he or she fears will be the ramifications.

The approach could also serve as a means of mourning the loss of loved ones due to death, divorce, or other circumstances. When a child experiences emotional withdrawal of a parent, intolerable stress within the larger home, or temporary loss due to traveling or hospitalization, he or she could use the second house as a retreat. Here the child could define and direct the interaction with family members rather then feeling helpless.

A second house might portray the benefits of becoming invested in alternative support systems or caring people who are able to supplement the parenting a child is getting at home. Nurturing, sources of appropriate limits, and models for identification can be depicted. The second home provides the means for developing a child's sense of values, needs, and fantasies about what is desirable and possible. The child can take from the old that which is valued, and reject or rework that which is not. Changing the ways family members relate to each other and discharging feelings becomes possible within a less threatening context. Afterward, the child has the choice of returning himself or his family to the "real" home.

The subtle variety of factors contributing to the usefulness of the two-house concept in play therapy suggests its value as standard equipment in the playroom.

SUMMARY

A case example is presented, demonstrating the potential for the use of two houses in play therapy to help children master conflicts resulting from separation trauma. Providing two houses stimulates the use in play of a metaphor representing the child's life situation. Different parts of the child and his or her conflicts are able to move back and forth symbolically, enabling the child to grieve, regroup, and accept available solutions to meet needs, and to create new, more successful substitutes.

The case of Emily demonstrates mastery on several levels:

1. The use of two houses to identify and express pent up fears of the home environment.
2. Conceptualization of a surrogate parent and second home as an alternate nurturing modality.
3. Regression in the service of the ego to work through feelings of fear, rejection, guilt, and anger.
4. Development of a new perception of the real mother and increased assertiveness to get her own needs met.
5. New growth facilitated by mastery of past traumas in the old house and identification with the new house and its parenting figures.

The possible implications of such a technique for children with a wide range of problems in different settings is discussed.

REFERENCES

Erikson, E. (1937) Configurations in play—Clinical notes. *Psychoanalytic Quarterly,* **6**(2), 139–213.

Fraiberg, S. (1962) A therapeutic approach to reactive ego disturbances in children in placement. *American Journal of Orthopsychiatry,* **32**(1), 18–31.

Greenacre, P. (1959) Play in relation to creative imagination. *Psychoanalytic Study of the Child,* **14**, 61–80.

Klein, M. (1961) *Narrative of a child analysis.* New York: Basic Books.

Littner, N. (1956) *Some traumatic effects of separation and placement.* New York: Child Welfare League of America.

Moustakas, C. (1953/1956) *Children in play therapy.* New York: McGraw-Hill.

PART FOUR

Play Therapy for Specific Childhood Disorders

The remaining chapters in this book represent the essence of the prescriptive play therapy approach: the modification of general therapeutic approaches for use with children who have special needs. The type of patient problems which may lead the therapist to alter his or her approach are themes or conflicts specific to a particular patient subgroup, the need to involve others in the child's treatment, and difficulty in managing certain patients within the confines of more traditional therapy sessions. The avenues for change open to the therapist include those discussed in Part 3 of this volume as well as: (1) changing the rules of general therapy technique, such as either relaxing or increasing the limits applied, (2) using alternative therapists, para-professionals, or the child's mother, (3) involving the child's parents, siblings, or peers in the therapy, and (4) using play techniques with groups not previously considered to be in need of therapy or considered inappropriate for a play therapy approach. As with the material presented in Part 3, the strategies discussed in each of the following chapters are not meant to be used in isolation but rather are to be viewed as variations of more general theoretical and methodological approaches to play therapy.

CHAPTER 16

Play Therapy for Victims of Child Abuse and Neglect

EBERHARD MANN
JOHN F. MCDERMOTT, JR.

INTRODUCTION

It is estimated that in the United States 1% of all children under the age of 18 years are physically and/or emotionally abused, neglected, or sexually exploited (Oliver, 1978). Most child victims suffer longstanding, serious psychological damage from the abuse or neglect. Mental deficiency (Martin, 1972; Morse et al., 1970) or multiple psychiatric symptoms—depression, hyperactivity, hyperaggressivity, bizarre behaviors, pseudomaturity, or educational difficulties (Martin & Beezeley, 1976) are common outcomes. Green (1978a) described several types of psychopathology observed in physically abused children who were seen in psychotherapy. He found an overall impairment of ego functioning associated with intellectual and cognitive defects, panic states resulting from inflicted and feared trauma, severe distortions of object relations with a lack of trust, impaired impulse control, and low self-concept, self-destructive behaviors, difficulties with separation, and difficulties in school adjustment.

Many of these behavioral and personality traits are also found in the child's parents, who often report history of abuse or neglect during their own childhoods. It is well known that abusive or neglectful parenting is often passed on across generations and that the roots for future distortions in parent–child relationships are laid in early childhood. This indicates that the psychosocial disturbances in abused and neglected children tend to become chronic if they are not treated.

Since child abuse and neglect is considered a symptom of parenting dysfunction, interventions have emphasized a change of the home environment for the child rather than direct treatment. However, a change in the home— either by treatment of the parents alone or foster home placement for the child—is usually not enough to relieve the child's emotional response to the abuse. Foster home placement adds another stress—separation from the youngster's family, which may even worsen behavioral problems. If the problems persist, the child may begin a journey through serial placements, a situation which deepens feelings of rejection. Persistent behavioral difficulties also interfere with school and peer experiences and fuel a sense of failure, isolation, and friendlessness.

It is remarkable that the child abuse literature hardly mentions the psychological treatment needs of children whereas there is a wealth of articles and books on the parents' problems and their treatment. Beezeley et al. (1976a) casually mention that "some abused children will need and benefit from traditional types of psychotherapy" but do not discuss which children should be selected for what kind of problems or for which form of psychotherapy.

There are several reasons for this therapeutic orphaning of the abused child. First, child abuse and neglect tend to be treated as a medical condition. Indeed, it is considered a medical emergency. Typical symptoms (physical and emotional injuries) lead to a diagnosis (abuse and neglect) and recognition of the cause (faulty parenting). The child is considered the innocent victim who needs immediate treatment for the suffered injuries and protection from further harm—either by altering the parents' abusive behavior or removing the child from the home with the hope that a safe environment will normalize him or her. Even if the key professionals working with the parents are concerned about the child's associated emotional problems, they are often unable to help because of the parents' resistance. Parents may have a need to scapegoat the child in order to preserve a sense of self-esteem. It is not they who failed as parents but their "monster child" who caused the misery. Confrontations and interpretations by the therapist are taken as another accusation of bad parenting. On the other hand, the parents' own need for nurturance may make them intensely jealous and competitive for the therapist's attention. To prevent them from terminating therapy prematurely, many therapists choose to focus on the parents alone.

Cohn (1979) evaluated 11 child abuse and neglect treatment programs and found that only three provided direct treatment to a small number of children. All of the children showed significant improvement, whereas success with the parents was infrequent.

Play Therapy for Child Abuse

Whereas the need for individual treatment of the abused child is becoming more clearly recognized, approaches to child therapy have been changing dramatically over the past two decades. An upsurge of new treatment modalities in the 1960s and 1970s included group therapy, behavior modification, psychopharmacology, and family therapy. Most of these modalities require active involvement of the parents in the treatment process. But because of the self-centered, destructive relationship of abusive parents with their children, joint treatment is often contraindicated (Malone, 1979). Play therapy had been the central form of treatment for children in the 1940s and 1950s. Perhaps because it was used for virtually all problems, it gave way to these new and more dramatic approaches. Fewer modern child therapists are expert with play therapy techniques than ever before. It now returns as a specific treatment of choice for certain conditions such as the effects of child abuse. It has been found useful, if not essential, to prevent crystalization and internalization of the effects of physical assault, rejection, and neglect, as well as distorted and disturbed parent–child interactions into the personality structure of the child (Green, 1978b; In & McDermott, 1976).

This chapter describes goals, strategies, and problems encountered in the play therapy of 25 abused and neglected children whom we have treated over the past four years at the Child Guidance Center of Kapiolani-Children's Medical Center in Honolulu, Hawaii. The children, ranging in ages from three to 12 years, were all referred from Child Protective Services. More than half came from foster homes, referred because behavioral problems endangered their continued placement.

The Goals of Play Therapy

The goal of play therapy is to help children master the multiple stresses of abuse and neglect and to correct or prevent deviations in future psychosocial development. Play is particularly useful, since most abused children, even more than children in general, express their innermost feelings and fantasies much more readily through action than verbalization. It permits the necessary distancing from the traumatic events and parents by the use of symbolic materials. To the abused child, adults are unpredictable and always potentially dangerous.

Although every child has individual ways of coping with an abusive environment, common areas of psychological trauma need to be defined and addressed. They can be summarized as follows:

1. Fear of physical assault or fear of abandonment leading to depression and anxiety. These trigger defenses of aggression, distrust, and problems with impulse control.
2. Failure to meet parents' distorted expectations leads to defective object relationships, struggles over dependency, internalization of a "bad child" self-image with poor self-esteem. It furthers the depression already present.
3. Difficulty achieving separation and autonomy. The child remains tied to "splitting" the self and others into all good or all bad, based on experiences of being alternately rewarded and rejected unpredictably and arbitrarily.
4. Multiple rejections, out-of-home placements, including hospitalizations, prolong and heighten separation anxiety and ambivalence over attachment to adult caretakers.

Indications

All preschool and early school age children who show emotional disturbance are candidates for play therapy specially designed for abused children. Ideally, play therapy should begin after the child's home environment has stabilized enough to prevent reabuse, or continued neglect. Concomitant—but not joint—treatment of the parents is critical. Unfortunately, many parents have difficulty changing; they may stop attacking the child but they may continue to scapegoat him, because he cannot live up to the projective identification they have assigned him. But even in such a situation, play therapy may still provide the child with an experience of a different, safe environment where he or she can separate an outer world from the parents' idiosyncratic demands even if he or she cannot escape them. If the child is in foster care, the foster parents should be counseled about the children's special difficulties, for example, the need for reenactment of an abusive situation, and ways they can avoid participating in this. The structured milieu of a residential treatment setting may enhance the work of play therapy with more disturbed children.

Contraindications

In our experience, there is one major contraindication to play therapy: It should not be attempted if it mobilizes so much rage in the parents that the child's safety is endangered. Let us address this issue with a case example.

Peter, a 5-year-old boy, was referred for hyperactivity, physical attacks on his mother and preschool peers (biting, kicking, and pulling hair), and poor language skills. He was the only child born to a single woman who had been deserted by her boyfriend when he learned of the pregnancy.

Mother herself was severely neglected and scapegoated during her childhood and at age 14 was thrown out of her home. Guilt over having displeased her parents, coupled with rage over her rejection, found their way into a pattern of highly ambivalent, hostile, dependent, and violent interpersonal relationships. Her own self-image of a worthless child was projected onto her son, Peter, whose every move from infancy was seen and felt as deliberately hurting and defying her. If he was sleeping, she felt ignored and woke him; if he cried, she felt unloved. When angry, she would scold, then hit him, or as her anger escalated, cover his face with pillows to "choke him dead." When he began school, the teacher reported abuse when Peter came to class with a black eye.

When mother brought Peter to the first therapy session, she looked more bruised than her son. Her face and arms showed scratch and bite marks; her ear lobes were swollen. She stated she was relieved to find help for her boy. Then she proceeded to describe her suffering with the child. She portrayed him as an adultlike sadist, who spent his time thinking how best to torture her. During this time she held Peter tightly embraced on her lap, while he struggled to get away. Even when he began pulling her hair she did not loosen her grip, but actually lowered her head, bringing it closer to Peter's reach.

Because mother seemed unable to separate her own emotional needs from those of her child, individual psychotherapy for both mother and son by different therapists was recommended. Although mother agreed, she was very suspicious of the child's therapist's intentions. She demanded to know in detail what happened in play therapy. She feared that her son would "lie" and pretend to be a good child, putting her in a bad light. Her fears mounted rapidly until she lost control and severely battered Peter after his third therapy visit.

The case of Peter demonstrates that for children whose parents cannot tolerate any separation from their child, individual therapy may increase risk of abuse—regardless of whether therapeutic changes take place or not.

METHOD

In previous decades, play therapy was considered the treatment of choice for almost every young child seen in a guidance clinic. This is as unrealistic as notions of using family therapy as the universal treatment modality for all children's problems (McDermott & Char, 1974). As mentioned, play therapy now seems specifically indicated for abused and neglected children if the selection of play materials and strategies is designed to deal with their specific problems and is finely tuned to their therapeutic needs, centered around the reenactment in displacement, and the search for new and more adaptive solutions.

The Setting

Since many abused or neglected children have attention deficits and impulse control problems, they automatically act on feelings stemming from violent experiences rather than verbalizing them. To allow safe expression of motoric activity, a separate playroom is needed—it cannot be combined with an office as a play corner. It should be relatively plain, well-carpeted, and contain only the selection of toys chosen for the therapy session. The table and chairs should be easily movable, as the work of play therapy is sometimes better done on the floor. The walls should be washable and decorations limited to inexpensive, easily replaceable, relatively indestructible, and safe enough to be used even as "weapons." Plastic materials are best. Since all these children, over from the usual drawing materials. The room should be large enough to allow the child to withdraw to a corner when he cannot tolerate physical closeness with the therapist. Windows should be made from safety glass and be lockable. In summary, if the playroom contains too much fixed furniture, stacks of toys, bookshelves, telephones, much of the therapist's effort may go toward repeatedly placing limits to prevent injury or property destruction; frustration of the therapist over chaos in his office in such a situation is inevitable.

Play Materials

The choice of toys made available depends on the child's age and stage in therapy, as well as the fact he has been abused or neglected. They should be inexpensive, easily replaceable, relatively indestructible, and safe enough to be used even as "weapons." Plastic materials are best. Since all these children, regardless of age, will deal with family conflicts in play, toys should encourage and facilitate expression of their experiences and fantasies; a dollhouse with conventional rooms, furniture, and people is the most suitably structured and appropriate play material. The use of hand puppets presents problems. Children are less free to shift roles—a necessary defense and therapeutic resolution of conflict over self and parent—as they can with multiple doll figures. If in puppet play they begin to regress massively and attack the therapist, who hides barely disguised behind a puppet, the resulting loss of control and guilt becomes very stressful to the child. In addition, the therapist finds it difficult to decide when to stop the "assault," which in turn confuses and frightens the child.

Most abused children are very concrete and easily confused if only ambiguous play materials such as clay, papier-mâché, or even paper and pencil for drawings are available. They often react with increased anxiety, feeling that they are expected to perform a certain task such as producing a painting or a clay model. We avoid these materials at the beginning of therapy. We also do not use toys which carry both an explicit and powerful symbolic meaning of their own, such as war materials (soldiers, tanks, guns, and cannons). They may indeed elicit conflicts over aggression, but the play may take an endless repetitive ritualistic form without dealing with the more complex family relationships.

Many abused and neglected children need to sense that a safe distance exists between them and the adult therapist. Direct verbal communication is often too threatening. We have found a pair of play telephones as an excellent way to ease communication by distance and displacement in the next stage of therapy when the child shifts from more nonverbal dollhouse play to a more direct interaction which is, nevertheless, still play.

For preschool children, the dollhouse and the telephone are usually sufficient for the entire course of therapy. But for latency-age children, painting, clay materials, or structured competitive games with simple rules may become important in later stages. They should be introduced after the child shows improvement in impulse control, and is ready to delay immediate gratification in return for mastering a project such as drawing or building something, or even testing him- or herself in a game of checkers or cards with the therapist. Any game may be used as long as it permits successful mastery. To do so it must be simple. Complex games such as chess or Monopoly usually require too much attention to the intricate process of the game itself. Berlin (1977) has described in detail the use of checkers in play therapy as a means of therapeutic communication with nonverbal school age children, for whom the learning of rules, pride in accomplishment, and a sense of competency becomes a major developmental task.

Engaging the Abused Child in Play Therapy

Traditionally, play therapy has been found most useful for children whose emotional distress does not seriously impair object relationships or reality testing. The child should be able to play out conflicts creatively with a capacity toward increased self-awareness, which then helps him or her to modify patterns of relationships in a more adaptive, independent way. The parents, of course, should be supportive of the child's strivings to separate and individuate from them.

Abused and neglected children do not fit this model. They are often children with serious deficiencies in impulse control, reality testing, and object relationships and are often thought not to benefit greatly from psychodynamic play therapy (Carek, 1979). We have found that this is a myth. But indeed, play techniques must be sharply modified, sometimes in a way which would be considered nontherapeutic with nonabused children. Let us consider the various special strategies needed to prepare and engage these children in play therapy.

Teaching How to Play. Some children have never learned to play. They are fixated or regressed to a primitive level, unimaginative, inhibited, confused, and unable to use toys purposefully. Sometimes they are even unable to identify them.

CASE EXAMPLE

Amy, four years old, had been in foster care for three months after two episodes of physical abuse which had resulted in skull and rib fractures. Amy was brought to therapy because of poor verbalization, withdrawal, and uncontrollable screaming whenever her foster mother was out of sight. During the first two short therapy sessions, Amy could not tolerate her foster mother's departure. Sitting on her lap, Amy looked at the toys with interest, but would not touch them, even when they were offered by her foster mother. The therapist held a few toys in his own hands, calling them by name—"dolly," "chair," etc. Then he placed them near Amy simply to make them available to her. In the second session, Amy walked to the play table. She picked up a small doll figure, gazed at it intensely, shook it, smelled it, and put it in her mouth as an infant might begin an examination of a new object. As Amy became deeply involved in this, her foster mother was able to leave her chair slowly and walk to the door without any sign of panic in Amy. Soon the therapist placed another doll in front of Amy, gave it a name and Amy exchanged it for the first one. In subsequent sessions more objects were identified and accepted. Amy began to name the objects, imitating the therapist. She became comfortable enough to reach for toys which the therapist offered. The next step was easier—to introduce some concrete, simple play, for example, placing the doll in a chair: "The dolly sits in the chair," was quickly imitated by Amy. During the eighth session, she suddenly threw a doll on the floor, shouting: "Bad Dolly!" This was the beginning of the expression of her own experience and perception of the abuse through imaginative play.

Feeding. For most children, toys and games provide enough "fun" to overcome their reluctance to see a doctor to help them with "problems." Not so for many abused and/or neglected children, who have been deprived of basic physical nurturance and are unable to play for fun. For them, food is the strongest reinforcer—stealing, hiding, or hoarding food as substitution for parental love is a frequent symptom.

Although Gardner (1979) has pointed out the risk of *perpetuating* a pathological pattern if the therapist compensates a lack of genuine affection for the child ("the real thing") with food as a symbol of love, we have found that we often cannot work effectively without it and that we can use it therapeutically.

CASE EXAMPLE

Six-year-old Wendy, who had been living in foster care for six months, came to therapy because of continued stealing of candy from stores, nightly trips to the foster parents' refrigerator to take bread, hamburger meat, or whatever she could find to hoard under her bed, in drawers, and in her schoolbag. The foster family was distraught at Wendy's behavior, as they provided regular meals and food she liked.

Wendy had been raised by two alcoholic parents who had frequently left her unsupervised and unfed, and they had encouraged her to go begging from age three. When neighbors found Wendy alone at home for several days with the parents nowhere to be found, she was placed in a foster home. In therapy, Wendy presented herself as a bossy, impulsive, and oppositional little girl, given to swearing, pounding the table, and throwing the toys if any of her demands were not met instantly. All her attention focused on the candy jar. She would not talk or play unless she received a candy. The therapist told her that he would make a deal. He would give her a candy now and then decide, together with her, when to give another one. Wendy stuffed the first candy in the pocket of her pants. Then she agreed that she would answer one question per candy. This type of bargaining continued for three sessions, but the agreements became more complex without threatening her fear of helplessness if she was not in control. She received one candy for a picture drawing; one candy for a 10-minute play with the dollhouse. Later the candy exchange could be stretched out over time, for example, the number could be "scored" until the end of the session when she received the total earned. With the help of such predictability, Wendy began to feel safe enough to delay gratification. She didn't need to spend all her time and energy on provisions for survival. In the meantime, the dollhouse play began to identify her conflicts. She always played mother, who locked all the children up to "have a good time with daddy." Mother did not care if the children were "starving to death." The therapist, taking the child's role, was scolded, ignored, or laughed at when he cried that he was hungry and lonely. One day, the therapist-child decided to run away to look for "other parents," knocking at the dollhouse door. Wendy suddenly shifted from a "bad mother" to a "good mother," insisting that she cook for the "baby." Now both Wendy and the therapist provided real, though symbolic, food served on toy dishes. Gradually, the therapist, still playing the child, could demand from Wendy, still playing the ideal mother, other signs of affection—being cuddled, sung to, talked to and finally listened to. After another two months, Wendy cautiously switched roles and became the baby, who could accept the "ideal mother's" care, with food losing its significance in therapy. At home the stealing and hoarding of food stopped.

Providing Object Constancy.   Another important special favor useful with many of these children is permitting them to take home a small toy; this keeps a concrete link with the therapist. Multiple rejections in the past have made them distrustful, and they watch suspiciously for signs which would indicate that the therapist might "forget" them. Having their own set of toys in the office or always finding their own pictures on the wall will help to reassure them that they remain in the therapist's mind as a real person. Changes in appointments or cancellations without careful preparation may result in intense feelings of disappointment, withdrawal, or rage and should be avoided as long as these children show little tolerance for handling unpredictability.

Tolerating Dependency and Regression.   With nonabused, neurotic children, play therapy attempts to re-create and resolve conflicts from a solid foundation of ego strength. Prolonged regression and dependence on the therapist is discouraged. The situation is quite different for abused and neglected children, whose dependency needs, similar to those of their parents, have never been met and can become quite overwhelming once the initial stance of distance and distrust has been given up. Expecting independent functioning from those children too early will lead to disaster as it is perceived as just another rejection. At times these children may appear quite competent and autonomous on the surface. They carry out seemingly mature responsibilities in the home; they cook, clean the house, watch siblings, and cater to their parents when they are sick. They are overly perceptive of their parents' emotions and do their best to make them feel good. This "role reversal," in which the child assumes a parenting function and adjusts his or her behaviors, often quite skillfully, to the demands of others, often interferes severely with the development of a sense of self. These children often impress the observer as "nonpersons" because of their chameleonlike, mechanical adaptation to different environments.

CASE EXAMPLE

Eight-year-old Lisa was referred because of insomnia, frequent nightmares, excessive daydreaming, poor school performance, and withdrawal. She had no friends, stating that she was frightened because her classmates were out to hurt her. Lisa had been abused by her mother with frequent beatings which left marks but did not break bones. Although the beatings had stopped a year ago, after mother began to receive homemaking support from Child Protective Services, her views of Lisa as a "dumb and obstinate crybaby" had not changed, and verbal abuse continued unabated. Mother spent much time in bed with hypochondriacal complaints, while Lisa cared for the household and a six-year-old sister. Lisa's father, who reportedly had a good relationship with his daughter, was rarely home from business travel.

In the beginning of therapy, Lisa was withdrawn and would not engage in spontaneous play. She was hypersensitive to the therapist's own behavior; for example, when he coughed, she would remark: "I hope you aren't sick" or "Are you alright?" She followed suggestions to the letter, but was unable to take the initiative in play. Explicit permission had to be given each time before she would use the dollhouse. The therapist asked Lisa to show him what she did at home. Using the dollhouse, she became grimly efficient at scrubbing floors, bathing a baby, feeding a sick mother, massaging her, and asking whether she felt better. To establish a working relationship with Lisa, the therapist couldn't question her supermothering in the beginning. After several weeks, the therapist shifted tactics. He played the role of a child who had fallen sick and needed mother to take care of him. At first, Lisa appeared confused, exclaiming "Lisa *never* gets sick." The therapist replied that the doll-child was not Lisa but another girl named "Jenny." Lisa then proceeded to play "Jenny's" mother, who shouted angrily that Jenny was a good-for-nothing." The therapist said that Jenny was still very small and needed to be taken care of. If Jenny's mother was too ill to do it, another grown-up to help take care of her had to be found. Lisa asked the therapist whether he would like to be that person. She then insisted on playing Jenny herself, because she did not like Lisa. She wanted to be a baby. From then on, Lisa regressed in the therapy sessions to an infant, who wanted to be held, rocked, undressed, and diapered. She spoke babytalk, became demanding, and resisted any suggestions to "grow up." As Jenny, she could be irresponsible, moody, and aggressive without fear of retaliation (her repressed rage and depression over the beatings from her mother, the chores at home, and the father's absence became quite evident). The therapist became concerned that these regressed behaviors in play would spill over at home and further stress Lisa's relationship with her mother. Therefore, he tried to keep the Jenny role strictly within a context of "pretending," terminating the game five minutes before the end of the session to have "talk time," time to relate to Lisa at an appropriate age level. Lisa was quite capable of differentiating between the office play and the reality at home, where she could not act out her dependent fantasies. For eight weeks she clung tenaciously to her Jenny-baby-play, which was tolerated by the therapist. He left it up to Lisa to decide when she was ready to proceed to the next stage. One day she announced that Jenny had a "birthday"—her third—and that she was inviting her best friend from school for the party, her first autonomous decision.

THE STAGES OF THERAPY—A CASE DISCUSSION

Now that we have discussed techniques to engage the abused and/or neglected child in play therapy, let us put the treatment process into context. In most instances, four treatment phases can be distinguished:

Phase I   :   Establishing rapport and learning how to play.
Phase II :   Regression and abreaction of the trauma.
Phase III: The testing of real relationships, developing impulse control and self-esteem.
Phase IV: Termination.

The following detailed case discussion will illustrate these stages of treatment. Afterward, we will consider the special problems encountered in work with these children.

Background

Seven-year-old Denny was referred by his foster family for bizarre behavior—talking to imaginary "friends," explosive violent outbursts during which he would throw anything in his reach, bedwetting, and inability to relate to peers in school.

Denny was the youngest of three children born to a drug-addicted mother and an alcoholic father who beat his wife, but not the children. Because of the stormy marital situation, mother tried to abort Denny when pregnant; shortly after his birth, she tried to commit suicide. Mother herself had been raised by physically abusive, alcoholic parents. After recovery from her depression, mother took care of Denny until he was four years old. She described him as an overly irritable infant who screamed through the night, was fussy with food, and did not gain weight appropriately. In his toddler years, he had severe temper tantrums, hurting himself by head banging. His motor development was above normal, but he did not develop speech until he was three. He used only single words. When Denny was three-and-a-half years old, mother got divorced. In a fit of depression, she cut her wrists in front of the children and choked Denny until he was blue. The incident remained unknown to the authorities. When Denny was four years old, mother sought psychiatric help for him, since his "weird" and destructive behaviors had become unmanageable. Residential treatment was recommended for the child, who was diagnosed schizophrenic. Surprisingly, mother was found to be basically caring; she experienced considerable guilt over her negative perceptions of Denny, blaming herself for having caused his "mental illness." Her personality style was dependent and emotionally labile and her household and interpersonal relationships were chaotic.

Remaining in residential care for three years, Denny learned basic self-help skills and developed meaningful speech in simple communications with adults; daily aggressive outbursts and attacks on small children were reduced to rare occasions and usually occurred when Denny was confused or frightened in an unstructured peer group activity. When under stress, Denny would withdraw into a fantasy world full of spacecraft and animals, but rarely people.

With the cooperation of his mother, Denny was discharged into foster care when he was capable of relating to adults. Further psychotherapy was recommended. His discharge diagnosis was "Borderline Disorder."

Phases of the Treatment Process

Phase I: Establishing rapport and learning how to play (Months 1–3).   It took three months of weekly sessions for Denny to establish even a superficial relationship with the therapist. Although he had no difficulty from the beginning separating from his foster parents, he ignored and avoided the therapist in the playroom, calling out his name only when he needed a toy or crayon. He drew repetitive pictures of spacemen who were always at war with each other. If the therapist tried to engage him in conversation about his drawings he would stand up, hold out his arms to keep his distance from the therapist and began to talk to an imaginary friend, "Superman Talo." Frustrated at their lack of communication, the therapist thought of the use of antipsychotic medication to reduce these "autistic-like" behaviors and gain access to him. Instead he decided to try to join Denny in his inner world. He was convinced that Denny's avoidance of him and even human doll figures was related to extreme fear of contact because of past experiences of violence. He began to express his interest in "getting to know Talo." A breakthrough came in the twelfth session when Denny announced that "Talo" was coming to visit the "city." He made the city himself, using the dollhouse with its doll figures, a jail made from blocks, a movie house, and a restaurant. This was the beginning of his relationship with human symbols and a use of actual play.

Phase II: Regression and abreaction of the trauma (Month 4–7).   Talo, a ferocious monster that Denny made out of paper, spelled disaster for the city. He spit fire, created devastating earthquakes, or threw nuclear bombs, destroying houses and killing helpless people over and over again. Talo always stayed a safe distance from retaliation, which appeared in the form of rockets which the therapist set up in the city. The destruction became so noisy when Denny screamed and laughed hysterically at all the dead bodies, that others in adjacent offices began complaining. Denny's therapist became concerned that Denny might decompensate into a psychotic episode; however, he tried to structure things to contain the fantasy play within the office. Five minutes before the end of the session, he introduced "talk time" appropriate for an eight-year-old boy (while the games were called those of the two-year-old). Both these ages reflected parts of Denny, the way he felt at different times.

This helped Denny to reconstitute quickly. The therapist, knowing Denny's terror, his fear of violence and annihilation, began to play the role of a boy doll who was in near panic because of Talo's attacks. The boy wanted a strong friend who could protect him. Denny took up the suggestion, and Talo and the boy "Andy" became allies. Though equipped with Talo's magical powers, Andy was also a human boy so he could enter the city in disguise.

Until now, the therapist had avoided any interpretations of the play content except for identifying feelings of terror in the people and their desperate need to find a way to feel safe. After endowing Andy—a real person—with extraordinary powers, Talo began to disappear from Denny's private fantasy and had no further imaginary conversations with him.

Andy, now with Talo's power, was very skillful and sophisticated in his attacks. He would charm the people in the city saying "How are you? I hope you are fine!" and then smash their heads in. He began to differentiate between people, some who were "OK"—sending them to jail for their own safety and "people who cannot be trusted." He singled out a woman doll figure. She would approach Andy with a seductive embrace, tell him that she loved him and in the process attempt to strangle him to death. (This was a fairly accurate replay of what had happened when Denny was three years old.) Andy fought back and tried to kill her in self-defense. This scene was repeated over several weeks; while Andy was choking to death, the therapist encouraged him to shout "Stop it" rather than killing her right away, in order to find out whether she could listen. Gradually, Andy became more and more articulate. He would, for example, say: "Stop it, you scare me, it hurts," after which the woman would apologize and withdraw. The therapist continued to avoid any direct references to Denny's mother. The experience remained in displacement so that he would not react with withdrawal and termination of the game. Once Denny had mastered his fear of attack through Andy, the dollhouse play became more relaxed amd dealt with more usual activities such as family visits to the restaurant, going to school, and even learning.

The end of this phase of therapy came when Denny announced that he was tired of these "two-year-old games." He wanted to learn chess. At this point, the foster parents and schoolteacher (Denny attended a class for emotionally handicapped children) reported that Denny's bizarre behaviors had almost ceased. He still withdrew into daydreaming in confusing social situations, but was eagerly imitating adult behavior and attitudes.

Phase III: Impulse control and self-image. (Months 8–14) The testing of real relationships. Denny learned the moves of the different chess figures very rapidly. Even though chess is not usually used in play therapy, it was felt important to agree to Denny's choice of a new game and level of functioning. The new aspect of this game was, of course, that Denny had to interact with the therapist directly. He was impatient, and needed to win at all cost, changing rules and cheating openly. He was hungry for praise and hypersensitive to criticism; he would throw the game off the table if the therapist tried to teach him a better move. The therapist did not challenge Denny, in order to keep up his interest in the game, and, of course, lost each time much to Denny's delight. He called the therapist "dumb" and "mental." But he was simply projecting his own feelings of inadequacy. At the same time, he seriously inquired whether he had hurt the therapist's feelings. He was puzzled that the therapist did not "hate" him like his mother had when he was "mean."

The inability to integrate good and bad aspects of one's self-concept is common with abused children; this "split" of either good or bad feelings about oneself is projected on other people. If Denny felt good, the therapist was a friend; if Denny felt bad, he became an enemy. Through the chess play, the therapist could model and demonstrate learning from mistakes, that losing was frustrating but not "bad," that certain actions might be "dumb and mental," but they did not make the whole person hateful, and that feelings could get hurt, but that did not mean rejection. By now, Denny's relationship to the therapist had become sufficiently important for him to begin to assimilate some of his attitudes. Slowly gaining more self-confidence, Denny was able to postpone gratification. He began to reconcile and integrate complex feelings about himself and others and could better appraise social relationships. At this stage of therapy, play and games lost some of their significance—and talking prevailed. For the first time he talked about the importance of friends. He could verbalize disappointment and hurt when they teased him. But he was also aware that he made them angry by calling them names, and this was something which was in his power to change. During the fourteenth month of therapy, Denny felt safe enough to talk about his mother, whom he regularly visited. He reported that he had told her to "Stop being so weak and cry all the time." When she replied, "How could you say something like that to your own mother?" Denny had responded: "I just don't like it, that's why, I'm sorry if it hurts you, but that's how I feel." In school, Denny was "promoted" to a regular class; with improved impulse control, motivation, and peer relationships, special education was unnecessary.

Phase IV: Termination (Month 15–16).　The process of termination of therapy naturally was filled with small signs of regression in Denny at the prospect of separation. For a short period, Denny resumed some of his bizarre behaviors: He tried to reinvite his imaginary superpowered friend Talo into the sessions; at home there was an unprovoked attack on two foster siblings. This time, the therapist did not so readily allow Denny to regress, but insisted on focusing on age-appropriate sharing of sadness. Denny bounced back fairly rapidly. It was important for him to be remembered, and little gifts and a photograph were exchanged. Another link was set up—follow-up phone calls scheduled every month for the first year.

Follow-Up.　Denny's therapy sessions were terminated two years ago. He is now 11 years old, attends a regular class, and has average grades. He lives in the same foster home, but has regular contacts with his mother, who has remarried and divorced, continuing her chaotic lifestyle. However, Denny has a realistic view of her capacity as a mother. "She loves me the best she can." Bedwetting, aggression, and withdrawal into bizarre fantasies have ceased. He still has some problems with peers and often self-consciously avoids contact unless activities are structured by adults.

SPECIAL PROBLEMS IN TREATMENT OF ABUSE AND NEGLECT: CASE MATERIAL

Post-Traumatic Reactions

Little has been written about the emotional sequelae of violent trauma in children. Terr (1981), who studied the psychological effects on nonabused children of the Chowchilla schoolbus kidnapping (see Chapter 17), found that fear of further trauma, traumatic dreams, and repetitive reenactment of attitudes, fears, and actions during the incident persisted long after the dangerous situation was over. Green (1978b), in his work with abused children, found them preoccupied with violent fantasies and suffering, periodically, from acute anxiety states in anticipation of further trauma.

The child who is assaulted by the parent on whose care he is so dependent may have to be on constant guard to prevent attack. Hypervigilance and startle reactions are common in these children. Expectations of being hurt may become generalized; any person, including peers, may be perceived as dangerous; if anyone approaches the child he may attack them to defend himself against an expected injury. For many abused children the violent interactions with their parents became the principal or only relationship they know. In order to stay in contact they may provoke abuse over and over and develop a self-destructive, masochistic, relationship pattern. Others may identify with the powerful aggressor to ward off feelings of helplessness and anxiety, and appear tough, controlling, and violent like their parents.

Reenactment of sadomasochistic patterns or identification with the aggressor may perpetuate abuse-seeking behavior in real life, even after the abuse has stopped. The goal of play therapy is first to help these children master their "traumato-phobia" and then give up patterns which are likely to invite abuse or rejection.

Most children who come to therapy will, at one time or another, display fears that the therapist will hurt or abandon them just like their parents did. Therefore it is important that, from the beginning, the therapist reassure the child that he or she will not be physically harmed. The therapist should set limits—no one is to be hurt. On the other hand, conflicts over aggression can be freely and safely expressed with the dollhouse figures.

Often, helping children master their fears of trauma constitutes the first stage of therapy. The therapist should allow the children to replay the experience of the trauma, verbalize for them the feelings associated with their play and help them gradually differentiate the world around them in a more realistic way rather than indiscriminantly generalizing fears of trauma.

CASE EXAMPLE

John, a nine-year-old boy who had been severely abused periodically since age two by his alcoholic father, was finally placed in his maternal grandmother's home when he suffered a broken arm during one of his father's explosive outbursts. His mother was not only unable to protect her son, but also received frequent beatings herself. John had been placed in a class for emotionally handicapped children because of his assaultive behavior. In grandmother's house, he attacked the younger children with little or no provocation, usually in front of grandmother.

On his first visit to the clinic, John, a rather frail-looking youngster, greeted the therapist by flexing his muscles and demonstrating karate kicks. He asked whether the therapist wanted to fight. The therapist explained the playroom rule, which did not permit him to hit John nor John to hit him. However, by using the toys, both could learn how to fight appropriately. In the first two sessions, John's play was disorganized and destructive. He would pile up toys in a heap and fire at them with blocks, shouting "Got you!" Some blocks seemed directed toward the therapist, usually accompanied by a wary expression on John's face as if he expected a counterattack. Without commenting on the testing behavior, the therapist suggested that John might want to set up some of the toy people and see whether he could hit them with the blocks. For the next two months, the people destruction game continued. The doll figures were maimed, killed, and buried. They were dismissed as "stupid things." Separating the strong people from the weak, John chose an adult male figure (father) and boy child figure (himself) as the aggressors; the victims were all male children; the women were passive observers. John, identifying with his father, proceeded to reenact the actual incidents at home. He continued to choose the role of attacker, but the victim with the broken arm also seemed to be him. With the help of the therapist, John began to verbalize both the aggressor's and victim's feelings. The aggressor was "mad," "strong," and "mean." The victim was "dumb" and "scared" and "very mad inside." John's feelings of vulnerability surfaced when the father figure shifted the attack to his ally—the boy child. When the therapist pointed out that the boy child must feel very scared and cheated, John became increasingly anxious. He did not want to return to therapy and accused the therapist of wanting to hurt him. Transferring onto the therapist the image of parents is common in the therapeutic process. But whereas the therapist could not promise John safe conduct with his parents, he could reassure him that he was protected from violence in the office; more importantly, in the office it was safe to express the frightening feelings of rage, fear, insecurity, and sadness over the loss of his father.

Emotional abreaction in a supportive atmosphere often relieves the paralyzing anxiety of these children. When this is mastered, its symptoms—expressed in hyperactivity, impulsivity, and aggressivity—often diminish and work can proceed to improve the child's self-esteem and distorted object relations. Unfortunately, many abused children have been treated with stimulant medication alone for their hyperactivity (often they are diagnosed as MBD, like John, who had received Ritalin for two years without improvement). These drugs do not relieve posttraumatic anxiety; they may even reinforce the child's feeling that there is something wrong with him or her which he or she cannot change. If used at all, there should be careful and specific diagnostic indications, and they should be combined with ongoing psychotherapy.

Failure to Meet Parents' Expectations

Abusive parents have an intense, highly ambivalent, and hostile dependent attachment to their children (Gladston, 1979). The child is expected to fulfill the parents' unmet needs for emotional well-being. The parents, unable to contain their ambivalence, lash out at the child at the slightest disappointment. Failing to meet the parents' expectations, the child incorporates an image of "badness," as well as a persistent longing for acceptance, which is constantly frustrated by the parents' angry rejection. Anxiety, depression, poor self-esteem, and the same ambivalent, dependent object relationships are the emotional consequences. As Green (1978b) points out, the use of primitive defenses, for example, denial, projection, and especially splitting, allows children to maintain a fantasy of having a good parent. The badness is projected onto other persons or themselves, and everyone is rigidly classified as either all good or all bad. This "splitting" prevents them from integrating lovable and hateful aspects within themselves and others. It interferes with their ability to assess realistically the behavior of their parents or others, or the effects of their own behaviors on others. After mastery of traumatic reactions in the initial stage of therapy, as previously described, emphasis must be placed on improving the child's feelings of self-worth. Mature coping skills for handling depression and anxiety and a firmer sense of identity separate from the parents' shortcomings and distorted expectations are developed through resolution of the fixed tendency to split persons into good or bad, rewarding or depriving, rather than acknowledging that everyone has good and bad in them. This is a slow and difficult process. The following case example demonstrates the long process of working through these conflicts.

Case Example

Eight-year-old Albert was referred to the clinic after cutting his arms with a knife, crying that he wanted to be dead. Since age three, he had repeatedly been beaten by the father, who thought of him as "retarded." When Albert was seven, two of his younger sisters accused the father of sexually abusing them. Father denied the charge, and claimed that Albert was the "rapist." He told the school and neighbors to watch his son closely—he was a sex maniac. Three months before the referral, Albert, while being beaten by the father, had threatened to "kill" him with a knife. One month later his father died from a chronic kidney ailment. Since then, Albert had repeatedly called himself a murderer. His mother, although assuring Albert that he had not caused his father's death, became severely depressed. In school Albert was described as a loner, with explosive aggressive outbursts following minor provocations. He had been suspended twice for hurting other children.

During the first few therapy sessions, Albert was virtually mute. He repetitiously set up blocks and knocked them over to bury the dolls he had placed behind them. If they were not completely covered, he piled more blocks over them. The therapist was uneasy because he could not elicit any verbalizations from Albert, and commented that the scene looked like a graveyard. Albert responded: "That's right. That's where killers belong." Then Albert looked up abruptly and asked, "Are you going to kill me?" Albert did not believe that there was not a hidden plot, that nobody would get hurt in the office. Over and over he searched for weapons and accused the therapist of having deadly rays in his wristwatch. Albert identified the therapist with his powerful and feared father, but he also projected his own murderous impulses onto the therapist, resulting in simultaneous fear and the need to be punished, or "killed." Albert became more and more provocative, interpreting the therapist's nonviolent responses as rejection, until he called out in despair in one session: "If you love me, why don't you kill me?" Subsequently, in play, the therapist began to clarify and differentiate Albert's confused and conflicting feelings. Albert assumed the role of a bad child who needed to be locked up in jail and should be shot. The therapist translated these wishes and feelings into words. "Wanting to kill" was equated with with a feeling of "being mad, so mad that it feels like you want to kill somebody." However, the therapist was an adult who could contain such an impulse. He could even tolerate the "bad child" voicing such anger. The therapist was not worried he would die from the child's "bad thoughts"—his murderous wishes or angry verbalizations. In reality, Albert had *not* killed his father. Getting to this point took about six months.

After Albert had separated the therapist from the image of his father, he began to idealize him. Suddenly he shifted from a difficult to a "perfect" child. He brought gifts to the therapist and tried every way to please him. He became extremely possessive and jealous of the therapist's attention. He would depreciate the therapist's other patients and anxiously inquire whether they were "better kids" than he was. In play, only two dolls, the therapist (adult) and Albert (child) would interact; all other figures were eliminated. If the therapist could not meet Albert's enormous demands for attention and approval, Albert would fall into a rage; however, these angry outbursts were verbal and no longer expressed in violent behavior. Disappointment and frustration over unmet demands were dealt with by playing out situations which did not allow for immediate gratification. For example, the "adult" doll had to go on a short trip, saying how sad he was that he could not take the "child" doll with him.

He inquired how the child felt. Albert (the "child" doll) said that he too was sad, and even afraid the therapist ("adult" doll) might not come back. The therapist asked what the boy could do about his sad feelings. Albert mentioned that he could cry, write a letter, or make phone calls. He could also "smash up" his sister which would surely make the adult doll come back. Albert was complimented for thinking of so many possibilities and discussed each one in turn, its pros and cons. He said Albert should try one. Albert chose the telephone.

Albert's ability to master such a painful situation and to consider alternative behaviors with which to deal with his feelings marked a major advance in therapy. It signified the beginning of a change in self-image from a helpless victim of his own impulses and fears to a person who was in control of his thoughts and emotions and was capable of making "good" and "bad" choices. This was different than being either a "good" or a "bad" person.

It was time to shore up impulse control and improve Albert's self-image. Age-appropriate projects were now made available in the playroom. Initially, Albert was convinced he would fail and gave up easily in building a simple model car or plane. He would destroy them because they looked "ugly" or wouldn't take them home because he was convinced that his family would laugh at them. In time he became more confident and less afraid of failure. The therapist always acknowledged that he had similar feelings of frustration and couldn't do everything right. But this hardly made either him or Albert a worthless or loathsome person.

During the final stage of therapy (in the second year), Albert wanted to play competitive games like checkers. Aggression channeled into competition, winning and losing rather than kill-or-be-killed were totally new experiences for him. At the same time, he began to express sadness that his father had never played with him. He began to realize that his father was different from other fathers. It was unfair! But it was nothing he could change. He began to see his father as a person who had problems of his own that kept him from being happy, and the way he treated his son was more the result of his problems than anything Albert had done.

Six months after termination of therapy, Albert was doing well in school. He had several good friends and no longer found himself in constant fights.

Deprivation and Emptiness (Neglect)

Neglectful parents are different, and so are their children. In contrast to the intense pathological parent–child relationship in abusive families in which the child often represents a projective identification of a "bad" person or self, neglectful parents are unable to "endow the child with a personal value" (Gladston, 1979). These children suffer from a lack of attention, which in severe cases leads to understimulation, global developmental delays, apathy, and difficulties in interpersonal attachments.

Establishing a working therapeutic relationship may take a very long time because of such little responsiveness from the child. As in the case of Wendy, described earlier, food or candy is useful to engage the child in therapy and may have to be used extensively. Once an attachment has formed, regression and infantile clinging becomes intense and longlasting. Premature attempts to promote autonomy are met with fierce resistance or renewed withdrawal—deep depression from the threat of abandonment. The relationship with the therapist is often marked by manipulation and attempts at exploitation to defend against this abandonment depression.

To reach a true therapeutic alliance, the relationship with the therapist must become so important and safe enough for the neglected child that he is willing to take the enormous risk of giving up his self-protective, narcissistic preoccupation. The early play activities should be designed to attract the child's interest and provide pleasure. They should not be threatened with interpretation of the meanings of the play.

Continued Separation Fears

Many abused children must be hospitalized for treatment of their injuries or they may be placed in foster care if their home situation is considered too dangerous to warrant a safe return. These changes in placement compound the psychological reactions to the abuse. Anxiety, guilt, and depression over separation from parents are common. The children may interpret placement as punishment, rejection, and confirmation of their "badness." Martin and Beezeley (1976b) found that the degree of psychiatric disturbance correlated most highly with the child's perception of the impermanence of his current home.

To help the child adjust to his present life situation, these issues must be addressed in therapy.

CASE EXAMPLE

Mark, a five-year-old boy, was referred to therapy because he did not adjust to his foster home, even though he had done well in a residential treatment setting within three months of his placement there. He had been removed from his mother by court order after she had attempted to stab him. She was diagnosed as chronic schizophrenic and was following a delusional command to "get rid of the devil." During his stay in the residential treatment center, Mark, an extremely bright and verbal boy, had reenacted the incident and apparently had accepted that his mother was "crazy." He refused to see her and was looking forward to living with his foster parents, whom he had met while in the residential program. But once in the foster home, he began to wet the bed, steal food and money, and throw severe temper tantrums. He often wandered off for hours for no reason. The foster parents indicated that they might not be able to keep him if his behavior continued. He was taken into play therapy.

In play therapy, a repetitive theme immediately developed. Mark built a house of blocks over and over again; however, it was built on shaky ground, collapsing each time and burying everybody except for one boy who was left out in the "cold, cold winter." Since Mark was an exceptionally bright youngster, the therapist could deal with his fear of being abandoned fairly rapidly. To cope with his abandonment anxiety, Mark developed fantasies of power. He would grow up into a "big man." Just like the doll he decided would live at the very "end of the world." There he built a fortress where he would live all by himself. The fortress withstood all kinds of natural disasters, tornadoes, and hurricanes, but when people came to visit, the owner of the castle would always hide.

In therapy, Mark's frightening feelings of helplessness at having no real control over his future had to be acknowledged, while at the same time better coping skills for his distress had to be suggested. Rather than simply withdrawing into fantasy, he could develop age appropriate skills in games and sports and make friends, if only he could trust his capacity to learn to be a real five-year-old boy.

Another major theme in therapy was Mark's need for self-punishment, which he perpetuated with passive–aggressive provocations in the foster home. He believed that he had been stabbed and sent away because he was "bad like the devil." Whereas in direct conversation Mark refused to talk about his mother, his play revealed his guilt over the loss of his mother. It began one day when he decided to get married in his "castle." The bride was a mirror image of his mother. One day the husband went to the movies to "have some fun" without telling the wife. The wife was very upset and lonely and when he came home she stabbed him with a knife. She said she had been badly hurt and he should never leave her again. It was apparent that Mark's own developmental pull toward autonomy conflicted with his mother's symbiotic attachment to him. New and alternative solutions had to be offered to help Mark out of this dilemma. The therapist gradually shifted the roles of husband and wife to the real ones—a mentally ill mother and her son. Because mother was sick, she could not care for Mark, even though she loved him. The decision that Mark had to live in the foster home had been made by a judge, who "has a say over little people." It had nothing to do with anything Mark was or had done. After one year of therapy, Mark could writer letters to his mother, telling her that he loved her and hoped that she would get well enough to take care of him again some day. He also could let her know that he was proud of going to school and had made new friends. He was able to tell his friends that he lived in a foster home because his mother needed help for her own problems.

Countertransference Reactions

When working with abused and neglected children, the therapist must be constantly in touch with his own feelings and reactions which might interfere with the treatment process. In the beginning there is often a tendency to overidentify with the child, especially if the therapist has had little contact with the parents. Anger and disgust with adults who mistreat children may evoke pity and rescue fantasies which do not fit the child's real needs and neglect the positive aspects of the bond between the child and his parents. The therapist attempting to be a better parent leaves the child confused, anxious, and more depressed because of the message that the most significant people in his life—his parents, of whom he is part, are bad.

Rescue feelings are often quickly shattered when the child enters the regressive—dependent phase in therapy. Suddenly, the therapist may be overwhelmed by the demands for attention and nurturance which alternate with angry outbursts when he or she cannot meet the child's demands. Feelings of inadequacy, frustration, and hopelessness are then common. Watch for danger signals—feelings of relief when an appointment has been canceled or frequent glances at your watch in hope that the therapy hour is almost over. Various changes in approach signal countertransference problems: The therapist may want to terminate therapy; he or she may try to push the child too fast to a more independent level of functioning, perhaps by making concrete behavioral suggestions (e.g., a star chart for not swearing); he or she may decide the best approach might be to work with caretakers "on" the child. In any case, the child is not permitted to master his emotional illness at a tolerable, appropriate pace.

Since most of the play of these children is full of violent themes, therapists who have conflicts over aggression may be frightened of losing control or of overreacting in a punitive way; they may thus participate in the reenactment of the abusive rejecting cycle.

Once the therapist in the long treatment process has felt some gratification from positive changes in the child, he or she may have difficulties loosening the intense relationship with the child, who will then have more difficulties generalizing newly gained skills in interpersonal relationships to his or her daily social setting.

To counteract the negative influence of the therapist's own emotional reactions, regular case discussions with colleagues are helpful if not essential. They should permit the therapist to ventilate feelings freely and help him or her recognize the limitations of therapist involvement in the overall treatment of abused children and their families.

SUMMARY AND CONCLUSIONS

The few publications dealing with the outcome of psychotherapy for abused and/or neglected children confirm our impression that most children benefit significantly from treatment.

Beezeley et al. (1976b) found that children who remained in play therapy for at least one year showed significant gains in their ability to trust adults, delay gratification, and verbalize feelings. Their self-esteem and capacity to experience pleasure improved. Positive changes were most marked and rapid if the child was young and seen within a therapeutic preschool setting, if the parents "permitted" the child to make changes, and if the therapist could influence the environment, that is, home and school.

Similarly, Green (1978b) reported that 15 out of 16 children who remained in therapy at least nine months exhibited significant improvement in impulse control, cognitive functioning, and object relations. He considered the prognosis poorer if the child was young at the onset of the abuse. Generally he found that development deviations and degree of psychopathology were more severe in these youngsters than in children who were abused at a later age.

In our experience, all 25 children, with the exception of one psychotic boy, improved (as judged by parents, foster parents, school, and therapist) in areas of behavioral symptom control, social relationships, school performance, and self-esteem if they remained in weekly therapy for at least one year. The preschooler's improvement depended more on stabilization of the environment than did improvement with latency children, of whom many showed persistent gains over a two-year follow-up period even if their home environment remained less than ideal. Their social network was wider- mainly through school—and provided a variety of different, successful experiences which they could not attain at home.

We have found no short cut to the effective treatment of the serious psychological problems of these children. Although controlled studies are not yet available to compare the outcome of treated and untreated groups of children, the persistent psychopathology of many youngsters in which the focus is limited to environmental protection and manipulation indicates that individual treatment of the child is essential for improvement. Those children who were followed for two years after termination of treatment retained most gains observed in treatment. However, more longitudinal studies are needed to assess whether they will master new developmental crises such as adolescence, marriage, and parenthood, or whether the stresses of identity formation, mature heterosexual relationships, or childrearing will lead to a regression influenced by earlier abusive experiences.

Abuse and neglect produce serious and devastating damage to the child's personality development, which is rarely corrected by simply providing a safe environment. Behavioral disorders, impulse problems, disturbed object relationships, anxiety, depression, poor self-esteem, and cognitive deficiencies are the frequent psychological reactions which have been recognized by professionals over the last 20 years. Yet they have not been given much psychotherapeutic attention. A few programs which provide individual psychotherapy to abused children have reported significant improvement of behavioral symptoms and resumption of personality development. To help children work through their inner conflicts and their relationships with others, psychodynamically oriented play therapy appears to be the most useful modality. It is specifically indicated for abused and/or neglected children and can be easily tailored to their particular needs and fears. Playing in a dollhouse quickly reveals the child's fears, fantasies, and coping skills and permits the therapist to help the child sort out and clarify conflicted feelings, correct misperceptions, and promote more mature, adaptive, coping mechanisms. For older children, structured games can be utilized to help with mastery of impulses and enhance a sense of competency.

The special needs of abused and neglected children require adjustment of traditional play therapy techniques. Some children may first have to be taught how to play. Because of their distrust in adults, an inordinate amount of time must be spent in establishing a therapeutic relationship; food may be needed to engage the child in therapy.

Once a relationship has been established, rage at unmet needs for nurturance tends to come to the fore with great intensity—and a prolonged phase of regression and dependence must be tolerated. Acute traumatic reactions are seen in the seemingly endless repetition of the violent acts; if handled by a therapist who offers alternative solutions, they can be mastered.

Only then, the therapeutic focus can shift to improve self-esteem, help the child develop a realistic view of him or herself in relationship to others, and foster a sense of identity separate from his parents' unrealistic expectations. Lastly, the therapist helps the child adjust to the givens of his present situation, which may include placement away from home.

The outcome of play therapy is encouraging enough to command it for a much larger group of abused and/or neglected children. It may serve to interrupt a vicious cycle in which victims of abuse grow into abusers themselves. Long-term follow-up will be necessary to determine whether the initial gains in therapy help the child master late developmental stages such as adolescence, marriage, and parenting. Meanwhile, special training in the use of play therapy for workers who deal with these children is necessary.

REFERENCES

Beezeley, P., Martin, H. P., & Alexander, H. (1976a) Comprehensive family oriented therapy. In R. E. Helfer & C. H. Kempe (Eds.), *Child abuse and neglect: The family and the community.* Cambridge, Mass: Ballinger. Pp. 169–194.

Beezeley, P., Martin, H. P., & Kempe, R. (1976b) Psychotherapy. In H. P. Martin (Ed.), *The abused child: A multidisciplinary approach to developmental issues and treatment.* Cambridge, Mass: Ballinger. Pp. 201–214.

Berlin, J. B. (1977) Play therapy: Checkers as a means of communication with children and adolescents. In P. P. Oswald (Ed.), *Communication and social interaction.* New York: Grune and Stratton. Pp. 227–236.

Carek, D. J. (1979) Individual psychodynamically oriented therapy. In J. D. Noshpitz

& S. I. Harrison (Eds.) *Basic handbook of child psychiatry*, vol. III, New York: Basic Books. Pp. 35–57.

Cohn, A. H. (1979) An evaluation of three demonstration child abuse and neglect treatment programs. *Journal of the American Academy of Child Psychiatry*, **18**, 283–291.

Gardner, R. A. (1979) Helping children cooperate in therapy. In J. D. Noshpitz & S. I. Harrison (Eds.), *Basic handbook of child psychiatry*, vol. III. New York: Basic Books. Pp. 414–433.

Gladston, R. (1979) Disorders of early parenthood: Neglect, deprivation, exploitation and abuse of little children. In J. D. Noshpitz (Ed.), *Basic handbook of child psychiatry*, vol. II, 581–593. New York: Basic Books. Pp. 581–593.

Green, A. H. (1978a) Psychopathology of abused children. *Journal of the American Academy of Child Psychiatry*, **17**(1), 92–103.

Green, A. H. (1978b) Psychiatric treatment of abused children. *Journal of the American Academy of Child Psychiatry*, **17**, 356–371.

In, P. A., & McDermott, J. F., Jr. (1976) The treatment of child abuse: Play therapy with a 4-year-old child. *Journal of the American Academy of Child Psychiatry*, **15**, 430–440.

Malone, C. A. (1979) Child psychiatry and family therapy: An overview. *Journal of the American Academy of Child Psychiatry*, **18**, 4–21.

Martin, H. P. (1972) The child and his development. In C. H. Kemp & R. E. Helfer (Eds.), *Helping the battered child and his family*. Philadelphia: Lippincott. Pp. 94–103.

Martin, H. P., & Beezeley, P. (1976) Personality of abused children. In H. P. Martin (Ed.), *The abused child: A multidisciplinary approach to developmental issues and treatment*. Cambridge, Mass: Ballinger. Pp. 105–111.

McDermott, J. F., Jr., & Char, W. F. (1974) The undeclared war between child psychiatry and family therapy. *Journal of the American Academy of Child Psychiatry*, **13**, 422–436.

Morse, C. W., Sahler, O. J., & Friedman, S. B. (1970) A three-year follow-up study of abused and neglected children. *American Journal of Diseases in Children*, **120**, 439–446.

Oliver, J. E. (1978) The epidemiology of child abuse. In S. M. Smith (Ed.), *The maltreatment of children*. Baltimore: University Book Press. Pp. 95–119.

Terr, L. C. (1981) Psychic trauma in children: Observations following the Chowchilla school bus kidnapping. *American Journal of Psychiatry*, **138**, 14–19.

CHAPTER 17

Play Therapy and Psychic Trauma: A Preliminary Report

LENORE C. TERR

INTRODUCTION

Posttraumatic play is a newly defined type of play observed in children who have undergone a psychic trauma. A traumatic experience is one which is so sudden, unanticipated, and intense that ordinary coping mechanisms and defenses are insufficient to prevent the child from being overwhelmed with anxiety. Posttraumatic play was first observed and described in 23 schoolbus kidnapping victims of Chowchilla, California (Terr, 1979, 1981). The concept was further elaborated and confirmed in a study of 12 infants and children and one adult who had played repetitively following separate and individual traumatic experiences (Terr, 1981).

There are 11 currently defined characteristics of posttraumatic play:

1. Compulsive repetition
2. Unconscious link between the play and the traumatic event
3. Literalness of play with simple defenses only
4. Failure to relieve anxiety
5. Wide age range
6. Varying lag time prior to its development
7. Carrying power to nontraumatized youngsters
8. Contagion to new generations of children
9. Danger
10. Use of doodling, talking, typing, and audio duplication as modes of repeated play
11. Possibility of therapeutically retracing posttraumatic play to an earlier trauma.

Because of the recent observations which led to the delineation of this type of play, only preliminary speculation can be offered about its potential therapeutic uses. Few of the children upon whom the original observations were made were available for psychiatric treatment because of distances, unwillingness, and parental, financial, and/or time constraints. In this chapter, six traumatized children from my own clinical files will be presented to illustrate both the potential uses of posttraumatic play in psychotherapy and the techniques of play therapy for severely stressed youngsters. Clinical examples from other authors will be employed to illustrate particular techniques; the reader is asked to bear in mind that when these examples are used, the patients had not been considered by those authors to have indulged in "posttraumatic play."

This chapter is divided into two sections: (1) the therapeutic uses of posttraumatic play, and (2) the use of play therapy for psychically traumatized youngsters.

THERAPEUTIC USES OF POSTTRAUMATIC PLAY

It is very unusual to observe posttraumatic fantasy play directly in the office or playroom. More commonly, the outpatient therapist may observe the reproduction of posttraumatic artwork or storytelling. The therapist will usually hear about, but not directly observe, the posttraumatic fantasy play from parents, concerned teachers, fellow victims, and perhaps reluctantly, from some child victims. There are two reasons why posttraumatic fantasy play is so often excluded by the child from the therapy session: (1) its monotonous ritualization, and (2) its secrecy.

The monotonous ritualization of posttraumatic play requires that its "context" (Schwartzman, 1978) or its "configuration" (Erikson, 1937) remain fixed; that is, the play must be played the same way each time it is enacted. The therapists's presence and the therapeutic setting "spoil" the context of play. Furthermore, the fantasies in posttraumatic play are secret. The best example of posttraumatic child's play in fiction, Boyer's *The Secret Game* (1950), which was later made into the movie *Jeux Interdits* (Clement, 1952), demonstrates the private and nakedly aggressive nature of such "games." The child victim prohibits adult onlookers from his play even though other children are often drawn into it.

Mary, a schoolbus kidnapping victim of Chowchilla whom I saw when she was five and again when she was nine, illustrates the ritualization and secrecy which often prevent the therapist from directly observing posttraumatic play. Mary had been extremely frightened when her schoolbus was taken at gunpoint ("When the men held the guns, I though they'd shoot me in the bus"), and when she had been buried 16 hours in the underground truck trailer ("I thought the 'hole' was just down in the ground. I heard them put on dirt and I started crying. I wouldn't go to sleep or nothing. I thought they [the kidnappers] would come in there too. The 'hole' was the scariest part!")

Toward the end of her interview at age five, she confided, "There is a cement place at my grandma's which is like a hole. I put clothes in it and my Barbie dolls, I pretend they're stuck in the hole." Mary could see no relationship between her play and her fear of being buried alive. The more I tried to discuss the play with her, the more reluctant Mary became to admit that she had indeed played this game at all. My attempt at therapeutic intervention was promptly dropped. Mary's specific play context (Grandma's cement hole, Barbie dolls, Barbie clothes) made spontaneous indulgence in such play impossible in the elementary school classroom where we spoke. Mary's secrecy about her play took precedence over her willingness to consider an outsider's questions or insights.

Four years later, I asked Mary about her old games with Barbie dolls. She had moved several times in the intervening years and had long since lost access to Grandma's "cement place." "I used to bury Barbies. I played it a long time—in Mississippi. I played it until I returned to Chowchilla [last year]. I just bury it. I pretend it's dead. I put catsup on the arm. She got shot and she died. I must have played it three years. It didn't do nothin' to me. I thought it was fun. I didn't want to play other things."

Mary's play, secret, fixed, and uninterpretable in the first session had continued unabated for three years! The context had gradually shifted away from Grandma's cement place, and the text had gradually included shooting and blood, but Mary's considerable anxiety had not been relieved by her repeated attempts to play it out alone. Only a new move into the physical custody of a different parent stopped the perpetual recurrence of Mary's "Burying Barbies" game.

Four psychotherapeutic techniques utilizing observation of or knowledge about posttraumatic play will be outlined: (1) therapeutic reconstruction utilizing knowledge about the play, (2) therapeutic interpretation based upon observation of the play in the office or playroom, (3) therapeutic interpretation of posttraumatic play observed in residential treatment settings, and (4) therapeutic intervention related to observation of posttraumatic artwork, stories, or recordings.

Therapeutic Reconstruction Utilizing Knowledge about Posttraumatic Play

A therapist who learns from a child, other children, a parent, or a teacher about repeated, monotonous, atypical, "strange" play must suspect a past psychic trauma. An example of such a therapeutic reconstruction follows.

I had just recently begun seeing Andrew (age seven) for a short course of once weekly sessions because of negative behavior, whining, and unhappiness at school, when his mother phoned me. "He's been putting little Tony [his two-year-old brother] in a box!"

When I asked Andrew about it, he reluctantly corroborated his mother's story. He could think of no reason for his behavior other than that it was "fun." I then asked Andrew if anyone had ever put him in a box and frightened him.

"Not a box, a clothes dryer," Andrew answered. "Jeremy and his friends bet me five bucks that I could get into a dryer. When I got in they banged the door shut and left. I thought I would die in there. I punched and punched the door. Almost broke my hand. I screamed. Nobody came. Finally I got out. And they never paid me the five bucks!"

Andrew and I spent two psychotherapy sessions talking about his anxiety in the clothes dryer. His play did not recur, nor did he complain of repeated dreams. The trauma had been fairly recent and short-lived. According to his mother, there had been no sign of further posttraumatic behavior in the four years following the interpretation of Andrew's play episodes.

Therapeutic Intervention Based Upon Outpatient Observation of Posttraumatic Play

The opportunities to observe spontaneous posttraumatic play directly in outpatient settings are quite limited. Erik Erikson, however, includes an excellent example in *Childhood and Society* (1950). Sam, a five-year-old child with seizures precipitated by "unknown psychic stimulus," had witnessed his grandmother's heart attack and the subsequent removal of her body in a coffin when he was three years old. A play group had previously been prescribed for Sam, where it was noticed that the "otherwise vigorous boy would, in dreamy concentration, build innumerable variations of oblong boxes, the openings of which he would carefully barricade." Two years after Sam's grandmother's death, Erikson held his first psychotherapeutic interview with the child. They played dominoes, and Erikson won consistently. The child hit Erikson hard in the face with a rubber doll and then rearranged the dominoes hurriedly into a box. Erickson noted,

"The dominoes all faced inward." I said, "If you wanted to see the dots on your blocks, you would have to be inside that little box, like a dead person in a coffin."
"Yes," he whispered.
"This must mean that you are afraid you may have to die because you hit me."
Breathlessly, "Must I?"
"Of course not. But you must have thought that you did make your grandmother die and therefore had to die yourself. That's why you built those big boxes in your school, just as you build this little one today. In fact, you must have thought you were going to die every time you had one of those attacks."
"Yes. . . ." (pp. 23–28)

Therapeutic Interpretation of Posttraumatic Play Observed in Residential Settings

In a residential treatment setting, the therapist has the opportunity to observe the spontaneous emergence and perpetuation of posttraumatic fantasy play. The institutionalized child will carry on with his play in much the same fashion as the noninstitutionalized child would secretly play at home or at school. Anna Freud and Dorothy Burlingham's (1942) four-year-old Bertie lived at the Hamstead Nurseries following his father's death from a bomb during an air raid and his mother's hospitalization with a psychotic condition. The authors relate,

A war game of a different kind was played by Bertie (4) at the time when he still refused to admit the truth of his father's death. He was ill in bed at the time of the spring raids, had a whole tray full of paper houses on his bed, and played undefatigably. He would build the houses, cover them with their roofs, then throw them down with small marbles which were his bombs. Whereas in the other children's game, any number of people were "killed" and in the end everything was left in bits and pieces, the point in Bertie's play was that all his people were always saved in time and all his houses were invariably built up again. The other children repeated incidents of a more impersonal kind in their games: they played active and embellished versions of events which had actually happened. This served the purpose of relief and abreaction. Bertie's play, on the other hand, had the opposite intention; he wanted to deny the reality of what had happened. Since the denial was never completely successful, the play had to be repeated incessantly—it became compulsive. The games of the other children remained transitory. Bertie stopped playing in his way when, half a year later, he at last gave up his denial and was able to tell his story. "My father has been killed and my mother has gone to the hospital." (pp. 196–197)

Therapeutic Interpretation Based upon Posttraumatic Play Variants—Art Production, Storytelling, and Audio Duplication

Variations upon the posttraumatic play theme lend themselves well to outpatient interpretation. The ritualized play can be duplicated easily in the therapist's office because art, stories, or tapes are similar to those in the child's milieu.

Louis (eight years old), illustrates the wealth of art material which can be used for interpretation. Unfortunately the 90-minute session I had with Louis did not have sufficient therapeutic impact to quell his need for posttraumatic doodling. Louis is an educationally handicapped hispanic child who was kidnapped in the Chowchilla schoolbus incident. For the entire year after his terrifying experience, Louis doodled pictures of trucks, trailers, and vans on his schoolbooks, work sheets, and papers. He could not read by the end of the third grade when I interviewed him. "I need glasses," he explained. As he spoke with me, he continually drew pictures. "I thought the hole [actually a buried truck trailer] was a trailer or one of those trucks. [He drew them.] It had two wheels. I draw it a lot. I draw another one almost every day. After the kidnapping was coming, I drew and drew one of those pictures. Sometimes I draw people in the trucks. Sometimes I make drivers, and I scratch through his face." Louis went on to draw a picture of himself with no arms. He said, "They're shooting me right in the heart." He drew another truck, this one "with a papaya to hit the men over the head." He drew a different truck, this time with the driver scratched out, a pile of dirt on top of a huge supporting stake in the process of falling down, and two tiny armless children, one black and one white, inside the trailer. (Louis had originally moved a supporting stake in the buried truck trailer causing the roof partially to collapse. For many children, this was their most intensely frightening moment of the entire kidnapping. There were some feeble passive into active defenses in his art work, but much of the doodling was a direct repetition of the traumatic experience.

Louis's anger and sense of helplessness were discussed with him in that single 90-minute interview about nine months after the kidnapping, but the interpretation had little effect. Four years after the kidnapping, Louis's teacher reported that the doodling had continued, "His work sheets and papers are covered with trucks."

Newman (1976) includes several interesting pieces of posttraumatic children's art in her article on the Buffalo Creek flood victims. There was no mention of therapeutic intervention in Newman's study, but if such work were produced in a therapeutic rather than an investigative setting, psychiatric interpretations might be at least partially effective in reducing anxiety and the sense of helplessness.

Posttraumatic storytelling is another variant of posttraumatic play which can be observed and interpreted in the therapeutic setting. Richard Gardner's Mutual Storytelling Technique (1971, 1979) seems particularly applicable in cases of psychic trauma. Gardner (1971) tells of Chris (age five) who had been previously tied down and hospitalized several times for correction of a hare lip, cleft palate, and bilateral inguinal hernias. Prior to beginning his eight-month course of therapy with Gardner, Chris had spent hours fantasizing in isolation. Gardner encouraged Chris to tell stories into the tape recorder. Most likely these stories were the same as the fantasies Chris daydreamed at home. The child told tales of flowers, plants, or men who died, were mutilated, and then eaten. Gardner, in turn, told stories to Chris about plant doctors and human doctors who meant to help children. For weeks, Chris repeated the same stories monotonously, but then he began to incorporate more possibilities for coping into his stories. On his last day of treatment, Chris told a flower story with no mutilations or death, a sign to Gardner that he had at least in part mastered the psychic traumas he had undergone. (I have some misgivings about therapies which finish as the child still plays repetitious posttraumatic games. Gardner saw Chris briefly 14 months later because he had been teased about his repaired hare lip and had become depressed. Two of Chris' stories from that time are cited by Gardner; both are about damaged plants or damaged plant-products [wood].)

The mutual storytelling technique is only one of several ways that children's stories and audio duplications can be interpreted therapeutically. Posttraumatic stories can be interpreted directly to the child by the therapist. Tape recordings can be made by the child in the therapist's office, or they can be brought in from home and later interpreted in the psychotherapeutic setting.

THE USE OF PLAY THERAPY FOR PSYCHICALLY TRAUMATIZED CHILDREN

In this section I will no longer consider spontaneously originating posttraumatic play but rather the types of play therapy which may be useful in posttraumatic stress disorders of childhood (APA, 1980). Long-term follow-up studies, when available, will determine whether the effects of trauma yield to psychotherapy. My experience to date indicates that brief psychotherapy fails to heal the deep psychological wounds following trauma.

Release Therapy (Abreactive Treatment)

In several landmark papers on play and on childhood psychic trauma, David Levy (1938, 1939, 1945) suggested "release therapy," a treatment which allows children to abreact without receiving direct psychotherapeutic interpretation. The definition of psychic trauma of Levy and others at that time was far broader and more inclusive than the present one suggested by Anna Freud (1967). Even so, Levy's abreactive treatment remains currently applicable to external situations which have had a stressful, if not "traumatic," effect. Levy (1938) saw Paul (two years, two months) for stammering which had developed after two instances in which a nursery school peer had scratched and hit him without eliciting any counteraggression. Levy worked with Paul only four times during which he allowed Paul to break up pieces of clay, to place them between his own and Levy's lips, and to run a train over Levy's notes. Later Levy showed Paul two dolls and told the child that one doll was Paul, the other Paul's playmate. At first Paul could not let his doll hit the other, but in the third session he hit the peer-doll, threw it on the floor, and stepped on it. He then played further with clay and water, eventually throwing objects and trying to squirt the therapist. After this session, the stammering ceased. The fourth session involved more free activity along the lines of the third session. Paul was seen by Levy for a one-year and a two-year follow-up, and on both occasions he was asymptomatic. The reader will note that Levy never directly interpreted Paul's feelings to him, but he simply let him play them out. He states (1939) "In release therapy the interpretive function of the therapist is reduced to a minimum and may be absent, especially in children 2, 3 and 4."

Psychotherapy Utilizing Spontaneous Play

Erik Erikson (1950) provides us with some of the professional literature's most beautifully told examples of spontaneous child's play and its interpretation. In *Childhood and Society,* he tells of Mary, age three, who had been born with six digits and had one removed at age six months. Her mother had minimized the scar when Mary asked about it, saying, "It's just a mosquito bite." Mary had suffered a recent series of nightmares. She had also exhibited anxiety attacks in the play group she had recently joined. Her mother told Erikson that just recently Mary's father had lost his job and had refused to let Mary participate in his morning bathroom grooming operations.

In her second session with Erikson, Mary spontaneously engaged in two play activities which clearly related to her anxieties. First she enclosed a cow with blocks, a "close fitting stable [which] looks like a hand—with a sixth finger." She then slyly abandoned Erikson in his office, sat in his waiting room, and explicitly ordered him several times to "sthay in there!" In this way, Mary spontaneously corrected for her banishment from her father's bathroom. Erikson did not directly interpret Mary's play to the child, but he prescribed a course of action to her parents based on his interpretation of her play. He recommended truthfulness from her parents in regard to the scar on her hand and to any questions she asked about her genitals. He suggested more activity, more play with peers, and less intervention by parents during her nightmares, saying, "perhaps she needed to fight her dreams out." Mary was seen one more time by Erikson and she had improved remarkably (pp. 195–207).

Psychotherapy Utilizing Preset or Prearranged Play

Preset or prearranged play therapy, which Levy (1939) termed "control play," allows the traumatized child to "find" toys which the therapist believes are particularly applicable to the child's terrifying experience. The child spontaneously takes over and plays with the items the therapist has provided. Such play may look a great deal like spontaneous posttraumatic play, but it is important to remember that the therapist, not the child, sets the play context.

For example, MacLean (1977) just happened to have a complete set of animals including a toy leopard (Does the reader have one?) when a four-year-old boy, who had been attacked in a pet shop by a leopard, came to him for psychotherapy. During 24 sessions over an eight-month period, the boy played leopard in each session. MacLean states, "one major theme that progressed throughout all the sessions was the reenactment in play of the traumatic event" (p. 73). MacLean noted that the elements of play which he interpreted were reenactment, transference, defenses, and affects. MacLean states that the child was asymptomatic when discharged from therapy, although he still "played leopard" at the last session.

Stanley Shapiro (1973) set up a play situation for a four-and-a-half-year-old girl's "brief psychoanalysis." She had unexpectedly witnessed her mother's abrupt delivery of a stillborn baby in an upstairs hallway. Shapiro writes, "To facilitate the emergence of her notions about blood, I provided a doctor kit complete with thermometer, stethoscope, syringe, and tongue blade. In addition, prominently displayed in the playroom was red paint, some of which was spilled on absorbent paper towels. There also were, of course, dolls and a plastic bottle" (p. 261).

Play Therapy Utilizing Corrective Dénouement

I have found corrective dénouement play to be successful in brief intervention with traumatized children. It is a newly coined phrase by which I indicate that the therapist helps the child to find, in retrospect, a solution which might have avoided the trauma or stopped the assault altogether. This "answer" or dé-nouement is the sort of possibility that children try to find retrospectively and magically in their omen formations (Terr, 1979), but in the case of corrective dénouement play, the solution provided is real, not magical. This permits the child–victim to realize (1) that he could not have avoided the traumatic event because he did not know how and (2) that he now has the coping skills to deal with a similar event should it occur in the future. Dénouement play relieves both guilt and fear.

Obviously, in order for a corrective dénouement to be offered within the play context, the trauma must have been one in which such a solution is possible. Large-scale natural disasters, catastrophic illness, or random unpro-voked attacks cannot be reworked in any such way.

The example of Betsy (age nine) will be presented because her traumatic experience is the type of small-scale disaster which lent itself to corrective-dénouement play. Betsy had lived with her divorced mother and for several months with a strange, frightening "roomer," Ed. Her mother confided to Betsy that she had recently learned that Ed was being sought in another state for robbery. Because her mother was afraid to ask Ed to leave, she sent Betsy for a few days' safekeeping to her grandmother's house. Unfortunately, Betsy's grandmother had just purchased a beautiful new car, which the little girl and the old woman were afraid Ed might want to steal.

Early one morning, in response to a ring of the doorbell, Betsy's grand-mother looked outside and saw Ed waiting. "Betsy, call the operator and get the police!" demanded Grandmother.

Betsy did not know how: "I didn't understand."

The grandmother, now irritated, grumbled, "Never mind, you're no help," and opened the door. Ed came in, ate breakfast, and announced he would help Grandmother drive Betsy to school in the new car. As they left Betsy off at her school, she caught a final glimpse of her grandmother. The old woman was found murdered that afternoon. Her car had been taken and wrecked. When Ed was apprehended by the police, he shot himself to death.

Betsy saw her grandmother's ransacked living room, but was barred from the kitchen where the body was found. She had a recurring, terrifying dream of her own death in the first few weeks after the murder. During the daytime, she repeatedly went over in her mind the morning scene in which her grand-mother accused her, "You're no help!"

The child was brought to me by her social worker within one week of the murder. She came for treatment first weekly and later twice monthly for nine months. When her father was given legal custody, her treatment was transferred to a social worker nearer to her home. In the first week of treatment, Betsy was terrified that Ed would come back to kill her, but after she learned that Ed had committed suicide, her sense of guilt remained a serious problem. She suffered because she had survived and had failed to protect her grandmother. She told me in her first interview, "Mom wanted to catch Ed [at stealing] and wanted me to go to Grandma's. She wanted me there to protect Grandma. I was being sent to help Grandma until Mom got secret papers to the police. Mom wanted me to go in case something happened to her . . . I stayed one night. I thought something would happen!"

In the second interview Betsy reflected about pictures in her mind "only when I expect it" of the morning of the murder. "When I get to that time in the morning—the phone—it was light out. . . . She said, 'You're no help.' I think I had other ways I could have saved Grandma. What are those lights on your phone?"

"Would you like to play a little with the phone?" I asked. I set the phone line on hold, so that she could play. "How *would* you call the police?"

Betsy looked stricken.

"Of course, no one ever told you, so you could not have known what to do." I showed Betsy how to dial the operator and call the police.

"What if Ed walked in right then and interrupted?"

"You could leave the line open, so that the operator could trace the call and send the police anyway."

"How do you do that? Could I try?"

We played out the scenario several times. Betsy still looked very concerned. "I wish I had known how to help Grandma better."

"Your Grandmother might have protected you, too, in some ways!" I shifted the emphasis.

"How?" Betsy stared unbelieving.

I stood up and barricaded my door with a chair. I then dialed operator for the police. I moved Betsy and myself to a corner of the room away from the door. I showed Betsy how we might crouch together away from any gunfire. I explained that adults learn such things from books, movies, and the way armies are trained.

Betsy looked amazed and relieved. She had never conceived that her grandmother had had any options that fatal morning. She had accepted the entire responsibility onto her nine-year-old shoulders.

The corrective dénouement which Betsy was offered in play and in words served as a long-lasting therapeutic measure. In the months that followed that session, Betsy had few daydreams about the morning before the murder. Her nightmares rarely occurred. She remained emotionally vulnerable from the experience. Her sense of the future was foreshortened (Terr, 1982). When asked four months after the murder how long she imagined herself living, she answered, "Till I'm 12." She giggled. "I don't know, I just said that—I don't know. It's possible more bad will happen. But I'm not thinking that. I won't get married. I don't like boys except my Dad and my foster Dad. I couldn't have kids unless I was married, so I wouldn't have kids. I'd like to be a *telephone operator* [emphasis added] or a beautician."

Telephones have been particularly successful adjuncts to therapy for two other children who were kidnapping victims within their own families. Neither child, Wanda, five years old, or Emanuel, eight years old, had known how to phone "collect" at the time that their noncustodial parents had taken them away. Both children played-out collect calling only once in their psychotherapy sessions and both expressed relief that they knew that there was an effective way they could tell their custodial parents where they were. Both of these children had been afraid to go outside for fear that they would be "stolen" again. After the telephone "game," each was satisfied that if stolen, he or she could be retrieved. Parenthetically, both children had immediate confidence in their ability to sneak to a phone unseen. No instructions were required.

SUMMARY

In this chapter I have defined posttraumatic play and have suggested some uses of spontaneous posttraumatic play, stories, or art work in the psychotherapist's office or in residential treatment. I have outlined four types of play therapy that appear particularly suitable for children suffering from psychic trauma: abreactional play therapy, interpretive free-play therapy, interpretive prearranged play therapy, and corrective dénouement play therapy.

In my opinion play methods are only partly successful following psychic trauma. The traumatized child needs to verbalize as well as to play. This is why the observation of posttraumatic play or simply the knowledge about posttraumatic play can be so useful. It provides a focus for psychotherapeutic reconstruction—a verbal technique. It also allows for "prescriptions" to the parents which bypass direct therapy with the child.

Those cases in which play therapy alone can be expected to succeed are those in which the trauma is limited and without extensive intrusion past the child's coping and defense mechanisms. In those very unfortunate cases in which the trauma has been of disastrous proportions, neither play therapy nor insight-directed verbal treatments may be enough to reverse the damage or to limit the child's increased vulnerability to stress.

REFERENCES

APA (1980) *Diagnostic and Stastical Manual-III.* Washington, D.C.: American Psychiatric Association.

Boyer, E. (1950) *The secret game.* New York: Harcourt, Brace.

Clement, R. (1952) *Jeux Interdits* (available through Janus Films, New York).

Erikson, E. (Homburger) (1937) Configurations in play. *Psychoanalytic Quarterly*, **6**, 139–214.

Erikson, E. (1950) *Childhood and society.* New York: Norton.

Freud, A., & Burlingham, D. (1942) War and children. Report 12 in *The writings of Anna Freud*, Vol. 3. New York: International Universities Press, 1973. Pp. 143–211.

Freud, A. (1967) Comments on trauma. In S. Furst (Ed.), *Psychic trauma*, New York: Basic Books. Pp. 235–245.

Gardner, R. (1971) *Therapeutic communication with children: The mutual storytelling technique.* New York: Science House.

Gardner, R. (1979) Helping children cooperate in therapy. In J. Noshpitz (Ed.), *Basic handbook of child psychiatry*, Vol. 4. Pp. 414–433.

Levy, D. (1938) Release therapy in young children. *Psychiatry*, **1**, 387–390.

Levy, D. (1939) Release therapy. *American Journal of Orthopsychiatry*, **9**, 713–736.

Levy, D. (1945) Psychic trauma of operations in children and a note on combat neurosis. *American Journal of Diseases of Children*, **69**, 7–25.

Lifton R., & Olson E. (1976) The human meaning of total disaster. *Psychiatry*, **39**, 1–18.

MacLean, G. (1977) Psychic trauma and traumatic neurosis: Play therapy with a four-year-old boy. *Canadian Psychiatric Association Journal*, **22**, 71–76.

Newman, C. J. (1976) Children of disaster: Clinical observations at Buffalo Creek. *American Journal of Psychiatry*, **133**, 306–312.

Schwartzman, H. (Ed.) (1978) *Transformations: The anthropology of children's play*, New York: Plenum Press.

Shapiro, S. (1973) Preventive analysis following a trauma: A 4½-year-old girl witnesses a stillbirth. *Psychoanalytic Study of the Child*, **28**, 249–285.

Terr, L. (1979) Children of Chowchilla: A study of psychic trauma. *Psychoanalytic Study of the Child*, **34**, 547–623.

Terr, L. (1981) Psychic trauma in children: Observations following the Chowchilla schoolbus kidnapping. *American Journal of Psychiatry*, **138**, 14–19.

Terr, L. (1981) Forbidden games: Post-traumatic child's play. *Journal of the American Academy of Child Psychiatry*, **20**, 741–760.

Terr, L. (1982) Time sense following psychic trauma: A clinical study of ten adults and twenty children. Presented at the annual meeting, American Orthopsychiatric Association, San Francisco.

Terr, L. (1982) Chowchilla revisited: the effects of psychic trauma four years after the kidnapping of a schoolbus. Presented at the annual meeting, American Academy of Child Psychiatry, Washington, D.C.

CHAPTER 18

Play Therapy with Children of Divorced Parents

ALLAN E. MENDELL

INTRODUCTION

Concern by clinicians about the impact of divorce on children who are referred for psychotherapeutic help has been buttressed by recent statistical psychological studies. Kalter (1977), Kalter & Rembar, (in press) found that one-third of the children referred to a typical university psychiatric clinic (University of Michigan, Ann Arbor) were children of divorced parents, almost twice the prevalence of children of divorced parents in the normal population. Kelly and Wallerstein (1975, 1976, 1977) found that in a "nonclinic" population in California, 44% of the preschool children (two and a half to six years old) studied at the time of divorce "were found to be in significantly deteriorated psychological condition at the follow-up a year later," with similar worrisome statistical findings for the early- and late-latency age groups. This finding was accentuated by Kalter and Rembar (in press) who discovered in their clinical sample, a population of children two-thirds of whom had experienced parental separation more than five years previously, that "the pain of parental divorce, and its particular expressions, was still all too poignantly vivid." Kalter suggests that "children whose parents divorce may be especially vulnerable to the types of developmental conflicts that eventuate in psychiatric referral."

In agreement with Kalter's suggestion, I believe it most useful to think of divorce in terms of "developmental interference." "A 'developmental interference' can be defined as whatever disturbs the typical unfolding of development" (Nagera, 1966), particularly gross environmental deprivations or demands which are not commensurate with the child's immature ego capacity to comply or cope with them. Divorce can be such a situation for the child because it deprives him or her of a personal relationship, usually with the father, necessary for the successful negotiation of phase-appropriate tasks. Also, the trauma of parental hostilities and the sudden loss of one parent from the home may overtax the young child's emotional and cognitive abilities. The degree to which the divorce is a developmental interference will, of course, depend on such factors as the following:

1. The child's age and developmental level obtained prior to the divorce.
2. The nature of the child's environment and developmental interferences prior to the time of the divorce.
3. The constitutional strengths of the child.
4. The maturity of the parents and their ability to keep the child out of marital and divorce hostilities.
5. The psychopathology versus relative health of the custodial parent (usually the mother), and her ability to be supportive and emotionally available to the child rather than neglectful of the child or using him or her as an object for her own emotional needs.
6. The availability and relative health and maturity of the noncustodial parent.
7. The support available in terms of other family members and members of the community.
8. The availability of someone familiar and trusted by the child to, in some ways, take over the functions of the missing parent.

Again, Kalter and Rembar (1981) and Kelly and Wallerstein (1975, 1976, 1977) have offered statistical and observational evidence of the importance of the developmental level of the child at the time of the divorce in determining how disturbance will manifest itself. Most significantly, Kalter found evidence of a "mild cumulative deficit effect" (the younger the child at the time of divorce, the greater the disturbance). He also found that marital dissolution very early in a child's life, two and a half years or younger, was associated with separation related difficulties during latency; divorce during the oedipal phase was associated with a dramatic sex-linked effect in adolescence, a surprising inhibition of aggression in boys, and a "time-bomb effect" in girls of problematic aggression combined with academic problems. Kelly and Wallerstein found that younger preschool children were more likely to regress in the face of parental separation; older latency-age children had a better ability to tolerate and express painful affects; but children in all age groups reacted to parental divorce with rage, sadness, self-blame, evidence of narcissistic injury, fears of abandonment and rejection, and a shaken sense of security and identity.

Thus, divorce may function as a developmental interference at an earlier or later stage in a child's development, predisposing him or her to the development of a certain character structure or certain neurotic conflicts, but the child will most likely not come to the attention of a psychotherapist until (and if) he or she manifests the type of behavior that most frequently results in a referral to a psychiatric clinic, namely, problems with aggression or school-related problems when the child reaches latency age; delinquent behavior, sexual acting out, or drug abuse in adolescence. For the younger child, play therapy may be one component of the treatment.

METHOD

In my view, play therapy is an important component in an overall, integrated treatment approach for disturbed children which includes work with the parent or parents, and, at times, school personnel and other important people in the child's environment. Sometimes in working with children on whom the effect of parental divorce is the main concern, play therapy is not necessary or even indicated. Kelly and Wallerstein (1977) found that in some cases short-term, supportive, educational, crisis-oriented work with the parents initiated shortly after the time of the divorce was successful in significantly ameliorating the effect of divorce on the child. Chethik and Kalter are currently assessing the efficacy of group work with divorced parents. At times, marital conflicts and other personal conflicts may be displaced onto the child in such a way that treatment of the "parent–child relationship," via "parent guidance" with the custodial parent may be the most strategic mode of intervention (Kelly & Wallerstein, 1977). At other times, when the child is fortunate enough to have supportive and sensitive parents, crisis-oriented educational and supportive individual work with the child may be indicated, especially if the child has the cognitive and emotional capability of utilizing such information (Kelly and Wallerstein). In this regard, educational books and games may be used fruitfully (Gardner, 1976). However, in the typical psychiatric clinic population, the majority of children of divorced parents are referred several years after the divorce has occurred (Kalter, 1977, in press) and the effects upon the child's personality are more entrenched and enmeshed with the internal sequelae of other environmental influences interacting with the child's developing personality. Usually, parental pathology is such that long-term work with the custodial parent in the form of "parent guidance" and focal psychotherapy on issues pertaining directly to the parent–child relationship is a necessary adjunct. Analytically oriented play therapy is the best format for allowing a child's fantasies to unfold in the context of a "safe" environment and a trusting relationship developed over time so that the nature of the child's conflicts and personality structure may be understood by therapist and child via interpretation and appropriate environmental interventions may be made via parent guidance. When this approach has been taken, certain themes related to divorce have been observed by myself and other analytically oriented therapists. Play therapy allows for such a process because, in the words of Mort Chethik (1981), "In my experience with young children, the process of 'talking' is often a foreign language that many children learn, in order to manage the world of adults; play is their natural and affective language, and an expression of their affective life." A brief enumeration and description of these themes, necessarily incomplete, will be the subject of the remaining part of this section.

Grieving

Divorce involves the partial loss of a relationship (usually with the father, although frequently the child will have to sustain diminished availability of both parents, as the mother may have to work or be otherwise preoccupied, i.e., depressed). Nevertheless, the loss is a permanent one. The ability of the child to mourn a permanent loss is a subject of dispute. When writing of an adults' ability to react to the death of a loved one, Freud (1917) used the term "mourning" to mean "that reaction to loss in which the lost object is gradually decathected by the painful and prolonged work of remembering and reality testing" (Wolfenstein, 1966). Some observers (Nagera, 1970; Wolfenstein, 1966) state that such a process is not possible until adulthood. Furman (1964) proposes that attainment of the phallic level of development is a prerequisite along with the availability of a supportive environment to enable the child to tolerate the concomitant pain; Bowlby (1960, 1980) points to the manifestations of "protest, despair, and denial" in very young children separated from their mothers as similar to "pathological mourning" in adults. However, there is no dispute that all children show evidence of grieving in reaction to such loss, when the term "grieving" is used as proposed by Tessman (1978) to denote "the affective state of sadness, pain, and desolation when unrequited longing for the absent person is paramount."

Deutsch (1937) noticed that children tend to take flight from the suffering entailed in grieving. She proposed that the ego of the child is not sufficiently developed to bear the strain of mourning and therefore tries to circumvent the process through infantile regression (as observed by Kelly & Wallerstein, 1975) or by the mobilization of primitive defenses such as omission of affect. Denial and fantasy (Wolfenstein, 1966; Gardner, 1976) are employed by the child to buttress the repression of painful affects by failing to recognize the reality of the situation. Also, "splitting of the ego" (Wolfenstein, 1966) is common in that the child may give verbal evidence that he or she is cognitively aware of the nature of the loss yet emotionally refuses to accept the loss. This is particularly manifest in children of divorce by fantasies of reunion and reconciliation (to be described as follows), and defiant refusal to accept a stepparent as a substitute. The use of these defensive mechanisms took a curious twist in the case of James, to be recounted, in that initially he maintained that his father was "dead" in order to avoid the painful realization that his divorced father lived close by, but totally ignored him. (When eventually confronted with the fact that his father wasn't dead, he started making up stories of incredible rendezvouses with his father—even seeing him on TV!) Deutsch (1937), Wolfenstein (1966), Furman (1964), Gardner (1976), and Tessman (1978), unanimously stress the importance of helping the child tolerate and express the pain, anger, sadness, and fear associated with grief over the loss of a parent, so that the child, as an adult, will not suffer the constriction of affect associated with trying to avoid painful feelings, or burdened by neurotic attempts to complete the aborted mourning process. As Deutsch eloquently stated, "In any case, the expediency of the flight from the suffering of grief is but a temporary gain because, as we have seen, the necessity to mourn persists in the psychic apparatus."

The child is not a finished product. The multitude of developmental processes cannot come to a halt in order for the child to do the work of mourning (decathexis of the lost relationship and replacement with the realization of a new reality). The child, under the press of developmental needs, may precipitously latch onto a new relationship or else re-create or hold onto the lost relationship through fantasy (Nagera, 1970). The regression that the child undergoes upon the loss of an important relationship may not only serve as a defensive avoidance of painful affect, but also be a manifestation of the inability to negotiate a certain developmental state without the presence of the necessary developmental object relationship. In this regard, Chethik and Kalter (1980) speak of the role of the therapist as a "developmental facilitator." They found in their clinical work with children of divorce that "the psychotherapeutic process appears to allow them a new opportunity, with a 'new object' to complete many of the developmental tasks interfered with by the divorce." Thus, a boy may undertake for the first time phallic competitive activity with the therapist, or a girl may flirt with the therapist to obtain narcissistic supplies that she was unable to receive from her father. "It often seemed that these children, rather than dealing primarily with entrenched neurotic conflicts, were 'starved' for someone who could facilitate tasks interrupted by the divorce." James and Madeleine, whose cases will be recounted, seemed to convey the impression that they "would do anything" in order to "keep" the therapist as a replacement for the lost object. (In these two cases, I term the phenomenon "oedipal object hunger," indicating the oral, need-fulfilling, as well as the oedipal determinants of the behavior.) However, it is important to keep in mind that the therapist can only be a *"partial* replacement object," and cannot, in reality, take the place of a "real" parent. Thus, it is incumbent on the therapist to confront the child gently with this reality and help the child deal with the pain of the unrequited desire for the lost relationship. In this manner, the therapist may simultaneously enable the child to complete interrupted developmental tasks without aborting the grief process.

Finally, Furman (1964) stresses the importance of a conducive home environment for nurturing the development in the child of the ability to tolerate the grieving process. This is often difficult to achieve in the aftermath of divorce when the custodial parent is still experiencing bitter feelings toward the departed spouse and may have difficulty dealing with his or her own feelings of anger, pain, loss, and rejection. Through parent guidance, the therapist may help the mother learn to tolerate her own feelings so that she may support the child in the expression of his or her affects. The case of James provides an example of this.

Reunion Fantasies

As Nagera (1970) points out, the child's tendency to maintain or recreate the lost object relationship is evidence of the child's inability to complete the mourning process. Sometimes the fantasy will lie dormant or be fostered in secret for years because it conflicts with the child's knowledge of reality (Tessman, 1978), only to appear in the open (sometimes in idealized form) when provoked by a threatening, external event such as remarriage of one of the parents or disappointment with a stepparent. Sometimes, under the impact of object loss, the child will regress to primitive modes of thinking and problem solving, using magical gestures to hold onto or bring about the return of the lost relationship. (James would attempt, in the transference, to "hold on" to the therapist, preventing him from terminating a session on time, by imprisoning him in a make-believe cage.) Sometimes the fantasied reunion is acted out in displacement by overly seductive behavior with males. (The cases of both Madeleine and James illustrate this point flagrantly.)

Lohr et al. (unpublished) distinguish the reconciliation fantasy as a special type of reunion fantasy. They use the term "reconciliation fantasy" to denote "the child's wish for a continuation of the parental ties to one another as well as to the self." Kelly and Wallerstein (1976) found this type of fantasy to be widespread and persistent in their sample of latency-age children. Several authors (Lohr et al., Tessman, 1978; Gardner, 1976) report that reconciliation fantasies may be fueled by the parents' unresolved attachments which may be manifested by continued sexual involvement or quarrels over issues involving the children, such as custody, visitation rights, child support, and more subtle battles over who is the better parent. Guilt may be a factor contributing to endurance of reconciliation fantasies as the child wishes to undo the parental separation for which he or she may feel responsible. The child may experience the lack of an intact parental unit as a narcissistic injury, and may seek to reestablish the integrity of this unit in an attempt to restore an intact sense of self. (Both James and Madeleine consistently depicted their families as intact families in their fantasy play with drawings and puppets.)

Fear of Abandonment and the Issue of Blame

As stated previously, as the result of divorce, the child may be relatively abandoned by both parents. One parent has been removed from the home, while the other must often devote more of (usually) her attention to other matters. Thus, the child is precipitously and forcefully confronted with the fragility of his or her world. The security provided by an intact parental unit is taken for granted by most children of intact families (fortunately); however, children of divorce can never again feel that security. There is always the possibility, even if not spoken (and sometimes it is spoken!), that "If daddy can be extruded, so can I"; and "If daddy can abandon me, so can mommy." Kelly and Wallerstein (1975) found that in some preschool children, the mother was perceived as a frightening, powerful, threatening figure who could banish family members at whom she was angry and cause them to disappear. At times, a little girl may angrily hold her mother responsible for the double narcissistic insult of depriving her of a father and a penis. (See the case of Madeleine.) Kelly and Wallerstein (1975) also found that the older preschool children tended to blame themselves, feeling that if only they had behaved better or had not had "naughty" feelings the tragedy would have been avoided. A younger child, still under the sway of magical thought processes and preoedipal omnipotent fantasies, may hold his intense rageful feelings or sensuous desires or neediness responsible, leading to a conviction that these feelings are bad and must be controlled. (Thus, James' aversion to the "body book" and the expression of angry feelings recounted in the case illustration.) The child is often caught up in conflicts of loyalty between parents or may feel guilty about accepting a stepparent, experiencing this as a betrayal of the idealized departed parent (Tessman, 1978). A child may also feel guilty about displaying the departed parent as the "oedipal victor," and fear retaliation from an imagined, angry, returning rival.

One of the consequences of divorce is that the child must face and learn to deal with diminished narcissistic and material supplies. (Madeleine, in her fantasy play, must seduce the mean and stingy Count Count into sharing his possessions which she then must bring home to share with her mother. In real life, her father refused to send child-support money or visit regularly, and Madeleine became extremely adept at avoiding waste and helping mother watch her money.) The child may employ other methods of ensuring the continuity of supplies. The child who thinks his or her "bad" behavior was responsible for the divorce, may continue the "bad" behavior in order to maintain the illusion of control (Gardner, 1976). In the case illustration, Madeleine becomes very accomplished at "mothering" her mother in order to assure herself of her mother's continued ability as a reliable source of narcissistic supplies.

Problems of Identification

"Identification is defined as a transformation of the self, whereby the self becomes similar to the external object" (Chethik et al., unpublished). A person's "sense of self" owes a great deal to identification with parental objects early in childhood. The process of identification in normal development is fostered in part by the natural daily separations from the object, that is through identification the child can, in a sense, keep the longed-for, absent object with him. Thus, "it is through identification that the child seeks to minimize his vulnerability to objects" (Chethik et al., unpublished). Identification with parental figures plays an important role in the development of superego, ego ideal, and sexual identity.

Chethik et al. (unpublished) have noticed that it is a common phenomenon for children to try to retain the departed, divorced parent through the process of identification. They have found that under the impact of the stress of acute family disruption, a number of children, "struggling with the acute aspects of the loss, 'become' the lost object. This is usually a transient symptom picture, a partial identification, and a component of an acute grief process." However, this defensive identification can become fixed, especially if the custodial parent has a need for the child to assume some aspects of the departed spouse in order to continue the marital battle (this time with the child), or re-engage in family conflicts from his or her own childhood. (Madeleine's mother allows her to take over her departed father's role by sleeping and showering with her; James' mother complains about his whininess, irresponsibility, and hangdog demeanor in the same fashion that she complained about these attributes in her ex-husband.)

Neubauer (1960) observes that the absence of a parent during the oedipal stage of development has a pathogenic potential for superego formation and sexual identification. In the course of development of the superego, the child learns to renounce immediate instinctual gratification in order to please the parent. Wolfenstein (1966) points out that at times the child's good behavior may be predicated on a type of "bargain" that if he is "good" nothing bad will happen. When the parent leaves, the child may feel that the bargain has been abrogated, and, consequently, angrily rejects previously internalized standards. The case illustrations provide dramatic examples of the sexual confusions, as well as the lack of proper superego prohibition, which can result from an absence of the oedipal father: Madeleine attempts to acquire the therapist's penis; James assumes a negative-oedipal position toward the therapist in fantasy, attempting to have a baby by him and set up house with him.

The preceding discussion has highlighted themes that commonly arise in play therapy with children of divorced parents. The following case illustrations will serve to highlight some of those themes. Each child was seen two times per week for play therapy, and the parent one time per week in parent guidance for a period of approximately one year.

CASE MATERIAL

Madeleine *

Madeleine, six and a half years old, was brought in by her mother at the urging of Madeleine's schoolteacher, who was quite concerned about "bizarre behavior" in class, which consisted of a short attention span, easy distrac-

* Grateful acknowledgment is made to Dr. Harvey Falit, M.D., for his help as supervisor of this case.

tibility, poor frustration tolerance, a tendency to "go into a daze," and a propensity for becoming easily excited (as manifested by jumping, spastic flapping of her arms, or crawling on the ground to the accompaniment of self-produced, high-pitched squeals). Madeleine's insightful teacher did not feel that Madeleine was hyperkinetic, but rather was reacting to the constant feuding between Madeleine's parents, divorced when Madeleine was two and a half years old.

Madeleine's mother presented herself in the disconcerting manner of a 46-year-old hysteric. An imposing and ungainly lady by virtue of her size, she also had an intellect and wit which could be used in a devastating fashion, principally to the detriment of her most recent ex-husband, Madeleine's father, but also occasionally against the therapist or for the categorical abuse of manhood in general. When this lady spoke, one had the feeling that it was best to hold on tight and wait in suspense to see where the torrents of words, storms of emotion, and abrupt shifts in content would carry her. The scrambled, unfocused account of her life revealed childhood memories of a remote, idealized father, and a mother whom she described as narcissistic, uncaring, and always at odds with her. Her stormy history included three marriages, three divorces, and three suicide attempts by drug overdose (none during Madeleine's lifetime).

The pregnancy with Madeleine was planned. In fact, mother's third marriage was planned for the purpose of conception. At age 39, mother decided she wanted to have a child before she got too old to have one. In a separate interview (I met with Madeleine's father once during the initial evaluation period and did not see him subsequently), Madeleine's father stated, "She enticed me to marry her with promises that things would get better and promised me that if she had a child she wouldn't ask me for child support if we got divorced." (Father was an alcoholic and had been involved in a stormy two-year relationship with the mother prior to the marriage.) Father was not present at Madeleine's delivery, and mother was "shocked" when she came home from the hospital with the baby to find that father had moved out. Father was in and out of the house for the next two and a half years until the separation and divorce were made final. The relationship continued its stormy course with outbreaks of violence that included physical blows, threats with knives, and attempts to run each other over with a car. During this period, mother started her affair with a married man, Bob, which has lasted off and on to this day. Since the divorce, Madeleine's mother and father have continued to have violent disputes over child support payments and visitation rights.

Mother has been working to support herself and her daughter since Madeleine was 11 months old. As a result, Madeleine has been taken care of by babysitters and teachers for most of her life. However, as a compensation to this, Madeleine's mother has invested a great deal in the relationship with her daughter, and spends almost every available moment with her. Most of mother's hard-earned money goes to such things as private schooling for Madeleine, psychotherapy for Madeleine, and ballet and horseback riding lessons for Madeleine.

At the time of the evaluation, Madeleine presented a much more disturbed history than she presented in person. Thoughts of organically based behavioral problems and possibly a seizure disorder were considered and then immediately rejected when Madeleine was seen in the flesh. She presented herself as an adorable, yet seductive, little girl who was obviously intelligent, imaginative, and able to engage in prolonged object-related fantasy play without evidence of attention deficits or poor frustration tolerance. A neurological screening exam for hard and soft neurological signs was negative. The most noticeable pathological characteristic was extreme object hunger, especially "oedipal object hunger."

Because it was hard to imagine a girl emerging from such a chaotic and disturbed family environment without developing a severe personality disturbance, she was initially given a diagnosis of "Childhood neurotic disorder with question of borderline characteristics." However, there was never any behavioral evidence of "borderline" features and easy reversibility of her most severe symptoms ruled out pathology of either an organic or "borderline" nature. Within a few weeks of the start of therapy, all of Madeleine's behavioral problems at school had ceased, never to reoccur during the course of therapy. By the end of the semester Madeleine was not only one of the most academically outstanding pupils of her class, but was also one of the most popular. She had two very close, special friends among her classmates.

1. *Course of Treatment: Parent Guidance.*   At the beginning of therapy, it became apparent that aside from continuing an intense, heated, sadomasochistic relationship with her ex-husband, mother maintained a very interesting relationship with her married boyfriend, Bob. When mother started her affair with Bob (Madeleine was approximately one year old), she was just one of Bob's many lovers and continued in this fashion until she prevailed upon him to move in with her. Madeleine was five and a half years old. During this period of time, Madeleine referred to both her father and Bob as "daddy." However, Bob, described as a person who usually clams up and withdraws when angry, soon began to get into heated arguments with mother and was consequently kicked out of the house after a period of only two months. However, once out of the house, he and mother were able to reestablish a friendly, "working" relationship which consisted of his coming over and slipping into bed with mother at 3:00 every morning. Madeleine would usually join them. Madeleine was able to describe in subsequent therapy sessions how exciting it was to be "squashed" between mommy and Bob as they all "rolled around in bed together." The threesome would also frequently bathe together and walk around the house in the nude. When mom was asked if Madeleine exhibited excited behavior when she was around Bob in the nude, mom wanted to know what I meant by "excited." When I described the symptoms Madeleine displayed at school, the excited jumping up and down, the shrieking and spastic flapping of her hands, mother explained, "Yes, she acts that way when she's around any man, whether clothed or not." (Madeleine subsequently verified this in therapy at excited moments.) Mother was soon able to see that Madeleine was

being sexually overstimulated by Bob, but refused to accept the fact that she, herself, could be sexually stimulating her daughter. Although an extremely intelligent woman, mother's judgment was severely hindered by her overidentification with Madeleine: "At the end of a hard day, Madeleine and I both need to regress (by getting in bed together)." Consequently, although she subsequently required that Bob be fully dressed when not in bed, and instructed Madeleine to stay in her own room in the early mornings, she still allowed Madeleine to get in bed with her when she was alone. However, this was apparently enough to help Madeleine keep her cool in school.

Mother's overidentification with Madeleine and her need to use Madeleine inappropriately as a mother and a spouse was a dominant focus of the parent guidance. Although mother was not able, during the course of parent guidance, to compensate for her need to use Madeleine in this fashion, she was increasingly able to identify episodes in which she looked to her daughter for inappropriate mothering, felt guilty about it, and attempted to make appropriate changes. She was able to tolerate separating from Madeleine enough to let her spend an occasional night at a friend's house, although as mother stated, "It's not easy; when Madeleine spends the night out I can't sleep." Mother was eventually able to acknowledge that Madeleine had emotional needs separate from hers. Mother related how she was initially shocked when Madeleine started telling her words that she learned at school of which mother did not know the meaning. It was an earth-shattering experience for mother to realize that Madeleine could know things that mother didn't know. Mother realized that her inability to differentiate her feelings from Madeleine's made it difficult to tolerate painful, sad, and angry feelings in her daughter. Eventually, mother was able to tolerate and support some appropriate expression of these affects on the part of her daughter without feeling totally rejected and a failure as a mother. She was able to link her need for mothering to the fact that she perceived her own mother as narcissistic and uncaring. Although mother came to feel increasingly conflicted about her intensive use of Madeleine to satisfy her own needs, she was unable to follow up on advice to seek her own therapy. However, six months after termination, she contacted the therapist to inform him that she was getting involved in group therapy specifically for divorced parents.

Another major focus of the parent guidance was mother's volatile relationship with the father. Her tendency to use splitting as a defense made it extremely hard for her to work out any type of cooperative parenting relationship with her ex-husband. At the onset of therapy, mother viewed her ex-husband as a homicidal maniac who was out to kidnap her daughter, although there was never any evidence that he had abused Madeleine in any way other than to be unreliable in regard to visitation and child-support payments. Mother was afraid to take legal action against her husband because she feared that he would somehow win, despite his huge arrearage in child-support payments. Rather, she used discontinuation of visitation as a means of coercing child-support payments from him.

Thus, the therapist had an important role to play as an "auxiliary ego" not only in helping the mother establish boundaries between herself and her daughter, but also by helping her deal more realistically with her ex-husband. Again, mother had to separate her feelings from Madeleine's in order to recognize that her daughter needed and desired an ongoing relationship with her father. The therapist resisted mother's pleas to "talk sense" to Madeleine's father as this would have circumvented the need for mother to learn to deal with him effectively herself. Conjoint sessions were ruled out by both parents, and might have endangered the therapist's fragile alliance with the mother had they been carried out. Mother then tried to evade the necessity of dealing rationally with her ex-husband by having him deal directly with Madeleine as far as setting up visitation times. It was necessary for the therapist to point out that she was placing Madeleine in a difficult test of loyalties, and once again putting her in the role of the parent (it's a parental responsibility to work out visitation responsibilities). Mother was finally able to confront the ex-husband with her determination that reliable visitation was a paternal responsibility as much as were child support payments. Father's response to this was to lose interest in visitation, a result intended by the mother, but also indicative of father's use of Madeleine as a tool of warfare against mother; he had little genuine fatherly interest. By the time of termination, mother had hired a lawyer to seek legal redress for the overdue child support payments.

Course of Treatment: Work with the Child.   The themes that would occupy us for the 11-month course of therapy were vividly present in the first session. Madeleine was escorted by her mother to the treatment room. Madeleine objected strenuously to her mother's leaving, folding her arms, stamping her feet, and running in and out of the room in an excited manner. When I pointed out the toys in the room for her to play with, she looked at the two examiners (myself and a male medical student) as if she had noticed us for the first time. She smiled and appeared to be quite interested in us. In a vexatious manner, she told us she was "furious" at her mother. However, what she was angry about was a "secret." She then danced around the chair in an excited manner, but finally settled down in the chair and started to build a car with Legos. When asked if it had been explained to her why she was here, she replied that it was her idea to come, not her mother's, but that she had forgotten the reason. She got along with her mother and had no problems in school, but was worried about a friend who was behind in reading. When asked about her father, she admitted forthrightly that she was angry at him because he threw her mother down on the concrete once. She denied being scared; she was just angry. We then played a game with the puppets. She took the bear and I the lion. As the bear, she went to the honey tree and shared her honey with me. We then brought the honey home to mother, who paid us increasingly large amounts for it. We then went to Count's castle. He was a Count who liked to count everything: people, eyes, and everything. He was a rather stingy fellow, but could be seduced into letting us spend the night. The lion and bear crawled into bed and snuggled up to one another and slept together "because they are friends." We then stole Count Count's furniture and took it home to mommy who rewarded us with more money. We were then able to seduce Count Count into giving us food, which we took to mommy. The bear then cuddled the lion in a protective and nurturing fashion and they went to sleep. After this, I asked Madeleine to draw a picture. She drew a rather phallic looking fish and explained that this fish married another fish and then they had babies. When I told Madeleine that I would be meeting with her father, she anxiously remarked that she was afraid that I would be mugged. When we left the room to meet her mother, Madeleine, excited and giggling, hid behind a chair and said she didn't want to go. As mother insisted it was time to go, she ran back to me and gave me a hug, and then walked down the hall with her mother, gesturing angrily and stamping her foot.

Thus, dramatically evident in the first session were: (1) Madeleine's oedipal object hunger, (2) her view of men as possessing some special "goodies" that had to be stolen or procured by seduction and then shared with mommy, (3) her anger at mother for depriving her of the oedipal object, (4) hints of over-stimulation at home, (5) anxiety about separation from mother, (6) battles with mother for autonomy (whose idea was it to come to therapy!), (7) a protective, nurturing attitude toward her mother (and therapist), who can't protect and provide for themselves, and (8) an intense need to please (followed the therapist's every instruction) in order that she not be rejected.

During the initial sessions the excitement level was high and resultant anxiety and concern for mother were just beneath the surface. Madeleine seemed never to tire of the Count Count game, and would excitedly crawl around on the furniture and jump around the room, giggling the whole time. There were frequent requests to go to the bathroom and check to see how mommy was doing. She would make attempts to sit in the therapist's lap and jump on his back for a piggyback ride. Madeleine was informed that this was "excited" behavior that interfered with our ability to do therapy as well as schoolwork, and had to be controlled. Madeleine was able to connect her excited behavior in therapy to her behavior around Bob, with whom she was "in love." Because of her intense need to please me, she was able to control her excited behavior. Her need to check with her mother was reduced by interpretations that she was afraid her mother might leave her. After one month of therapy, Madeleine's teacher informed me that Madeleine's overexcited behavior had ceased, her schoolwork was improved, but she still looked depressed and distracted. At six weeks, mother informed me that Madeleine no longer evidenced a desire to get in bed with her and Bob and did not reciprocate as enthusiastically as in the past to Bob's overtures to hug and kiss her. (This coincided with mother's decision to have these behaviors curbed. Thus this change in Madeleine's behavior may have been partially due to a change in the signals that mother and Bob were giving her.) At this point, Madeleine expressed a desire to quit therapy because it was "frustrating." When I commiserated with her about how indeed it must be frustrating for Madeleine to curb her excitement and her desire to have me as a father, Madeleine let loose with agonizing howls of "I'm bored, bored, bored, bored!" (Boredom is a common response to situations where one is not allowed to gratify one's desires.)

Madeleine then commenced work on a "snowflake book." She drew "families" of snowflakes. The father snowflake was usually the biggest. I wondered out loud if the father's being biggest meant he was the most important. Madeleine denied that she felt this way, stating that "everyone is equally important." I wondered if she sometimes felt her family was different because her father didn't live with them. She denied that her family was different. "All families are the same. It doesn't matter whether or not you have a father." Shortly after, an event occurred which made this the therapist's most memorable session. It started sedately enough with Madeleine busily painting a lace doily that she had brought with her. She then started talking to me in a "secret language," that I soon figured out was English with an "r" positioned at the beginning of each word. I started responding to her in the secret "r" language, which she responded to in an excited manner. She started frantically looking through the drawers of the desk while I observed out loud that she was a girl who liked to explore and see what was inside of things. Madeleine enthusiastically agreed to this astute observation with a gleeful "Yes, I do," and drooling, suddenly turned around and lunged at me, placing both her hands firmly on my crotch. It took quite a bit of effort to dislocate her hands. She then suggested that we play "treasure hunt." She started hiding the clues while I composed myself. She then excitedly observed me as I uncovered the clues and found the treasure chest at the end filled with coins and pebbles. I commented that I knew what other treasure she was interested in; she wanted to explore what was inside my pants. She denied this. I pointed out that she had just put her hands on my penis. She denied this, claiming that she had put her hands on my leg. I pointed out that lots of little girls were interested in men and their penises. She started screaming, "I'm bored! I'm bored!" I insisted that lots of girls are curious about the differences between boys and girls. She informed me that there weren't any differences. I insisted that boys had penises and girls had vaginas. She opened my coat pocket and, indicating the empty contents, stated, "See, there aren't any differences." I persisted that boys had penises and girls didn't, and sometimes it was hard to admit this. She finally acquiesced with, "Well, aside from that there aren't any differences!" It was clear from this that Madeleine felt that daddies were more important because they had penises, and she was a deprived little girl because she didn't have a daddy or a penis. In order to compensate for this painful reality, she had to deny strenuously the differences, yet she could not contain her intense longing. It was this incident which convinced me at a relatively early stage in my training that penis envy did indeed exist.

Subsequent to this session, Madeleine's outbursts of overexcited behavior ceased. This was probably in part due to an increased conscientiousness on my part not to do anything which might excite Madeleine (such as speaking the "secret" language), as well as increased vigilance on mother's part. Shortly after this, when mother observed Madeleine playfully spank a friend's father on the buttocks, she severely reprimanded her. A couple of months later, when Madeleine was taken out to a resturant in honor of her birthday, a middle-aged man, quite taken by her appearance, inquired in a childish, seductive tone of voice if she would be his date. Madeleine replied in a stern, no-nonsense manner, "Cut that out." (A bit of an "overdetermined" response. This type of rigid reaction formation is common in the initial stages of the development of superego prohibitions.)

Interpretations about Madeleine's sadness at not having a reliable father, her desire for her therapist to fill that role, and her frustration over his not being able to were made *ad nauseum,* as Madeleine continued to bring projects into therapy for me to help her with in a fatherly manner. We focused on Madeleine's need to please me so that I would like her and never leave her. Madeleine always took pains in therapy to be exceedingly neat and orderly and even helped the male janitor clean the rooms while she was waiting during her mother's sessions.

In March, the representative theme of the puppet play consisted of a mother trying to soothe her little boy who is afraid that when mother goes to the store she might not ever come back. Mother reassures the boy by letting him accompany her and by buying him a pet lion that becomes his constant companion. The lion was seen to represent Madeleine's desire for the "father-therapist–penis."

In April, Madeleine suddenly became concerned about termination when I was called out of the room for an emergency. She was afraid that I would leave her unexpectedly as her father had done. Madeleine was also able to talk about how her father had been kicked out of the house and even jailed for his bad behavior. She expressed fears that her mother might leave her when she's particularly angry and naughty. When it came time for my vacation in May, Madeleine quite openly talked to me, her mother, and her teacher about how sad she was that I was going away and how much she would miss me. The therapist suggested to her that these feelings were related to those she felt about her father. She stated in response, "You know, when a person goes away on vacation, it may be good for that person, but it's bad for the person that's left behind." When I expressed her wish for me to stay, she replied, "No, no. You've had this plan for a long time."

When I returned from my vacation, mother informed me that Madeleine was reluctant to return to therapy, stating, "I didn't miss him as much as I thought I would." When I interpreted Madeleine's anger at me for leaving, she denied it, but then launched into a tirade against her father, "that little nurd!" for being so unreliable, "he's never on time for his visits! He disappears for months without telling anybody! He comes over without asking if it's all right first! He doesn't pay his child support which is my money for getting me things I need! He never listens to me when I talk! He takes me to cheap resturants!"

Later in the summer, mother and father were again arguing, and mother was threatening to cut off visitation. The attorney stepped in to mediate, and Madeleine was to tell the attorney her wishes in private as part of the decision-making process. Madeleine informed the attorney that her father was "in violation of the law," and that she was angry at him, but also she still loved him and wanted him to visit on Wednesdays and Sundays.

It was at about this time that Madeleine decided to clean out her locker. Aside from keeping her old friends the bear, lion, and horse puppets, she decided to give away all other "oedipal" and "preoedipal" toys. She gave up the Fisher-Price dollhouse, dolls, clay, building blocks, and mommy, daddy, girl, and boy puppets. She kept paper, scissors, drawing materials, and Legos. At the same time, she was cleaning out her room at home. As mother was helping her clean and put old things in the basement, Madeleine informed her mother that she was angry at some of the things that daddy did, but that she still loved him. She also informed her mother that she felt the same way about her!

As mother continued to have problems with her former husband and was also experiencing severe financial problems, she increasingly turned to Madeleine for more mothering. Ironically, Madeleine did a good job of mothering. Madeleine helped look for the cheapest brands in the store to help mother save money. When mother sprained her ankle, Madeleine assured her that she would be all right. Mother asked Madeleine's opinion about a strange phone call from a drunken old boyfriend she had received in the middle of the night; Madeleine appropriately informed mother that it was a "weird" conversation. When, on a visit to the mother's family in Kansas, grandmother started berating mother for the manner in which she disciplined Madeleine, Madeleine retorted to the grandmother in her mother's defense, "How will I grow up to be a big girl if my mother doesn't correct me?" Mother took Madeleine along with her to a posttherapy checkup for a carcinoma of the uterus which had been successfully excised five years previously. The doctor had a long talk with Madeleine about how her mother was out of danger. Madeleine developed migraine headaches.

In therapy, following her first migraine, Madeleine expressed a fear that the horse she used for horseback riding lessons would fall down under her weight and die. We then played with the puppets. She had her horse puppet give my lion puppet a ride. The horse became excited, but also exhausted. I commented what a heavy burden it must be. I talked about how sometimes children's worries about their mothers could be heavy burdens and cause migraine headaches.

I informed mother that Madeleine was becoming "prematurely mature" because of mother's need to use Madeleine as a mother. I pointed out that although Madeleine was becoming very good at mothering, becoming a strong, sensible, and compassionate person, she was also paying the price in terms of migraine headaches. Mother was disinclined to heed me until one day shortly afterward, Madeleine exclaimed in exasperation to her mother, "How can I talk to you about my problems when you're always talking to me about yours?" Mother then realized that by using Madeleine as a mother, she was abrogating her own responsibility as a mother. Madeleine had two migraine headaches in quick succession thereafter, but did not have any more for the rest of the course of the therapy.

Madeleine started another book, in therapy, about birds. The stories consisted of a mother bird feeding its young and then the young gradually learning to fly and finally leaving the nest for good.

Termination.   One month into the school year after 10 months of therapy, the decision was made to terminate in six weeks. The decision was made because after reentering school, none of Madeleine's presenting symptoms returned. She was an excellent student with excellent peer relationships and no overt behavior problems. (She did continue to wet her bed occasionally at night, but this was not an occasion of concern to either Madeleine or her mother, and it did not prevent Madeleine from spending nights out with friends and spending nights out camping.) It was felt that Madeleine's oedipal problems had been resolved and that she was firmly into latency. It was true that an unhealthy symbiotic relationship still existed between mother and daughter, but Madeleine was coping as an auxiliary ego to a "borderline" mother as best could be expected. It was felt that no further progress could be made with Madeleine in therapy unless mother was willing to engage in her own therapy, which she was not.

With the announcement of termination, Madeleine was finally able to display anger at me, "I don't give a damn when therapy ends!" When I sympathized with her anger, however, it quickly dissipated. Madeline explained that what she meant was that she could stay in therapy two years if it was necessary. Madeleine was quite open about expressing her sadness at termination, and was on the verge of tears several times. She informed her teacher and her mother of her sadness and angrily demanded of her mother, "How could you get me involved in therapy without consulting me?" Thus, she blamed her mother for the end of therapy as she blamed her for the lack of father and the lack of a penis.

During the early part of the termination phase, there was a mild increase in flirtatious behavior, a mild regression, as if to try to hold onto me by a return of the initial symptoms. However, when Madeleine was trying to tell me of a risqué song that was being sung at school, she was genuinely embarrassed and finally had to write the words on a sheet of paper because she couldn't say "There's a place in France where naked ladies dance." This was testimony to the strength of reaction formation and the firmness of her move into latency.

Typically, in the confusion of the morning hours, mother would frequently get mad at Madeleine for some misbehavior and overreact by giving her a spanking. There would usually follow an intense, heated exchange, then a period of stubborn silence which ended in an emotional mutual apology and affectionate hugging and kissing before Madeleine was dropped off at school because neither could stand the insecurity of parting from the other in anger.

There was a dramatic change in this behavior during the termination period. One morning, Madeleine was thrown on the couch and spanked for having her shoes on the wrong feet. Madeleine met her mother's attempts at an apology with stony silence, and when they arrived at school, she merely said, "good-bye." When she was picked up at school, she quietly gave her mother an apology unaccompanied by hugs and kisses. The following day, Madeleine presented her mother with a written "scroll of independence for kids," which commented that kids have certain rights to food, clothing, and shelter from their parents, and the right to wear their shoes on the wrong feet! However, she subsequently came up with a "scroll of independence for parents," which stipulated that parents had a duty to love and care for their kids and never leave; and parents do have a right to correct their children when their shoes are on the wrong feet, without nagging! Madeleine was able to talk in therapy about her fears that her mother might leave her if she got angry, but was then quickly able to reassure herself that this would not happen. Subsequently, the next time Madeleine was punished by being sent to her room, she gave her mother the following letter upon her release, "Side one—you're a mean mommy. Side two—I hate you (for awhile)." Mother was able to tell Madeleine that it was OK to feel angry when being punished.

During termination, mother announced plans to have Bob move in "permanently" in January. I suggested that mother was trying to find a replacement for her relationship with me. Mother denied this. However, she asked Madeleine's opinion, as usual, and Madeleine was able to give a reality-based response. Madeleine asked her mother what made her think this time would be any different from last time. Mother explained that she and Bob weren't arguing as much. Madeleine replied, "Yeah, when he moves in, that's when you'll start arguing again!" Madeleine was also concerned about what Bob would do with his family. She didn't feel that it was right for him to leave them, as her father had left her.

On her last session, Madeleine presented me with a picture of herself as a ballerina and a postcard of geese flying south for the winter. After she closed her locker for the last time, she turned to me, nervously shook my hand, and with a subdued but firm voice, said, "Goodbye, Dr. Mendell."

Formulation.   The case of Madeleine certainly is in agreement with the finding of Kalter and Rembar (in press), that "separation and subsequent divorce during the child's earliest years was associated with a significantly higher incidence of non-aggressive disturbances in the parent–child relationship in both the boy and girl latency groups."

Madeleine apparently was endowed from birth with sufficient ego capacity and experienced good enough motherhood during early infancy to weather the chaos of her family environment without suffering severe early pathology. Partially because of the absence of a father from age two and a half onward, there was no one to protect Madeleine from forming a symbiotic relationship with a "borderline" mother. Because of the loss of the father, which may have coincided with the discovery that she didn't have a penis, Madeleine developed an intense anger at her mother for depriving her of a father and a penis. The projection of this anger, coupled with the reality that mother was absent daily for long periods of time, heightened Madeleine's separation anxiety. This led to an intensification of the oedipal conflict and a developmental arrest at this stage. Dad and Bob served as remote, mysterious, highly exciting and desirable oedipal objects. Madeleine's projected anger and constant fear of retaliation by object loss were compensated by clinging to her mother and desiring to please and "mother" her. Mother, because of overidentification with Madeleine used poor judgment in allowing Madeleine to be sexually overstimulated. This resulted in the presenting symptom picture. The therapist served as a "developmental facilitator" for the child, helping to master oedipal issues (penis envy and separation anxiety), so that she could pass on to latency. The therapist served as an auxiliary ego to the mother, helping to create conditions in the home environment that would not obstruct Madeleine's developmental progress.

At the end of therapy, Madeleine had strengthened her ego resources to the point where she gained control over her impulses. She was an intelligent, resourceful girl with a better than average ability to effectively articulate her feelings. I believe that potential danger lies in Madeleine's tendency to somatize, and her being struck prematurely with the job of parenting her childlike mother. Madeleine may well grow up to be an extremely competent and successful person with ulcers and migraine headaches.

James *

James, six years old, was referred by his mother who was concerned because he "doesn't provide enough space for others both physically and emotionally"; "He is totally uninhibited about everything"; "You can be walking down the sidewalk and he'll be all over your feet"; "He's constantly into other people's stuff"; "He doesn't do what he's told to do, unless it's a stranger." Mother was despairing of her ability to set and enforce limits with James, and was concerned that if he didn't learn to control himself he would someday wind up in trouble with the law.

The living arrangements of the family were rather complex. Bo and Amy, James' parents, were divorced in February 1978, after a seven-month separation. Amy, James, and James' brother, Kerry, age 13, remained in the house in which Bo grew up and which is owned by Bo's parents. After Bo departed, Amy's brother, Dave, moved in while Amy and James started spending three to four nights a week on the farm of Amy's boyfriend, Terry, who was formally Bo's "best friend." Kerry has preferred to remain at the house with Uncle Dave. If the reader finds this confusing, he or she has a small inkling of how the situation must have been experienced by James.

* Grateful acknowledgment is made to Mort Chethik for his help as supervisor of the case.

Amy is a "tough lady." Her typical dress consists of jeans and a sweatshirt. She has a deep voice and a rugged, masculine appearance. Although a very intelligent, capable, and resourceful woman, she chooses to work at a relatively low paying job as a newspaper distributor with an annual income of about $9,000. Her chief concerns, as far as relating on a personal level, are that people be honest, responsible, and reliable (as she is, indeed, herself).

Amy is herself a child of divorce. Although her parents' divorce did not occur until she was 13 years old, her family never contained a person called "father." For the first three years of her life, Amy's only exposure to her Navy-enlisted father was in the nature of a photograph set on the mantel. She learned to refer to him as "Rickey," as everyone else did. When he returned home from the service she continued to call him Rickey and all her younger brothers and sisters followed suit. When Amy was age 10, her family moved away from the city, but Rickey continued to live in the city with his own mother during the week in order to keep his job as a mailman. When Amy was 13, her parents were divorced. She recalls a painful scene when her father kidnapped her six-month-old little sister (who was subsequently returned) and threw her protesting mother to the ground as she watched frozen to the spot with terror. She recalled trembling with fear in the judge's chambers as the insensitive, imposing man asked each child which parent they wished to live with. She recalled how she felt undesirable, "a fifth wheel," because her father and paternal grandmother made it clear that they preferred her two younger brothers to her.

Amy was the oldest of five children, two boys and three girls. After the divorce, Amy was responsible for taking care of the horde, as her mother had to work. She states that they were a poor family (her mother earned less than a dollar an hour), but that they were not conscious of their state of indigence, because, living in a small town, other people knew them and looked out for them. The grocer would sell them surplus at reduced prices, the rich man who owned the town gave them secondhand furniture and clothes, the landlord, when evicting them for nonpayment of rent (because the father would send no money), sympathetically helped them pack and relocate. Amy worked on a horse farm during the summer and before and after school. She had to take her entourage of siblings everywhere she went, but she didn't let it stop her. She recalled horseback riding with four children tucked on the horse in front of her. She never truly experienced an adolescence, as her teenage years were consumed with school, work, horses, and siblings. However, she did not experience these years as drudgery, but rather developed a sense of ability to survive, make do, and trust in people and even fate to help out in a pinch. The only outrageous thing she felt she had to tolerate was sharing a room with a sister who was not yet toilet trained and who would smear feces over her belongings.

Amy stated that she was attracted to Bo because he was like "clock-work" in his dependability and was a handy person to have around because of his considerable abilities as a mechanic. Their married life was happy until Bo injured his back accidentally at work and handled his depression by drinking and sitting in front of the TV all day. She became disgusted, returning home from work to find her husband drunk and irritable, the house a mess, and Kerry, their son, dirty and unkempt. She began to browbeat and castigate her husband just as she had noticed his mother had done before her, which further weakened his already demolished self-esteem. Bo continued to drink after returning to work. "It was like living with a tornado. He always came home angry. I learned to avoid him. He took his anger out on Kerry. He didn't physically beat him, but emotionally beat him. Kerry learned to run upstairs and hide when he heard his father's car coming."

One day, Bo came home unexpectedly early from work and announced that he was moving out that day. Bo lived for various periods of time in his car and with his mother until finally getting an apartment of his own. Several months after the divorce, Terry, Bo's "best friend," arranged to meet with Amy ostensibly to negotiate a reconciliation. Terry and Amy began to see each other. After several months of dating, Amy and James started spending nights at Terry's family farm where he lived in order to help care for his dying mother.

Developmental History.   Amy did not greet the discovery of her fourth pregnancy (she had had two previous miscarriages) with shouts of joy. She was contemplating leaving her husband, and Kerry, at age five, no longer required constant looking after. Now she felt trapped into another five years of supervising a preschooler in a marriage she did not want. The pregnancy and delivery were without complications. All of James' developmental milestones were normal except for toilet training. Mother made no attempt to toilet train him until age three and a half "because I was lazy." Although mother previously had strong feelings about cleaning up her little sister's feces, she states that she did not mind cleaning up after James. Amy then proceeded to toilet train James in two days using the "how to toilet train your child in one day" technique.

Kerry, who is six years James' senior, has consistently served as a foil for James. At the onset of therapy, James was described as messy, rambunctious, undependable, disrespectful, and aggressive. Kerry was self-reliant, dependable, quiet, concerned, and controlled. Mother stated that, although she made no verbal mention of it to the kids, they could probably detect that she preferred Kerry, who is a "little goody like I was when I was a kid." She added that if she had to choose between keeping Kerry and James, she would keep James because he needed her more than Kerry did. (This is, indeed, the actual living arrangement when mother stays with her boyfriend.) However, approximately two months into the treatment, the contrast began to take on a different slant. Whereas James was seen as assertive (even if overly so) and able to make his needs known, mother became concerned that Kerry was prematurely adultlike, seclusive, quiet, and depressed. She felt that Kerry was responding to the neglect of his father in a manner reminiscent of the way her younger brother responded to her father's departure at the time of her parents' divorce.

She feared that Kerry would end up an awkward, painfully shy, introverted person like her brother. She subsequently accepted the recommendation of treatment for Kerry.

Amy described Bo as always being more interested in Kerry than James. Whereas he would seek out Kerry to help him do mechanical work around the house, James was generally left to observe. Subsequent to the divorce, Bo has had little contact with the children even though his workplace is a couple of blocks from their home. He has frequently disappointed both children by failing to show up for scheduled visitations and forgetting them on birthdays and holidays.

Father, a tall, lanky man with long red hair and resembling Kerry remarkably, was seen briefly. He presented a disheveled appearance and a disorganized manner. He failed to show up for a scheduled appointment with me and finally appeared several months later because of my repeated insistence. Amy accurately described him as a "sad, little puppy dog with his tail between his legs, looking to be kicked around." He claimed ruefully that he had been neglectful in regard to visitations because of depression over financial difficulties and promised to rectify the situation immediately by going straightaway to seek James and Kerry after the session. Months later, father had still not been heard from by the kids. At the time of the initiation of James' therapy, James appeared to have made a cathexis of Terry, mother's boyfriend, to whom he referred as "father." He referred to Bo as "dead."

Course of Treatment: Parent Guidance.   At the onset of treatment, Amy appeared to be a phallic, intrusive, restrictive, and castrating woman who was threatened by the budding masculinity of her oedipal-aged child. During the summer months, mother kept James with her at all times, even on the job distributing newspapers, during which time she expected him to sit quietly in the van for hours. Mother's approach to containing James' behavior was to be "as tough as an Army sargeant and as persistent as a bulldog." Also, James had no one of his age to play with. I saw my first goal in parent guidance to be getting James out of mom's constant surveillance. I did this by convincing mom that James was lonely because he had no playmates and that his aggression was partially secondary to the intimidation of living in a world of giants (adults). Mother, after initial resistance, finally agreed to enroll James in a summer day camp.

With the entry of Kerry into treatment with another therapist, mother expressed concerns over Kerry's propensity to make friends with genuinely obnoxious characters and abandon the friendships that she had actively promoted for him. She also revealed worries over Kerry's inability to protect himself and assert his rights against the bullying neighborhood gang and the paper route customers who evaded paying him. She described the heavy-handed and intrusive ways in which she stepped into these situations on his behalf. Mother was able to make intelligent use of ensuing discussions about the teenager's need for autonomy to get a more objective perspective of her own intrusive, controlling style. This culminated in a session midway through treatment when Amy was discussing a running disagreement she had with Kerry about how to handle one of the family's puppies, Lynn. Kerry was training Lynn to take the place of her mother, Mooch, who used to accompany him on his newspaper deliveries until she became very ill and died a month previously. Amy repeatedly cautioned Kerry to keep the dog leashed to the wagon as she was not yet trained well enough or mature enough to keep herself out of trouble and danger. A couple of weeks later, Amy was driving home from work and spotted Kerry on his route; she noticed that Lynn was not leashed to the wagon, as she had directed. However, she also noticed that Lynn was behaving in an intelligent manner, not running out in front of cars or interfering with people strolling by. She then stated with self-deprecating remorse that she realized that in some ways "Kerry is more mature than I am." "He knows when to let go and I don't. I try to do things for people whether they need it or not. I would have hung onto that dog until it died." In the same session, she recalled times when she had been fiercely and inappropriately angry and wondered where the anger came from. She also commented on an incident in which James was greatly relieved and offered profuse claims of love for his mother when she did not punish him for a mistake he made which was a genuine mistake and not an act of willful disobedience. Mother remarked, "My kids must think I'm a real ogre."

Simultaneously, mother was also working on her own feelings of sadness and fears of abandonment. She had taken James and Kerry to see a Walt Disney movie, *Song of the South.* In the movie, a young boy is deserted by his father, who goes off to the city on business. The boy becomes attached to Uncle Remus, the famous storyteller, who was cathected as a father substitute. When Uncle Remus must leave, the boy is injured by a bull when he blindly chases after Uncle Remus to prevent his departure. The boy, in a coma, is finally revived by Uncle Remus' stories and is joyfully reunited with his father in the end. Mother noted that both James and Kerry were in tears during the movie. She felt she had done the boys incalculable harm by allowing them to see the movie, and swore in remorse that she would never have taken them to see it if she had been aware of the content. I reassured Amy that she had by no means harmed her children; rather, part of the function of therapy was to allow the boys to tolerate the sadness they experienced as a result of their father's abandonment.

This led to a tearful recounting of the miserable feelings and frightening experiences that were associated with her own father's departure at the time of her parents' divorce. She revealed how worthless she felt when her father made it clear that he desired visitation with the boys and youngest girls, but not with her. Despite this, she stated that if her father was down and out and needed help, she would welcome the opportunity to take him in. Subsequently, the illness and death of the family dog, Mooch, gave us an opportunity to deal further with Amy's tendency to avoid and suppress painful affects. Upon first discovering that Mooch had a terminal illness, Amy's immediate urge was to have the dog secretly taken away and put to sleep without James' or Kerry's knowledge. However, she was persuaded to talk with Kerry, and acceded to his request to keep Mooch around the house until she showed signs of being in pain. Mooch soon thereafter died in her sleep. Mother was able to appreciate Kerry's wisdom in wishing for a mourning period to deal with the pain of Mooch's death. By acquiring the ability to recognize her own sad and fearful feelings of abandonment, Amy was able to tolerate them in her own children and help them deal with painful feelings appropriately.

Course of Treatment: Work with the Child. As is usual, one can look back on the first session and detect most of the themes that would dominate the course of therapy. When James entered the treatment room for the first time, he noticed with dismay and panic that "there are no toys here." I explained to James that each child had a locker and that his toys were in his new locker. I demonstrated how the combination lock worked, and he greeted the sight of the toys with great excitement, particularly the yellow truck (trucks being highly valued by all members of his family). He then became fascinated by the Play-Doh. He mixed the different colors together, squished it up, flattened it out, playfully tried to smear it on my face, stuck it in his mouth, pretending to eat it, and remarked how good it smelled. He then decided that we should bake cakes and was careful to divide the Play-Doh into equal portions for the two of us. At times his excitement became so great he would drool all over himself, me, and everything around him. He then decided to make a bird's nest and told me a story about a small bluejay whose mother pecked him all the time. When I asked if his mother had told him why he was coming here, he replied that he had been told he was coming to talk with me. I explained that I was a worry doctor who helped kids with worries. In response, he told me he had a dream the other night that some man attacked his mommy and daddy. It was scary. He could not elaborate further on the dream. When asked who was the daddy in the dream, Terry or Bo, he replied "Terry." When I replied that it seemed like Terry acted like his daddy in real life, whereas his real daddy didn't, he agreed and added that he had an "Uncle David that acted like his real uncle, too." He told me what big muscles his Uncle David had, as big around as the building block container, and he was taller than me, and able to lift up trucks with his bare hands while changing tires. He commented on my size. "Mom said I was coming to see a short doctor," he giggled. James then started giving orders and directives about how I should help pick up in a certain way, because I had made part of the mess.

While we were doing this, he told me a story about how he and his "father" Terry had climbed a steep mountain 1½ miles "tall." A man had been hung upside down on this mountain a few days ago. The man was then thrown down the mountain with cables and had his head split open and died. He then told me how he had been walking on the hill and almost slipped and cracked his skull. I commented on how scary that sounded, and he replied, "No, it was fun. I was alright and we waved to my mother." He then had me set up the soldiers and dinosaurs and had great fun charging the soldiers with the woolly mammoths. He then had the soldiers separated into piles, one pile for each elephant to have for his dinner. The elephants were a family consisting of a boy, a mother, a baby, and a sister. There was no father. Next, the dinosaurs formed a circle with their tails toward the center in order to protect them, because the elephants like to come and eat their tails. One elephant tried to attack the circle, but the dinosaurs flicked their tails and knocked the elephant sky high. He then took the yellow truck and started careening around the room with it, taking pleasure in making near miss sweeps at the dinosaurs. He then had me load the dinosaurs on the back of the truck to take them to a burial spot that was marked by an American flag. Time was up, and James, protesting reluctantly, helped me pick up. He ran ahead out of the room and greeted his mother with a "boo."

Thus, in the first session, we see a fear of being denied what is rightfully his (toys), accompanied by poorly modulated excitement as a result of subsequent gratification. There is a regression to oral and anal sadistic modes (drooling, smearing, eating Play-Doh) in the light of castration anxiety (getting his head cracked open, his tail eaten), and insecurity about the permanence of relationships (who his real father is, his reluctance to leave the session). There is a hint of the relationship between him and his mother (the baby bluejay whose mother pecks at him all day). His controlling style (ordering me around) may have been a manifestation of identification with the aggressor, a way of expressing his reactive hostility over the fear of abandonment, and a way of "holding on" in an attempt to prevent the feared abandonment. Oedipal concerns are evident in his dream about some man (himself?) killing his mommy and daddy. We also see signs of fantasies of phallic prowess (powerful dinosaur tails), and phallic identification (Uncle Dave's muscles and truck). But above all, we see in the preceding vignette a situation in which a therapist could develop a troublesome countertransference reaction toward this drooling, aggressive typhoon in human form.

This therapist was less than saintlike. His first task of the therapy was to learn to recognize and deal with his own anger toward a child who ordered him around and smeared and drooled all over with the explanation, "I act this way because I like you." Interpretations about his anger at me or his overexcitement had little effect. Limit setting statements about how that behavior wasn't allowed and how it interfered with therapy met with temporary restraint but was followed at the end of the session by a slap on my butt or a poke at my penis as he left the room giggling. The therapist's attempts to confront James' obnoxious behavior by addressing him with "Yes, boss" only thinly veiled the therapist's hostility and caused a reactive increase in James' controlling behavior. At times, the therapist's anger clearly broke through; for example, on one occasion during the daily battle to determine who would open the toy locker, the therapist indignantly exclaimed, "It's your therapy, you open the locker!" Finally, some success was achieved in dealing with both the therapist's and the patient's anger when the therapist empathically portrayed the sentiment underlying James' aggressive behavior. When James ordered me around, let me know that something I had built was no good, or when he wanted to smear Play-Doh on me, I would say with a pouting expression, "You know, I feel like pooh; everything I do is pooh; you treat me like pooh." James would feel sorry for me and assure me that I was "better than pooh," and immediately act more considerately. From there, it was easy to make interpretations such as, "You know, when little boys' fathers leave them and ignore them, sometimes they feel like pooh. Sometimes they feel that their fathers left because they were bad, like pooh, and fear that others will leave them or not like them for the same reason." I pointed out that he was trying to make feel the way he felt and was angry at me beceause I couldn't be his father and gratify him. These interpretations appeared to have the effect of subduing the aggressive aspects of James' "messy" and "controlling" behavior, and at times, James even acknowledged their correctness by means of a sad, quiet attention to my remarks, followed by a simple "Yes."

However, aside from the aggressive component, James' behavior also contained an unmodulated libidinal component. James' excitement over smearing was genuine, probably as a result of the sustained body contact with his feces and the pleasurable contact surrounding his diaper training which was prolonged because his late toilet training. Observations about how he was a boy who was excited by messiness and pooh merely served to escalate his behavior, and sage advice about how this behavior was maladaptive outside of therapy merely served to make him feel bad about it. However, some means of dealing with James' sexual excitement had to be found, as James would introduce words like "doo-doo," "ass," "butt," "weenus," "pee-pee," and "fuck" into therapy and become quite carried away with giggly excitement. He had to make frequent trips to the bathroom to discharge his excitement. In order to help bind this excitement as well as the aggression, a "body book" * was introduced into the therapy. I suggested to James that since he was a boy with lots of concern about the body that we make a book about it. Initially he objected, but then he became intrigued. The first entry was "horse's ass" (pictorially represented with a drawing of a horse and an arrow pointing to the rear), as James had spent the previous session pretending that balls of clay were horses' asses, which he could cut up, being careful to wipe the "blood" off his scissors, and then deceptively sell as deer meat to store customers. This led to a discussion about how he, in anger, made "horses' asses" out of people by fooling them and he felt like a "horse's ass" because he was mistreated or abandoned. This led to an angry denunciation of Terry as a "horse's ass" because Terry called him an "ass" when he was angry at James. James then volunteered the next word for the book, which was "weenus." This was accompanied by a drawing by James of an upright penis shooting pee into the air which he labeled "yellow," writing the word himself with great satisfaction. He then decided he wanted to label the next page "butt," with an accompanying

---

* Credit for this idea must go to Mort Chethik, my supervisor on the case.

illustration of vertically situated buttocks with an irregular lump of "dukey" posed on top. On the fourth page, he had me write the word "body," and drew an outline of a body which he later decided was a "skeleton." On the fifth page, he had me write the word "hand," and then traced my hand. He told me he thought of three "good things—horse's ass, body, and hand." I wondered if he thought "weenus" and "butt" were bad, to which he replied, "Yes." I started to write the word "bad" on pages two and three, but he objected, so I wrote the word "bad," and then crossed it out, explaining that a lot of people thought these parts were bad, but they really were just normal parts of the body. He giggled back that they "stunk." I corrected him, saying that they didn't stink, although the things that came out of them might stink. Nevertheless, he insisted that I write "pee-pee u" on the page. Thus, the "body book," for a limited time, served as a structure to discuss and help organize his primitive excitement and aggression. Subsequently, however, when I suggested his returning to the body book when he was showing signs of getting carried away by "dirty words," he would object adamantly, but cease his excited behavior. It seemed that by physically pushing aside the body book, he was able to "push aside" temporarily his "excited body feelings," but apparently the excitement was too strong for him to face the prospect of dealing with them even in this structured way. Later, in the therapy, we were able to discuss sexual issues in an unexcited manner, as long as I did not bring up the term "body book." Outside of therapy, James was reported, by the third to fourth month of treatment, to be behaving appropriately at school and at home. During the remainder of therapy, oedipal themes predominated, giving ample opportunity to deal with James' ambivalent feelings (longing and anger) toward the father figures in his life (Bo, Terry, and the therapist), as well as his tendency to defend against these feelings by regression to the anal mode.

James brought a small, plastic Lassie dog to therapy. Lassie went on all types of oedipal exploits, saving helpless kittens by "biting off the butt" of the mean hunter, and dismembering a dangerous octopus. James built a "bar" for Lassie which was identified as the bar that Terry frequents. Lassie evidently liked this bar, but James stated that he hated Terry's bar because it was "smelly and noisy."

James brought a Rudolph puppet that he made out of construction paper. Rudolph had a doe-friend named Flamingo. James played that he was a ferocious bull guarding the sleeping pair as a malevolent tiger puppet (played by me) snuck up on them. My hand was almost separated from my arm as James ferociously swept down on the tiger puppet. James got so excited playing the part of the bull that the play had to be stopped. James then identified the bull as the bull from *The Song of the South.* Thus, I was able to interpret that James' silly, excited bull feelings were a cover for angry, killing bull feelings that a boy feels toward a father who has left him. Similarly, he was angry at me for not being his father.

At Christmas, James decided to make a Christmas book which contained family-oriented drawings. He drew a fireplace with stockings and a Christmas tree with presents around it. There were presents and stockings for the dogs, cats, James, Kerry, Uncle David, Terry, father, and mother. By father, he meant Bo; Terry was his "friend." When I commented on this change, that he used to call Terry his father; he indignantly replied, "I'm a big boy now, I don't have to call Terry my father." He went on to talk about how he wanted to have Christmas at home, and that he was sure that Bo would be there. I commented on what a sad little boy he would be if Bo didn't show up, and he replied, "Yes, I'll be sad, even if he only gives me rocks." James started mentioning to his mother, outside of therapy, that he wanted Bo to come for Christmas and that he would be sad if he did not come. He bought Bo a tool set and made him a Christmas ornament at school. Bo made arrangements with mother to visit the children at a time when mother would be away. However, Bo failed to show up at the prearranged time, but managed to show up at a time two days later when only Kerry was at home. He left James a check for $5.00, but failed to take James' presents with him. The presents sat under the tree unclaimed for about two weeks before they were finally put away

After the Christmas break, James informed me that he had received a $5,000 dollar check from his dad. However, he admitted that he had not seen his father at Christmas. I commented on how sad this was, and he agreed that, indeed, it was. He told me that Santa Claus had left him only four presents, because he was a bad boy who threw rocks and broke things. I talked about how sometimes boys felt that they were bad when their fathers did not visit them around Christmas time. In response to this, James became silly and started calling me "grouchy, garrulous Mendell." He informed me that my brains had fallen out of my rear end and had poop all over them. I pointed out how he got silly "pooh" feelings when he was hurt and angry. He was sad and angry at his father for not showing up at Christmas, and he was angry at me for talking about these painful feelings and not being more like a father. He met these interpretations with silence.

The next few sessions consisted of James' involvement in competitive and cooperative phallic activity, such as target practice with a ball or building a log cabin. We talked about how these activities were similar to what he did with Terry, and wished he could do with his father. James would show me how to make things like a wooden airplane which he brought in from home. We talked about how it was nice to be the big boy who was doing the teaching for a change rather than the little boy who always had to be shown how to do things. He talked about how his brother Kerry shows him how to do lots of things at home, and I noted how Kerry was becoming more and more like a father, as Terry was becoming less involved with James.

One session, James brought his Snoopy puppet from home. The Snoopy and horse puppets (played by James) fetched logs while the lion and tiger puppets (played by the therapist) used them to construct a house. Soon, it developed that this was a family. Snoopy and the horse were parents, the lion and tiger were children. After the house was completed, the mother and father decided that the house was only big enough for two, and kicked the kids out to sleep in the cold. The children (me) pouted and complained about how mean and unfair the parents were. The parents, in response, beat up the kids and took off to their farm. There, the parents kissed and hugged one another and ignored the kids. They discovered vast amounts of gold on the farm. They kept all the gold for themselves and gave 25 cents to each of the kids. I complained about how mean and stingy the parents were. At this point, the parents suddenly became the best parents in the world. They brought their children gifts and gave them hugs and kisses. Father showed the kids how to make model planes and gave them flying lessons. There were plenty of crashes, but everything got fixed up. Each member of the family got a pile of gold and they all went off to the store to buy each other gifts. Mother got a new dress. James exclaimed, "She looks just beautiful. She usually wears jeans." Father got a new tie. Older brother got a bicycle. The younger brother got a "bunny rabbit to help him sleep at night." A skunk and bear came along and tried to spoil things, but father beat them up. I talked about how kids sometimes feel they have the meanest parents in the world and at other times feel their parents are the nicest, and the best. James replied with a wholehearted "Yes." As the session came to a close, James noted that he did not got "wild and excited this time"; we had discussed previously that usually he gets excited at the end of the sessions because he feels angry and scared as if he is being kicked out. I believe the session reveals the temporary satisfaction obtained by the fantasy of an intact, happy family. Also, it demonstrates James' new appreciation of mother as a feminine object of oedipal desires.

On James' birthday in early March, he pulled out of his pockets an old water pistol and a small McDonald's frisbee. He explained that his father got him these for his birthday, as his father does not have a lot of money to spend on presents. After the session, he told his mother that these were presents from me. (In reality, I had gotten him a birthday card which he largely ignored throughout the session.) It turned out that James' father completely forgot or ignored his birthday. In subsequent sessions, James became more demanding. Over my objections, he took things home from the session. I commented on how he was a boy who felt cheated without a father and who thought he could make up for the loss by getting presents or taking things.

For a later session in March, James brought in three more puppets so that we had two horses, two lions, a tiger, a bear, and a Snoopy for a total of seven. He informed me that this was an "all male family." He then proceeded to play out his fantasy of killing off the mother so that he could be alone with father (the negative oedipal fantasy). The horses were parents, the two lions were "younger brothers," and the rest were "older brothers." The parents then announced that they were going to the store, and brought back model airplanes as birthday presents for the two younger brothers. Everybody took turns hugging one another. When the kids asked for help building the planes, the parents replied that they would provide "pins and stuff," but the kids should build the planes themselves. Then the parents built big, fancy "Z" planes and took turns giving all the kids rides. Afterward, the mother took off in the plane alone; she started acting silly and crashed. She was killed. The father and two younger brothers went out looking for her and found her body. The father (James) suggested they could put her back together, as they previously put back together an airplane that had crashed and broken to pieces. The father instructed that his bridle should be taken off his nose and put on the nose of the mother. This brought the mother back to life, and the bridle was returned to the father. James was quite adamant that the bridle not be left on the mother. (Thus, the males must symbolically relinquish the phallus, or the reins, in order to undo the consequences of their anger toward mother. Fortunately, the loss is not a permanent one.) We then repeated the sequence, this time with the older brothers getting the presents. I talked about how we just had a birthday party for James, but this time the father was there, unlike James' real birthday. He acknowledged his wish that he could have a regular birthday and a regular family with both his mommy and daddy. He then decided he wanted to use the toy phone to call his father, but then changed his mind and called Kerry. He asked Kerry to bring over some metallic red paint, and Kerry immediately agreed and made the delivery. Then he telephoned his daddy and asked him to bring over some bicycle parts and some wheels. James insisted on paying the father $10.00 even though the father offered to bring it over for free. I pointed out how James felt he had to pay his father, but not pay Kerry, and maybe that was because his father did not bring him presents and ignored his birthday, often using a lack of money as an excuse. James sadly agreed. I pointed out how Kerry was acting like his father in many ways, to which James added, "Yeah, he helped me pay for my bicycle which I got for my birthday." At the end of the session, James took my pen from me, stating that he was going to take it with him. I again pointed out how he was angry at me for not being more like a father, and that he wanted presents from me in order to make up for his missing father. He agreed to give the pen back on the condition that I stop talking about his father.

Termination. After one year of therapy, a premature termination was planned, because, unfortunately, the therapist's training program was coming to an end and he was moving to a distant city. Events conspired to make the termination even more traumatic than necessary. Because of the condition of economic depression in the area, it was necessary for Terry and Uncle Dave to make plans to move far away to seek employment. Shortly after this, Amy gave permission to the local Friend of the Court to begin the process of pressuring Bo to pay the huge amount of child support arrearage that he owed. Bo responded by having his parents, who owned the house in which James' family dwelled, serve them an eviction notice. The only ameliorating factor in this catastrophe, and quite a significant factor, was Amy's newfound ability to tolerate painful affects, and thus be a reassuring, sensitive support to her children. Her ability to understand their anger and panic, and her reassurance that they had the wherewithal to take care of themselves and that she would

never abandon them made the situation far less catastrophic than it otherwise
would have been. It was eventually decided that the case would be transferred
to another therapist, after a summer break, to help James integrate the traumatic impact of these events.

With the news of Terry's possible departure, James underwent a marked
regression, both in and out of therapy. At home, James again became more
oppositional and sarcastic. At school, he was isolated at his own desk because
of his distracting and distractable nature. His teachers reported that, although
he was getting his work done (by taking it home to complete it), he appeared
to be preoccupied and to have difficulties concentrating. In therapy, his sessions regained some of their original "wild" flavor. Again, scatological words
fouled the air, as the messy triumverate of giggling, drooling, and smearing
reigned supreme. I was threatened by the prospect of chairs hurtled through
space if I so much as opened my mouth.

I was forced to begin one session with James by giving him a firm lecture
concerning what I would and would not tolerate (angry words falling in the
former category, and violent acts in the latter). Later in that session, James
started playing like he was a puppy dog retrieving a ball for me. I commented
that he felt like a poor little puppy who had been chastised and now he was
bringing me presents in order to assuage my anger. He informed me that he
saw his father on TV today playing golf. I commiserated with him that he
missed his father, and that perhaps he felt his father did not visit him because
he acted badly at times. James suggested we play a doggy game. I was the
father and he was the "little boy dog." He barked for danger to signal that
there was a bear or a shark coming and we would scamper into the doghouse
(under the table) together. James barked the all clear signal, but suddenly the
puppy was dying. I had to give him an oral medicine, but he still felt sick. He
announced that he was pregnant and about to deliver. He positioned himself
prone on the floor with his rear protruding into the air and started grunting as
if about to defecate. I explained to James that a lot of boys think that babies
come out like BM's, but that is not the case. He suggested that they come out
of the stomach, so I proceeded to give James an enlightening sexual anatomy
lesson. After the lesson, James, with a disgusted look on his face, stated that he
did not want to be a girl: "It's much better to be a boy." I explained to James
that sometimes little boys want to give their fathers a present, like the baby
that his mother could give his father. Perhaps he wanted to give me a present
because he felt he had been bad and I was angry and he wanted to make up
for it. (This graphic depiction of a negative oedipal fantasy was not the first
time that James evidenced some sex role confusion. In the Lassie episodes
recounted previously, Lassie eventually beame a "Lassie-Laddie" dog, half
male and half female.)

Two weeks later, when I introduced the subject of termination, James had
already calmed down somewhat. James' immediate reaction was to ask if he
could start therapy again "when it begins again." I told him that decision was
up to him and his mother, and that was something we could talk about, but

that it would have to be with someone else. He speculated that I would have another kid, so I explained that I was moving out of town. He pouted and said, "Awwww." He threw some pens around the room in a playful way, the whole time pouting in a very cute fashion. He turned over a chair and giggled. I commented on how he was again showing me how he acted silly when he was sad and angry. He probably felt bad the way he felt when his father left. He decided to make a fort out of the capsized chairs. We were cats preyed upon by hungry wolves. We had to get in the fort to protect ourselves. James went out on forays against the wolves to defend me, using his fangs to mangle them. Then James took a tool set (the trash can) and fixed up a car so we could drive away. As the driver, he got a bit excited, driving recklessly, and ended up getting shot in the chest. After I had taken the bullet out, he decided that it would be better if I drove. We went to the store and bought some stewed wolves' meat. We took it home and James cooked it. We then ate it. It was delicious. Thus, James displayed his willingness to do anything, even marry me, give me a baby, protect me, and set up house with me in order to keep me as a functional father substitute.

James began to bring magazines about fishing to therapy. He bragged about all the fancy equipment he had and the tremendous fish he had caught in order to impress me with his phallic prowess, proving that he was worthy enough to keep me from leaving. He brought more coloring books and puppets from home to put in his toy locker, as if to deny that we would soon be parting. When I confronted James about this behavior and interpreted his neediness, he told me to "shut up," imprisoned me in a cage to keep me from leaving, and excoriated me with a make-believe whip to punish me for the impending abandonment.

In subsequent sessions, James would try to provoke me by hitting me or would threaten to walk out of sessions if I continued to bring up the painful feelings he had about termination and how it was similar to the previous loss of the relationship with his father. His belligerent actions and threats were interpreted as a "negative identification" (Chethik, unpublished) with his father. If he was threatened with abandonment, he would get kicked out or leave the way his father did.

James again introduced sexual words into therapy and stuffed puppets into one another, explaining that they were "pregnant." When I tried to explore his sexual concerns, he warned me to "shut up." He searched in his locker for the "body book" and tore it to shreds. I pointed out to him that he obviously still felt his "sexy" feelings were bad, and perhaps responsible for his father's abandoning him and my leaving. I explained that the "sexy" feelings were something that all boys and girls had, and that he could not get rid of them by tearing up the "body book"; this would be something with which he would have to deal with his next therapist.

When James' father succeeded in getting his parents to evict his children from their house, James could no longer defend himself from his painful feelings about his father. He had to deal with them. He was able to talk with his mother about how he now "hated" his father. In therapy, he angrily threw blocks into a box exclaiming that he was angry and that he had been hurt.

Shortly after this, he wandered away from Terry's farm in order to walk home to see his brother, quite a distance away. He got lost, scared himself, and was rescued by his mother and Terry. He explained that he thought Kerry was angry at him for an argument they had the other day. In response to this, brother Kerry started spending more time with James in order to reassure him that he was in no danger of being rejected by his brother as well. In therapy, James repetitively played out a fantasy of children wandering through a forest inhabited by a vicious wolf. The parents were ineffective in protecting the children and were eaten themselves. In some versions of the fantasy, the children also fell victim to the wolf, in other versions the children vanquish the wolf and find their way to a new home. Thus, by means of play, James was able to work out his fears concerning the reliability of adults and his ability to take care of himself. This, along with the "wandering off" episode, revealed his fear that he might be left alone to fend for himself. Mother was able to reassure James with concrete, detailed accounts of moving to a new home, and pointed out, in a sensitive fashion, that she had had the same experience as a child.

Although James had come a long way in his ability to tolerate painful affects, he was not able to make it through our final session. The "good-bye feelings" literally gave him a stomachache and a headache. He had to return to his mother to lie in her lap. When I bid him a final good-bye, he was able to lift his arm weakly to shake hands with me.

Formulation.   The case of James is a touching account of the heroic effort of three "children of divorce" (Amy, Kerry, and James), to deal with the pain of parental divorce. Amy dealt with the narcissistic injury of loss of the father and the sense she experienced of being devalued because she was not a boy, by becoming a combination mother and father to her siblings, and later, to her own children. In an effort to regain her lost father, she chose relationships with men (Bo and Terry) who were like her father in that they were alcoholics and would eventually abandon her. Her anger at her hurt was manifest in a castrating and controlling attitude toward males that was evident in her presenting complaints about James. However, mother's ability to utilize parent guidance as a form of "focal psychotherapy" to help her reexperience and tolerate the pain of her own childhood, allowed her to be sensitive and supportive to her own children.

Kerry, James' brother, reacted to the divorce by becoming depressed and isolated. He identified with the father in both positive ways (his interest in mechanics) and negative ways (feelings of worthlessness and incompetence). Loyalty conflicts prevented him from accepting Terry as a partial father substitute as James had.

James, four and a half when his father left, was in the midst of traversing the oedipal stage when he was given a vivid illustration of the vulnerability of men. He reacted by regressing to the excessively libidinally charged anal mode of interacting (his mother had tended to his needs for anal cleanliness until he was three and a half years old). He dealt with his anger and insecurity by trying to control people in a sadistic manner. The therapist served as a "developmental facilitator" who allowed him to renegotiate partially some of the conflicts of the oedipal stage. The therapist also allowed James the opportunity to learn to tolerate the emotional pain associated with grieving the lost relationship with his father. Unfortunately, the process was interrupted prematurely and at a particularly traumatic time so that James will have to continue with another therapist.

SUMMARY

Divorce is a painful process for all children and will have sequelae reflective of the child's stage of development at the time of the divorce, the child's constitutional strengths and previous personality makeup, and the child's environment. I have recounted various themes which commonly occur in the course of play therapy with children of divorced parents. The cases of James and Madeleine dramatically illustrate the "hunger" felt by some children of divorce for an "object" with which to complete interrupted developmental processes. The therapist can best serve such children as a "developmental facilitator" who helps the child renegotiate necessary developmental tasks while simulataneously helping the child tolerate the pain of grieving the lost relationship.

REFERENCES

Bowlby, J. (1960) Grief and mourning in infancy and early childhood. *Psychoanalytic study of the child,* **15.**

Bowlby, J. (1980) *Attachment and loss,* Vol. III. *Loss, sadness, and depression.* New York: Basic Books.

Chethik, M. (unpublished) Play and the players: Some thoughts on the therapeutic process with children. Presented to Michigan Psychoanalytic Society, May 21, 1981.

Chethik, M., Dolin, N., Davies, D., Lohr, R., & Darrow, S. (unpublished) Children and divorce: The negative identification.

Chethik, M., & Kalter, N. (1980) Developmental arrest following divorce: The role of the therapist as developmental facilitator. *Journal of the American Academy of Child Psychiatry,* **19,** 281–288.

Deutsch, H. (1937) Absence of grief. *Psychoanalytic Quarterly,* **6,** 12–22.

Furman, R. (1964) Death and the young child. *Psychoanalytic Study of the Child,* **19,** 321–333.

Gardner, R. (1976) *Psychotherapy with children of divorce.* New York: Jason Aronson.

Kalter, N. (1977) Children of divorce in an outpatient psychiatric population. *American Journal of Orthopsychiatry*, **44** (1).

Kalter, N., & Rembar, J. (1981) The significance of a child's age at the time of parental divorce. *American Journal of Orthopsychiatry.*

Kelly, J., & Wallerstein, J. (1975) The effects of parental divorce: Experience of the preschool child. *Journal of the American Academy of Child Psychiatry*, **14**, 600–616.

Kelly, J., & Wallerstein, J. (1976) The effects of parental divorce: Experiences of the child in early latency. *American Journal of Orthopsychiatry*, **46** (1).

Kelly, J., & Wallerstein, J. (1976) The effects of parental divorce: Experiences of the child in later latency." *American Journal of Orthopsychiatry*, **46** (2).

Kelly, J., & Wallerstein, J. (1977) Divorce counseling: A community service for families in the midst of divorce. *American Journal of Orthopsychiatry*, **47** (1).

Lohr, R., Chethik, M., Press, S., & Solyom, A. (unpublished) Impact of divorce on children: Vicissitudes and therapeutic implications of the reconciliation fantasy.

Lohr, R., Darrow, D., Chethik, M., Davies, D., & Dolin, N. (unpublished) Childhood and divorce: Interferences in future object relationships.

Nagera, H. (1966) Early childhood disturbances, the infantile neurosis, and the adult disturbances: Problems of a developmental psychoanalytic psychology. *The psychoanalytic study of the child,* Monograph **No. 2.** New York: International Universities Press.

Nagera, H. (1970) Children's reactions to the death of important objects: A developmental approach. *Psychoanalytic Study of the Child*, **25**, 360–400.

Neubauer, P.B. (1960) The one-parent child and his oedipal development. *Psychoanalytic study of the Child*, **15**, 286–309.

Tessman, L.H. (1978) *Children of parting parents.* New York: Jason Aronson.

Wolfenstein, M. (1966) How is mourning possible? *Psychoanalytic Study of the Child*, **21**, 93–126.

CHAPTER 19

Treating Oedipal Problems with the Mutual Storytelling Technique

RICHARD A. GARDNER

INTRODUCTION

I have found my Mutual Storytelling Technique to be useful in the treatment of a wide variety of childhood disorders. In this chapter I discuss its value in the treatment of children's oedipal problems. I first discuss the basic technique, then, my own concept of oedipal problems, with regard to my agreement and disagreement with the most commonly held views of classical psychoanalysts. Last, I present a case vignette, including a verbatim interchange with a child (taken from a videotape), to demonstrate the use of this technique in the treatment of oedipal problems.

THE MUTUAL STORYTELLING TECHNIQUE

The Mutual Storytelling Technique is one proposed solution to the question of how the therapist can use a child's self-created stories therapeutically. In this method the child tells a self-created story, then the therapist surmises its psychodynamic meaning and creates a responding story. The therapist's story includes the same characters in a similar setting but introduces healthier adaptations and resolutions of the conflicts that have been exhibited in the child's story. Because the therapist is speaking in the child's own language, there is a greater chance that the message will be "heard" and incorporated into the child's psychic structure. Resistances are thereby circumvented and a therapeutic message is received without the child being burdened by psychoanalytic interpretations which are often alien. Direct, anxiety-provoking confrontations, so reminiscent of the child's experiences with parents and teachers, are avoided.

Although play-therapy material traditionally used for eliciting self-created fantasies can certainly be used with the Mutual Storytelling Technique, I have found the audio and the videotape recorders to be especially useful. Traditional material has an intrinsic problem, in that it consists of reality stimuli that tend to channel and even contaminate the child's fantasies. The tape recorder is less likely to produce such contaminations of the child's fantasies and almost asks to be spoken into. Children generally enjoy listening to their stories when an audiotape recorder is used, and if the examiner has a videotape recorder available, there is the enhanced attraction of the child's viewing him- or herself on TV.

I begin by asking the child if he or she would like to be guest of honor on a make-believe television program on which stories are told. If the child agrees—and few decline the honor—the recorder is turned on and I begin:

Good morning boys and girls, ladies and gentlemen. I'm happy to welcome you once again to Dr. Gardner's "Make-up-a-Story Television Program." On this program we invite children to see how good they are at making up stories. It's against the rules to tell any stories about anything that really happened to you or anyone you know. The story cannot be about anything you've seen on television, heard on the radio, or read in books. Naturally, the more adventure or excitement the story has, the more fun it will be to watch on television afterward. After you finish your story, you tell us the moral or lesson of your story. And everyone knows that every good story has a lesson or moral. Then Dr. Gardner will make up a story and he'll tell the lesson or moral of his story.

And now, I'm very happy to tell you that we have a new boy (girl) who is with us for the first time today. Can you tell us your name, young man (lady)?

I then ask the child a series of brief questions that can be answered by single words or brief phrases, such as age, address, school, grade, and teacher. These "easy" questions diminish the child's anxiety about the more unstructured themes involved in "making up a story." The child is then told: "Now that we've heard a few things about you, we're all interested in hearing the story *you* have for us today. You're on the air!" At this point, most children begin telling a story, usually with the traditional "Once upon a time . . ." beginning. While the child is engaged in telling the story, I jot down notes which not only help in analyzing the child's story but also serve as a basis for my own. When the child has finished telling the story, I ask for its lesson or moral. The lesson or moral can provide me with information regarding which of the various themes in the story will be the most useful to focus on.

Following the presentation of the child's story (or while the child is presenting it), I try to determine the inappropriate or maladaptive themes. I surmise which figure(s) symbolizes the patient or various aspects of his or her personality and which represent significant figures in the child's environment. Sometimes questions to the child will help me gain insight into the meaning of the various symbols. For example, I might ask, "Was the bear in your story a man or a lady?" "Was the fish in your story a child or adult?" and "Why was the cow so mad at the bull?" I then create a story of my own, using the same characters in a similar setting, but introduce what I consider to be healthier modes of adaptation and healthier methods of resolution than those revealed in the child's story. Generally, after completing my story I will ask the child to try to figure out the lesson or moral of my story. This helps me determine whether my message has been understood and has "hit home." If the child is not successful in ascertaining the moral of my story, I then present it. When my story is completed I generally try to engage the child in a discussion of its meaning to the degree that the child is capable of gaining insight and/or referring it to him- or herself. If the child does not have the interest or the capacity for such insights, I do not press for them because I believe that the important therapeutic element is to get across a principle—and that this principle, per se, can contribute significantly to therapeutic change and alteration of behavior. Elsewhere (Gardner 1969, 1970a,b, 1971a, 1972a,b, 1973a, 1974a, b, c, 1975a, b, c, 1979a, b, 1980, 1981) I have described the use of the technique in the treatment of a wide variety of psychiatric disturbances of childhood. In addition, those interested in a more thorough description of the details of utilizing the technique (especially with regard to story analysis) might wish to consult this author's full-length text on the subject (Gardner, 1971b).

OEDIPAL PROBLEMS IN CHILDHOOD

The Etiology of Oedipal Problems

Freud's theory of the Oedipus complex was derived from the analysis of adults Freud considered neurotic, and some of whom we today would consider psychotic. Freud published only one article on the treatment of a child, the case of Little Hans (1909), and even here he was not the therapist. Rather, the boy's father treated him under Freud's supervision. In the three-and-a-half-month course of treatment, Freud saw the boy only once. Freud believed that sexual attraction toward the opposite-sexed parent and jealous rivalry against the same-sexed parent universally appeared in children between the ages of about three to five. The healthy child then gives up (resolves) the sexual quest at five and enters into a six-year period of relative sexual quiescence the latency period. Freud believed further that failure to resolve the Oedipus complex successfully was a central contributing factor in the development of all neuroses. My own experience over the 25 years that I have worked intensively with children is that only a small fraction, less than 5%, exhibit oedipal problems. The remainder have difficulties that are unrelated (or only remotely related) to oedipal difficulties. And when oedipal problems are present, there are usually specific factors in the family constellation that are directly contributing to the development of such. They do not arise naturally, as Freud would have us believe, but are the result of very specific family patterns that are conducive to the development of such symptomatology.

To elaborate, I believe there is a biological sexual instinct that attracts every human being to members of the opposite sex. From birth to puberty this drive is not particularly strong. Although weak and poorly formulated during the prepubertal period, it nevertheless exhibits itself through behavior that I consider manifestations of *oedipal interest.* A normal boy may speak on occasion of wishing to marry his mother and get rid of his father. These comments may even have a mildly sexual component such as "and then Mommy and I will sleep in bed together." I believe that the possessive, more than the genital-sexual, interest predominates here. The child is primarily interested in a little more affection and attention undiluted by the rival.

In a setting where the child is not receiving the affection, nurture, support, interest, guidance, protection, and generalized physical gratifications (such as stroking, warmth, and rocking) necessary for healthy growth and development, he or she may become obsessed with obtaining such satisfactions and develop one or more of a wide variety of symptoms that are attempts to deal with such frustrations. One possible constellation of symptoms are the kinds of sexual urges, preoccupations, and fantasies that Freud referred to as oedipal. The instinctive sexual urges, which are normally mild and relatively dormant, have the *potential* for intensive expression even as early as birth. Getting little gratification from the parents, the child may develop a host of fantasies in which frustrated love is requited and the rival is removed. Such fantasies follow the principle that the more one is deprived, the more one craves and the more jealous one becomes of those who have what one desires. Such manifestations can appropriately be called oedipal problems in the classical sense. The foundation for the development of neurosis is formed not, as Freud would say, through the failure to resolve successfully one's sexual frustrations regarding the parent of the opposite sex but through the failure to come to terms with the more basic deprivations from which the child is suffering.

The Alleviation of Oedipal Problems

Freud used the term *resolution* to refer to the dissolution of oedipal problems between the ages of five and a half and six. I prefer to use the term *alleviation* because I do not believe that oedipal involvements and interests are ever completely resolved. At best Oedipus problems can be alleviated. For Freud, the resolution of the oedipal complex comes about partly via natural developmental processes. He compared oedipal resolution to the loss of the milk teeth and the growth of the permanent teeth. In addition to natural psychobiological processes, Freud believed that the boy's fear that his father would castrate him contributed to the development of the superego and subsequent suppression and repression of sexual fantasies toward the mother (Freud, 1924). Freud believed that the therapist's role in helping children to alleviate oedipal problems was to foster resignation to the fact that the boy cannot gratify his sexual-genital cravings toward his mother. However, he is consoled with the hope that someday he may get a suitable substitute. Basically he is asked to forestall gratification in this area for many years.

My therapeutic approach to oedipal difficulties reflects my concept of the oedipus complex itself: the problems to be alleviated relate to the general problem of emotional deprivation and not specifically to such factors as parental seduction and/or paternal threats of castration (which are prominent in Freud's theory of the development of oedipal problems). Therefore, I consider the improvement in the parent–child relationship crucial to the alleviation of oedipal problems in children. An attempt is made to improve the boy's relationship with his mother so that he will obtain the gratifications that are due in childhood and will be less obsessed with gaining them in neurotic ways. A similar approach is used with girls exhibiting oedipal problems in their relationships with their fathers. In addition, such children are helped to accept the fact that they cannot completely possess either of their parents and that the affection and attention of each of them must be *shared* with other members of the family. This sharing concept is an important one to impart. The child must be helped to appreciate that no one can possess another person completely: The father shares the mother with the children; the mother shares the father with the children; and the child has no choice but to share the mother and father with the siblings. In the context of such sharing, children must be reassured that, although they may not get as much as they might want, they will still get something. In addition, they must be helped to gain gratifications from others during the present time. Whatever deficiencies may exist in the parent–child relationship can be compensated for to some degree by satisfactions in other relationships. It is a well-known therapeutic principle that if one is going to take something away from a patient, one does well to provide substitute gratifications at that time, that is, gratifications which are healthier and more adaptive. My approach does not involve suggesting to the child that he wait. To wait for his possessive gratifications may appear to consume an endless number of years. Rather, he has the potential to gain some of these satisfactions in the present and he is given the hope that as he grows older he will have greater autonomy to acquire the more exclusive type of possessive relationship enjoyed by his father. Space does not permit a more detailed description of other factors involved in the treatment of oedipal problems. The reader who is interested in more detailed discussions of this issue might wish to refer to other publications of mine on the subject (Gardner 1968, 1973b, 1975a, 1976).

THE TREATMENT OF OEDIPAL PROBLEMS: CLINICAL EXAMPLE

The way in which the Mutual Storytelling Technique can be useful in the treatment of oedipal problems is well demonstrated in the case of Frank, a seven-and-a-half-year-old boy, who was referred for psychotherapy because of generalized immature behavior and poor school performance. Both his teacher and his parents described him as being silly to the point where he rarely took things seriously. He was ever trying to avoid responsibility and typically took the path of least resistance. Most often he would deny responsibility for any unacceptable behavior and was always blaming others. Not taking school work seriously and rarely doing homework, his grades were suffering. He played well with younger children but did not get along with children his own age because of his low frustration tolerance, impulsivity, and inability to place himself in other children's situations to the degree appropriate for his age.

Although there was nothing in the presenting symptoms to suggest that Frank was suffering with oedipal problems, many of the stories he told centered on the theme of rivalry with the father figure for possessive control of the mother figure. In addition, castration anticipations and fears, symbolically presented, were common. As mentioned, when I do see oedipal problems, there are generally specific factors in the family situation that are conducive to the development of this typical reaction pattern. Frank's family situation is an excellent example. His father, an obstetrician, was away for significant periods from the time of his birth right up until Frank began treatment. In the early years this was associated with his residency training and in later years with the building of his practice. Frank and his two younger brothers were left alone with his mother. Although she was by no means seductive, the long periods of being alone with his mother provided Frank with opportunities for intimacy (physical and social, but not sexual) that other boys do not usually have. His father exhibited slightly effeminate gestures, but there was no sign of homosexuality. (The significance of this will be discussed subsequently.)

Frank was born with undescended testicles which required frequent examination. Often, it was his father who conducted the examinations and reported his findings to the consulting urologist. In addition, at the age of three, an inguinal hernia was found and this, too, was periodically examined by Frank's father. Frank's appreciation that his father's work as an obstetrician and gynecologist involved extensive manipulation of the genital region of people who lacked external genitalia was conducive, I believe, to Frank's viewing his father as a "castrator." Frank's father did, indeed, operate on women in the genital region and it is easy to see how Frank could have viewed his father as having castration potential.

We, see then, three factors in Frank's family situation that were conducive to the development of oedipal problems:

1. The long absences of Frank's father from the home allowed Frank an unusual degree of intimacy with and possessive gratification from his mother.

2. The father's occupation as an obstetrician and gynecologist—an occupation in which the father literally performed operations on the genitalia of people who already lacked a penis and testes—contributed to the father being viewed as a potential castrator.

3. The frequent examination by his father of Frank's own genitalia also could have induced castration anxieties in that such examination was indeed performed to assess Frank's readiness for surgery in that area.

On the Rorschach test, Frank often saw as female those blots traditionally seen by boys as male. In addition, there was some evidence for identification with the stereotyped passive female. This, I believe, was the result of the long contact alone with his mother, depriving Frank of opportunities for more masculine identification models. In addition, the somewhat definite, albeit slight, effeminate gestures of his father probably played some role in this feminine identification problem. However, the Rorschach and TAT did not reveal a complete absence of masculine identification. Rather, a sex-role confusion was evident. Oedipal themes were also apparent. On one TAT card, Frank related this story:

> Now his father dies. . . . He and his mother went to the funeral and after to the Greek hall to eat something. He got shrimp cocktail and she ate the same. Then they went home and got into bed and thought about their husband and father. His mother had him before she married his father and so he loves his mother more than his father.

This was the story Frank told during the third month of treatment:

PATIENT: Once there was three little peanuts and a nutcracker lived down the block. And every day when they went outside, the nutcracker would try to crack them open. So they said they'd have to move from their mother's house because the nutcracker lived right down the block. So they moved. So they found a house that was sold to them and they had a new house. They had a mansion. But the nutcracker moved right across the street from them.

THERAPIST: Wow.

PATIENT: And every time they went out in the street to play again, the nutcracker would come out and try to crack them open. So one day the nutcracker came to the door and looked in the window and saw them playing cards. So he shut the window real fast. And then right there was a metal monster eater and he just loved nutcrackers. He gobbled the nutcracker up and there was never a nutcracker again. The end.

THERAPIST: What did he do?

PATIENT: He liked metal and especially nutcrackers. He ate the nutcracker whole and there was a happy ending and they never were aware of the nutcracker again. So that's the end of the story. The end. Good-bye.

THERAPIST: Okay. And the lesson of that story?

PATIENT: Ah, think smart and you'll be smart.

THERAPIST: And what was the smart thinking here?

PATIENT: Uh, they put a metal monster eater right underneath the window.

The three peanuts, as the protagonists of the story, symbolize the patient and his two younger brothers. The nutcracker, who lives down the block, represents Frank's father. He is already out of the home and Frank has gratified his oedipal wishes to possess his mother completely. However, the nutcracker, castrator that he is, is obsessed with the notion of cracking the three peanuts. Their attempts to elude him prove unsuccessful as he pursues them to their new home. Interestingly, it is a mansion—implying that Frank has the wherewithal to live with his mother in "high style." The problem of the nutcracker's relentless pursuit is solved by the peanuts' engaging the services of a "metal monster eater" who "just loved nutcrackers." The story ends with his gobbling up the nutcracker and "there was never a nutcracker again. The End." Finally, "there was a happy ending and they never were aware of the nutcracker again." Now all is well with the world. Frank gains complete possession of his mother and his father is not only removed from the house but is completely obliterated assuaging, thereby, Frank's castration fears.

It was with this understanding of Frank's story that I told mine:

THERAPIST: Okay. Now it's time for me to tell my story. Now my story may start like your story, but different things happen very quickly. Once upon a time there were three peanuts. And these peanuts lived in a neighborhood where they lived with their mother.

PATIENT: Yeah.

THERAPIST: They also lived with their father.

PATIENT: Yeah, uh huh.

THERAPIST: (Looking at patient) In my story, the father is a nutcracker! (At this point, the patient looks up toward the therapist, somewhat incredulously.)

THERAPIST: That's my story.

PATIENT: Uh, huh.

THERAPIST: And the three peanuts are very upset because they think that their father wants to crack them. So they said to him one day, "Are you going to try to crack us? Are you going to try to crack us open?" (Patient now rolling his kneesocks down.) And the father said, "No, but at times you boys get me angry and I sometimes feel mad at you. But I don't have any desire to crack you or crumble you up or get rid of you that way." (Patient now rolling his kneesocks up.)

PATIENT: Or throw you out of the window or throw you on the concrete floor or make you smashed. (Patient now laughs nervously.)

THERAPIST: "No, I'm not going to do that."

PATIENT: (In a reassured tone) Uh, huh.

THERAPIST: He said, "However, you boys sometimes get me angry." They said, "Yeah, we know that we sometimes get you angry." And (turning toward the patient) do you know when the boys would sometimes get the father angry?

PATIENT: When?

THERAPIST: What kinds of things do you think they did that would get the father angry?

PATIENT: (Now bends over, puts his elbows on his knees, and supports his chin in his cupped hands): Let's see now. They would do things that the father didn't tell them to do? (Patient now resumes his original position of facing the examiner.)

THERAPIST: Like what?

PATIENT: Like, when he wanted them to clean his car and they wouldn't do it.

THERAPIST: Yeah, that would be the kind of thing that would get him angry. One of the things that would get him angry was when they would want the mother all to themselves, and they wouldn't want him to spend any time with the mother. You know, that would get him angry sometimes, when they would say, "We don't want you around. We don't want you to be with Mommy all the time. We don't want you to be with her. Things like that." He said, "That's the kind of thing that gets me angry." (Patient now tying his shoelaces.) And they said, "Well, that's the kind of thing that makes us think you want to get rid of us. That you want to kill us. That you want to get rid of us. That you want to crack us up and get rid of us, and then have Mommy all to yourself." You see the father and the three boys were kind of rivals. (Therapist now turns to patient.) Do you know what *rival* means?

PATIENT: Uh, huh.

THERAPIST: What does rival mean?

PATIENT: I don't know.

THERAPIST: They were kind of fighting for the mother to have time with her. Each wanted the mother all to themselves. The father wanted the mother a lot of times and the boys wanted her. The boys wanted to have her to take care of them, to teach them things, and to read books with them, and things. (Patient now stops tying his shoelaces and interlocks the fingers of one hand with the other.) And the father said, "I get angry at you when you want her all to yourself." And they said, "And we get angry at you, because we don't want you around. We want her all to ourselves." They were kind of fighting for her. So what do you think happened?

PATIENT: (Now resting hands in his lap) I think the father got so mad that he cracked them open.

THERAPIST: (Shaking his head negatively) No way! No. What they decided to do was . . . they realized that the father shouldn't have the mother all to himself, because the boys were still part of the family. And that the boys shouldn't have the mother all to themselves because the father was still part of the family. So they decided to compromise. And they decided that they will *share* the mother. That sometimes the boys will have time with the mother (patient now takes his hand out of his lap and slaps his thighs) and sometimes with the father. (Patient now puts his hands on his thighs.) Now this still made the boys feel a little bit sad, because they didn't have their mother all they wanted to. (Patient now whistling and flapping the palms of his hands on his thighs.) So what did they do then?

PATIENT: They had a whole day with the mother and didn't let the father have
. . . no . . . they had a whole week with the father (patient now moving his
hands toward his groin area). No (patient now rubbing his penis), and
had a whole week with the mother (still rubbing his penis) and then the
father had a whole week with the mother.

THERAPIST: That was one way. Sharing. That's one thing they can do. (Patient
still rubbing himself.) And another thing that made the boys feel better
was to spend time with their friends. When they weren't with their . . .

PATIENT: . . . mother . . .

THERAPIST: mother, they could spend time with their friends. And also, another thing (patient still rubbing his penis), was they knew that when they
grew up they would have (patient now grasps his penis with his left hand
and pulls up his shirt with his right hand) a lady. Each one would get
married. Or live with somebody, or have a girlfriend. Something like that.
(Patient now pulls his pants forward, at the belt level, with his left hand
and puts his right hand inside and starts stroking his penis.) And then
they would not feel so jealous of the father, you know. (Patient now pulls
his right hand out of his pants and strokes his penis from the outside).
Because they would have . . .

PATIENT: (Slapping his both hands now on his thighs with an air of certainty)
. . . a lady of their own.

THERAPIST: . . . a lady of their own. (Both the patient and the therapist's
statement, "a lady of their own" was said simultaneously. It was clear that
the patient knew exactly what words the therapist was going to say and so
they both made exact statement simultaneously.) Right!

PATIENT: (Laughing with a sigh or relief) Uh, huh. (Patient again moves both
hands toward the groin and rub the penis area.)

THERAPIST: And that's exactly what happened. (Patient still rubbing penis.)
And what do you think the lessons of that story are?

PATIENT: Uh (patient still holding penis and laughing nervously).

THERAPIST: What are the lessons?

PATIENT: Let me see. (Patient now removes hands from groin and puts them
on top of his head.) Share.

THERAPIST: Share.

PATIENT: Share with other people.

THERAPIST: Right. And is there any other lesson?

PATIENT: (Hands now clasped behind his head) . . . and you'll get along
together.

THERAPIST: Share, and you'll get along together. Any other lesson?

PATIENT: (Hands on top of head, nodding negatively) No.

THERAPIST: There's another lesson. What you can't have in one place, you can
have in another. Like they couldn't have the mother all the time, but they

could have friends: boys and girls that they played with in the street or in the home . . .

PATIENT: (Interrupting) Did they have a busy street?

THERAPIST: Yeah. There were a lot of kids around.

PATIENT: Were there a lot of cars? (The patient then removes his hands from his head and imitates moving cars with buzzing sounds.)

THERAPIST: Yeah. But they had quiet streets too in that area. If there weren't friends in their neighborhood, they would go elsewhere. And also, if you can't have something now there's always the hope that you can get it in the future. You know?

PATIENT: Yeah. (Patient now playing with his wristwatch.)

THERAPIST: And then they could have a girl all their own. Anything you want to say?

PATIENT: No.

THERAPIST: Do you like this game?

PATIENT: (While clasping his hands) Yeah.

THERAPIST: Do you want to watch this?

PATIENT: (With an excited expression on his face, while still clapping his hands) Yeah!

THERAPIST: Okay. Let's watch this. Do you want to have your mother come in and see it?

PATIENT: (Still excited) Yeah.

THERAPIST: Let's do that. (Both arise.)

In creating responding stories, the therapist often has a conflict. If the therapist retains the original symbol used by the child, pathological elements may have to be retained. On the other hand, to dispense with such symbols entirely may rob the therapist of rich symbolism that significantly enhances the impact of the therapeutic communications. I generally will retain the symbol and make sure, in the course of my responding story, to emphasize the healthy element associated with it and to deemphasize, ignore, or directly negate the unhealthy aspects of the symbol. In my responding story here I purposely retained the nutcracker symbol because I considered the advantages to far outweigh the disadvantages. However, after informing the patient that the father was a nutcracker, I quickly emphasized the point that he has the *potential* for castration but that he does not use his power. Rather, I focused on behavior manifested by the peanuts that might cause the father to be angry and studiously avoided any possibility that the anger could reach such proportions that castration, symbolic or otherwise, could possibly occur.

In addition, at the beginning of my story, I make it quite clear that the father lives with the peanuts. This is in contradistinction to the father in Frank's story who has already been ejected from the household. In my story the problem with the father is worked out through discussion rather than acting out. In Frank's story the father is already removed and the father is a castrator. In mine, the father is present, is not a castrator, and engages in meaningful communication to discuss problems with his peanut sons.

The main point that I make in my responding story is that it is not a question of *either* the father or the peanuts having full possession of the mother. Rather, they can *share*. Sometimes the peanuts spend time with the mother, sometimes the father spends time with the mother, and sometimes all of them spend time with her. And, when the father is with the mother, the peanuts can still spend time with others in their neighborhood to compensate for their loss. In addition, they are provided with the hope that when they get older they will have more opportunity for greater possession of an appropriate female peanut.

According to Freud, the Oedipus complex naturally passes like the milk teeth that give way to the permanent teeth. In addition, fears of the father castrating the child contribute to the development of the superego which suppresses and repressess the boy's possessive, sexual longings for the mother. Lastly, the boy is consoled with the fact that someday he will have a female of his own. Most therapists agree that it is very difficult to take something away from patients without offering something in return. In Freud's formulation, the boy is consoled with the knowledge that someday he will have a female of his own. For the child of five, this future is like a million years away and is not likely to serve well as a meaningful consolation.

In the kind of oedipal resolution I propose, the boy is not asked to give up entirely his *present* desires for possessive involvement with his mother. Rather, he is advised to share her with his father. It is certainly easier to share a prized possession than to give it up entirely. In addition, the boy is given the consolation that there are opportunities with others at the present time. Lastly, he is also told about future possibilities.

In the course of telling my responding story, the patient continuously rubbed his genital area and pulled his pants tightly against his penis. It became apparent that he had an erection and that the prospect of possessive opportunities with a female were sexually titillating. Frank's response was clear evidence that my story was indeed dealing with issues that were most important for him and that my message was a most meaningful one. The vignette is an excellent demonstration of a situation in which the therapist knows that his responding story is indeed being received with interest and receptivity and that it is touching on important psychological issues.

CONCLUDING COMMENTS

Although oedipal problems, in the classical sense, are not in my opinion frequently seen in childhood, there are some children who undeniably exhibit such symptomotology. The danger for the therapist is that he or she will interpret the presence of oedipal problems in occasional children to prove a generalized theory about the existence of such problems in all children and thereby presume an oedipal role in the development of all neurotic symp-tomotology. We do well to place oedipal problems in proper perspective, as one of many symtomatic manifestations that can result from parental depriva-tion and other types of parent–child difficulty. The therapeutic alleviation of such problems, then, should focus on the alleviation of the intrafamiliar prob-lems that are contributing to the development of the oedipal symptoms. The approach to the child, as part of a therapeutic approach that involves the parents as well in varying capacities, should be multifaceted. As shown in this chapter, the Mutual Storytelling Technique can be useful as one part of such a therapeutic program.

REFERENCES

Freud, S. (1909) A phobia in a five-year-old boy. In *Collected Papers*, Vol. 3. New York: Basic Books, 1959. Pp. 149–289.

Freud, S. (1924) The passing of the Oedipus complex. In *Collected Papers*, Vol. 2. New York: Basic Books, 1959. Pp. 269–276.

Gardner, R. A. (1968) The Mutual Storytelling Technique: Use in alleviating child-hood oedipal problems. *Contemporary Psychoanalysis*, **4**, 161–177.

Gardner, R. A. (1969) Mutual storytelling as a technique in child psychotherapy and psychoanalysis. In J. Masserman (Ed.), *Science and psychoanalysis*, Vol. XIV. New York: Grune and Stratton. Pp. 123–135.

Gardner, R. A. (1970a) Die Technik des wechselseitigen Geschichtenerzählens bei der behandlung eines Kindes mit psychogenem Husten. In C. J. Hogrefe (Ed.), *Fort-schritte der Psychoanalyse, Internationales Jahrbuch zur Weiterentwicklung der Psychoanalyse*, Vol. 4. Göttingen: Verlag für Psychologie. Pp. 159–173.

Gardner, R. A, (1970b) The mutual storytelling technique: Use in the treatment of a child with post-traumatic neurosis. *American Journal of Psychotherapy*, **24**, 419–439.

Gardner, R. A. (1971a) Mutual storytelling: A technique in child psychotherapy. *Acta Paedopsychiatrica*, **38**, 253–262.

Gardner, R. A. (1971b) *Therapeutic communication with children: The mutual storytell-ing technique*. New York: Jason Aronson.

Gardner, R. A. (1972a) "Once upon a time there was a doorknob and everybody used to make him all dirty with their fingerprints . . ." *Psychology Today*, **5**, (10), 67–92.

Gardner, R. A. (1972b) The mutual storytelling technique in the treatment of anger inhibition problems. *International Journal of Child Psychotherapy*, 1 (1), 34–64.

Gardner, R.A. (1973a) *The Mutual Storytelling Technique* (12 one-hour cassette tapes). Cresskill, N.J.: Creative Therapeutics.

Gardner, R. A. (1973b) *Understanding children—A parent's guide to child rearing*. Cresskill, N.J.: Creative Therapeutics.

Gardner, R. A. (1974a) Dramatized storytelling in child psychotherapy. *Acta Paedo-psychiatrica*, **41** (3), 110–116.

Gardner, R. A. (1974b) La technique de la narration mutuelle d'historettes. *Médecine et Hygiène* (Geneva), **32**, 1180–1181.

Gardner, R. A. (1977c) The Mutual Storytelling Technique in the treatment of psychogenic problems secondary to minimal brain dysfunction. *Journal of Learning Disabilities,* **7**, 135–143.

Gardner, R. A. (1975a) *Psychotherapeutic approaches to the resistant child.* New York: Jason Aronson.

Gardner, R. A. (1975b) Psychotherapy in minimal brain dysfunction. In J. Masserman (Ed.), *Current psychiatric therapies,* Vol. XV. New York: Grune and Stratton. Pp. 25–38.

Gardner, R. A. (1975c) Techniques for involving the child with MBD in meaningful psychotherapy. *Journal of Learning Disabilities,* **8** (5), 16–26.

Gardner, R. A. (1976) *Psychotherapy with children of divorce.* New York: Jason Aronson.

Gardner, R. A. (1979a) Helping children cooperate in therapy. In J. Noshpitz (Ed.), *Basic handbook of child psychiatry,* Vol. III. New York: Basic Books. Pp. 414–433.

Gardner, R. A. (1979b) Psychogenic difficulties secondary to MBD. In J. Noshpitz (Ed.), *Basic handbook of child psychiatry,* Vol. III. New York: Basic Books. Pp. 614–628.

Gardner, R. A. (1980) The Mutual Storytelling Technique. In R. Herink (Ed.), *The psychotherapy handbook.* New York: New American Library. Pp. 408–411.

Gardner, R. A. (1981) The Mutual Storytelling Technique and dramatization of the therapeutic communication. In G. Schattner & R. Courtney (Eds.), *Drama in therapy.* New York: Drama Book Specialists.

CHAPTER 20

Play Therapy with Cross-Gender Identified Children

GEORGE A. REKERS

INTRODUCTION

Cross-gender identification is a relatively rare psychological disorder which typically is detected first in observations of the child's play between the ages of two and eight years of age (Rosen, Rekers, & Friar, 1977). This compulsive, excessive, and persistent pattern of cross-gender play is distinguished from the occasional exploration and adaptive flexibility of sex-typed play of normal boys and girls (Rekers, Rosen, Lovaas, & Bentler, 1978; Rekers, Sanders, Strauss, Rasbury & Mead, in press). Boys outnumbered girls as much as 20 to 1 in the rate of referral to child clinicians for therapy for cross-gender identification (Rekers, 1981b), paralleling the finding that adulthood gender dysphoria and sexual deviations appear more frequently in males than females (Green & Money, 1969; Money & Ehrhardt, 1972; Stoller, 1968b). The psychodiagnosis and treatment of these childhood gender disorders in boys and girls is critical because they place the child at high risk for the adulthood psychological problems of transsexualism, transvestism, and some forms of homosexuality (Green, 1974; Rekers, 1977b; 1978b; 1982a,b; Rekers, Bentler, Rosen, & Lovaas, 1977; Rekers & Mead, 1980; Rekers, Rosen, Lovaas, & Bentler, 1978; Rosen, Rekers, & Bentler, 1978; Zuger, 1978).

Gender Identity Disorders in Boys

The play of cross-gender identified boys is a chronic pattern including high frequencies of the following kinds of feminine sex-typed features: (1) play with baby dolls, female dolls, and accessories; (2) play with actual or toy cosmetic sets, including lipstick, eyeliner, and manicure items; (3) play with feminine jewelry, including bracelets, necklaces, rings, and earrings; and (4) actual or improvised cross-dressing into female attire, including the wearing of dresses, wigs, women's high-heeled shoes, and female undergarments such as bras and underpanties (Bates & Bentler, 1973; Bates, Bentler, & Thompson, 1973; Green, Fuller, Rutley, & Hendler, 1972; Rekers, 1972; 1975; Rekers & Yates, 1976; Zuger, 1966). The role playing of these boys also often involves feminine behavioral characteristics such as the use of an artificially high-pitched vocal inflection, predominantly feminine speech content as compared to masculine content, and various effeminate gestures, mannerisms, and gait (Bentler, Rekers, & Rosen, 1979; Rekers, Lovaas, & Low, 1974; Rekers, Willis, Yates, Rosen, & Low, 1977), as compared to normal boys (Rekers, Amaro-Plotkin, & Low, 1977; Rekers & Rudy, 1978; Rekers, Sanders, & Strauss, 1981). The presence of these strongly feminine stereotypic play characteristics is accompanied by a general avoidance of masculine sex-typed play, avoidance of same-aged boy peers for playmates, and habitual choice of a female role in fantasy play (Bates & Bentler, 1973; Bates, Skilbeck, Smith, & Bentler, 1974; Bentler et al., 1979; Rekers, 1977a; Rekers & Milner, 1978; 1979; Rosen et al., 1977).

Cross-gender identification in boys is a severe disorder in which the boy manifests any combination of two or more of these feminine play patterns and also evidences a wish to be or fantasy that one is a female (Green, 1974; Greenson, 1968; Rekers, 1972; Stoller, 1968a,b). This feminine identification is typically evidenced by a chronic, stated desire or preference to be a girl or a mother and to bear children and breast-feed infants and/or to have his penis removed. These boys are typically normal physically (Rekers, Crandall, Rosen, & Bentler, 1979).

Gender Identity Disorders in Girls

Although relatively less research has been published on cross-gender identification in girls, this disorder can be clinically differentiated from a normal "tomboy" phase in childhood (see an extended review of the literature and a discussion of the clinical issues by Rekers & Mead, 1980). The deviant play pattern includes a chronic rejection of stereotypic feminine toys, female cosmetic items, jewelry, and dresses, coupled with a preoccupation with masculine sex-typed toys and clothing. For example, one cross-gender identified girl habitually drew a mustache and beard on her face, play-acted shaving of the face, avoided play with girls, and adopted male roles in fantasy play (Rekers & Mead, 1979a). Accompanying these boyish play features is often a masculine appearance in gestures, mannerisms, and walk, as well as a deliberate projection of the voice into lower, gruffer sounds (Rekers & Mead, 1979a, 1980). Exaggeratedly "masculine" aggressiveness is similarly observed in some cases.

This rigid adherence to a masculine stereotype in play in the case of cross-gender identification, is accompanied by the girl's expressed desire to be a boy. This is evidenced, occasionally, by the girl's insistence upon being called by a boy's name or nickname.

A Social Learning Theoretical Framework for Therapy

Although biological abnormalties may be potential contributing etiological factors in some rare cases (e.g., Evans, 1972; Hutt, 1978; Money & Ehrhardt, 1972; Zuger, 1970), social learning variables have been considered to be the primary source for deviance in sex-role development (Litin, Griffin, & Johnson, 1956; Lukianowicz, 1959; Mead & Rekers, 1979; Meyer-Bahlberg, 1977; Money, Hampson, & Hampson, 1955; Pauly, 1969; Rekers, Mead, Rosen, & Brigham, in press; Rosen & Rekers, 1980; Stoller, 1969). The etiology of cross-gender identification disorders is not completely understood (Bentler, 1976; Money, 1970a, b; Rosen, 1969; Zuger, 1970a,b). However, the prospective longitudinal data available (Bakwin, 1968; Green, 1974; Lebovitz, 1972; Zuger, 1966, 1970a, 1978; Zuger & Taylor, 1969) indicates that boyhood effeminate play behavior is fairly predictive of male homosexuality and related sexual identity problems. Feminine play is also retrospectively reported to be a prominant feature in the childhood histories of adult male homosexuals (Bieber et al., 1962; Evans, 1969; Holemon & Winokur, 1965; Whitam, 1977), adult male transsexuals (Benjamin, 1966; Bentler, 1976; Green, 1974; Green & Money, 1969; Money & Primrose, 1968; Walinder, 1967; Zuger, 1966), and adult transvestites (Prince & Brentler, 1972). Therefore, considering all the literature, the best prognosis would indicate that the gender identity disturbed boy is at high risk for transsexualism, transvestism, or homosexuality (Rekers, Bentler, Rosen, & Lovaas, 1977).

Theoretically, then, early identification and early intervention for childhood gender identity problems could constitute a preventative treatment for the adult conditions of transvestism, transsexualism, and some forms of homosexuality (Rekers, 1977b; Rekers, Bentler, Rosen, & Lovaas, 1977; Rekers, Rosen, Lovaas, & Bentler, 1978; Rosen, Rekers, & Bentler, 1978). Several uncontrolled case studies have reported environmentally induced changes in childhood gender role play behavior (Bates, Skilbeck, Smith, & Bentler, 1975; Bentler, 1968; Dupont, 1968; Green, 1974; Green & Fuller, 1973; Green, Newman, & Stoller, 1972; Myrick, 1970; Stoller, 1970-1971), and the intrasubject replication studies by Rekers and colleagues demonstrate that sex-typed play behavior in gender-disturbed children is, in part, a function of stimulus control and reinforcement control (Rekers, 1972, 1975, 1979; Rekers & Lovaas, 1974; Rekers, Lovaas, & Low, 1974; Rekers, & Varni, 1977a, b, Rekers, Willis, Yates, Rosen, & Low, 1977; Rekers, Yates, Willis, Rosen, & Taubman, 1976). Therefore, a social learning approach to play therapy with gender-disturbed children is the most promising intervention indicated by the currently available literature.

METHOD

The sex-typed masculine and feminine play behaviors in gender-disturbed children are characterized by stimulus specificity and response specificity. Rekers (1972, 1975) investigated various potential discriminative stimuli for masculine and feminine sex-typed play in boys with cross-gender identification. An ABA reversal design was used to demonstrate that the presence of the child, mother or father, or a female or male stranger produced reliable intra-subject changes in sex-typed play.

Two different toy tables were placed in a playroom. For example, the "dress-up" table had both masculine and feminine clothing and grooming toys on it. The feminine toys consisted of a wig, a pair of small high-heeled shoes, a long-sleeved dress (child's size), a play cosmetic set of lipstick and manicure items, and a set of feminine bracelets, necklaces, rings, and earrings. The masculine toys were a plastic football helmet, a sea captain's hat, an army helmet, an army fatigue shirt, an army belt with hatchet holder and canteen holder, and a play electric razor. These two sets of toys had been sex-typed by a number of child development studies (Brown, 1956; Lefkowitz, 1962; Rabban, 1950; Sutton-Smith, et al., 1963)

The "affect" table also had masculine and feminine sex-typed toys (Brown, 1956; Hartley & Hardesty, 1964; Rabban, 1950; Rosenberg & Sutton-Smith, 1959, 1964; Sutton-Smith et al., 1963; Walker, 1964) and provided the opportunity for sex-typed affect expression—either maternal nurturance with toys such as baby dolls or masculine assertive play such as hunting activity.

Rekers (1975) found that all the gender-disturbed boys played predominantly feminine while alone in the playroom. For each child, at least one observer-present condition was found in which the boy played predominantly masculine, although no single environmental condition was consistently discriminative for masculine play across children. For example, one boy played exclusively feminine each time his mother observed him, but played predominantly masculine each time his father observed him. But another boy played predominantly feminine in all conditions except when a male stranger observed him play with the "affect" table toys. Therefore, sex-typed play was a function of an interaction of the social situation and the type of play response related to the two sets of toys.

Individual Play Assessment

The clinician should be aware that the boy's sex-typed behavior is potentially different in the presence of his father, his mother, a male therapist, or a female therapist. This can be assessed systematically in the individual case (e.g., Rekers & Lovaas, 1974) to design the appropriate method of play therapy for the individual child client. If, for example, the gender-disturbed boy plays predominantly feminine in the presence of the mother or a female clinician but not in the presence of a male clinician, it would be appropriate to shape appropriate sex-typed play in sessions with a female therapist and/or with the mother, but not with a male therapist (see Rekers, 1977a). Multiple assessment methods should be used for the initial diagnosis of childhood cross-gender identification (Rekers, 1981a; Rosen, Rekers, & Friar, 1977) to assist in formulating a therapeutic strategy for the individual child. This complete testing should include systematic behavioral observations of sex-typed behavioral mannerisms and gestures during play (Rekers, Amaro-Plotkin, & Low, 1977; Rekers & Mead, 1979b; Rekers & Rudy, 1978).

Individualized Play Therapy Method

Because of the stimulus specificity and response specificity of sex-typed play behaviors in gender-disturbed children and because therapy effects have tended to be situation specific and response specific, play therapy procedures need to be designed in ways to provide generalization and maintenance of the therapeutic effects (Rekers, 1977a). Whereas some of the more complex techniques of discrimination training and behavior shaping for sex-typed gestures and mannerisms require the skills of professional therapists, some objectives of social-learning-based play therapy can best be accomplished by training the child's parent to be his or her play therapist. Theoretically, the properly trained parent can extend the therapeutic intervention to the *in vivo* environment of the home, thereby promoting greater treatment generalization.

Play Therapy Sessions

To increase appropriate sex-typed behavior in the cross-gender identified child, the therapist can train the parents in social reinforcement techniques (Rekers, 1982b). To do this, the therapist can demonstrate the play therapy technique while the parents watch from behind a one-way mirror or while the parents watch in the room. Verbal instructions can be given to the parent on how to reinforce appropriate sex-typed play by attending to it and giving verbal reinforcement and how to decrease inappropriate and compulsive cross–sex-typed play by ignoring it (putting it on "extinction" in social learning terminology). The therapist should closely observe and supervise the parents' acquisition of behavior-shaping skills in the play setting by asking the parent to join in the play session in the clinic.

Intervention for Play Pattern. A series of intrasubject replication studies have been conducted whereby a parent guardian, or other adult is trained to apply social reinforcement procedures in clinic play sessions with gender-disturbed children (Rekers, 1977a). Rekers and his colleagues developed a set of therapeutic procedures in which the therapist or parent was present with the child in a playroom supplied with the sex-typed toys described by Rabban (1950) which were placed on a small table. The parent is given a "bug-in-the-ear" device which allows the therapist to communicate directly to the parent without the child's overhearing the conversation. The therapist observes from behind a one-way mirror. The parent is given a large magazine to hold and then given specific instructions to attend to the child's appropriate sex-typed verbal and play behavior by smiling and complimenting the child's play, and to ignore sex-inappropriate behavior by picking up the magazine to read. With the "bug-in-the-ear" device, the therapist verbally reinforces the parent for correct responses and gradually fades out prompting instructions. ABA reversal, intrasubject replication designs have demonstrated that these procedures are successful in decreasing compulsive feminine play and verbal behavior and in increasing appropriate masculine play in boys (Rekers & Lovaas, 1974; Rekers, Yates, Willis, Rosen, & Taubman, 1976; Rekers, 1972, 1979).

The intrasubject studies by Rekers found that the play therapy treatment effects using these procedures tended to be specific to the particular stimulus environment in which they were introduced. Generalization of these treatment effects occurred in environments most similar to the treatment environment. For this reason, Rekers et al. (1976) introduced a variation on this technique in which a series of similar treatment procedures were introduced in different environments. For example, a variety of different therapy rooms were used as well as a variety of therapists including both the child's mother and father. This revision in the treatment procedures reduced the stimulus specificity of the treatment effects. In addition, the child was asked to play alone with the therapy toys in the clinic room while his parents waited just outside the playroom wearing the "bug-in-the-ear" device. The therapist observed the child's solitary play from behind the one-way mirror and when the child initiated compulsive feminine play, his parent was immediately instructed to enter the playroom and to repeat a verbal prompt requesting that the son not play with the feminine toys.

Rekers and Varni (1977a,b) developed another modification of this procedure whereby the young child was taught to monitor his own role play using a wrist counter (the type commonly used to keep golf scores). The child was instructed on how to use the wrist counter and told that although he could play with any toy while alone in the playroom, that he could press the counter only when playing with "boys' toys." The therapist verbally labeled each toy in the room as being either a "boys' toy" or a "girls' toy." The child was allowed to use the "bug-in-the-ear" device for some of the sessions to allow the therapist to prompt him from the observation room. For example, the therapist would say, "OK, Brian, you played just with the boys' toys for the last few minutes, you can press the wrist counter now." This behavioral cueing procedure was gradually faded out to maximize the probable therapeutic outcome. The therapist also evaluated a self-reinforcement contingency for selected sessions. The child was told that after the play session he could give himself cookies in exchange for points he had accumulated on his wrist counter.

With this self-control procedure in the play therapy session, it is possible to train the parent to conduct similar sessions in the home environment, allowing the boy to take the wrist counter with him in his normal living surroundings.

Rekers and Mead (1979a) used an intrasubject replication design to demonstrate the effectiveness of this kind of self-monitoring procedure and behavioral prompting technique in the case of an eight-year-old girl with a cross-gender identification. Self-monitoring during play therapy sessions in the clinic resulted in a high, stable rate of appropriate sex-typed play, and this effect was demonstrated to generalize to a different set of sex-typed toys over time.

Intervention for Sex-Typed Speech. For some cross-gender identified boys, one of the most socially salient aspects of their disturbance is their use of a high, "feminine" vocal inflection which occurs with predominantly "feminine" speech content in their verbalization. Rekers, Lovaas, and Low (1974) experimentally evaluated a behavioral play therapy procedure in which appropriate sex-typed voice inflection and speech content were socially reinforced. The therapist and child had access to a chalkboard in the clinic playroom. The boy would regularly tell elaborate fantasized stories with extensive feminine content while he drew pictures on the chalk board. Using an ABA reversal design, the therapist differentially reinforced appropriate sex-typed speech. If the boy asked questions regarding masculine or neutral topics, the therapist gave short, nonleading, direct answers that expressed positive interest. When the boy talked about feminine topics, the therapist withdrew all social attention. And if the boy asked why the therapist was not attending to him, the therapist would make a statement expressing disinterest: "I'm not interested in that." Feminine speech content decreased, masculine speech content increased, and a generalized suppression effect was obtained whereby the feminine speech inflection also decreased. These effects were demonstrated by tape-recording the play therapy sessions and having independent observers behaviorally code all statements by the boys in the categories of "feminine vocal inflection," "feminine speech content," "masculine speech content," and "neutral speech."

Intervention for Cross-Gender Mannerisms. Sex differences have been found in normal children at various ages in the occurrence of certain body gestures and arm movement mannerisms (Rekers, Amaro-Plotkin, & Low, 1977; Rekers, & Rudy, 1978; Rekers, Sanders, & Strauss, 1981). Cross-gender identified children often display the sex-typed body gestures and mannerisms more typical of the opposite sex. In addition, some of the "effeminate" body gestures and mannerisms of cross-gender identified boys are actually caricatures of feminine mannerisms. That is, the "effeminate" gestures in the cross-gender identified boy are exaggerations of feminine standing, sitting, or walking behaviors and these exaggeratedly "feminine" gestures actually occur at higher frequency rates in cross-gender identified boys than they do in a normal girl population. These gestures, therefore, become a source of social peer ridicule for the cross-gender identified child. They are highly socially salient and they occur at high frequency rates in the play of these children. Therefore, play therapy procedures are necessary to decrease these atypical body gestures and mannerisms.

A behavioral play therapy technique incorporating a response-cost and verbal-prompt procedure was developed to decrease a gender-disturbed boy's cross-gender mannerisms (Rekers, Yates, Willis, Rosen, & Taubman, 1976). "Flexed elbow," and "feminine running" were behaviorally recorded while the child participated in the game of throwing a tennis ball at a target. The child was given a number of tokens at the beginning of each therapy session. Each feminine gesture was explained to him and he was told that he would lose one token for each instance of a "flexed elbow" or "feminine running." In addition, the therapist trained the child in appropriate running movements by modeling the behavior and then asking the child to imitate, using manual guidance where necessary. The therapist used these techniques in the clinic, and instructed the parents on how to use these techniques in the home. These procedures resulted in a decrease in these feminine mannerisms to a sufficient degree that the boy ceased to appear effeminate.

In a subsequent study (Rekers, Willis, Yates, Rosen, & Low, 1977), an additional procedure was incorporated in the play therapy session in order to provide discrimination training with the videotape feedback procedure. In our clinical experience, it appears that some children have an initial difficulty in discriminating the cross-gender mannerisms in their own repertoire. This procedure was suggested by a gender-disturbed boy's own expressed concern that he was really unaware of the things he did that resulted in the peer ostracism he was experiencing at school. Observations in the clinic playroom confirmed that he was unaware of which of his mannerisms were perceived as "feminine" or "masculine." Working in the clinic playroom, we therefore developed (1) procedures to assess his ability to discriminate his own cross-gender mannerisms, (2) procedures to train him how to discriminate those mannerisms, and (3) play therapy procedures designed to decrease the occurrence of those mannerisms.

First, the therapist explained the target mannerisms of "finger extension," "hand clasp," "hyperextension," "limp wrist," and "flutters" to the boy (definitions in Rekers, Willis, et al., 1977). The therapist guided the boy manually through the movements that constituted each target behavior. The therapist then told the boy that he could earn one penny for each mannerism he could correctly identify on a five-minute segment of the videotape of himself playing. Alternating test sessions with training sessions, the therapist systematically trained the boy to be able to discriminate each of his feminine mannerisms on the videotape sequences.

After this training feedback was completed, play therapy sessions were conducted in which a response-cost and verbal-prompt procedure was introduced contingent upon the occurrence of one of those mannerisms—for example, "limping the wrist." The intrasubject study data indicated that limping the wrist decreased, with concurrent decreases in other feminine mannerisms.

This play therapy procedure resulted in a more rapid decrease of cross-gender mannerisms as compared to previous cases (Rekers, 1972; Rekers & Lovaas, 1974; Rekers et al, 1974; Rekers et al., 1976). The relatively more efficient play therapy intervention results may have been a joint function of (1) the prior self-observation training, (2) the more easily discriminable contingency for a single subclass of mannerisms treated on a one-at-time basis, and (3) the addition of the verbal cueing procedure which provided a clearer connection between the response and the feedback. More research is needed to determine the relative effectiveness of various behavioral techniques for teaching a child to discriminate particular complex behaviors prior to the introduction of contingencies for their occurrence.

Intervention for Athletic Participation.   A specific set of play therapy procedures in a park setting has been developed to shape athletic behaviors in cross-gender identified boys (Rekers et al., 1974; Rekers, Willis et al., 1977; Rekers, 1979). Cross-gender identified boys are typically ostracized from their peer group and they have accumulated a behavioral deficit in certain game participation skills due to extended periods of time avoiding gender-appropriate play with their peers. Therefore, play therapy procedures were provided in various athletic skills such as throwing a football, socking a playground ball, kicking a kickball, and shooting baskets. The acquisition of these skills enabled these boys to gain social reinforcement from their own peer group and it also provided competing responses to the compulsive feminine play behavior pattern typical of their maladjustment pattern.

Therapy training is provided in one skill at a time and after substantial improvement has been demonstrated in the initial skill according to a pre-established criterion, training is then provided for a second skill. Following a multiple-baseline design, a number of children have been trained in several skills each. The therapist takes the child to a park setting and models the target behavior. He then reinforces successive approximation of the desired responses with verbal praise and candy. To monitor progress, test sessions are interspersed at regular intervals between training sessions. For example, the percentage of successful throws is recorded, and a measure of motivation is calculated as the percentage of time during which the boy attempts the behavior during the test session.

The play therapy sessions are designed in a way to help desensitize the boy's fears with the goal of helping the child to learn that playing ball can be intrinsically enjoyable. Wherever possible, the father is invited to participate in the training sessions. Emphasis is upon establishing a nonthreatening play session in which the task is never too difficult to induce feelings of failure.

Using these play therapy procedures in a park setting, one boy attained a level of competence that allowed him to compete with his peers without feelings of failure and accompanying anxiety. Another boy became involved in neighborhood athletic play and began to imagine himself as a professional football player. Yet another boy succeeded to the extent of being elected captain of the school kickball team (Rekers, 1977a).

CASE ILLUSTRATION

Rekers and Lovaas (1974) reported the detailed intrasubject study of a 4-year, 11-month-old boy, Kraig. Kraig came from an intact family, including a normal brother eight years old and a sister nine months of age. He had been referred by a psychiatric authority on gender identity problems who described him as one of the "most severe cases" that he had assessed. Kraig had a history of cross-dressing from the age of two years. He had chronically been playing with cosmetic items of his mother and grandmother. He frequently improvised in cross-dressing—for example, using a mop or towel over his head for long hair, or a long t-shirt for a dress—if feminine clothing was unavailable. He had a notable ability to imitate many subtle feminine behaviors. He continuously displayed pronounced feminine mannerisms, gestures, and gait; and he used an exaggerated feminine voice inflection coupled with high rates of feminine content in his speech. At the same time, he avoided all "rough-and-tumble" games of boys his age in his immediate neighborhood. He consistently avoided playing with his brother, other boys, and he declined to defend himself among his peers. He strongly preferred to play with girls and with one neighborhood girl in particular. But even when playing house with her, he invariably insisted on playing the part of the "mother" while assigning the part of "father" to one of the girls. This led to peer relationship problems even with the girls in his neighborhood. Overall, Kraig was compulsive and rigid in the extent to which he insisted upon being a girl and in his refusal of all contact with masculine activities.

In baseline play sessions, it was observed that Kraig played nearly exclusively with feminine sex-typed toys while alone in the playroom, in the presence of his mother, and in the presence of male and female therapists. He played predominantly with the masculine toys only in the presence of his father.

In the play therapy research studies with this boy, the experimental procedure followed the ABABABA reversal, intrasubject replication design, in which A represented a baseline and reversal condition in which no differential reinforcement was given and B represented the play therapy sessions. With sex-typed toys in the playroom, the boy and mother were introduced into the playroom with the mother wearing "bug-in-the-ear" device. When the mother attended to masculine play and verbal behavior by smiling and complimenting the boy's play, the masculine behavior increased. When she ignored feminine play behaviors by picking up the magazine to "read," the feminine behavior became extinguished. The therapist verbally instructed and reinforced the mother for her correct differential reinforcement of the boy. These instructions and praise to the mother were gradually faded out. The intrasubject replication design demonstrated that these procedures were successful in decreasing compulsive feminine play and verbal behavior. The results suggested that appropriate masculine play and verbal behavior did exist in the gender-disturbed boys' behavioral repertoire prior to treatment. The rapid change to masculine behavior with these play therapy procedures suggested that the change in the boy's play represented discrimination of the reinforcement contingency rather than the more complex process of response acquisition (learning).

After these clinic play therapy procedures successfully resulted in appropriate sex-typed play in the boy, treatment was extended to the home setting where the parent was carefully monitored to reinforce appropriate sex-typed behavior and to suppress compulsive feminine sex-typed play.

Follow-up data three years after the treatment began and also ten years after the conclusion of treatment have demonstrated that Kraig now has a normal gender identity as a male and is indistinguishable from other boys his age in terms of sex-typed play behavior. In addition, Kraig now enjoys normal peer relationships and peer acceptance as a teenage boy. The follow-up evaluations were conducted by independent clinical psychologists. The durability of the play therapy effects appear to be a function of the mother's acquired skills in the social learning therapy techniques which, in effect, extended the treatment program indefinitely on an informal basis throughout Kraig's environment over time. This published case constitutes the first experimentally demonstrated effective treatment for cross-gender identification in children, and shows promise as a technique for the prevention of adult transsexualism or similar adult sexual deviation.

SUMMARY AND CONCLUSIONS

These behavioral play therapy procedures have resulted in adaptive changes in sex-role behaviors in the numerous cases of gender-disturbed children reported by Rekers and his colleagues. Similar results have been reported by Bates and his colleagues, although they did not use the kind of intrasubject replication designs to demonstrate therapeutic effectiveness that were used by Rekers and his colleagues (Bates, Skilbeck, Smith & Bentler, 1975). More than 50 children have been treated by these two independent treatment teams with similar positive outcomes. The long-term follow-up by Rekers and his colleagues incorporates the use of independent clinical psychological evaluations of the children at periodic points after treatment. Preliminary results indicate that permanent cognitive change in terms of gender identity has been a function of overt, nonverbal gender behavior changes instituted by these play therapy procedures. To the extent that gender identity can be measured by the child's own spontaneous statements to independent clinicians and by means of the projective testing and other personality testing that have been employed, we now entertain the tentative conclusion that an effective preventative treatment has been isolated for the adult conditions of transvestism, transsexualism, and effeminate male homosexuality.

Scientifically speaking, the follow-up data of Rekers and his colleagues will be compared to outcome data on gender-disturbed children who have been followed through adolescence and early adulthood without treatment (see Green, 1974; Green & Money, 1961; Zuger, 1978).

Because of the difficulties in treating adulthood cases of transsexualism, transvestism, and some cases of homosexuality, the preferred clinical strategy should be early identification and early intervention with behavioral play therapy procedures. Our research to date encourages us to have a realistic optimism that behavioral play therapy procedures can constitute the preventative treatment needed for these individuals with cross-gender identification. Until more follow-up data are available, however, it remains wise to hold several reservations. First, although the reversals in gender identification from a feminine identification to a masculine one in these children have held up into adolescence, these changes may or may not continue into adulthood. Second, we have not yet determined the extent to which these profound changes in childhood may or may not affect changes in future preference for sex mates. It is theoretically possible that adult sexual preference is a response that is independent of the ones that we have treated in childhood. Third, there remains the theoretical possibility that the gender-behavior changes achieved through behavioral play therapy in childhood may not be predictive of normal gender adjustment in adulthood if these treatment procedures simply produced a shift in cross-gender behavior from the overt mode to the covert level of private fantasy. To the extent possible, our independent clinical evaluations of these children as they reach adolescence have incorporated measures of the intrapsychic concerns, wishes, and fantasies of the individuals as they grow up, in addition to reports of overt behavior and stated sexual preferences. There are, however, research design limitations upon the accessibility of the necessary data to determine the complete adulthood outcome of these cases.

Nevertheless, the intrasubject studies completed in childhood and the follow-up data, to date, have demonstrated very comprehensive changes in these cross-gender identified children which have had durable effects over time. No other therapeutic intervention procedure in childhood has been experimentally demonstrated to have this same effectiveness. With the current state of knowledge, therefore, the most ethically appropriate intervention for a cross-gender identified child would be these play therapy procedures based upon a social-learning theoretical framework (Rekers, 1977, 1978a, 1980, 1981a; Rekers, Bentler, Rosen, & Lovaas, 1977; Rekers & Jurich, in press; Rekers, Rosen, Lovaas, & Bentler, 1978; Rosen, Rekers, & Bentler, 1978).

REFERENCES

Bakwin, H. (1968) Deviant gender-role behavior in children: Relation to homosexuality. *Pediatrics,* **41,** 620–629.

Bates, J. E., & Bentler, P. M. (1973) Play activities of normal and effeminate boys. *Developmental Psychology,* **9,** 20–27.

Bates, J. E., Bentler, P. M., & Thompson, S. (1973) Measurement of deviant gender development in boys. *Child Development,* **44,** 591–598.

Bates, J. E., Skilbeck, W. M., Smith, K. V. R., & Bentler, P. M. (1974) Gender role abnormalities in boys: An analysis of clinical ratings. *Journal of Abnormal Child Psychology,* **2,** 1–16.

Bates, J. E., Skilbeck. W. M., Smith, K. V. R., & Bentler, P. M. (1975) Intervention with families of gender-disturbed boys. *American Journal of Orthopsychiatry,* **45,** 150–157.

Benjamin, H. (1966) *The transsexual phenomenon.* New York: The Julian Press.

Bentler, P. M. (1976) A typology of transsexualism: Gender identity theory and data *Archives of Sexual Behavior,* **5,** 567–584

Bentler, P. M., Rekers, G. A., & Rosen, A. C. (1979) Congruence of childhood sex-role identity and behavior disturbances. *Child: Care, Health and Development,* **5**(4), 267–284.

Bieber, I., Dain, H. J., Dince, P. R., Drellich, M. G., Grand, H. G., Gundlach, R. H., Kremer, M. W., Rifkin, A. H., Wilbur, C. B., & Bieber, T. B. (1962) *Homosexuality: A psychoanalytic study.* New York: Basic Books.

Brown, D. G. (1956) Sex-role preference in young children. *Psychological Monographs: General and Applied,* **70**(14, Whole No. 421), 1–19.

Dupont, H. (1968) Social learning theory and the treatment of transvestite behavior in an eight-year-old boy. *Psychotherapy: Theory, Research, and Practice,* **5,** 44–45.

Evans, R. B. (1969) Childhood parental relationships of homosexual men. *Journal of Consulting and Clinical Psychology,* **33,** 129–135.

Evans, R. B. (1972) Physical and biochemical characteristics of homosexual men. *Journal of Consulting and Clinical Psychology,* **39,** 140–147.

Green, R. (1974) *Sexual identity conflict in child and adults.* New York: Basic Books.

Green, R., & Fuller, M. (1973) Family doll play and female identity in pre-adolescent males. *American Journal of Orthopsychiatry,* **43,** 123–127.

Green, R., Fuller, M., Rutley, B. R., & Hendler, J. (1972) Playroom toy preferences of fifteen masculine and fifteen feminine boys. *Behavior Therapy,* **3,** 425–429.

Green, R., & Money, J. (1961) Effeminacy in prepubertal boys: Summary of eleven cases of recommendations for case management. *Pediatrics,* **27,** 286–291.

Green, R., & Money, J. (Eds.) (1969) *Transsexualism and sex reassignment.* Baltimore: Johns Hopkins University Press.

Green, R., Newman, L. E., & Stoller, R. J. (1972) Treatment of boyhood "transsexualism"—An interim report of four years' experience. *Archives of General Psychiatry,* **26,** 213–217.

Greenson, R. R. (1968) Dis-identifying from mother: Its special importance for the boy. *International Journal of Psycho-Analysis,* **49,** 370–374.

Hartley, R. E., & Hardesty, F. P. (1964) Children's perceptions of sex roles in child-hood. *Journal of Genetic Psychology*, **105**, 43–51.

Holeman, E. R., & Winokur, G. (1965) Effeminate homosexuality: A disease of child-hood. *American Journal of Orthopsychiatry*, **35**, 48–56.

Hutt, C. (1978) Biological bases of psychological sex differences. *American Journal of Diseases in Childhood*, **132**, 170–177.

Lebovitz, P. S. (1972) Feminine behavior in boys: Aspects of its outcome. *American Journal of Psychiatry*, **128**, 1283–1289.

Lefkowitz, M. M. *Some Relationships between Sex Role preferences of Children and other Parent Child Variables Psychological Reports*, 1962. Vol. 10 43–53

Litin, E. M., Giffin, M. E., & Johnson, A. M. (1956) Parental influence in unusual sexual behavior in children. *Psychoanalytic Quarterly*, **25**, 37–55.

Lukianowicz, N. (1959) Transvestism and psychosis. *Psychiatria et Neurologia*, **138**, 64–77.

Mead, S. L., & Rekers, G. A. (1979) The role of the father in normal psycho-sexual development. *Psychological Reports*, **45**, 923–931.

Meyer-Bahlburg, H. F. L. (1977) Sex hormones and male homosexuality in compara-tive perspective. *Archives of Sexual Behavior*, **6**, 297–325.

Money, J. (1970a) Critique of Dr. Zuger's manuscript. *Psychosomatic Medicine*, **32**, 463–465.

Money, J. (1970b) Sexual dimorphism and homosexual gender identity. *Psychological Bulletin*, **74**, 425–440.

Money, J., & Ehrhardt, A. A. (1972) *Man and woman, boy and girl.* Baltimore: John Hopkins Press.

Money, J., Hampson, J. G., & Hampson, J. L. (1955) An examination of some basic sexual concepts: Evidence of human hermaphroditism. *Bulletin of the Johns Hopkins Hospital*, **97**, 301–319.

Money, J., & Primrose, C. (1968) Sexual dimorphism and dissociation in the psychol-ogy of male transsexuals. *Journal of Nervous and Mental Disease*, **147**, 472–486.

Myrick, R. D. (1970) The counselor–consultant and the effeminate boy. *Personnel and Guidance Journal*, **48**, 355–361.

Pauly, I. (1969) Adult manifestations of male transsexualism. In R. Green & J. Money (Eds), *Transsexualism and sex reassignment.* Baltimore: John Hopkins University Press.

Prince, C. V., & Bentler, P. M. (1972) A survey of 504 cases of transvestism. *Psychologi-cal Reports*, **31**, 903–917.

Rabban, M. (1950) Sex-role identification in young children in two diverse social groups. *Genetic Psychology Monographs*, **42**, 81–158.

Rekers, G. A. (1972) Pathological sex-role development in boys: Behavioral treatment and assessment. (Doctoral dissertation, University of California, Los Angeles.) *Dissertation Abstracts International*, **33**, 3321B. (University Microfilms No. 72-33, 978).

Rekers, G. A. (1975) Stimulus control over sex-typed play in cross-gender identified boys. *Journal of Experimental Child Psychology.* **20**, 136–148.

Rekers, G. A. (1977a) Assessment and treatment of childhood gender problems. In B.

B. Lahey & A. E. Kazdin (Eds.) *Advances in clinical child psychology* (vol. I). New York: Plenum.

Rekers, G. A. (1977b) Atypical gender development and psychosocial adjustment. *Journal of Applied Behavior Analysis,* **10,** 559–571.

Rekers, G. A. (1978a) A priori values and research on homosexuality. *American Psychologist,* **33,** 510–512.

Rekers, G. A. (1978b) Sexual problems: Behavior modification. In B. B. Wolman (Ed.) *Handbook of treatment of mental disorders in childhood and adolescence.* Englewood Cliffs, N.J. Prentice-Hall.

Rekers, G. A. (1979) Sex-role behavior change: Intrasubject studies of boyhood gender disturbance. *The Journal of Psychology,* **103,** 255–269.

Rekers, G. A. (1980) Therapies dealing with the child's sexual difficulties. In Jean-Marc Samson (Ed.), *Enfance et Sexualite/Childhood and Sexuality.* Montreal & Paris: Les Editions Etudes Vivantes.

Rekers, G. A. (1981a) Childhood sexual identity disorders. *Medical Aspects of Human Sexuality,* **15**(3), 141–142.

Rekers, G. A. (1981b) Psychosexual and gender problems. In E. J. Mash & L. G. Terdal (Eds.) *Behavioral assessment of childhood disorders.* New York: Guilford Press.

Rekers, G. A. (1982a,) *Growing up straight: What every families should know about homosexuality.* Chicago: Moody Press.

Rekers, G. A. (1982b,) *Shaping your child's sexual identity.* Grand Rapids, Mich: Baker Book House.

Rekers, G. A., Amaro-Plotkin, H., & Low, B. P. (1977) Sex-typed mannerisms in normal boys and girls as a function of sex and age. *Child Development,* **48,** 275–278.

Rekers, G. A., Bentler, P. M., Rosen, A. C., & Lovaas, O. I. (1977) Child gender disturbances: A clinical rationale for intervention. *Psychotherapy: Theory, Research, and Practice,* **14,** 2–11.

Rekers, G. A., Crandall, B. F., Rosen, A. C., & Bentler, P. M. (1979) Genetic and physical studies of male children with psychological gender disturbances. *Psychological Medicine,* **9,** 373–375.

Rekers, G. A., & Jurich, A. P. (In press) Development of problems of puberty and sex roles in adolescents. In C. Eugene Walker & Michael C. Roberts (Eds.), *Handbook of clinical child psychology.* New York: John Wiley and Sons.

Rekers, G. A., & Lovaas, O. I. (1974) Behavioral treatment of deviant sex-role behaviors in a male child. *Journal of Applied Behavior Analysis,* **7,** 173–190.

Rekers, G. A., Lovaas, O., & Low, B. P. (1974) The behavioral treatment of a "transsexual" preadolescent boy. *Journal of Abnormal Child Psychology,* **2,** 99–116.

Rekers, G. A. & Mead, S. (1979a) Early intervention for female sexual identity disturbance: Self-monitoring of play behavior. *Journal of Abnormal Child Psychology,* **7**(4), 405–423.

Rekers, G. A., & Mead, S. (1979b) Human sex differences in carrying behaviors: A replication and extension. *Perceptual and Motor Skills,* **48,** 625–626.

Rekers, G. A., & Mead, S. (1980) Female sex-role deviance: Early identification and development intervention. *Journal of Clinical Child Psychology,* **9**(3), 199–203.

Rekers, G. A., Mead, S. L., Rosen, A. C., & Brigham, S. L. (In press) Family correlates of male childhood gender disturbance. *The Journal of Genetic Psychology.*

Rekers, G. A., & Milner, G. C. (1978) Sexual identity disorders in childhood and adolescence. *Journal of the Florida Medical Association,* **65,** 962–964.

Rekers, G. A., & Milner, G. C. (1979) How to diagnose and manage childhood sexual disorders. *Behavioral Medicine,* **6**(4), 18–21.

Rekers, G. A., Rosen, A. C., Lovaas, O. I., & Bentler, P. M. (1978) Sex-role stereotypy and professional intervention for childhood gender disturbances. *Professional Psychology,* **9,** 127–136.

Rekers, G. A., & Rudy, J. P. (1978) Differentiation of childhood body gestures. *Perceptual and Motor Skills,* **46,** 839–845.

Rekers, G. A., Sanders, J. A., & Strauss, C. C. (1981) Developmental differentiation of adolescent body gestures. *Journal of Genetic Psychology,* **138**(1), 123–131.

Rekers, G. A., Sanders, J. A., Strauss, C. C., Rasbury, W. C., & Mead, S. L. (In press) Differentiation of adolescent activity participation. *The Journal of Genetic Psychology..*

Rekers, G. A., & Varni, J. W. (1977a) Self-monitoring and self-reinforcement processes in a pre-transsexual boy. *Behavior Research and Therapy,* **15,** 177–180.

Rekers, G. A., & Varni, J. W. (1977b) Self-regulation of gender-role behaviors: A case study. *Journal of Behavioral Therapy and Experimental Psychiatry,* **8,** 427–432.

Rekers, G. A., Willis, T. J., Yates, C. E., Rosen, A. C., & Low, B. P. (1977) Assessment of childhood gender behavior change. *Journal of Child Psychology and Psychiatry,* **18,** 53–65.

Rekers, G. A., & Yates, C. E. (1976) Sex-typed play in feminoid boys vs. normal boys and girls. *Journal of Abnormal Child Psychology,* **4,** 1–8.

Rekers, G. A., Yates, C. E., Willis, T. J., Rosen, A. C., & Taubman, M. (1976) Childhood gender identity change: Operant control over sex-typed play and mannerisms. *Journal of Behavior Therapy and Experimental Psychiatry,* **7,** 51–57.

Rosen, A. C. (1969) The intersex: Gender identity, genetics, and mental health. In A. Plog & R. Edgerton (Eds.), *Changing perspectives in mental illness.* New York: Holt.

Rosen, A. C., & Rekers, G. A. (1980) Toward a taxonomic framework for variables of sex and gender. *Genetic Psychology Monographs,* **102,** 191–218.

Rosen. A. C., Rekers, G. A., & Bentler, P. M. (1978) Ethical issues in the treatment of children. *Journal of Social Issues,* **34**(2), 122–136.

Rosen, A. C., Rekers, G. A., & Friar, L. R. (1977) Theoretical and diagnostic issues in child gender disturbances. *The Journal of Sex Research,* **13**(2), 89–103.

Rosenberg, B. G., & Sutton-Smith, B. (1959) The measurement of masculinity and femininity in children. *Child Development,* **30,** 373–380.

Rosenberg, B. G., & Sutton-Smith, B. (1964) The measurement of masculinity and femininity in children: An extension and revalidation. *Journal of Genetic Psychology,* **104,** 259–264.

Stoller, R. J. (1968a) Male childhood transsexualism. *Journal of the American Academy of Child Psychiatry,* **7,** 193–209.

Stoller, R. J. (1968b) *Sex and gender: The development of masculinity and femininity.* New York: Science House.

Stoller, R. J. (1969) Parental influences in male transsexualism. In R. Green & J. Money (Eds.) *Transsexualism and sex reassignment.* Baltimore: John Hopkins University Press.

Stoller, R. J. (1970-1971) Psychotherapy of extremely feminine boys. *International Journal of Psychiatry,* **9,** 278–280.

Sutton-Smith, B., Rosenberg, B. G., & Morgan, E. R. (1963) Development of sex differences in play choices during preadolescence. *Child Development,* **34,** 119–126.

Walinder, J. (1967) *Transsexualism: A study of forty-three cases.* Goteborg: Scandinavian University Books.

Walker, R. N. (1964) Measuring masculinity and femininity in children's game choices. *Child Development,* **35,** 961–971.

Whitam, F. L. (1977) Childhood indicators of male homosexuality. *Archives of Sexual Behavior,* **6,** 89–96.

Zuger, B. (1966) Effeminate behavior present in boys from early childhood: I. The clinical syndrome and follow-up studies. *Journal of Pediatrics,* **69,** 1098–1107.

Zuger, B. (1970a) Gender role determination: A critical review of the evidence from hermaphroditism. *Psychosomatic Medicine,* **32,** 449–467.

Zuger, B. (1970b) The role of familial factors in persistent effeminate behavior in boys. *American Journal of Psychiatry,* **126,** 1167–1170.

Zuger, B. (1978) Effeminate behavior present in boys from childhood. Ten additional years of follow-up. *Comprehensive Psychiatry,* **19,** 363–369.

Zuger, B., & Taylor, P. (1969) Effeminate behavior present in boys from early childhood: II. Comparison with similar symptoms in non-effeminate boys. *Pediatrics,* **44,** 375–380.

CHAPTER 21

Play Therapy with the
Aggressive, Acting-Out Child

BRENT WILLOCK

INTRODUCTION

This chapter concerns a population of children who are notoriously difficult to
work with in play therapy or any other therapeutic modality. Diagnostically
they are known as antisocial character disorders, primary behavior disorders,
delinquents, predelinquents, and so forth. At times their behavior is described
as psychopathic or sociopathic. According to the latest nosology of the American Psychiatric Association (1980), they are classified as aggressive conduct
disorders and divided into a socialized and an undersocialized subtype. This
DSM-III system captures the idea that there is significant variation among
aggressive, conduct-disordered children and it is not incompatible with the
concept of a continuum of aggressive conduct disorders varying in terms of
severity of disturbance (Willock, 1982). A possible shortcoming of the DSM-
III terminology is the implication that the primitive aggressivity characteristic
of the most disturbed of these children is primarily due to their not having
learned the appropriate mores of civilized society, their not having grasped
enough of the basics of socialization to make it beyond the first rung on the
ladder of moral development. Whereas such implications have some descriptive validity, they could also be dynamically misleading to the extent that the
concept "undersocialized" may mask the degree to which so many of these
children are doggedly *antisocial.* It is not simply that they lack good social
bonding or attachment. They are frequently committed to maintaining quali-
tatively negative bonds, provocatively defying social conventions, and actively
thwarting attempts to establish more positive relationships with them.

I would like to express my sincere gratitude to Dr. David Klein, Research Associate on the Child
Analytic Study Program at the Children's Psychiatric Hospital, University of Michigan Medical
Center, for having contributed clinical data to a recent study on hyperaggressive children, and
again for having given his permission for this material to be utilized in this chapter as a case
illustration.

Although diagnostic issues are important, one might say that it is not so much by their nosological labels that these children are known, but by their violently disruptive behavior and their extreme resistance to remedial efforts. Again and again one finds statements in the literature attesting not only to the difficulty of treating these youngsters, but also to the inadequacy of traditional psychodynamic formulations and modes of intervention. For example, Berman (1964) noted that "the concepts which guide us in treatment are of no avail" (p. 24), and Schmideberg (1959) asserted: "Conventional psychotherapeutic techniques are not applicable with this type of patient" (p. 300). The harsh reality of clinical experience with this population was summed up by Berman (1964) with a simple statement: "Attempts to treat these patients almost always fail" (p. 24).

The conclusions of these seasoned clinicians concerning the difficulties encountered in trying to treat hyperaggressive children tend to be echoed in the research literature. Studies of treatment outcome suggest that few of these children benefit from the individual therapies typically provided (Levitt, 1971) and that even residential treatment facilities have little success in effecting long-term behavioral changes (Teuber & Powers, 1953; Meltzoff & Kornreich, 1970). Given such difficult courses of treatment and such frequently disappointing outcomes, it is not completely surprising to hear that of all such children referred for treatment, only a small fraction are actually offered it (Bahm, Chandler, & Eisenberg, 1961).

The Treatment Approach

The therapeutic approach which will be described in this chapter is a very intensive one consisting of long-term, individual psychotherapy integrated into an intensive milieu treatment program composed of special education, activites therapy (occupational, recreational, and music therapy), and intensive child-care work. Although this chapter focuses on the play therapy rather than the total milieu treatment, it must be emphasized that the comprehensive resources of a good residential treatment center are essential for working with such severely disturbed children. Usually a variety of interventions of lesser intensity have already been attempted in the child's home community prior to his or her referral for residential treatment. For example, the school may have initiated consultations with psychologists, social workers, and psychiatrists. These evaluations may have led to counseling or therapy for the child, and perhaps for the parents as well. The child may have been placed in a special classroom for emotionally impaired students, put on a behavior modification program, and so forth. When these interventions failed to produce the desired results, the child may have been suspended from school with increasing frequency, or restricted to half-day attendance. The child's cumulative nonresponsiveness to the school's efforts, indeed his or her progressively worsening behavior, may have culminated in school personnel feeling "burnt out" and consequently willing to do just about anything to get rid of the child rather than endure another day of his or her defiance and unmanageable violence (fighting and threatening, tearing up papers, throwing books, overturning desks, hurling chairs, etc.). The school and the child's parents are likely to see residential treatment as a last hope or, to the extent that they feel beyond hope, they may see it as a way of getting rid of the child.

The psychotherapeutic framework which will be discussed is basically a psychoanalytically oriented one, although such a description requires elaboration. These are by no means simply neurotic patients; nor do they resemble any other population traditionally considered well-suited to a psychoanalytically oriented approach. In fact, as Tooley (1974) noted, "By any mode of assessing accessibility to psychotherapy these children would be judged the poorest of risks" (p. 341). The material which they present in therapy is not what a psychodynamically oriented psychotherapist is typically looking for or expecting. Instead, these children are prone to spewing forth a seemingly endless barrage of abuse and resistance, replete with exceedingly graphic obscenities, fisticuffs, spit, flailing arms and legs, flying toys and ashtrays. Rather than "talking about feelings," they would generally prefer to overturn furniture and trash their therapists' offices.

The psychotherapist's interventions may also seem remote from the usual *modus operandi* of a psychodynamically oriented psychotherapist. Traditional treatises on technique typically say little about the appropriate mode of intervention when a patient precipitously adopts the single-minded aim of destroying the therapist's office or inflicting bodily harm upon the therapist. It may seem most unanalytic for a therapist to experience a surge of adrenalin, leap out of his or her chair, and struggle with great intensity in order to restrain the patient in such a way that flailing arms and legs are immobilized while somehow remaining a sufficient distance from the patient's mouth so as not to be the recipient of teeth and spit, all the while trying to ensure that the patient's wrists, elbows, shoulders, and so forth do not become dislocated or fractured. What remains analytic in all this turbulence is the therapist's attempt to make sense of the behavior, to understand the nature of the child's ego dysfunction as completely as possible, and ultimately, to find nonthreatening ways of communicating this understanding to the child so as to alleviate the underlying anxieties which propel his or her aggressive acting out.

This agenda for the therapeutic enterprise may seem to many to exceed what anyone ever meant to encompass by the optimistic concept of "the widening scope of psychoanalytically oriented psychotherapy." Yet the aim of this chapter is to suggest that these children are not beyond the reach of psychotherapeutic intervention and that individual psychotherapy has an important role to play as an integral component in the total treatment approach. Although psychotherapy is only one element in the therapeutic armamentarium, the psychodynamic perspective on which it is based can serve as a framework that informs, pervades, and encourages all other approaches to the child.

More than thirty years have passed since Redl and Wineman (1951, 1952) published their landmark books on the treatment of hyperaggressive children. They presented a vivid portrait of these youngsters and a design for working with them in residential treatment which stressed the therapeutic possibilities of activities programming and life-space interviews. Because they believed at the time that these children were essentially "below the grip of the psychiatric interview" (1951, p. 277), their writings, although they continue to be essential reading for anyone working with these children, are less directly suited to the particular needs of individual psychotherapists. In the three decades since their groundbreaking experiment, little has been added to the clinical literature to fill this gap. We hope this chapter will help with this necessary project.

The Aggressive, Acting-out Character Style

Behind their defiant, "tough guy" façades, hyperaggressive children tend to feel basically unappreciated, unwanted, and unloved. They may believe that they do not have whatever it takes to engage and sustain the concerned interest of others. This lack of a basic sense of valued connectedness with important others constitutes a fundamental area of narcissistic vulnerability in the child's personality.

Beyond feeling unimportant and unloved, these children also believe that there is something essentially unloveable about themselves. They harbor the fear that in the eyes of the world they are not merely insignificant and worthless, but utterly repulsive as well. This abysmally negative self-image constitutes a second facet of their core narcissistic vulnerability. I refer to these two aspects of self-structure as *the disregarded and the devalued self.*

Much of the explosive behavior which typifies the hyperaggressive child can be understood in terms of this underlying narcissistic vulnerability. In order to ward off the anxiety, the anger, and the depression which are associated with the disregarded and the devalued self, these children adopt an angrily alienated, "I don't care" attitude ("I don't care about you. I don't care what you think about me.")—a posture which they may reinforce by indulging in blatantly antisocial activities. The younger the child, the less hardened this defense will be, and consequently, the younger child will be more prone to noisy outbursts of aggression every time he or she imagines something to signify that he or she is unloved or no good. Because the young child's character armor is less consolidated, he or she will also be somewhat more accessible to therapeutic efforts.

The question arises as to the origins of this core narcissistic vulnerability. Typically these children have experienced some degree of inadequate parenting, ranging from insufficient, unempathic parenting combined with harsh physical punishment, all the way down to the grosser forms of neglect and abuse. The developmental timing, intensity, frequency, and duration of these traumatic experiences are important factors in determining the specific characterological outcomes.

In many cases the deficiencies in the parental "protective barrier" (Bergman & Escalona, 1949; Boyer, 1971) may have created stresses for these children to contend with right from the beginning of their lives, forcing them to develop precociously whatever self-protective mechanisms they might have had in their innate armamentarium. One body of research suggests that hyper-aggressive children may be constitutionally endowed with very active, aggressive, out-turning temperaments (Glover, 1960; Michaels, 1955; Soddy, 1960; Stott, Marston, & Neill, 1975; Thomas, Chess, & Birch, 1968). Deficiencies in parenting may call forth unusually pronounced manifestations of these response tendencies as the child tries to register an angry protest and simultaneously counter his or her feeling of being threatened and vulnerable by mobilizing fighting instincts in order to give him or herself at least some sensation of power. The cumulative effect of all these experiences could be the consolidation of a feeling in these children of being excessively on their own and needing to rely upon their own self-preservative instincts in order to provide themselves with a modicum of security.

Whatever the extent and cumulative effects of the early nonoptimal or traumatic experiences may have been, in the subsequent course of socialization, and frequently in its earliest phases during the second year of life, the child typically experiences some pronounced narcissistic injury in relation to his or her parents at a time when he or she would ordinarily have been developing a more positive, idealized sense of the parents as powerful protectors, guides, and love objects (Eissler, 1950). This narcissistic insult might center around a major disappointment, lack of adequate protection, abuse, or loss of parental attention through divorce, birth of a sibling, or parental depression. Such experience increases the child's sense of being unprotected, unloved, and unloveable. It interferes with the development of positive attitudes toward adults and helps consolidate a stance of angry alienation in relation to the adult world.

Because the traumatic experiences occur so early, the child remains in many ways fixated at a developmental phase where danger situations are relatively undifferentiated (Eissler, 1950), particularly in those areas involving a threat to the self (the disregarded and the devalued self). Minor and imaginary threats or "slights" are readily taken to be major, real dangers. Criticism of one aspect of the child's behavior is felt to be a total condemnation of the basic self. Feeling so vulnerable, the child feels it necessary to maintain a constant readiness to call upon primitive, aggressive security operations in order to defend against such "attacks."

Whereas the child's aggressivity over the years gets him or her into a great deal of trouble, he or she also feels it be be the most reliable defense. He or she will not, therefore, be trustingly disposed toward anyone who suggests such behavior ought to stop on account of it's being maladaptive and inappropriate. Having learned to ward off old hurts and frustrated dependency longings with a feisty, counterdependent, "tough guy" attitude, any therapist offering what amounts to an intimate, caring relationship will inevitably be regarded with uneasy suspicion. Whereas the therapist may perceive him- or herself as manifesting interest in the child by attempting to engage him or her in meaningful dialogue, the patient is more likely to see the therapist's "damn questions" as dangerous attempts to tamper with his or her precarious controls over "the floodgates of the past" (Redl & Wineman, 1951). The therapist is thus confronted with a patient who is threatened by and consequently rejecting of the therapeutic situation. The following section will address some of these problems and how they can be approached therapeutically in light of the etiological considerations and the phenomenological and psychodynamic meanings outlined previously.

METHOD

Technical Aspects

Play therapy typically depends upon the child expressing various configurations of impulse and defense through combinations of verbalization and play, and permitting the therapist to make sympathetic observations, inquiries, or interpretations. The child responds to the therapist's interventions either by producing further significant material or by becoming more defensive. The therapist may then comment upon the child's response, and so the therapeutic dialogue proceeds. Unfortunately, hyperaggressive children, as Tooley (1974) noted, have little capacity for expressive or reflective verbalization, or for dramatic, imaginative play. Furthermore, they tend to feel intensely threatened by the slightest inquiry or observation on the part of the therapist. They thus present severe obstacles to the viability of play therapy as a means of helping them

The following vignette will illustrate some of these difficulties. It is taken from an early session in Tyrone's treatment with his new therapist. Tyrone was an 11-year-old hyperaggressive boy who had previously been in treatment for two years with another therapist who noted in his transfer summary that Tyrone had made very little, if any, progress. One piece of historical material relevant to understanding this sequence of play is that Tyrone had been adopted at birth, and shortly afterward his parents had conceived three (female) children in fairly rapid succession.

Tyrone approached the dollhouse and began to portray a newlywed couple excitedly looking forward to the prospect of "humping" and making a baby. His play was driven and proceeded at a fast tempo. When the dolls began to have sexual intercourse, Tyrone could not resist introducing himself into the play as the giant. He pulled down his pants to "hump" the female doll with his erect penis, then passed her over to his therapist. Rather than participate in the manner Tyrone was suggesting, the therapist remarked that thinking about sexual things made Tyrone so excited that he could not stick with the play. Tyrone responded by putting his clothes back on and continuing his story, although, not before turning his backside to his therapist to point and say, "This is my asshole!"

After making two babies, the couple adopted a third. "That's me," Tyrone stated. "That's Tyrone?" the therapist inquired. "No," Tyrone replied. "I'm the one they had. They adopted the girl." Evidently Tyrone's attempt at defensive reversal (making himself the natural child and "demoting" the daughter to adoptive status) after having touched upon this area of conflict was insufficient to contain the anxiety which had been aroused, and so he made a quick regressive shift to wild acting up which combined sexual, aggressive, and "babyish" behavior. He darted into the secretarial pool shouting, "Pussy!" From behind a desk he fired staples at his therapist and threatened to throw a cup of coffee on him if he kept approaching. The therapist stopped and tried to talk, but Tyrone threw the coffee anyway. When the therapist succeeded in getting Tyrone back to the treatment room, Tyrone scrambled under the desk where he began to crayon provocatively on the walls. He made it difficult for his therapist to stop this messy acting out by hiding the crayons in his mouth whenever his therapist tried to take them away.

This vignette illustrates the enormous difficulty these children have in maintaining any kind of a safe area in which they can talk or play out their concerns. Sublimated play activities too easily break down into raw enactments of sex and violence, and the displacement barrier between "the producer" of the play and the play figures is also so weak that the direct personal relevance of the material cannot be safely disguised and distanced for long. Threatened with what Redl and Wineman (1951) referred to as "case history flooding," these children flee from the anxiety-arousing material and throw themselves into a whirlwind of provocative acting out. At this they are exceedingly adept. It enables them to feel perversely in control as they turn the tables so that the therapist becomes the one with the difficult control problems while the child indulges in an orgy of acting out, excitedly flooding the therapist with a torrent of wildly driven behavior. By a total commitment to creating chaos and struggle, the child makes it all but impossible for the therapist to address any of the truly salient issues in a therapeutic manner.

As the therapist becomes more familiar with the child and the nature of his or her disorder, he or she may come to realize that even at times as unwieldy as those portrayed, it may not be inappropriate to gently but firmly interpret the meaning of the child's behavior, even at the same time that physical restraint is applied, and even though such conditions do not seem in any way to resemble optimal textbook circumstances for interpretive work. Thus, for example, as Tyrone's obstreperous crayoning began to become less frantic and more repetitive—that is, when it was no longer so necessary for binding his initial rush of anxiety and was beginning to take on secondary gain as a good way to provoke and frustrate the therapist—at that point the therapist could begin to interpret how all this wild and regressive action served to defend against frightening feelings, that evidently even to begin talking about his concerns about being adopted and then having three sisters come along, was very, very upsetting, so much so that he believed it simply was not safe to discuss and was therefore willing to do just about anything he could to get far away from those feelings, even if he had to act in a way that he knew was not right. While making such comments, the therapist must be attuned to how the child is reacting, being careful not to flood him with interpretation and being ready to step back if the child becomes too anxious. In terms of countertransference (or simply negative counterreactions) the therapist who has just had a cup of coffee poured on his white shirt needs to be careful that he does not use interpretation as a means of getting back at the child—hitting him with an overwhelming interpretation which throws him back into the anxiety-laden material that he was frantically struggling to avoid, rather than supporting and clarifying things for him.

Because these children have such problems in symbolically communicating their concerns, they usually abandon the attempt to do so. They feel safer in more structured activities that are less likely to activate such intense drives and anxieties. They may thus prefer to play board games or cards. With many other kinds of patients, a therapist might want to discourage such games since they do not facilitate the portrayal of the child's inner world the way other play modalities do, and some children want to play them largely for this reason, as a form of resistance to the therapeutic process. However, as the dollhouse vignette showed, other more revealing modalities of play are often too threatening for the hyperaggressive child. Rather than stimulating a gradual unfolding of therapeutic material and interaction, they may trigger wild acting out. Expecting the child to participate in such play may increase his or her fear and consequent avoidance of the therapeutic situation. The therapist may therefore welcome the child's suggestion that they play checkers or rummy. He or she may even propose this to a child, for example, to one who is refusing to come to therapy after having had a number of upsetting sessions like the one previously described. The game then serves as a vehicle for interaction and a buffer against threatening intimacy. It helps the child to stay in the treatment room, keep his or her behavior within reasonable bounds, and not dread the prospect of therapy. Of course, if playing games permitted no more than this, one could scarcely call the experience psychotherapy. Fortunately, this is not the case. The games can help to set the stage for meaningful interaction. Often they make it possible for the child to look forward to sessions with a modicum of pleasureable feeling—and this may enable him or her to tolerate some of the more difficult aspects of treatment.

Needless to say, since hyperaggressive children are so narcissistically vulnerable, even these structured games do not guarantee smooth interaction. Games inevitably bring up issues of winning and losing which are very threatening for these children because of their profound problems with self-esteem regulation. The following vignette from the beginning phase in the treatment of Luis, a 12-year-old hyperaggressive child, illustrates many of these problems. In his therapy, games had quickly become established as the major modality for interaction. Luis consistently maintained a fiercely competitive stance. When capturing a chess piece, he would often knock it halfway across the room. He cursed his therapist for being too slow as well as for "always rushing" him. He accused him of cheating, not instructing, and trying to show off. Any attempts to discuss these charges met with angry shouts to get on with the game.

One day when his therapist won a game, Luis threw all the men on the floor. Proclaiming himself to be the winner, he ordered his therapist to pick them up. Eventually he grudgingly agreed to participate with his therapist in picking the pieces up. However, when his therapist began to take the lead in the next game, Luis leaped up furiously, his eyes brimming with tears of frustration and rage. He cursed his way downstairs and burst onto the ward, declaring his intention to "break his [therapist's] ass." Seizing a pool cue, he charged back up to his therapist's office. The door was closed since the therapist had left but Luis assaulted the door anyway with feet, fists, pool cue, and curses.

This incident captures much of the essence of the explosive character pathology which brought Luis to treatment. Losing the game evidently engendered a traumatic loss of self-esteem, an intolerable sense of humiliation, powerlessness, and vulnerability. To repair the narcissistic injury, to restore a feeling of security and well-being, he had to deny the unbearable reality and reverse the situation, aggressively proclaiming himself to be the victor and ordering his therapist in a most demeaning manner to pick the mess up. This defensive maneuver helped Luis to achieve some psychic equilibration, but the resulting state was so unstable that the therapist's advance in the next game constituted an overwhelming stress to which Luis could only react with tears, flight, and a furious, armed attack. Being beaten was so intolerable that he had to reverse his experience of the situation and literally try to "beat" his therapist.

The element of violence in this vignette also raises the issue of the necessity, when working with violent children, to take certain precautions with regard to safety of property and person. If the therapist conducts treatment in his or her own office, it should not contain highly cherished objects that could be destroyed easily. The therapist will be able to relax more and concentrate more fully upon the patient if he or she works in a playroom with few and relatively indestructible furnishings. The therapist should not wear clothing so fine that if it were torn or smeared with ink, irreparable damage would be done to his ability to cathect the patient positively. Male therapists usually opt to leave their neckties elsewhere during sessions with these children since they are too easily grabbed and pulled, sometimes beyond the ability to resume their former shape. In working with children with particularly weak controls and particularly strong, primitive sadism, one needs to bear in mind that a small metal truck or an ashtray can do serious damage if thrown at one's head. Such children are also not above delivering an unexpectedly swift blow to the therapist's genitals. Knowing that such events are possible, the therapist will be less likely to be caught completely off guard should they occur and may be in a better position to prevent serious injuries. A female colleague, undoubtedly tired of bruised, sore shins from her work with an extremely violent girl, prepared for a stormy phase of treatment by wearing shin pads underneath her slacks. This was an unusual measure, but certainly an understandable one. During periods of treatment when aggressive acting out is especially severe, a more common practice is for therapists to have a member of the ward staff waiting outside the treatment room to assist in restraining the child or to escort the child back to the ward to settle.

We hope these cautionary suggestions will not frighten or turn off any person who might otherwise be interested in treating these children. The purpose of mentioning these very concrete realities is to facilitate work which is difficult but not impossible and which can ultimately be a rewarding experience for both parties. It is just that one may never reach that point if one's therapeutic optimism is repeatedly crushed by experiences such as: "I'm not surprised that he'd try to knock my glasses off my face. But that he actually stomped on them!" Knowing that he well might, a therapist might take precautionary measures a little more quickly than usual.

After an explosive session like the one with Luis described previously, the therapist will likely realize that it is important to comment upon any signs that the patient is becoming anxious, angry, tense, or in any other way upset during the course of the game. The patient will typically react angrily to any such observations, threatening the therapist with dire consequences should he or she continue talking. Nonetheless, it is usually prudent for the therapist to firmly, albeit sympathetically, insist (and explain) that they should discuss the feelings and thoughts which are disturbing the child before they become so strong that the child cannot stop him- or herself from throwing the game and everything else onto the floor, then storming off, thereby ending their work together and leaving the child feeling badly about his or her loss of control. By doing so, the therapist functions as the child's auxiliary ego/superego, providing him or her with important warning signals. In Luis' case, the success of this therapeutic strategy was pleasantly evident after several months when Luis began to make remarks during games like, "I can tell I'm really angry 'cause I'm cussing so much!" These comments indicated that he was beginning to integrate this observing, warning function into his own ego, rather than ignoring his mounting tension until it had increased beyond the point of no return.

In some cases, not even board games suffice to help the child feel that therapy is a safe place. Trying to get such a child to stay in, or even come to, the treatment room can become a major technical problem. At a certain phase in Tyrone's treatment, for example, he began acting up the minute his therapist arrived to pick him up for therapy. He demanded to have his sessions outside and would pay no attention to his therapist's attempts to explain why it was better to have therapy in the same place at regularly scheduled times. Even if he finally did go to the treatment room, he usually ran out during the course of the session. Frequently he even ran out of the hospital, and when his therapist caught up with him outside, Tyrone would fight no holds barred against any attempt to get him to go back inside.

Ultimately the therapist felt it necessary to negotiate a compromise, acknowledging with Tyrone that for some reason it seemed too threatening for him to stay in the treatment room, whether because of his fear that he would be surrendering too easily, or that talking would be too scary, or for some other reasons. They agreed to alternate one session outdoors (weather permitting) with one session in the regular treatment room. Needless to say, Tyrone continued testing this therapeutic contract in every conceivable way (e.g., "Let's have our session outside again today since the weather's so nice and it may not be for my next outdoors session two days from now. After that, I promise I'll come to the treatment room for two sessions in a row.") When the therapist insisted that they stick to *their* agreement and explained the reasons why, Tyrone was able to keep to the contract.

In psychoanalysis, the "fundamental rule" is for the patient to say everything that comes to mind. Obviously with these children the fundamental rule is much more basic, namely to stay in the room for the allotted time. The child's agreement to do so, despite occasional resistance, can be seen as the beginning of a therapeutic alliance, albeit on a very basic level. To illustrate this idea further, Tyrone's testing sometimes seemed to have the quality of a game, a relatively light-hearted teasing/testing of his therapist rather than an all out argument about their arrangement (as had previously been the case). At these more playful times, his demanding and complaining cleared up relatively quickly in response to his therapist's firm uncorruptibility, with Tyrone's protest mellowing into a smile as if he at least partly appreciated not getting his way when to do so would sabotage the long-range agreement which, at some level, he seemed to know represented an important alliance (and that his basic problem had always been his inability to sustain a progressive alliance with anyone).

The preceding vignette can also be seen as an illustration of the need to find an appropriate balance between frustration and gratification with these children who are so ready to see adults as depriving, unloving, and hateful. If the special parameter enables the child to participate in treatment, then eventually it should be possible to suggest to the child that he is no longer so much in need of such special arrangements, that he has grown considerably in terms of his ability to tolerate some frustration of his wishes, and to express his feelings in words, etc. The child may then be ready to agree, for example, that only one of his three weekly sessions needs to be outside, or that when fall comes they can phase this parameter out entirely. The child's capacity to agree to such progressive modifications in the therapeutic contract in the direction of the regular "basic rule" represents important strengthening of the therapeutic alliance.

The Play Behind the Action

It is possible to apply some findings from recent psychoanalytically oriented developmental research to our understanding of the significance of certain patterns of problematic behavior manifested by hyperaggressive children in play therapy. For example, family observations by Tooley (1974, 1977) suggested that mothers of aggresive-children-to-be do not keep a close enough eye upon their children as they go through the highly mobile phase of toddlerhood and that they consequently fail to protect their offspring from excessive hurts as they run, climb, and explore the world (cf. Settlage, 1977). One can easily imagine that children who are relatively neglected with regard to appropriate supervision (and soothing after their many bumps and falls) might come to feel that their parents do not care enough to keep a loving, watchful eye on them (the disregarded self). When hyperaggressive children are seen in psychotherapy, one can observe certain behaviors which can be understood as attempts to test for and elicit the type of hovering, mildly anxious, parental concern with its warnings, prohibitions, and physical interventions that a toddler would ordinarily get from his lovingly attentive parent. For example, 12-year-old Tyrone constantly got himself into the most precarious and dangerous of predicaments. No ledge was too high or too narrow for him to climb and crawl along. His daredevil feats had staff contantly amazed, alarmed, and anxious about his safety. Tyrone himself acted as if he were totally unconcerned about the possibility of hurting himself. When his therapist cautioned him not to pursue his skateboard should it go onto the road or into the path of a car, Tyrone denied that he should consider his own safety because the skateboard was worth 20 dollars. It was a long time before he could express the perverse satisfaction he derived from the anxious concern which he stimulated in his therapist. "I had you scared out of your pants!" he asserted with sadistic glee after coming down from a tall wire fence he had scaled. When he was able to admit this, it also became possible for him to begin acknowledging that he, too, was sometimes a bit scared by the situations into which he got himself. Tyrone did not instantly stop climbing to dangerous heights, but he did begin to ask questions like, "What would happen to me if I fell? Would I break a leg? . . . Will you stand under me so you can catch me just in case I fall?" Thus even though he continued to indulge some of these exploratory, thrill-seeking impulses, his behavior was no longer quite so driven, provocative, and dangerous. It had come to have a slightly more cooperative, interpersonally responsive quality as he became able to ask more openly for closer supervision and guidance.

It thus seems that hyperaggressive children in therapy have a conviction that their transference parent figures will not care enough to watch out for their safety and that they must therefore coerce them to do so by engaging in behaviors with compelling stimulus/arousal value. This style of forcing close caretaking while acting as if that were the last thing they wanted can be understood as a form of masked dependency. To consider some of the provocative, counterphobic behaviors of these children in light of such hypotheses opens up various interpretive possibilities and helps to free the therapist from getting exclusively tied up in anxieties and negative feelings about children who just will not mind, who seem to have no concern for their own safety, and so forth.

It is not only by getting themselves into dangerous situations that aggressive children attempt to elicit concerned behavioral monitoring akin to what a toddler's good mother would show; during toddlerhood, mothers of aggressive-children-to-be may also fail to protect their offspring from pursuing courses of action likely to make other people furious at them, for example, knocking over a lamp, spilling coffee on grandmother, urinating on daddy's lap (Tooley, 1974). During psychotherapy, aggressive children may try to obtain this type of helpful guidance from their therapists. Initially, and depending upon the degree of disturbance, such motivation may be vigorously denied and the behavior may simply appear to be aggressively provocative. For example, the child may regressively indulge in throwing objects around the treatment room, giving no indication that he or she would like to be prevented from doing this, except perhaps for a brief smile or excited laugh that may occasionally slip out when the therapist actually moves to stop this destructive acting out. Further along in treatment, these children may express their longings for good toddler parenting in less hostile disguise, even making a game out of it. During a phase of treatment lasting several weeks, Tod began to progress from actually messing and destroying things in his therapist's office to more playfully attempting to firm up his image of a concerned parental figure who would reliably limit him from indulging in actions which could lead to hostile rejection. He began asking his therapist: "Would you get mad if I looked in your desk drawers? . . . Or dumped things all over the floor? . . . Would you get mad if I went back to school without escort? . . . If I broke the 'Exit' sign? . . . Would you be firm with me if I knocked down the shelf? . . . What would you do if I . . . ?" Climbing onto his therapist's desk, he insisted that the therapist name those objects he could not walk on (not the dictaphone, not the ashtray, not those papers) as opposed to those places where he could place his feet! In this rather striking behavior for an 11-year-old "tough guy" it is easy to discern his need to create a regressive, reassuring situation in which he could feel he was getting a very particular type of parental concern.

Another good example of developmental research which can be applied usefully to increasing our understanding of certain behaviors of hyperaggressive children has been done by Kleeman (1973). He discussed a developmental line related to the mastery of separation anxiety and the integration of autonomy which can be observed during the second year of life in a sequence of play proceeding from active peek-a-boo to object tossing, being chased, hiding, early hide-and-seek, the bye-bye gesture, verbal bye-bye, and other uses of language. The steps in this series of games connote increasing levels of confidence that the object is still there and that reunion will occur, thus expressing and contributing to the growth of basic trust. In therapy with aggressive children, one can observe initially driven, defiant efforts at running away from the therapist mellow gradually into increasingly playful games of chase, hiding, hide-and-seek, and even bye-bye type games. The initially driven, antisocial quality of their "play" reflects the fact that for aggressive children this developmental line is fraught with additional anxiety and aggression due to the child's conviction that for some reason he cannot count on being able to engage and sustain his caretaker's interest in playing such developmentally important games.

Central to the second year of life are issues of separation from mother and separate functioning, or "holding on and letting go" (Erikson, 1950). While at first glance the aggressive child might seem to be running away from the therapist, defying him or her and the whole therapy business, the child may actually be trying to "hold on" to the therapist's attention in a very controlling manner. In many cases, if the therapist does not play this unacknowledged game of "chase me" (hoping perhaps to extinguish it by nonreinforcement) the child will escalate the implicit demand to be pursued and held by adding various increasingly provocative, destructive elements to the game. He or she may, for example, steal the secretary's cigarette lighter, block and overflow the toilet, head for the copying machine to press the button to make 999 copies of nothing, and so on. The therapist is likely to learn that if he or she does not play the proper part in the game by pursuing the patient, he or she may be faced with some very undesirable consequences.

It is a relief for both patient and therapist when the child can finally trust that the therapist does care about him or her so that rather than really running away, the patient can simply hide in a relatively obvious place and enjoy watching the therapist come looking. The therapist may add to such fun by wondering aloud where the patient could possibly be, etc. It can be quite striking to see how even some of the most defiant "tough guys" can come to enjoy such "nonsensical" verbalizations as part of the game. The following vignette further illustrates this type of progression from antisocial acting out to play. When Tyrone's therapist accompanied Tyrone back to his classroom after their sessions, Tyrone typically announced his arrival by pounding and kicking the classroom door in an abusively impatient manner. His therapist, initially shocked by such displays of aggression, would speak to Tyrone about his need to be more patient, about the inappropriateness of such behavior. He also physically intervened at times to stop Tyrone from continuing these actions. As Tyrone's general level of hostility and defiance began to diminish and progressive forces in his personality began to increase, he was able to create a new game in which he would knock on his teacher's door, then playfully hide, sometimes excitedly telling his therapist to inform his teacher that he had "run away." It was obvious that Tyrone just wanted to enjoy his teacher's surprised concern a little before popping out of his hiding place to get some additional enjoyment from his teacher's further "surprise" at such an "unexpected" reunion. It was a delight for everyone to see Tyrone's previously driven, joyless behavior evolving into this humorous game.

In sum, much of the action which dominates play therapy with hyperaggressive children can be understood as a manifestation of arrested and distorted development in the sphere of object relationships and, more particularly, in the development of interactive play. During psychotherapy one sees driven, aggressivized, and sometimes sexualized manifestations of this blocked play development. If treatment continues long enough, one can observe these issues being worked through such that healthier versions of early developmental play emerge as the child returns to where he or she got stuck and eventually begins to progress along a more normal developmental track. Understanding some of the apparently unsocialized or antisocial behaviors of these children and their relative inability to play in terms of blocked play development can open up avenues of interpretation for therapists whose interventions might otherwise be restricted to behavioral management.

CASE ILLUSTRATION

Presenting Problem and Family Background

Sean was referred for psychiatric evaluation at the age of 10, shortly after he and some friends had been apprehended by the police for breaking into a building, kicking holes in the walls, and setting a number of fires with cigarette lighters stolen from a nearby store. This particularly alarming incident occurred within a context of generally problematic fucntioning. Sean's academic performance had been deteriorating over the past year. School personnel reported that he would not follow directions and he had been expelled from the school lunchroom because he was always fighting with other children. His mother also reported that Sean would not listen to her and that he was given to violent outbursts during which he would slam doors and smash toys. She was also worried about Sean's fantasies of stealing a gun from a relative in order to shoot his mother, his eight-year-old brother, and himself. It also appeared that Sean's mother was inappropriately seductive with him and was having difficulties setting appropriate limits around the nature of his physical contact with her. During the course of the evaluation, Sean ran away from home, although this was apparently a brief episode.

Sean's mother had become pregnant, and therefore married, in her midteens. Several months later her husband was drafted and sent to Vietnam. He reacted to this stressful turn of events by sexually acting out in a manner which strained the marriage. After his tour of duty, Sean's mother and father lived together for a few months until Sean's mother decided to leave her husband and go stay with her grandparents. One reason Sean's mother left her husband was that he had spanked Sean so hard for wetting his pants that he bruised his buttocks. Sean was one-and-a-half years old and he had a brother who was three months old at the time of this separation.

Sean formed a strong postive attachment with his grandfather, but this was frequently stressed by separations. Sean's living situation was repeatedly disrupted by his being shuttled back and forth between his grandparents' and his mother's home. Sometimes the reason Sean's mother sent the boys off to their grandparents was her fear of her own abusive potential and, indeed, she had hit Sean a number of times. When Sean was seven, his mother remarried, but a year later Sean lost this stepfather through another divorce. Babysitters played a large role in Sean's upbringing, although the boys inevitably managed to drive all sitters away with their unruly behavior. Thus Sean's life prior to treatment had consisted of many separations and losses, harsh physical punishment, and inadequate parenting from an immature, overwhelmed mother.

Because of the serious and deteriorating nature of Sean's clinical picture, it was recommended that he be admitted to a residential facility which could provide intensive psychotherapy for Sean as well as parent guidance for his mother and family therapy at a later date.

Course of the Psychotherapy

The following description of Sean's psychotherapy is necessarily highly condensed. Its purpose is to provide some sense of the process of long-term treatment and to demonstrate the relevance of some of the theoretical concepts presented earlier, in terms of how they manifest themselves and are to some extent resolved during the course of intensive, psychoanalytically oriented psychotherapy.

Early Manifestations of the Disregarded and the Devalued Self.   Much of Sean's therapy was composed of complaints that the staff in general, and his therapist in particular, were not caring for him properly. In his very first session, he complained that the child-care workers were weird and mean. He had asked a couple of them to supervise him so that he could play kickball, but they had informed him they were too busy. When he checked back 20 minutes later, they were still "just sitting around doing nothing." There seemed to be no doubt in his mind that they just were not interested in him.

A few weeks later, after Sean had become accustomed to the pattern of spending weekdays at the hospital and weekends at home, he asked his therapist why he had not asked him how his weekend had been, emphasizing that "everyone else" had asked. He clearly feared that his therapist's failure to inquire was indicative of a profound lack of concern.

Sean's complaints revealed his underlying worry that adults just don't care about him, that somchow he doesn't have whatever it takes to engage the concerned interest of his supposed caretakers. This negative expectation, which he carries with him into all new situations and relationships, reflects that aspect of self-structure which I called the disregarded self. Sean himself articulated this basic outlook when talking to his mother about his suicidal/homicidal thoughts prior to hospitalization. He told her that he felt like he was a bother to the whole world. At the hospital, it was apparent that he was continuing to worry that no one would ever really want to be bothered with him.

Related to his conviction that staff were not genuinely interested in him was Sean's belief that all the other children had nicer therapists. As early as his second session, he complained that his doctor was the only one who did not give toys to his patients. (Sean's therapist did provide him with a drawer full of play materials but, like most therapists, he would not allow these toys to be taken from the treatment room.) Sean's chronic complaint about not having enough toys reflected his feeling of being disregarded relative to other children and seemed related to his intense sibling rivalry. At home he used to beat up his younger brother, frequently giving him a bloody nose or mouth, while in therapy he tried to steal or smash the toys which his therapist kept in separate drawers for his other patients, Sean's transference siblings, whom he hated openly.

That facet of self-structure which I termed the devalued self was also strikingly apparent from the beginning of Sean's treatment. In his second session, for example, he asked his therapist if he liked fishing. His therapist wondered why this question was important to him. Sean replied that if his therapist did not like fishing, then Sean would not like him. When questioned about this reasoning, Sean said that it would not really matter if his therapist didn't like to fish, but what would matter was if his therapist considered fishing to be gross, disgusting, and stupid. Then Sean definitely would not like him. He was evidently worried that if he were to reveal what was meaningful and important to him, others would consider *him* to be gross, disgusting, and stupid, and would turn away with revulsion and contempt.

Sean's view of himself as repugnant and unloveable was also apparent in one session in which he was trying to build a truck out of Lego blocks. Frustrated that his production kept falling apart, he finally cursed it as "shit on display" that everyone could smell. Although Sean would undoubtedly have liked to believe that he was merely describing a contemptible object "out there," his description clearly reflected how he was feeling about himself—that he was a no good, yucky kid who couldn't do anything right, that anything he made could only be a reflection of the contemptible object he was, and that everyone would necessarily be repulsed by him and his products alike. It is not surprising that he would not want to acknowledge such a grossly devalued self-image and that he would desperately try to externalize it onto other people and things. During the next several months of therapy, in session after session, Sean characteristically stormed out of the treatment room yelling at the top of his lungs so that everyone could hear that his therapist was an ass, an asshole, and shit. It was a long time before Sean was able to begin dropping this aggressive, externalizing defense and admit, for example, that he could see no reason why his therapist would not dislike *him.*

Play with Toys.   Sean did not often use toys to enact fantasies although sometimes he did enjoy playing out (and, less frequently, drawing) explosive battle scenes. Sadistic anal themes were clearly in evidence. In one war, for example, a toy tank blasted a cannon. The cannon yelped "like a dog." Sean explained that dogs yelp like that when shot in the rear end with a BB gun. During another war he informed his therapist that the army sometimes shot people not to kill them, but to make them suffer, for example, by shooting them in the rear end. These anal sadistic themes were strongly reminiscent of the abusive toilet training which Sean had suffered at the hands of his father who beat him for wetting his pants until his buttocks were bruised.

Another time, while playing a "Battleship" game, Sean made it impossible for his therapist to say anything by drowning him out with obscenities. Finally his therapist commented that all this cursing and shouting seemed like a way of hitting with words. Sean seemed to hear this and he quieted down. Then he told his therapist that he would really like to thrash him once, to beat his ass. Refusing to elaborate this confirmatory material, he returned to hollering, "Asshole!" His therapist pointed out that he seemed to be trying to beat his ass with words, with curses. Sean began to put the Battleship game away, but then started pounding on it, so hard that he almost broke it. His therapist observed that a guy might want to beat things up when he feels he's been treated unfairly. "You've got it right!" Sean replied, in an unusually direct confirmation.

The Anger, the Depression, and the Play Behind the Action.   After he had been in treatment for about two months, Sean's sessions became extremely stormy. He would typically greet his therapist with a "Fuck you," or by calling him an asshole, underscoring his hostile provocation by giving him the finger. He would climb on top of the toy cabinet and kick it, overturn chairs, and threaten to break valuable objects like the dictaphone. In addition to his habitual cursing at his therapist, he began picking up the telephone to curse at whoever happened to be talking on the line. For a finale, he often made a huge mess, then ran out, perhaps returning for a moment to turn out the lights, spit into the room, and hurl a few more obscenities at his therapist. His therapist attempted to interpret this whirlwind of destructive acting out as Sean's way of stirring up excitement in order to get away from his thoughts about not getting any new toys and to get away from other empty feelings he had inside.

One day after Sean had stormed out of his session, his therapist overheard him saying to another member of the staff, "Why doesn't my doctor hold me like John's doctor does? Anything I do he doesn't grab me." In subsequent sessions, Sean's therapist was able to use this information. He told Sean that he could see that he wanted him to chase him and hold him and fight with him. Then they would really be far away from all those empty feelings that hurt so much inside. Sean seemed to hear this and calmed down for awhile, but then began to escalate again, throwing various objects at his therapist.

When Sean cursed on the telephone, his therapist interpreted that he certainly could not be ignored when he was behaving like that, and that was probably why he was doing it—to get attention and to get far away from his feelings of emptiness. He also interpreted many other meanings of Sean's acting out. For example, he pointed out how Sean wanted him to clean up the huge messes he made, just like a mother would do. Despite the accuracy of these interpretations, Sean's aggressivity, with occasional ebbings, generally increased. It seemed as if in addition to all the meanings of this behavior which his therapist was interpreting, Sean was bound and determined to do whatever was necessary to get his therapist to hold him. He finally succeeded in forcing his therapist to do this one day by running into the secretary's office and overturning chairs. When he headed for the typewriter, his therapist grabbed hold of him for fear that he might do serious damage. Sean, somewhat surprised, commented, "You're not hurting me." His therapist assured him that he was not trying to. Sean was soon able to confess that he did not like it when his therapist did not stop him from throwing and breaking things. They returned to the treatment room, but in a few minutes Sean ran into the secretary's office again. His therapist went after him and took hold of him, telling him to cut this out and that he was getting angry. Sean did not struggle hard and there was a sense that the whole thing was a game, unlike other times when the hostile, attacking quality predominated. Sean was even able to verbally confirm his "hidden agenda" by saying to his therapist, "I finally got you to hold me!"

Thus it appeared (as discussed in the theoretical section) that Sean felt a peremptory need to engage his therapist in action, to get him to chase him, stop him from throwing and breaking things, physically intervene, and hold him. It was as if he was saying via his behavior that words were not going to be an effective medium for reaching him and limiting his aggressivity. In so doing, he appeared to be expressing needs, frustrated developmental needs, from a preverbal period, likely from toddlerhood. Sean's repetitive drive to get his therapist to intervene physically brings to mind Winnicott's (1965) view that traumatic experience from the preverbal period is best, and perhaps only, communicated through action. Evidently during Sean's toddlerhood his mother was not available to attend to him, guide him, and help him to find constructive and appropriate channels for expressing his new energies and capacities. Instead, as she expressed it to the family therapist, she was so lost in her own depression that she was not very attuned to what was going on with Sean.

Needless to say, the concerns which propelled Sean's driven acting out were not instantly resolved by his "victory" in getting his therapist to hold him and stop his inappropriate impulsivity. Instead, these and other closely related themes continued to be addressed for the next several months. The cumulative impact of Sean's destructive acting out ultimately made it necessary for Sean's therapist to decide to move their sessions from his office down to one of the regular treatment rooms where there was little that could be damaged. Sean insisted that the door be left open, and seemed to enjoy the fact that his therapist felt the need to sit near the doorway to prevent Sean from running into the hallway. At a much later date he referred to this function of his therapist as "protection." Presumably he meant that he felt his therapist was striving to see that Sean did not pursue certain courses of action that could result in his getting in trouble, getting other people mad at him, or hurting himself. Protective interference one might call it.

Sean continued to hurl toys about the new treatment room and, with the door now being open, he could also throw objects out into the hall. His therapist interpreted this behavior to Sean as a form of play, likening it to the way a baby in a playpen or crib throws a toy on the floor. When his parent retrieves the object, the baby laughs and giggles. The baby then throws something else, his parent smiles and retrieves it, and so on. Sean declared that he never played that game when he was a baby, insisting that he just slept all day long. His therapist agreed that he may not have had much opportunity to play such games because his mother had been so tired and so wrapped up in her own concerns. Later on, when Sean demanded in session after session over a period of several weeks that his therapist play pool with him, his therapist interpreted that when he was little he must have wondered why his mother would not play with him more. He suggested that this very old concern lay behind Sean's current insistent demands to play pool.

Sean and his therapist were ultimately asked to leave the floor where the treatment rooms were located because of a concern that Sean's throwing objects out into the hall might hurt passers-by. Despite his therapist's attempts to run protective interference, Sean had still managed to alienate people with his object tossing and his lack of inhibition with regard to lashing out at passers-by with insults, threats, farts, and even an occasional kick. The process whereby Sean was moved first from his therapist's office to a treatment room, then from the treatment room to the ward, can be seen as a miniversion of the process by which these children are so frequently extruded right out of treatment institutions. Fortunately for Sean, he had a therapist, and his therapist had enough institutional support, so that these extrusions could be partial ones that merely resulted in some modifications in certain aspects of the treatment.

Sean's demands to play pool, came at a time when therapy was already being conducted in the ward's large dayroom where he had the privilege of playing ping-pong with his therapist. His therapist could therefore interpret that Sean's demands to play pool were also part of his old feeling that he never got enough, that people did not like him enough. He suggested to Sean that if he were to play pool with him, then soon Sean would be feeling that was not enough. He would still have those empty, unloved feelings, and would keep asking for more, and keep being dissatisfied, unless he could really talk about those feelings and come to understand them and work them through.

Sometimes Sean acted out by scribbling or writing "dirty words" on the walls, again enjoying this fairly reliable method of getting his therapist to intervene in a physical manner. His therapist interpreted how Sean's early development had been interfered with by his parents' divorce and the birth of his brother and that when he had seen his brother getting all kinds of attention from his mother, he undoubtedly felt that he was losing out and that he needed to figure out ways of securing his mother's attention, even if he had to resort to making a ruckus in order to ensure that he at least got a good dose of negative attention. Initially Sean reacted to any of these interpretations about his early relationship with his mother as if he were being attacked, and he responded in kind, shouting and hurling various objects at his therapist, or running away. Gradually, however, as his therapist sensitively worked out ways of communicating with Sean so as to minimize his sense of threat, Sean became increasingly able to hear these interpretations and sometimes he could even smile or laugh at their obvious timeliness and accuracy.

Signs of Progress.   During this working-through period, there were increasingly frequent signs that Sean's hostile, defiant stance was beginning to soften. He had put his therapist's therapeutic commitment through many harsh trials, yet it had not faltered. His therapist had not retaliated, nor had he lost interest or come to think poorly of Sean. He continued throughout to communicate clearly his intention of working to help Sean to understand the significance of his actions, to find more constructive ways of expressing his feelings, and to work through his fears and conflicts. Thus Sean's belief that he would necessarily be disregarded and devalued by any important adult was challenged and he began to understand something of the origins of these negative convictions, all of which made his antisocial stance less necessary and freed up his potential for developing a more positive relationship with his therapist (and others).

Initially Sean had found it necessary to act as if he did not care what his therapist thought of him. However, as he began to realize that his therapist might not despise him and that he might even consider him to be a worthwhile and even likable or at least potentially likable person, then he began to be able to allow himself to stop his defensive denial and begin to show that he did care about what his therapist thought of him. Thus he began to say that he would like to resume meeting in his therapist's office. He regretted having acted up so much and expressed concern that his therapist might be "disappointed" in him for having been so noisy and destructive. The idea that another person might be disappointed in him appeared to be a new concept for Sean. Previously he could only consider his own disappointment that his therapist (and others) were not doing enough for him. This new capacity, to be concerned about his therapist's disappointment in him, also implied that he could now believe that his therapist might be displeased with one aspect of his behavior without it meaning complete condemnation of his total self.

Not only did Sean express such regrets and hopes for a better future, but he also showed signs of committing himself to improving his image in his therapist's eyes. For example, he brought it to his therapist's attention that he had never stolen his keys the way some other patients had, and that he hadn't even stolen the jar of paint which he had once claimed to have stolen (back in the days when he was committed to being just about as bad as he could be). He even declared that he was tired of being "the bad guy." He shared a New Year's resolution he had made not to "throw hairies" during therapy, and he expressed pride when he eventually could reflect back upon a considerable period of time during which he had not indulged in such wild acting out. When he slipped back to his former ways, for example, by throwing something, he was sometimes able to take steps to prevent the usual escalation by reminding himself to "Be mature!" and saying to that old part of himself, "Get out, you delinquent!" Thus he was also beginning to show signs of being able to bear criticizing a part of himself without feeling that such criticism meant he was totally worthless "shit on display."

Sean's attitude and behavior also reflected a growing commitment to a more cooperative, mutually satisfying therapeutic relationship. After a quiet session of listening to records, he observed that they had not talked very much but that it had been fun for him. He wondered if his therapist had also enjoyed it. Back when he was convinced that his therapist couldn't possibly enjoy being with him, he would not have had any concern about his therapist enjoying the sessions. At most in those days he could aspire to make their sessions "not boring" by keeping the action revved up to an attention-grabbing level of "excitement," but the idea of their having a nice relaxed time together was scarcely conceivable. Now, Sean was also beginning to show a new respect for the formal structure of therapy, occasionally arriving a minute or two early or waiting out the last few minutes of a session despite his urge to walk out. There were even some signs that he was beginning to identify with his therapist's analytic perspective, as when he voluntarily told his therapist about a fight he got mixed up in, and spontaneously wondered *why* he had become involved.

Outcome. In the last few months of Sean's inpatient treatment, paralleling the progressive changes noted previously, one could also observe a shift in the content of Sean's material, from preoedipal, dyadic entanglement to more neurotic-like, phallic–oedipal material. Just as the previously noted progressive changes were mixed in with continuing aggressive acting out and defiance, so too were these phallic–oedipal strivings and conflicts mixed in with the older anal preoccupations and struggles. In short, preoedipal fixations in Sean's personality continued to exert a regressive influence upon the healthier developmental strivings which were beginning to emerge.

Nonetheless, after one year of residential treatment, Sean's therapist, and the whole treatment team, felt that Sean had improved sufficiently to return to his home and to public school. It was also felt that he needed to continue his psychotherapy on an outpatient basis. His therapist was able to continue working with Sean three times per week, and with his mother on a less frequent basis.

I had followed Sean's treatment during his inpatient stay as part of a larger study I was conducting on hyperaggressive children, but I did not follow the subsequent course of his outpatient therapy. I understand, however, that treatment continued for another year and a half and that progress was slow but reasonably sure and Sean's adjustment in the community was relatively good.

When treatment did end, it was unfortunately not an ideal, mutually agreed upon decision among child, parent, and therapist. Rather it had become necessary for the therapist to firmly confront Sean's mother on a circumscribed but important area of acting out in her own life which bore directly upon Sean's treatment. At this point his mother decided to terminate treatment. Thus whereas Sean had clearly benefited from both the inpatient and the outpatient phases of his treatment, due to the premature termination one would have to be somewhat more guarded prognostically than had Sean had the opportunity to achieve a more secure resolution of his characterological difficulties. To be optimistic, one might say that since Sean had had over two and a half years of helpful treatment, there is at least some foundation for hoping that if his current level of adjustment were to deteriorate, or if it simply proved unsatisfactory in view of the developmental tasks of his adolescence, then both he and his mother might be favorably disposed toward seeking further treatment.

SUMMARY AND CONCLUSIONS

One purpose of this chapter has been to fan the sparks of optimism concerning the treatability of hyperaggressive children. As mentioned earlier, working with these children can drive almost any therapist to the brink of burn out, if not beyond. For those who would turn to the clinical literature at such times in search of possible solutions to their therapeutic dilemma, there often do not seem to be quite enough solid guideposts to take hold of to sustain the long, uphill journey. We hope this chapter may have provided some useful insights and some sense that the path, while difficult, does not go endlessly uphill, or endlessly nowhere, but that it really can lead somewhere better, and that the severe obstacles encountered along the way—the chaos, the violence, and the defiance—are not without meaning.

Shields (1962) discussed how a delinquent child, when first admitted to a residential facility, may be relatively obedient and pleasant, to the point that one might wonder how he or she could ever have been described as impulsive, aggressive, sullen, cunning, and depraved. He believed that many institutions try to prolong this initial phase by encouragement and reassurance, and that "No attempt is made nor opportunity given for a thoroughgoing investigation into the nature of his real predicament" (p. 135). Consequently, when the child returns to a normal environment and ordinary family life, he or she tends to break down rapidly. The residential stay may have served to temporarily remove certain environmental stresses and perhaps to teach the child some new skills, but the underlying explosive, antisocial core and profound narcissistic vulnerabilities would not have been therapeutically engaged and worked through. These aspects of his or her personality persist, perhaps in a dissociated state. They constitute a dangerous potential which may readily reemerge at some future time when the child no longer has the ego supportive benefits of the tightly structured residential milieu. Obviously the approach advocated in this chapter consists of a very thorough exploration of the child's psychological situation, including the defensive, dynamic, and developmental features evident in his or her behavior. Such an uncovering or insight-oriented approach is also very much concerned with ego support and ego building, even though these two approaches are often talked about as if they were mutually exclusive.

Needless to say, this form of treatment is not only difficult but it is also very costly since the individual psychotherapy is only one component of the intensive, long-term residential treatment program. This financial factor is especially important in an increasingly stressful political-economic era when military expenditures are given ever greater priority over human welfare needs, raising the threat that it may become increasingly unlikely for these children to receive the treatment they need. These economic forces will undoubtedly lead to ingenious efforts to devise therapeutic technologies to circumvent the necessity of providing the child with an opportunity for a serious investigation into the nature of his or her predicament. Whereas these treatments may have the beneficial effect of, say, temporarily stopping the child from throwing books at a teacher and making a shambles of the classroom, the "cure" may not be long-lasting, and when the child is no longer a child, he or she may graduate to weapons more lethal than books, with tragic results that may shoot holes into and make a shambles out of the narrowly conceived cost–benefit analyses which served to short-circuit the necessary long-term, intensive treatment—treatment that the child and his family needed to have and that society needed them to have.

This section began with a statement about fanning sparks of optimism and has led to some serious concerns of an apparently opposite emotional valence. In a way though, quite apart from the economic considerations, such contrasting emotions are really part and parcel of the work with hyperaggressive children. New insights may help to maintain therapeutic hope and may lead to further useful insights, all of which may help to balance the negative counterreactions which inevitably arise in the course of working with obstreperous, destructive, acting-out children, but those stressful counterreactions will still arise. Play therapy with aggressive, acting-out children is therefore an undeniably difficult process, but it can also be an exciting and ultimately rewarding endeavor having highly significant benefits for the child and for all those destined to share his or her life space.

REFERENCES

American Psychiatric Association. (1980) *Diagnostic and statistical manual of mental disorders,* 3rd ed. Washington, D.C.: American Psychiatric Association.

Bahm, A. K., Chandler, C., & Eisenberg, L. (1961) Diagnostic characteristics related to service in psychiatric clinics for children. Paper presented at the 38th annual convention of the American Orthopsychiatric Association, Munich.

Bergman, P., & Escalona, S. (1949) Unusual sensitivities in very young children. *Psychoanalytic Study of the Child,* **3/4,** 333–352.

Berman, S. (1964) Techniques of treatment of a form of juvenile delinquency, the antiocial character disorder. *Journal of the American Academy of Child Psychiatry,* **2,** 24–52.

Boyer, L. B. (1971) Interactions among stimulus barrier, maternal protective barrier, innate drive tensions, and maternal overstimulation. In S. C. Feinstein, P. L. Giovancchini, & A. A. Miller (Eds.), *Adolescent psychiatry,* Vol. 1, New York: Basic Books.

Eissler, K. R. (1950) Ego-psychological implications of the psychoanalytic treatment of delinquents. *Psychoanalytic Study of the Child,* **5,** 97–121.

Erikson, E. H. (1950) *Childhood and society.* New York: Norton.

Glover, E. (1960) *The roots of crime: Selected papers on psychoanalysis,* vol. 2. New York: International Universities Press.

Kleeman, J. A. (1973) The peek-a-boo game: Its evolution and associated behavior, especially bye-bye and shame expression during the second year. *Journal of the American Academy of Child Psychiatry,* **12,** 1–23.

Levitt, E. E. (1971) Research on psychotherapy with children. In A. E. Bergin & S. L. Garfield (Eds.) *Handbook of psychotherapy and behavior change.* New York: Wiley.

Meltzoff, J., & Kornreich, M. (1970) *Research in psychotherapy.* New York: Atherton Press.

Michaels, J. J. (1955) *Disorders of character: Persistent enuresis, juvenile delinquency, and psychopathic personality.* Springfield, Ill.: Charles C. Thomas.

Redl, F., & Wineman, D. (1951) *Children Who Hate: The disorganization and breakdown of behavior controls.* New York: Free Press.

Redl, F., & Wineman, D. (1952) *Controls from within: Techniques for the treatment of the aggressive child.* New York: Free Press.

Schmideberg, M. (1959) Panel discussion, In B. Karpman (Ed.), *Symposia on child and juvenile delinquency.* Presented at the American Orthopsychiatric Association. Washington, D.C.: Psychodynamic Monograph Series.

Settlage, C. F. (1977) The psychoanalytic understanding of narcissistic and borderline personality disorders: Advances in developmental theory. *Journal of the American Psychoanalytic Association,* **25,** 805–833.

Shields, R. W. (1962) *A cure for delinquents: The treatment of maladjustment.* London: Heineman.

Soddy, K. (1960) *Clinical child-psychiatry.* London: Bailliere, Tindall, and Cox.

Stott, D. H., Marston, N. C., & Neill, S. J. (1975) *Taxonomy of behavior disturbance.* London: University of London Press.

Teuber, H. L., & Powers, E. (1953) Evaluation therapy in a delinquency prevention program. *Psychiatric Treatment*, **21**, 138–147.

Thomas, A., Chess, S., & Birch, H. G. (1968) *Temperament and behavior disorders in children*. New York: New York University Press.

Tooley K. M. (1974) Words, actions, and "acting out": Their role in the pathology of violent children. *International Review of Psychoanalysis*, **1**, 341–351.

Tooley, K. M. (1977) "Johnny I Hardly Knew Ye": Toward a revision of the theory of male psychosexual development. *American Journal of Orthopsychiatry*, **47**, 184–195.

Willock, B. (1982) Psychotherapy with hyperaggressive children. In E. T. Nickerson & K. S. O'Laughlin (Eds.), *Helping through action: Readings in action-oriented therapies*. Amherst, Mass.: Human Resources Press.

Winnicott, D. W. (1965) *The maturational processes and the facilitating environment*. London: Hogarth.

CHAPTER 22

Play Therapy for Borderline Children

RUDOLF EKSTEIN

INTRODUCTION

An eight-year-old boy comes for treatment; according to the parents he is out of control at home, in constant struggle with the younger sister, and full of violent rage against the mother. The father, a man also given to rage, tries to defend him.

The first sessions are uneventful. He puts plastic houses together, fills a playhouse with furniture but without parents, creates a domestic who lives and eats outside the house, and he keeps as far away from any expression of direct concern for his home situation as possible. His parents, he suggests, brought him here because he is not a good boy. The only wish he has is that I document him as a good little boy. He takes to me in a positive way and starts to look forward to the hours. After a few weeks of seeming avoidance he finds a way to get to me. He wants to use the tape recorder in order to tell a science fiction story and has me introduce him to an invisible radio audience. He tells a story of violence and murder, a space struggle, reminiscent of the space child whom I described 30 years ago (Ekstein & Wright, 1952). At the beginning and end of each hour he allows some participation on the part of the therapist. I am to introduce him and sign off at the end. The dialogue is minimal and most of what is said is directed to an unknown, nonexistent audience, really just a monologue. I may listen but I may not comment and I am merely used as a radio announcer. The cassette tape, filled with his story, brings him to comment about me in the end. He speaks now about his liking for me, and suggests that we develop a television script together, actually a videotape that he wants to produce for the trade. I am to be the manager, someone who might correct the script, but he himself is to be the main actor, the hero. He wants to be Superboy, to live somewhere in outer space, and come to Earth when the world calls him for a rescue mission. My modest questions concerning parents, friends of Superboy, and schools where he trains are bypassed while he develops the script. He is at first Superbaby in a Supership (a Supermommy?) on a faraway star. He becomes the Superboy, growing up like a fish in water and he, like the fish, does not need mother or father. In astonishment

I remember that our space child (Ekstein & Wright, 1952) had an almost identical fantasy. He puts on his Superboy suit which gives him the power to fly through the air and he lands on (Mother?) Earth. The landing place, however, is not a town or some flat land but is a mountainside, Mt. St. Helens in Oregon. It is the fire spitting mountain, rumbling from the earthquake. Would Superboy be devoured? Will his strength be greater than the earthshaking volcano (that enraged, rejecting mother)?

I will stop the clinical vignette here in order to use this illustration to get to the task of defining the concept of borderline conditions in childhood.

In 1954 we stated our task of understanding the borderland between psychotic and neurotic conditions as well as normal states of mind as follows (Ekstein & Wallerstein, 1954):

> He who ventures to accompany the borderline or psychotic child into the *terrain of his inner world* will find his journeys beset with many special hazards and bewildering phenomena. We refer not to *the fluid landscape* or to the archaic figures which emerge, coalesce and disappear, only to rise again in more monstrous display. For despite the dimness of the landscape, some maps have already been charted and reports of previous travelers are available for aid. However, even the most seasoned traveller will be puzzled by phenomena of *arrival and departure in this world of fantasy.* Once having communicated his readiness to embark upon these journeys in whatever guise the child requires, the traveler cannot but wonder at the exact moment and at the startling abruptness with which the voyages commence and terminate. Nor can he help but speculate that a knowledgeable grasp of *the time table* might provide him not only with more adequate preparation for the journey, but with the means for affecting the course and destination of his young guide as well.
>
> We describe children whose adjustment was marginally located in their use of both neurotic and psychotic mechanisms, a clinical group described as borderline, as schizophrenic-like, as severely neurotic, as acting out, and the like. Certainly, these children did not fit the kind of ideal classification that Kraepelin strived for, that researcher dedicated to thoroughness and excellence, and whose classification for psychotic disorders, whose delineation of the symptomatology has dominated diagnostic classification systems for a long period of time. A marked and frequent, often abrupt fluctuation in ego states as they emerge during the treatment process characterizes the patient group of concern to us. (p. 344)

My patient plays, without knowing, into a more recently developed metaphoric language of mine which uses, for the description of borderline states and disturbances, metaphors from geography. I speak about the borders between different countries when speaking of these "space children," lost in global wars and often fantasized as taking place in outer space and at times in inner psychological space. I am describing trips which also go into different time space: tomorrow, yesterday, millions of years ago, millions of years from now, but very rarely to the "here and now," which is avoided by such patients.

This child leads us from the megalomania of the Superbaby to the omnipotence of the Superboy floating somewhere in outer space. He is neither at home, in school or in this or that city, but coming to Earth on dangerous territory far away from people and without parents. He has landed on the fire spitting, devouring surface of a mountain that has come to life. The fantasy is certainly not the one that accompanied eight-year-old little boys in the days when I grew up. There is no Hans Christian Andersen or the Brothers Grimm. At best, as I try to look for similar fantasies, I recall the science fiction novels of Jules Verne which are much nearer to reality testing than some of the science fiction films of today, characterizing as they do, not only the advanced state of science but also the fantasy life of many of our patients.

I am not referring to dreams, but to active fantasy life in the waking state. In a recent communication (Ekstein, 1981) concerning dreams of children, I suggested that younger children do not differentiate well between dreams, daydreams, or fantasies. Frequently their dreams are more mindful of wish-fulfillment fantasies or of anxiety daydreams. There is a subtle connection between the play of children, their daydreams, and fantasies, respectively, and their dreams as they recall them in the therapeutic session.

METHOD

The Annotation of Play Behavior

One might well say that this child brings me a script for a movie, something that he plays with me, dividing the roles between us. He is to be the television star or the movie hero while I am to be the manager who will help him to have a more perfect script. The script that we have developed in active interpersonal play, the cassette being the up-to-date toy, travels into the past. It deals with the current situation and also allows predictions concerning his adaptive capacity as we look into the future. We play movie making together as we move through time and space and between time and space. The *script*, developed by the patient and annotated by me, could be treated like a dream, and directly interpreted. Melanie Klein (1932) suggested that the play of the child be interpreted like a dream, a view that I do not fully hold, as will be indicated in the discussion of my own way of dealing with the play material.

Superboy, as he comes down to Earth on his rescue mission, can be seen as a modern, postindustrial Oedipus. He gains his strength from spaceships, electronic devices, television sets, and other hardware. He comes down to Mother Earth, Jocasta, in the shape of Mt. St. Helens, in order to save her from the raging bull, the father figure who is to do violence to her. Superboy's rage is projected onto the dangerous father and at the same time the father is seen as helpless and weak, unable to withstand the strength carried by magic thinking and by timeless yearning for the mother. Ready for the rescue mission, he finds, however, the mother responding to the rage. He encounters counterrage, a fire breathing volcano, moving lava masses, and terrible devouring danger. The yearning for the mother, the good breast, the promise of milk and honey, turns into poison, the bad breast, a devouring fury, a deadly vampire. He must overcome the fire and the danger and feels deadly rage against her. He finds himself divided between eternal longing and bitter hate. An Oscar Wilde (1898) phrase, "each man kills the things he loves," characterizes the inner dilemma of my patient.

This is the nightmarish reality of my patient. The question now is how to enter such landscape, so different from the usual play of children his age who are embattled in neurotic conflict, but who are much nearer to reality testing. How are we to cross the border and venture out into a land where the brutal forces of untamed nature, the magic paranoid fantasies of the child and the "encounters of the third kind" are ruling? They are much nearer to the primary process than to the secondary process where reality testing becomes a part of problem solving and preparing productive solutions.

The play language of the child, his way of writing scripts, has to be "annotated"—that is, interpreted in such a way that the child can understand it, is not frightened, and is allowed to keep the process going. He must have the choice of remaining in the fantasy life of the borderline condition or at times taking forays into the social situation which we sometimes believe is the "real" one. But what we must consider is the special language maintained in order to prevail over his struggle for some kind of integrity and primitive identity.

I regret the loneliness of the Superboy who must travel alone to an unknown destination, to encounter a landing on Mother Earth which puts him right into that situation and moment where Mother Earth is most dangerous. Why does he, the Superboy, have no home, no kind parents, no friends? Why must he struggle all alone? The child reassures me that Superboy has lost his parents. They are dead. But somehow, maybe they are not dead and they will come to life again and will also be rescued. Here is the rescue mission again. Must Superboy rescue his parents? Or, is he afraid of his parents? We must never attack the role the boy has chosen, the identity that he must borrow from the science fiction films of our world. Rather, our annotations, like footnotes to an obscure work of the Middle Ages, are hints offered in such a way as to show him that we try to understand him; we must not impose on him a quality of insight that he cannot yet accept or comprehend.

Transitions Between the Reality of Play and the Reality of the Adult World

At times he switches from the science fiction movies and suddenly tells me that he had a terrible struggle with his mother. Some incident occurred and she would not allow him to use the same bathroom she uses. He should go to the other bathroom in the home. He always leaves her bathroom messy. He feels so angry and enraged that he wishes she were dead and he could kill her. He says that when I speak to his parents I should never mention this terrible secret of his. We understand each other and at that moment we almost travel in the usual world, his social world. He is willing to face the conflict, look at this rage that he cannot understand as well as his mother's rage and complaints that he has messed up her bathroom. He just thinks of the room, the bathroom. The nice, warm water is a symbolic representation of being reunited with her and undisturbed by the threatening sibling. The father may come to his rescue and try to calm the mother down. We have here an interesting version, as mentioned before, of a little would-be Oedipus who yearns for the mother. He wants to keep her out of danger, kill the father, but finds himself in a kind of alliance with the father, ready to kill the mother. It is as if Oedipus and Laius would unite to kill Jocasta. Instead of direct interpretation I offer metaphors, and we remain within the mythology, the private mythology the child has chosen in order to convey his problem to us. This is his secret and he can bring it to us only in his secret language. His play is a myth, an image of his inner life and, of course, it has truth in it. Behind the facade of the movie script is the suffering of a little boy who cannot contain his rage, his frustrations, and disappointments. His current solution is to become a mythical hero. And we know of the heroes of old; they never really win. Mythology of old is always a tragedy.

In mythology the hero of the tragedy dies. He may be resurrected centuries later as was Prometheus. First the gods punished him, and later, the ruling goddess, Pallas Athena, instituted a torch parade each year to honor Prometheus. Prometheus wanted to save the world of humans from the angry gods and brought the people the secret of fire; as Freud (1932) suggests, this marked the beginning of civilization based on the taming of fire.

My little patient in his private myth is a hero doomed to lose. He once said how much he likes to come to his hours with me and confirms that I have chosen my role well. I sought a form of interpretation that would allow him to see me not as an intruder or an educator, not as a person who forces him out of his fantasy world, but as simply one who annotates. That is, to make things more understandable rather than insisting on change. I am referring, of course, to the language of metaphor, a form of therapeutic communication which I have discussed at length in other communications. Metaphor allows a special relationship to develop between the child and the therapist.

There is a time in the life of the child when our way of building a bridge between his mind and ours is often carried by fairy tales and children's stories. We bring these stories to the child and allow him to use them as a bridge between inner and outer world, between himself and the parents, himself and the community. The time will come, usually in elementary school, when he will turn the play around. The initiative is not ours now, but his. He brings his fairy tales, his private mythology to us. Educators and therapists who think differently might want to modify this behavior, to counter his fairy tales with "fairy tales about the real world," a phrase used by Richard Gardner (1972). There may be moments when we want to do that. But in our case I am not concerned with behavior modification. I am concerned with building a bridge between soul and soul, between me and the child. I want to understand his mythology rather than force him to translate this mythology prematurely into concepts that allow for reality testing, that seem to be sociology or education. But we aspire to gain insight into the psyche—into the soul—rather than see the psychic mechanisms which rule the mind of the child as he ventures into the borderline world and invites us to follow him and understand him. We do not want him to be prematurely frightened into social tasks that he cannot resolve.

In another communication (Ekstein, 1980), also about borderline conditions in childhood and adolescence, I spoke about the need to help the patient gain a passport to cross borders between mental states—normal, neurotic, borderline, and psychotic states. But in order to make it possible for the patient to achieve the freedom of traveling, like free association, we must first have a passport of our own. And I suppose it is not enough to be well-analyzed to travel into the land of Oz, or into the Wonderland of Alice.

I believe therapists who work with such children, perhaps with all children or adolescents, not only should know the technical and theoretical literature but also should be concerned with fairy tales and children's stories, with mythology and religious myths of all countries, of all persuasions. Behind the language of faith, the language of magic, the language of hope, and the language of despair is psychological truth. We must learn this language and thus identify with the suffering of the child, with the meaning of his private mythology. In turn, at times he will internalize that part of us that wishes to understand him, that speaks his language. Then he may ask how to translate into our language, a language that he knows exists, a language that will help him venture out of his island of despair and secret, often forbidden longings to the mainland where the rest of us usually reside.

SUMMARY

My little patient has occasionally taken small excursions here to my land, to my usual way of talking. He comes across the bridge that we have built together and he looks around, but not for long. He withdraws to his land where it is safer even though it is at times lonely. In his fantasy life he is usually a hermit, a little Henry David Thoreau who must withdraw to Walden Pond, the land of the monologue. As soon as he, like his great predecessor, leaves Walden and comes to the city, he faces danger.

Skinner (1958) once wrote about *Walden II*, a world free of the fantasy of Thoreau but full of the conviction that conditioning will make this world safe. Thoreau or our child patient would need to give up the Walden fantasy and accept the reality of the postindustrial society. In my *Walden III* (Ekstein, 1974), metaphoric language rules, a language that builds a bridge between consciousness and preconscious, a security system by means of which we can turn the power of the unconscious away from being in endless danger of a Mt. St. Helens into a source of creativity. Could we then look at the play of the borderline child as one which reflects the conflict between the regressive and the adaptive, between the anxieties and fears of old, the trauma of birth and the trauma of growing, between the forces of growth and adaptation? Psychotherapy, that is, play therapy with such children is then the means to turn thesis and antithesis into synthesis, a combination of unconsciously fed creative fantasy and adaptive reality testing guided by new ego strength.

REFERENCES

Ekstein, R. (1974) Towards Walden III. *Journal of Loma Linda University School of Medicine,* **28,** 2, 5–17.

Ekstein, R. (1980) Borderline states and ego disturbances. In G. P. Sholevar et al., (Eds.), *Treatment of emotional disorders in children and adolescents.* New York: Spectrum Publications. Pp. 403–413.

Ekstein, R. (1981) Some thoughts concerning the clinical use of children's dreams. *Bulletin of the Menninger Clinic,* **45,** 2, 115–124.

Ekstein, R. & Wallerstein, R. (1954) Observations on the psychology of borderline and psychotic children. *Psychoanalytic Study of the Child,* **9,** 344–369.

Ekstein, R., & Wright, D. (1952) The space child. *Bulletin of the Menninger Clinic,* **16,** 211–224.

Freud, S. (1932) The acquisiton and control of fire. *The Standard Edition of the Complete Psychological Works of Sigmund Freud.* Volume XXII. London: Hogarth. Pp. 187–193.

Gardner, R. (1972) *Dr. Gardner's stories about the real world.* Englewood Cliffs, N. J.: Prentice-Hall.

Klein, M. (1932) *The psycho-analysis of children.* London: Hogarth.

Skinner, B. F. (1958) *Walden II.* New York: Macmillan.

Wilde, O. (1898) The ballad of reading goal. *Collected works of Oscar Wilde.* New York: Greystone Press.

CHAPTER 23

Play Therapy with Learning Disabled Children

LOUISE F. GUERNEY

INTRODUCTION

Until relatively recently in the history of education, it was assumed that a child with adequate vision, hearing, intellectual capacities, and a grasp of the official language (e.g., English) would learn without difficulty. Learning problems not explained by a deficiency in one of these areas were typically attributed to psychological causes (e.g., inadequate motivation or indifferent parents). However, recent advances have identified factors other than these which also contribute to adequate learning. Intactness of the peripheral and central nervous systems is required as well as certain psychic processes, for example, interest in the adult world (Johnson & Myklebust, 1967). *Learning disabilities*, in the current use of the term, is meant to apply only to problems in learning attributable to central nervous system dysfunction. Although the sense organs are intact, intellectual development measures are average or better, and in fact no major psychological disturbances exist, the learning disabled still fail to learn important academic and life skills. Problems in the central nervous system which interfere with sensorimotor processes seem to be at the base of learning disabilities. These problems can be very narrow, for instance, difficulties in auditory memory only, or affect many areas, including motor coordination and balance.

One of the early terms for designating children with neurogenically based learning difficulties was *minimal brain damage*. Because the term implied the presence of actual damage to an intact brain, it was abandoned in favor of the *perceptually impaired,* and somewhat later, *minimal cerebral or minimal brain dysfunction* (Clements & Peters, 1962).

Further description of the learning disabled frequently includes problems in attending and in impulse control. In fact, the latest term which appears in the DSM III 1980 is *Attention Deficit Disorder* (ADD). ADD is merely descriptive of the problem, as is the term *learning disability,* but many consider it preferable because it covers more than the problems of learning per se. Attention deficits may affect all facets of behavior, for example, listening to others, sustained play, or relationships of the child to space.

Whereas disputes continue about the labels and definition of this childhood difficulty, its incidence, and persistence into adult life, in this chapter we will adhere to the term *learning disabilities* (from here on LD), and in so doing will consider it to apply only to children with neurogenically based learning problems. This would exclude learning deficits due to poor teaching, early childhood illness, school phobia, or other nonphysical factors.

Hyperactivity

A number of LD children tend to suffer also from motor restlessness and motor hyperactivity (hyperkinesis). Therefore, it seems appropriate here to describe how this disorder relates to LD. Since all of these terms seem to be bandied about rather indiscriminately, it will be important for the student of play therapy techniques to have some clarity about the children for whom the play therapy methods to be described are considered appropriate.

The term *hyperactivity syndrome,* which has been replaced in the latest diagnostic terminology by the label *ADD with hyperactivity* DSM III, is applied to children who also display hyperkinesis and in whom no other basis for hyperkinesis exists. (This is a controversial issue, since the single symptom of hyperkinesis can be present in organic brain disease as well as in disorders and dysfunctions, e.g., ADD). Since it is the hyperkinesis that is most immediately apparent and the most troublesome to others, it tends to dominate in the assessments of these children. There are some hyperkinetic children who do not have academic difficulties, but most typically they evidence the following complex of behaviors: motor restlessness, impulsivity, short attention span, learning difficulties, and emotional lability (O'Malley & Eisenberg, 1973). Generally the term is restricted for use with children manifesting these behaviors and in whom organic pathology is absent.

Secondary Problems of LD Children

Researchers and practitioners concerned with LD children have consistently identified the presence of secondary problems in the areas of emotional and social adjustment (Bryan & Pearl, 1979; Ross & Ross, 1976; Wender, 1971). These problems are not part of the primary problem, but rather are outgrowths of the effects of the primary problem on the children's lives. Children's reactions to the experience of failure in school and in tasks at home can create these problems and also exacerbate the neurogenically based learning deficits. Because LD children see themselves as unable to achieve in spite of what might be heroic but nonetheless unsuccessful efforts, they assume that they are inferior and that they, unlike others, have little power to bring about desirable outcomes. Thus, they manifest poor self-concepts. Research on the locus of control indicates that LD children can become victims of "learned helplessness" (Dweck & Reppuci, 1973). This is demonstrated by the childrens' feelings that unless the work is easy or they receive external support of some sort, they are helpless to deal effectively with the learning environment. Such feelings of helplessness tend to be circular, that is, as the children feel it is useless to make attempts at mastery, they fall further behind, which brings them more negative feedback, which in turn reinforces the idea that they are failures. Parents and teachers learn to share in these views and further reinforce them (Bryan & Pearl, 1979).

Researchers examining intrinsic versus extrinsic motivation in LD children found that LD children are more dependent on external reinforcement because of earlier failure. Researchers concluded that delay in experiencing success creates further delay in experiencing the good inner feelings of efficacy which accompany competent interactions with the environment (Lincoln & Chazan, 1979).

As noted by Bryan and Pearl (1979), remediation on academic material only is not enough to overcome these attitudes of defeat and poor self-concept; "It appears that simply providing special education services will not offset the low teacher/mother (and child) expectations for learning disabled children." They recommend as a necessary intervention in this process the training of LD children to expect success by giving them projects which will result in success whenever they dare to try rather than rewarding them only for finished, complex products.

Children with LD seem to have relatively low social status in relation to normal children. This is apparently attributable to their poor ability at mastering the usual social cues and the fact that teachers devote more time to assisting them on purely academic tasks in contrast to "their more purely social or non-academic interactions with comparison children" (Serafica & Harway, 1979, p. 229).

These kinds of secondary relationship problems further lead to self-competence and self-confidence problems (Wender, 1971). Thus, the tasks for interventionists attempting to help LD children are greater than remediation of the learning deficits. Unless the LD child can be identified and his or her deficits overcome before environmental feedback takes on a negative tone, effects are likely to be destructive on the developing concept of self in relation to the social and learning environments.

Incidence

Various estimates have been made of the number of learning disabled children in the population at large. Of those with the hyperactivity syndrome, about 5% appears to be the most common figure offered (Arnold, 1973; O'Malley & Eisenberg, 1973; Wender, 1971). Figures which encompass the broader definition of learning disabled tend to be from about 5 to 10%. This would represent a sizable portion of American children. Some treatment centers estimate that the number of children that they see for diagnosis or treatment of LD and/or hyperactivity represent about half of their clientele. If this is even roughly accurate, it is certainly an inescapable fact that many of the children seen for presenting symptoms of underachievement, maladaptive social behavior, or other psychological problems are members of the great body of the learning disabled. Any clinician attempting to offer play therapy must recognize that when social and/or behavioral problems are the referring symptoms, the environmentally induced neuroses and intrapsychic conflicts presented may be secondary to neurological impairment (Freeman & Cornwall, 1980).

In describing play therapy, then, we will discuss its use with the broadest category of the learning disabled; this classification includes problems in learning to master academic work, limit motor activity, focus and refocus attention appropriately, master elementary motor coordination tasks (tying shoes, balancing bike, etc.), communicate verbally in appropriate ways, relate appropriately to peers, family, and teachers, be appropriate in emotional expression, and have some degree of diminished self-esteem and self-confidence. The reader should bear in mind that problems in some of the areas could occur at either extreme—too much (hyperkinetic) or too little (as in hypokinetic or underactive children)—or in slower speech development or excessive, compulsive-like verbalizing and noise making. Lest the reader feel that the LD classification can be applied to most clinical cases, it is important to remember that these behaviors have neurogenic origins. Thus, they may be considered behavioral manifestations of, or perhaps adaptations to, neurological dysfunctions of some type which interfere with the more usual cognitive processes.

Appropriateness of Play Therapy

It would appear that there is a clear need for intervention directed toward these secondary consequences or concomitants of learning deficits. Play therapy would seem very appropriate because its goals are to provide the child with a positive growth experience in the presence of a supportive adult. Thus, the child is able to discover internal strengths that cannot be revealed in situations where he or she must be guarded because of the evaluative aspects typically present in real life.

The opportunity to fantasize, as one example of an option provided in play therapy, permits the child to practice behaviors and experience successes that would be impossible in real life. However, such experiences do seem to promote more mature, adaptive behavior in real life (Singer, 1974; Speers, 1976) and assist in cognitive development (Yawkey, 1980).

Although LD children, particularly the hyperactive ones, are generally regarded as concrete in their thinking (O'Malley & Eisenberg, 1973; Wender,

1971), they are nonetheless capable of fantasizing as well as engaging in more realistic play, for example, ball games. Whereas Guerney (1979) observed less use of fantasy play by hyperactive-LD children in play therapy, Thompson and Wade (1974), in an empirical study of play, found that hyperactive children actually used more fantasy under certain play conditions than did normal children.

PLAY THERAPY TECHNIQUES FOR LEARNING DISABLED CHILDREN

History of Play Therapy with LD Children

The literature on child therapy tends to show a paucity of nonmedical interventions on behalf of the learning disabled which are not directed toward modification of specific behaviors. Goals of play therapy tend to be broader. Rather than trying to increase the child's attention span for arithmetic, as might the behavioral therapist, the play therapist of any persuasion will generally have a broader goal, such as increasing the child's ability to deal appropriately with his or her feelings or relating more appropriately to authority figures. Thus, comparison among the various therapeutic approaches is difficult when it comes to goal attainment (Pumfrey & Elliott, 1970). Most play therapists, however, will also aim to reduce the number and degree of specific symptoms or inappropriate behaviors. However, at this time there seem to be no studies which compare the effectiveness of behavioral and play therapy with the learning disabled. There are few reports on the use of play therapy with the learning disabled, most particularly with hyperactive children.

The question of treatment for the learning disabled with hyperkinesis has been raging for a long time (Connors, 1974; Wender, 1971). Since the use of stimulant drugs is often dramatically effective in reducing symptoms of hyperactivity, it is sometimes espoused as the treatment of choice, generally with recommendations for augmentation of parent counseling and modification of the environment at home and at school (O'Malley & Eisenberg, 1973). However, strong voices are heard against the employment of medication, particularly on the part of some parents. Advocates of the nonpharmaceutical strategy stress the importance of managing the child's environment—both social and physical, particularly dietary—so as to reduce excessive behaviors and increase attention span (Feingold, 1975). Strategists from the behavior modification school of therapy (Meichenbaum & Goodman, 1971; Patterson, Jones, Whittier, & Wright, 1965) address very specific behaviors only. They believe that this approach not only has the advantage of eliminating the use of medication, but also provides the means by which the child and his caregivers acquire new, more adaptive behaviors. Even advocates of the medical approach state that drugs are not an end in themselves: "They do not produce learning, they make it possible to learn . . . all of the treatment modalities must be included if the child is to benefit completely" (O'Malley & Eisenberg, 1973, p. 101).

The use of play therapy with learning disabled children does not require the clinician to take a position on the primacy of medical intervention or on the etiology of the problems presented. The play therapist can proceed to undertake therapy because of the developmental value of the play therapy experience for the child. Play in a special physical and interpersonal environment can permit learning disabled children to succeed and develop a feeling of satisfaction with themselves and their competences. The world of learning disabled children typically provides limited or at least very selective positive feedback as a result of the children's incompetence in important task areas. They may stop trying since they feel they have little effect. Permitting the child to master situations that are labeled "play" as opposed to "real" should make the threat of evaluation less heavy (Abramowitz, 1976; Dorfman, 1958).

Because of the previous lack of sophistication and current discrimination problems in relation to learning disabilities as a discrete diagnostic entity, it is certain that many children who have entered play therapy over the years have been learning disabled although unlabeled as such. In her 1947 book, *Play Therapy* (Axline, 1947), Virginia Axline (the developer of child-centered or nondirective play therapy, as it is also called) described a child who would probably be labeled LD in today's terminology. Axline described Emma as having an I.Q. of 112 and possessing a poor school record. She disliked school, was a behavior problem there, fought with and tantalized other children, and failed to respond to correction. She was labeled "maladjusted, antisocial, and a behavior problem" (p. 273) prior to successful completion of therapy.

Antisocial, impulsive, underachieving children who exhibited no blatant manifestations of brain damage or other organicity were referred for play therapy along with other children. However, as early as 1961, Ginott, in his book *Group Psychotherapy with Children* (1961), recognized that hyperactive children represented a special group among his nondirective play therapy clients. He considered hyperactivity the "hallmark of the *brain-injured* child, one who experiences forced responsiveness to stimuli." Some of the other behaviors he ascribed to brain damage are also currently classified under learning disability problems: "poor motor control, perseveration, social and emotional ineptness, and over-reaction to minutiae."

Ginott found the basic nondirective play therapy approach very suitable for these children. However, he did suggest that some of the stimulating toy materials—primarily finger paints and running water—be eliminated. He recommended instead toys which have focusing potential, for example, building blocks, sawing, driving nails, and shooting toy rifles. These "give form and direction to the disorganized urges of these children. . . . In an atmosphere of wise encouragement, the children's frustration tolerance will be enhanced and they will become able to focus energies on projects and goals, both in and out of the playroom" (pp. 55–58).

Types of Play Therapy Reported in Use with LD Children and Their Effects

For this section, descriptions of the types of play therapy and the reported effects will be presented in the order of frequency with which they appear in the literature. The first section includes the few empirical studies reported. Because all happen to have employed the nondirective play therapy approach, both individual and group formats, that method will be described in relation to the studies. Next in frequency of reported use are group therapy methods of various kinds for which there are no empirical data, followed by two reported individual approaches. A section on the use of parents as therapists will follow. In actual quantity, the number of reports on parents as therapists is the same as some of the other approaches. However, since the concept of parents as therapists introduces a new dimension into the treatment, which requires discussion, it will appear last.

The reader should bear in mind that the therapies and empirical findings reported here have been selected because their explicit application to LD children has been reported, or they have been used with children exhibiting problems which fall into the current definition of LD but the label or an equivalent one was not necessarily used. For example, the studies by Bills (1950a,b) of below-grade readers of average intelligence have been included because the subjects share the features of LD children, that is, academic deficit despite normal intelligence with no other organic pathology.

Nondirective Play Therapy.   Nondirective play therapy has been described in Chapter 2 of this book. Let us briefly review what the approach entails. In nondirective play therapy, children are given permission to express themselves verbally in any way they choose. Limits are placed on destructive *actions.* It is the child's responsibility to monitor his or her own behavior to stay within the limits, which are rigidly enforced. Toys are unstructured for the most part, that is, they can be used in many ways, for example, clay, paints, puppets, and building materials. No directions are given the child as to how or what he or she should play or talk about; the child leads the way. The therapist accepts the child's direction and expression and responds empathically. When offered extended acceptance and permitted freedom to exercise control over him- or herself, the child will drop undesirable behaviors and move toward more mature ones.

Studies Conducted.   Bills (1950a) was able to demonstrate that maladjusted third grade children with below-grade reading levels improved significantly in reading ability following six sessions of individual nondirective play therapy and three group sessions with all of the target children together. Reading tests were administered six weeks prior to therapy, immediately before and after therapy, and six weeks following the end of therapy. Thus, the children served as their own controls. When he repeated the study in the same way (Bills, 1950b) with *well-adjusted* below-grade readers, the same increase in reading was not attained. Bills posited that the improvement in personal adjustment accounted for the gains in the maladjusted children. In other words, deficits resulting from secondary adjustment problems were removed, but primary deficits were not.

Fisher (1953) also obtained improved reading in underachieving, delinquent boys with nondirective play therapy. This improvement was significantly better than progress made by a no-treatment control group.

Moulin (1970) conducted a study with 126 under-achieving school children in grades one through three. Ninety percent were black. He divided the number into treatment and control groups, further dividing the latter into small therapy groups by random assignment. Prior to treatment, he assessed the children with the California Short Form of Mental Maturity Test, the Illinois Test of Psycholinguistic Abilities, and the Children's Apperception Test (a personality test) for which he obtained a T-score (developmental level). He found significant differences between control and treatment children on tests of nonverbal ability, such as, visual–motor encoding. Even though significant gains on several others tests (e.g., vocabulary), were made by the treatment children, these did not significantly surpass those of the control group. Moulin concluded that the method was worth pursuing to increase attention span and other nonverbal skills.

GROUP PLAY THERAPY. Ginott (1961) makes a powerful case for the use of group play therapy as the preferred treatment for many young children. He sees "social hunger" as the crucial variable that indicates whether group therapy should be the treatment of choice. "The assumption is that the child will show toward the therapist and group members some of the same behavior which he shows toward his parents and siblings." Via the group interactions, these behaviors can be modified as needed to lead to more acceptable social status. Although, as mentioned earlier, Ginott (1961) did not discriminate LD children from the more grossly brain damaged, he did not exclude the brain damaged from groups, and seemed to deal with LD children regularly for treatment of impulsiveness, aggression, withdrawal, and other behaviors that frequently accompany basic neurological impairments.

Although he did not use the term LD, Kaczkowski (1979) recommends a group play therapy approach which utilizes both structured materials and a structured leader approach for children "who are frustrated or emotionally upset because he or she functions in some activities at a level below peers." Puppets, figurines, or animal reproductions are used to help children examine their behavior in social situations. The play serves as a medium for helping a child to learn about self, to set realistic levels of aspiration, to form relationships with others, and to examine the role of the classroom milieu on behavior. The counselor and the group assist the child in examining the consequences of behavior and in reviewing alternative ways of solving problems.

Millman (1974) describes the use of "game-like situations with groups of neurologically impaired children for the purposes of providing gratification in cooperating with peers." The major goal in such group games would be to provide the child with a social environment that would "teach appropriate behavior to the child whose repertoire does not include such behavior" (p. 27). In such a therapy, the game atmosphere, under the management of a therapist, would tend to facilitate acquisition of new behaviors.

OTHER PLAY THERAPY APPROACHES.   Gardner (1975) recommends the use of the Mutual Storytelling Technique as a structured play therapy device. The child tells a story and the therapist tells one of his own, using the child's characters and the child's words, which conveys understanding of the child's dynamics and encourages the development of insight. Gardner also recommends the use of the Talking, Feeling, and Doing Game which he developed for promoting expression and insight. This method, of course, would be directed toward the emotional problems of the child, secondary to remediation of the learning deficits per se.

Goldberg (1980) describes a method of play therapy with the use of the game Battling Tops (now also called Battling Space Ships), in which tops are spun and collide in a bowl-shaped area. Goldberg points out that when the "game is used with the cerebral dysfunctional child, special attention is given to the role of success experiences and curbs on impulsive behavior" (p. 206). With children who have motor deficits and/or attention problems, Goldberg has found that setting up the mastery of the game to provide success experiences will lead to greater motivation and eventually autonomy. Instruction and expectations for careful focusing are included. Goldberg has found that continued sessions with the game help to diminish undesirable aspects of behavior. "The impulsive child becomes more reflective, the depressed child more hopeful, vital, and energetic, and the obsessive or inhibited child becomes less restricted and more able to express affect at the tops' collisions" (p. 209). However, Goldberg cautions that the Battling Tops approach must be viewed as only one therapeutic modality and not a total regimen.

PARENTS AS PLAY THERAPISTS.   Currently an active area of play therapy with the learning disabled is in that of Filial Therapy (Guerney, 1964). This is a method of teaching parents to be the play therapists with their LD children under the close supervision of professionals (Guerney, 1979) using the nondirective play therapy approach (Axline, 1969; Ginott, 1961).

The typical format for the play session is used with little change. One modification has been introduced for hyperkinetic children. Structuring for the playroom is done in very positive terms rather than as prohibitions. For example, typically, children are told rules of the playroom in negative terms— "In here you may not write on the blackboard with crayons." For the hyperactive children whose impulsiveness often prohibits full processing of instructions, the rule would be stated, "You may write on the easel, drawing paper, etc., with crayons." Thus, the child is provided with positive, direct guidance to acceptable behaviors. Parents are fully instructed in the methods of conducting play sessions with demonstrations and feedback on their performance. Part of this instruction involves teaching parents about the nature of the LD and/or hyperactivity syndrome so that they can appreciate the importance of the language and structuring they use.

However, it should be understood that the Filial approach is used to reduce secondary symptoms and not to change the basic neurological picture. Insofar as nondirective therapy is able to have an impact on the development of cognitive control and organization of one's behavior, there may be indirect improvement in the child's learning, but primarily the expected changes involve adjustment in the home, school, community, increased self-control, and decreased fearfulness.

Concerned with the lack of support and knowledge typically provided for parents of LD children, Harrell and Dewitt (1981) set up a Filial Therapy program to increase the competence of mothers. In addition to conducting play sessions at home on a weekly basis, parents were taught principles of behavior modification so as to help their children change some specific behaviors. Parents in a control group did none of these things during the four-month period of the treatment. Preliminary findings from the experimental evaluation of the treatment versus control participants suggest positive changes for the treatment group.

A senior school psychologist in Long Beach, California, has devised a ten-week modification of Filial Therapy which he describes in his book on the method, *Are You Listening to Your Child?* (Kraft, 1973). Kraft uses the method with the entire gamut of school psychological problems, and reports on a case of minimal brain dysfunction. The child is a five-year-old girl with a "mild coordination handicap." In this short period, with a very accepting mother conducting the nondirective play sessions at home, the child worked out her fear of handling clay, improved her coordination, even learned how to swing on a swing, and noticeably reduced her dependency on her mother.

Jernberg (1979) also reports using parents as play therapists in her Theraplay approach (see Chapter 6) with LD children, as well as with other categories of childhood problems. As with Filial Therapy, transfer of the appropriate aspects of parent behavior in the play sessions to the home is prescribed by the supervising therapists and in fact generalization is reported to take place. Jernberg (1979) presents a case of a 16-year-old LD boy whose father administered the treatment with very successful results. Trust and intimacy were developed as the father was taught to interact with his son in the therapy sessions in "fun," physical ways, for example, wrestling. The adolescent's academic work and overall behavior improved as did his relationship with his father.

ILLUSTRATIVE CASE EXAMPLE: NONDIRECTIVE PLAY THERAPY ADMINISTERED BY A MOTHER.   A case report follows of the use of play therapy with an LD child by his mother. A treatment report using a parent/therapist was chosen to provide the reader with an opportunity to become acquainted with this less common modality. However, the outcome of therapy, and to a great extent the process as well, would be similar if a professional therapist were administering the treatment.

M. was a seven-year-old boy residing in an upper-middle class community which held high achievement expectations for children. M.'s father was a successful professional, and his mother a former business executive who now stayed at home to care for M. and his younger brother, age three. This was the mother's choice, since she had regretted not having had more time with M. when he was an infant and she was still employed. In fact, she postulated that perhaps his learning and other difficulties were a result of some possible (but not actually known) negative experiences with the live-in child-care worker who had looked after him.

M. was having problems with schoolwork, particularly arithmetic and handwriting. M. was awkward in his physical movements, and "nonphysical" in his interests and abilities. He had no friends. When he was referred at the end of the second grade, he was feigning illnesses to stay home from school. He and his parents, most often his mother, had many disagreeable experiences in relation to M.'s homework. He was given extra homework because of his poor performance in the classroom. His parents insisted on neat, correct papers, which M. could rarely produce. Unfortunately for M., an occasional correct performance convinced both parents and teachers that he could do it "if he wanted to." (This is a common misinterpretation of the LD child's erratic performances, which are part of the typical LD picture.)

M. was referred by the guidance counselor to a university psychological clinic for diagnostic work. He was found to have superior intelligence. A diagnosis was made of LD, which was confirmed by a neurologist who identified the impairment as particularly severe in the area of motor functioning.

While the diagnosis permitted the family to feel less punitive to themselves and M. about the problem, it did not really help them deal with it any more effectively. Play therapy was recommended to be administered by the mother (the father begged off because of erratic professional hours) under the supervision of a staff psychologist.

Mrs. W. joined a Filial Therapy group with five other mothers, two of whom had LD children. All were trained to conduct play sessions at home on a weekly basis. Supervised sessions were held at the clinic once every three weeks to be certain that the mother followed the methods, to observe the mother–child interactions, and to track the progress of M. in play therapy.

At first, M. demonstrated an enormous amount of helplessness, which he managed via great dependence on Mrs. W. She reinforced this by always having wonderful ideas for him. The play session rules required her to permit M. to lead the way. This frustrated both M. and Mrs. W. at first because they had not yet developed alternative approaches. A typical exchange in session three follows:

M.: I don't know what colors to make things. What color shall I make this?

MRS. W.: You want to know what color to make that.

M.: Yes. (He looks to her and waits.)

MRS. W.: You want me to tell you.

M.: Yes (with annoyance).

Mrs. W.: (Starts to take the "lead" under the pressure.) Well, what color should a duck be? Would it be blue?

M.: No . . . but would it be orange or yellow?

Mrs. W.: I think yellow would be better. (M. uses yellow and then quickly switches to orange.)

It was discussed in the Filial group following the session how M. appeared to feel both helpless and resentful toward his mother for providing help, which he usually demonstrated by countering her suggestions. Mrs. W. was rehearsed on how to address his feelings of helplessness and demands for help, while remaining in the nondirective model. An example of a typical exchange after Mrs. W. learned to let M. keep the lead would be:

M.: What color should I make this?

Mrs. W.: You want to check it out with me before you do it.

M.: Should it be blue or purple?

Mrs. W.: Both those colors seem okay, but you want to make sure that you get the one that is *most* right.

M.: Right.

Mrs. W.: In here you may select any color *you* think is best, and whether it seems right to *me* is not important. (Structuring for him.)

M.: I think I'll use red. (Takes full advantage of the freedom and chooses an unusual color, and then looks to Mrs. W. to see if she'll "correct" him.)

Mrs. W.: You want it red and that's what you're making it! (Warmly with a smile.)

Permitted to make choices without having to be accountable to his mother for the "right ones," M. makes decisions and even permits himself to be a little daring with colors, demonstrating to himself and his mother that he has that kind of "power."

In many other ways, M. worked out his conflict between the safe, dependent route and perhaps riskier independent alternatives. Since his mother was not disapproving in the play sessions but instead was accepting of his decisions, he learned to rely on himself.

Since the mother was also learning through the sessions that M. was capable of moving on his own, she pulled back in real life as well, and as M. attempted to transfer some of his felt "power" to other situations, she was able to be supportive.

The homework battle was the first outside area to be tackled. M. took full responsibility for it, with Mrs. W. exercising magnificent control not to monitor him. If she had to go out for the evening, she had M. put his homework on his night table so that she could see that he had it. But she demonstrated conviction about trusting M. by not allowing herself even a peek at it. Other group members reinforced her, and frankly admired her ability to pull back and give M. the space he now seemed willing to fill.

While the sensorimotor problems continued, since maturation seemed to be the only possible thing to alter them significantly, M. became willing to try new tasks, did not give up at the slightest obstacle, persevered and got up to grade level in arithmetic. He became less clinging and fearful so that he was willing to join other children in the neighborhood for games, except baseball. M. was given 24 half-hour play sessions by his mother at home, and 10 demonstration sessions with her at the clinic.

Since the mother was the therapist, early progress was probably a little slower in play sessions. However, the transfer to the home was accelerated because the mother was simultaneously changing her controlling behaviors. Such parallel movement with the use of a professional play therapist (with or without a counselor to talk to the mother as well) would be much more difficult to attain. Because the mother could see directly that change was needed and could participate in promoting it, she increased her efforts.

SUMMARY AND CONCLUSIONS

Children whose difficulties with mastering academic and life skills stem not from mental retardation, organic brain pathology, primary emotional disturbance, family disorganization, or other traditional bases for learning problems, have only begun to emerge as a clinical entity from the nebulous mass of developmental disabilities. Progress in understanding the basis for these children's problems with learning, that of neurological impairment, has made it possible to identify a rather sizable group whose learning difficulties are most parsimoniously explained as neurogenic in origin. However, the overt manifestations of the neurological impairments are in inadequate academic, perceptual–motor, social, and emotional behaviors. Methods of direct treatment of the neurological deficits per se are either nonexistent, unproved, or very controversial. Thus, therapeutic approaches aimed at each of the behavioral problem areas remain those currently viewed as most appropriate for treating the learning disabled. Treatments ranging from drill in academic performances to social skills and impulse control training are employed. Among those demonstrated to be most useful for dealing with the emotional and social behavioral problems is play therapy. Although very little appears in the literature on the use of play therapy with LD children exclusively, it is highly probable, because of the relative recency of the LD diagnosis, and the tendency to refer children for treatment for the major behavioral complaint without regard to its etiology, that many LD children are and have been treated on a regular basis via play therapy—and successfully! Successful case reports have been published using structured, nondirective, individual, and group approaches with both professionals and parents as the therapists in treating symptoms stemming from LD.

Since the diagnosis of LD is most likely to be applied with certainty after children have entered school, and to produce the most predictable effects in school, it is surprising that more reports of play therapy have not appeared in the literature from school service personnel. Nickerson (1973) makes a case for the "application of play therapy in the school setting" as a means of remediating inadequate development and learning as a result of "the lack of adequate sensory equipment and/or neurological impairment" (p. 361). Nickerson does not provide case illustrations of success with this group, nor does she prescribe any particular type of play therapy. But she stresses that the method has a place in the school where many of the children's problems are manifested and are of concern to teachers and pupil service personnel. What little experimental evidence does exist for the efficacy of play therapy with children who could be labeled LD includes a study that actually demonstrates, in a limited way, improvement in reading achievement (Bills, 1950a) and in encoding (Moulin, 1970)—performance areas outside of those for which play therapy more typically is purported to be effective. This suggests that perhaps it would be fruitful again to explore empirically the impact of play therapies on the full range of problem manifestations of the learning disabled child.

Since the problems of LD children are manifested in the home as well as the school, parents are going to be involved firsthand in trying to manage them. Parents as play therapists could provide the parent involvement schools seek in relation to resolving children's difficulties (Berman, 1979; Kraft, 1973). The advantages of such parent involvement are many, outstanding of which is the potential for the parent to offer the support, acceptance, and assistance in self-regulation provided by the play therapist and to generalize these therapeutic behaviors to the home.

The problems manifested by LD children tend to generate negative feedback from the interpersonal environment; this tends to further exacerbate their learning and other deficits. Empirical evidence of these phenomena have already been cited in this chapter. It is critical, therefore, that primary care providers, including teachers, be made aware of the need for maintained positive support and develop the attitudes and skills required to provide it. Knowledge of play therapy, all approaches of which seek to build feelings of self-competence and self-confidence, would seem to provide a means for acquiring the necessary tools. When not feasible for primary care givers to serve as therapists or when appropriate supervision is not available to them, referrals to professionals for play therapy would be desirable. Since neither help with academic deficits nor medication is sufficient to overcome the multiple problems of LD children, psychotherapeutic approaches, including behavioral therapy and play therapy, should be included more frequently in treatment plans. Further, comparative research needs to be conducted to determine which therapy is most appropriate for different types of LD problem patterns.

Play therapy seems to hold greater promise for having genuine impact, even on some of the primary manifestations of the neurological impairments such as encoding problems (Moulin, 1970), than the limited number of publications on this population would indicate. It is likely that most play therapists have been reporting their activities in terms of the secondary behaviors exhibited, for example, aggression, rather than in relation to neurological impairments.

REFERENCES

Abramowitz, C. V. (1976) The effectiveness of group psychotherapy with children. *Archives General Psychiatry,* **33,** 320–326.

Arnold, L. E. (1973) Is this label necessary? *Journal of School Health,* **43,** 510–514.

Axline, V. (1947) Play therapy: A way of understanding and helping reading problems. *Childhood Education,* **26,** 156–161.

Axline, V. (1969) *Play therapy.* New York: Ballantine Books.

Berman, A. (1979) Parenting learning disabled children. *Journal of Clinical Child Psychology,* **8,** 245–249.

Bills, R. E. (1950a) Non-directed play therapy with retarded readers. *Journal of Consulting Psychology,* **14,** 140–149.

Bills, R. E. (1950b) Play therapy with well adjusted readers. *Journal of Consulting Psychology,* **14,** 246–249.

Bryan, T., & Pearl, R. (1979) Self-concepts and locus of control of learning disabled children. *Journal of Clinical Child Psychology,* **3,** 223–226.

Clements, S., & Peters, J. (1962) Minimal brain dysfunctions in the school age child. *Archives General Psychiatry,* **6,** 185–197.

Connors, C. K. (Ed.) (1974) *Clinical use of stimulant drugs on children: Proceedings of a symposium at Key Biscayne, Florida.* New York: American Elsevier.

Dorfman, E. (1958) Personality outcomes of client-centered child therapy. *Psychological Monographs,* **72**(3), whole no. 456.

DSM-III. (1980) R. Spitzer & J. Williams (Eds.), *Diagnostic and statistical manual of mental disorders.* Washington, D.C.: American Psychiatric Association.

Dweck, C., & Reppuci, N. (1973) Learned helplessness and reinforcement responsibility in children. *Journal of Personality and Social Psychology,* **25,** 109–116.

Feingold, B. (1975) *Why your child is hyperactive.* New York: Random House.

Fisher, B. (1953) Group therapy with retarded readers. *Journal of Educational Psychology,* **44,** 356–360.

Freeman, D., & Cornwall, T. (1980) Hyperactivity and neurosis. *American Journal of Orthopsychiatry,* **50.**

Gardner, R. (1975) Techniques for involving the child with MBD in meaningful psychotherapy. *Journal of Learning Disabilities,* **8,** 272–282.

Ginott, H. (1961) *Group psychotherapy with children.* New York: McGraw-Hill.

Goldberg, T. (1980) Battling tops: A modality in child psychotherapy. *Journal of Clinical Child Psychology,* **9,** 206–209.

Guerney, B. G., Jr. (1964) Filial therapy: Description and rationale. *Journal of Consulting Psychology,* **28,** 303–310.

Guerney, L. (1979) Play therapy with learning disabled children. *Journal of Clinical Child Psychology,* **9,** 242–244.

Harrell, J., & Dewitt, M. (1981) *An intervention program to increase parental competence of mothers with learning disabled children.* Paper presented at the meeting of the American Educational Research Association in Los Angeles, April.

Jernberg, A. (1979) *Theraplay.* San Francisco: Jossey-Bass.

Johnson, D., & Myklebust, H. (1967) *Learning disabilities.* New York: Grune and Stratton.

Kaczkowski, H. (1979) Group work with children. *Elementary School Guidance Counseling,* **14,** 44–51.

Kraft, A. (1973) *Are you listening to your child?* New York: Walker and Co.

Lincoln, A., & Chazan, S. (1979) Perceived competence and intrinsic motivation in learning disabled children. *Journal of Clinical Child Psychology,* **8,** 213–216.

Meichenbaum, D. H., & Goodman, J. (1971) Training impulsive children to talk to themselves: A means of developing self-control. *Journal of Abnormal Psychology,* **77,** 115–126.

Millman, H. (1970) Minimal Brain Dysfunction in Children. Evaluation and Treatment *Journal of Learning Disabilities vol. 3,* 89–99

Moulin, E. K. (1970) The effects of client-centered group counseling play media on the intelligence, achievement, and psycholinguistics of underachieving primary school children. *Elementary School Guidance Counselor,* **98.**

Nickerson, E. (1973) The application of play therapy to a school setting. *Psychology in the Schools,* **10,** 361–365.

O'Malley, J., & Eisenberg, L. (1973) The hyperactive child. In S. Waltzer & P. Wolff (Eds.), *Minimal cerebral dysfunction in children.* New York: Grune and Stratton.

Patterson, G. R., Jones, R., Whittier, J., & Wright, M. A. (1965) A behavior modification technique for the hyperactive child. *Behavior Research and Therapy,* **2,** 217–226.

Pumfrey, P., & Elliott, C.E. (1970) Play therapy, social adjustment, and reading attainment. *Educational Research,* **12,** 183–193.

Ross, D., & Ross, S. (1976) *Hyperactivity: Research, theory, and action.* New York: John Wiley & Sons.

Serafica, F., & Harway, N. (1979) Social relations and self-esteem of children with learning disabilities. *Journal of Clinical Child Psychology,* **3,** 227–233.

Singer, J. (Ed.) (1974) *The child's world of make believe.* New York: Academic Press.

Slavson, S. R. (1943) *An introduction to group therapy.* New York: International Universities Press.

Slavson, S. R., & Shiffer, M. (1974) *Group psychotherapies for children.* New York: International Universities Press.

Speers, R. (1976) Play: An essential component of development. *Children in Contemporary Society,* **9,** 61–62.

Thompson, A. R., & Wade, M. G. (1974) Real play and fantasy play as modified by social and environmental complexity in normal and hyperactive children. *Therapeutic Recreation Journal,* 161–167.

Wender, P. (1971) *Minimal brain dysfunction in children.* New York: Wiley-Interscience.

Yawkey, T. (1980) An investigation of imaginative play and aural language development in young children, five, six, and seven. In D. Williamson (Ed.), *Play in human settlements.* London: Croonhelm Publishers.

CHAPTER 24

Play Therapy for Mentally Retarded and Developmentally Disabled Children

HENRY LELAND

INTRODUCTION

The mentally retarded or developmentally disabled (MR/DD) child who demonstrates sufficient maladaptive behavior (Coulter & Morrow, 1978) that community agencies, schools, or families become concerned, needs the type of treatment usually included under the rubrics of psychotherapy or play therapy. This chapter will discuss some of the broad implications of the concept of therapy with MR/DD populations as they apply to children who require help in changing behaviors which make their survival in community programs or in the home otherwise untenable. I will outline some of the broad principles of play therapy based on a previous book (Leland & Smith, 1965). The chapter will also review some of the more recent developments in this area. These new developments concern moving away from the doctor–patient service model in favor of working with groups of individuals and the utilization of a different type of professional personnel in interdisciplinary settings. Finally, I will discuss some of the factors relating to the child in the home, recognizing that if we are to be successful in our efforts to modify the behavior of these children, the utilization of the concept of a total milieu must also be applied.

Our approach is based on three general assumptions. First, there is an unwritten law that the less children are able to function or to evolve appropriate coping skills when left to their own devices, the greater the need for directed intervention (Sherwood, 1980). One has to recognize that the MR/DD child has a great deal of difficulty in utilizing the cues and stimuli of the surrounding environment and that this difficulty creates very real problems in the overall ability to make appropriate coping decisions. (Edmonson, Leland, deJung, & Leach, 1967; Edmonson, Leland, & Leach, 1970). This failure to make appropriate coping decisions is often the basis for the child's clinical referral, since children who are included in play therapy or other forms of psychological intervention usually have demonstrated a large number of coping failures within the community. The various community resources represented by clinical services are typically the last resort of a parent attempting to deal with the problem behavior of their child. Thus, the clinical situation has to deal with a child who is not only demonstrating maladaptive behavior and inappropriate coping responses, but one who has also been demonstrating such behaviors over a period of time and already has a history of failure experiences and inappropriate social interactions. In the face of this history one cannot expect these children to come freely into a therapeutic situation and be able to develop insights into their problems. Such ability would imply awareness of his or her behavior or that such awareness could easily develop; this would be inconsistent with the diagnosis of mental retardation. If children we considered retarded behave in that manner, it is not appropriate to expect that they will gain awareness of the basis of their behaviors, primarily because they have had little or no history of success experiences or opportunities to relate behaviors to their consequences. Understanding must come through the therapeutic process and the more retarded the child appears in the therapy sessions the greater the amount of directed play and directed intrusions must come from the therapists.

The *basic* procedure is:

1. The child does something (recognizing that even nothing is "something")
2. The therapist intervenes, asking what the child is doing
3. If the child responds in any manner (e.g. words, noises, gestures etc.) the behavior is allowed to continue with the therapist providing the necessary description of the activity, e.g. "you are building with blocks" or "you are making this sound" (and the therapist then imitates the sound)
4. If the child fails to respond in any manner, the therapist intrudes, stops the activity explaining that it can't continue until the child gives some kind of response

This general pattern is followed throughout the sessions with variations based on the four different types of play therapy I will discuss as follows.

A second major principle is that regardless of what the therapist feels about social standards, cultural mores, and so forth, the particular differences that are present in the child's environment cannot be expected to be carried as his or her personal cross. Rather, children, because of their retardation, must be brought to a level which will permit them to live in their environment regardless of its nature. The therapist does not attempt to remake the child "in his own image," and in fact, has a major responsibility not to introduce so many new variables (even though they may be considered positive in the broad sense of social standards) that the therapy only adds to the child's confusion. Children must be able to interact appropriately with their own family or within the social environment in which they live. The therapist must have cognizance of the social forces present in the community from which the client comes and must avoid disrupting the social ecology of the child. Play therapy does not have to be considered a long-term, highly involved procedure; in fact it should be a relatively short-term, direct procedure which leads to the modification of one or two very specific high-priority behaviors which are causing a great deal of difficulty and putting the child's social survival in jeopardy. Again, it must be emphasized that were the child surviving properly, he or she would not have been brought into clinical services.

On a practical basis we usually advocate blocks of 12 sessions. The basic pattern is:

1. Meet with the referring party and obtain as clear a description of the problem behaviors as possible.
2. If a regular clinical assessment (including an Adaptive Behavior evaluation) has not been done, it should be arranged.
3. Meet with the parents and obtain their view of the situation.
4. If the priority needs of the client are not clear, or if the client is otherwise untestable, a Play Diagnostic session is arranged (Leland & Smith, 1965; Deutsch, 1978).
5. Immediate Play Therapy goals are established based on Steps 2 and/or 4. These goals are minimal and designed for possible achievement within a period of 12 sessions.
6. At the end of the 12 sessions, new meetings are held, current behaviors are reviewed, and if continued Play Therapy is required, new goals are developed and the process continues.

Third, it is recognized that children tend to learn primarily from each other. Without this, the processes of imitation may be as valuable as any other intervention from the therapist. Therefore, the therapy may often occur better within groups of children than on an individual basis. There are also instances when a more individual approach might be valuable. These decisions must be based on the expressed needs of the children, and the types of behaviors which have to be changed. If groups are used, they should be kept to a maximum of four clients. Also at least one therapy assistant should be used (older or more mature peers can also help the progress of a group [Sherwood, 1980]).

Manipulation of Structure

The atmosphere of the therapeutic setting and the approaches of the therapists are extremely important in the change processes we are trying to establish. This general idea is best represented by the concept of structure. The presence or absence of an organized system of therapeutic procedures and materials literally becomes the keystone of the whole therapeutic process. Where there is a tightly organized, well-developed plan of procedures and methods, we would say that the process was highly structured. Where there is a less-developed plan, not as tightly organized, and where the methods or procedures are not strictly followed, we would say that this is lacking in structure or to use the terminology we are employing, unstructured. Structure is defined as the degree of preconception of form or order found in the therapeutic field.

The key to the psychotherapeutic process with MR/DD children is the modification of behavior and the key to the modification of behavior is the manipulation and control of the structure or the order and form surrounding the child during the play therapy. Insofar as we are dealing with that aspect of retarded behavior related to coping (which is thus tied into both cognition and learning), the amount of organization and form which a therapist must use is very closely related to the level of behavior that requires modification.

Manipulation of structure becomes more than just a manipulation of the child's therapeutic milieu. What is attempted in play therapy, that which makes it therapy rather than just another behavior modification process, is that the child is put into the kinds of life situations which are causing the greatest difficulty with adaptive behavior. The recommendation for psychotherapy grows out of specific behaviors and not out of a vague group of emotional patterns or diagnostic labels. A child should not be recommended for psychotherapy just because he or she is described as "aggressive" or "acting out" or some other such phrase, nor because he or she would be described as brain damaged or schizophrenic. Rather, the child should be recommended for psychotherapy because there are certain specific behaviors which are manifested regularly as the result of environmental stimuli. These behaviors disturb the surrounding environment, make the child extremely visible in that environment, and subject the family to pressures to remove the child from that environment. It is the role of the therapist to try to determine what these specific behaviors are, and what specific cognitive style the child uses in attempting to cope with environmental stimuli, recognizing that the particular coping model which the child evolves is also part of the mental retardation.

The therapist must determine which behaviors seem to be the key sources of the environmental upsets surrounding the child, the child's level of development, both socially and intellectually, and the child's previous level of training and experience. Then the therapist can establish a pattern of approach which will take these developmental elements as a guide for the therapeutic procedure. The therapist attempts to set up situations most consistent with the developmental and experiential level of the child and elects a structural pattern which will give cues and guides as to different types of behavioral options.

One of the key elements of reward in the play therapy situation is the child's ability to maintain permission to carry out behaviors of his or her own choice. The question of manipulating structure centers around how much the child is to be rewarded with permission for certain behaviors and how much he or she is to be punished by having these behaviors blocked. If the child has a mode of coping with environmental needs which is inconsistent with the expectations and critical demands of the social milieu, these behaviors must be stopped. If this particular mode continues, the therapist must interfere with the child's choice of behavior, must intrude until the child, in order to avoid this intrusion, is willing to modify the behavior. However, if the mode of coping that the child chooses is consistent with the critical demands of society, the therapist rewards him or her by permitting the behavior to continue, thus giving the child a sense of self in that a freely chosen behavioral mode has been rewarded instead of being intruded upon.

This approach to play therapy centers around the need of MR/DD children to utilize environmental cues appropriately and to make social decisions based on these cues. This is an area which readily yields itself to training. The function of play therapy becomes a form of reeducation of modes of adaptation which are considered to be reversible aspects of mental retardation (Leland, Shellhaas, Nihira, & Foster, 1968). One cannot use the same therapeutic process with all retarded children, but must select a type of process based on the amount of structure to be introduced, dependent on the needs of these children. We have arranged these into four general types.* Children with different coping problems have to have a different type of therapeutic approach; a single approach to play therapy cannot be utilized.

The play therapeutic process must be modified in terms of developmental needs of the client and this seems to be best accomplished by dealing either with the level of structure found in the various materials utilized in play therapy or in the amount of organization and preconception associated with the therapist. Specific behaviors which violate the critical demands of the child's environment can be changed and in the long run, make the child a more livable person and more likely to remain in the community.

Goals, Limits, and Procedures

The goals of play therapy with retarded children are varied but they generally center around attempts to raise the level of functioning and control of behavior. It is hoped that children will learn to do more things, to improve cognitive ability, and through increased ability, to deal with critical situations so that they will be happier and more useful people. Any planned or "goal directed" attempt to create behavioral change, as long as an effort has been made to establish a close interpersonal relationship between the client and the therapist, as long as an effort has been made to create an organized treatment setting, and as long as the processes of communication are emphasized, should be considered psychotherapy. Differences in materials and procedures will produce different therapeutic results.

The personality changes sought in MR/DD individuals are those which will make them more able to conform to the demands of the community. They

---

*A thorough discussion of this approach to the therapeutic process appeared in Leland and Smith (1965, now in the process of revision) and what appears here and below is a brief overview.

should be able to take from their environment, as does the normal child, the cues which act as guides to learning in both the behavioral and intellectual spheres. We find, for example, questions on standard psychometric trests for information which, in terms of the standardization, a child must have before entering school. This information could be learned in school but is expected to be gained before entering into any kind of formal learning situation. This knowledge has to come from the milieu. It may have been presented by such sources as television, peers, or logic, but whatever the source, the milieu has produced sufficient cues that the child knows for example, that a dog has four legs, *though no one has upended a dog and explained it.*

Retarded children seem to be blocked in this area. They do not draw on the information which the culture provides. Everything they know they have had to learn either through very arduous struggle or by having had it taught in a very painstaking manner. The reasons for this blockage are varied. But regardless of the cause, the result is that the child's functional level has been lowered by inability to use minimal cues as a guide to expected behaviors.

When the child seems to be an "invisible" part of the surrounding community, accepted for him- or herself at whatever level of functioning, he or she is not constantly being made aware of deficiencies. He or she seems to be able to develop a suitable adjustment. Some children break down later, in adult life, due to changes in social relationships, but this is easier to handle if the child had a sense of belonging. Children who are not able to feel part of the day-to-day world, who feel that they have nothing to say about their future, rather that they are in the hands of forces which are both frightening and out of their area of control, become disturbed and need special treatment over and above the processes utilized to deal with the abnormal level of mental development.

The behavior changes in which we are most interested are related to the development of a consciousness of social stimuli and once aware of these stimuli, an ability to utilize behavioral options. This produces a pattern of behavior which is both socially acceptable and personally rewarding. There is no easy formula because children have different demands and requirements based on the image they have of themselves, the image they have of the people around them, their families, their friends, and their peers, as well as the rest of their life experiences.

The psychotherapy goals for the mental subnormal are those which tend to accelerate their ability to mature and to learn. We need ways of replacing faulty learning and conditioning new learning in an effort to reorder the ways the clients use the knowledge they already have. This can be accomplished if the therapist is aware of the principles whereby children learn. He or she can arrange therapy procedures and approaches in keeping with the growth and developmental patterns of the client or group of clients and thus be in a position to accelerate these growth patterns. The client must constantly be aware of what he or she is doing in the play session and be willing to indicate this awareness by either responding to the therapist actively or behaving in a manner that the therapist knows this awareness had been achieved. This requires an emphasis on cognitive processes. The child has to intellectualize in order to achieve recognition and approbation from the therapist. This process can be described as *forcing the child to think*. Therefore, beside the freedom from intolerable disappointment which the psychotherapeutic process should represent, it must also represent an introduction to social and individual responsibility. If children behave in more socially acceptable ways they are less likely to run into disappointments than if they behave in less socially acceptable ways. With this realization comes improved cognition and with improved cognition comes higher functioning. Thus, the technique of "forcing the child to think" becomes a way of accelerating growth and developmental processes. There may be instances in which the child is overly resistant to this approach and in those cases additional modes of intrusion must be sought.

Part of the maladaption is due to a general lack of understanding that rules and regulations are not aimed specifically at the child, but rather around the needs of the social order. When a child is scolded for stepping off into the street rather than waiting at a stop sign or looking for cars, this is not a personal rejection or attack but rather the way society functions so that both children and cars can exist in the same world. For this reason the therapist has a responsibility of establishing *limits*. Limits must be conceived (1) in terms of the relationship of the client to the therapist (this may reach the point of personal safety); (2) in terms of the relationship of the client to materials utilized in the play; and (3) in terms of the time and place (setting). These limits are, however, in a broader sense, most related to the child's understanding that in spite of the fact that the therapist has imposed limits, the child is still accepted, still "loved" by the therapist and these limits are not a punishment but rather are a means of increasing his or her freedom within the therapy situation.

Concerning the third type of limits (time and place) there are some additional factors. "Time" refers to the limits set on the therapy session. Here we have an inescapable limit in the sense that time passes regardless of what else occurs. This can be used to help the child realize that there are many forces in nature, or things in society which, as far as he or she is concerned, are immutable. However, though unchangeable, it nonetheless provides continuity and whereas it stops one session, it also starts the next.

"Place" refers to the playroom or play therapy setting and is considered a limit in the sense that it is usually the only place that the child interacts with the therapist as a *therapist*. Both the child and the therapist must be aware of the special roles and relationships the setting provides. Thus, some things are possible in the playroom that are not permitted outside. The playroom becomes the source of freedom and the therapist helps the use of this freedom constructively. For this reason we have suggested that "dirty" activities (e.g., sand, water, paints etc.) and "clean" activities (e.g., games, trucks, etc.) be done in different rooms. The use of two different rooms for "dirty" versus "clean" activities also helps establish the fact that these are different places to do different types of things. Also, the room and the therapist become united in the child's mind and they come to symbolize both the freedom of activity and the source of models.

TECHNIQUE

The Four Basic Technical Variations

We use the following four different types of play therapy (Deutsch & Leland, 1976, 1977):

1. Unstructured materials with unstructured therapeutic approaches (U-U).
2. Unstructured materials with structured therapeutic approaches (U-S).
3. Structured materials with unstructured approaches (S-U).
4. Structured materials with structured therapeutic approach (S-S).

The U-U process is the most primitive. It demands the least from the patient in terms of previous cognitive development or present cognitive ability. We differentiate between the two because, in terms of psychological problems, the previous level of cognitive development may not necessarily be representative of present functioning ability. We do not imply that this form of play therapy be used only with the most severely retarded. The level of measured intelligence is not important. Rather we are interested in the level of functional behavior. The child whose behavior indicates a lack of consciousness of self, who seems too impulsive, or who appears to be "driven" to act out feelings of hostility, destructiveness, or general aggressiveness without seeming to have a basis for this behavior, or conversely who is withdrawn and rejects the environment or major portions of it, seemingly without cognitive basis, is best served by a therapeutic process in which the structure has been, if not eliminated, at least modified to such an extent that it appears to the child as if there were no structure.

The importance of unstructured materials lies in the clients greater ability to control, create, change, and develop play activity with them. They can learn that they are people capable of creating and controlling materials. This paves the way for learning that they can control themselves and eventually allows them to interact with others. They can learn that they are not necessarily dangerously destructive and they can see that their impulses have been destructive primarily to themselves. They can learn that their ideas and efforts can produce tangible differences in reality, for example, the change in the size or shape of a piece of clay is due to their behavior. The client does not destroy unstructured materials, some may get used up, but such materials are thought of as being expendable and the concept of destruction does not enter into it. If the client tears a piece of clay in two, it is not destroyed but is simply in two pieces which can be recombined. They may become aware of the fact that it was they who created the two pieces and in a psychological sense, produced new material from what existed previously.

The materials we have in mind are those which do not have any particular preconceived function or value unto themselves. Materials such as sand, water, blocks, beads, string, finger paint, clay, paper, crayons, pipe cleaners, snow, scraps of wood, and various similar objects, either provided by the therapist or brought into the playroom (in this case, the "dirty" room), by the clients, may serve as unstructured materials.

The indications for U-U therapy and the therapist's tasks become clearer if we think of the specific goals. The therapist's tasks are based on fairly clear criteria for choosing between two major modes of responding to the client. One, a positive response which is reinforcing, or two, a negative response which is blocking or intruding. The decision of how to respond is based on the basic goals of this form of play therapy. These goals are threefold. The first is recognition of self. This refers to the child's gaining a sense of control over the environment, realizing the freedom to follow personal ideas, and gaining a sense of being a real person. It is the primary goal because the child must be encouraged to develop motivation for growth and become able to deal with more challenging problems. The child with no awareness of self is completely unable to utilize any of the growth-producing elements of the environment.

The second goal involves gaining understanding that impulses can be controlled. This is a form of conditioning whereby the client becomes aware of ability to control sudden intense drives. These children have been unable to direct their behavior in a socially acceptable manner in the past and this fact has given rise to frustration, guilt, and a lack of self-concept which has been partially responsible for the presence of the emotional disorder.

The third goal is training to live within social boundaries. These boundaries in an unstructured situation are slight, but they are reflective of greater limits which society imposes. This is a matter of learning to respond to the behavior of others in a controlled manner and learning to contribute to mutually conceived projects in group situations. These children usually have been unable to work through their own problems with the resources they have available and so have not had sufficient psychic energy to participate with their peers or society. They tend to reject their peers, to fight when intruded upon, and generally behave in a way disruptive to any sort of social activity.

The next of the four procedures is that which utilizes unstructured materials with a structured therapeutic approach (U-S). This method is not new to the therapeutic field and is found in the activities of the art therapist, music therapist, recreation therapist, and other similar workers. One of the differences is the relationship between the client and the therapist. When this relationship is close and warm, the therapist is able to play the role of a model. When the relationship is not based on an interchange of feelings, but facilitates a setting in which the patient feels safe to carry out behaviors, this is usually described as activity therapy but not given the title of psychotherapy. We are not claiming that psychotherapy is defined only by the procedures we have described, but rather that these kinds of playroom activities must set up the interpersonal relationship between therapist and client which is required for psychotherapy to take place. The important factor is the concept that the client is able to translate desires into socially acceptable behavior by learning to anticipate what would be acceptable to the therapist. This prejudgment comes both from what he or she has observed the therapist doing and what, based on previous experience and insight, he or she judged that the therapist expected to be done. The therapist functions as a representation of the more democentric aspects of society and becomes a model upon which the client may test behavior. It should be underlined that the end product is not of great importance, but the general procedures followed by the client in attempting to create a product are important. Thus, it does not matter how good a bowl emerges from the clay, but it does matter that the client is able to sufficiently control the behavior, the impulses, and the general acting out tendencies to make a bowl. We can understand this if we remember the times children will go out to play, will call it "going out to play," but will nonetheless get a hammer and some nails and start making something. They feel that while they are making these things they are playing. What is important is that the activity itself takes on significance because they feel that they are producing a product, but the efforts to create the product serves the function of play in terms of building imagination, helping develop creativity, and improving understanding of the surrounding world.

The approach of the therapist is much more structured or preconceived. The session is planned, and the kinds of activities are established and not left to free choice, and the materials are prepared in advance. The therapist tries to induce the child to use the materials (how they are used doesn't matter), and then they discuss what the client is doing. The therapist must always relate the activity to the preconceived goals and look for emotional loadings which can be converted into cognitive understanding.

The first goal of the U-S method is the development of an improved self-concept. We have already established recognition of self (in the U-U method), but the U-S method unites self-image with objective reality in terms of actual ability, and becomes a form of improving self-concept by giving self-confidence where it is lacking, or bringing it to the reality level where it seems to be distorted. This goal is important if the child is to be able to live in the community at his or her level. These types of children must have a self-concept consistent with their ability but not so self-deprecating that they cannot function up to their potential. Rather it must permit them to recognize that there are many things which cannot do, but also that there are many things which they can do, and when this recognition has been established and accepted it can be said that the therapy has been successful.

The second goal for this type of therapy involves improved impulse control.

Children who realize that impulses can be controlled may find this knowledge a two-edged sword in that they may still have a problem in controlling their impulses; they know that they can control them and thus may feel guilty and upset because they do not. This is a process whereby the feelings of social unease increase because the children are not doing something they know they can do. Play therapy improves impulse control by increasing understanding that the basic desires can be satisfied in a socially acceptable manner. It is not the desires themselves that are at fault but rather the knowledge of what to do about them.

The third goal involves the improvement of ability to interact socially. Having learned that there are limits in society, children have to learn where the limits are imposed, how they are imposed, and the difference between major limits and minor limits. This is related to social reality. The first impression on learning that there are limits is that it is as great a crime to walk on the grass as it is to steal a ball. Both are treated as equal sins, both are treated with equal daring if the child decides to be hostile. Here the improvement of ability to interact socially will help in learning to make the appropriate differentiations within the social requirements.

The third of the four procedures utilizes structured materials with a generally unstructured approach (S-U). The materials and approach, the indications for the psychotherapy, and the goals are all similar to traditional play therapy procedures (Axline, 1947). We define this method as involving, as do the traditional precepts of play therapy, toys which have a preconceived construct as to their use, in a situation where the therapist has no preconception as to what the child should play. The setting in the S-U situation is more narrowly conceived than in the usual play therapy room, the toys are also more narrowly conceived, but in general the method can be thought of as primarily aimed at inviting thematic play; the S-U method is also usually done in the "clean" room.

The materials for this type of play are trucks, dolls, guns, dollhouses, telephones, tools, bop bags, and general toys with specific play functions such as jigsaw puzzles and dishes. Any item of that type is appropriate with the provision that it is large enough to be handled by brain damaged children, and simple enough that the complexities of operation will not overwhelm the child and negate the thematic aspects.

The goals of the S-U method are first to help children build secure relationships with things and people at the level of understanding that a more democentric, more expressive interaction with the environment can be more gratifying than the egocentric, self-contained attitudes and behaviors which they had previously adopted. This is gained through the expression in play of the conflicts and hostilities which they feel and through associations which the therapist helps provide concerning acceptable means of expressing feelings without destroying the environment or the interpersonal relationship.

The second goal is to help children deal with social and cultural realities in terms of the fact that they are in a position to create some joy and gratification in their environment if they will learn to deal with the reality of society and not constantly run contrary to expectations and demands.

The third goal attempts to help children evaluate their past experiences in the light of new attitudes, to aid in their development, and to establish personal goals in terms of a realistic level of aspiration and a realistic consciousness of self. It may be argued that a child with little ability or potential is a preconceived failure in this kind of therapy. However, if a child is at a sufficiently high functional level to be brought into the S-U type of therapy, he or she has sufficient potential to contribute socially at various levels; the understanding of these levels will enhance his or her personality rather than increase the frustration.

The fourth procedure utilizes structured materials with a structured therapeutic approach (S-S). This form is based on the premise that many personality aberrations are due to an awareness of an inability to function at a level equal to that of his or her peers. This assumption does not require that the child have a knowledge of all of the ramifications of the disturbance, but rather, observation that he or she is not performing as well, in important areas, as his or her peers. Thus, if a child feels that if he or she could tell time he or she could compete, then the S-S type of therapy may very specifically take time out to teach telling of time. Therapists would not necessarily agree with the child that this was the source of the problem, but having taught telling time the therapist would help the child understand that there were still problems and that possibly they could find alternative ways of working them through.

The materials utilized for this method must be definite, highly structured, with an emphasis either on production of cognitive content or production of creative expression. The end product is important as are the consequences of the behavior.

Each session is conceived in advance; the therapist sets the scene, continually making sure that the client remains in the kind of situation which the therapist has contrived. This may take one play session or it may take a number of sessions. The therapist must maintain rapport and patient contact by participating in the activities so that the two of them are trying to deal with the problem together, rather than the child finding him- or herself isolated. At no time should the therapist set up a problem and then psychologically go away, leaving the client to work it out alone. Rather they must attempt to work it through together, permitting the client to feel that he or she has an ally, although the final solutions must come from the patient and not the therapist. The three goals are: (1) the improvement of the level of social maturity through the development of improved cognitive function; (2) the development of understanding on the part of the child as to how to fit into the milieu and gain personal acceptance; and (3) the building of realistic levels of aspiration including a sense of "rules" and a sense of achievement.

The forms of play therapy which have been briefly outlined are, in effect, forms of behavior required for survival in the community. Society seems to structure itself around MR/DD persons in terms of these U-U, U-S, S-U, and S-S situations. Less-structured aspects of community living face individuals daily with unstructured stimuli (e.g., rain, wind), in an unstructured relationship to the community. Particular demands are not placed upon them but they must, nonetheless, respond properly (e.g., get out of the weather or wear proper clothing). More structured situations present highly structured stimuli in structured relationship to the community, and individuals are not free to make decisions but instead must go along with the decisions society has already made, (e.g., stoplights). If the child learns through play to cope with these problems in a controlled manner, he or she may carry this learning into daily living as an adolescent and an adult. The major gains from play therapy include the ability to know the critical demands of the community and the experience of successful dealings with these demands. This creates a personality pattern which is acceptable to the community; the individual can then be permitted to remain and to contribute to it (Shellhaas & Nihira, 1969).

Individual or Group

One of the factors of which the therapist must be constantly aware is not how the child plays but how he or she plays in relation to other children. Modes of play and peer interaction considered unacceptable in some areas of the community may be very acceptable in other areas, and it is part of the responsibility of a successful play therapy program to maintain the ability of the child to survive among his or her own peers and in his or her own community. Therefore, for the therapist to intrude with a model of behavior inconsistent with the child's personal model as found in the home and neighborhood would, in the long run, be destructive to the child even though it may modify certain behaviors.

The first question is whether the child successfully plays in a group in a manner consistent with the demands of his or her peers and community. If so, then regardless of what types of learning disabilities or school delays which have emerged, play therapy as we have described it should not be treatment of choice. Rather than approach the child as though we were dealing with a pathological problem it is better to approach the difficulty as an educational and cultural question which may not even be posed as a problem but merely as a different way of behaving.

If on the other hand, the child emerges as not being able to interact with peers, as having different or peculiar behavior modes in relation to peers, and is rejected by them as well as by the more dominant community elements, then there is a strong possibility that the child should be in group therapy (where the peers themselves may be valuable adjuncts to the therapy process, Sherwood, 1980).

The question is a matter of knowing what play experiences are required to permit retarded children to function with more "normal" children so that a larger community of learning can be achieved.

It is to be expected that children will emerge whose maladaptive behavior is intolerable to their peers. These children will have a combination of learning disabilities including some evidence of retardation and a definite impairment in their adaptive behavior (Grossman, 1977). Typically, small play groups aimed at modifying a set of similar behaviors can be easily formed. Two types of play therapy groups can evolve: One based on the convenience of the therapist in which all of the children have similar needs and it is a matter of dealing with these needs on a group basis rather than on an individual basis, and the other where it is felt that certain types of peer interactions will speed up and support the therapy process through imitation and counterimitation. In the first instance, a small group of three or four youngsters, all of whom have the same presenting difficulty, can be brought into a similar group procedure usually at the S-U or U-S level (these two forms being more readily adaptable to group procedures than either the U-U or S-S levels). The therapist and cotherapist or therapy assistant may, by developing patterns of mutual intrusion and by setting up certain types of limits, help the group achieve the necessary behavior modification. This is a slow process, MR/DD children tend more toward "parallel" play than group play. But when progress is made it is usually very effective.

The other alternative is based on the fact that it is often valuable to mix groups of children with different coping modes, (e.g., aggressive versus withdrawn or passive) because the children learn somewhat more readily from each other through imitating those behaviors which seem to be successful and rejecting those which seem to cause punishment or intrusion (Leland, Walker, & Toboada, 1959). This group experience can progress to a very highly specialized group approach somewhat resembling the S-S level. It will ease the delivery of service problems by dealing with more children at one time than on a one-to-one basis, but it should be recognized that this reason is secondary to meeting the unique needs of the concerned children.

Aspects of Service Delivery

Training. If the types of group experiences we have described are to be possible, it is obvious that a greater number of play therapists have to be available. It is illogical to conceptualize, at this time, a vast increase in the number of doctoral-level psychologists or other individuals doing play therapy at a highly professional level. The requirements for these individuals and the expansion of programs and services is such that most persons currently trained at this level are not giving direct service but rather find themselves in various administrative capacities where they are planning, organizing, and managing programs. We thus face the contradiction that the individual trained to provide the service is not providing it, while at the same time the needs for such services are increasing. The answer is obviously not to take highly trained people out of the planning, administrative, and organizing roles, because the development of innovative programs and the total expansion of service, training, and research programs is dependent on that level of training and understanding. The answer would seem to lie in the other direction, that is, beginning to train an increasingly large number of technician-level personnel who can take on more and more responsibility in the service areas under the supervision of the more highly trained individuals. Here one deals with a service-training paradigm which says that where there is an organized body of knowledge with a well-organized set of procedures and which experiences a relatively small impact from each specific decision, a relatively untrained person can perform. Where the knowledge and procedures are vague and the impact of decisions is great (e.g., a decision to institutionalize a child) then the services must be performed by a more highly trained or more competent individual (Sutter, Leland & Barclay, 1969). It is very feasible to train a large number of subprofessional individuals to carry out the kinds of play therapy procedures which we have described. There is an organized body of knowledge with fairly well-organized procedures surrounding it and the individual decisions do not have a decisive impact on the child. This would seem to be a ready-made situation for a subprofessional who could step in under the supervision of a more highly trained person and carry out the actual play therapy processes. In point of fact, groups of such individuals who might be described as play therapy aides become even more effective and are able to provide some of the requirements of one-to-one interaction while dealing with increasingly large groups of children who require this type of help.

With this problem in mind we have set up a procedure which has been relatively successful. The senior therapist sets up the therapy group and may carry three or four of the sessions to ensure that the clients have a fairly clear understanding of the limits and in general have begun to be part of a more concise and definite play therapy process, regardless of the method being used. At this point lesser trained individuals are introduced into the therapy sessions and are maintained as cotherapists for an additional one or two sessions so that there may be several people in a therapy session with varying backgrounds. At the end of that period the senior therapist retires and the junior therapists continue to maintain the sessions, still working together under the supervision of the senior therapist but now with full responsibility for the management of the cases and the establishment of the therapeutic procedures. It has been demonstrated that this type of transfer works very smoothly, that there is little difficulty in making the transition, in fact, less difficulty than under other circumstances because the patients do not develop the kind of fixed loyalty or transfer of affections which sometimes occurs in one-to-one relationships.

If one of the cotherapists is to be in charge, he or she should be introduced from the beginning as a cotherapist so that any specific problems which may arise around building initial rapport can be handled. This gives the lesser trained therapists more confidence in their ability to deal with the problems.

The relationship between the cotherapists and the senior therapist becomes the key to success in this type of approach. One of the more effective ways of providing such supervision, taking into consideration time limitations, and so forth, is the establishment of teaching seminars whereby the supervision is provided not only by the senior therapist leading such a seminar, but also by all of the other participating cotherapists discussing, questioning, and dealing with varying modes of approach. It would be possible for many different modes to emerge, all of which could be dealt with logically and consistently apropos the behavior of the child, so that the most appropriate mode could be chosen. This type of supervision permits immediate review of the therapeutic interactions without making overwhelming demands on time. The supervisory sessions have to be based on the evolution of procedures and the logical understanding of why certain procedures work with some children. The main criteria should be whatever works.

Therefore, if the senior therapist can evolve a training program around a group of junior therapists who can follow specific concepts on a session-by-session basis, and who receive intervening supervision so as to improve their understanding, and if they can learn to transmit this to the child both through standard therapy procedures and expressive emotional responses, it is possible to reach a larger number of children with a larger number of personnel.

This type of program has been developed as part of an interdisciplinary training program at the Nisonger Center, Ohio. The further advantages of interdisciplinary training are that the therapy aides can also bring their personal skills to bear on the client goals. Thus, nursing, social work, communication, or child development students, for example, can all add to the play therapy through their previous training. This is one of the major responsibilities of the Nisonger Center, as a university affiliated facility of the Ohio State University.

Working with Parents. Another aspect of improving the delivery of services includes teaching the parent how to encourage certain behavior modes whereby the child can move from maladaptive coping into more adaptive coping within the broad aspects of the home situation. This is a matter of working through with the parents what aspects of the child's behavior they feel must be changed above all else. The parents can learn procedures which might permit changes by reinforcing certain behaviors and intruding on or punishing others. The child is given an opportunity for a broad pattern of continuity from what he or she has learned in play therapy on through to the home (though the parent does not necessarily do what the therapist does). Typically the parent does not have time, considering the requirements of housekeeping, a job, and so on, to devote the kind of attention to all aspects of the child's behavior as is done in therapy. What can be done though, is that the parents can become aware that they have established procedures with which to respond to those specific behaviors that are most annoying to them, and which they can effect with various interventions. Finally, the parents can become rewarding individuals instead of the continually punishing individuals that the parents of retarded children often tend to become.

One aspect of parental involvement in play therapy is the possibility of initiating more directed play within the home situation. It is a matter of systematically teaching the child how to play and indicating what things he should be playing with and under what modes. This is not an attempt to limit creativity by the parent coming and saying, "Okay play with your trucks now," but rather a very systematic effort saying "This is a truck," "It has four wheels," "They go around," and "You play with it in the following manner, here." The child may or may not wish to play with it at that time, and the parent should permit choices, but at least an effort will have been made to improve understanding of what playing with a truck implies. Quite often this is the instruction that has been lacking; it is assumed that one knows how to play with a truck. They may not play with it at the moment the parent discusses it, simply because children do not always do things at the moment their parents tell them to, but usually they will come back and play with it later when it can be their decision and the play activity will thus move forward. This feeling that they are doing something that their mother wants them to do, that she has shown them how to do, and that other children around them do, adds to their repertoire of successful experiences and they begin to achieve the same aspects of self-confidence and self-concept which become the elementary goals in the more intensive forms of play therapy. Thus, parents can play a very clear-cut and facilitative role without being therapists themselves.

CONCLUSION

In this chapter we have described some patterns which should emerge in attempting play therapy with the mentally retarded; I have pointed out that the main impetus of play therapy has to do with the function of structure within the child's environment; and the main function of the therapist becomes the manipulation of that structure in helping to modify the child's behavior. I have further pointed out that whereas play therapy is a regular and necessary part of the procedure of dealing with emotionally disturbed, mentally retarded, or developmentally disabled children, the kinds of procedure used must nonetheless take into consideration the level of disturbance or the level of retardation. We have suggested four particular kinds of procedures which have been successful for us.

I have also discussed a model for the development of therapy aides, with particular emphasis on interdisciplinary approaches. And I have underlined the importance of including the parents or family in the therapeutic milieu of the atypical child so that the whole process can move forward at a more rapid and successful pace.

The area of behavior modification and intervention into the behavior of the mentally retarded child is one which still requires a great deal more study and research in establishing an organized mode for such intervention. I have not given specific case illustrations because the chapter is already long and the illustrations would consume a great deal of additional space. There are two video presentations available through the Nisonger Center, 1580 Cannon Drive, Columbus, Ohio 43210 (Deutsch & Leland, 1976; 1977), which demonstrate the program in action.

Play therapy with the mentally retarded is somewhat different than play therapy with children of higher mentalities, where the major emphasis is on learning to cope with situations—with the basic assumption that they are already aware that the situations exist. This difference does require different therapeutic approaches and different training for the clinical psychologists involved (Leland, Smith, & Barclay, 1970). However, the results are rewarding both for the child and for the therapist and will carry us a long way toward improving the total mental health and learning potential of the children.

REFERENCES

Axline, V. M. (1947) *Play therapy.* Boston: Houghton Mifflin.

Coulter, W. A., & Morrow, H. W. (Eds.) (1978) *Adaptive behavior: Concepts and measurement.* New York: Grune and Stratton.

Deutsch, M. (1978) *The development of a diagnostic play procedure for developmentally disabled children.* Unpublished doctoral dissertation. The Ohio State University, Columbus.

Deutsch, M., & Leland, H. (1976) *Play therapy with developmentally delayed children.* Television Tape 1-058, Nisonger Center, The Ohio State University, Columbus.

Deutsch, M., & Leland, H. (1977) *Play therapy with developmentally delayed children.* Television Tape 1-059, Nisonger Center, The Ohio State University, Columbus.

Edmonson, B., Leland, H., deJung, J. E., & Leach, E. M. (1967) Increasing social cue interpretations (visual decoding) by retarded adolescents through training. *American Journal of Mental Deficiency,* **71**(6), 1017–1024.

Edmonson, B., Leland, H., & Leach, E. M. (1970) Social inference training of retarded adolescents. *Education and Training of the Mentally Retarded,* **5**(4), 169–176.

Grossman, H. J. (Ed.) (1977) *Manual on terminology and classification in mental retardation,* rev. ed., Washington, D.C.: American Association on Mental Deficiency.

Leland, H., & Smith, D. (1965) *Play therapy with mentally subnormal children.* New York: Grune and Stratton.

Leland, H., Walker, J., & Toboada, A. N. (1959) Group play therapy with a group of post-nursery male retardates, *American Journal of Mental Deficiency,* **63**(5), 848–851.

Leland, H., Smith, D. E., & Barclay, A. (1970) Report of the workshop on the training of clinical child psychologists in mental retardation, *Mental Retardation,* **8**(4), 24–28.

Leland, H., Nihira, K., Foster, R., & Shellhaas, M. (1968) The demonstration and measurement of adaptive behavior. In B. W. Richards (Ed.), *Proceedings of the First Congress of the International Association for the Scientific Study of Mental Deficiency.* Surrey, England: Michael Jackson Publishing Co.

Shellhaas, M., & Nihira, K. (1969) Factor analysis of reasons retardates are referred to an institution. *American Journal of Mental Deficiency,* **74**(2), 171–179.

Sherwood, S. (1980) *Play psychotherapy with socially maladaptive mentally retarded children using same-age and younger-age peers as therapists.* Unpublished Doctoral Dissertation, The Ohio State University, Columbus.

Sutter, E., Leland, H., & Barclay, A. (Eds.) (1969) Report of the workshop on the role of subprofessionals in clinical child psychology and mental retardation. Washington, D.C.: American Psychological Association, Section 1, Division 12.

CHAPTER 25

Play Therapy with the Physically Handicapped

MARION K. SALOMON

INTRODUCTION

Psychological Problems of Physically Handicapped Children

It has long been known that physical handicaps impose psychological burdens on children and their families. Physically handicapped children must cope with stresses stemming from frequent hospitalizations, their families' and friends' discomfort with their conditions, and distortions in body image. In addition, there are the realistic restrictions imposed by the particular disability, as well as the usual range of potential psychological problems independent of the handicap. It is not surprising, then, that physically disabled children frequently benefit from psychological treatment.

The impact of a handicapping condition will vary with many factors; for example, whether the condition affects the personal appearance (Abt, 1971), whether the handicap is congenital or acquired (Greenberg, 1974), and whether the defect is mild, moderate, or severe, although trivial disabilities may cause intense conflict (Abt, 1971). In addition, the child's age is a significant variable. As Magrab and Calcagno (1978) point out, during infancy, the development of trust toward adult caretakers may be disrupted by frequent separations due to hospitalization. In addition to separation from parents, hospitals often provide painful, unpleasant, or frightening experiences—enforced passivity, injections, IV's, medicines, operations—which may be expected to make the preschool child less ready to trust and confide in the adults who permit or perform these procedures.

Parents of handicapped preschoolers may tend to overprotect and overindulge their children; the children, in turn, often blame themselves and their parents for their illnesses, feeling that they may be suffering retribution for some known or unknown transgressions. Children of school age who should be developing new skills and peer relationships may find that they are hindered by extra restrictions and dependency on adults as a result of their chronic conditions.

Often, disabled children's families contribute to their problems. Parents exhibit disappointment, resentment, and overattention with respect to their handicapped offspring, whose siblings may feel ashamed and guilty about their resentment (Magrab & Calcagno, 1978). The process of socialization may be adversely affected by the parents' withholding or overindulging in affection, by their difficulties in establishing appropriate rewards and punishments, and by their failing to provide the child with realistic models for identification and imitation (Magrab & Calcagno, 1978). The resulting family configuration inhibits and distorts emotional growth.

In one particularly interesting report, Lussier (1980) discusses a handicapped child whose primary problem was parental rather than physical. A 12-year-old boy with arms only six inches long, he proved to be much more in need of his mother's acceptance than of normal arms. He felt that his body was complete and self-sufficient as it was, and that his mother had failed to acknowledge this and to offer him sufficient encouragement. (The therapist admitted that he, too, did not see his client as physically complete at first.) The boy resisted surgery to fit artificial arms, since this threatened to change the image of the body he had known from birth. In this case, although the physical disability was a prominent one, the child had coped with it adequately. His major difficulty concerned the significant adults in his life, who did not share his attitudes.

Society's emphasis on physical beauty and strong, healthy bodies exacerbates the problems of the handicapped. Much research has focused on the attitudes of others toward disabled people, and many investigators have found that the handicapped are viewed less favorably than are the nondisabled (Donaldson, 1980). An unusual physical appearance or a sensory or motor impairment gives the handicapped individual a body clearly at odds with cultural norms and may result in tremendous self-consciousness and a poor body image. Not surprisingly, the handicapped are often found to be lonely and suspicious of others (Abt, 1971). Physical disability has frequently been linked with feelings of inferiority, shame, guilt, bitterness, envy, and self-pity; although no one attitude is invariably exhibited by the handicapped, they are commonly seen to be immature and to be subject to primitive fixations and stereotyped activities (Greenberg, 1974).

Many forms of maladjustment are discussed in the literature. Some disabled youngsters see all of their problems as stemming from their handicaps. They hold the conviction that, if not for their disabilities, all of their difficulties would disappear (Yorke, 1980). A child holding such beliefs may be unwilling to develop interpersonal skills or to examine family conflicts, since these may give evidence that problems exist independent of the disability. On the other hand, the feeling that they would be perfect if not for their handicaps may cause children to develop strong drives to overcome their disabilities in the expectation that they may then be capable of extraordinary achievements. If they fail to reach their almost unattainable goals and find themselves able to achieve only modest success, they may suffer complete loss of self-confidence.

Other disabled children ignore their own handicaps completely, denying that there is any interference with normal functioning (Greenberg, 1974). This disability denial seems to involve the rejection of the disabled part of the individual, and may cause children to refuse to discuss their handicaps with their therapists. They, too, may set unrealistic personal goals, thus increasing the likelihood of failure.

Another common reaction to physical disability, especially in older children and in those whose handicap is acquired rather than congenital, is despair, which fosters the need for revenge (Greenberg, 1974). (Those who become severely disabled often go through mourning for the lost body part or function [Vargo, 1978].) Blame of others, or self-blame and the resulting depression, must then be dealt with by the therapist. These negative emotions may threaten the rehabilitation team of psychologists, occupational therapists, physical therapists, and the rest, who prefer to work with patients who are well-motivated to strive cheerfully toward therapeutic goals. Under these circumstances, the child may find that expressions of despair or anger are unacceptable to professionals and may feel encouraged by them to deny these negative feelings. When a child is physically handicapped and of normal intelligence, tendencies to deny emotion may be increased by strong pressures to develop intellectual abilities. In order to increase the child's self-esteem and marketable skills, parents, professionals, and the child may emphasize academic attainments at the expense of emotional development, reinforcing denial of the disability.

Certainly there is no necessary relationship between physical handicap and psychological distress. Some physically normal children are maladjusted, and some severely disabled children are not. However, handicapped children do have the added stresses discussed above, and may often benefit from therapy designed to help them cope with their unusually difficult situations.

Play Therapy as Treatment

Many types of therapeutic intervention are possible for use with physically handicapped children, but the basic principles of play therapy would seem to make it especially appropriate for many of these youngsters. (The principles discussed as follows are taken from Axline [1947].)

1.   The therapist must develop a friendly relationship and good rapport with the child and must show acceptance of the client. Frequently, disabled children have little experience with nonjudgmental adults. They have histories of failure to meet normal expectations and they are likely to have received more than their share of negative evaluations, critical judgments, and discouraged and discouraging remarks. For example, Kogan, Tyler, and Turner (1974) found that over a two-year period, mothers and physical therapists of

cerebral palsied preschoolers showed a gradual decrease in acceptance and warmth toward the children; this tendency was most marked for those young-sters who failed to achieve independent walking by the end of the study. Presumably, this decrease in affection was at least partly due to the adults' disappointment that anticipated improvement was not as great or as rapid as they had initially hoped.

Even when their relationships with handicapped children are at their most positive, adults engaged in special education and therapeutic programs are trying to change the children, with varying degrees of cooperation from the youngsters. This focus on goal-oriented activity necessitates a degree of adult control over the child. Disabled children may, therefore, be in even greater need of unconditional positive regard and permissive attitudes than nondis-abled children are.

2. Play therapy, unlike some other forms of intervention, emphasizes the recognition and reflection of feelings. The therapist tries to understand the feelings which the child is expressing through play, and to help the child comprehend these attitudes and emotions. This approach can be of particular benefit to the physically handicapped youngster. Parents often overprotect such children, shielding them from anything unpleasant including the expres-sion of unacceptable feelings. As discussed previously, health professionals, too, may discourage overt displays of depression and anger, feeling that these reflect badly on their programs and hinder the child's progress. Society's atti-tude toward the handicapped requires that they strive harder and be more cheerful than other people; their hopefulness and extraordinary determination to succeed are expected to help them overcome enormous obstacles. Disabled children may thus have no opportunity to display and to recognize their own feelings of despair and rage. The disability denial mentioned previously fre-quently accompanies a physical handicap. Play therapy provides the handi-capped child with an adult capable of understanding, accepting, and reflecting his feelings. The honesty and lack of bias inherent in this situation, at its best, provide the child with the feedback which nonhandicapped children can get from peers and from many different adults.

Physically handicapped children may tend to be more passive than other children, to initiate and explore less, and to show greater dependence on adults. A vivid example of this is provided by Hopkins (1977), who describes the case of an eight-year-old goy who had been severely affected by a congeni-tal, life-threatening illness. Although his physical health had improved, he was emotionally unresponsive and listless at the time of referral. The therapist found that his passivity came not from physical weakness, but from the fear of letting his body be "the container of precious emotional vitality." The author reports significant gains in academic performance and energy level after thera-peutic intervention.

3. Play therapy might be the treatment of choice for passive, dependent children because it is an approach which views children as active participants

in their own development. The therapist gives the child the opportunity to solve problems, and believes that the young client is capable of taking this responsibility. The entire course of the therapeutic intervention is led by the child, who determines both the direction and the speed of the therapy. The physically handicapped child, used to being guided and led by adults, is suddenly the decision maker, working with an adult who respects the youngster's ability to direct his or her own actions. The disabled child's feelings of competence and self-worth may well be enhanced by this opportunity to take responsibility.

The basic principles of play therapy thus make it an excellent technique for use with physically handicapped children. The friendly, accepting, nonjudgmental therapist, the recognition and reflection of feelings which are often denied expression in other settings, and the encouragement for the child to take the initiative may be especially beneficial for the disabled child.

Despite the many advantages which play therapy may offer the physically handicapped it has been used with this group very infrequently. One possible reason for this is offered by Cowen and Trippe (1963), who point out that therapy with the nondisabled depends on the ability to communicate, to move about, and to manipulate objects, the latter two functions being especially important for play therapy. Often, these abilities are impaired in handicapped people, and as a result, therapists and researchers may feel that the usual therapeutic methods are inappropriate for them. They may then choose not to undertake or to study play therapy—or any other form of therapeutic intervention—with handicapped groups. When play therapy has been employed with disabled children, reports of its effectiveness have seldom presented sufficient data for the reader to evaluate the results.

In an early study, Axline (1947) reports the case of a six-year-old boy with a constricted throat. During the course of the therapy, the child gradually learned to cope with his mother's rejection, to consider his foster family as his own, and to abandon the nursing bottles and rubber feeding tubes which he no longer needed for eating. Subsequent to this study, Cruikshank and Cowen (1948) employed a nondirective play therapy group with five physically handicapped children in a public day school. As several authors have pointed out (e.g., Cowen & Trippe, 1963), handicapped children are often isolated and ostracized and may be deprived of opportunities to form friendships and participate in group play. Group play therapy can offer such children the added advantage of social inclusion. In this case, on the basis of pre- and posttherapy "essay type reports" completed by teachers and parents, the researchers (Cowen & Cruikshank, 1949) concluded that three of the five children showed considerable improvement in social adjustment, while one showed slight improvement and one showed no indication of gain. As the investigators themselves point out, this study is limited by the absence of pre- and posttherapy objective measures, by the lack of a follow-up study to determine the stability of the reported gains, and by the lack of a control group.

Cowen and Trippe (1963) summarize several case histories and research reports on play therapy with blind children. In general, these youngsters appear to have gained insight and personal satisfaction from their therapeutic experiences, although no formal evaluative data are presented.

In a detailed discussion of play therapy with one physically handicapped, retarded boy, Moustakas (1959) found that the child, initially indifferent to toys and unresponsive to other children, developed interest in the materials available in the playroom. He learned to imitate the other children who sometimes joined him, and occasionally played cooperatively with them. His ability to express his feelings and his organizational skills also improved.

In a more recent study (Irwin & McWilliams, 1974), 11 children with cleft palates participated in weekly group therapy for eight months. Unlike the play therapy sessions mentioned in the previous reports, these included only dramatic puppet play and pantomime. The children, aged three to six, frequently showed themes of oral aggression and fear of bodily injury in their play; large biting animals, doctors, nurses, and surgery were dramatized intensely and repeatedly. The authors report that the children shifted from passive roles as victims of injury to more active roles as medical personnel during the course of the therapy. As this study suggests, when a handicap is mild and its negative effects are focused narrowly in one area of functioning, a few specific materials and play techniques may be used exclusively during the therapeutic sessions. These may be very effective in eliciting the children's concerns relating to their handicapping conditions.

Play therapy also has been utilized successfully with children suffering from severe physical limitations. Salomon and Garner (1978) discuss the treatment of a four-year-old boy of normal intelligence and verbal ability, but with a physical handicap which precluded his manipulating all but the smallest and lightest play materials. The child's skill in communicating with the therapist and in using vicarious experiences allowed him to participate fully in therapy, although he was unable to move about the playroom or to handle most of the toys available in it. During the course of the therapy, the boy gradually showed greater independence and increasingly demanded the opportunity to do things for himself. He also became freer to discuss his annoyance at his physical restrictions and his fear of the frequent hospital procedures to which he was subjected.

Positive results have also been reported when parents of physically handicapped children have served as their play therapists. Guerney (1979) discusses this form of intervention—which she labels "Filial Therapy"—with learning disabled children, although she states that it has been used effectively with those with mild cerebral palsy, too. The author has chosen to use parents as therapists because she feels that parents can best transfer their children's therapeutic gains to other settings; in addition, the permissive and empathetic parent–therapists are especially influential in reshaping their own children's self-images. Finally, the children come to see their parents as adults who care about how children feel and not just about how they perform. Guerney reports that children's negative feelings about themselves become more positive, and that the youngsters become more independent and self-controlled as a result of therapeutic intervention.

Several authors have discussed play therapy with hospitalized children. Although many of the reported results are based on nonhandicapped people, the findings of these studies are relevant here because the physically handicapped child typically spends a relatively large proportion of time preparing for hospital procedures, undergoing them, and recovering from them. The child may thus find it especially beneficial to have the opportunity to express in a therapeutic setting feelings regarding the hospital stay. Play specialists can help children cope with hospitalization by aiding them in reducing stress, by eliciting information relevant to medical treatment, and by communicating facts about illness, hospital equipment, and routines (Jolly, 1979).

Plank (1962), in an early study of children in hospitals, discusses the use of dramatic play to prepare children for medical and surgical procedures and to help them deal with troubling events after surgery. The play therapy room is provided with actual equipment anesthesia masks, caps, gowns, bandages, stethoscopes—as well as toy replicas of syringes and plastic intravenous set-ups to attach to doll carriages. The play specialist occasionally takes a didactic role, and aided by drawings, conveys medical information to the child.

A similar approach is taken by Azarnoff (1974), who describes a play therapy program for children in inpatient and outpatient clinics. Her playroom includes small models of x-ray machines, wheelchairs, and beds on wheels. Real x-ray negatives are compared with paper Halloween skeletons, and models of the heart, with Valentine hearts. Children dramatize the roles of nurse and doctor, explore medical equipment and supplies, and try out various behavior patterns (e.g., resisting an injection and then bravely enduring it). Because it is felt that some children need to escape from the hospital atmosphere, art materials, records, and books with nonhospital themes are provided, too. The playroom staff—trained in psychology, early education, or special education—meets regularly with physicians, occupational and physical therapists, and laboratory technicians to exchange information and plan programs.

Play intervention projects in hospitals may have great benefits for the children who participate in them. However, there is little evaluative data on these programs presented in the literature, and the few available findings are not uniformly positive. For example, Clatworthy (1978) reports that among children hospitalized for three days, those participating in therapeutic play maintained the same anxiety level on admission and discharge; the children who did not have play therapy showed an increase in anxiety over the same period. In contrast, Hackett (1978) finds no significant difference in psychological adjustment between children who have had play therapy before cardiac surgery and those who have not. In this case, 25 children aged one to 15 and hospitalized for heart surgery were randomly assigned to experimental or control groups. The experimental subjects had two sessions of structural play therapy designed to provide emotional release and behavioral rehearsal to prepare the children for surgery. Their mothers had two counseling sessions, designed to decrease maternal anxiety and overprotectiveness, and to improve the mothers' methods of disciplining their children. The only significant finding was that after the intervention, the mothers disciplined their children more than the control mothers did.

In summary, it is not possible at this time to reach any firm conclusions about the efficacy of play therapy in helping children to cope with hospitalization. The play intervention programs described in the literature vary in degree of structure, in number of sessions offered, in extent of parental involvement, in children's presenting medical complaints, and in success rate. Perhaps future studies will be able to isolate those factors necessary for therapeutic effectiveness in this area. It does appear, however, that play therapy has the potential for aiding children in hospitals in coping with stress; handicapped children, hospitalized more frequently than others, may thus find this form of therapy of particular benefit.

METHOD

Adapting Play Therapy to the Physically Handicapped

Procedural Modification.   Modifications in and additions to the usual play therapy procedures may be necessary or desirable if this form of intervention is to be used with the physically handicapped. Each disability will impose its own restrictions on the methods utilized in the play therapy room, and will suggest other adaptations which, although not essential, are particularly effective with the individual handicapped client.

One valuable addition to the basic play intervention program for almost all disabled children is the use of an interdisciplinary team approach. Frequently, the physically handicapped child has regular contact with occupational, physical, and speech therapists, with social workers, special education teachers, and medical specialists. Input from these people will help the play therapist set relevant goals for the client and choose appropriate materials and activities for the playroom. These professionals can also give feedback to the play therapist regarding the effectiveness of the intervention and its transfer to other settings; the child's success at achieving separation from the mother, or in taking the initiative in therapy, or in controlling impulsivity, will be tested outside the playroom, and the information thus obtained can be used to plan future play therapy sessions. The play therapist, too, is often able to provide information which will improve the client's interactions with other interdisciplinary team members. The freedom to express fear, anger, and grief in play therapy may make it easier for the child to deal with the practical aspects of coping with handicaps during occupational or speech therapy. For all of these reasons, then, it is usually of great benefit to include other disciplines when one is doing play therapy with a physically handicapped child.

A second desirable addition to therapeutic interaction with a disabled child is the provision of psychological support for other family members. As discussed previously, handicapped children add a great deal of stress and many burdens to their families. Their parents may feel guilt and shame, have extra financial obligations and child care responsibilities, and experience social isolation (Cowen & Trippe, 1963). Psychotherapy with parents should help them to form better relationships with their children and to resolve their own conflicts. Parents may also need education in the practical matters of day-to-day living with their exceptional child, and might benefit from guidelines concerning any limitations or restrictions. Siblings, too, may find it helpful to have some form of psychological support to enable them to cope with their additional difficulties. Family members may benefit from many different types of intervention—support groups, therapy groups, instructional groups, individual counseling, or behavior therapy. Detailed discussion of all these is beyond the scope of this chapter. However, the play therapist may find that one or more of the various forms of support services should be made available to the family of the physically handicapped child.

Modifications Based on Level of Play Development.   The play behaviors of physically disabled children may be very different from those of normal children, and a play intervention program should take these differences into account. According to Piaget (1951), there are three main stages in the development of play. During the first, which ordinarily characterizes children from birth to about two years, play is sensorimotor; a major task of this period is the development of object permanence, the conviction that things exist independent of one's perception of them. From age two to about age seven, children are less dependent on the actual objects present during their play; symbols and fantasy are commonly used during this period. From about age eight, normal children are capable of role playing, in which they take another person's point of view; in addition, games with rules are often played at this stage. Each of the stages incorporates the concepts and skills of the previous one(s); an impairment in an earlier stage will have a harmful effect on the child's later play behavior, as well.

Some physical handicaps tend to disrupt the normal development of sensorimotor play. The blind child cannot see the available materials and play area, and is limited by lack of vision; the crippled child often cannot explore, imitate, test hypotheses, or construct objects as other children do (Hart, 1976). As a result, sensorimotor knowledge of the world is restricted. Salomon and Garner (1978) reported on one severely crippled four-year-old child of normal intelligence who still had only a tentative concept of object permanence; he seemed unsure that people or toys which were out of sight would reappear. Apparently, his almost complete immobility resulted in a lack of opportunity to have the usual sensorimotor experiences and a consequent delay in this child's awareness of the permanence of objects. Similarly, Fraiberg (1971) found that childhood blindness resulted in impaired human object relations, poor adaptive hand behavior, and immature gross motor development; however, the blind children in this study improved significantly when they were given increased tactile stimulation and when they were taught how to grasp objects and how to reach toward sounds on cue.

Many handicapped children have not had adequate opportunity to see their surroundings from different vantage points, to notice that things appear to change size and shape as one looks at them from different angles and distances, to experiment with various weights, textures, and physical properties of objects. Since their knowledge of the concrete world is limited, such children may experience difficulty in achieving the more abstract levels of play; symbolism and fantasy may be slow to develop.

It has been suggested, too (Sheridan, 1975), that handicapped children frequently lack drive and concentration, that in learning new skills they persevere too much or tend to relax and regress, and that they do not seek outside help when it would be appropriate to do so. Many authors (e.g., Hart, 1976; Hunter, 1976; Hewson, McConkey, & Jeffree, 1980; Sheridan, 1975) recommend that disabled children be taught sensorimotor play, that they receive step-by-step instruction in working with concrete materials, in exploring the physical environment, in discovering the relevant features of their surroundings, and in generalizing from them. In the Hewson et al. study, one five-year-old boy, severely handicapped both mentally and physically, participated in an individualized program designed first to increase his interaction with toys, and later, to encourage imaginative play and to extend his ability to plan his actions. Using a highly structured sequence of play activities, the child made significant improvements in fine-motor coordination, imaginative play, and organizational ability; he also learned to enjoy exploring his environment. In this case, a structured approach led to advances in sensorimotor play and then in symbolic, fantasy play; these positive changes were evident during free play as well.

The play therapist considering intervention with a physically handicapped client must take into account the child's level of play development. Surely, the ability to participate in imaginative play, to symbolize and fantasize, are necessary prerequisites for the type of play therapy described by Axline and Moustakas. The child who merely constructs objects without ever seeing them as representative of real structures, who moves dolls and blocks about without considering them as possible people and vehicles, who makes marks on paper with crayons or paint without being able to view them as anything but marks on paper, will not succeed at symbolizing his difficulties with the use of toys and transferring newly gained insights to other situations. Incomplete mastery of sensorimotor play may cause deficiencies in more sophisticated, abstract types of play. Before attempting to engage children in symbolic, therapeutic play, one should ascertain that they have had sufficient sensorimotor input to enable them to perform at the required level. There is some evidence that the basic play skills can be taught, and, in some cases, it may be decided that a structured, didactic program must be completed before therapy is begun. On the other hand, other forms of therapy, more directive or behaviorally oriented, may be more appropriate for such clients.

Even for those handicapped children whose sensorimotor input has been adequate, there are often deficiencies in imaginative play. Deaf children, not physically restricted by poor vision or crippling illness, are presumably able to explore their environments much as hearing children do during the sensorimotor period. However, during the preoperational stage (about ages two to seven), when language and a shared system of symbols gain importance, hearing-impaired children show less-mature play patterns than do the normally hearing, engaging in relatively little make-believe play and object substitution, and interacting less with their peers (Darbyshire, 1977). (In this study, high socioeconomic status, the acquisition of a hearing aid by age two, and early language training were associated with comparatively mature play patterns.) In a review of several studies of the play development of the hearing-impaired, Higginbotham, Baker, and Neill (1980) concluded that these children engaged in less symbolic solitary play and less cooperative and dramatic play than normally hearing children did; they attributed these deficiencies to the restricted social interaction experienced by the deaf and hard-of-hearing. Lubin and Sherrill (1980) found that deaf children, ages three to five, were significantly poorer than hearing children on motor creativity, as measured by the Torrance Test of Thinking Creatively in Action and Movement. (The children were asked to use objects in as many ways as possible, and to move like various objects.) Twenty days of "guided movement exploration" led to improved performance for the hearing-impaired subjects.

In summary, the ability of deaf and hard-of-hearing children to participate in symbolic, imaginative, and interactive play seems to be limited, compared to that of hearing children. Again, there are some indications that these forms of play can be taught, and the play therapist may wish to provide training in imaginative play for those clients demonstrating lacks in this area. This training should probably not be undertaken by nondirective therapists themselves, who might not wish to begin relationships with clients with a didactic stance. Alternatively, other types of therapy may be chosen for these children. In addition to the problems of hearing-impaired children discussed previously, deficiencies in symbolic play of handicapped children in general may be caused by an overemphasis on toys that encourage sensory training and concept formation—for example, nesting toys, pegboards, stringing beads—and the consequent neglect of the more traditional toys—dolls, everyday household objects, wheeled toys—which would stimulate vocabulary, social understanding, and make-believe play (Sheridan, 1975). Play development programs should make use of both types of toys to ensure that handicapped children derive maximum benefit from their training.

Technical Modifications.   Having ascertained that a particular physically handicapped child is capable of imaginative play, the play therapist must then consider whether the usual play therapy techniques are appropriate. Even such ordinarily straightforward matters as when and how to begin and end each session and where to position oneself and the client may be complicated by the child's physical limitations. For example, in the case of the severely crippled four-year-old boy described earlier (Salomon & Garner, 1978), the child's mother placed him on the floor at the beginning of each session to assure that he would not slide off a chair inadvertently; his position remained unchanged during the entire session. Language was used to a much greater extent than would be the case with most young children. This boy used verbal means to direct the therapist in arranging materials, to play at sports vicariously, and to show his superiority to other, less verbal youngsters in situations in which other children would be expected to use their physical capacities. Since this child was unable to leave the therapy room unaided, the termination procedure was modified; at a time previously arranged with the therapist, the client's mother knocked on the door and then waited five minutes, to prepare the child for the end of the session.

Clearly, as this case demonstrates, therapeutic techniques with the exceptional child may differ considerably from those with nonhandicapped children. In many cases, despite the child's need to develop autonomy, the therapist must do things for the client and allow the youngster to lean on him or her (Moustakas, 1959). Parents and other adults may also take a much more active role than is usual.

Other modifications in therapeutic technique are discussed by Cowen and Cruikshank (1948) in their report on group therapy with physically handicapped children; the authors found that the usual methods of setting and enforcing limits had to be changed with these clients. The children needed extra limitations to protect them from physical injury, and the therapist could not allow delay in citing and enforcing the rules. For these reasons the therapist had to be especially careful to see that the children felt accepted in the therapy room. The authors also found that the entire therapeutic intervention was disrupted and lengthened because these clients were absent more frequently than most nonhandicapped children would be.

Adaptive Play Materials.   Suggestions from other professionals are often helpful when one is choosing playthings, setting up the therapy room, and devising methods to allow physically handicapped children to participate fully in the activities offered. For example, Hunter (1976), a special education teacher, suggests that cerebral palsied children have paint brushes taped to their hands or elbows if they wish to paint but cannot grasp objects; she also recommends the use of hats, pocketbooks, and scarves for dressing up, since these are relatively easy to handle.

Finnie (1975), in her excellent volume on cerebral palsied children, offers many useful suggestions for positioning the child and choosing appropriate toys. For example, she recommends large colored balls to catch a child's interest; heavy balls for ataxic and athetoid children who are too uncoordinated to keep light ones from rolling away; smaller solid balls for the spastic who cannot lift heavy objects; beanbags or balls and bats attached by elastic if the child cannot grasp a ball at all. Many types of toys can be adapted for use with the handicapped in order to allow them to participate as fully as possible in play therapy.

SUMMARY

In summary, if a physically handicapped child is to benefit from a play intervention program, the therapist must often have considerable ingenuity in selecting toys and arranging equipment. She or he must also be prepared to deal with extra, but legitimate, dependency needs and possible disruptions in the normal development of imaginative play. As in therapy with other children, the client's family may benefit from counseling, but here, the family's need for support and information is even greater than usual. An interdisciplinary team approach can be of value in treating the multiple problems presented by the handicapped child.

Play therapy, modified to suit the individual needs of the disabled client, has great potential as a method of helping the child cope both with problems caused by his or her handicap and with difficulties independent of it. Although it is certainly not the only type of therapy which can be of benefit, play therapy can be of value to physically handicapped children because it includes a positive, accepting relationship between therapist and client, because it allows the client autonomy, and because it emphasizes the reflection of feelings. All of these factors make play therapy particularly suited for use with the handicapped.

If this form of intervention is to become a more effective and more widely used therapeutic procedure, however, it is essential that therapists or researchers collect data and report their results, compare procedures and conduct follow-up studies. The literature on play therapy is in need of precise descriptions of technique and objective measures of outcome; without these, the usefulness of play therapy cannot be evaluated, and specific therapeutic methods cannot be improved.

REFERENCES

Abt, L. E. (1971) The psychology of physical handicap: A statement of some principles. In R. L. Noland (Ed.), *Counseling parents of the ill and handicapped.* Springfield, Ill.: Charles C. Thomas.

Axline, V. M. (1947) *Play therapy.* New York: Ballantine.

Azarnoff, P. (1974) Mediating the trauma of serious illness and hospitalization in children. *Children Today,* **3,** 12–17.

Clatworthy, S. M. (1978) The effect of therapeutic play on the anxiety behaviors of hospitalized children. Doctoral dissertation, Boston University School of Education. *Dissertation Abstracts International,* **38**(12-B), 6142.

Cowen, E. L., & Cruikshank, W. M. (1948) Group therapy with physically handicapped children: II. Evaluation. *Journal of Educational Psychology,* **39,** 281–297.

Cowen, E. L., & Trippe, M. J. (1963) Psychotherapy and play techniques with the exceptional child and youth. In W. M. Cruikshank (Ed.), *Psychology of exceptional children and youth,* 2nd ed. Englewood Cliffs, N.J.: Prentice-Hall.

Cruikshank, W. M., & Cowen, E. L. (1948) Group therapy with physically handicapped children: I. Report of study. *Journal of Educational Psychology,* **39,** 193–215.

Darbyshire, J. O. (1977) Play patterns in young children with impaired hearing. *Volta Review,* **79,** 19–26.

Donaldson, J. (1980) Changing attitudes toward handicapped persons: A review and analysis of research. *Exceptional Children,* **46,** 504–514.

Finnie, N. R. (1975) *Handling the young cerebral palsied child at home,* 2nd ed. New York: Dutton.

Fraiberg, S. (1971) Intervention in infancy: A program for blind infants. *Journal of the American Academy of Child Psychiatry,* **10,** 381–405.

Greenberg, R. (1974) Psychiatric aspects of physical disability in children and adolescents. In S. C. Feinstein & P. L. Giovacchini (Eds.), *Adolescent psychiatry,* vol III.

Guerney, L. F. (1979) Play therapy with learning disabled children. *Journal of Clinical Child Psychology,* **8,** 242–244.

Hackett, J. M. (1978) Preoperative psychological preparation for children undergoing cardiac surgery (Doctoral dissertation, California School of Professional Psychology, San Diego, 1976). *Dissertation Abstracts International,* 1978, **38**(9-B), 4457–4458.

Hart, V. (1976) The special child and his play behaviors. *The Publication: Children in Contemporary Society,* **9**(67), 81–82.

Hewson, S., McConkey, R., & Jeffree, D. (1980) The relationship between structured and free play in the development of a mentally handicapped child: A case study. *Child: Care, Health and Development,* **6,** 73–82.

Higginbotham, D. J., Baker, B. M., & Neill, R. D. (1980) Assessing the social participation and cognitive play abilities of hearing-impaired preschoolers. *Volta Review,* **82,** 261–270.

Hopkins, J. (1977) Living under the threat of death: The impact of a congenital illness on an eight-year-old boy. *Journal of child psychotherapy,* **4,** 5–21.

Hunter, L. (1976) Teaching play to the physically handicapped. *The Publication: Children in Contemporary Society,* **9**(71), 81.

Irwin, E. C., & McWilliams, B. J. (1974) Play therapy for children with cleft palates. *Children Today,* **3,** 18–22.

Jolly, H. (1979) The work of the play specialists in Charing Cross Hospital, London. *Journal of the Association for the Care of Children in Hospitals,* **6,** 4–10.

Kogan, K. L., Tyler, N., & Turner, P. (1974) The process of interpersonal adaptation between mothers and their cerebral palsied children. *Developmental Medicine and Child Neurology,* **16,** 518–527.

Lubin, E., & Sherrill, C. (1980) Motor creativity of preschool deaf children. *American Annals of the Deaf,* **125,** 460–466.

Lussier, A. (1980) The physical handicap and the body ego. *International Journal of Psycho-Analysis,* **61,** 179–185.

Magrab, P. R., & Calcagno, P. L. (1978) Psychological impact of chronic pediatric conditions. In P. R. Magrab (Ed.), *Psychological management of pediatric problems,* Vol. I: *Early Life conditions and chronic diseases.* Baltimore: University Park Press.

Moustakas, C. E., (1959) *Psychotherapy with children: The living relationship.* New York: Harper & Row.

Piaget, J. (1951) *Play, dreams and imitation in childhood.* New York: Norton.

Plank, E. N. (1962) *Working with children in hospitals: A guide for the professional team.* Cleveland: Case Western Reserve University Press.

Salomon, M. K., & Garner, A. M. (1978) Use of play materials in treating a severely handicapped child. *Child: Care, Health and Development,* **4,** 131–140.

Sheridan, M. D. (1975) The importance of spontaneous play in the fundamental learning of handicapped children. *Child: Care, Health and Development,* **1,** 3–17.

Vargo, J. W. (1978) Some psychological effects of physical disability. *American Journal of Occupational Therapy,* **32,** 31–34.

Yorke, C. (1980) Some comments on the psychoanalytic treatment of patients with physical disabilities. *International Journal of Psycho-Analysis,* **61,** 187–193.

Author Index

Subject Index

Psychology and Psychiatry in Courts and Corrections: Controversy and Change
  by Ellsworth A. Fersch, Jr.
Restricted Environmental Stimulation: Research and Clinical Applications
  by Peter Suedfeld
Personal Construct Psychology: Psychotherapy and Personality
  edited by Alvin W. Landfield and Larry M. Leitner
Mothers, Grandmothers, and Daughters: Personality and Child Care in
Three-Generation Families
  by Bertram J. Cohler and Henry U. Grunebaum
Further Explorations in Personality
  edited by A. I. Rabin, Joel Aronoff, Andrew M. Barclay, and Robert A. Zucker
Hypnosis and Relaxation: Modern Verification of an Old Equation
  by William E. Edmonston, Jr.
Handbook of Clinical Behavior Therapy
  edited by Samuel M. Turner, Karen S. Calhoun, and Henry E. Adams
Handbook of Clinical Neuropsychology
  edited by Susan B. Filskov and Thomas J. Boll
The Course of Alcoholism: Four Years After Treatment
  by J. Michael Polich, David J. Armor, and Harriet B. Braiker
Handbook of Innovative Psychotherapies
  edited by Raymond J. Corsini
The Role of the Father in Child Development (Second Edition)
  edited by Michael E. Lamb
Behavioral Medicine: Clinical Applications
  by Susan S. Pinkerton, Howard Hughes, and W. W. Wenrich
Handbook for the Practice of Pediatric Psychology
  edited by June M. Tuma
Change Through Interaction: Social Psychological Processes of Counseling and
Psychotherapy
  by Stanley R. Strong and Charles D. Claiborn
Drugs and Behavior (Second Edition)
  by Fred Leavitt
Handbook of Research Methods in Clinical Psychology
  edited by Philip C. Kendall and James N. Butcher
A Social Psychology of Developing Adults
  by Thomas O. Blank
Women in the Middle Years: Current Knowledge and Directions for Research and Policy
  edited by Janet Zollinger Giele
Loneliness: A Sourcebook of Current Theory, Research and Therapy
  edited by Letitia Anne Peplau and Daniel Perlman
Hyperactivity: Current Issues, Research, and Theory (Second Edition)
  by Dorothea M. Ross and Sheila A. Ross
Review of Human Development
  *edited by Tiffany M. Field, Aletha Huston, Herbert C. Quay, Lillian Troll,
  and Gordon E. Finley*
Agoraphobia: Multiple Perspectives on Theory and Treatment
  edited by Dianne L. Chambless and Alan J. Goldstein
Handbook of Play Therapy
  edited by Charles E. Schaefer and Kevin J. O'Connor